£2.95

4/7/3

LENTEN

REFLECTIONS

LENTEN

REFLECTIONS

Tony Philpot

Tony Philpot is parish priest of Our Lady and the English Martyrs, Cambridge. He also co-ordinates a voluntary group of priests in the Catholic Church called the 'Jesus Caritas Fraternity', which is an international brotherhood founded on the example and writings of Charles de Foucauld.

First published 1990 in Great Britain by
KEVIN MAYHEW LTD
Rattlesden, Bury St Edmunds
Suffolk IP30 0SZ

ISBN 0 86209 125 X

Cover design by Graham Johnstone
Typesetting by Saxon Printing Ltd, Derby
Printed and bound in Great Britain by
The Five Castles Press Limited, Ipswich, Suffolk

CONTENTS

WEEK ONE

John 1:1 – 18

In the beginning was the Word, and the Word was with God, and the Word was God. He was in the beginning with God; all things were made through him, and without him was not anything made that was made. In him was life, and the life was the light of men. The light shines in the darkness, and the darkness has not overcome it.

There was a man sent from God, whose name was John. He came for testimony, to bear witness to the light, that all might believe through him. He was not the light, but came to bear witness to the light.

The true light that enlightens every man was coming into the world. He was in the world, and the world was made through him, yet the world knew him not. He came to his own home, and his own people received him not. But to all who received him, who believed in his name, he gave power to become children of God; who were born, not of blood nor of the will of the flesh nor of the will of man, but of God.

And the Word became flesh and dwelt among us, full of grace and truth; we have beheld his glory, glory as of the only Son from the Father. (John bore witness to him, and cried, "This was he of whom I said, 'He who comes after me ranks before me, for he was before me'.") And from his fullness have we all received, grace upon grace. For the law was given through Moses; grace and truth came through Jesus Christ. No one has ever seen God; the only Son, who is in the bosom of the Father, he has made him known.

Matthew, Mark and Luke begin their Gospels on the soil, and among the people, of the Holy Land. Matthew starts with a family tree; Mark with a Jewish preacher; Luke with a childless Judaean couple. There is something reassuring and familiar about all this. It's as though they were coming to meet us on our own ground, with ordinary, human beginnings to their story.

But John begins his Gospel outside time. He begins it in the mind and heart of God, who was there before there was any world, or any time. You get the feeling, after the other three Gospels, that the centre of gravity suddenly shifts. Where, after all, he is asking, is reality rooted? In the experience of us, of men and women? Or – much more difficult for us to grasp – in the being of God himself, in his will and in his intention?

Where does our story start, the story of the Passion? I am quite convinced that it starts in the unfathomable mercy of God. God made this material universe of ours, one way or another, out of nothing (let's not concern ourselves with the details, whether it was a Big Bang or not… in the end, it makes little difference). And then God made us human beings (let's not concern ourselves with the details, whether it was a slow process or a quick one… in the end, it makes little difference). The main thing is that he made us, and gave us extraordinary gifts of spirit and self-determination, so that we could be, quite consciously, the stewards of his creation; so that we could detect the spark of immortality he had planted in us. And yet, in the very act of creating, he already knew – he must have known – what ambiguous creatures we would be and are. He knew our capacity for waywardness as well as our capacity for love. And already, all that time ago, he was planning our rescue. That is the incredible thing.

This is a far cry, isn't it, from the blood and sweat of Calvary; from the panic of Peter, and the cynicism of Pilate, and the kangaroo courts, and the midday heat and the final prayer of the Good Thief? And yet none of this, in all its detail, none of those things we recall with reverence now, could have taken place without that decision in principle which the Father took at the beginning of time; really, outside time.

Here, then, is the unanswerable question. Why has God this clinging affection for our human race, this unquenchable desire and determination to bring it home to himself? It's a desire which causes God (who is immortal and invisible) to get entangled, himself, in our affairs; to take our flesh, to suffer our condition, to die our death. It seems out of all proportion, doesn't it? Christianity is founded on a breach in the logic of things. How right God is to say, 'My ways are not your ways, my thoughts are not your thoughts.'

I don't understand it because I am not God: I can't see with his eyes or love with his heart. I can only say this: that it seems to me as though, having made us in his own image and likeness – having made us basically spiritual, in other words – he has invested so much in us that he cannot afford to let us go. We are now worth saving at any price – even the price of his Son. And so, 'The Word became flesh, and dwelt among us.'

St John's perspective is right: he sees the story of Christ's passion and death from God's point of view. 'The true light that enlightens every man was coming into the world. He was in the world, and the world was made through him, yet the world knew him not.'

Against this background – that of the eternal plan of God – the story of Our Lord's passion and death has a really awesome quality. If it were a Greek tragedy you were reading, and not the Gospel of Jesus Christ, it would make you hold your breath. Surely, now, after Good Friday, you would say, God must finally obliterate humanity. The only question is, when will he do it? When will Nemesis strike? Because we have taken his divine and sinless Son, his Messenger, and rejected him and mocked him, abused and tortured him, priced him at 30 silver pieces and killed him. 'He came to his own home and his own people received him not.'

I don't know what you can say about a humanity like this. That it's incurably vicious? That it's fatally accident-prone? Because we couldn't have got it more wrong. This is a disaster of cosmic proportions. The crucifixion is like the distillation of all the blindness, foolishness, narrow-mindedness, stubbornness and cruelty: all the dark underside of the human character is here to see.

It is at this point that the Father shows us how different he is from us. 'My ways are not your ways, my thoughts are not your thoughts.' Thank God for that. Because instead of bringing down on humanity the hammer of annihilation, which is what you would have done or I would have done, God takes the cosmic disaster and turns it into a cosmic victory.

For in God's book, you win not by muscle but by love. The love of Christ proves stronger than anything that can be done to him. You have to match on the one hand the *realpolitik* of Annas and Caiaphas, the supercilious might of Rome and Pilate's tribunal, the sadistic cruelty of the mercenary soldiers... against on the other hand Christ's heroism, integrity, self-sacrifice, enduring forgiveness, implicit trust in his Father. Our world says, regretfully, that the nails and the spear win, the meek and innocent man loses. But God replies, 'You're wrong. The weakness of God is stronger than men. My power is made perfect in weakness.' And so Good Friday is followed by Easter Sunday, the crucifixion by the resurrection.

That's why the cross becomes our flag, our standard. We place it on the rooftree of our churches, we install it at the top of mountains; we put it on walls and on desks; we incorporate it in a hundred different logos and emblems and badges, so that, to use an Old Testament expression, it is constantly before our eyes. We are the people who do not believe that might is right. We are the people, to quote St Paul, who believe that God's strength is made perfect in our weakness. You can imagine nothing weaker than Jesus – rejected by the people, sentenced by the occupying power, scourged and crucified. Yet out of this dreadful mess comes the resurrection.

And out of it, too, comes a message from the Father to us. Two messages, in fact. One is, 'You are precious in my eyes. When you look round at the human race, and the pits it digs for itself, and the black passages in its history, you may be tempted to say "We are an unlovable lot." It isn't so. In spite of everything, I love you. So, lift up your heads, claim your dignity – and treat one another with that same dignity.' And the other is, 'Remember where the moral victory lies: not with the bully-boy, the manipulator and the trickster; but with the man or woman of integrity.' And the moral victory is the real victory.

Discussion Topics overleaf.

Discussion Topics

1. There are two ways of thinking of Jesus:
    – as God the Son, Second Person of the Trinity, who came down to earth at the annunciation and took a human body and soul, so that he could die and rise for us;
    – as Jesus of Nazareth, the human son of Mary, to whom the Word of God was united, so that we can rightly say 'Christ is divine.'
    One point of view starts with the divinity of Christ; the other with his humanity. Which do you find easiest?
2. Do we, as Christians, really believe that love is the strongest force? There have been times, after all, when the Church was in a dominant position. At those times she would try to legislate, or even persecute, her enemies out of existence. How do you feel: is it naive not to use muscle, in a good cause? In the name of truth, are all weapons fair?
3. It is wrong to be conceited and smug. But if God loves me as much as he says (and proves, by the sending of Jesus), then I shouldn't treat myself with contempt: I *am* worth something, I *do* have an importance and a dignity. Where is the line between proper love of self, and pure big-headedness?

WEEK TWO

Romans 5:1 – 11

Therefore, since we are justified by faith, we have peace with God through our Lord Jesus Christ. Through him we have obtained access to this grace in which we stand, and we rejoice in our hope of sharing the glory of God. More than that, we rejoice in our sufferings, knowing that suffering produces endurance, and endurance produces character, and character produces hope, and hope does not disappoint us, because God's love has been poured into our hearts through the Holy Spirit which has been given to us.

While we were still weak, at the right time Christ died for the ungodly. Why, one will hardly die for a righteous man – though perhaps for a good man one will dare even to die. But God shows his love for us in that while we were yet sinners Christ died for us. Since, therefore, we are now justified by his blood, much more shall we be saved by him from the wrath of God. For if while we were enemies we were reconciled to God by the death of his Son, much more, now that we are reconciled, shall we be saved by his life. Not only so, but we also rejoice in God through our Lord Jesus Christ, through whom we have now received our reconciliation.

You can hear the story of Christ's Passion on two levels. One is the purely human level. He was an innocent but brave man who fell foul of the forces of the Establishment, and paid the penalty. He annoyed and challenged the religious authorities of his own people. He called their bluff, showed them up before the ordinary folk. They responded as best they knew how – by blackmailing the Roman Governor into disposing of him, getting rid of him, crucifying him. A story, then, about power, and the misuse of it. We're quite at home with the story told on this level – not exactly comfortable with it, because it is a tale of corruption and cruel cynicism on a large scale: but still, we find it all only too familiar, easy to understand.

There is, however, another level which is infinitely more important. It is the level of Christian belief. Here there is another scene, underlying the first. Here the initiative shifts dramatically. We see Christ sacrificing himself, giving himself up for our sake. In this scene, Annas and Caiaphas and Pilate are unimportant; they could have been any other set of interlocking authorities, in any other century. What matters is *why* this heroic self-sacrifice was necessary. What was *really* going on on Good Friday? So we are going to think about the crucifixion in what you might call a theological way. You may think this takes us a long way away from the pain, and the heartbreak, and the tragedy of a very human event. I'll try not to be too technical. After all, we're still dealing with the most loving and caring action in the history of the planet. I certainly don't want to lose sight of that!

From the beginning of time, mankind had carried the burden of its own sin. Conscious, or semi-conscious, of insulting and offending God in so many ways, the human race was impotent to do anything about it. The load of guilt lay upon us like some huge undigested lump; where to put it? What to do with it? How could we ever express to God in an adequate way our regret, our sorrow, our resolution to live henceforth in the light of his face? How could humanity ever unite sufficiently to speak with one voice about all this? It was totally beyond any human capacity. It looked like an alienation which would simply go on and on.

The coming of Jesus is like a watershed: it marks the start of a mended, healed relationship between the human race and God. It is as if God put into *our* hands the means of making the vital gesture which was needed. He allowed the Word, the eternal Son of God, to be human. At last, here was someone with hands and heart free enough to stand before the Father, and by an act more eloquent than any words, express our collective longing. Longing to be forgiven. Longing to be given the means of fighting evil. Longing not to feel separated any more. Longing to be God's intimate family in a way which hadn't been possible since the shadowy, sketchy, mysterious dawn of the Garden of Eden.

I am saying that this gesture of the crucifixion was the appropriate way of atoning for sin. That's a huge thing to say. How could anything so grim be appropriate? Is the Father such a heartless and exacting taskmaster? Or are we rather dealing with what Newman calls, in his hymn, 'O Wisest love'? Without the loving, voluntarily-accepted death of the cross, there could have been no resurrection. And we needed the resurrection more than anything else in the whole history of the world. The resurrection is for us, literally, a matter of life and death.

Still, the first thought that comes to mind is inevitably this: 'Sin must be a truly appalling thing, to need this kind of recompense. It must be much worse than ever I thought. It can't just be a joke for cracking in pubs, or an old-fashioned myth to be seen as some sort of peasant hang-up. It must be real, and ghastly, and sordid beyond words: because the crucifixion was real, and ghastly, and sordid beyond words.'

This is right. Sin is the greatest of all disasters. To offend

God is the ultimate evil. God is the source and inventor of everything that is true or good. To fly in his teeth is to launch yourself into the darkness, like a space-craft perpetually off-course. John, in his Gospel and in his letters, is almost obsessed with this theme of light and darkness. 'In him was life, and the life was the light of men. The light shines in the darkness, and the darkness has not overcome it.' 'This is the message we have heard from him and proclaim to you, that God is light and in him is no darkness at all. If we say we have fellowship with him while we walk in darkness, we lie and do not live according to the truth.' John would be the first to tell us: 'Sin isn't only offensive to God, who deserves better of us than that; it is also self-defeating. It is the ultimate choice of nothing.'

Sin comes from inside us. Matthew relates two sayings of Jesus which are very powerful. 'Out of the abundance of the heart,' says Christ, 'the mouth speaks. The good man out of his good treasure brings forth good, and the evil man out of his evil treasure brings forth evil.' And again, 'Do you not see that whatever goes into the mouth passes into the stomach, and so passes on? But what comes out of the mouth proceeds from the heart, and this defiles a man. For out of the heart come evil thoughts, murder, adultery, fornication, theft, false witness, slander.' Three times Jesus uses that word 'heart'. Your heart is, symbolically, the fount of love. It can also be the fount of ill-will. Sin is the conscious choice, the conscious willing of what you know in your heart to be wrong. Here is the fatal ambiguity of man – that he is capable of this choice, this willing.

A picturesque description might be this: that I was made to be a unit, a harmonious whole. When my free choice goes on the spree, one way, and my conscience goes the other way, I am split in half. I lose my unity. I lose, in every sense, my integrity. And the splitting of me is a grave affair. After all, the splitting of the atom, deceptively small, has cosmic results. So does sin.

Two things occur to me as a result of all this. One is that we should have the self-confidence to consult our conscience, to listen to our conscience, to take notice of it. It isn't an absurd and truncated piece of outmoded equipment: it is what gives you your dignity as a human being and a child of God. It is the deepest part of you that is accessible. It is what makes you who you are, so treat it with respect!

The other is this: you know that very human trick of pushing things under the carpet? We do this with things that just aren't tolerable. We do it with things we cannot bear to look at. Psychologists have more technical terms to describe it, this operation, but even without professional terminology we know what it is, don't we, from our own experience? I find that sometimes people do this with their sins. Some people are constitutionally incapable of ever saying, 'I was wrong', or, 'It was my fault'! They find this 'shadow' side of their life unbearable to contemplate. I would be like this myself... *if* I didn't believe that the crucifixion of Jesus had been a success. But it was a success in this sense, that it achieved what it set out to achieve, which was my forgiveness, and yours. So now I can take the risk of bringing my sinfulness out into the light of day, and looking at it, and not panicking at what I see. It has been allowed for, and atoned for; it is something from which I can recover.

Paul sums it up beautifully in the text from Romans quoted above. 'For if while we were enemies we were reconciled to God by the death of his Son, much more, now that we are reconciled, shall we be saved by his life.'

Discussion Topics overleaf.

Discussion Topics

1. Do you think of sin as the breaking of an external regulation? Or more as a fatal division *inside* you, because instinct and conscience are pulling you in opposite directions? Could a person commit a sin by accident?
2. Some people find it hard to make a moral assessment of their life-style. Do you? Do you think that our human situations are so complicated that analysing them as 'right' and 'wrong' is too simple?
3. Do you think of sin as a regrettable but normal part of life? After all, there have always been dishonesties, injustices, infidelities, cruelties. Or do you see the sinfulness of man as a horrible and unnecessary blight, like the Plague: something to be fought and opposed; something to feel impatient about?
4. To live a happy and fulfilled life, do you need a well-functioning conscience? And if so, does it need training or informing? Or do you think it should work by itself?

WEEK THREE

Matthew 27:27 – 50

Then the soldiers of the governor took Jesus into the praetorium and they gathered the whole battalion before him. And they stripped him and put a scarlet robe upon him, and plaiting a crown of thorns they put it on his head, and put a reed in his right hand. And kneeling before him they mocked him, saying, "Hail, King of the Jews!" And they spat upon him, and took the reed and struck him on the head. And when they had mocked him, they stripped him of the robe, and put his own clothes on him, and led him away to crucify him.

As they went out, they came upon a man of Cyrene, Simon by name; this man they compelled to carry his cross. And when they came to a place called Golgotha (which means the place of a skull), they offered him wine to drink, mingled with gall; but when he tasted it, he would not drink it. And when they had crucified him, they divided his garments among them by casting lots; then they sat down and kept watch over him there. And over his head they put the charge against him, which read, "This is Jesus the King of the Jews." Then two robbers were crucified with him, one on the right and one on the *left. And those who passed by derided him, wagging their heads and saying, "You who would destroy the temple and build it in three days, save yourself! If you are the Son of God, come down from the cross." So also the chief priests, with the scribes and elders, mocked him, saying, "He saved others; he cannot save himself. He is the King of Israel; let him come down now from the cross, and we will believe in him. He trusts in God; let God deliver him now, if he desires him; for he said, 'I am the Son of God'." And the robbers who were crucified with him also reviled him in the same way.*

Now from the sixth hour there was darkness over all the land until the ninth hour. And about the ninth hour Jesus cried with a loud voice, "Eli, Eli, lama sabach-thani?" that is, "My God, my God, why hast thou forsaken me?" And some of the bystanders hearing it said, "This man is calling Elijah." And one of them at once ran and took a sponge, filled it with vinegar, and put it on a reed, and gave it to him to drink. But the others said, "Wait, let us see whether Elijah will come to save him." And Jesus cried again with a loud voice and yielded up his spirit.

There is an hour of the afternoon when it is quite easy to go to sleep. In Latin countries they build this custom into their day. You don't have to be shifty or secretive about it. It's part of life. Everybody's life.

So I was probably being very obstinate and stubborn one day in August, not long ago. I was attending a conference in a Latin American country. The afternoon was beautifully quiet, and most of my colleagues had wisely retired to their rooms. I decided to take advantage of the peace and the silence, and to try to pray a little before the uproar of debate and translation broke out again. I wasn't being pious: just stubbornly different, I suppose.

So I went into the chapel. It was a very simple building, with whitewashed adobe walls and a thatched roof. The roof, I might say, leaked whenever it rained, which was often. But just for the moment it wasn't raining. The earth between the palm trees outside, and in the banana plantations, was steaming in the hot sun, cicadas were whirring away in the bushes, and little lizards were chasing each other up the walls by the altar. There was a torrent of birdsong in the trees.

And suddenly my eyes were riveted on the crucifix which was hanging there on the wall. It wasn't beautiful, graceful, aesthetic, like the kind of carved crucifix you might buy in an Alpine village, or like the exquisite ivory ones the Spaniards used to make. It was plaster, heavy and crude, too big, and painted in primary colours. And what caught my attention most of all were the knees of Christ.

The knees were depicted as cut and bleeding. This makes sense, doesn't it, from what we know? Our Lord had been scourged. He had been forced, in a gravely weakened state, to carry the cross through the streets of Jerusalem and up the hill of execution. The guards who escorted him were anything but gentle. It would be astonishing if he had managed to make this journey without falling, without grazing and bruising his knees.

But I'd never before seen a crucifix which took particular account of the knees of Christ. And this one, by some trick of association, made me think of the times I had hurt my knees. Times as a small boy when I was learning to ride a bicycle, but hadn't yet learned how to dismount. Times in the playground when I had tripped and fallen. Times when my leg had come into violent contact with somebody else's football boot.

The remedy was always the same. I searched out my mother, or a teacher, or some other sympathetic adult, and demanded attention. 'Look what's happened.' It was, after all, a fundamental right of man to have his knee inspected, washed and plastered up before it was pronounced usable again. There was a ritual to be gone through with knees. It was often through our knees, wasn't it, that our parents reassured us, 'I still love you; I do care what happens to you.' A lot of human affection, a lot of tenderness, was expressed in the careful sponging, the kissing better, the dabbing with bits of lint and disinfectant. The care was often out of proportion to the injury. In retrospect it might all seem very sentimental. But how important it was. And is.

There is a legend which isn't scriptural, but which is part of the devotional treasury of Catholics, that Jesus' own Mother met him on the way to Calvary. She would have been conscious of those knees of his. They would have symbolised for her as nothing else the brutality, the gross cruelty of the whole affair. Because he was going to be crucified, his knees didn't matter any longer. Indeed, his feelings didn't matter either. He'd crossed the invisible line between being a person, deserving consideration, and a thing, to be disposed of. He had crossed it when Pilate had washed his hands and handed him over: remember what Matthew tells us in his Gospel... 'They gathered the whole battalion before him. And they stripped him and put a scarlet robe upon him, and plaiting a crown of thorns they put it on his head, and put a reed in his right hand. And kneeling before him they mocked him.' Feelings didn't matter any more. On the Way of the Cross those physically nearest to him, the mercenary soldiers entrusted with his execution, saw him as a job to be finished before tea, so to speak. Here is a large part of the horror of Good Friday. It's that the time for tenderness is over. And when you say that, you have said the final 'No' to somebody else's humanity.

Maybe because I was in Latin America, and because

there were some very poor people just at the end of the drive, my thoughts moved to them, and folk like them. That for many people in the world, too, the time for tenderness is over. They can expect no pity, no reassurance, from anyone. I thought of husbands and fathers picked out of ditches in El Salvador, and whole populations starving on the march in Mozambique, and refugees in wretched camps on the Thai border. How easily we accept that our world is a cruel place. The edge of our indignation is quickly blunted.

It seemed to me then, and it is still my conviction, that the showing of tenderness is very near the heart of what it means to be Christian. And to be part of any system which has renounced tenderness in the name of expediency is the opposite of being Christian. Some people might say that this was absurdly naive; that a certain number of people have to suffer, and that's that. 'But one of them, Caiaphas, who was High Priest that year, said to them, "You know nothing at all; you do not understand that it is expedient for you that one man should die for the people, and that the whole nation should not perish".' Tired, mature, worldly-wise, John's reporting of the dialogue in the Council has a disturbingly modern ring.

At my conference were priests whose people were being massacred by drug-traffickers, shot as a deterrent to others by government troops, tortured as a matter of course before interrogation in the downtown barracks, thrown off their miserable strips of land to make room for highways and high-tech farms, systematically deprived of all medical help unless they could pay for it.

Once upon a time we could have said, with a sigh that exempted us from all responsibility, 'Well, at least, there's none of that going on here.' It's not so easy today, though. So many of the levers of power, political and economic, do lie in unexpected places. We need a worldly wisdom to match that of Caiaphas, but for a different and opposite purpose. We need it to ensure that wherever our influence spreads, there will be tenderness, there will be regard for the individual, there will be respect for human dignity, no man or woman will be expendable, no person will be treated like a thing.

The same Christ who was crucified is on record, in this same Gospel of Matthew from which the extract above is taken, as saying this: that the Kingdom of Heaven will go to those who are tender: feeding the hungry and thirsty, caring for the stranger, the sick, the imprisoned. When we say to him, 'Lord, when did we do this?', he will reply, 'Truly I say to you, as you did it to one of the least of these my brethren, you did it to me.'

Discussion Topics

1. Do you agree that a prisoner condemned to death ceases to be regarded as a person, and just becomes – for others – a 'thing'? Is any crime big or bad enough to justify this, do you think?

2. Every night, we have instant TV news of distant horrors. Do you find your compassion gets exhausted? Have we, each of us, a limited quantity of feeling to spend on others? Or, in a Christian, are pity and mercy and sympathy always available? Should they be?

3. In the modern world, where is the greatest need for sustained tenderness? Which is most important for you – problem-solving, or individual acts of kindness?

WEEK FOUR

2 Corinthians 1:3 – 11

Blessed be the God and Father of our Lord Jesus Christ, the Father of mercies and God of all comfort, who comforts us in all our affliction, so that we may be able to comfort those who are in any affliction, with the comfort with which we ourselves are comforted by God. For as we share abundantly in Christ's sufferings, so through Christ we share abundantly in comfort too. If we are afflicted, it is for your comfort and salvation; and if we are comforted, it is for your comfort, which you experience when you patiently endure the same sufferings that we suffer. Our hope for you is unshaken; for we know that as you share in our sufferings, you will also share in our comfort.

For we do not want you to be ignorant, brethren, of the affliction we experienced in Asia; for we were so utterly, unbearably crushed that we despaired of life itself. Why, we felt that we had received the sentence of death; but that was to make us rely not on ourselves but on God who raises the dead; he delivered us from so deadly a peril, and he will deliver us; on him we have set our hope that he will deliver us again. You also must help us by prayer, so that many will give thanks on our behalf for the blessing granted us in answer to many prayers.

Suffering of some sort is the lot of every man, every woman. This isn't a morbid reflection, it is an experienced fact. It may be physical suffering – injury or illness; it may be mental suffering – anxiety or depression; it may be spiritual suffering – guilt, or crumbling faith. But suffering of some sort is part of the business of being alive. We don't need anyone to prove that to us. Every one of us carries some kind of a cross: more or less willingly, perhaps determined not to make a fuss about it, saying to ourselves and to others, 'What I have to put up with is absolutely nothing compared with what happens in some parts of the world.' So, not complaining... but still suffering.

The reaction of the Christian, when these times of suffering come, is to pray. We may pray a straight prayer of asking: 'Please, God, may this thing go away and leave me in peace.' We may try to resign ourselves to what is unavoidable: 'God, whatever you want is all right by me – but give me more strength, give me some understanding.' We may pray in exasperation a great cry of reproach, like one of the great woman saints of Christian Europe: 'God, if this is how you treat your friends, no wonder you have so few.' But one way or another, we pray.

And as we pray, we begin to sense that we are treading in someone's footsteps. The trail is already blazed. Someone has been there first, and left some signposts. And that is Christ. Because in his Passion he underwent all those things – physical, mental and spiritual suffering. And in his Passion he prayed all those prayers: 'My Father, if it be possible, let this cup pass from me.' 'Nevertheless, not as I will, but as thou wilt.' 'My God, my God, why hast thou forsaken me?'

The suffering of Jesus is a great mystery. The intensity of it. The depth of love and obedience which prompted it. The self-emptying it involved. For this was no play-acting, as some twisted forms of early Christianity maintained. Our Lord could not hold part of himself aloof from pain and misery. He was consumed by it, just as we, on a smaller scale, are consumed by ours. Part of the mystery is this, that the Word made flesh could, as Paul said to the Philippians, empty himself, taking the form of a servant. That he could take a human frame, and being man, submit to the annihilation which is, to all appearances, the fate of every man. How could God the Son do this?

Whatever the answer, the *fact* is a great comfort to me. That Christ has pre-suffered my sufferings. He knows, then, the blackness of them, the grimness of them, the sameness and monotony of them, even the progressive horror of them. There is no feeling which is foreign to him, even the sense of being to blame. Remember the scene in front of Pilate's Palace, with the people, the *ordinary* people, who had welcomed him on Palm Sunday, holding him guilty, seeing him as the great betrayer, demanding his death. Not just scribes and Pharisees, but ones he had reckoned as his friends, they blamed him. How would you or I feel at such a moment? We would feel guilty. Paul said to the Corinthians, 'For our sake he made him sin who knew no sin.'

What makes sense of the total sacrifice of the cross? What could reasonably underlie that awful experience, do you think? Surely, the only explanation is Christ's total resolve to crack the problem of human suffering, to roll it back. And he started with the definitive, ultimate, worst of all human sufferings, which is the loss of eternal life. To protect us from that was his prime objective. To do it he had to penetrate evil to its heart. No cosmetic solution would do. Loss of eternal life is perpetual separation from God; for you and me this would be the final disaster, the loss of meaning to our very existence. To rescue us from this, Jesus voluntarily experiences, on the cross, deep separation from his Father. He plumbs the depths of the thing he is saving us from.

There is a legend – only a legend – that when St Peter

was in Rome, the persecution by the Emperor Nero got so bad that Peter lost his nerve; he packed up and moved out, leaving the City walls on the south side and taking the road to Naples. He had gone a very short distance when he saw someone coming towards him, and as the figure got closer he realised that it was Jesus. Breathless with astonishment he stopped him, and asked, 'Where are you going, Lord?' and Jesus looked at him and said, 'I'm going to Rome, to be crucified again.' Which, as you may guess, shamed Peter into turning back himself, and facing the persecution with new courage. They built a church there, to mark the spot. The church is a reminder of something far more important than the legend. The fact that sometimes, in our flight from suffering, we meet Jesus going the other way – right into the heart of our suffering in order to save us from it.

So suffering, which in my own experience, is sordid, non-productive, a complete waste, begins to take on a new light. Christ links it to love. He shows me how it can express love and create good where previously there was none. I know there is an awful danger of sounding glib about suffering, producing packaged solutions to other people's problems, smug little stereotyped words of comfort which give no comfort at all. And I really don't mean to do that. But as a Christian I still want to say this: I know that even my suffering can be redemptive. Isaiah describes it when he talks about the Suffering Servant who was to come. 'When he makes himself an offering for sin, he shall see the fruit of the travail of his soul.' Christ puts a value on my suffering too: he has raised it up, joined it on to his, given it a saving power for my poor world. 'In my flesh,' again Paul, this time to the Colossians, 'I complete what is lacking in Christ's afflictions for the sake of his Body, that is the Church.'

All right: it is easy enough to talk about suffering when you are not suffering: easy to philosophise about it. At the time, it is hell. Noble thoughts are hard to have. But when I cry out to Christ, risen from the dead, enthroned at his Father's right hand and beyond the reach of suffering, I am nevertheless calling on someone who is marked by what he has been through. Marked physically, perhaps, by the nails and the spear; but, more important, marked personally. The recollection of Gethsemane, of the approach of Judas, of that series of trials, of the final dread-filled confrontation with the crowd, is still on him. The experience of the scourging and the crowning with thorns and the Way of the Cross has not been blotted out, annulled, by the resurrection. He remembers being crucified, and what it was like, with the thieves on either side. So that I am talking to one who can enter into *my* sufferings, small by comparison to his, but still maximum-endurable for me, maybe more than maximum. He knows what it's like. I do not have to spell it out.

Paul wrote his letter to the Corinthians, part of which is given above, as a seasoned sufferer. It is hard to think of a pain, physical, mental, nervous, which he hadn't undergone. He lived under constant threat. He was aware of a large number of ingenious enemies out there on the edge of his life. Paranoia would have been easy for Paul: to see plots and risks and dangers everywhere. Each day, quite objectively, could turn out badly, with stoning or arrest or imprisonment. To be a travelling preacher of the Gospel, back in the first century, was perilous in the extreme. He was scorched, frozen, worn out, let down, disappointed, locked up, beaten, shipwrecked, and eventually executed. And yet he could talk about 'the God of all comfort, who comforts us in all our affliction.' And he could say, 'As we share abundantly in Christ's sufferings, so through Christ we share abundantly in comfort too.' He talks about one of the real low-points of his life, on one of his journeys through Turkey; and he realises now that the sheer hopelessness of it all was to make him rely not on himself, but on God who raises the dead.

Here, I suspect, is the heart of the matter. Our education teaches us to be self-reliant, to be in charge, to be in control of our lives. How deprived we feel if, say, we are sent to hospital! It isn't just that our strength seems to have evaporated. It's also being at the mercy of other people, however well-intentioned, however skilled. It's letting other people make decisions for us. And being told only what is good for us to know, and no more – that sort of thing. Trusting is hard. Surrendering yourself to a process governed by others is agony. It is not in our nature.

And this is the nerve God touches in our suffering. 'Trust me,' he says. 'Against all appearances, and against all the odds. Trust me. Unless you become like little children you cannot enter the Kingdom of Heaven.' And the most notable thing about little children is that they trust their parents. They haven't yet learned to distrust.

Every moment of distress, every hard experience, contains a direct invitation from the Father to trust him. And if, quite out of character, we accept his invitation, and surrender ourselves to him, we find to our astonishment that we are not alone. In the heart of our suffering we find Jesus Christ, and he enables us to say, with him, 'Father, into your hands I commend my spirit.'

Discussion Topics

1. Does suffering bring you closer to God, or make you feel far away from him?
2. Are there some kinds of suffering which make you panic, in case God's strength cannot cope with them, and his Providence is unable to hold you up, sustain you?
3. When you realise that Our Lord has been through the total mill of human suffering, mental and physical, does that change the way you feel about him now? Do you feel that he is immensely wise *because* of his suffering?

Week Five

Luke 11:37 – 54

While he was speaking, a Pharisee asked him to dine with him; so he went in and sat at table. The Pharisee was astonished to see that he did not first wash before dinner. And the Lord said to him, "Now you Pharisees cleanse the outside of the cup and of the dish, but inside you are full of extortion and wickedness. You fools! Did not he who made the outside make the inside also? But give for alms those things which are within; and behold, everything is clean for you.

"But woe to you Pharisees! for you tithe mint and rue and every herb, and neglect justice and the love of God; these you ought to have done, without neglecting the others. Woe to you Pharisees! for you love the best seat in the synagogues and salutations in the market places. Woe to you! for you are like graves which are not seen, and men walk over them without knowing it."

One of the lawyers answered him, "Teacher, in saying this you reproach us also." And he said, "Woe to you lawyers also! for you load men with burdens hard to bear, and you yourselves do not touch the burdens with one of your fingers. Woe to you! for you build the tombs of the prophets whom your fathers killed. So you are witnesses and consent to the deeds of your fathers; for they killed them, and you build their tombs. Therefore also the Wisdom of God said, 'I will send them prophets and apostles, some of whom they will kill and persecute,' that the blood of all the prophets, shed from the foundation of the world, may be required of this generation, from the blood of Abel to the blood of Zechariah, who perished between the altar and the sanctuary. Yes, I tell you it shall be required of this generation. Woe to you lawyers! for you have taken away the key of knowledge; you did not enter yourselves and you hindered those who were entering."

As he went away from there, the scribes and the Pharisees began to press him hard, and to provoke him to speak of many things, lying in wait for him, to catch at something he might say.

Christ, says Paul, is the first-born from the dead; the first of many brothers. He is the leader of the whole of humanity, and the property of us all: we call him 'Our Lord', and that's correct.

So it is that you will find black ebony statues of Jesus, and pictures of Japanese babies in the stable at Bethlehem. There's a blond British Jesus in stained glass at Ely; and in one cathedral high in the Andes, an oil-painting of a perfect Amerindian Holy Family in the house at Nazareth. It is right that it should be so. No race has a monopoly of Jesus. Christ is no one's exclusive property.

But having said that, we have also to say that God did become man at a particular moment in history, in a particular place, as a member of an identifiable society. He could have done it otherwise, but this was the way he chose. He chose to belong to a subject race. He chose to be a man who worked with his hands, not a professional. He chose to have roots in the distant provinces, not the capital. See how the picture builds up. He chose very humble friends and companions.

It would be fair to say that Jesus was a poor man. Not in the sense of being destitute – there is no evidence for that – but in the sense of being powerless: one of the 'anawim', the great ruck of the Hebrew population, little ones, the ordinary folk. Being without pull, without influence, without recourse, without any say in how your life will develop, or the terms of your employment – these things are real poverty. Now of course it is wrong to read the social attitudes of 20th century Western Europe into first century Palestine. People did not feel the same grievances that we feel, and their perception of justice was different. But allowing for that, Jesus was still a poor man: one of the anonymous thousands who were without clout and without consequence.

The poor were ripe for manipulation by the learned. Listen to how Jesus describes it. 'Woe to you lawyers also, for you load men with burdens hard to bear, and you yourselves do not touch the burden with one of your fingers.' (Luke 11:46) It is clear from the Gospels that the scribes, the Pharisees, the High Priests, Pilate and Herod all looked down on the poor for different reasons. Because they were unclean, bad observers of the Law; because they were prone to revolt and had to be kept quiet; because they were so easily exploited. 'They who devour widows' houses, and for a pretence make long prayers. They will receive the greater condemnation.' (Luke 20:47) So there is grievance there, isn't there? Our Lord sides consistently with the defenceless against the fast talkers and the smooth operators.

Jesus had power, but it was power that sprang from his

integrity. He wasn't clergy, so to speak; he had no qualifications, no human mandate. Yet, 'No man ever spoke as this man speaks,' and the crowds listened to him and followed him 'because he spoke with authority.'

The harshest words in the Gospel are reserved for the articulate, the controllers of society. 'Whitened sepulchres' he calls the scribes in Matthew's Gospel; 'Go and tell Herod, that fox...'; and to Pilate, when Jesus is on trial for his life, 'You would have no power over me unless it had been given you from above.'

With his disciples he is quite uncompromising when it comes to power. At the Last Supper, when a dispute arose among them, which of them was to be regarded as the greatest, he says to them, 'The kings of the Gentiles exercise lordship over them; and those in authority over them are called benefactors. But not so with you; rather let the greatest among you become as the youngest, and the leader as one who serves.' And to the mother of James and John, who attempted some insider-dealing on behalf of her sons, 'Places on my right and my left are not mine to give' – as if to say, 'This is a subject which bores me, because it isn't relevant.' It wasn't relevant because, as he was to say to Pilate, 'My kingship is not of this world; if my kingship were of this world, my servants would fight, that I might not be handed over to the Jews; but my kingship is not from the world.' Jostling for position makes no sense, if there is no earthly rule in prospect: and for Jesus, there simply never was.

And once you begin to think along these lines, other things come to mind. Like, for example, the temptations in the desert. Early in his public life, Our Lord is offered a short cut to success: all the kingdoms of the world, with the authority and glory to go with them. A good springboard, you would say, for preaching the Gospel. But no: this isn't the way it is to be, for Our Lord has come to preach the Good News to the poor, and he has set his sights on the captives, the blind, the oppressed, and you can't help these from a great height; only from their own level can you speak to them.

When the Pharisees and the High Priests decided that he should be eliminated, it was as a poor man that they targeted and victimised him. He had no powerful friends to speak for him, and his disciples were easily intimidated. He was vulnerable to the classic forms of persecution. They put agents on the fringes of the crowds he addressed, who made notes of the things he said, reported him to the authorities, compiled a dossier on him, jotting down incriminating words and phrases; so that when the time came for his trial, they could say, 'This man said....' When they handed him over to Pilate, it was really on the grounds that he was a public nuisance: 'He stirs up the people, stops them paying taxes, entitles himself king.' All these are ways in which, through the ages, poor people have been nailed and enmeshed. And yet the irony of it was that if Jesus had been willing to aspire to earthly power, the Jewish people would have supported him in his bid. They could not conceive of a Messiah without nationalistic power; the refusal to accept this was Christ's death warrant.

It was as a poor man that Our Lord was executed. He was humiliated and treated like a slave. He was crucified partly as a warning to others: 'This is what happens if you fail to stay in line, if you buck the system.' And the psalm he quoted with his dying breath contains this act of faith: 'The Lord has never despised nor scorned the poverty of the poor. From him he has not hidden his face, but he heard the poor man when he cried.'

I believe that the great division in today's world is not between East and West, but between the powerful and the powerless. And as I read the Gospel I see Jesus unmistakably ranging himself on the side of the powerless. He does this both in his life and in his death. It is not that he was preaching anarchy or trying to destroy authority, civil or religious; on the contrary, 'Render to Caesar the things that are Caesar's,' and, 'The scribes occupy the seat of Moses, so you must do what they say.' It was simply that he judged those in power very strictly, applied stern principles of fairness to them. The softest spot in his heart was reserved for the beggars, the lepers, the sinners and the no-hopers; and for the thief on the cross at his side he has the most beautiful promise in the whole of scripture: 'This day you will be with me in Paradise.'

There are two lessons here for our world. The first is that if we are deeply committed to Christ, naked ambition is beside the point, because worldly distinction is an illusion. In terms of eternity, it doesn't count. It will be good, then, if we can – even if it falls to us to accept office, and serve the public – remain aloof and detached from the honour it brings. This demands of us a radical conversion, one which, it must be admitted, the Christian world as a whole has never yet managed to make.

The second is this: that there are millions of helpless people in our world. They correspond to the widows and the orphans, the lepers and the blind beggars, the Samaritans and the publicans of Jesus' time. These people are precious to God; woe betide us if through our agency or lack of interest they are ill-treated or victimised. Christ never preached material equality. But he did preach justice. And in our planet today there is a lot of injustice. You and I must work out for ourselves just where we fit into this kaleidoscope of power and powerlessness, of influence and helplessness. We should look at our world with the critical eye of Christ, for only his eye is sure and accurate.

Discussion Topics overleaf.

Discussion Topics

1. Do you find it significant that Jesus was poor, working-class, relatively uneducated, without social leverage or political power? Does this look to you like a deliberate choice?
2. If I am a real disciple of Jesus, how should I think about and relate to the poorest and humblest citizens of my world?
3. What would Jesus say today to the presidents and prime ministers of the world? To the tycoons and captains of industry? To the religious leaders?
4. Where do you see yourself fitting into the spectrum of power and powerlessness, influence and helplessness, justice and injustice?

WEEK SIX

Romans 8:28 – 39

We know that in everything God works for good with those who love him, who are called according to his purpose. For those whom he fore-knew he also predestined to be conformed to the image of his Son, in order that he might be the first-born among many brethren. And those whom he predestined he also called; and those whom he called he also justified; and those whom he justified he also glorified.

What then shall we say to this? If God is for us, who is against us? He who did not spare his own Son but gave him up for us all, will he not also give us all things with him? Who shall bring any charge against God's elect? It is God who justifies; who is to condemn? Is it Christ Jesus, who died, yes, who was raised from the dead, who is at the right hand of God, who indeed intercedes for us? Who shall separate us from the love of Christ? Shall tribulation, or distress, or persecution, or famine, or nakedness, or peril, or sword? As it is written,

"For thy sake we are being killed all the day long;
We are regarded as sheep to be slaughtered."
No, in all these things we are more than conquerors

through him who loved us. For I am sure that neither death, nor life, nor angels, nor principalities, nor things present, nor things to come, nor powers, nor height, nor depth, nor anything else in all creation, will be able to separate us from the love of God in Christ Jesus our Lord.

When Jesus was dying on the cross, the centurion pierced his side with a spear and, John tells us, water and blood flowed out. With this detail, John is reminding us of something hugely important. The water *of baptism* gets its power from the crucifixion. So does the *Blood of Christ* received in the eucharist. The life of Christians today is thus intimately linked to the sacrifice of Christ on the cross.

And when John says that Our Lord bowed his head and gave up his spirit, he is saying two things. One – simply, that Our Lord died. But also that from the cross he sent his Holy Spirit into the world. The Spirit who lives in our hearts. The Spirit who enables us to believe. The Spirit who triggers off prayer in us, who prays inside us. The Spirit who is the soul and the life of Christians, and of the whole Church – he was breathed forth from the cross. That's what John is saying: *the cross gives life.*

John writes about the crucifixion, but he already knows about the resurrection when he writes. And he knows the effect the resurrection will have on the followers of Jesus. Baptism and the eucharist will unite them to the risen Christ. As he writes, these things are already happening, all round him.

Yes, for all of us, but more consciously for those of us who belong, in whatever way, to the Church, the resurrection is a continuing experience. When I am baptized into God's family, I experience the resurrection. When I am fed and forgiven by God, I experience the resurrection. When the word of scripture finds a home in me, and inspires me, I experience the resurrection. It is going on all the time. The resurrection is ours. Why? Because, as Paul says in the passage from Romans quoted above, we are conformed to the image of Jesus. He is our elder brother. Where he goes, we follow.

So all the priorities of the pagan world are stood on their head. Things which previously looked so frightening – tribulation, distress, persecution, famine, nakedness, peril, sword, death itself – all these things are paper tigers. Because Jesus Christ takes us by the hand, as his younger brothers and sisters, and says, 'Stay close to me, and I will take you through all this, and bring you safely out the other side. Because I've been there, and I know the way.' In all these things, then, we are more than conquerors. Nothing to fear.

When, as a priest, I have to officiate at a funeral, I can still be profoundly moved. Even after 30 years, I am not proof against emotion. Especially if it is the funeral of a child, or of someone badly needed by their family and desperately missed; or of the victim of a sudden, tragic death. And yet, with the sadness, there goes a deep conviction. I know that there is something so noble and so deep about the human spirit that it cannot be disposed of at a graveside or in a crematorium. You can't snuff out a human consciousness, a human intelligence, just like that.

That's a pretty unformed hunch, you might say: just a gut-feeling. In fact it is the resurrection of Christ which gives shape to this feeling. It is fascinating to listen to the words of people much nearer to the Easter experience than we are: some of our forefathers in faith. Leo the Great, for instance, writing in the fifth century: 'By dying, Christ submitted to the laws of the underworld, but by rising again he destroyed their power; and so he broke the uninterrupted sequence of death and made temporary what was eternal.'

'Made temporary what was eternal.' Do I really mean that? Do I really mean that a funeral, which looks so permanent and final, is only a temporary arrangement? Yes, that is exactly what I do mean. 'I am the resurrection and the life,' says Jesus, 'He who believes in me, even if he is dead, shall live, and all who live and believe in me, will never die.'

Our Christian ancestors caught and relayed the full power of this fundamental Christian teaching. Listen to Augustine, writing just before Leo: 'Who can doubt that he will give the saints (that's us) his life, since he has already given them his death? Why is human weakness slow to believe that men will one day live with God?' And another preacher, an anonymous one, puts these words into the mouth of Christ: 'I command you, awake, sleeper. I have not made you to be held a prisoner in the underworld. Arise from the dead: I am the life of the dead. Arise, O Man, work of my hands, arise, you who were fashioned in my image. Rise, let us go hence; for you in me and I in you, together we are one undivided person.'

What a totally liberating thing this is: to know that the tide of life is stronger than the tide of death, because by the cross and resurrection of Christ, God has turned the tide.

In the Gospel account he turns the tide with faultless timing. The resurrection does not become apparent immediately after the death of Jesus. God leaves time for the dust to settle. The body is buried, and the sabbath comes. The sabbath gives time to the High Priests and the scribes to breathe a sigh of relief: their major irritant and threat is gone for good. It gives time to Pilate to congratulate himself on having done the only politically possible thing, and having avoided an uprising with very little bloodshed. It gives time to the apostles to bite on the hard bullet of despair, and wonder how to refashion their shattered lives. It gives time to the other disciples of Jesus, like the ones he would meet on the road to Emmaus, to share their overwhelming disappointment: 'We had thought he was the one who would save Israel.' It gives time to all these people to come regretfully or otherwise to this conclusion: as far as Jesus was concerned, Calvary was the last word. Finis, the end.

Then, and only then, does God prove them all wrong. In the dawning of Easter Sunday comes the dawning realisation. It spreads like the ripples on a pond. He is alive. Why look among the dead for one who is alive? He has appeared to Simon. He has appeared to the eleven apostles. He is again a power to be reckoned with, but this time indestructible.

And Paul, in his letters, doesn't stop with the resurrection. Writing to the Romans he assures them of the *continuing* care of Our Lord for them, and for all his people. Christ was raised from the dead, and now he is at the right hand of God, interceding for us. A startling thought: that the Son of God holds my interests, my welfare, my eternal destiny, close to his heart, and intercedes for me. Looking back he can see me far, far behind him on the trail – an indifferent disciple, only intermittently faithful, easily tempted off course by the siren voices of my world – but still his brother; and therefore beloved. Neither death, nor life, nor angels, nor principalities, nor things present, nor things to come, nor powers, nor height, nor depth, nor anything else in all creation, will break that bond.

Discussion Topics overleaf.

Discussion Topics

1. How, thinking of the resurrection, would you as a
    Christian comfort a bereaved and lonely person?
2. When you think of Jesus, do you always do so in
    terms of the Gospel images – the crib, Nazareth,
    Galilee, Jerusalem, Calvary – or can you relate to him
    as he is *now*, enthroned at his Father's right hand,
    Lord, interceding for us, because he has risen from
    the dead?
3. The Good News of the Gospel is above all the good
    news of the resurrection. The liturgy we celebrate is
    above all a celebration of Easter. In your experience,
    do sermons and services in church reflect the
    colossal hope, joy and relief contained in the words
    'he is not here – he has risen'?
4. Do you agree with this statement: that the
    resurrection shows above all that our God is a God of
    life, not death; that he loves life, loves giving life;
    and therefore anything *we* can do to give life,
    enhance the quality of people's lives, struggle with
    them against the threats of death and misery... all
    this is a way of prolonging the resurrection into our
    age?

Footprint

Western Canada Handbook

Matthew Gardner & Alison Bigg

If I had known what it was like I wouldn't have been content with a mere visit. I 'd have been born here.

Stephen Butler Leacock,
My Discovery of the West

1st edition

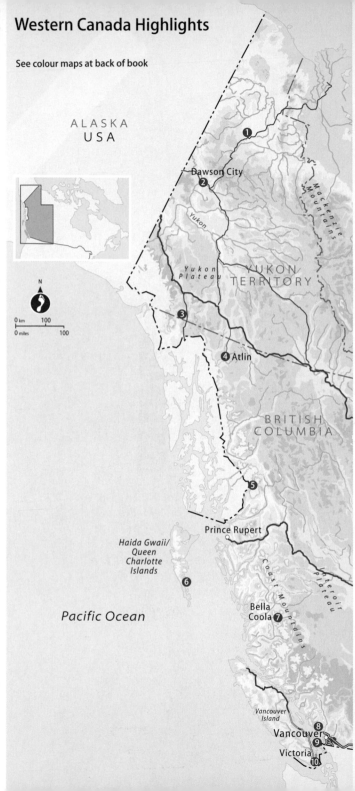

Western Canada Highlights

See colour maps at back of book

1 Dempster Highway
The last great frontier road to the frozen north

2 Dawson City
Site of history's biggest Gold Rush, preserved as a living Wild West museum

3 Tatshenshini whitewater rafting
The ultimate trip down a pristine river

4 Atlin
A remote, ramshackle frontier-style village in a stunning setting

5 Bear Glacier
Eerie blue ice-tongue, lapping at a road lined with icefields, waterfalls and hanging glaciers

6 Gwaii Haanas National Park
Haida villages and totem stands on this remote and magical island

7 Bella Coola
Gateway to a wildlife-filled wilderness, reached via the breathtaking Discovery Passage

8 UBC Museum of Anthropology
An overwhelming collection of Northwest Coast Native carvings

9 Cortes Island
The quintessential Gulf Island: beautiful, laid-back and friendly

ALASKA USA

Dawson City

Yukon

Yukon Plateau

YUKON TERRITORY

Mackenzie Mountains

BRITISH COLUMBIA

Prince Rupert

Haida Gwaii/ Queen Charlotte Islands

Pacific Ocean

Coast Mountains

Plateau

Bella Coola

Vancouver Island

Vancouver

Victoria

N

0 km   100
0 miles   100

⑩ Victoria Inner Harbour
Atmospheric, picturesque and lined with grand buildings

⑪ Fraser Canyon
A tumultuous canyon of churning water, and a road that clings to the sheer rock face

⑫ Naramata
A charming base for enjoying the Okanagan's climate, wineries, orchards and beaches

⑬ Nelson, Kaslo and New Denver
Three pretty, old mining towns in a beautiful area offering great outdoor pursuits

⑭ Waterton Lakes National Park
Landscapes and Prairie views, and hiking to rival the Rockies

⑮ Calgary Stampede
The ultimate Wild West extravaganza: 10 days of non-stop hoe-down

⑯ Drumheller
Mind-boggling Badlands scenery coupled with one of the world's finest dinosaur museums

⑰ Icefields Parkway
230 km of lofty snow-capped peaks and vast glaciers

Contents

The Yukon

Northern British Colombia

Alberta

Canadian Rockies

South Interior BC

Vancouver Island

Vancouver

A foot in the door

Amethyst Lakes (right) The lakes mirror the
wilderness mountains of Jasper National Park
Science World (below) A suitably futuristic venue for
Vancouver's science museum

The Drumheller Badlands (above)
Forbidding yet fascinating, this bizarre
landscape entwines sandstone,
mudstone and ironstone
Stanley Park (right) The largest
urban park in Canada breathes life
into Vancouver
Dempster Highway (previous
page) Driving along this 740-km
frontier road into the chill of the Arctic
circle is not for the faint hearted

Introducing Western Canada

Take an area bigger than Mexico and sprinkle sparingly with fewer people than there are in Switzerland, tucking almost all of them into one small corner. Now cover the vast remaining wilderness with row upon row of lofty ice-capped mountains, huge lakes and mighty rivers, heavily treed forests, broad valleys and plateaux, and wide-open prairie-land. For sheer variety, throw in some bizarre moonscape Badlands, steep-sided canyons, glaciers and icefields, Arctic tundra, even the odd patch of cactus-dotted desert. Now decorate the edge with a lush, convoluted, weather-beaten coastline punctuated by long, narrow fjords and coated with islands of all shapes and sizes. Leave in the melting pot of modern history for little more than a century, and serve: Western Canada.

The essence of this Brave New World is its freshness and sheer size. It is one of the last easily accessible places to experience the planet in its wild and pristine state, where ancient trees still stand firm against fields, roads and cities, and numerous creatures have the space to survive. Nature still reigns supreme here, and she flaunts her versatility and overwhelming beauty as if in celebration.

With a few notable exceptions, the region's small towns are undeserving of their surroundings, choked with the downside of newness: strip-malls, megastores and tasteless chain restaurants. This land's history is above all in the culture of the First Nations and the many gold rushes. The people, however, display a distinctive 'West Coast' character. Humbled and clearly delighted by their sublime surroundings, Western Canadians tend to be polite, friendly, cheerful and laid-back. Politically liberal, they're tolerant of homosexuality and marijuana, opposed to oppression, war and the corporate culture. They favour fresh, organic food, smoke little, and take full advantage of the exceptional scope for outdoor pursuits their home offers. All this makes travel here easy, safe and relaxing. Thanks to the weak dollar, it's also surprisingly affordable.

Highlights

Slices of life Say 'Western Canada' and most people conjure images of moose and snow-capped peaks. Wildlife and mountain scenery abound, but there are many less obvious and equally rewarding slices to this pie. For starters, Vancouver, the obvious point of entry, is a genuine meeting place of East and West, with cosmopolitan neighbourhoods great beaches and a location to die for. Victoria's mild climate belies the frozen north cliché, adding gorgeous flower gardens to its English-style picturesque charm. In summer, the whole coast is a playground for kayakers, sailors and beach-bums, with plenty of whale-watching and some of the world's best diving. On the Gulf Islands, an exceptionally laid-back pace has attracted an unusual blend of artists, hippies, eccentrics, draft-dodgers and pot-growers. The biggest surprise is the Okanagan, which gets more sun and higher temperatures than most famous resorts to the south. Hills covered in wineries, orchards and sagebrush slope down to beaches heaving with bronzed bathers. A spirit similar to the Gulf Islands is also found in the West Kootenays, which harbours a string of attractive former mining communities plus the odd ghost town and several hot springs. To the east there's cowboy culture, Badlands, Buffalo jumps and dinosaurs. To the north, frontier roads built for goldrushers lead through increasingly broad horizons to the Yukon. Here the sun shines at midnight, northern lights dance, the landscape explodes into colour in late summer and strange volcano-shaped frost heaves dot the icy plains.

Cowboys & Indians Before the European takeover, half of Canada's entire aboriginal population lived in a relatively small area on the Pacific Northwest Coast, speaking over 16 distinct languages. These were North America's most highly evolved civilizations, their complex social structures supporting a whole class of skilled artists whose works are considered as fine as those of any aboriginal people in the world. As well as experiencing first hand the increasingly respected spiritual, ecological and holistic beliefs of the region's First Nations, there are endless opportunities to witness some superb carving. Remote abandoned villages flanked by rows of totem poles can be visited, along with sites where Plains Indians drove thousands of buffalo over a cliff face, or etched the mysterious symbols of their vision quests onto scattered rocks. All are welcome at First Nations' pow-wows to celebrate the games, gambling, food, drumming and dancing of a living culture.

For those more attracted to the cowboy side of things, Southern Alberta and the Cariboo are still the real McCoy, with working ranches offering visitors the chance to get on a horse, don a big hat, ride the dusty plateau, and help out at a branding. There are big annual rodeos in venues like Vancouver and Williams Lake, but the ultimate cowboy hoe-down is the 10-day Calgary Stampede.

The Wild West Western Canada's modern era may date back little more than a century, but that's a century of vibrant history nonetheless. The West was won by adventurers and pioneers, their stories the stuff of legend and boys-own annuals. Explorers travelling by foot and canoe cut across great swathes of unknown, uncharted land; the prototype 'mounties' marched halfway across the world's second largest country to confront a bunch of liquor-peddling outlaws; and a series of gold rushes, including the greatest stampede of all time, led hundreds of thousands of hopefuls on an epic quest to the northwest hinterland. Such events are still so recent that their strong flavour lingers in the communities they helped to create. Upstaging the ghost towns and reconstructed 'living museums' is Dawson City, the ultimate boomtown, which has been preserved in its Wild West condition, complete with boardwalk streets, clapboard houses and saloons.

Totem poles *(left)* Originally totems portrayed actual characters, often enemies of the family, who were depicted to provoke ridicule and contempt from those passing by

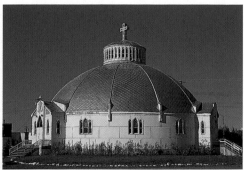

Igloo church *(top)* This unusual house of worship in Inuvik is a remote example of Canada's communion of cultures
Lassoing in Alberta *(above)* Cowboys and country and western are the name of the game in Alberta
Nisga'a Lava Bed Park *(left)* This striking longhouse at Vetter Creek is the park headquarters
Elk *(next page)* You are most likely to see elk wandering through campgrounds in the Rockies or grazing in northern wetlands

Whistler *(right) As the largest ski area in North America,
Whistler flags the way for international competitions*
Black bear *(below) These timid animals are fast on their
feet, travelling at speeds of up to 55 kmph*

Killer whales *(above) These
year-round residents of the West
Coast can often be seen from the
shore of Vancouver Island*
Lake Louise *(right) Taking a
leisurely trip across the Rockies'
star attraction*
Kaslo *(next page) The ruggedly
beautiful West Kootenays are not on
the way to anywhere*

In the raw

The Rocky Mountains range is one of the natural wonders of the world. Its jagged **Happy trails**
peaks, sheer rock walls, alpine meadows, tumbling waterfalls and pristine aquamarine lakes make visitors want to laugh, cry, drool, and never leave. Yet in Western Canada, a handful of other ranges dare to rival the Rockies' supremacy, and a dozen parks
offer scenery to challenge anything you'll see there, with far fewer people. The way to
explore this wonderland is by hiking. Well-maintained trails of all lengths lead deeper
into the wilderness, accessing even more knee-trembling views. Taking a tent and
camping in the bush is an essential part of the experience. Equally celebrated hikes
lead past ancient trees through the rugged temperate rainforests of Vancouver Island.
If your legs aren't up to the challenge, let a horse do the work.

In winter, the endless mountains provide Western Canada with ski hills that are **Off piste**
cheaper, less crowded and more numerous than anything the Alps has to offer, covering the full spectrum from vast world-class resorts like Whistler, to friendly little local
hills that are unlikely to intimidate even a beginner. This region has pioneered
snowboarding from the start, and has some of the best backcountry, cat- and
heli-skiing in the world. There's also ice-skating, dog-sledding, ice-climbing,
snow-mobiling, tobogganing, and ice-fishing. Certain waterfall-fed canyons in the
Rockies are at their best in winter, when they're transformed into eerie sculpted
palaces of blue ice.

For anyone interested in outdoor pursuits, this is a high-adrenalin heaven. Mountain **Convivial**
bikers will find some of the most exciting terrain of their lives. Places like Squamish **pursuits**
offer hundreds of challenging routes for rock climbers in sublime surroundings.
Mountaineers will find remote peaks that nobody has yet conquered. Caving, wind-
surfing, paragliding, bungee-jumping… it's all here. Even the golf courses are gaining
international recognition.

As for water sports, both the kayak and canoe were invented by Canada's First
Nations. Sea-kayaking is still the ultimate way to explore the hundreds of little islands
that surround Vancouver Island, camping alone in remote spots. For maximum
excitement, there are whitewater rafting trips down several crazy rivers. And the
Georgia Strait region has been named the world's second best destination for scuba
diving, thanks to its clear water and abundant, oversized marine life.

Western Canada is dominated by its charismatic animal population. In the mountain **Of moose**
parks, it's not unusual for a giant elk or two to saunter calmly through the camp- **& men**
ground; bighorn sheep hang around in clusters by the roadside, trying to provoke
accidents and black bears scurry around eating berries, trying to ignore the humans. If
you're lucky (or unlucky), you'll see one of their brown cousins.

With some planning, more extensive wildlife encounters are possible. Brackendale
receives the world's biggest annual congregation of bald eagles. In late summer,
rivers and creeks turn red as millions of salmon battle their way from ocean to birthplace. Each spring, some 24,000 grey whales migrate along the West Coast, and orca
(killer whales) are easily seen, even from Downtown Victoria. Out in remote forests,
the intrepid seek a glimpse of rarer creatures: cougars, wolverines, lynx and bobcats,
the elusive white kermodei bear.

Essentials

Planning your trip

Where to go

Western Canada is vast, so if your time is limited you'll need to home in on exactly what you want from your trip. If you try to squeeze in too much you'll end up spending all your time on the road.

Vancouver is far and away the easiest, most convenient starting point, and also represents a great year-round destination in its own right. If you want to concentrate on the Rockies, however, you would be well advised to arrive in Calgary. The direction in which you should travel the loops described below depends a lot on timing. Combining this and the following section with the calendar of events on page 42 will hopefully help you to get the most out of your trip.

One week With just a week, you definitely have to focus on one area. For a taste of the Gulf Islands plus two very different but equally enticing towns, hop from Vancouver to Victoria via Galiano and Salt Spring Islands. You might have time to squeeze in a hike along the East Sooke or Juan de Fuca trails. For the best of outdoor pursuits, take the Sea to Sky Highway (No 99) from Vancouver to the Coast Mountains around Squamish, Garibaldi Park and Whistler. Those with their own wheels could return via the dramatic Fraser Canyon. For big trees, whale-watching, hot springs, endless beaches, sea kayaking and a lively seaside scene, head straight to Tofino from Vancouver. And if you move fast, you might be able to squeeze in a trip to Gabriola Island from Nanaimo.

Alternatively, fly into Calgary and spend the whole week in the Rockies. Concentrate on Banff, Lake Louise and Yoho, but try to drive as far north as the Columbia Icefield. If you are lured to the north, you could take an internal flight to Whitehorse, hire a vehicle and drive a wonderfully scenic loop of the Yukon, including Kluane National Park, the Top of the World Highway, Dawson City, the Dempster Highway as far as the Tombstone Mountains, then back to Whitehorse on the Klondike Highway.

Two or three weeks With two weeks or more, you could combine the above Gulf Islands and Tofino trips. Between the two, Chemainus is worth a stop. Return to Vancouver via Nanaimo, or if time allows continue north to Courtenay, catch a ferry to Powell River, and drive south along the Sunshine Coast. Alternatively, combine either of these coastal trips with a week in the Coast Mountains. Depending on how much driving you want to do and how fast you move, it would also be possible to see a lot of British Columbia's Southern Interior. From Vancouver, take the Sea to Sky Highway or Fraser Canyon routes to Salmon Arm, then spend some time in the wineries, orchards and beaches of the Okanagan, returning via Highway 3. Or continue on Highway 1 to Revelstoke, head south through the West Kootenays, and back on Highway 3, maybe getting a taste of the Okanagan on the way. With an open-jaw ticket flying out of Calgary, you could get a taste of the Coast Mountains, Okanagan or West Kootenays *and* the Rockies.

From Calgary, you could easily spend all of your time in the Rockies. Work north from Banff to the Columbia icefield, then on the way back down do the Lake Louise-Yoho-Kootenay Park loop. A great longer loop, also offering a taste of BC, would involve driving the whole Icefields Parkway to Jasper, then heading west to Mount Robson, south to Kamloops via Wells Gray Park, then back on Highway 1 via Revelstoke and Yoho Park. Should a spare day or two arise, take the excursion from Calgary to the Badlands and Dinosaur Museum at Drumheller. The Yukon loop described above would make a great two- or three-week trip. If time allows, add a short canoe trip, or a diversion to Haines, Alaska or Atlin, BC.

This is the right amount of time to do justice to Western Canada. You could do the **coastal loop** described above (Gulf Islands-Victoria-Tofino-Courtenay-Sunshine Coast), then take an interesting tour of the **Southern Interior** including, for example, the Coast Mountains and Okanagan. Or work to the north of Vancouver Island, take the **Inside Passage** up the ruggedly beautiful West Coast to Prince Rupert; visit Haida Gwaii (Queen Charlotte Islands) and take a kayak tour to abandoned First Nations villages and stands of totem poles; then hurry across on the Yellowhead Highway to Mount Robson and Jasper; drive through the Rockies to Banff, then back to Vancouver taking in whatever parts of the Southern Interior most appeal. The even more ambitious could continue north from Prince Rupert to Skagway on an Alaska ferry, do the above tour of the Yukon, then drive south on the Cassiar Highway, taking a diversion to see the glaciers on the way to Stewart.

Here's a dream **inland loop** to think about: drive Highway 3 to Osoyoos, then head north through the Okanagan Valley to Vernon; head east to Nakusp, do the West Kootenays loop of New Denver-Slocan Valley-Nelson-Kaslo-New Denver, then return to Nakusp and continue north to Revelstoke; drive east to the Rockies, then north up the Icefields Parkway to Jasper; return to Vancouver via Mount Robson, Wells Gray Park, Kamloops, and the Sea to Sky Highway.

For an **Alberta-based loop**, drive from Calgary to Drumheller, south to the Dinosaur Park, then Lethbridge, and take in Head-Smashed-In Buffalo Jump, Cardston and Waterton Lakes Park; then cross the Crowsnest Pass and head north through the East or West Kootenays, finally looping back to the Rockies. A month in the **Yukon** would allow you to do some hikes in Kluane National Park and the Tombstone Mountains, and take a longer canoe trip such as the two-week paddle up the Yukon River, or drive the Dempster Highway to Inuvik and take a trip further into the frozen North.

With this amount of time you can afford to be ambitious. Try to combine those elements presented above in a way that gives you a taste of everything. The following are some of the highlights you could include, presented as a giant clockwise loop. Spend some time in **Vancouver**. Be sure to visit the UBC Museum of Anthropology. Cross to **Vancouver Island**, taking in a couple of the Gulf Islands. In Victoria, you can enjoy the gardens, the Inner Harbour, and the Museum of BC. Maybe take a diversion west to have dinner at Sooke and hike either the East Sooke or Juan de Fuca trail. Head to Pacific Rim National Park, maybe stopping in Chemainus and Gabriola Island. From Tofino do the whale-watching/hot springs cove tour, hike through old-growth forest on Meares Island, go beach-combing on Long Beach and kayaking in either Clayoquot or Barkley Sound. Think about reserving a place on the tough but popular West Coast Trail. Back on the East Coast, go hiking in Strathcona Provincial Park, and visit Denman and Hornby or preferably Quadra and Cortes Islands. Snorkel with the salmon at Campbell River. Head to the north of the island and go killer whale-watching from Telegraph Cove. If you're ambitious you could do the Cape Scott hike from near Port Hardy.

Take the Inside Passage to **Prince Rupert** and the north. Visit **Haida Gwaii** (Queen Charlotte Islands) for an eye-opening introduction to the Haida First Nation. Either take an Alaska ferry north to Skagway, or drive east. If choosing the latter, take a diversion up the Nass Valley from Terrace to see the Nisga'a Memorial Lava Bed Park. Visit the First Nations sites around the Hazeltons, then backtrack to take the spectacular **Cassiar Highway** north. Be sure to take the detour to Stewart to see the Bear Glacier. In season, go to Hyder to see bears fishing for salmon. In the **Yukon**, drive the loop described above, taking detours to Atlin, Haines, the Dempster at least as far as the Tombstone Mountains, and maybe to quaint Keno City. Be sure to do at least one canoe trip as well as rafting the Tatshenshini River. Spend some time in the Gold Rush capital of Dawson City.

If you take the ferry to Skagway, drive south from the Yukon on the Cassiar, otherwise, for variety, take the less interesting **Alaska Highway**, stopping at the wonderful

Liard Hot Springs. On either road, drive south to Jasper and spend at least a month in the **Rockies**, including the Yoho-Golden-Radium-Kootenay loop. For the best of **Alberta**, head over to **Calgary** and do the loop mentioned above through Drumheller, Dinosaur Park, Lethbridge, Head-Smashed-In Buffalo Jump, Cardston and Waterton Lakes Park. From there you could head up through Kananaskis Country back to Calgary, or over the Crowsnest Pass into BC.

Either way, it is impossible to see all the highlights of BC's **Southern Interior**, and even taking in a few will involve a lot of backtracking. If you don't mind lots of driving, here's a dream route from Waterton Lakes: follow Highway 3 west, stopping to enjoy Fernie and maybe Fort Steele. At Creston, take the scenic route up the East Shore of Kootenay Lake, and make a diversion to **Nelson**, which is worth a few days. Backtrack northeast to Kaslo, then through Sandon to New Denver and north to Nakusp, where you can enjoy the hot springs. Continue north to **Revelstoke** and west to Salmon Arm and the **Shuswap**. In season, be sure to catch the salmon run up Adams River. Head south through the **Okanagan Valley** to Osoyoos or Keremeos, maybe spending some time in Cathedral Park close to the latter. Take Highway 3 west to Hope, then loop up the **Fraser Canyon** to Lillooet and down the Sea to Sky Highway, finishing off with the glorious **Coast Mountains** before returning to **Vancouver**.

A winter loop Visitors coming to Western Canada in winter are here to ski or snowboard. Bearing that in mind, here's a loop that takes in most of the best hills. Start in Vancouver, which has three hills, and drive the two hours to North America's number one resort at **Whistler** (or save this for last). Back in Vancouver, head east on Highway 3 to the Okanagan, where there are good hills close to **Penticton**, **Kelowna** and **Vernon**. Continue north to pick up Highway 1 at Salmon Arm, then east to **Revelstoke** and **Rogers Pass**, two areas particularly noted for their backcountry, cat- and heli-skiing. Then follows a trio of excellent hills: the Kicking Horse Resort at **Golden**, **Lake Louise** and **Sunshine Village** close to Banff. There's also first-class Nordic skiing at **Canmore**.

Double back and through Kootenay Park to Highway 95, where **Invermere** and **Kimberley** both have good hills. Far better is **Fernie**, well worth the 87-km diversion east from Cranbrook. Backcountry fiends should head west again to the **Creston-Salmo Pass**, and then **Whitewater** is on the Salmo-Nelson road. The area around Kaslo is regarded by experts as one of *the* backcountry skiing Meccas, with plenty of operators offering cat- and heli-skiing at resorts such as Retallack. Head west again on Highway 3, taking a diversion to the unmissable ski-bum village of Rossland and Red Mountain. There's good Nordic skiing nearby at Nancy Greene and Poulson Passes. On the way back to Vancouver, you can grab one last cross-country excursion in Manning Park.

When to go

Canada's high season is between Victoria Day (third Monday in May) and Labour Day (first Monday in September), with many sights and visitor centres remaining closed for the rest of the year. Most hikes in the Rockies and other mountain regions are only snow-free between July and September. At these times prices for accommodation are naturally higher, and it is usually advisable to book ahead. Ferries to Vancouver Island and the Gulf Islands, and the longer passages up the West Coast, tend to be overly burdened at these times and should also be booked ahead. An advantage of the summer months is the extended hours of daylight, especially up in the Yukon, where the sun barely sets at all around the summer solstice (June 21).

The height of summer has its disadvantages, however. Many places are booked solid and overrun with tourists. The Rockies in particular are packed to capacity, and gaggles of motor-homes clog the highways north, where short nights also prevent you from seeing the wonderful northern lights. The best time for both these areas is mid-August to September when trails are still open and the larches are turning golden in the mountains, while in the Yukon the onset of autumn brings the most spectacular colours. Spring is a good time for visitors concentrating on the coast as the blossoms are out in Victoria and Vancouver, and the whales are migrating past Tofino.

Winter in Canada is a different matter entirely. Tourism is still very much alive, but attracting a different group of people: those who come to ski. Canada offers some of the best, most affordable skiing in the world, as well as many other snowbound activities. Most sights are closed in winter and transportation is slow and arduous. Late February to March are the best months for skiing, as

Climate table ◀

	Average temp (°C)			
	Jan	*Apr*	*Jul*	*Oct*
Banff	-9	3	15	5
Calgary	-9	4	16	6
Castlegar	-2	8	20	8
Edmonton	-13	4	16	5
Inuvik	-28	-13	14	-7
Jasper	-10	4	16	6
Kamloops	-4	9	21	9
Kelowna	-4	8	19	7
Lethbridge	-8	6	18	7
Port Hardy	3	7	14	9
Prince George	-9	5	15	5
Prince Rupert	1	6	13	8
Vancouver	3	9	17	10
Victoria	3	8	16	10
Whitehorse	-18	0	14	1

Essentials

the days are getting longer and warmer but the snow is still at its best. Vancouver has its own hills, and makes an excellent year-round destination.

Climate

The weather in Western Canada, particularly BC, is extremely changeable and very much a local affair. Each region has an exact relation to its surrounding topography meaning more or less rain. The Okanagan and Thompson Valleys, for instance, are so dry as to be nearly desert, yet can get very cold in winter. At the other extreme, the West Coast receives copious amounts of rain year-round, but is blessed with Canada's mildest winters and earliest springs. Weather in the mountains is liable to change dramatically several times within a single day, running the full gamut from blazing sunshine to snow, even in July. As a rule, the further north you go the harsher the winters, but Alberta shares the inordinately cold winters of the Prairies to the east. Many roads close entirely during the winter, notably most of the Icefields Parkway from Banff to Jasper.

Calendar

See also the list of festivals on page 43

January: bald eagles congregate in Brackendale near Squamish.
Late February to March: best skiing.
March to April: best time to see the migration of 22,000 Pacific grey whales past the West Coast. Victoria and Vancouver gardens in full spring bloom.
July to mid-September: best time to see orca whales, especially in Johnstone Strait near Telegraph Cove. Also best time for mountain hiking.
Late August to September: stunning autumn colours in the Yukon.
September to October: peak of the salmon run.

Tours and tour operators

There are countless companies offering tours in Western Canada, most of them specializing in various outdoor pursuits. Operators can be found via the more general websites listed below under Finding out more, but for an excellent overview with many links, check out **www.adventuretours-bc.com**

Adventure tours

About the most comprehensive operator is *Kanata Adventure Specialists*, www.canadian-adventures.com Among other activities, they offer horse riding, canoe, kayak, hiking, biking, rafting, bear- or whale-watching, dog-sledding and skiing trips in BC and the Yukon. *Nomads Exploration Company*, T1800-7272952, www.nomadsexploration.com, run 3-, 7- and 10-day ecofriendly trips from Vancouver to the Rockies, featuring hiking, rafting and sightseeing. *Ecosummer Expeditions*, T6740102, www.ecosummer.com, run a number of extended, intelligently chosen trips that take in some of the best locations and activities in BC and the Yukon/Alaska.

Bus tours   The best cheap way to get around BC is with *Moose Travel Network*, T1888-3884881, www.moosenetwork.com This is the only jump-on-jump-off bus company in the province. Mini-coaches leave Vancouver hostels three times weekly for the 'West Loop', a circuit that follows the Sea to Sky Highway route to Kamloops, north past Wells Gray Park to Mount Robson and Jasper, south through the Rockies to Banff and possibly Calgary, then back west via Revelstoke and the Okanagan. An unlimited pass costing $420 makes for great flexibility, and is open to all ages. *Maverick*, T1800-6676301, www.mavericktours.bc.ca, offer a broad range of bus tours to key destinations, lasting one to 14 days.

Canoe &   *Great Expeditions*, T604-2572040, www.greatexpeditions.com, run kayak, canoe
kayak tours   and sailing tours to all the best places, such as the Queen Charlottes, Johnstone Strait, Gulf Islands, etc. *Kingfisher Wilderness Adventure*, T1866-5464347, www.kingisher-adventure.com, run kayak tours to the same spots.

Climbing tours   *Slipstream*, T1800-2177467, www.slipstreamadventures.com, specialize in backcountry trekking and rock-climbing/mountaineering tours.

Cycling tours   *Canusa Cycle Tours*, T1800-9387986, www.canusacycletours.com, offer lots of good options for beginners or experts, mostly around the Rockies, with accommodation in tents or hotels. Prices average at about $150 per person per day. *Fernie Fat-Tire Adventures*, T1888-4237849, www.ferniefattire.com, run excellent cycle tours of BC and the Rockies, with additional activities possible, starting at $95 per person per day.

Golf tours   *BC Golf Safaris*, T1866-7232747, www.bcgolfsafaris.com, and *Golf Central*, T1866-3804653, www.golfcentraltours.com, specialize in package tours to golfing centres around Vancouver, Victoria, Vancouver Island, Whistler and the Okanagan.

Motorcycle   *Pacific Motorcycle Adventure Tours*, T1877-8839842, www.pacificmotorcycle.
tours   com, have lots of good suggested routes for groups or individuals, as well as custom tours and rentals. *Coastline Custom Tours*, T1866-3380344, www.coastlinemc.com, run more expensive and structured tours on Harleys and BMWs.

Seniors   *Senior Tours Canada*, T1800-2683492, www.seniortours.ca, operate 14-day escorted bus tours of BC and the Rockies for about $3,350.

Sightseeing   The most comprehensive tour operator in Western Canada is *Brewster*, T1877-7915500,
tours   www.brewster.ca, who offer all manner of independent or guided tours and packages, with multiple starting points and destinations, travelling by car, coach or train. *Uniglobe Pacific Travel*, T1888-5235232, www.funtravel.com, offer an interesting range of summer and winter packages; anything from golf to kayaking to silviculture.

Ski & snow-   *Canadian Mountain Experience*, T1888-8675448, www.canadianmountain.com,
board tours   specialize in winter packages throughout BC and the Rockies. *Traxxx Snow Tours*, www.traxxx.com, operate nine-day ski and snowboard tours from Whistler, taking in all the best hills in BC for $1,500, not including accommodation and meals.

Canadian Mountain Holidays, T1800-6610252, www.cmhhike.com, organize hikes from remote lodges in spectacular areas reached by helicopter.

West Coast Women Adventures, www.westcoastwomen.ca, specialize in tours of BC for women over 30, featuring hiking, biking, kayaking, rafting, horse riding and wineries.

Walking tours

Women-only tours

Finding out more

There are no Canadian Tourist Board offices overseas, though in the UK you can request brochures for any province from *Visit Canada*, PO Box 5396, Northampton, NN1 2FA, UK, T0906-8715000.
Tourism British Columbia offices are at 802-865 Hornby St, Vancouver, V6Z 2G3.
www.hellobc.com The official BC site, with accommodation, attractions and a great festivals and events page.
www.travelalberta.com The official Alberta site.
www.touryukon.com The official Yukon site.
www.canadavacationplanner.com A useful overall information page for accommodation, tour operators, attractions, etc.
www.MyBC.com A horribly commercial site, but useful for current listings.
www.infocan.gc.ca The official government site. A bit bland but useful for nitty gritty information.
www.cs.cmu.edu/Unofficial/Canadiana Canadian resources page with lots of factual information.
www.parkscanada.pch.gc.ca The official Parks Canada site.
www.atlas.gc.ca Great site for Canadian maps.
www.bbcanada.com A general site for B&Bs.
www.yellowpages.ca, and **www.canada411.com** Useful for finding phone numbers and addresses.
www.britishcolumbia.com A very useful sight for gleaning more information about even the smallest BC destinations.

Language

Canadians consider themselves as having no accent at all, and by and large they are easier to understand than just about any other English-speaking nation. What exceptions there are tend to be on the East Coast, notably Newfoundland.

Disabled travellers

Disabled travellers should call ahead to make arrangements with hotels and restaurants, many of which will go out of their way to be helpful. Being such a young country, Canada has a relatively high proportion of modern buildings, which tend to be wheelchair friendly. Many national and provincial parks have wheelchair-accessible interpretive centres and trails. For more information, contact the *Canadian Paraplegic Association*, T604-3243611, www.canparaplegic.org Information on accessible transportation around Canada can be found at www.accesstotravel.gc.ca *Freedom Rentals*, 4996 Westminster Av, Delta, Vancouver, T604-9524499, www.wheelchair vanrentals.com, rent out wheelchair-accessible vans for about $150 per day, $900 per week. *Abilities Magazine* is a cross-disability lifestyle magazine published by the *Canadian Abilities Foundation*, www.enablelink.org

For disabled travel in Vancouver, see page 113

Essentials

Gay and lesbian travellers

Canadians are generally tolerant of homosexuality, though as everywhere exceptions exist. Be more wary in 'red-neck' communities, especially in Northern BC, Alberta and logging and mining towns. Places like the Gulf Islands and West Kootenays are especially tolerant, and Vancouver's West End has a flourishing gay scene. For general information and links, check out **www.gaycanada.com** An excellent site for listings of all kinds of gay-friendly businesses across the country is **www.purpleroofs.com**

Student travellers

Most sights in Canada offer a discounted price for students. *ISIC* cards are widely accepted as proof of ID. Most of Canada's hostels are affiliated to Hostelling International (HI), with reductions for members.

Travelling with children

Canada is generally a safe country that presents few worries for people taking their kids. There are no poisonous animals, crime levels are low, and there's plenty of space and countryside to enjoy. The only potential problem is the huge distances that often have to be covered in this vast country.

Flying with kids Inform the airline in advance that you're travelling with a baby or toddler, and check out the facilities when booking as these vary with each aircraft. *British Airways* now has a special seat for under-2s. Pushchairs can be taken on as hand luggage or stored in the hold. Skycots are also available. Take snacks and toys for in-flight entertainment, and remember that swallowing food or drinks during take-off and landing will help prevent ear problems.

Eating out with kids Eating out with children is rarely a problem in Canada. As in most respects, people tend to be relaxed and tolerant. High chairs are usually available on request, especially in so-called family restaurants.

Women travellers

See also Women-only tours, page 23 There are few if any countries in the world that are safer for women travellers than Canada. Naturally the usual precautions need to be taken in cities and larger towns, such as avoiding quiet unlit streets and parks at night. In more 'red-neck' logging and mining communities, or in sports-oriented places like Whistler, a surfeit of pumped-up males may result in more attention than most women would want, but even here the problem is more one of irritation than danger.

Working in Canada

Non-Canadian residents need a permit to work legally in Canada. To get one you must first have an offer of employment. *Human Resources and Development Canada*, T1800-6226232, www.hrdc-drhc.gc.ca, must confirm this. You then have to apply to *Citizenship and Immigration Canada*, www.cic.gc.ca, for the permit. Performing artists can sometimes work legally without the permit. People without permits tend to have the best luck waiting at tables in Vancouver or picking fruit in the Okanagan. Pay for the latter can be reasonable if you are very fast. Another (and legal) option is *Willing Workers on Organic Farms* (wwoof-ing). See Where to stay, page 35, for details.

Canadian embassies abroad

Australia *High Commission:*
Commonwealth Avenue, Canberra, ACT
2600, T02-62704000, T02-6273-3285.
Austria: *Laurenzenberg 2, A-1010 Vienna,*
F01-531383000, F01-531-38-3905
Belgium *Avenue de Tervueren 2, 1040*
Brussels, T02-7410611, F02-7410643.
Denmark *Kristen Bernikowsgade 1,*
Copenhagen K, DK-1105,
T33-483200, F33-483220.
France *35-37 Avenue Montaigne, 75008,*
Paris, T01-93227930, F01-44432999.
Germany *Friedrichstrasse 95, 10117,*
Berlin, T4930-203120, F4930-20312121.
Ireland *65 St Stephen's Green, Dublin 2,*
T01-4174100, F01-417 4101.
Italy *Via Zara 30, 00198 Rome, T06-*
445982443, F06-445982905.
Japan *7-3-38 Akasaka, Minato-ku*
Tokyo 107-8503, T03-54126200,
F03-54126247.

Netherlands *Sophialaan 7, 2514JP, The*
Hague, T070-3111600, F070-3111620.
New Zealand *High Commission: 3rd*
Floor, 61 Molesworth Street, Thorndon,
Wellington, T04-4739577.
Norway *Wergelandsveien 7*
0244 Oslo, T22995300, F22995301.
South Africa *High Commission: 19th Floor,*
Reserve Bank Building, 60 St George's Mall,
Capetown 8001, T21-4235240, F21-4234893.
Sweden *Tegelbacken 4, Box 16 129*
S-103 23, Stockholm, T46-84533000,
F46-8242491.
Switzerland *Kirchenfeldstrasse 88,*
CH-3005 Bern, T31-3573200, F31-3573210.
UK *High Commission: Macdonald House,*
1 Grosvenor Square, London W1K 4AB,
T020-72586600, F020-72586333.
USA *501 Pennsylvania Av NW,*
Washington DC 20001, T202-6821740,
F202-6827701.

For individual
websites and further
details, go to
www.dfait-maeci.gc.ca
/english/missions/pdf

Essentials

Before you travel

Getting in

Visa regulations are subject to change, so it is essential to check with your local Cana-   **Visas**
dian embassy or consulate before leaving home. Citizens of the EU, Scandinavia and
most Commonwealth countries do not need an entry visa, just a full valid passport. US
citizens only need proof of citizenship and residence, such as a driving licence. All visitors have to fill out a waiver form, which you will be given on the plane or at the border.
If you don't know where you'll be staying just write 'touring', though immigration officers may then ask for an idea of your schedule. They will also decide the length of stay
permitted, up to a maximum of six months. You may have to show proof of sufficient
funds, such as a credit card or $300 per week of your proposed stay. If you wish to
extend your stay beyond the allotted time, send a written application to the nearest
Canada Immigration Centre well before the end of your authorized time limit.

It's a good idea to take out some form of travel insurance, wherever you're travelling   **Insurance**
from. This should cover you for theft or loss of possessions and money, the cost of all
medical and dental treatment, cancellation of flights, delays in travel arrangements,
accidents, missed departures, lost baggage, lost passport and personal liability and
legal expenses. Find out whether your policy pays medical expenses directly to the
hospital or doctor, or whether you have to pay and then reclaim the money later. In the
latter case, be sure to keep all medical bills, and if you have anything stolen get a copy
of the police report as you will need this to substantiate your claim.

There are a variety of policies to choose from, so it's best to shop around to get the
best price. Your travel agent can advise you on deals available. *Columbus Direct*,
T0207-3750011, is one of the most competitive British companies. *STA Travel* and

other reputable student travel organizations also offer good-value travel policies. Travellers from the United States should check their existing insurance policies as they may already be covered for travel in Canada. Otherwise, try the *International Student Insurance Service* (ISIS), which is available through *STA Travel*, T1800-7770112, www.sta-travel.com Other recommended North American companies include *Travel Guard*, T1800-8261300; *Access America*, T1800-2848300; *Travel Insurance Services*, T1800-9371387; *Travel Assistance International*, T1800-8212828; and *Council Travel*, T1888-2686245.

Of particular importance for travel in Canada is that many policies exclude so-called 'dangerous activities' or charge a higher premium for them. This may include scuba diving, skiing and even trekking. Be sure to read the small print.

Older travellers should be aware that that some companies will not cover people over 65 years old, or may charge high premiums. *Age Concern*, T01883-346964, usually have the best deals for seniors.

Customs   The **duty-free** allowance for people over 19 (18 in Alberta) is 1.4 litres of liquor or 24 355-ml bottles of beer, plus 200 cigarettes and 50 cigars. **Dogs and cats** from the United States, more than three months of age, must be accompanied by a vet's certificate to show that the animal has been vaccinated against rabies during the preceding 36 months. For details contact *Canada Food Inspection*, T1888-7326222, www.inspection.gc.ca **Weapons** and self-defense sprays such as mace are prohibited entry into Canada. **Firearms** such as hunting rifles must be declared. For information call T1800-7314000.

Vaccinations   No vaccinations are necessary for travel in Canada. See also Health, page 49.

What to take

For health and first aid accessories, see page 49   Canada's weather is extremely changeable, so bring clothes for all occasions. It can be blisteringly hot in summer, but in the mountains it could snow at any time of year. For hiking and other outdoor pursuits bring plenty of layers of thin synthetic fibres, preferably long-sleeved for protection against the armies of bugs (which are also less attracted to light colours); a good pair of boots and waterproof clothing are equally important. Other gear depends on your sporting interests. A camera is essential, and binoculars can be useful for spotting wildlife. Many situations call for a tent, sleeping bag and lightweight camp-stove. A Swiss Army knife, flashlight/torch and compass are also key items. Visitors staying in hostels may want to bring a sleeping sheet and padlock, though such things are usually supplied. Everything you could possibly need can be bought in Canada, probably at a lower price than you'll find at home.

Money

Currency   The Canadian currency is the dollar ($), divided into 100 cents (c). Coins come in denominations of 1c (penny), 5c (nickel), 10c (dime), 25c (quarter), $1 (called a 'loonie' because it carries a picture of a loon, a common Canadian bird), and $2 (called a 'toonie'). Banknotes come in denominations of $5 (blue), $10 (purple), $20 (green), $50 (pink) and $100 (brown).

Banks   Almost every small town in Canada has a branch of at least one of the big Canadian banks, which tend to offer the best exchange rates: *Bank of Montréal*, *CIBC*, *Royal Bank*, *Scotiabank* and *TD Bank*. The most important exceptions are the Gulf Islands, many of which do not even have an ATM. The minimum opening hours for banks are

Exchange rates

Prices given in the book are in Canadian dollars unless otherwise specified.

UK£1 = Can$2.29
US$1 = Can$1.47
Euro 1= Can$1.58
Aus$1 = Can$0.58

Mon-Fri 1000-1500, but they're usually open until 1630. Outside these hours, money can be changed at **bureaux de change**, found in most city centres, airports and major train stations. Avoid changing money or cheques in hotels, whose rates are usually poor.

Most hotels, shops and restaurants in Canada accept *Access/MasterCard* and *Visa* credit cards, though this is not to be **Credit cards & ATMs** relied upon in rural areas and at smaller establishments. ATMs (cashpoints) are just about everywhere in Canada, and almost all of them will give Canadian cash on one of the above credit cards. If you have lost your credit card call: *VISA*: T1800-3368472; *MasterCard*: T1800-3613361.

While the credit card/ATM combo makes for greatest convenience, travellers' **Travellers'** cheques remain the safest way to carry money. These are available for a small com- **cheques** mission from all major banks. *American Express (Amex)*, *Visa* and *Thomas Cook* cheques are widely accepted and the most commonly issued by banks. You'll normally have to pay commission again when you cash each cheque. No commission is payable on *Amex* cheques cashed at *Amex* offices. Canadian dollar travellers' cheques are recommended as many hotels and even restaurants will accept them as currency. Keep a record of the cheque numbers and the cheques you've cashed separate from the cheques themselves so that you can get a full refund of all uncashed cheques should you lose them.

The quickest way to have money sent to you in case of an emergency is to have it wired **Money** to the nearest bank via *Western Union*, T0800-833833, or *Moneygram*, T0800-894887. **transfers** Charges are on a sliding scale so it will cost proportionately less to wire out more money. Money can also be wired by *Thomas Cook* or *American Express*, though this can take a day or two.

Almost everything in Canada is subject to the federal **Goods and Services Tax** (GST) **Taxes** of 7%. A **rebate** can be claimed on accommodation expenditure and goods taken out of the country within 60 days. This can add up to a considerable amount, so remember to keep your **receipts**. Rebate forms are available from visitor centres, hotels, shops, airports and Canadian embassies. Claims can also be made at the duty-free shops of certain US border crossings. For more information call T1800-6684748, or T902-4325608 outside Canada. In British Columbia (but not Alberta, the Yukon or NWT) most goods and services carry a **Provincial Sales Tax** (PST) of 7%. In addition there is a **hotel rooms' tax** of up to 10%. None of these taxes are included in the original price, meaning everything you buy ends up costing more than you expect (up to 24% more for accommodation).

The cost of living is considerably lower in Canada than in the UK or US. Things that will **Cost of living** cost a pound in England will often cost a dollar in Canada. Notable exceptions are luxuries like beer and cigarettes which are roughly on a par with the UK and therefore more expensive than they are in the US. Petrol (gas) is cheaper than in the UK but more expensive than the US. An average basic salary in Canada is around $25-30,000. Rent averages at around $500-700 per month, though this varies dramatically.

Essentials

Cost of travelling Canada is not a budget destination, but the weakness of the Canadian dollar makes it reasonably affordable for those coming from the United States or Britain. Apart from accommodation, the single biggest expense is travel, due to the vast distances that need to be covered. Petrol (gas) gets considerably more expensive the further north you go. Accommodation and restaurant prices tend to be higher in popular destinations such as Whistler and Banff, and during the summer months (or winter at ski resorts).

The minimum daily budget required for those staying in hostels or camping, travelling by bus and hitching, and cooking their own meals, will be roughly $50-70 per day. If you start staying in cheaper motels or B&Bs and eating out occasionally that will rise to $80-100 per day. Those staying in slightly more upmarket accommodation, eating out daily and visiting attractions can expect to pay around $100-120. If you want to hire a car, take ferries, eat well, and go on the odd excursion, the cost will rise considerably. The best way to budget is to move around less and camp a lot. In destinations like the Rockies, this is also about the best way to experience the country. Single travellers will have to pay more than half the cost of a double room in most places, and should budget on spending around 60% of what a couple would spend.

Getting there

Air

Other than visitors from the United States, who have the option of driving, the only feasible way of getting to Canada is by air. The best-served city in the west is Vancouver, though visitors focusing on the Rockies may want to fly into Calgary or Edmonton.

Buying a ticket There are so many outlets for buying plane tickets these days that finding the best deal can be a lengthy process. Fares fluctuate mainly according to season. Prices are highest in the summer peak season, from July to September. The shoulder season either side of these months is cheaper, but the best deals can be found in winter, with the obvious exception of Christmas and the New Year. It is advisable to start looking for your ticket early, as some of the cheapest tickets have to be bought months in advance, and the most popular flights sell out quickly. On the other hand, those with the flexibility to leave at a moment's notice can often snap up unbelievable last-minute bargains. Mid-week flights are usually slightly cheaper. The best way to find a good deal is on the internet, though in the UK the Sunday papers, or London's *Time Out* and *Evening Standard* are also good places to look.

Official cheap flight tickets are known as budget fares, Apex, super-Apex, advance-purchase tickets, or whatever a particular airline chooses to call them. Unofficial discounted tickets are not sold directly by airlines but are released through selected travel agents. They are usually as low or lower than the official budget-price tickets.

Return tickets are usually a lot cheaper than buying two one-way tickets. The cheapest often limit your stay to two or three weeks. Cheaper flights often involve changing planes in the USA, so shop around with American airlines. Most travel agents offer 'open jaw' tickets that allow you to fly into one city and out from another, though this usually precludes you from the best deals. When buying a ticket, make sure you check the route, the duration of the journey, stopovers allowed, any travel restrictions such as minimum and maximum periods away, and cancellation penalties.

When buying cheap tickets through small lesser-known agencies, avoid paying too much money in advance, and you can check with the airline directly to make sure your reservation has been made. It may be safer to choose a well-known agent such as *STA*, which has offices worldwide, or *Trailfinders* in the UK, *Council Travel* in the US.

◀

Airlines flying from the UK and the rest of Europe

Air Canada, T0870-5247226, www.aircanada.ca 14 flights per week from London Heathrow to Vancouver, seven per week from Heathrow and Frankfurt to Calgary.
British Airways, T08457-799977, www.british-airways.com Seven flights per week from London Heathrow to Vancouver and Calgary.
KLM, T0870-5074074. Seven flights per week from Amsterdam to Vancouver.
Lufthansa, T0845-7737747, www.lufthansa.com Seven flights per week from Frankfurt to Vancouver.

Airlines flying from the USA

American Airlines, T1800-7763000, www.americanair.com
Continetal Airlines, T1800-2310856, www.flycontinental.com
Delta Airlines, T1800-2414141, www.delta-air.com
Northwest Airlines, T1800-4474747, www.nwa.com
TWA, T1800-2212000, www.twa.com
United Airlines, T1800-5382929, www.ual.com

Airlines flying from Australia and New Zealand

Air Canada, T1800-221015, www.aircanada.ca Three flights per week from Melbourne
Qantas, T13-1211 in Aus; T0800-808767 in NZ, www.qantas.com.au
Air New Zealand, T09-3573000, www.airnz.com 2 flights per day from Auckland.

Flights from London average about £500 return in the low season, £750 in the high season. You can get one for as little as £350-400, and at peak times they rise to over £1,000. Prices are roughly the same from Frankfurt and Amsterdam as they are from London. Availability is rarely a problem except at times like Christmas.

There are no direct flights from any other European cities or from Israel or South Africa. Flights from Israel are often via Los Angeles and take around 22 hours. It is faster to fly from Capetown via Frankfurt (35 hours) than from Johannesburg via New York City (40 hours).

Road

The main highways into Western Canada from the United States are Highway 5 from Seattle to Vancouver, a three-hour drive; Highway 395 from Spokane to Grand Forks; Highway 93 from Kalispell, Montana to Cranbrook; and Highway 15 from Great Falls, Montana to Lethbridge, Alberta. Traffic jams and long queues are not uncommon at the very busy Peace Arch Border Crossing on Highway 5, especially at weekends, in summer, and on Canadian or US holidays. Note that San Francisco to Vancouver is about 19 hours' drive. Once in Canada, the TransCanada Highway (Highway 1) runs right across the country. *Greyhound*, T1800-2312222, run 6 daily buses from Seattle to Vancouver, a 3½-4½-hour trip costing $22 one-way, $40 return. *Quickshuttle*, T9404428, www.quickshuttle.com has 8 daily services from Seattle's Downtown and airport, arriving at the *Holiday Inn*, 1110 Howe Street, Downtown Vancouver. The journey takes 3 hours 45 minutes, costing $39 single, $70 return for adults; $27 single, $49 return for students; and $21 single, $38 return for children.

Essentials

▶ ## Discount travel agents in the UK

Council Travel, 28a Poland Street,
London W1V 3DB, T020-7437 7767,
www.destinations-group.com
STA Travel, 86 Old Brompton Road,
London SW7 3LH, T020-7361 6161,
www.statravel.co.uk

Specialists in low-cost student/
youth flights with branches
throughout the country.
Trailfinders, 194 Kensington High Street,
London W8 6FT, T020-7730 3402,
www.trailfinders.co.uk.

Discount travel agents in the USA

Air Brokers International, 323 Geary
Street, Tsuite 411, San Francisco, CA94102,
T1800-8833273, www.airbrokers.com
Consolidator and specialist in RTW and
Circle Pacific tickets.
Council Travel, 205 E 42nd Street, New
York, NY 10017, T1888-2686245,
www.counciltravel.com
Student/budget agency with branches
in many other US cities.
Discount Airfares Worldwide On-line,

www.etn.nl/discount.htm   A hub of
consolidator and discount agent links.
STA Travel, 5900 Wiltshire Boulevard,
Suite 2110, Los Angeles, CA 90036,
T1800-7770112,
www.sta-travel.com   Discount student/
youth travel company with branches in NY,
San Francisco, Boston, Miami, Chicago,
Seattle and Washington. DC.
Travelocity, www.travelocity.com
Online consolidator.

Discount travel agents in Australia and New Zealand

Flight Centre, 82 Elizabeth Street, Sydney,
T13-1600; 205 Queen Street, Auckland,
T09-3096171, www.flightcentre.com.au
Also branches in other towns and cities.
STA Travel, 702 Harris Street, Ultimo,
Sydney, and 256 Flinders Street,

Melbourne, T1300-360960, 10 High Street,
Auckland, T09-3666673,
www.statravel.com.au   Also in major
towns and university campuses.
Travel.com.au, 80 Clarence Street, Sydney,
T02-92901500, www.travel.com.au

Sea

A number of American-run ferries run to Victoria, including **MV Coho**, T3862202, from Port Angeles, US$8 single, $30 return; **Victoria Clipper**, T3828100, from Seattle, US$75; and **Washington State Ferries**, T3811551, Anacortes (San Juan Island), US$11 single, $29.75 return. **Alaska Marine Highway**, T1800-4782268, run ferries to Prince Rupert from several Alaskan towns such as Juneau, and the Yukon can be easily accessed by road from Skagway, Alaska. Many cruise ships also arrive in Vancouver and Victoria throughout the summer.

Train

Amtrak, T1800-8727245, run one daily train from Seattle to Vancouver, leaving at 0745, arriving 1140. US$23-35 one-way, depending how far ahead you book.

Touching down

Electricity The current in Canada is 110V AC, 60 cycle. Plugs have two flat parallel prongs and sometimes a third that is cylindrical.
Emergencies For all emergency services dial 911.
Laundry Most towns have launderettes (here called laundromats). The average cost for a wash and tumble dry is about $2.50-3.
Time Canada as a whole has six time zones. Western Canada has just two: Pacific Time, which covers most of BC and the Yukon, is generally eight hours behind Greenwich Mean Time; Mountain Time, used in Alberta and the NWT, is seven hours behind GMT.

Toilets Public toilets are found at train and bus stations and tend to be free and clean. All places selling food are required by law to have a washroom. Public toilets are almost extinct in town centres.
Weights and measures Imperial and metric systems are both used in Canada. Distances are always in kilometres. Shorter measurements tend to be in inches rather than centimetres. Drinks are served in pints, though this is nominal rather than fixed, and the size of a pint can vary dramatically. Weights can be in pounds or kilos, often both. Hectares and acres are also both used.

Touching down

Airport information

Vancouver, T604-2077077, www.yvr.ca Terminal facilities include a Visitor Information desk on the Arrivals floor (level 2), and an Airport Information desk (which operates a lost and found service) one floor up in the Departure Lounge, along with most of the shops and services. There are plenty of phones and ATMs dotted around, and the corridor linking the two terminals has a children's play area and nursery. There is a hotel right in the airport and several others a short taxi ride away. Car rental companies are found in the main indoor car park. For more details see page 37. **Calgary**, T403-7351372, and **Edmonton**, T780-8908382, airports are smaller, but have all the usual facilities including Visitor Information desks, car hire, ATMs and bureaux de change, left luggage, shops, restaurants and bars.

All passengers departing from Vancouver airport have to purchase an Air Improvement Fee ticket, which is $5 for BC/Yukon, $10 for other parts of North America, $15 elsewhere. They can be bought from machines or airport booths and must be presented at security. **Airport tax**

Tourist information

Visitor Information Centres can be found in almost every Canadian town. Their addresses, phone numbers and opening hours are listed in the relevant sections of this book. Opening hours vary depending on the time of year. Many are summer-only, which usually means mid-May to mid-September. The level of helpfulness of these offices varies dramatically, but they tend to be well stocked with leaflets and the very useful publications put out by the provincial tourist boards. In **British Columbia** this includes the indispensable *Approved Accommodation* brochure; *Vacation Guides* for each region; the extremely informative *Outdoor and Adventure* brochure; and others for freshwater and saltwater fishing. **Alberta** produces an *Accommodation Guide* and a separate *Campground Guide*, a very useful *Vacation Guide* full of attractions and *For Tourist Board websites see Finding out more, page 23*

Essentials

▶ **Overseas embassies and high commissions in Canada**

Australia, 710-50 O'Connor,
T613-2360841, F613-2364376,
www.ahc-ottawa.org
Austria, 455 Wilbrod St, Ottawa, T613-
7891444, F613-7893431, www.austro.org
Belgium, 80 Elgin St, Ottawa,
T613-2367267, F613-2367882,
www.diplobel.org/canada
Denmark, 450-47 Clarence St, Ottawa,
T613-5621811, F613-5621812,
www.tradecomm.com/danish
France, 42 Promenade Sussex,
T613-7891795, F613-5623790,
www.amab-ottawa.fr
Germany, 1 Waverley St, Ottawa,
T613-2321101, F613-5949330,
www.germanembassyottawa.org
Israel, 1005-50 O'Connor St, Ottawa,
T613-5676450, F613-2378865,
www.israelca.org
Italy, 275 Slater St, T2322401, F2331484,
www.italyincanada.com
Japan, 80-1177 W Hastings St, Vancouver,
T604-6845868, F604-6846939,

www.vancouver.ca.emb-japan.go.ip
Netherlands, 350 Albert St, Ottawa,
T613-2375030, F613-2376471,
www.netherlandsembassy.ca
New Zealand, 727-99 Bank St,
Ottawa, T613-2385991,
F613-2385707,
www.nzhcottawa.org
Norway, 90 Sparks St, Ottawa,
T613-2386571, F613-2382765,
www.emb-norway.ca
South Africa, 15 Sussex Dr, Ottawa,
T613-7440330, F613-7411639,
www.docuweb.ca/SouthAfrica
Sweden, 377 Dalhousie St, Ottawa,
T613-2418553, F613-2412277,
www.swedishembassy.ca
Switzerland, 5 Marlborough Av, Ottawa,
T613-2351837, F613-5631394,
www.eda.admin.ch/canada
UK, 80 Elgin St, Ottawa, T613-2372008,
F613-2322533, www.britain-in-canada.org
US, 490 Sussex Dr, Ottawa, T613-2385335,
F613-6883082, www.usembassycanada.gov

operators, and some regional brochures. The **Yukon** produces an attractive brochure called *Places to go on Yukon Time*, as well as a *Vacation Guide*. Look out also for the excellent *Visitor Guide* put out by the Yukon First Nations Tourism Association, and the privately printed, whimsical (and free) *Guide to the Goldfields*.

Most Information Centres will provide information on local transport and attractions, and sell relevant books and souvenirs. Many also produce self-guiding Heritage Walking Tour maps of their towns, and have picture books of local B&Bs. *Parks Canada* operates its own offices, usually in conjunction with the local tourist board. These tend to be excellent facilities, especially the ones in the Rockies.

Local customs and laws

Politeness Canadians are generally liberal, broad-minded people, with few rules that are likely to trip up the visitor. Politeness is a way of life; people don't jump queues or lose their tempers over trivialities, drivers rarely honk their horns, and many junctions have four-way stops instead of traffic-lights, where vehicles leave in the order in which they arrived.

Religion Outside the major urban centres, Western Canada is overwhelmingly dominated by European descendants, so finding a place of worship is often impossible for non-Christians, especially in remote areas. In cities, the best place to start looking is the Yellow Pages, or at www.411.ca Your nearest **Catholic** church can be found at www.alapadre.net/chcanada A useful all-round site is www.catholiccanada.com The United Church, Canada's largest **Protestant** denomination, can be visited at www.uccan.org A number of **Gospel** churches are represented by www.agcof canada.com The **Reformed** Church's site is www.prca.org The Canadian **Jewish** Congress, www.cjc.ca, provides a

How big is your footprint?

Western Canada is one of the most unspoilt regions left on earth, and by following a few simple rules we can help keep it that way.

- *Only light fires in designated places and always make sure they're out when you leave.*
- *Practise 'no trace' camping: pack it in, pack it out.*
- *In the bush, use outhouses or bury your waste far from water, and burn the paper.*
- *Keep soap, detergent and toothpaste away from lakes and streams.*
- *Never feed wildlife, and use facilities to keep food/litter away from bears.*

- *Avoid confronting animals in the wild.*
- *Respect all fishing and hunting rules.*
- *Always stick to designated trails, and don't pick flowers or plants.*
- *Respect the wishes and privacy of Native Canadians.*
- *Think about using a sailboat or canoe instead of a motorboat; taking a dog-sled tour instead of a snowmobile; hiking into the mountains instead of taking a helicopter.*
- *A number of companies, particularly those coming from the US, and some lodges are listed on www.ecotourism.org*

Essentials

list of all synagogues, while a useful list of regional Jewish resources is found at www.hareshima.com/regional/Canada **Muslims** can find their closest mosque at www.islamicfinder.org There is an Islam Information Centre at 3127 Kingsway, Vancouver, T604-4347526, www.al-huda.ca A useful all-round site is www.islam.ca All Canadian **Hindu**, **Sikh**, **Buddhist** and **Jain** temples are listed at www.mandirnet.org/canada_list Useful sites for general info are www.hindunet.org, and www.buddhismcanada.com

Smoking On the West Coast generally, people are more health- and diet-conscious, more sports-oriented and smoke less than elsewhere. Lighting up is illegal in most public places, such as buses, cinemas, etc. A BC provincial law banning smoking altogether in restaurants was introduced for the first day of the new millennium. When this legislation was lifted recently, 97% of BC's restaurants chose to retain the policy. Even many bars and nightclubs have a no-smoking rule. While still illegal and not something you should indulge in publicly, the attitude towards smoking marijuana is far more relaxed in BC than almost anywhere in the world.

Tipping West Coast Canadians take tipping very seriously. In restaurants the customary tip is 15%. Bars and pubs usually have waiter/waitress service, and these too are tipped 10-15%. Even if you buy your drink at the bar, you are expected to leave a tip, usually change but still 10% or so. Taxi drivers and hairdressers should also be tipped 10-15%. Naturally, this all depends on service.

Responsible tourism

Hiking Always stick to the trails when hiking. Taking short cuts leads to unnecessary destruction of vegetation, some of which, like alpine moss and lichens, take centuries to grow. Never pick wildflowers. Where no outhouses are available, bury waste and toilet paper in the ground away from paths and at least 30 m from a water source.

Fire Every summer, Canada experiences at least a few forest fires that rage out of control destroying vast tracts of land. Keep an eye out for fire bans, never light a fire other than in the designated place, never leave a fire burning, and be especially careful when extinguishing cigarettes; one spark taken by the wind to the tinder-dry brush is all it takes.

First Nations   Another key aspect of Canada's appeal that could easily lead to abuse concerns its First Nations. Most of us are interested in native culture, because it offers a heady whiff of something essential that we have lost in our own societies: a relationship with the Earth, a sense of the interconnectedness and sacred quality of all things, an ability to live off the land without trashing it, and so on. But what starts off as respect and curiosity can lead to false assumptions, stereotyping and condescension. Canada's native populations are still alive and evolving, and do not necessarily enjoy the attention of tourists. Please respect any First Nations sights such as burial grounds that are held as sacred and off-limits to outsiders, and never photograph a Native American without first asking their permission.

Wildlife   Never feed any wild animals; observe them but don't approach them. In the Rockies in particular, herds of big-horn sheep hang out by roadsides where they know they will be given hand-outs by irresponsible tourists. Whale-watching and bear-watching tours are major draws in Canada, and most operators are respectful towards the animals; still, there will always be the odd unscrupulous guide who oversteps the line. Don't encourage them. Visitors who come to Canada to hunt or fish should be aware of and respect the laws and limitations; they are there to protect the future of the species.

Bears   Like most animals, bears are always on the look-out for easy food, and have a prodigious sense of smell. For this reason, the correct disposal of litter and storage of foodstuffs is a key issue. Brutal but true is the expression 'A fed bear is a dead bear': bears that dine well once due to a camper's laziness will keep coming back until they eventually have to be put down. For the same reason, avoid getting into confrontational situations with bears while hiking; you are, after all, on the bear's turf. See page 478.

Safety

Few countries in the world are as safe as Canada. Even here, common sense should prevail in cities. Avoid walking alone in remote, unlit streets or parks after dark. Elsewhere the biggest danger is from wildlife, though there are no poisonous animals to worry about. Never approach wild animals, even the ones deemed safe. More people are injured annually by elk than bears.

Where to stay

Hotels   Most of the big American four-star hotel franchises are represented in major Canadian towns. Often the luxury seems to be shallow, with inflated prices paid for prestige, service, and facilities that you may not necessarily use. Certainly the rooms are rarely any bigger or more impressive than elsewhere. We have tried to mention only those with a degree of character or genuine class. Usually the most impressive buildings are owned by the *Fairmont* chain. These are the hotels that were constructed by the Canadian Pacific Railway (CPR) at the turn of the last century, and tend to resemble French châteaux.

Lodges & resorts   These two words are extremely vague. Resorts tend to dominate touristy areas, especially those by the water, such as Tofino. They can be motels or hotels in disguise, or offer cabins, huts or chalets, which can be quaint but faded. If you get the chance and can afford it, try to stay in one of the gorgeous log constructions for which the West Coast is famous. Lodges are often found in remote spots, and may be associated with hunting or fishing outfitters. Traditionally, a lodge will be a big central building with rooms, and probably cabins scattered around the grounds, but these days it can mean almost anything.

Price categories

◀

The price codes used for accommodation in this book refer to the following:
LL *(over $280)* - **L** *($220-280) Prestigious and upmarket hotels with all services, facilities and the best locations.*
AL *($180-220)* - **A** *($140-180) Most so-called resorts and lodges that line the beaches in places like Tofino, and almost anything in touristy places like Banff or Whistler are in this price range.*
B *($100-140) Most of the mid-range chain hotel and motels fall into this*

category, as do the nicer B&B rooms. Facilities might include a pool or hot tub.
C *($75-100) For this price you can get a reasonable motel room in the mid-range chains with agreeable if predictable decor, a TV, fridge and bath. You could also get a nice en suite room in a B&B.*
D *($50-75) The cheapest standard motels with little luxury or aesthetic appeal or a private room in a hostel.*
E *($25-50) Very basic; dormitory bed in a hostel.*

Essentials

Motels The Canadian accommodation scene is dominated by cheap to mid-range motels, often belonging to a franchise, with identical furnishings everywhere you go. In small towns they are often the only choice. Of the budget chains, *Comfort Inn* seems to be the most reliable. In descriptions of these establishments the word 'standard' means that the room is dull and functional but clean and acceptable, with an en suite bathroom and a reasonable bed. You can usually expect to get a TV, small fridge and coffee maker. Facilities such as saunas, hot tubs, fitness rooms and indoor pools are often small and disappointing.

B&Bs For about the same price, you can usually find an attractively furnished room in a B&B, with breakfast thrown in. In terms of aesthetics and value for money there is no comparison and if you want to meet Canadians on their own ground this is an excellent option. Note that continental breakfast often amounts to no more than a cup of coffee and a muffin, whereas full breakfast means something cooked, plus cereal, fruit, tea or coffee, etc.

Working farms & ranches In a similar but more exotic vein, there are plenty of working farms and ranches that provide accommodation, particularly in Alberta and the Cariboo. For more details contact the *BC Guest Ranchers' Association*, T3746836, www.guestranches.com, and check the BC and Alberta *Accommodation Guides*.

Hostels Almost all Canadian towns have a hostel. Many of these are run by, or at least affiliated to, *Hostelling International* (HI), with a reduced fee for members. For information and reservations call T604-6847111, www.hihostels.bc.ca in BC; T403-2835551, www.hostellingintl.ca/alberta in Alberta. There is no age limit. A typical hostel has dormitories with 4 or more beds, usually single-sex, plus a few private rooms for couples and families. Facilities include shared washrooms with showers, a common room with TV and sometimes games and a library, a kitchen/dining room, and lockers. Many organize activities or tours. Almost all are clean, friendly, a bit noisy and great for gleaning information and meeting fellow travellers. In the Rockies, a string of HI hostels enjoy locations second only to the campgrounds, making them a great budget option. A number of other West Coast hostels are regulated by the *Pacific Rim Hostelling Network*. For information call Moni at T1800-8611366.

A number of budget options can be found at **www.budgetbeds.com** Long-term budget travellers may also want to look into *WWOOF Canada: Willing Workers On Organic Farms*. The deal varies from place to place, but generally entails working 4-6 hours per day for room and board. A booklet listing 300 places costs $30. Call T250-3544417, or visit www.wwoof.ca

Essentials

Campgrounds Camping is the cheapest option, and even if money is not an issue, this is often the way to go. Canada's main appeal is, after all, its countryside. What better way to enjoy it than to be immersed in it? Where the scenery is wildest, camping is frequently the only choice. Those who want their luxury as well might consider hiring an **RV** (Recreational Vehicle). The drawback is that campgrounds which cater to RVs with pull-through sites and hook-ups often resemble car parks, with few trees and no privacy. Campsites in big towns tend to be far removed, expensive and ugly, making a hostel a much better bet.

The best campgrounds are those within **provincial parks**. As they're not driven by profits, these tend to have considerably more spacious and spaced-out sites, with plenty of trees and privacy. The busier ones often have shower facilities and hot running water, but those seeking calm will gravitate towards the small campgrounds that have no facilities beyond an outhouse and a water pump. Even cheaper than these are **forestry campgrounds**, intended for use by tree-planters and loggers, and almost always situated off the beaten track on logging roads. Their locations are marked on regional forestry maps (available at information centres). The nominal fee is hardly ever collected. Another possibility is '**guerilla camping**', which means finding out-of-the-way spots where you can pitch your tent for free, or sleep in the back of your van, without being bothered. Much of Canada is remote enough to make this possible. Logging roads are always a good place to look (and you may stumble on a forestry site). Note that guerilla camping is impossible in the Rockies. Anyone interested in this approach might want to buy K and C Copeland's *Camp Free in BC*, Voice in the Wilderness Press. Volume 1 covers the south, Volume 2 the north.

Getting around

Air

If you are short of time and want to cover a lot of ground quickly, Canada's extensive network of internal flights, mostly operated by *Air Canada*, www.aircanada.ca, its subsidiaries *Air Jazz* and *Air Tango*, and *West Jet*, www.westjet.ca, is the way to go. Many mid-sized towns such as Kelowna, Kamloops, Cranbrook, Castlegar, Prince George and Prince Rupert have an airport, and some communities in the north are only linked to the outside world by air. For those who have more time than money, however, the road is preferable as internal flights are relatively expensive. To give an idea, a one-way to Kamloops from Vancouver with *Air Canada Jazz* costs $69 with 10 days' notice, $89 with five days, and $109 with three days. Returns are double. A single from Vancouver to Calgary with *Air Canada Tango*, www.flytango.com, costs about $200.

Ferry

On the West Coast, ferries are a way of life, almost all of them operated by *BC Ferries*. The main routes are those connecting Vancouver with Victoria and Nanaimo on Vancouver Island, and those servicing the Gulf Islands. Sailings on all these services are fairly regular. Details are given in the text. Vehicles can be taken on all but a few minor crossings and bikes can be taken on all. If using the ferries, you'll need to pick up the latest timetable, though they can be confusing and subject to short-notice changes. If in doubt, ask a local. In summer, especially during Canadian and US holidays, long waits are common.

BC Ferries also operate two very popular long-distance routes which provide excellent means of accessing the north, and can be treated as cheap but beautifully scenic cruises in their own right. These are the *Inside Passage* to Prince Rupert, and the *Discovery Coast Passage* to Bella Coola. Both leave from Port Hardy at the northern tip of Vancouver Island. In addition, a number of ferries provide essential links across lakes in BC's Southern Interior. The longest and most important of these are in the West Kootenays, crossing the Arrow Lakes near Nakusp and Kootenay Lake near Nelson. Formerly free, these services are now subject to a fee.

Two other services worth mentioning are privately run boats that provide a popular means of accessing some very remote coastal spots around Vancouver Island. The *MV Lady Rose* out of Port Alberni runs to Bamfield, Ucluelet and Barkley Sound. The *MV Uchuck III* out of Gold River runs to Nootka Sound, Tahsis and Yuquot. Both will take and launch kayaks, an invaluable service.

Road

Canada's highways rarely compare to the soulless, multi-lane, high-speed motorways found in some countries. Particularly in BC, where there are always mountains to be crossed, roads tend to be scenic but tortuous, with steep up and down sections, and only stretches of dual carriageway for overtaking. Driving in Canada is mostly relaxed and pleasurable; road rage is alien to the Canadian psyche; roundabouts are practically unheard-of and even traffic lights are often replaced with four-way stops. The greatest hazard in cities tends to come from bus drivers.

For transport information throughout Canada, visit www.tc.gc.ca

To drive in Canada you must have a current driving licence. Foreign licences are valid for visitors. If bringing in your own vehicle, you should also have your registration or ownership documents. Make sure you are adequately insured. Throughout Canada you **drive on the right**, and seat-belts are compulsory. **Speed limits** are from 90 to 110 kmph on the open road, usually 50 kmph in communities. The police advise people to drive with lights on even during the day. Many places mentioned in this book are reached via forestry/logging roads, which tend to be dirt or gravel, and often in very poor condition. It is advisable to have four-wheel drive, all-wheel drive, or at least front-wheel drive for these roads. Where active logging signs are on display, proceed with extreme caution, think about changing your plans, and ideally contact the logging company in question to enquire about current status. Logging trucks are giant, frightening beasts that have difficulty slowing down. If you see one coming, get as far off the road as you safely can.

Rules & regulations
Visit the Canadian Automobile Association site at www.caa.ca

The only real way to see Canada is by driving yourself. Much of what is exceptional about the country is off the beaten track, in places where there is no public transport. If you can afford it, we strongly recommend hiring a vehicle, preferably one you can sleep in. If this seems too expensive, consider renting a small, basic car or a motorbike, and camping in a tent, which will reduce your accommodation expenses to almost nothing. Details of rental agencies are given in the transport sections of Vancouver, Calgary, Edmonton and Whitehorse. Ask the main multinational companies in your own country about possible fly-drive deals, which can work out cheaper. Before hiring a vehicle, be sure to check exactly what is included in the price. For example, there is often a mileage limit beyond which a penalty is payable. Check also what the insurance covers, especially regarding foresty roads.

Hiring a vehicle

The next best option is the network of buses mostly operated by *Greyhound*, T1800-6618747, www.greyhound.ca, or *Laidlaw*, T3854411, www.grayline.ca, on Vancouver Island. Buses tend to service only those towns that are on or close to the TransCanada and Yellowhead highways. Getting from *Greyhound* depots to sights is often impossible or means paying for a taxi.

Bus

Essentials

Hitching Safe as Canada is, hitchhiking always carries a certain risk, and cannot be recommended for lone women travellers. Having said that, it is a pretty reliable form of travel and, in certain areas, such as the Gulf Islands or the West Kootenays, hitching is a way of life, and is often the only way for those without a vehicle to get around.

Maps A number of cheap fold-out maps of the individual provinces or cities are available, but the map we recommend is the Rand McNally, *BC and Alberta Road Atlas*, which comes in a ring-binder. Its provincial maps are 1:1,100,000, with key areas like the Southern Interior and Rockies also covered by 1:250,000 maps. At the back are decent maps of the key towns and cities, with additional city centre maps of the most important. There's even the bonus of a Yukon map, meaning it covers the whole region dealt with in this book. *BC Parks* produce a number of blue maps of their provincial parks which are extremely useful and free (so far). *Parks Canada* also distribute very useful free maps/hiking guides. For the Rockies they sell two 1:200,000 maps – one for Banff, Yoho and Kootenay, one for Jasper – which are recommended as an overview. Those who really want to get off the beaten track could invest in a *Backcountry Mapbook* (2001), Mussio Ventures, $16. These cover areas like the Kootenays, Central BC, Cariboo, or Kamloops/Okanagan, showing all the secondary and forestry roads, with full details on free and forestry campsites, hot springs, and other useful features.

Train

Canada's once integral and proud railway system has been ground down to nearly nothing by inefficiency and the modern world's obsession with the automobile. These days the train is a good way to cover large distances across the country, though it is both slower, less frequent and more expensive than the bus. Of the many smaller lines that operated until quite recently, only *VIA Rail's* Malahat service between Victoria and Courtenay on Vancouver Island will keep running.

Keeping in touch

Communications

Internet As the internet and email are assuming ever-greater importance in our lives, cyber cafés are springing up everywhere, Canada being no exception. Look in each town's directory section for locations of internet access. All but the smallest Canadian towns have some kind of public access. If they don't, you can head for the municipal library, which will usuakoffer free internet access, though you may have to register in advance to get a slot. Otherwise charges vary, averaging about $1 for every 15-20 minutes. In big cities it can be considerably cheaper.

Post Most towns have *Canada Post* offices, which are usually open Monday-Friday
www.canadapost.ca 0900-1700. It is often more convenient to send post from one of the major drug stores/chemists. Costs for a standard letter are 48c within Canada, 65c to the US, and $1.25 anywhere else. Prices for packages depend on exact destination and weight. Within BC this is roughly $4.95 for 1 kg then 25c for every additional 500 g. To Eastern Canada it is roughly $8 then 45c for every extra 500 g. It is considerably cheaper to send parcels abroad as 'small packages'. To the US this includes anything up to 1 kg. By surface this is $7.40, rising 65c with every extra 500 g. By air it's $9.90 then $1.50 per extra 500 g. To Europe, a small package can be up to 2 kg. By land 1 kg is $9.50, 2 kg = $13.55; by air 1 kg = $21.30, 2 kg = $38.55. To Australia and New Zealand is $28 up to 1.5 kg by land, then $4 per 500 g; $44.45 by air up to 1.5 kg then $9 per extra 500 g.

Note that international mail can take up to two weeks to arrive. In Canada, Poste Restante is known as General Delivery. In smaller towns, regular post offices will hold General Delivery. In big towns this should be addressed to the main Post Office, whose address will be given in the text. Fax services are generally available at post offices.

In Canada as elsewhere, the advent of the mobile phone has led to a decrease in the number of public phones, but these are still pretty numerous. Most take coins and credit cards. Local calls are free from personal phones, with a charge of 35c at pay phones for an unlimited amount of time. Any long-distance numbers beginning with 800, 888, 877, or 777 are free in North America. There is no charge for calling 411 for **directory enquiries**. To reach an **operator**, dial 0. For normal long distance and international calls it works out much cheaper to buy one of the many cards available from newsagents and gas stations. Those from *7-11* are reliable. For international calls, ask for one with no connection fee. **Long-distance calls** within the country have to be preceded by 1 then the 3-digit code, which is 250 for most of BC, 604 for Vancouver, the Sunshine Coast and Sea to Sky Highway, 403 for most of Alberta, 780 for the Edmonton region and 867 for the Yukon.

Telephone
Dial 911 for police and emergencies

The international code for Canada is 011

Essentials

Media

There are two **national newspapers** in Canada. The *Globe and Mail* is a broadsheet that appeals to a more intellectual and liberal-minded readership. The *National Post* is a more right-of-centre and populist broadsheet. British Columbia has *The Province* and the *Vancouver Sun,* the first along the same lines as the *National Post*, the second a tabloid that, while hardly highbrow, is less trashy than some.

Newspapers & magazines

   Foreign newspapers and magazines, including *USA Today,* the *International Herald Tribune* as well as weekend editions such as *The Observer* are available in larger newsagents in Vancouver, Calgary and Edmonton.

The best way to get an idea of the Canadian psyche is to tune in to **CBC Radio One**. This is mostly talk radio, where current issues and all manner of topics are discussed from a Canadian angle in a very Canadian way. The news is broadcast every 30 minutes, with an extended national news at 1700, and world news at 1800. Shows in the morning are provincial, those in the afternoon are national. *Cross-country Check-up* (Sun, 1300-1500) and the provincial *BC Almanac* (weekdays at noon) are phone-in shows where people talk about key current issues. In this they give a very real sense of the attitudes and preoccupations that unite a vast, underpopulated land made up of small rural communities where people are still largely bound to the land. BC's *Sad Goat* (Mon-Fri 1400-1600), is also a phone-in show, but more light-hearted and often silly. Other shows to listen out for are: *Definitely not the Opera* (Sat 1400-1700), a pop culture magazine usually good for new Canadian music; *Vinyl Café* (Sun 1200), which gives a good idea of Canadian humour; *Tapestries* (Sun 1500), which deals with spiritual and metaphysical matters; and *Quirks and Quarks* (Sat 1200), an intelligent magazine about science. **CBC Radio Two** is mostly dedicated to classical music.

Radio & TV

   In comparison, Canadian television tells you very little about the country beyond its obvious proximity to the United States. There are only two Canadian channels, one national (**CBC**), the other provincial (**BCTV** in BC, for example). Even these have ads and are dominated by US content. Otherwise, those with satellite usually have the standard 60 or 70 US channels. Still, you might be able to catch the odd comedy show that is very Canadian. *Kids in the Hall* is a frequently repeated favourite; *SCTV* similarly features lots of whacky sketches, and launched the career of many a famous Candian comic, such as John Candy, Rick Moranis, Martin Short, etc. The current show in favour is *This Hour has 22 Minutes* (CBC, Fri 2000), which is satirical, fast-moving, and does a good job of sending up politicians and those neighbours to the south. Nothing of note is produced on the West Coast, unless you count the *X-Files* which were all filmed in Vancouver, or the 1970s series called the *Beachcombers*, filmed on the Sunshine Coast.

Restaurant coding

Expensive: over $20
Mid-range: $10-20
Cheap: $5-10
Seriously cheap: under $5
Prices refer to the average cost of a main course.

Food and drink

In Canadian cities you can find any kind of food you want, and to a very high standard. A predominance of international ethnic cuisines have filled the gap left by any lack of national culinary identity. In smaller communities, however, especially further north, you're most likely to experience 'family' restaurants, serving variations on meat-and-potato dishes, 'Chinese' restaurants of dubious authenticity, and pizza.

Cuisine   While Canada as a whole has little in the way of national dishes, the West Coast does have something of a culinary identity. **Pacific Rim** cuisine covers regions as far apart as BC, Japan, California and Australia. The common denominators are an emphasis on healthy dishes made from fresh, local produce, and a reluctance to overcook the flavours out of food. The ultimate example is sushi, which brings in another key factor: seafood. Vancouver Island in particular is a major source of fresh oysters, mussels and crab.

Under this broad umbrella, **West Coast** cuisine has taken many elements from traditional native cooking. Salmon is used extensively, often cooked on cedar planks or alder grills. Fresh wild game such as caribou and buffalo is also featured, often flavoured with local berries. Barbecuing and smoking are very common. It has become very fashionable to prepare different ethnic cuisines in a West Coast manner, often rendering them more healthy as a result by cutting down on fat and using only fresh ingredients. The best city restaurants offer **fusion cuisine**, where all international boundaries are broken down.

Alberta is famed for the quality of its beef, so if you like steak, this is the place to indulge. Many restaurants specify that their steak is Alberta AAA, the best of the best. **Vegetarians**, on the other hand, are well catered for in cities and more bohemian areas such as the Gulf Islands and West Kootenays. The more you move into the red-neck communities further north, however, the harder it gets to avoid the meat-and-potatoes mentality.

Eating out   Restaurants in major towns tend to stay open late. The smaller the town, the earlier everything will close. Most towns will have an expensive so-called 'fine-dining' establishment. This usually means old-style European, predominantly French, cooking, with the emphasis on steak and seafood. Where many types of ethnic cuisine are available, we have attempted not to favour any particular kind but to search out those whose quality, ambience and value are worthy of recommendation. The majority of these will fit into the mid-range category, with main courses costing $10-20.

There are certain chains which sadly dominate the Canadian market, and sometimes they represent the only choice. We have only mentioned them in the text if they are in some way exceptional, but if you find one you like, you're pretty much guaranteed that it will be everywhere you go. *Earl's* is the best of the bunch. They tend to cover most popular food types, offering decent portions of good food in attractive interiors. We recommend the shrimp and pesto pizza, washed down with a pint of their own *Albino Rhino* ale. *Milestone's* is in a similar vein, though with less character. *The Keg* is a ubiquitous but reliable steakhouse, while *Kelly O'Briens* offers good portions of predictable staples, reasonable prices, and beer. All too often, in places like Cranbrook, you're stuck with the dull 'family' restaurants that specialize in big, reasonably priced breakfasts: *Denny's*, *White Spot*, *Smitty's*, they're all basically the same. Don't bother with their coffee. All the American fast-food outlets are here. For something fast, filling, cheap and not unhealthy, it's hard to beat *Subway*, who will make your sandwich exactly how you want it.

Canada has not been exempt from the world-wide obsession with phoney Irish-style pubs, and has more than a few English-style boozers too. A typical Canadian pub has a pool table, TV sets screening sporting events, bad music, predic- table food and several locals propping up the bar, probably playing *keno* (a lottery game). In Vancouver the best establishments are often called bistros.

Drinks & bars

One of the things that separates the red-necks from the rest is the beer they drink. Sadly, most of the beer sold in Canada is tasteless, weak, watery lager, such as *Molson*, *Kokanee*, *Canadian* and *Old Stock*. Yet Canada has some of the best breweries in the world, and has gone a long way with the concept of microbreweries, which produce small-batch, carefully crafted beers using natural ingredients. All styles of beer are available, served carbonated and chilled. Hand-pumps and warm beer are unheard of. Breweries to look out for, whatever your preference, are *Big Rock* (Calgary), *Nelson* (West Kootenays), *Yukon* (Whitehorse), *Tree* (Kelowna) and *Sleemans* (Guelph, Ontario). *Granville Island* (Vancouver) and *Okanagan Spring* (Kelowna) are also reliable. Very small breweries we recommend include *Raven* (Vancouver), *Crannog* (Shuswap), *Salt Spring*. Individual beers to look out for are *Black Bear* (Kamloops) and *Natureland*. Connoisseurs should be sure to try a range of beers brewed in Québec by *Unibroue*, and only available bottled (with a champagne-style cork). The best are *Maudite* and *Fin du Monde*.

While in Canada, you should also make a point of trying some BC wines, the best of which are made in the Okanagan. The region specializes in German-style whites, sparkling wines, pinot noir, and the sweet and sophisticated ice-wine. See page 227 for more details. It's hard to recommend specific wineries, but *Tinhorn Creek* and *Red Rooster* never disappoint. For a cheap but reliable red, you can't go wrong with a bottle of *Mission Hill Vintner's* Reserve Merlot or Cabernet.

People in Western Canada take their coffee seriously. Locally brewed examples to look out for include *Kicking Horse* (Invermere, East Kootenays), *Oso Negro* (West Kootenays), *Salt Spring* (Southern Gulf Islands) and *Bean Around the World* (Vancouver).

Coffee

Shopping

Canada has its share of tacky souvenirs, usually featuring moose, grizzlies or maple leaves, but a bottle of authentic **maple syrup** makes a nice gift, or you can buy **smoked salmon** (which will keep) in a hand-crafted cedar box, decorated in Native Northwest Coast style. The most popular items among tourists are works by Canada's various **First Nations**, such as the Inuit or Haida. These include carvings in gold, silver, wood and argillite (a black slate-like rock), jewellery, masks, paintings and prints, clothing, mocassins, beadwork, dream-catchers and much more. The cheapest places to buy these artworks is where they were made, such as Haida Gwaii (Queen Charlotte Islands). There is a lot of mass-produced rubbish sold to tourists, so be sure to shop around to get an idea of just how exquisite good native art can be. If you want the real thing, it can be found in Vancouver and Victoria, but don't expect it to be cheap.

Remember to keep your receipts so that you can claim back the tax Most things are cheaper in Alberta where there is no PST (see page 27)

Essentials

▶ **Calendar of events**

January *Brackendale Winter Eagles Festival*, near Squamish, celebrating the biggest annual gathering of bald eagles in the world.

February *Vancouver International Boat Festival*, the largest boat show in Western Canada.

All Native Basketball Tournament, held in Prince Rupert, is a massive and popular event that celebrated its 43rd year in 2002.

March *Pacific Rim Whale Festival*, features various events held around the park and Tofino, to celebrate the annual migration of thousands of grey whales.

April *Telus World Ski and Snowboard Festival*, held in Whistler. The biggest annual winter sports event in North America, featuring the world snowboarding championship.

May *Spring Wine Festival* Held throughout the Okanagan.

June *International Jazz Festival* In Vancouver.

JazzFest International in Victoria. *International Jazz Festival* in Calgary. *Jazz City International Festival* in Edmonton.

Yukon International Storytelling Festival in Whitehorse.

Commisioner's Potlatch, an important native celebration held in Whitehorse.

Dawson City Music Festival, one of the best, most friendly of all.

July *Vancouver International Comedy Festival*

Celebration of Light, held from late-July to early-August in Vancouver, is a two-week international fireworks competition.

Festival of the Arts, a month-long event on Saltspring Island.

Sandfest in Parksville, features the World Sandcastle Competition.

Streetfest, in Nelson involves a lot of outdoor entertainers.

Williams Lake Stampede, on the weekend closest to 1 July, is one of the biggest and (first held in 1919) oldest of its kind in BC.

Banff Festival of the Arts, runs throughout the summer, showcasing young artists in various media.

Calgary Stampede is a 10-day cowboy extravaganza.

Folk Music Festival, in Calgary.

Buffalo Days Pow Wow, Head-Smashed-In Buffalo Jump.

Klondike Days A celebration of the pioneer era held in Edmonton.

Street Performers Festival, in Edmonton. *Great Northern Arts Festival*, in Inuvik, is a 10-day bonanza featuring over 100 artists from north of the Arctic Circle.

August *Victoria Fringe Theatre Festival* The most important festival of its kind in BC, and Victoria's major event.

Filberg Festival held in Comox, Vancouver Island. A massive four-day expo of the best arts and crafts in BC.

Kamloops Pow Wow, one of the best in the country.

Peach Festival, in Penticton, is a massive party.

Ironman Triathlon, also in Penticton, is a very serious event.

Jazzfest, in Kaslo, enjoys one of the most spectacular locations of any festival.

Edmonton Folk Music Festival, *Edmonton Fringe Theatre Festival* is massive.

Squamish Days, a loggers' sports festival. If you want to see one such event, this is the one.

September *Vancouver Fringe Festival*, Vancouver International Film Festival *Sandcastle Festival*, Harrison Hot Springs. *Fall Wine Festival*, held in late September/early October throughout the Okanagan.

October *Vancouver International Film Festival*

Non-aboriginal **arts and crafts** are also exceptionally fine and often extremely good value given the workmanship involved. Regions such as the Gulf Islands and West Kootenays are overrun with artists and artisans, but Vancouver's Granville Island is the best place to see a wide range of works. Visitors to Alberta may want to buy some authentic **cowboy boots**, a stetson hat or a set of chaps. Music lovers should take advantage of the fact that Canada is one of the cheapest places in the world for **CDs**. It could also be better for certain items of **sporting equipment** than your home country.

Entertainment and nightlife

Most towns in Canada will have a cinema, theatre, museum and art gallery, but the standard and choice is predictably much higher in the cities, particularly Vancouver. The main Canadian spectator sport is ice hockey, but you could also go to see baseball, Canadian football, basketball or even curling. For details on spectator sports, see under Entertainment for each town. The nightlife in Vancouver is not as good as it should be, but there is still plenty of choice, and the DJs here are as up to the moment as anywhere. Clubs tend to operate from 2100 to a disappointing 0200, and most bars are shut by 0100. Don't expect too much of the nightlife scene in small-town Canada.

Holidays and festivals

New Year's Day; Good Friday; Easter Monday; Victoria Day, third Monday in May; Canada Day, 1 July; Labour Day, first Monday in September; Thanksgiving, second Monday in October; Remembrance Day, 11 November; Christmas Day; Boxing Day.

National holidays
See box, opposite

Alberta: *Family Day*, third Monday in **February**; Alberta Heritage Day, first Monday in **August**.
BC: *British Columbia Day*, first Monday in **August**.
Yukon: *Discovery Day*, third Monday in **August**.

Provincial holidays

Sport and special interest travel

Many people visit Western Canada because they know that most of the adventure sports known to man are available here at a level that is barely equalled anywhere else. Those who enjoy more genteel activities such as golf and bird-watching are also being drawn in ever-growing numbers by Canada's great outdoors. Countless specialist tour operators are on hand to offer guidance up to any level (see page 21 and under individual areas throughout the book). A great place to find out more about these activities is in British Columbia's extremely useful *Outdoor and Adventure Guide*, available from any Visitor Centre.

Basketball, ice hockey, baseball, lacrosse and Trivial Pursuit were all invented in Canada

Western Canada is crossed by one of the most important migratory routes in the world, with thousands of geese, swans, ducks, waterfowl and other birds passing through each year. The major spots for seeing them are mentioned throughout the text. One is the stretch of coast between **Parksville and Qualicum Bay**, where 18 of the top 100 species most sought by birders are spotted. **Courtenay** is one of the best places for trumpeter swans, while **Brackendale**, close to Squamish, enjoys the world's highest number of visiting bald eagles. **Vaseux Lake Park** south of Penticton is also highly regarded by birders. On the whole, though, you're more likely to see birds in the Yukon. **Marsh Lake** to the southeast of Whitehorse, for instance, is a major staging area for waterfowl.

Bird-watching

The most rewarding area for caving is close to **Nootka Sound** on Vancouver Island's west coast. Experts could research a wealth of systems in the **Zeballos** region, but the

Caving

most commonly visited is **Upana Caves Recreation Area**. Further south on the island are the more commercial **Horne Lake Caves**. Also easily visited are **Cody Caves** near Ainsworth Hot Springs, and **Nakimu Caves** near Glacier National Park. Worth looking into is the **Crowsnest Pass** region of southwestern Alberta. For more information, contact the *BC Speleological Federation*, BCSF@cancaver.ca

Canoeing　Northern BC and the Yukon are overflowing with world-class canoeing. Some of the most accessible spots are **Murtle Lake** in Wells Gray Provincial Park, **Bowron Lakes** in the Cariboo, and the **Powell Forest Canoe Route** on the Sunshine Coast. The **Stikine River** further north is a rugged option that probably requires a guide. If you want to make canoeing the focus of your holiday, however, the Yukon is the place to go. The province's most popular trip is the two-week journey down the **Yukon River** from Whitehorse to Dawson City, which is suitable even for beginners. The **Nisutlin**, **Teslin** and **Wolf** rivers, all ending at Teslin Lake, are also firm favourites. For experts, the most exciting area is the remote **Peel Wilderness**, and the pristine **Snake**, **Wind** and **Bonnet Plume** rivers. Yet further north, the majority of visitors to Ivvavik National Park are there to canoe the **Firth River**. The standard guide is *Ken Madsen's Paddling in the Yukon*. If going without a guide, always wear a lifejacket, and carry a bailing bucket, throw-rope and whistle in the canoe. Avoid paddling in the afternoon on larger lakes. For more details contact the *Recreational Canoeing Association of BC*, T4371140, or check out two useful sites at **www.bccanoe.com** and **www.canoebc.ca**

Climbing　The best area for climbing is Squamish. The granite monolith known as the **Stawamus**
& moun-　**Chief** is the most famous location, with over 250 routes, but there are plenty of other
taineering　sites nearby, including the **Smoke Bluffs Rock Climbing Park**. Professionals also rate **Bugaboos Provincial Park** in the East Kootenays, an area of astounding natural beauty. **Skaha Bluffs** near Penticton in the Okanagan is also recommended. For climbing and mountaineering, the Rockies is an obvious destination. Canmore is home of the *Alpine Club of Canada*, and has some nice cliffs at *Grassi Lakes*. Hard-core mountaineers might want to take on North America's highest peaks in the *St Elias Range* which runs through the Yukon and Alaska. For more information contact: *Federation of Mountain Clubs of BC*, T604-8787007, www.alpineclubofcanada.ca;　*BC Mountaineering Club*, T604-2689502; the *Association of Canadian Mountain Guides*, T6782885, www.acmg.ca

Cycling　Canada can be a wonderful country to explore by cycle, but remember how vast the distances are and try to stick to lesser-used roads. An excellent trip is the 287 km down the **Icefields Parkway** from Jasper to Banff, through the heart of the Rockies. This could be extended by adding the loop that takes you through **Yoho** and **Kootenay** national parks. A beautiful road trip could also be made around the West Kootenays, following the **Nelson-Kaslo-New Denver-Slocan Valley** loop, for instance. For the more adventurous, the **Yukon** would be a superb region to explore by bike, with many old mining roads to explore, and lots of (admittedly long) scenic loops.

　　BC's outdoor enthusiasts take their **mountain biking** very seriously. There are some first-class trails on **Vancouver's North Shore**, and also around towns like Kamloops, Kelowna and Williams Lake. The best overall region is the Kootenays, particularly Rossland, Fernie, Nelson and Kaslo. The best location in Northern BC is **Babine Mountain Recreation Area** near Smithers. For information, always go to a bike shop rather than the Information Centre.

Fishing　**Freshwater**　In Canada you're never far from a lake or river renowned for its fishing. Particularly popular is the interlakes region of the **Cariboo**, with over 125 lakes within an hour's drive along Highway 24. **Princeton** on Highway 3 is also close to some 50 trout-fishing lakes. Many lakes around **Kamloops** are equally noted for trout, while **Kootenay Lake** is renowned for the world's largest strain of rainbow trouts. If you want to catch a whopper, try battling the giant sturgeon of the **Fraser River**. For salmon fishing, the **Nass**, **Skeena** and **Stikine** rivers in Northern BC are all excellent. A freshwater licence is required to fish in BC's lakes and rivers. In addition, specific licences are required in all national parks. When buying your permit, ask for the *Freshwater Fishing Regulations Synopsis*, which details possession limits, and be sure to pick up *BC's Freshwater Fishing Guide* from any Information Centre. For details of outfitters, contact *BC Fishing Resorts and Outfitters Association*, T250-3746836.

Saltwater Vancouver Island is famous for its year-round salmon fishing, and halibut from April to August. Prime spots are **Campbell River** and the **Barkley** and **Clayoquot Sounds** in Pacific Rim National Park. Northern BC is also highly renowned by anglers, especially the waters around **Prince Rupert** and **Haida Gwaii**, **Bella Coola** and **Bella Bella**. A tidal waters sport fishing licence is required to fish in BC's waters, widely available at sports stores. *Fisheries and Oceans Canada* sets the regulations. For details call T604-6662828. Pick up the BC *Saltwater Fishing Planning Guide* at any Visitor Information Centre, or contact T604-6893438, www.sportfishing.bc.ca Any number of tour operators will take you out to the best spots and supply all equipment. The *Oak Bay Marine Group*, T1800-6637090, www.obmg.com, has seven destinations in key fishing areas, and a lot of experience.

Essentials

Golf

Golf is apparently Canada's most popular participation sport, played by 7.4% of the population. There are courses everywhere, including many around Vancouver and Victoria, but for a golf holiday the places to head for are **Whistler** and the **Okanagan**, both with demanding and scenic courses, some of which are designed by professionals like Jack Nicklaus.

In April 2003, the US Masters was won by Mike Weir, the first Canadian ever to win a golf major

Hiking

Western Canada has to be one of the world's best destinations for hiking and nobody should visit the area without attempting some of its superlative walks. The cream of the cream are to be found throughout the **Canadian Rockies**, including Waterton Lakes National Park in the Alberta section; the Coast Mountains of Garibaldi Park, Squamish and Whistler; the Purcell and Selkirk ranges of the West Kootenays; Kluane National Park in the Yukon, which contains Canada's highest peaks and is far less busy than the southern parks; and the Tombstone Mountains on the Dempster Highway. On top of this, some specific hikes can be recommended: the famous **West Coast Trail** in Pacific Rim National Park; the **Juan de Fuca** and **East Sooke** trails on Vancouver Island's south coast; the hard-core **Cape Scott Trail** at the Island's northern peak; or the 180-km **Sunshine Coast Trail**. For details of the very best hikes, we recommend *Gotta Hike BC* by Skye and Lake Nomad, Voice in the Wilderness Press, 2001. For more information, contact the *Outdoor Recreational Council of BC*, T7373058. The **TransCanada Trail** is an ambitious attempt to build a single trail right across the country. When completed, it will be the longest recreational trail in the world, and is destined to be a classic trek or cycle. In the meantime, whole stretches of the trail are in place, offering many hiking possibilities. For the latest information visit **www.tctrail.ca/registry**

Kayaking

Exceptional kayaking is available right in and around Vancouver, up **Indian Arm** or around **Bowen Island**. Even better are several locations around Vancouver Island, particularly the **Broken Group Islands** in Pacific Rim National Park; **Clayoquot Sound** and the area around Tofino; **Nootka Sound** further north; in **Johnstone Strait**; and around the **Gulf Islands**. **Desolation Sound Marine Park** at the end of the Sunshine Coast is also a prime spot. More remote sea kayaking can be found around **Bella Bella** on the Chilcotin Coast, including the Hakai Recreation Area, and around **Haida Gwaii** (the Queen Charlotte Islands). Almost all canoe trips in the Yukon could be handled in a kayak, which is a

▶ **Ski-hill vital statistics**

Nearest town	Hill	Area (ha)	Snowfall(cm)	Vertical drop(m)
Banff	Mt Norquay	66	300	503
Banff	Sunshine Valley	1,282	914	1,070
Courtenay	Mt Washington	607	900	505
Fernie	Fernie	1,012	875	857
Golden	Kicking Horse	1,619	360 cm	1,100
Invermere	Panorama	1,153	447	1,220
Kamloops	Sun Peaks	979	527	881
Kelowna	Big White	892	750	777
Kimberley	Kimberley	708	570	751
Lake Louise	Lake Louise	1,619	360	1,000
Nelson	Whitewater	405	1,200	396
Penticton	Apex	223	570	505
Revelstoke	Powder Springs	162	450	300
Rossland	Red Mountain	486	700	880
Vancouver	Cypress Mtn	101	622	538
Vancouver	Mt Seymour	24	300	330
Vancouver	Grouse Mtn	486	500	370
Vernon	Silver Star	583	700	760
Whistler	Whistler/ Blackcomb	2,862	900	1,609

more suitable vessel for some of the rougher rivers such as the **Alsek** and **Tatshenshini**. A good place to learn kayaking is *Strathcona Park Lodge* on Vancouver Island (see page 176), but most tour operators are happy to instruct beginners. Some useful contacts for more details are *Sea Kayak Association of BC*, T604-2909653; *Whitewater Kayaking Association of BC*, T604-5156379, www.whitewater.org and *Pacific International Kayak Association*, T604-5971122.

Essentials

Lifts	Runs	Beg	Int	Exp	Day pass	Comments
5	31	11%	45%	44%	$47	Small; steep and deep runs for experts
14	91	20%	50%	30%	$54	Huge snowpack, long season
8	50	25%	40%	35%	$44	Huge run; access to back country; fast-growing resort
10	97	30%	40%	30%	$54	Largely undiscovered; an aficionados favourite
8	38	25%	35%	40%	$40	Plenty of snow; vast area; brand new and still uncrowded
10	100	15%	55%	30%	$49	Big area, lots of runs, some very long
5	80	24%	30%	46%	$46	Native protests over land claims
13	105	18%	56%	26%	$48	Big tube park; night skiing; confusing resort
9	67	20%	45%	35%	$45	Skating, tobogganing
11	105	25%	45%	30%	$54	Huge, cold, amazing views; can get pass for all 3 hills
3	36	20%	40%	40%	$37	Access to large backcountry; lots of snow
5	60	16%	48%	36%	$61	Ice-skating trail; tube park
2	27	40%	40%	20%	$28	Cheap; lots of snow; cat-skiing; accessible backcountry
5	83	10%	45%	45%	$42	Close to a great town; ample expert terrain
5	23	30%	30%	40%	$36	Snowboard park; good for experts
4	21	40%	40%	20%	$22	3 snowboard parks; good for beginners
11	24	40%	40%	20%	$32	Vancouver's busiest; great views; nightskiing; lots of activities
9	107	20%	50%	30%	$45	Pretty, friendly and colourful resort
33	200	15%	55%	30%	$61	Big, famous, record-breaking; touristy, cliquey resort town

Rafting The most famous whitewater rafting trip in the west is down the **Tatshenshini** and **Alsek** rivers, which slice through the wilderness of Kluane National Park from the Yukon to BC. The **Fraser Canyon** is also great for rafting, with trips including the **Fraser** and **Thompson** rivers. Of many in the Rockies region, the **Kicking Horse** is renowned for its whitewater, while the **Columbia River** makes for a more sedate trip. The **Chilko River** in the Chilcotin is famous for the 19 km of non-stop rapids in the Lava Canyon.

Sailing   Canada's West Coast, with its hundreds of small islands and extensive marine life, is a Mecca for sailors. The **Gulf Islands** are an obvious prime spot, as are the **Sunshine Coast** and **Desolation Sound**. For something more rugged, follow the **Inside Passage** from Port Hardy to Prince Rupert. Experienced mariners could even cruise around **Haida Gwaii**. Marinas and boat supply stores stock nautical charts, sailing directions and tide and current tables. The *Canadian Hydrographic Service*, T3636358, sell charts and tide tables. Those sailing into Canadian waters must clear customs, or could obtain an advance CANPASS permit. In North America, call T1888-2267277. For information on boating regulations and safety practices, contact the *Canadian Coast Guard*, T1800-2676687, www.ccg-gcc.gc.ca The BC edition of the *Guide to Federal Small Craft Harbours* can be obtained from *Fisheries and Oceans Canada*, T604-6666271. Useful contacts are the *BC Sailing Association*, T604-7373126, and the *Canadian Yachting Association*, www.sailing.ca

Scuba diving   Thanks to its cold, clear water and abundant marine life, the **Georgia Strait** between the mainland and Vancouver Island's east coast has been named by no lesser an authority than the *Jacques Cousteau Society* as the second best region for scuba diving in the world, after the Red Sea. Many first-class sites are just north of Vancouver, including **Whytecliff Park** and **Porteau Cove**, which has a number of artificial reefs created by sunken ship-wrecks. **Powell River** on the Sunshine Coast is known as the 'Dive Capital of Canada'. Its attractions include an underwater bronze statue of a mermaid and 'The Hulks', a ring of sunken ships that form the world's longest breakwater. **Nanaimo** is renowned for its diving too, as is the **Discovery Passage** around Quadra Island, but Vancouver's most highly rated diving is out of **Port Hardy**, where the water is exceptionally clear. Experienced divers with their own gear can even dive down to a submerged village in Banff's Lake **Minnewanka**. Visibility is best between October and March, when it reaches up to 30 m. Contact the *Underwater Council of BC*, T604-6756964, www.ucbc.bc.ca

Skiing &   Whistler/Blackcomb is the most famous ski resort in Canada and is consistently voted the
snowboarding   best in North America. But BC is loaded with excellent hills that are less busy and expensive, and may be more suitable for beginners. A marvellous winter tour of Western Canada could be based on ski-hill hopping (see Where to go, page 18). There are three hills on **Vancouver's North Shore**. **Mount Washington** on Vancouver Island is one of the province's most popular, and is currently being upgraded. The Okanagan has a scattering of great hills, including Kelowna's massive **Big White** and Vernon's small but delightful **Silver Star**. In the Kootenays are a handful of gems highly recommended by resident experts, such as Rossland's **Red Mountain**, Nelson's **Whitewater**, and Fernie's **Alpine Resort**. Golden's **Kicking Horse** is a comparatively new resort and still expanding, but seems set to take the industry by storm. Of those in the Rockies, **Lake Louise** enjoys a vast terrain, and superb facilities, snow and views, while Banff's **Sunshine Village** has the deepest snow-pack of all. There are numerous factors to take into account when rating a ski hill. The data in the table on page 46 should help you to make a choice.

Naturally, there's more to skiing than downhill. The terms **cross-country** and **Nordic skiing** are virtually interchangeable, the first speaking for itself. Most ski hills also have a cross-country area, often with trails that are groomed and track-set, but some of the best skiing is to be found in unofficial areas where paths have been blazed by locals. Recommended spots include Manning Park, Poulson Pass and Nancy Greene near Rossland, the Salmo-Creston Pass on Highway 3, Rogers Pass on Highway 1, and Canmore. Experienced skiers often prefer **backcountry skiing** to downhill. Some of the best is to be found near Kaslo or at Rogers Pass. If you want the very best snow, you have to pay for it: a number of operators offer **cat-skiing** and **heli-skiing**. Again, the Kootenay region near Kaslo is especially renowned, but a number of operators in Northern BC also access vast areas of snow to die for. Shop around and consult the major ski magazines.

The best place for surfing in Western Canada is **Long Beach** in Pacific Rim National Park, though it doesn't compare with what's on offer in Australia and California. Only experienced surfers and strong swimmers should surf these waters, as the rip-tides are notoriously dangerous. Ask at the two board shops in Tofino for the best advice.

Surfing

In March and April, around 22,000 Pacific grey whales pass Vancouver Island's West Coast. **Tofino** and **Ucluelet** are the best places to pick up a tour. **Johnstone Strait** on the Island's northeast coast near Telegraph Cove is the best place to see pods of resident orca (killer whales), though they're also easily seen from Victoria. **Haida Gwaii** is great for seeing humpback whales in February, Pacific greys in spring, plus orcas and the odd blue or fin whale. There are plenty of reputable operators running whale-watching tours. When choosing one, bear in mind that the most important decision is whether you want to ride in an inflatable zodiac, which is a faster, wetter, more exciting trip, or a hard-shell boat, which is more sedate.

Whale-watching

A formidable holiday could easily focus on wine-tasting in the **Okanagan Valley**.

Wine-tasting

Health

Western Canada must be one of the safest places on Earth, it has good medical facilities and there are no prevalent diseases, so no vaccinations are required before entry. In fact, with its ample fresh air and water and lack of stress, Canada is a place to go for convalescence. Your greatest threat is probably from wildlife, particularly animals that seem innocuous such as elk and moose. During rutting season, around September, such animals can be particularly aggressive. Give all wildlife a wide berth. In 2003, only the second human death from rabies since 1985 was reported from British Columbia. This does not mean everyone needs rabies vaccine for Canada but if you are a keen worldwide traveller it is worth having a course of rabies vaccines.

See individual town and city directories for details of medical services

Make sure you are up to date with the most basic **vaccines** such as tetanus and polio. It is also wise to be up to date with hepatitis A vaccine and Typhoid even for this relatively safe destination.

The health service in Canada is maintained by provincial governments. Every citizen is obliged to pay health insurance, known as *Medicare*. Visitors should make sure their insurance covers all medical costs. In BC, the health system is being run down at an alarming rate. Hospitals are being closed in all but the major urban areas, leaving much of the population in a very precarious position. Visitors suffering from a condition that may need immediate care, such as those with serious allergies or diabetes, are advised to carry what they need in case of an emergency. Do not rely on the proximity of an open hospital.

Medical facilities

There are plenty of pharmacies throughout Canada stocking all the medical provisions you could possibly need. As elsewhere, many drugs are only available with a doctor's prescription. Pharmacists (chemists) are often large retail outlets that stay open late, some even 24 hours, especially in big cities.

What to take

Altitude sickness This can start with chest or head problems both caused by excess fluid. An early clue to brain swelling will be headache and a feeling of sickness. You may feel unusually short of breath. The best treatment is to descend. The best preventative is not to ascend too quickly. Consult an expedition medicine expert before you consider any medications.

Common complaints

Essentials

Hypothermia and frostbite To avoid frostbite and hypothermia, which is when your core temperature falls below 35°C, you should keep warm by wearing several layers of suitable clothing (see What to take, page 26). If you feel cold move about rather than just standing still.

Insect bites Canada's insects are vicious but carry no diseases. The tiny ticks that carry Lymes disease are too rare in Canada to worry about.

Sea sickness Even on short trips out to the islands, the movement of the sea can be unsettling. Try *Kwells* or other sea-sickness tablets.

Sun burn Avoid extensive exposure to the sun, wear a hat and sunglasses and use a high protection factor sun cream.

Water Tap water is safe to drink throughout the country. Drinking water from dubious sources, especially slow-moving streams, can lead to **giardia**, commonly known here as 'beaver fever'. The result is vomiting, diarrhoea, weakness and sometimes nasty eggy burps.

Sexual health   The range of visible and invisible diseases is awesome. Unprotected sex can spread HIV, Hepatitis B and C, Gonorrhea (green discharge), chlamydia (nothing to see but may cause painful urination and later female infertility), painful recurrent herpes, syphilis and warts, just to name a few. You can cut down the risk by using condoms, a femidom or avoiding sex altogether. Consider getting a sexual health check on your return home if you do have intercourse.

Adapted by **Dr Charlie Easmon** MBBS MRCP MSc Public Health DTM&H DOccMed Director of Travel Screening Services.

Vancouver

Introducing Vancouver

Far and away the most important urban centre in Western Canada, Vancouver is also one of the world's great post-modern cities. Its Downtown core is a delightfully eclectic hotchpotch of architecture, where sleek glass-and-chrome skyscrapers rub shoulders with the odd Gothic church, Victorian warehouse, and a handful of other delights and oddities.

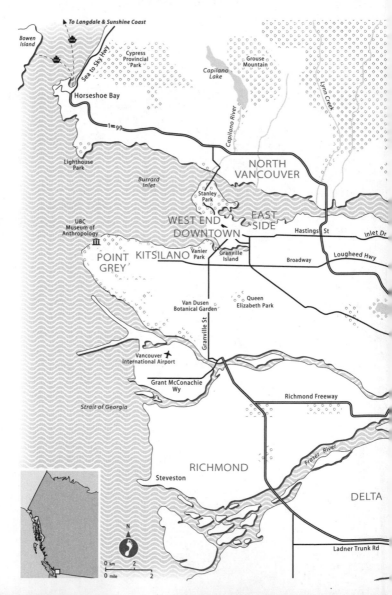

This fascinating city, which enjoys a magnificent mountain and ocean setting, is the northern hemisphere's answer to Rio de Janeiro. As well as providing a breathtaking backdrop, the Coast Mountains that loom over Downtown Vancouver also offer easily accessible world-class skiing, hiking and mountain-biking. Beaches, seawalls and ferry-buses are also an everyday part of city life, while some of the best kayaking, canoeing, sailing, scuba diving and whale-watching in the world are all within a stone's throw. Copious rainfall and a surprisingly mild climate means that abundant vegetation and some of the planet's largest trees adorn the city's many parks and forests.

The young, extremely cosmopolitan population of this vibrant city supports more restaurants, reads more, shops more, drinks more wine, spends more on sports equipment and smokes less than that of any other Canadian city. Such classic West Coast traits are complemented by a distinctive Pacific Rim character. Closer to Japan than it is to Britain, with 30% of its residents of Asian origin, this is a genuine meeting place of East and West, its strong oriental flavour having earnt it the nickname 'Lotus land'.

Vancouver

24 hours in Vancouver

If you only have one day to spend in Vancouver, you can start with coffee and breakfast at *The Naam* or *Sophie's Cosmic Café* in Kitsilano, and then take a bus to the **UBC Museum of Anthropology**. Heading back to Kits, walk along the beach, through **Vanier Park** to **Granville Island**. Spend some time in the art stores and Food Market before hopping on a bus to **Downtown**. There you could pop into the Art Gallery or Craft Museum, or stop for another coffee in the HBSC building. Be sure to see the Public Library, **Chinatown** (where you could stop for lunch) and **Gastown**, as you make your way to the SeaBus terminal. Cross the water to Lonsdale Quay, and catch a bus up to **Grouse Mountain**, where the Skyride Gondola will whisk you up to fabulous views. If time allows, go for a walk in **Capilano Park**, or check out the suspension bridge. Later, you can stroll to **Denman Street**, where there are plenty of spots for dinner and drinks. Walk back into town window-shopping along **Robson Street**. Over another drink, browse the *Georgia Strait* for a show or band and check out the night scene in **Yaletown**, eventually heading back to **Gastown** where the best clubs are.

Ins and outs

Getting there

Phone code: 604 (778 for numbers issued after 2001)

Colour map 1, grid C4

Population: City of Vancouver: 545,671; Greater Vancouver: nearly two million

For transport details see page 109

Vancouver International Airport (YVR), T2077077, www.yvr.ca, is located on Sea Island in the mouth of the Fraser River, 13 km from Downtown, adjacent to Richmond. Two very attractive terminals (see box page 55) cater to international and domestic flights. The International Terminal has all the usual facilities, including a useful BC **Visitor Information** desk on the Arrivals floor (level 2), and an Airport Information desk (which operates a lost and found service) one floor up in the departure lounge, along with most of the shops and services. There are plenty of phones and ATMs dotted around, and the corridor linking the 2 terminals has a children's play area and nursery.

Three forms of transport head Downtown from right outside the International terminal: the ***Airporter*** shuttle bus leaves every 15 mins, running to Downtown hotels, Canada Place and the bus station ($12 one-way, $18 return); **taxis** operate around the clock, charging $25-30 for the 25-min trip Downtown; a **limousine** costs $40 for up to 8 passengers. There are also direct services to Whistler and Victoria. The **city bus** leaves from the Domestic terminal (follow signs), and take sabout 45 mins, involving a transfer onto Bus No 98 B.

Trains and **long-distance buses** all leave from the VIA Rail Pacific Central Station, 1150 Station St, a short *SkyTrain* ride from Downtown. *BC Ferries* arrive from Victoria and the Southern Gulf Islands at Tsawwassan, about 30 km south of Vancouver. City buses run Downtown, with one transfer ($4). Ferries from Nanaimo in Central Vancouver Island arrive at Horseshoe Bay, some 15 km northwest on Hwy 99, with 2 direct buses Downtown ($3). About 1 million **cruise-ship** passengers pass through per year. Canada Place is the main terminus along with Ballantyne, 1 km east at 655 Centennial, connected by a free shuttle. Much effort is taken to ease connections between cruise ships and the airport or bus station.

Getting around

Unlike most North American cities, Vancouver's Downtown streets have names rather than numbers, making orientation more tricky. If in doubt look for the mountains to the north. Block numbering is divided into east and west by Ontario Street, which runs north-south just east of the Downtown core. So the address 39 W Broadway is in the block immediately west of Ontario, whereas 297 W 4th Av would be in the third block west. Most sights of interest are west. Unlike most cities built on a grid, the numbers of

◀

Airport art

Vancouver International Airport is packed with some wonderful pieces of art that provide a fine introduction to the West Coast. Before clearing the Arrivals Hall, have a look at the Spindle Whorl, *a giant version of a traditional Coast Salish art form. Carved out of red cedar, it is suspended from a wall of granite shingles over which water flows to suggest the rivers that are so integral a part of Salish life. On the Arrivals level of the International Terminal building is a pair of 6-m high* Welcome Figures, *carved from the same red cedar log in the Salish style. Nearby are four large Native Musqeuam weavings.*

Don't even think about leaving this building without going upstairs to see Bill Reid's exquisite Spirit of Haida Gwaii, the Jade Canoe. *This bronze casting with its distinctive green patina is considered to be the masterpiece of the man who reintroduced the genius of Northwest Coast Native carving to the world (see page 74). Behind it is* The Great Wave Wall, *a giant piece of glass art that changes constantly with the light to suggest the ocean. Dotted around the airport are display cases rotating artworks from galleries around town. Finally, outside the main entrance, set among a small forested area, is a set of three classic totem poles, the shape of things to come.*

Vancouver

avenues in Vancouver do not correspond directly to block numbers. To work out the block number from a numbered avenue, add 16. So 3400 Main St would be the block immediately south of 18th Av.

Many of Vancouver's attractions are concentrated within the Downtown peninsula, which is best explored **on foot**. *TransLink* operate a network of city **buses** that converge on Granville St Downtown, an elevated rail system called the **SkyTrain**, and a passenger ferry called the **SeaBus**. The same tickets are valid for all three. A couple of private **mini-ferries** also ply the waters of False Creek. Measures have been taken to make the city negotiable by **bike** (see page 110).

Vancouver's main **Visitor Information Centre** is at Plaza Level, Waterfront Centre, 200 Burrard St, T6832000, Open daily mid May-Sep 0800-1900, Oct-mid May Mon-Fri 0830-1700, Sat 0900-1700. The full range of facilities are offered, including currency exchange, travel info, photo albums of hotels and B&Bs, a reservation service, and tickets for events and excursions. They also carry information on most of southern BC. There is a tourist information desk at **Vancouver International Airport**, on the Arrivals floor (level 2), open daily year-round 0730-2330. Another is at the Peace Arch border crossing, open daily 0800-2000 mid-Sep to mid-May and 0900-1700 mid-May to mid-Sep. **Tourist information**

Make no mistake, Vancouver is a rainy city, with an average of 170 days of precipitation per year. Since local topography involves a jump from sea level to mountains within a few kilometres, not to mention proximity to the Pacific Ocean, Georgia Strait, and mountains of Vancouver Island and Washington's Olympia Range, the weather here is unpredictable to say the least. Forecasts are definitely not to be trusted. Having said that, a warm Pacific Ocean current combined with a strong air-flow originating near Hawaii help make Vancouver's climate the mildest in Canada. Spring flowers start blooming in early March, and winter snowfalls Downtown are rare enough to throw the city's motorists into confusion. For these reasons Vancouver has been called the Canadian city with the best climate and the worst weather. Like most of the country, unless you are looking for winter sports, there is no doubt that summer is the time to visit. **Climate**

▶ **Arriving at night**

Should you arrive in the small hours, rest assured that Vancouver airport is safe, with taxis running Downtown through the night. There is a hotel right in the airport, and several others a short ride away (see page 86). Almost all hotels in town have staff on duty 24 hours, or can cater for a late arrival if given warning. If you're hungry or thirsty, head for The Naam *at 2724 W 4th Avenue, which stays open through the night.*

History

Earliest remains of habitation in the Vancouver area date back some 10,000 years. More recently, the so-called Marpole civilization, 3,000-year distant ancestors of today's natives, already lived in large cedar plank houses, produced stone carvings and copper ornaments and navigated in dugout canoes. Most significant of several First Nations who inhabited Greater Vancouver when the Europeans arrived were the Squamish and the Musqueam. The Spanish commander Dionisio Galiano wrote of these villagers: "Their liveliness, grace and talent engaged all our attention. They displayed an unequalled affability together with a warlike disposition".

During the 1770s, when Captain James Cook arrived at Nootka Sound on Vancouver Island, the Pacific Coast was rife with European exploration. The Spanish, Russians, British, Dutch and French were all looking for the elusive Northwest Passage, a northern trade route to the Orient between the Pacific and Atlantic Coasts. First to venture into the Georgia Strait was Spanish navigator José María Narvaez, who believed Point Grey to be an island surrounded by other islands. The following year Cook's former apprentice, Captain Vancouver and the Spaniard Dionisio Alcalá Galiano both sailed up Burrard Inlet and Vancouver Island's East Coast. The Englishman spent just one day in the city that would come to bear his name.

Other than a brief and treacherous foray into the region by Simon Fraser (see page 443), the next appearance of a European on the scene came in the form of the Hudson's Bay Company, which established Fort Langley in 1827. Five years later 2,000 beaver pelts were shipped from the fort, and by the 1840s it was the biggest exporter of salted salmon on the coast. When gold was discovered on the Fraser River in 1858, the fears of American expansion created by the arrival of 25,000 prospectors caused the governor of Vancouver Island to declare the mainland a British colony, and 25 Royal Engineer 'sappers' were dispatched from England to show the flag and build a number of roads that have become the major thoroughfares. The giant trees that covered the whole area were chopped down at an alarming rate.

In 1867, Vancouver's first major industry was established when Edward Stamp opened a mill on the south shore of Burrard Inlet. Later to become the Hastings Mill, this has been called "the nucleus around which the city of Vancouver grew". But it could be that the real hub of the settlement soon officially called Granville Townsite was the saloon built around the same time by 'Gassy' Jack Deighton (see page 65), after whom it was originally called Gastown. Confederation also happened in 1867, and four years later BC agreed to join this new land called Canada on condition that a railway would be built to connect east and west. When the Canadian Pacific Railway finally arrived 15 years later, certain political wranglings led today's Downtown peninsula to be chosen as its terminus, and its name changed to Vancouver. Two months later the 'Great Fire' destroyed the ramshackle town in less than an hour, but rebuilding (this time in brick) began before the embers had stopped smoking and four years later the town's population had swollen from 400 to 13,000. It doubled again in the next decade, then exploded.

Incorporation finally came in 1886, followed by electricity the following year and the first streetcar three years later. By 1911 the population had reached over 120,000 and was doubling every five years. A period of untrammelled development, reflected by a series of buildings that replaced each other as the tallest in the British Empire, only came to an end with the Wall Street Crash of 1929. The next period of serious growth came in the mid-60s with a Downtown rejuvenation program that brought the Robson Square complex, BC Place, the renovation of Gastown, and the pedestrianization of Granville Street. In 1986 the city celebrated its 100th anniversary by hosting Expo '86, which attracted over 21 million visitors and led to a new wave of development and the construction of many landmark buildings such as Canada Place and the distinctive futuristic sphere that now houses Science World.

Most of BC's population lives in the suburban corridor between Vancouver and Chilliwack to the east, an area known as the Lower Mainland. As the focus of such a concentration of population, Vancouver's importance today in terms of travel, trade, industry and culture outweighs any other city west of Toronto.

Sights

The heart of a sprawling suburban corridor that contains half of the province's population, Vancouver's Downtown peninsula is relatively tiny, yet contains the bulk of the city's sights. While these include attractions like the Art Gallery and Science World, most interest comes from examples of architecture, like the Marine Building or Public Library, and neighbourhoods like Gastown, Chinatown and Yaletown. The city is kept alive after dark by the proximity of the West End, Canada's most densely populated neighbourhood, whose residents enjoy the luxury of the vast and largely undeveloped Stanley Park, which has its own attractions such as the Aquarium.

Across False Creek and English Bay to the south is the bulk of the City of Vancouver. The main attractions here are the market and arts and crafts of Granville Island, the museum complex of adjacent Vanier Park, and the more distant UBC Museum of Anthropology. There are also some great beaches and several distinctive neighbourhoods, such as Kitsilano, West Broadway, Commercial Drive or South Main. To the north of Downtown across Burrard Inlet, in a group of districts collectively known as the North Shore, the picturesque mountains that so gloriously frame the city also provide a series of rugged parks and canyons, ideal for skiing, hiking and exploring; for many people these represent Vancouver's most appealing feature.

Downtown Peninsula

With five giant white masts rising from its 'deck', and a powerful prow jutting out into Burrard Inlet, Canada Place really does look like a large ocean-going vessel, and begs comparisons with Sydney's famous Opera House. Built as the Canadian Pavilion for Expo '86, it now functions as a hotel, conference centre, and the main terminus for the thriving cruise-ship business, but its chief interest for travellers is the **IMAX theatre** inconveniently situated at the back. Over the road is the indispensable **Visitor Information Centre**.

Canada Place & around
The sights are ordered geographically, starting at Canada Place then following an anti-clockwise circle

Opposite, at 355 Burrard Street, is the **Marine Building**. Designed to be strikingly magnificent and to put Vancouver on the international shipping map, this was and perhaps still is the city's most notable building. Completed

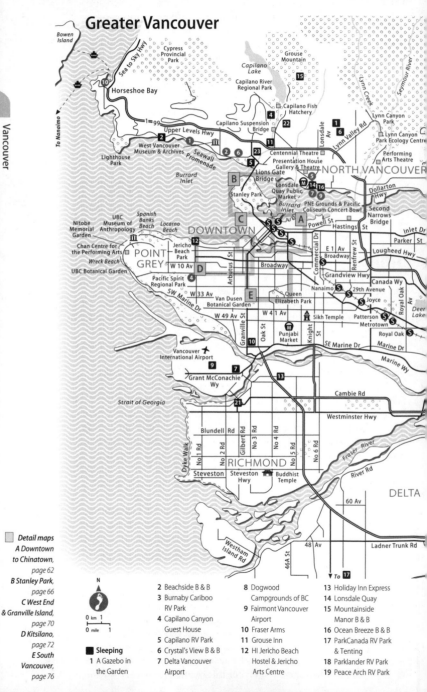

Greater Vancouver

Bowen Island

Cypress Provincial Park

Grouse Mountain

Capilano Lake

1=99

Horseshoe Bay

To Nanaimo

Capilano River Regional Park

Capilano Fish Hatchery

Upper Levels Hwy

Capilano Suspension Bridge

Lonsdale Av

Lynn Valley Rd

Lynn Canyon Park

Lynn Canyon Park Ecology Centre

West Vancouver Museum & Archives

Seawall Promenade

Centennial Theatre

Performing Arts Theatre

Lighthouse Park

Burrard Inlet

Presentation House Gallery & Theatre

NORTH VANCOUVER

Lions Gate Bridge

Stanley Park

Lonsdale Quay Public Market

Dollarton Hwy

UBC Museum of Anthropology

Spanish Banks Beach

Locarno Beach

Burrard Inlet

PNE Grounds & Pacific Coliseum Concert Bowl

Second Narrows Bridge

Nitobe Memorial Garden

DOWNTOWN

Powell St

Hastings St

Inlet Dr

Chan Centre for the Performing Arts

POINT GREY

Jericho Beach Park

W 10 Av

Arbutus St

Broadway

E 1 Av

Commercial Dr

Parker St

Wreck Beach

Grandview Hwy

Lougheed Hwy

UBC Botanical Garden

Pacific Spirit Regional Park

SW Marine Dr

W 33 Av

Van Dusen Botanical Garden

Queen Elizabeth Park

Nanaimo St

29th Avenue

Joyce

Canada Wy

Royal Oak Av

Deer Lake

W 49 Av

Granville St

Oak St

W 41 Av

Sikh Temple

Knight St

Patterson

Metrotown

Royal Oak

Vancouver International Airport

Punjabi Market

SE Marine Dr

Marine Dr

Strait of Georgia

Grant McConachie Wy

Marine Wy

Cambie Rd

Westminster Hwy

Blundell Rd

Dyke Walk

No 1 Rd

No 2 Rd

Gilbert Rd

No 3 Rd

No 4 Rd

No 5 Rd

No 6 Rd

Fraser River

River Rd

RICHMOND

Steveston

Steveston Hwy

Buddhist Temple

DELTA

60 Av

Westham Island Rd

48 Av

Ladner Trunk Rd

46A St

To

N

0 km 1
0 mile 1

Sleeping
1 A Gazebo in the Garden
2 Beachside B & B
3 Burnaby Cariboo RV Park
4 Capilano Canyon Guest House
5 Capilano RV Park
6 Crystal's View B & B
7 Delta Vancouver Airport
8 Dogwood Campgrounds of BC
9 Fairmont Vancouver Airport
10 Fraser Arms
11 Grouse Inn
12 HI Jericho Beach Hostel & Jericho Arts Centre
13 Holiday Inn Express
14 Lonsdale Quay
15 Mountainside Manor B & B
16 Ocean Breeze B & B
17 ParkCanada RV Park & Tenting
18 Parklander RV Park
19 Peace Arch RV Park

Vancouver

in 1930, with 26 storeys including three penthouse levels and four below ground, it remained the tallest building in the British Empire for more than a decade. Sir John Betjeman called it "the best art deco office building in the world". In keeping with the architects' vision of "some great crag rising from the sea", the relief frieze around its base and the brass surroundings of its double revolving doors are dotted with an array of marine flora and fauna. The sumptuous art deco façade is decorated with terracotta panels illustrating the discovery of the Pacific Ocean and the history of transport, including Zepellins, trains, and some famous ships like the *Golden Hind* and the *Resolution*. Over the main entrance, Captain Vancouver's ship *Discovery* is seen on the horizon, with Canada geese flying across the stylized sun rays. The lobby is designed to resemble a Mayan temple, overflowing with treasures and sumptuous details.

Just up the road at 601 West Cordova Street is the old **Canadian Pacific Railway (CPR) Station**. Built in 1914, this neoclassical beaux-arts-style building with its arches and white columned façade is now a terminus for the SeaBus and the Sky Train. The 1978 restoration retained many features of the original magnificent interior such as the high ceilings, woodworking and tile floor. Almost opposite, at 555 West Hastings Street is the **Lookout! Harbour Centre Tower** with its flying saucer-shaped top level. No longer the tallest building in BC, the observation deck here still gives the best close-up 360° views of the city, particularly striking at sunset on a clear day. In 50 seconds, glass-walled elevators on the outside of the building whisk you up the 167 m. From up there it is much easier to get a feeling for the layout and architecture of the city. The ticket is expensive but allows as many returns on the same day as you wish. ■ *Summer 0830-2130, winter 0900-2100. $9, $6 concessions. Guided tours included. T299-9000, ext 2626.* On the way to the Art Gallery, the **Pacific Mineral Museum**

Vancouver

20 Queen Anne
   Manor B & B
21 Richmond RV Park
21 Thistledown House B & B
22 Travelodge Lions Gate

● **Eating**
1 Beach House
2 Beach Side Café

3 Eiffel Café
4 La Notte
5 Moodyville's
6 Moustache Café
7 Raglan's Bistro
8 Raven
9 Rusty Gull
10 Ya Yas

has a big collection which includes meteorites, fossils and plenty of gems. There's a shop selling more of the same. ■ *$5, $4 concessions. 848 West Hastings, T6898021, www.pacificmineralmuseum.org*

Vancouver Art Gallery & around

Vancouver's original courthouse, an imposing neoclassical marble building, was designed in 1910 by Francis Rattenbury, the architect responsible for Victoria's Legislative Building and *Empress Hotel*. In 1983 it was renovated by Arthur Erickson (see Architecture, page 455), and today its four spacious floors house the largest art gallery in Western Canada. Of the 7,000 works in its collection, only the **Emily Carr Gallery** is a permanent fixture, but this justifies a visit in itself. The world's largest collection of works by this prominent Victoria artist (see Art and crafts, page 456) are rotated, and accompanied by a video on her life and art. Otherwise there are two major and one minor temporary exhibitions, usually of a contemporary nature. One of these will provide the focus for **Curator's tours** on Sunday at 1400; discussions in the *Philosophers' Cafe* on Thursday at 1900; occasional symposiums; and the *Open Studio*, where visitors and their kids are given material to create their own related pieces of art. There are also art courses and occasional concerts. The **Gallery Shop** is a great place for buying original crafts. The catacombs are said to house a ghost named Charlie, believed to be the spirit of William Charles Hopkinson, an immigration officer murdered there in 1914. ■ *Fri-Wed 1000-1730, Thu 1000-1900. Closed Mon Oct-May. $12.50, $9 seniors, $8 students, children under 12 free; suggested donation of $5 on Thu evenings. 750 Hornby St, T6624700, www.vanartgallery.bc.ca*

While renovating the old courthouse, Erickson designed the new **Provincial Law Courts** two blocks away on Hornby and Smithe. A steel-framed mass of sloping glass roofs and walls, it represents a radical departure from the tendency of courts to be closed off and intimidating. This one is so accessible you can literally walk on it. The building is part of the larger complex of **Robson Square**, whose landscaped public space is a favourite summer gathering spot.

East of the Art Gallery is the bizarre **Eatons** building, which resembles a space station or a slab of white cake, while to its west is one of Vancouver's most distinctive landmarks, the **Hotel Vancouver**. A typical example of the grand hotels erected across Canada by the Canadian Pacific Railway, this hulking Gothic castle sports a striking green copper roof, gargoyles, and some fine relief sculpture. It's worth wandering in to admire the opulent interior, and maybe stopping for a drink in the lounge.

Opposite, and all the more distinctive for its location amidst such towering edifices, is Vancouver's oldest surviving church, **Christ Church Cathedral** (finished in 1895). The Gothic Revival style of this buttressed sandstone building is reminiscent of English parish churches, featuring a steep gabled roof, and some impressive pointed-arch, stained-glass windows. While admiring these from the inside, note also the splendid timber framework. Next door is **Cathedral Place**, a marvellous staggered glass-and-granite edifice with fine details etched into its rock, and a roof that clearly pays homage to the *Hotel Vancouver* opposite. A neo-Gothic lobby full of art deco features leads to a lovely grassed courtyard and the small but extremely worthwhile **Canadian Craft and Design Museum**, whose innovative exhibits highlight artisan expertise in clay, glass, wood, metal and fibre. ■ *Mon-Sat 1000-1700, Sun 1200-1700, Thu 1000-2100. Closed Tue, Sep-May. $5, $3 concessions, by donation Thu after 1700. 639 Hornby St, T6878266.* The **HSBC Building** opposite has a towering atrium lobby

containing the world's largest pendulum, and one of Vancouver's best unofficial (and free) art galleries. It's also a relaxing place to stop for a coffee.
■ *Mon-Thu 0800-1630, Fri 0800-1700.*

A small triangle of land to the southwest, hemmed in by False Creek, Homer **Yaletown** and Nelson Streets, Yaletown was once Vancouver's rowdy warehouse district, with more saloons per acre than anywhere else in the world. As in so many similar quarters, but with a greater degree of success than most, these massive old brick buildings have inspired a recent renaissance, with architects and entrepreneurs falling over themselves to develop the kind of spacious apartments and trendy bars and restaurants that the young and upwardly mobile love to be seen to frequent. The result is not yet as attractive as it no doubt will be; many of the establishments walk a thin line between panache and pretentiousness, and the whole zone needs time to mellow into a genuine sense of style. Still, this is a fascinating area, well worth exploring at night, and some of the eating and watering holes are excellent (see page 87).

Back west on Robson Street, which is lined with exclusive boutiques and fancy **Vancouver** restaurants, is the incredible Vancouver Public Library. Despite architect **Public Library** Moshe Safdie's denials, its circular walls and tiered arches do bear an uncanny resemblance to the Roman Colosseum. Used to striking effect (along with many other Vancouver landmarks such as BC Place) in the Schwarzenegger film *The Sixth Day*, this post-modern masterpiece appears strangely ancient and futuristic at the same time. As well as the seven-level library itself, a square within a circle, the complex includes a 21-storey government building, and a pleasant shop-filled atrium spanned by a couple of elegant bridges.

Two blocks away at 646 Richards Street is the **Cathedral of our Lady of the Rosary**, a handsome Gothic Revival structure from the late 1880s. Key features include asymmetrical towers, the pointed arches of the windows and doorways, a vaulted ceiling and stained-glass windows. Of these, the oldest is found in the Lady Chapel to the left of the alter. Its octave of eight bells are still rung by hand each Sunday.

The world's largest air-supported dome when it opened in 1983, BC Place is **BC Place** known to Vancouverites as the 'marshmallow in bondage'. As well as a **Stadium** 60,000-seat venue for the city's major sports teams, it contains the **BC Sports Hall of Fame and Museum**, with hands-on displays highlighting the lives and achievements of the province's top athletes. ■ *1000-1700. $6, $4 concessions. T6875520. Robson St/Beatty, Stadium SkyTrain station, Bus No 2, 15 or 17 on Burrard, or No 5 on Granville.* Outside is the **Terry Fox Memorial**, a tribute to the local hero who died in 1981 attempting to run across the width of Canada to raise money for cancer research. It is a strange and unpopular brick, tile and steel structure intended to recall a Roman triumphal arch.

Sitting at the end of False Creek just off Main Street is another of Vancouver's **Science World** unusual structures, a giant silver golf ball that makes a suitably futuristic venue for Science World. Most of the interesting stuff is in the **Main Gallery** on level 2, where a wealth of interactive, mind-bending and thoroughly educational exhibits will keep anyone entertained for at least a couple of hours. The **Kidspace Gallery** has lots of hands-on stuff for younger children, while the **Sara Stern Search Gallery** does a good job of making environmental lessons fun. The Alcan **Omnimax** theatre upstairs has the edge over even the giant IMAXes by showing films on a huge dome screen with wraparound visuals and

Downtown to Chinatown

Vancouver

N

0 metres 100
0 yards 100

Related maps
A South
Vancouver,
page 76
B West End &
Granville Island,
page 70

■ Sleeping
1 Bosman's Motor *D1*
2 Cambie Hostal Gastown
   & Cambie Pub *C3*
3 Cambie Hostel Seymour *C2*
4 C & N Backpackers *E5*
5 Comfort Inn Downtown *D1*
6 Days Inn *B2*

7 Fairmont Waterfront *B3*
8 Global Village
   Backpackers *D1*
9 Jolly Taxpayer *B2*
10 Kingston *C2*
11 New Backpackers
   Hostel *C3*
12 Opus *E1*
13 Patricia *C6*
14 Sandman Inn *D3*
15 Sheraton Suites
   Le Soleil & Oritalia *B2*
16 St Regis *C2*
17 Victorian *C3*

18 YMCA *D3*

● Eating
1 Bacchus *C1*
2 Blakes *C4*
3 Bluewater Café &
   Raw Bar *E1*
4 Blunt Bros *C3*
5 Borgo Antico *B3*
6 Buddhist Vegetarian *C5*
7 Café Crêpe *C1*
8 Cioppino's
   Mediterranean
   Grill & Enoteca *E1*

9 Diva at the Met *B2*
10 Elbow Room *E1*
11 Glowbal Grill
   & Satay Bar *D1*
12 Guu *B1*
13 Hermitage *B1*
14 Homer St Café *D2*
15 Hon's Wun-Tun House *D5*
16 Incendio Pizzeria *C4*
17 Jewel of India *C5*
18 Joe Forte's Oyster
   House *B1*
19 Kam's *D5*
20 Kitto Japanese House *C1*

sound. Shows last 40 minutes. ■ *Mon-Fri 1000-1700, Sat-Sun 1000-1800. $12.75, $8.50 concessions; $17.75, $13.50 concessions with Omnimax; $13.50, $10.50 concessions for Omni max double bill. T4437440, www.scienceworld.bc.ca 1455 Quebec St. Sky Train, Bus No 3 or 8 on Granville or Hastings, or No19 on Pender. A ferry runs across False Creek from behind BC Place to Science World.*

Chinatown

In keeping with its East-meets-West persona (see box), Vancouver's bustling Chinatown is the third biggest in North America after New York and San Francisco. The restaurants here are as good and authentic as you'll ever find outside China. The streets are lined with noisy shops selling the kind of weird and wonderful ingredients only the Chinese would know how to cook. The most unmissable experience is the open-air **night market** at 200 Keefer Street and East Pender. ■ *Summer only, Fri-Sun 1830-2300.*

Chinatown's key sight is the **Dr Sun Yat-Sen Classical Chinese Garden**, the first authentic Ming Classical garden built since 1492, and the first ever outside China. It was created by 52 experts flown in, along with most of the raw materials, from Suzhou, China's 'City of Gardens'. This is a carefully planned world of symmetry and balance, simplicity and symbolism. Buildings, rocks, water and plants recreate a microcosm of the world. There are walls within walls, courtyards within courtyards, pavilions, halls, bridges and covered galleries. Hourly guided tours, included with admission, are essential for an understanding of the Taoist principles at work. Music events and art exhibitions are hosted in the summer. ■ *May to mid-Jun 1000-1800, mid-Jun to Aug 0930-1900, Sep 1000-1800, Oct-May 1000-1630. $7.50, $5 concessions. 578 Carrall St, T6897133. Bus No 19 or 22 east on Pender.*

▶ **East meets West**

Chinese immigrants played an important role in Vancouver's history but they have not always been made so welcome. The first Chinese settlers arrived in 1858, coming up from San Francisco during the Fraser Valley Gold Rush. In 1875 Queen Victoria gave assent to an act passed in the BC legislature to deny the vote to Chinese and First Nations people, a law that remained in effect for more than 70 years. During the 1880s, a great influx helped to build the BC section of the Canadian Pacific Railway, receiving half the wage of their white fellows, and often used as cannon fodder during dynamite blasting. Estimates are that three Chinese lives were lost for every kilometre of track laid in the almost impenetrable Fraser Canyon. Over 24 items of anti-Chinese legislation such as head- taxes were passed in BC between 1878 and 1913 alone, and public hostility also included rallies, campaigns and rampaging mobs.

Today Asians account for nearly one-third of Vancouver's population, and 38% of provincial exports now flow into the Pacific Rim. The Oriental community of Lotus land is in fact a rich multicultural mix in its own right, embracing immigrants from Hong Kong, Taiwan, China, The Philippines, Japan, South Korea, Malaysia and Singapore.

The **Chinese Cultural Centre**, an ugly concrete building with a colourful gate, contains a museum and archives. As well as temporary exhibits, the former has a permanent collection dedicated to the Chinese Canadian Military, and another called *From Generation to Generation*, which tells the story of Canadian Chinese from the Gold Rush to the present. ■ *Tue-Sun 1100-1700. $3, $2 concessions. 555 Columbia St, T6588865, www.cccvan.com The centre also runs tours of the district, Jun-Sep 1000-1400, $10, $8 seniors, $2.50 children.*

One local novelty that fails to live up to expectations is the **Sam Kee Building** at 8 West Pender. The story goes that when the city appropriated most of Chang Toy's 30-ft lot for street widening, his neighbour expected to get the remaining 6 ft at a bargain price. To frustrate him, Toy constructed the world's skinniest building and put a popular bath-house in the basement. Known as 'Slender on Pender', it is 6 ft wide, 100 ft long and 2 storeys high.

East Side Just a block north of Chinatown, and engaged in a strange tug-of-war with the overtly touristy Gastown on its other flank, is Vancouver's seediest quarter. Over a century ago, when the city's first streetcars connected Gastown to a newly emerging business district along Granville, Hastings Street entered a decline that has led to its current rating as Canada's lowest-income postal district. The blocks east of Cambie are lined with derelict buildings and closed shops, peopled by the city's many homeless, addicts, drug-dealers, and prostitutes. In particular, the corner of Hastings and Main has become notorious as the focal point for a sad and sleazy underworld, whose constant activity makes it the most continuously lively spot in the city. Newly elected mayor, Larry Campbell, has vowed to address the problems of this troubled district: North America's first walk-in injection site is due to open, and solutions are being sought for a long-term answer to the housing crisis.

In 1920 Houdini suspended himself from the roof of the Sun Tower

But this strangely compelling district is safe enough to wander through even at night, and contains some of the last remaining examples of neon from an era when Vancouver had some 18,000 neon signs; look out especially for the *Ovaltine Diner* at No 251 East Hastings and the *Only Café* at No 20. There are also some interesting buildings. The 19th-century French Classical-style **Dominion Building** at 207 West Hastings is one of the city's most attractive

Gassy Jack

◀

One of Vancouver's favourite historic characters is a garrulous Yorkshireman, 'Gassy' Jack Deighton. He first appeared on the scene running a bar in New Westminster that profited from the Cariboo Gold Rush traffic of 1862. But history remembers him best rowing across Burrard Inlet with his native wife, her mother and cousin, a yellow dog, two

chairs and a barrel of whisky. Knowing that the nearest drink was a 50-km row then 15-km walk away, he offered a bunch of thirsty workers at Stamp's Mill all the whisky they could drink if they helped him build a bar. Within 24 hours the Globe Saloon was finished, and soon became the focus of an area that came to be known as Gastown.

pieces of architecture, featuring an elaborately decorated red-brick and yellow terracotta veneer and a distinctive beaux-arts-style roof. In 1910 this was the British Empire's highest and most modern structure, and it stood opposite Vancouver's public focus, Victory Square, now run-down and nicknamed 'Pigeon Park'. Two years later its record height was topped by the nearby **Sun Tower** at 100 West Pender, named after the *Vancouver Sun*, whose offices it later housed. Just east of Main, on Cordova, is the **Firehall Arts Centre**, and **St James Anglican Church**, which combines touches of the Romanesque, Gothic, Byzantine and modern.

Keep walking north and you arrive in Gastown, another world again. The **Gastown** original site of Stamp's Mill, renamed Hastings Mill, and the famous saloon of 'Gassy' Jack Deighton, after whom the district was named (see box), this is the oldest part of Vancouver. Extensive renovations during the 1960s were designed to convert the run-down area into a tourist haven but mostly resulted in a string of tacky souvenir stores. There are, however, some handsome old red-brick buildings and cobbled streets, plus some of the city's best clubs, antique/curiosity stores and commercial art galleries.

The heart of Gastown is Water Street which contains the much-touted **Steam Clock**. In 1977 clockmaker Ray Saunders decided that the underground steam pipes used to heat local buildings could be used to power a clock, and built one to prove it. At 5 m tall, this isn't as imposing as you'd expect, though its four-sided glass face, 20-kg gold-plated pendulum, and Gothic-style roof are attractive enough. Every 15 minutes it entertains tourists by tooting and erupting in a cloud of steam.

Further east at the junction of Water, Powell and Alexander streets is the undeniably quaint **Maple Leaf Square**. A statue of Gassy Jack standing on a whisky barrel is a work of imagination on the part of sculptor Vern Simpson, as no one knows what the Yorkshireman looked like beyond a description of his 'muddy purple' complexion. Opposite the statue is the thin curved end of the wedge-shaped **Hotel Europe** (1909), the first reinforced-concrete building in Vancouver, and certainly one of its most charming constructions. Behind Gassy Jack is the site of his second saloon, built after the 1886 fire. Made from Chinese bricks used as ballast in sailing vessels, the **Byrne's Block** is Vancouver's oldest brick building. Secreted behind it is **Gaoler's Mews**, an atmospheric little courtyard full of trees, old-fashioned lampposts, ivy-covered walls, park benches and a sundial. A number of reinterpreted old buildings are dotted along these streets, many containing antique or art stores. Look out for the interesting filigree tower and steel-and-glass spire of the former **American Can Co** building at 611 Alexander, which also has a large atrium.

West End

Part of what gives Downtown Vancouver its perpetually vibrant character is the fact that the city's most populated area is immediately adjacent. Everything from Thurlow Street to Stanley Park, hemmed in to the north by the main drag of **Robson Street**, is known as the West End, a lively urban district. As well as being the most densely populated area in the country, it houses Western Canada's largest gay community. Most neighbourhood activity is focused on Denman and Davie Streets, both buzzing with restaurants and cafés. The local beach of choice is **Sunset Beach** on English Bay.

Most of the region's traditional buildings were replaced with over 200 high rises during the development boom of the 1960s. The best surviving block is **Barclay Heritage Square**, where a park-like setting contains nine historic houses built between 1890 and 1908. One 1893 home, furnished in Edwardian style, has been converted into **Roedde House Museum**. ■ *Admission by guided tour only. Phone for hours. $5, $3 concessions. 1415 Barclay St, T6847040, www.roeddehouse.org Bus No 5 to Broughton.*

Stanley Park

Stanley Park never closes. Isolated trails should be avoided after dark, especially by lone females

The first piece of business at the fledgling Vancouver's first city council meeting concerned a petition to lease a 1,000-acre (405 ha) military reserve from the federal government to be used as a park. Over a century later this evergreen oasis, the largest urban park in Canada, has been allowed to remain undeveloped, most of its space filled with second-growth but still giant cedar, hemlock and fir.

The main access roads are Davie Street/Beach Avenue to the west, Robson Street/Lagoon Drive in the centre, and Georgia Street, which dissects the park

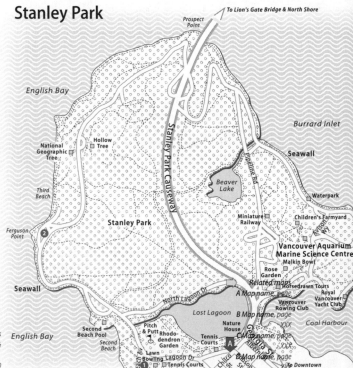

Stanley Park

To Lion's Gate Bridge & North Shore

Prospect Point

English Bay

Burrard Inlet

Seawall

National Geographic Tree

Hollow Tree

Third Beach

Beaver Lake

Waterpark

Stanley Park Causeway

Pipeline Rd

Ferguson Point

Stanley Park

Miniature Railway

Children's Farmyard

Vancouver Aquarium Marine Science Centre

Malkin Bowl

Rose Garden

Seawall

North Lagoon Dr

Lost Lagoon

Horsedrawn Tours

Royal Vancouver Yacht Club

Related maps

A Map name, page

Vancouver Rowing Club

B Map name, page

Coal Harbour

Second Beach Pool

Pitch & Putt

Rhododendron Garden

Second Beach

Nature House

Tennis Courts

Lawn Bowling

South Lagoon Dr

Tennis Courts

A

C Map name, page

B Map name, page

Chilco St

Alberni St

To Downtown

English Bay

Related maps
A West End & Granville Island , page 70

on its way to Lion's Gate Bridge and North Van. At the entrance to the park is the extensive **Lost Lagoon**, named by Native American poet Pauline Johnson. This is a haven for many birds including swans, ducks, geese and even the odd blue heron. The **Nature House** close to Georgia on its south shore offers ecological information and very useful maps. ■ *0900-1900 daily except Tue, www.stanleyparkecology.ca* The **Ecology Society**, T2578544, organize Sunday Discovery Walks ($5), birding, and various other walks/activities that are either free or cheap, and mainly aimed at kids.

Particularly in summer, activity focuses on the 9-km seawall which runs all round the park offering a variety of sea and mountain views. The best are from **Prospect Point** at the northern, most elevated, tip. It is a first-class walk, jog, roller-blade or bike ride. On one visit, Bill Clinton jogged the whole thing, with a posse of 30 black-suited bodyguards in tow. Equipment can be hired from a number of stores at the north end of Denman Street, where cyclists and roller-bladers must begin the circuit, which moves in an anti-clockwise direction. If you want to explore the coastline in the water, kayaks and canoes can be rented on Granville Island (see below). A couple of decent beaches hug the west side. **Second Beach**, close to the entrance, has a heated oceanside swimming pool. Just south, clustered around the splendid *Fish House Restaurant*, are tennis courts, lawn bowling, and an 18-hole pitch-and-putt golf course. ■ *$9.25, $7 concessions.* Adjacent to this is a **Rhododendron Garden** and a collection of many other ornamental trees, including azaleas, camellias, and magnolia.

The bulk of the park's interior is devoted to shaded walking paths which were once skid roads, used by early loggers to drag trees down to the water. One obvious highlight is the stump of one such monster now known as the **Hollow Tree**.

N

● Eating

0 metres 200
0 yards 200

1 Fish House
2 Tea House

Lighthouse Brockton Point

Totem Poles

9 O'Clock Gun

Hallelujah Point

Deadman's Island

Some 30 m from here down the path to **Third Beach** is a living cedar believed by *National Geographic* to be one of the largest trees (at almost 5 m across) and oldest cedars (roughly 1,000 years) in the world.

To protect this area from overuse, most of the park's infrastructure and attractions are concentrated on the narrow spit that juts out north of the sheltered Coal Harbour. Next door to the *Vancouver Rowing Club* is an information booth, and base of the one-hour horse-drawn tours that run every 20-30 mins from mid-May to Oct. ■ *$14.95, $9.95 concessions.* To the north is a **Rose Garden** and the **Malkin Bowl**, home to *Theatre Under the Stars* in July and August (T6870174). To the east on Avison Way is a parking area and the **Aquarium** (see below). Further north is a **Miniature Railway** and **Children's Farmyard**. ■ *Both open Apr-Sep 1100-1600 daily, Oct-Mar weekends only.* There's also a kids' Water Park.

Further round the shore of Coal Harbour, past the Royal Vancouver

Yacht Club, is the jutting-out Deadman's Island where the Coast Salish buried their dead. Brockton Point has a picturesque old **lighthouse** and a decent stand of Kwakiutl and Haida **totem poles**. The rumour that a bank robber buried $25,000 near here in 1942 no doubt prompted a $500 fine for digging in the park. A number of monuments around this spit celebrate a variety of characters, from Queen Victoria and David Oppenheimer to *Girl in a Wetsuit*. At the eastern point is the **9 O'Clock Gun**, a cannon fired each evening at that hour. The tradition that began a century ago to signal the end of the day's legal fishing has continued unbroken apart from the years of the Second World War and for a short period when it was 'kidnapped' by UBC engineering students.

■ *For more information call T2578400, www.parks.vancouver.bc.ca Bus No 135 daytime Mon-Sat, No 23 or 25 eve/Sun/hols. Parking anywhere in the park is $1 per 2 hrs or $3 for all day. A free shuttle bus runs right round the park every 15 mins from Jun to mid-Sep.*

Vancouver Aquarium Marine Science Centre

One of Vancouver's prime rainy-day activities, the Aquarium is even better when the sun shines, as the most exciting animals are outside. The seals, dolphins and otters, fascinating though they are to watch, are all utterly upstaged by a pair of giant and graceful white **beluga whales**. You can watch these extraordinary beings from the underwater viewing room downstairs, where a wealth of background information includes a video of the female giving birth.

The whales are best saved till last, though, as the other 20,000 creatures from the world's many seas tend to pale by comparison. Indoor highlights include the **Treasures of the BC Coast** gallery, with a giant Pacific octopus, coral, anemones, and some eerily beautiful jellyfish. Next door is a large collection of handsome frogs. The **Tropical** and **Amazon** galleries are worth exploring: as well as colourful fish there are caymans, anacondas, lizards, snakes and even birds. Before even entering the Aquarium, look out for Bill Reid's magnificent bronze sculpture of a killer whale, *The Chief of the Undersea World* (1984). ■ *Summer 0930-1900, winter 1000-1730. $14.95, $11.95 concessions, $8.95 children, under 3s free. T6593474, www.vanaqua.org Bus No 135 from Hastings. Free shuttle bus around the park in summer.*

Granville Island

Monday is a bad day to visit the island as most things are closed

When Vancouver was first founded, False Creek was five times the size it is today. Land has been reclaimed all around the water, much of it for Expo '86. Nowhere has this process been more successful than at Granville Island. Originally no more than a sand-bar, the area was built up into an industrial zone, then transformed into an attractive shopping and arts district, a magnet for tourists and locals, with an ambience similar to London's Covent Garden.

Though overwhelmingly popular and packed in summer, the island has not given in to tacky gift shops but remains the atmospheric domain of yachting repair shops and charter companies, restaurants and cafés, theatres and buskers, and most notably Vancouver's artist and artisan community. The highly renowned Emily Carr Institute of Art and Design is located here, and countless small, often excellent, arts and crafts shops are scattered around or clustered together in the **Net Loft** or on **Railspur Alley**.

Close to the road entrance, the **Kid's Market**, full of retail stores catering to children, is hard to miss. A couple of buildings away is the **Visitor Information Centre** which provides a *Visitors' Guide* with discount vouchers for many places, and a very useful map. ■ *0900-1800, T6665784.* Behind here, the **Waterpark** is an aquatic play area for kids, with multiple slides and a

◀

Vancouver for kids

Stanley Park: *Vancouver Aquarium, Miniature Railway, Children's Farmyard, Water Park, playground. See page 66.*
Science World: *see page 61.*
Granville Island: *Sport fishing, Model Ships and Model Trains Museums; Kid's Market, Waterpark. See page 68*
Vanier Park: *HR MacMillan Space Centre;*

Maritime Museum, International Children's Festival in May. See page 69
Playland Amusement Park at the PNE Grounds.
Vancouver Art Gallery: Open Studio, see page 60.
Capilano Suspension Bridge: see page 79.

playground. Though not strictly pedestrianized, the island is well geared to aimless strolling, with most vehicles crawling around in search of that elusive parking space. ■ *Open May-Sep*.

Meander at will, but be sure not to miss the **Public Market**. As well as a mouthwatering collection of international fast food stalls, the place is packed with every kind of fresh, innovative and tempting produce imaginable, from gourmet breads to seafood and sausages. The building itself is a fine lesson in the renovation of industrial structures, making great use of the natural lighting, large windows and doors, heavy timber and steel. The courtyard outside and adjacent bars are good places to watch the aquatic world float by. Nearby, **Granville Island Brewing Co**, Canada's first microbrewery, runs 40-minute tours daily. ■ *Tours at 1200, 1400 and 1600 cost $8.75, $2.50 concessions, including a decent round of tasters and a souvenir glass. The Taproom is open Tue-Sun 1200-1800, serving tapas-style dishes*.

It is best not to take vehicles across to the island; instead, take the ferry ($2) from the Aquatic Centre next to Burrard Bridge, or Bus No 50 from Granville Street and walk.

Tucked away in the Maritime Market are three museums rolled into one that represent one of Vancouver's most unexpected delights. Even if you have just a passing interest in fishing or models, go! All three collections are vast, world-class, and lovingly displayed. The Sport Fishing Museum has the world's largest displayed collections of Hardy reels and hand-tied fly plates, as well as a fine array of split-cane fly rods and many other notable pieces. The world's largest collection of model and toy trains lives upstairs, topped off by a fabulous O-scale working layout that has 5 lines on 4 levels running through an exquisitely detailed, hand-crafted landscape of mountain passes, trestles, tunnels and ocean shores that took 6 people 20,000 hours to complete. For most visitors, however, the highlight will be the extensive collection of model ships and submarines, with several dozen huge pieces that are all one-offs and demonstrate an obsessive attention to detail. One took a local modeller 18 years to complete! Such devotion is only matched by the enthusiasm of owner John Keith-King, for whom the whole project is clearly a labour of love. ■ *1000-1730. $6.50, $5 concessions, $3.50 children. 1502 Duranleau St, T6831939, www.sport fishingmuseum.ca, www.modelshipsmuseum.ca, www.modeltrainsmuseum.ca*

Granville Island Sport Fishing, Model Ships & Model Trains Museums

Vanier Park

East from Granville Island, a pleasant seawall path along **False Creek** connects a series of parks, marinas and small communities such as **Stamp's Landing**, a fine spot for a drink or meal. To the west of the island and Burrard

Vancouver

Bridge, where False Creek widens into English Bay, another footpath leads to the 12-ha Vanier Park. A popular summer hang-out, with ponds, trees, and plenty of lawn and beach, it also contains three fairly important sights.

The **Vancouver Museum** is housed in an interesting building whose shape was inspired by the hats of Haida natives, with a funky metal crab fountain

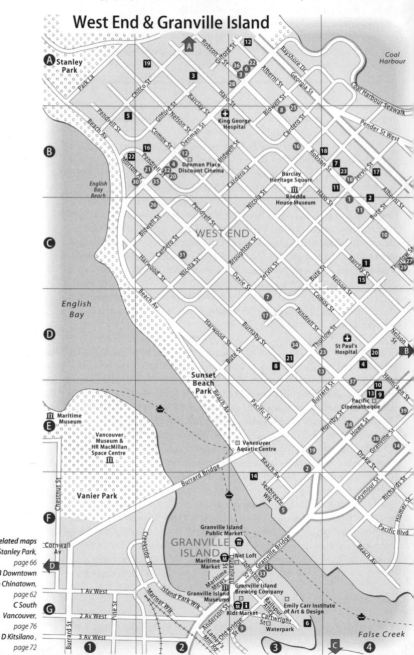

West End & Granville Island

Related maps
A Stanley Park,
    page 66
B Downtown
to Chinatown,
    page 62
C South
Vancouver,
    page 76
D Kitsilano ,
    page 72

outside. Devoted to the history of the city, a small collection of artefacts and recreated scenes tells the story of the first explorers and settlers. However, for most people, the real interest is more likely to reside in the temporary exhibits that home in on more unusual angles of the region's past. ■ *Fri-Wed 1000-1700, Thu 1000-2100, closed Mon in winter. $10, $8 seniors, $6 children, under 4s free. With Space Centre $17, $11 children. T7364431, www.vanmuseum.bc.ca Bus No 2 or 22 from Burrard, then walk, or ferry from the Aquatic Centre.*

In the same building is the considerably more upbeat **HR MacMillan Space Centre**. Its collection of interactive exhibits in the Cosmic Courtyard talk you through the Earth's geological composition, the nature of life in space, and the logistics of space travel. The **Planetarium** has a rather dated feel that adds greatly to its appeal, and it has been very popular since the 70s. It hosts a variety of 40-minute shows hourly in the afternoon. On Thursday-Saturday evenings are special laser shows set to the music of bands like Radiohead or Pink Floyd (■ *$9, $11 concessions*). The **GroundStation Canada Theatre** hosts 20-minute shows that are basically video-assisted lectures involving a few experiments designed to interest kids. Tickets include as many of these and the Planetarium shows as you want, plus one 15-minute ride in the **Virtual Voyages Simulator**. There is also an **Observatory** (free). ■ *Daily 1000-1700, closed Mon Sep-Jun. $12.75, $9.75 concessions, $8.75 children. T7387827, www.hrmacmillanspacecentre.com*

A short walk west is the **Maritime Museum**. The first thing you see upon entering is the RCMP *St Roch*. A video on its history recounts all the firsts achieved by this hardy little ship: the first to travel the treacherous and long-sought Northwest Passage, a 27-month journey from Vancouver to Halifax; first to make the same trip back via the faster, more northerly route; first to circumnavigate North America. This front part of the museum, with its distinctive steep

N

0 metres 100
0 yards 100

■ **Sleeping**
1 Amber Rose *C4*
2 Blue Horizon *C4*
3 Buchan *A2*
4 Burrard Motor Inn *D4*
5 English Bay Inn B & B *B1*
6 Granville Island & Dockside Brewing Co *G3*
7 Greenbriar *B4*
8 HI Vancouver Downtown *D3*
9 Inn at False Creek *E4*
10 Landis & Suites *E4*
11 Listel Vancouver *B4*
12 Lord Stanley Suites on the Park *A3*
13 Marriott Residence Inn *E4*
14 Meridian at 910 Beach *F3*
15 O Canada House B & B *C4*
16 Oceanside Apartment *B2*
17 Pacific Palisades *B4*
18 Riviera *B4*
19 Rosellen Suites at Stanley Park *A2*
20 Sheraton Vancouver Wall Centre *D4*
21 Sunset Inn Apartments *D3*
22 Sylvia *B1*
23 Tropicana Motor Inn *B4*

● **Eating**
1 A Taste of India *C4*
2 Bandi's *E3*
3 Bojangles Café *A3*
4 Brass Monkey *B2*
5 C *F3*
6 Café de Paris *A3*
7 Café Luxy *D3*
8 Capers *B3*
9 Cat's Meow *G3*
10 CinCin *C4*
11 Da Pasta Bar *C4*
12 Delilah's *B2*
13 Desalvio's *D3*
14 Fritz *E4*
15 Granville Island Coffee House *G3*
16 Gyoza King *B3*
17 Hamburger Mary's *D3*
18 Hon's Wun-Tun House *B4*
19 Il Giardino di Umberta *E3*
20 Indica *B2*
21 Just One Thai Bistro *B2*
22 Kafe Europa *A3*
23 Kam's Place *D4*
24 La Bodega Tapa Bar *E4*
25 Le Gavroche *A3*
26 Liliget Feast House *C2*
27 Olympia *C4*
28 Pancho's Mexican *A3*
29 Piccolo Mondo *C4*
30 Raincity Grill *B2*
31 Romano's Macaroni Grill *C2*
32 Sami's *B2*
33 Sand Bar *G3*
34 Stepho's Greek Taverna *D3*
35 Tanpopo *B2*
36 Tapastree *A3*

● **Bars**
37 Bin 941 *E4*
38 Morrissey Pub *E4*
39 Sugar Refinery *E4*

Vancouver

triangular shape, was actually built around the ship, which was lovingly restored to its original 1944 condition and can now be explored. Though this is the museum's highlight, there is much more to see, with lots of artefacts and stories, a fun exhibit on pirates, a hands-on area for kids, and some bigger remnants scattered over the lawn outside. There is usually also an interesting guest exhibit. ■ *Tue-Sat 1000-1700. Sun 1200- 1700. $8, $5.50 children and seniors, under 5s free. 1905 Ogden Av, Vanier Park. T2578300, www.vmm.bc.ca*

In the west of the park at 1150 Chestnut Street is the **City of Vancouver Archives**, a vast collection of old photos, books, maps, clippings and papers. ■ *Mon- Fri 0930-1730. Free. T7368561.*

Kitsilano Vanier Park leads seamlessly into **Kitsilano** (or Kits) **Beach**, a popular stretch of sand in the city, with great views of English Bay, Downtown and the Coast Mountains. **Kitsilano Outdoor Pool** is the biggest in Vancouver. ■ *22 May-12 Sep, 1200-2045 Mond-Fri, 1000- 2045 Sat-Sun. $4, $2.50 concessions, $1 children. T7310011. Bus No 2 or 22 south on Burrard to Cornwall then walk.* The adjacent **Kitsilano Showboat** is an outdoor theatre for summer productions.

In the 1960s Kitsilano was the main focus of Vancouver's sub-culture. By the 1980s, many of those hippies had got high-paying jobs, bought and

Related maps
A West End &
Granville Island,
page 70
B South
Vancouver,
page 76

N

0 metres   200
0 yards   200

■ **Sleeping**
1 Between Friends B & B *B5*
2 Camelot Inn B & B *C4*
3 Graeme's House B & B *D2*
4 Jericho Beach Hostel *C1, To...*
5 Maple House B & B *B5*
6 Mickey's Kits Beach Chalet *B4*

7 Penny Farthing Inn *C3*

● **Eating**
1 Annapurna *C5*
2 Bishop's *B3*
3 Capers *B4*
4 Deluxe Moderne Burger *C3*

5 Eatery *C2*
6 Greens & Gourmet *C3*
7 Lan's Vietnamese *C6*
8 Lumière *C3*
9 Maurya *C6*
10 Naam *B3*
11 Nyala *B2*
12 Ordinary Café *C6*

restored their houses, and helped turn Kits into Yuppieville. Reflecting this change, many of the old wooden town houses that used to grace the area have been torn down and replaced by condos. For all that, lots of character remains and the region's two main drags, **West Fourth** between Burrard and Mac-Donald (Bus No 4 or 7), and **West Broadway** between MacDonald and Alma (Bus No 10 or 16), offer some of the city's best browsing strips, with many interesting speciality stores, trendy hair studios, snowboard outlets and some decent restaurants. Weekend brunch here is a Vancouver institution, but parking can be a nightmare (try Fifth).

Point Grey

From Kitsilano, Fourth Avenue and the more scenic Point Grey Road lead west to the jutting nose of Point Grey, which has some of the city's best sand beaches (including the official nude beach), more wide-open park-land, and the University of British Columbia (UBC). Among the latter's attractions are the Museum of Anthropology (see below) and some botanical gardens. On the water near where Alma Street meets Point Grey Road is the **Hastings Mill Store**, Vancouver's oldest building, transported from its original site in

Gastown. Today it houses a museum with displays of First Nat- ions and pioneer artefacts. ■ *Mid- Jun to mid-Sep Tue-Sun 1100-1600, otherwise Sat-Sun 1300-1600. Donation. 1575 Alma St, T7341212. Bus No 9 Broadway or No 4, 7 or 44 to Alma and walk.*

From here a clutch of beaches and parks run almost uninterrupted around the edge of Point Grey. First of these is **Jericho Beach**, set in a large, very scenic park with a fine *Youth Hostel* (see Sleeping), a sailing school, and a bird sanctuary. Three unbroken kilometres connect it to **Locarno Beach**, a quiet area popular with families, and **Spanish Banks**, which has a beach café and warm, shallow water ideal for paddling. **Pacific Spirit Regional Park**, also known as the Endowment Lands, covers 35 sq km of forest criss-crossed with hiking, biking, and horse-riding trails. A wonderful trail leads right round its perimeter. From UBC, roughly where Marine Drive meets University Blvd, about 100 steps lead down through the forest to the 6-km strip of **Wreck Beach**. On a hot day as many as 10,000 sun-worshippers take advantage of its clothing-optional status, while wandering peddlars supply them with cold beers and food.

13 Pastis *B4*	● **Bars**	
14 Sausi's Lounge	19 Bimini's Tap House *C5*	
& Grill *C2*	20 Bin 942 *C6*	
15 Sophie's Cosmic	21 Fringe Café *C2*	
Café *B5*	22 Jeremiah's *B1*	
16 Tangerine *B4*	23 King's Head *B4*	
17 Velvet Café *C6*	24 Lou's Grill & Bistro *C2*	
18 Vij's *D6*	25 Truffles Bistro *B5*	

Vancouver

▶ ## Bill Reid

Born in Vancouver to a Haida mother and Scottish-American father, Bill Reid (1920-98) was a teenager before he was told about his native heritage. Though he only began investigating Haida arts at the age of 31, he was clearly to the manner born, and his carvings in gold, silver, argillite and wood, castings in bronze, and many book illustrations, have brought him recognition. In the words of Barry Mowatt, President of Vancouver's Inuit Gallery, "He is the pre-eminent West Coast native artist, who is responsible for re-creation of respect for the art of North West Coast people. He is probably the most important and significant native artist ever to have come to the world stage". Anthropologist Edmund Carpenter wrote: "I've followed Bill Reid's career for many years and come to believe that, in some strange way, the spirit of Haida art, once the lifeblood of an entire people, now survives within him, at a depth, and with an intensity, unrelated to any 'revival' or 'preservation', but deriving from primary sources and leading to daring innovations". While in Vancouver, it is essential to take in the works of this great artist, which are to be found at the airport, outside the aquarium, and above all in the UBC Museum of Anthropology.

Museum of Anthropology Founded in 1949, and situated on Native Musqueam land, this extraordinary museum is easily the best attraction in Vancouver. Designed by Arthur Erickson to echo the post- and-beam structures of Northwest Coast First Nations, its current home contains the world's finest collection of carvings by master craftsmen from many of these Nations, most notably the Haida of Haida Gwaii (Queen Charlotte Islands) and the Gitxsan and Nisga'a from the Skeena River region of Northern BC. The tone is set before you even enter by a pair of traditional but modern **Welcome Figures** and a set of fine red cedar K'san doors. Be sure to pick up a *Gallery Guide* at the Admissions Desk ($1.50). As well as providing a commentary to the exhibits, it gives a brief but excellent introduction to First Nations cultures, the stylistic differences between them, and an overview of their classic art forms: the carved façades of cedar plank houses, elaborate support posts, canoes, totem poles, bentwood boxes, bowls, baskets, blankets and robes.

Sculptures inside are grouped by general cultural area, and are informatively labelled. A ramp flanked by carvings mainly by the local Coast Salish groups quickly leads to the heart of the exhibition, the **Great Hall**. A 15-m-high wall of glass fills this vast space with ample natural light, whose constantly changing hues and shadows create a perfect atmosphere for the incredible collection of large carvings. Most of the pieces, such as the splendid house posts from Quattishe Village, date from the early-mid-19th century, but a surprising and encouraging number are very recent. Look out for the painted panels by Lyle Wilson, *Two Salmon, Beaver,* and *Killer Whale,* or *Wasco* by Jim Hart. The most exceptional pieces are by the late master **Bill Reid** (see box, above) such as *Bear* (1963), *Sea Wolf with Killer Whales* (1962) and a 7.5-m inshore cedar canoe (1985). Down the hall a natural light-filled rotunda houses his most exquisite masterpiece, *The Raven and the First Men* (1980), based, like so many of his works, on Haida mythology. Four adjacent cases contain many of Reid's earlier, smaller works.

The museum has such a large collection of smaller carvings in gold, silver, argillite and wood, that they are constantly rotated. Look out for the excellent late 19th-century silverwork of Charles Edenshaw, and the wonderful modern bronze sculptures of Dempsey Bob. Behind the Great Hall, visible through its vast windows, are a number of outdoor exhibits, including a large

Haida family dwelling, a smaller mortuary house, and a collection of 10 poles. There are fine views from here of the mountains and ocean.

Unbelievably, this is still only about half of what the museum has on display. The **Koerner Ceramics Gallery** features a collection of some 1,600 rare European ceramics. At least four galleries are devoted to temporary exhibitions. Then there are the **Visible Storage** galleries. In a relatively small space the museum makes over 14,000 objects accessible to the public: about 40% of its permanent collection. Quality pieces from all over the world, copious enough to fill another large museum, are grouped according to location and huddled together in crammed display cases or pull-out drawers. Again, Canadian aboriginal groups are well represented, including a good collection of Inuit tools and carvings. With so little space, each item bears just a number, referring you to a host of books that supply more detailed information than any casual visitor could want, reflecting the establishment's other role as a venue for anthropological research. The quantity of items is overwhelming. At least two visits are required to do the museum justice.

Save a bit of energy for the small gift shop in the lobby which is packed with splendid books, carvings, jewellery and prints.

■ *Summer daily 1000-1700, Tue until 2100. Winter Wed-Sun 1100-1700, Tue until 2100. $7, $5 seniors, $4 students, children under 6 free. Free entry Tue 1700-2100. Free tours daily at 1100 and 1400, plus 1800 on Tue. 6393 NW Marine Dr, T8225950, www.moa.ubc.ca Bus No 4 or 10 south on Granville then walk, or change to No 42 at Alma. Avoid coming by car as parking here is the most expensive in town and is limited to 2 hrs (which is not enough).*

Apart from the Museum of Anthropology, the University of British Columbia (UBC) has a number of other interesting buildings worth seeking out. The **Centre for Native Studies** has drawn much inspiration from the longhouses of the Coast Salish, especially the Great Hall, whose massive roof beams are supported by carved house posts in true West Coast style. The library contains a hotchpotch of styles, most interesting being the post-modern **Walter C Koerner Library** co-designed by Arthur Erickson in 1996. The **Asian Centre** at 1871 West Mall reflects the elegant simplicity of Japanese architecture. The **Geology Museum** at 6339 Stores Street, T8222449, has the usual collection of minerals, stones, and dinosaur bones.

University of British Columbia

A short stroll from the Museum of Anthropology is the **Nitobe Memorial Garden**, an authentic Japanese tea garden. It is a subtle experience, with every rock, tree and pool playing its part in the delicate harmony to create an ambience that encourages reflection and meditation. There are cherry blossoms in spring, Japanese irises in summer, and Japanese maples in autumn. Moving anti-clockwise, the garden apparently represents the stages of a person's life.

A further 3 km south on Marine Drive is the much more extensive but equally delightful **UBC Botanical Garden**, the oldest of its kind in Canada. Spread over 30 ha are a number of expertly maintained theme gardens. The Physick Garden is devoted to traditional medicinal plants from 16th-century Europe. The Food Garden includes a collection of fruit trees that have been cleverly twisted into various shapes, including a 'UBC'. This is as much an educational as an aesthetic experience, with well-labelled exhibits and regular lectures. The Gift Shop has many fine gardening-related products and plants for sale. ■ *Daily 1000-1800. Nitobe closed weekends in winter. $6 for both, $4.75 for Botanical Garden alone, $2.75 for Nitobe. Students $2. Free tours Wed and Sat 1300. 6804 SW Marine Dr, T8229666, www.hedgerows.com Bus No 4 or 10 south on Granville.*

South and East Vancouver

For those who know the city, the broad swath of Vancouver south of False Creek and Burrard Inlet is dotted with many small neighbourhoods which are more interesting and reveal more of what Vancouver is really about than the boutiques on Robson Street. This is where you go to savour shops, bars, restaurants and atmosphere. West Broadway contains pockets of activity other than the Kitsilano stretch. Once it moves far enough east from the seedy East Side district, Hastings Street loses little of its rough and ready nature, but becomes notably more multicultural and presentable, with some great cheap eateries and ethnic bakeries. It soon connects with **Commercial Drive** (Bus No 20), arguably Vancouver's most worthwhile

South Vancouver

Related maps
A West End &
Granville Island,
page 70
B Downtown to
Chinatown,
page 62
C Kitsilano,
page 72

0 metres 200
0 yards 200

■ **Sleeping**
1 Cambie Lodge *B2*
2 City Centre Motor *A3*
3 Columbia Cottage B&B *B2*

4 Douglas Guest House *B3*
5 Shaughnessy Village *B1*

● **Eating**
1 Afghan Horsemen *A2*
2 Amorous Oyster *B2*
3 Arirang House *A2*
4 Banana Leaf
Malaysian Cuisine *A2*
5 Habibi's *A1*

6 Kalamata Greek
Taverna *B3*
7 Locus Café *C3*
8 Maurya *A1*
9 Monsoon *B3*
10 Seasons in the Park *D3*
11 Sha-Lin Noodle
House *A2*
12 Slickity Jim's
Chat 'n' Chew *A3*

13 Tojo's *A2*
14 Tomato Fresh
Food Café *B2*
15 Vij's *A1*
16 Whip *A3*

● **Bars**
17 Main *D3*
18 Public Lounge *B3*

neighbourhood. Once known as Little Italy, 'The Drive' still has a number of little Italian coffee shops, but is now a much more widely cosmopolitan area, that also attracts many of the city's bohemian, artistic, alternative or just plain less wealthy citizens. There are no 'sights' as such, but it's a fascinating pleace to wander, eat, drink and people-watch. A neighbourhood beginning to move in the same direction, and maybe even more real as a result, is **Main Street** south of Sixth Avenue, known as **South Main**, or 'SoMa'. Trendy but gritty little cafés and restaurants are starting to appear, along with a wealth of antique and second-hand stores. Further south on Main between 48th and 50th Avenues is Vancouver's Indiatown, also known as the **Punjabi Market**. Here you will find all-you-can-eat buffets, Bollywood music, silk and gold, and even the odd *pan wallah* (seller of stuffed betel leaves). If in the area, seek out (so to speak) the splendid **Sikh Temple** at 8000 Ross Street, another Arthur Erickson special.

Queen Elizabeth Park Named in honour of the Queen Mother, this 53-ha park on Cambie and 33rd Avenue, is the former site of two basalt quarries, now converted into ornamental gardens, which make for very pleasant (and free) summer strolling. Along with an extensive rose garden, there is an arboretum said to contain a specimen of almost every tree found in Canada, including some rare species like the giant dogwood. There's also a roller rink, pitch-and-putt golf, tennis courts, and a nine-basket disk-golf course. Paths lead past a tai chi area and a bizarre **Henry Moore** sculpture to Vancouver's highest point (150 m), the peak of an extinct volcano, with good if rather obstructed views of the city below. Arguably the best vistas in town are reserved for patrons of the wonderfully romantic *Seasons in the Park* restaurant (see Eating), which once hosted a summit lunch for Bill Clinton and Boris Yeltsin. Nearby is the park's major draw, the **Bloedel Conservatory**, a giant triodetic dome that contains 500 varieties of exotic plants from tropical rainforest, sub-tropical and desert ecosystems, as well as floral displays that change with the seasons, and about 160 free-flying tropical birds. ■ *Apr-Sep Mon-Fri 0900-2000, Sat and Sun 1000-2100. Oct-Mar 1000-1730. $4, $3 concessions. T2578570. Bus No 15 on Burrard or Robson.*

VanDusen Botanical Garden This 22-ha garden contains over 7,500 different plants from around the world, including some rare species. Set around lakes, ponds and waterfalls, and dotted with sculptures, the 40-odd small, themed gardens are considerably more romantic and contemplative than those at UBC, and they feel bigger. As well as a few suggested walking routes, self-guided sheets change with the seasons to take visitors around the plants thriving at that time. Early spring is the best overall time. A perennial favourite with kids is the Elizabethan hedge maze. Courses and lectures on gardening and botany are offered all year. In December the gardens host the **Festival of Lights**. ■ *Daily 1000- 2100 Jun to mid-Aug, 1000-2000 May and mid-Aug to mid-Sep, 1000-1800 Apr and late Sep, 1000-1600 Oct-Mar. $5, $3.50 concessions, $2 children, family $11. 5251 Oak St and 37th Av, T8789274, www.vandusengarden.org Bus No 17 on Burrard or Pender.*

Richmond & Steveston South of the Fraser River, far from Downtown but close to the airport, **Richmond** is an ugly, flat, sprawling suburb of malls and megastores. A footpath stretches all around the peninsula offering incredible mountain views, but there are better places to walk. In its southwest corner is Steveston, which has been a fishing village for over a century and still has the largest commercial fishing fleet on Canada's Pacific shore. In 1901, when over 10,000 people crowded its boardwalks and saloons, the village's 50 or so canneries set a record by shipping out a staggering 16 million pounds of salmon. A reminder of those heady days is the **Gulf of Georgia Cannery National Historic Site**, nicknamed 'the Monster'. Tours of the site include the 'Journey Through Time' multimedia presentation, 10,000 artefacts, and machinery dating back to 1900. ■ *1000-1700, daily Jun-Aug, Thu-Mon Apr-May and Sep-Oct, pre-booked tours only Mar and Nov. $6.50, $5 concessions, $3.25 children. 12138 4th Av, T6649009, www.gulfof georgiacannery.com Bus No 401, 406 or 407 south on Howe.*

Nearby are the restored **Britannia Heritage Shipyards**, the oldest remaining structures on the Fraser River. When the boat comes in, the sea's bounty can be bought directly from the fishing boats at the public fish sales dock. At 3811 Moncton Street is the small **Steveston Museum**. Otherwise there is a salty seaside atmosphere to enjoy, though hordes of tourists can take the edge off the experience. The best strolling is along Bayview Street between No 1 Street and Third Avenue, where a number of outside tables at the many restaurants make for romantic dining on a summer evening.

Once you've come this far, it's worth considering a lengthy diversion to the incredible **Buddhist Temple**, justifiably vaunted as one of the finest examples of Chinese palatial architecture on the continent. The spectacular exterior, with golden porcelain tiles and flying dragons on the roof, and marble lions guarding the foot of the stairway, is only surpassed by the sumptuous interior with its many fine examples of Chinese craftsmanship. Outside is a Classical Chinese garden, twin gazebos, fountains, pools and sculptures, and a courtyard with a ceramic mural. Look out for the incense burner, the row of Tang Dynasty lanterns, and the 22-m long Seven Buddha Mural. Buddhist ceremonies, lectures and meditation classes are held, as well as art exhibitions. ■ *Daily 0930-1700. Free. T2742822, www.BuddhistTemple.org Bus No 403 on Howe (50 mins).*

Burnaby   Too far from the centre to be worth a special trip, the high-rise business suburb of Burnaby contains one of the city's most modern malls, *Metrotown*. **Burnaby Village Museum** is a reconstructed village from 1925 with over 30 full-scale buildings and costumed staff at work in traditional trades and activities. The highlight is a wooden-horse **carousel** from 1912. ■ *Daily 1100-1630, varies in winter. $7.50, $4.50 concessions, carousel $1. 6501 Deer Lake Av, Burnaby, T2936500. Bus No 144.* **Burnaby Mountain Conservation Area** offers good views and some decent bike trails. Nearby is **Simon Fraser University**, of interest to architecture buffs as it was mostly designed by Arthur Erickson. ■ *Bus No 135 from Hastings/Granville daytime Mon-Sat, No 35 Sun, evenings and holidays.*

Fort Langley   This restored version of the third Hudson's Bay Trading Post was built in 1839.
National   Historic buildings and costumed staff recapture the infancy of BC with artisan
Historic Site   demonstrations. ■ *Daily Mar-Oct 1000-1700. 23433 Mavis St, Fort Langley, 47 km east on the TransCanada, T5134777, www.parkscanada. gc.ca/langley Skytrain to Surrey Central Station then Bus No 502 to Langley Centre then No 507.* The **Canadian Museum of Flight and Transportation** has displays of aircraft and various aviation artefacts. ■ *Daily 1000-1600. $5, $4 concessions. Hangar No 3 Langley Airport, 5333 216th St, T5320035. Skytrain to Surrey Central Station, then Bus No 502 to Langley Centre, then No 511.*

Golden Ears   Vancouver also has on its doorstep the wild and remote Golden Ears Park.
Provincial Park   Located 41 km east on Highway 7, near the town of Maple Creek on the north side of the Fraser River, the park stretches north through the inaccessible peaks of the Coast Mountain Range to the southern boundary of Garibaldi Park near

Whistler. **Alouette Lake** is the popular summertime focus with three **beaches** for swimming and boating. Two large vehicle-accessible campgrounds on the water have all facilities but no hook-ups. Various long and short hiking and horse trails lead to viewpoints and waterfalls (see Sports, page 105).

North Shore

The North Shore – which includes the City and District of North Vancouver, the District of West Vancouver and a few smaller communities – is for many people the highlight of a visit to Vancouver. Those mountains that provide so stunning a backdrop to the Downtown make for excellent recreational possibilities including skiing, hiking, kayaking and mountain biking in a number of outstanding parks. Few cities have such expanses of semi-wilderness right on their doorstep.

Locals started canoeing across the water for a breath of fresh air as early as the 1880s, and one by one the major parks were established, often pioneered by skiers. But the North Shore only took off as a residential area after a British syndicate controlled by the Guinness Company bought over 1,600 ha of land there in 1931. To attract property buyers they built the **Lion's Gate Bridge** across the First Narrows at a cost of $6 mn. Modelled on San Francisco's Golden Gate, it was the Empire's longest suspension bridge in 1938. Today the area is mainly inhabited by the city's wealthy. West Van's inhabitants, 27% of whom are over 60, earn more per capita than those of any other district in Canada. For all that, there is little of interest for the visitor outside the major parks, though there are pleasant seawalls and beaches in Ambleside and Dundarave Parks, lots of small galleries, and a few decent neighbourhood pubs.

Lonsdale Quay Market

The obvious way to get to the North Shore is on the SeaBus ferry, a lovely jaunt across the water which, being part of the Vancouver Transit System, is only $2, or free if you have a transfer. It leaves from behind the Waterfront SkyTrain in the old CPR building, and docks at Lonsdale Quay Market, the North Shore's only real focal point. Local buses continue from here. The glazed and galleried interior of the market, a throwback to 19th-century industrial architecture, is well worth a look. Interesting as the market's craft and food stalls may be, however, this is no real alternative to Granville Island.

Capilano River Valley

The other main route to the North Shore is across the Lion's Gate Bridge from Stanley Park. Almost due north, Capilano Road runs parallel to the eponymous river, valley, and regional park all the way to the dammed Capilano Lake and beyond to Grouse Mountain. **Capilano Suspension Bridge** is Vancouver's oldest and most vaunted attraction. The current bridge is the fourth to span the 137 m across Capilano River 70 m below, which apparently makes it the longest and highest suspended footbridge in the world. The first was built in 1889 by land developer George Grant Mackay, who knew a beautiful spot when he saw one, and bought up 2,400 ha along the river. Beyond a small collection of totem poles, a diminutive First Nations carving shed and a few photos and artefacts, there is little to justify the entrance fee besides the admittedly astounding natural beauty and the short-lived excitement of walking across the bridge. Beyond is a patch of forest best described as manicured, with some very short trails through giant trees. The **Living Forest** interactive exhibit is aimed at kids, with lots of facts and displays of dead bugs. ■ *Summer 0830-dusk, Winter 0900-1700. $9.35, $6 concessions. Parking $3. 3735 Capilano Rd, T9857474, www.capbridge.com Bus No 246 from Georgia, or No 236 from Lonsdale Quay.*

▶ **Waiting for the Big One**

All the experts agree that Southwestern BC is overdue a big earthquake. The Cascadia Subduction Zone runs southwards along a 1,400-km fault line from Alaska down the west coast of the Queen Charlotte Islands and Vancouver Island to Oregon. Once every 20-50 years a major jolt releases the zone's built-up pressure. This last happened about 50 years ago when the area north of Courtenay on Vancouver Island was hit by a quake of 7.3 on the Richter scale.

For a free and more genuine taste of the valley's natural beauty, head up the road to the 160-ha **Capilano River Regional Park**. Access is from several car parks along Capilano Park Road, which heads west from Capilano Road shortly after the suspension bridge, or directly from the latter at Cleveland Dam. Sitting on Capilano Lake, and supplying much of Vancouver's drinking water, the dam offers fine views of the Coast Mountains. The park protects Capilano River as it heads south to Burrard Inlet, a journey followed by the 7.5-km one-way Capilano Pacific Trail, longest of 10 trails through forest of the unmanicured variety. Trail maps are available at car park info-boards or from information centres, and outline a number of pools and other river features to look out for. The park also contains the **Capilano Salmon Hatchery**, one of the best place to see them run. Information panels tell the whole story. ■ *Free. T6661790.*

Grouse
Mountain

Grouse Mountain is the most popular and easily reached ski hill on the North Shore, its lights seeming to hang from Vancouver's night-time skyline like Christmas tree decorations. Skiing here was pioneered as early as 1911 by Swedish immigrant Rudolph Verne, and took off after the 1924 construction of a toll road known as Skyline Drive. The first double chairlift in North America was built here in 1949. Today skiers and sightseers are whisked up to 1,100 m above sea level in about eight minutes by the **Skyride Gondola**. At the top are year-round panoramic views, 5-m chainsaw sculptures, and a host of activities and facilities. The atmosphere is wonderful between December and April when thousands of city-dwellers flock in to enjoy downhill skiing and snowboarding, ice skating, sleigh rides, 10 km of snowshoeing and 5 km of cross-country skiing (see Sports, page 105). In summer there is hiking (though not the best), mountain biking, paragliding, helicopter tours ($75-110), and horse-drawn carriage rides (the horses also come up in the gondolas). The *Theatre in the Sky* shows a 30-minute multimedia film that is free with the gondola pass.

Facilities at the lodge include all anyone could want apart from accommodation. There are fancy restaurants such as *The Observatory*, more basic cafeteria-style set-ups such as *Lupins* (see Eating, page 87), *and Bar 98*, the drinking spot with great views and pub-like food. In summer, you can walk to the *Hiwus Feasthouse* on Blue Grouse Lake. *Alpine Guest Services* in the lodge give information and will store bags. All manner of lessons are given and equipment hired. There's even an ATM machine. ■ *Gondola runs every 15 mins year-round, 0900-2200. $20, $18 seniors, $13 13-18 year olds, $8 5-12 year olds. T9840661, www.grousemtn.com   SeaBus then Bus No 236 from Lonsdale Quay.*

Cypress
Provincial Park

The next park west is Cypress, whose access road can be seen ascending the mountainous terrain in wide, drunken zig-zags. This has been a popular recreation site since the 1920s, and offers the same range of summer and winter activities as Grouse Mountain, though with less extensive facilities and thinner crowds. Some of the North Shore's best hikes are here (see Sports, page 105), leading to panoramic views that take in the city, Howe Sound, the lofty Mount Baker to the southeast, and the Gulf Islands, Georgia Strait and Vancouver Island to the west. Pick up a blue *BC Parks* map from the main information centre. ■ *T8789229, www.cypressmountain.com Shuttle bus from Lonsdale Quay or Horseshoe Bay.*

Lighthouse Park

Still further west, this small 75-ha park is one of the most accessible and best for strolling, and contains some of the most rugged forest on the North Shore, including one of the last remaining stands of old-growth Douglas firs. A number of short trails lead to arbutus trees, cliffs and the Point Atkinson Lighthouse, which has been staffed continuously since 1875. Today it can be seen but not reached. ■ *Free. Bus No 250 from Downtown.*

Bowen Island

Highway 1/99 swings north towards Squamish, soon passing **Horseshoe Bay** (Bus No 250 or 257 on Georgia), the terminal for ferries to Nanaimo and the Gulf Islands, and a surprisingly pretty village in its own right. The closest excursion to offer the visitor a taste of the more laid-back pace of life on the islands is Bowen Island, a mere 20-minutes away but already a different world, its 3,500 population characteristically including a large number of writers and artists. Services leave more or less hourly from 0600-2125 with a break for lunch. Weekday morning and early evening sailings are met by the island bus ($1.25).

Just off the ferry landing is the main centre of **Snug Cove**. The renovated *Union Steamship Company General Store*, now houses an **Information Centre**, where you can pick up a free copy of the *Bowen Island Book* brochure, with a map and a complete list of places to eat, accommodation and activities. Ask also for the free *Happy Island Historic Walking Tour*. This was the name given to the island by romancing couples who sailed over in the 1930s and 40s to visit the largest dance pavilion in BC. Nearby is *Doc Morgan's Inn*, a popular spot for a pint and pub food, with an outdoor patio and views of the marina and Cypress Mountain. Many people come for the fine boating and kayaking, which benefit greatly from the sheltered bays that surround the 50 sq-km island. **Mount Gardner** is an excellent 16-km return day-hike that is possible almost year-round (see Sports, page 105).

Lynn Valley

Moving east from the Lion's Gate Bridge and Lonsdale Quay, the nearest attraction is Lynn Valley, which is protected by a number of parks. The closest, reached via Lynn Valley Road (exit 19 from Highway 1, bus No 229 from Lonsdale Quay), is **Lynn Canyon Park**, 250 ha of relatively unspoilt forest. This was home to the tallest tree ever measured on the planet, a 120-m Douglas fir. The **Ecology Centre**, by the parking zone at 3663 Peters Road, has displays, films and information about the park, as well as a free map and guided walks. ■ *Daily 1000-1700 year round, but closed weekends Dec and Jan.* The 68-m suspension bridge that hovers 50 m above the rushing waters of Lynn Creek is free. Many hiking trails of varying length begin on the other side, including a 15-minute stroll to a wooden footbridge that crosses the creek at Twin Falls.

Longer hikes lead into two much bigger, more remote chunks of protected forest. At the very end of Lynn Valley Road (bus No 228 from Lonsdale Quay gets you closest) is **Lynn Headwaters Regional Park**, 4,685 ha of second-growth forest with 41 km of well-signed and maintained hiking trails, varying from short strolls along the creek to full-on backcountry treks (see Sports, page 105). A **Visitor Centre**, T4326350, is open in summer for information and trail maps. **Seymour Demonstration Forest** contains 5,600 ha of

Vancouver

interpretive trails through trees that are second-growth but still massive, their girth intended to show that with proper management logging need not result in ugly clear-cuts and sad tree-farms. The best of some 50 km of hiking and biking trails is the 22-km round-trip to the enormous, very dramatic **Seymour Dam**. There are also plenty of swimming holes to cool off in summer, and a 15-m-long Indian war canoe built in 1921. ■ *Generally open 0700-2100 in summer, 0800-1700 in winter. T9871273. Drivers follow Lillooet Rd north past Capilano College and cemetery.*

Mount Seymour Provincial Park Mount Seymour Road leaves Mount Seymour Parkway at the eastern end of the North Shore and climbs steeply up 1,000 vertical metres passing two stunning viewpoints, both worth a stop. Mount Seymour was first climbed in 1908, skiing first attempted by members of the Alpine Club in 1929, and the 3,508-ha park established in 1936. Other than the commercial ski hill, the park's semi-wilderness old-growth forest and sub-alpine wildflower meadows make for some excellent hiking (see Sports, page 105). Pick up a blue *BC Parks* map from the main information centre. **Flower Lake Loop** is a pleasant 1.5-km stroll through bog and ponds, a good place for spotting birds.

Deep Cove A lovely picturesque spot with views across the bay to snowy hills beyond, Deep Cove retains the unspoilt feel of a seaside village. As well as one of the best spots for kayaking and biking, it has a nice green park by the water, a few good restaurants, and the best neighbourhood pub in Vancouver. ■ *Take the SeaBus, then Bus No 229 to Phibbs Exchange then Bus No 211 or 212.*

Essentials

Sleeping

Downtown
■ *on map page 62*
Many Downtown hotels have surprisingly reasonable rates

Arriving in Vancouver without a reservation is rarely a problem

LL *Fairmont Waterfront*, 900 Canada Place Way, T6911991, www.thewaterfronthotel.com About the least stuffy and most comfortable of the big, waterfront hotels. Rooms are simple but tastefuly decorated, and most offer views of the harbour and North Shore mountain. Staff are helpful and attentive. Facilities include a heated outdoor pool, exercise room, steam rooms, hot tub, and a terrace with great views. **LL** *The Landis Hotel and Suites*, 1200 Hornby St, T6813555, www.landissuitesvancouver.com Vast 2-bedroom suites with well-equipped kitchens, patio-style dining rooms, big living rooms and simple but pleasant decor. Those on higher floors offer good city views. Facilities include an indoor pool, hot tub and exercise room. Continental breakfast included. Parking available. A great option for 2 couples or a family. **LL** *Opus*, 322 Davie St, Yaletown, T6426787, www.opushotel.com Brand new in 2002, this impossibly hip boutique hotel was designed to mirror Yaletown's upmarket urban chic. Rooms and suites follow 5 different designs with art, furnishings and amenities conspiring to create specific atmospheres from minimalist to retro to post-modern eclectic. Even the mirrors, wash basins and elevator are impressive. Facilities include a fitness room, a French brasserie with outdoor seating, a Zen garden courtyard and parking. **LL** *Sheraton Suites Le Soleil*, 567 Hornby St, T6323000, www.lesoleilhotel.com If money is no object and you want to be treated like royalty, this is the place. Every aspect of this hotel has been custom made to the highest standards with the emphasis on old-world luxury. Service is impeccable. Facilities include an indoor pool, fitness room, sauna and a fine restaurant that's as opulent as the hotel. **LL-L** *Sheraton Vancouver Wall Centre Hotel*, 1088 Burrard St, T3311000, www.sheratonvancouver.com This sleek, modern and aesthetically pleasing hotel is housed in the city's two tallest buildings. Rooms are a reasonable size, comfy and pleasant, with floor-to-ceiling windows making the most of great city views. Facilities include an indoor pool and hot tub. The restaurant, *Indigo*, is an upbeat, funky place. **L-B** *Marriott Residence Inn*, 1234 Hornby St, T6881234, www.residenceinn.com 1-room suites with big bed and windows, sitting area and kitchenette. Gym, indoor pool and sauna. Continental breakfast buffet included. Cheaper rooms a good deal. **AL** *The Meridian at 910 Beach*, 910 Beach Av, T6095100, www.910beach.com Pleasantly located on False Creek, *The Meridien* has studios and a variety of attractive, open-plan, fully equipped suites, some with patio or balcony. Floor-to-ceiling windows give views of the water and Granville Market or the city. There's a fitness centre, and continental breakfast is included in the price.

A *The Inn at False Creek*, 1135 Howe St, T6820229, www.qualityhotel.ca Best of a cluster of hotels, in an uninspiring, but conveniently central location. Rooms are well-equipped and good value, but nothing special. Extras include an outdoor pool and free passes to *Fitness World* a block away. **B** *Bosman's Motor Hotel*, 1060 Howe St, T6823171, www.bosmanshotel.com Outdoor pool, parking, rooms standard but pleasant and a reasonable size. **B** *Burrard Motor Inn*, 1100 Burrard, T6630366. Faded, rather dingy rooms, some with kitchenettes, redeemed by an inner garden courtyard. **B** *St Regis Hotel*, 602 Dunsmuir, T6811135, www.stregishotel.com Average, fair-sized rooms in a handy but potentially noisy Downtown spot. Good value. Free use of fitness room across road at BCIT. **B** *Sandman Inn*, 180 W Georgia, T6812211, www.sandmanhotels.com Standard rooms and some suites. Indoor pool, hot tub, parking. Good value. **B-D** *Victorian Hotel*, 514 Homer, T6816369, www.victorian-hotel.com Small but comfy rooms, some bigger, some with shared bath. Easily the classiest decor in its price range, with hardwood floors, good art, pastel shades, and tasteful bathrooms. Continental breakfast included. Great value. **B-D** *YWCA*, 733 Beatty St, T8955830, www.ywcahotel.com Private rooms for women or men with shared, semi-private or private bath. Shared kitchen, internet, laundry, coffee bar and restaurant. Rooms are very small and ordinary, but clean and professional. **C** *Comfort Inn Downtown*, 654 Nelson St, T6054333, www.comfortinndowntown.com Certainly the best deal in its range, this long-standing hotel has just been totally renovated in a hip retro 1950s style, with lots of black and white photos and neon signs. Continental breakfast and nightlife pass, but the real bonus is the central location and great price. **C** *Jolly Taxpayer*, 828 W Hastings St, T6813550. Small and basic rooms with toilets but shared bath. Good price, great location. Bigger family rooms available (**B**). 1 floor non-smoking. Continental breakfast. **C** *Kingston Hotel*, 757 Richards, T6849024, www.kingstonhotelvancouver.com Tiny but clean rooms, with or without bath. Continental breakfast and sauna. Bigger room for 4 people (**A**). Heavily booked due to price and location.

D-E *Global Village Backpackers*, 1018 Granville St, T6828226. This excellent hostel is centrally located in a colourful building with friendly staff. Dorms and private doubles, some with en suite bath. There's a common room with sofas, a pool table, licensed café and internet. Facilities include a big kitchen, laundry, lockers/storage room a TV room with free movies, and a travel desk for booking tours. Patio for smokers. Pub crawls 5 days a week. Will be serving cheap breakfast. **D-E** *HI Vancouver Central*, 1025 Granville St, T6855335. A brand new and very central hostel. Dorms and private rooms. Common room, express kitchen (microwaves, no stove), shared bath, lockers, trips arranged. **E** *The Cambie Hostel Gastown*, 300 Cambie St, T6846466, www.cambiehostels.com Well run and handily situated, this popular backpacker hostel has 142 beds, mostly in dorms. It common rooms are a good place to meet travellers and pick up information. Free breakfast, no kitchen but the popular, down-to-earth pub downstairs has a cheap restaurant and there's an excellent bakery next door. **E** *The Cambie Hostel Seymour*, 515 Seymour St, T6847757. Very small rooms with 2 beds or private double bed for couples. No dorms. Small kitchen, common room, laundry. Quieter location than above. Various ski/hockey packages. Coin-op internet, storage but no lockers. **E-F** *The New Backpackers Hostel*,

There is an excellent choice of hostels in town for budget travellers, but the better ones fill up fast in the summer

347 W Pender, T6880112. The cheapest in town, but only for the desperate or hardcore budgeters. Everything is small and grungy, and there aren't enough showers and toilets to go round. Tiny TV room and kitchen (which costs extra), lockers, laundry.

West End &
Robson Street
■ *on map, page 70*

LL-L *Listel Vancouver*, 1300 Robson, T6848461, www.listel-vancouver.com Impressively beautiful and stylish throughout. Rooms are thoughtfully equipped with big windows, beds, and TVs. 'Museum rooms' are decorated with First Nations' art and exquisite hand-carved furnishings. Each of the 'Gallery rooms' has been conceived by a different designer and they feature chaises longues by the windows. There's a fitness centre and a hot tub. Personal and attentive service. Highly recommended. **L-AL** *Lord Stanley Suites on the Park*, 1889 Alberni St, T6889299, www.lordstanley.com Rather small but fully equipped suites close to Stanley Park and the marina, with views or balconies. Exercise room and sauna. Continental breakfast included. **AL-B** *O Canada House B&B*, 1114 Barclay St, T6880555, www.ocanadahouse.com 7 en suite rooms, some with fireplaces, in an 1897 Queen Anne house tastefully decorated with period antiques. Sherry in the front parlour in the evenings. **AL** *Pacific Palisades*, 1277 Robson, T6880461, www.pacific palisadeshotel.com Decoration in rooms and throughout is bright, with vibrant greens and yellows, stripes and spots, and plenty of funky pieces of art. Rooms are big and comfortable with first-rate furnishings. Indoor pool, health-club, sauna and whirlpool are about the best in town. Free wine-tasting from 1700-1800. Suites (**L**) have balcony and sleep 4. *Zin Restaurant* shares the hotel's sense of colour, style and eclecticism. **AL** *Rosellen Suites at Stanley Park*, 2030 Barclay St, T6894807, www.rosellensuites.com Fully equipped 1- and 2-bedroom suites with kitchens and fireplaces, pleasant. Can sleep up to 6 ($15 extra per person). Free entry to nearby health club and aquatic centre.

A *Amber House B&B*, 1137 Barclay St, T6822900. 4 en suite rooms in a romantically decorated, restored 1904 house. **A** *Blue Horizon Hotel*, 1225 Robson, T6884461, www.bluehorizonhotel.com Large, plain but well-appointed rooms with balconies and good views on 2 sides. Those with 2 beds ($10 more) sleep 4 and are much bigger. Small pool, hot tub, sauna and fitness centre. Good value. **A** *English Bay Inn B&B*, 1968 Comox St, T6838002, www.englishbayinn.com 6 en suite rooms. Attractive and comfortable rooms, big breakfast. **A** *Greenbriar Hotel*, 1393 Robson St, T6834558. Good value suites with full kitchen. Can sleep 4 ($5 extra per person). Free parking. **A** *Oceanside Apartment Hotel*, 1847 Pendrell St, T6825641, www.oceanside-hotel.com Fairly spacious and pleasant suites with small kitchen. Can sleep 4. **A** *Riviera Hotel*, 1431 Robson St, T6851301, www.riviera onrobson.com Fairly small but neat and fully equipped suites, very heavily booked. **A** *Sunset Inn Apartment Hotel*, 1111 Burnaby St, T6848763, www.sunset inn.com Well- located and reasonable rooms and suites, all with kitchen and balconies. Worth paying a bit extra for the suites, which also have living-rooms.

B *Tropicana Motor Inn*, 1361 Robson, T6875724. Good value suites with small kitchens, unaesthetic decor, but quality TVs. Higher floors offer good views of the metropolis. Sauna, indoor swimming pool and parking. Can sleep 4 ($10 extra per person). **B-C** *Sylvia Hotel*, 1154 Gilford St, T6819321, www.sylviahotel.com A fine, historic, vine-covered building, open continuously since 1912 and the tallest in the West End until the mid-50s. Rooms are nothing special, though some offer views of Stanley Park next door. Heavily booked due to price and location. Suites (**A**) are much bigger, have kitchenettes, and can sleep 4 ($15 extra per person). **C** *The Buchan Hotel*, 1906 Haro St, T6855354, www.buchanhotel.com Small and basic rooms with tiny en suite or shared baths. Price is the only plus. **D-E** *HI Vancouver Downtown*, 1114 Burnaby St, T6844565, www.hihostels.ca 4-bed dorms and simple private rooms with shared bath. Clean and professional with top-notch facilities including a TV room, library, games room with pool-table, laundry, lockers, storage room, dining room, and large kitchen. Many cheap activities arranged, such as tours, kayaking and club nights. Convenient location. Reservations highly recommended. Free shuttle from bus/train station.

D *City Centre Motor Hotel*, 2111 Main St (at 6th Av), T8767166. Close to SkyTrain and Science World, a short bus ride from Downtown. Standard motel rooms at very reasonable prices. **D** *Patricia Hotel*, 403 E Hastings, T2554301. The best budget option in town, housed in a nicely renovated 1914 building enlivened with many plants and surprisingly classy given the seedy area. Rooms are simple, clean, and comfy, with en suite baths. Some have fine views. Price includes a huge breakfast at a café down the street. Smoking on every floor but the 5th. Off-season weekly rates available. Staff on duty 24 hrs. **D** *Waldorf*, 1489 Hastings at Commercial, T2537141. Faded but reasonably priced rooms over a pub a short bus ride from Downtown. Small bath with shower only. **E** *C&N Backpackers Hostel*, 927 Main St, T6822441, www.cnnbackpackers.com Handy location close to bus station/skytrain. 4-bed dorms and private rooms with shared bath. Bike rentals.

East Side
■ *on maps, pages 58 & 76*

L-A *Beachside B&B*, 4208 Evergreen Av, West Van, T9227773, www.beach.bc.ca Attractive house right on the beach close to Lighthouse Park. 3 luxurious en suite rooms or suites with TV and VCR, some with their own jacuzzi, views, garden patio, kitchen or fireplace. Very stylish. **L-A** *Crystal's View B&B*, 420 Tempe Cr, T9873952, www.bc-bedand breakfast.com Large, sumptuously decorated en suite rooms, some with jacuzzi, balcony and views. Guest sitting room and patio with winning views of the city. **L-A** *Thistledown House B&B*, 3910 Capilano Rd, T9867173, www.thistle-down.com Tastefully decorated 1920s heritage home set in gardens. 5 en suite rooms. Deck, guest lounge, full breakfast. **AL-A** *Queen Anne Manor B&B*, 4606 Wickenden Rd, Deep Cove, T9293239, www.n-vancouver.com Victorian-style home, sumptuously decorated and furnished. 2 sitting rooms, 1 with TV, 1 with library. 2 rooms and a suite, a bit twee.

North Shore
■ *on map, page 58*

   A-B *A Gazebo in the Garden*, 310 St James Rd E, T9833331, www.agazebointhegarden.com Beautiful prairie-style heritage home decorated with antiques and set in a stunning garden. 4 comfy en suite rooms with TVs. Full breakfast. **A-B** *Capilano Canyon Guest House*, 4085 Capilano Rd, T9878582, www.capilanocanyonrt.com 3 rooms with shared bath, overlooking the Canyon. **A-B** *Lonsdale Quay Hotel*, 123 Carrie Cates Ct, T9866111, www.lonsdalequayhotel.com Boutique hotel whose best feature is its location right by the SeaBus and market. **A-B** *Ocean Breeze B&B*, 462 1st St E, T9880546, www.oceanbreezevancouver.com Slightly small and twee en suite rooms with TV. Full breakfast, very handy location close to SeaBus.

   B *Grouse Inn*, 1633 Capilano Rd, T9887101, www.grouseinn.com About the best value of a clutch of standard motels on this busy stretch of road. Continental breakfast, outdoor pool, free parking. **B-C** *Mountainside Manor B&B*, 5909 Nancy Greene Way, T9909772, www.vancouver-bc.com/MountainsideManor Unusual, elegant home en route to Grouse Mountain. Light and airy interior with guest lounge, large deck and lovely garden. 4 pleasant rooms with en suite or private bath. **B-D** *Travelodge Lions Gate*, 2060 Marine Dr, T9855311, www.lionsgatetravelodge.com Standard motel with outdoor pool. Good location and price.

LL-AL *Granville Island Hotel*, 1253 Johnstone St, T6837373, www.granville islandhotel.com Varied but decent rooms, some with balconies. Glassed-in hot tub, steam room, lounge and restaurant. **A** *Camelot Inn B&B*, 2212 Larch St, T7396941, www.camelotinnvancouver.com 4 en suite rooms in an attractive 1912 house with hardwood floors and tasteful furnishings. **A-B** *Penny Farthing Inn*, 2855 6th Av, T7399002, www.pennyfarthinginn.com 4 plush and comfy rooms with TV, VCR and CD players. Guest living room and 3 patios.

Kitsilano & around
■ *on map page 72*

B&Bs tend to be in attractive, quiet residential areas such as the West End, Kitsilano or Mount Pleasant

   B *Maple House B&B*, 1533 Maple St, T7395833, www.maplehouse.com Fairly nice rooms in a 1900 home that enjoys a fine location close to Kits Beach and Vanier Park. **B** *Mickey's Kits Beach Chalet*, 2146 1st Av, T7393342. 6 pleasant and bright rooms, 4 with en suite, 2 with balconies. Quiet spot close to Kits beach, friendly and helpful host.

Vancouver

C *Between Friends B&B*, 1916 Arbutus, T7345082. 3 small but very nice rooms. One is en suite, but the nicest has a balcony and skylight. Pleasant sitting room and friendly hostess. **C** *Graeme's House B&B*, 2735 Waterloo St, T7321488, www.graemewebster.com 3 rooms in a pretty heritage house with lots of interesting features plus a deck and beautiful flower garden. Close to the most interesting section of Broadway.

D-E *HI Jericho Beach Hostel*, 1515 Discovery St, T2243208, www.hihostels.ca Built in the 1930s as a barracks for Jericho Air Station, this vast and interesting building is now the largest hostel in Canada, with 288 dorm beds and 10 private rooms, all with shared bath. All the usual top-notch facilities are here: a massive kitchen and dining-room, TV room, games room with pool table, library, laundry, big lockers, storage room, bike rental for $20 per day. Open 24 hrs, with an information desk in summer. Free or cheap tours and hikes, even activities like sailing. The main factor here is the location, a beautiful and quiet spot right on the beach, but a long way from town. A free shuttle runs to and from the Downtown HI Hostel and bus station 7 times per day 0700-1345 in winter, 0800-1600 in Summer with an extra 4 from 1800-2200. Dorms are very long but divided up into 4-bed alcoves. Sleeping bags not allowed to avoid bed bugs. Take bus No 4 (UBC).

Mount Pleasant
■ *on map page 76*

This quiet, well-to-do residential area centred around City Hall and Vancouver General Hospital has a number of decent B&Bs. **B** *Columbia Cottage B&B*, 205 W 14th Av, T8745327. 5 small but attractive en suite rooms on a quiet street. Pretty art deco living room, nice gardens, full vegetarian breakfast, friendly owner. **B** *Douglas Guest House*, 456 W 13th Av, T8723060, www.dougwin.com 8 fairly large rooms/suites, with en suite in all but 2 and TVs. Elegant decor, small common room, dining room in a glassed-in sun room with patio. **B-C** *Cambie Lodge*, 446 W 13th Av, T8724753, www.cambielodge.com 9 rooms, en suite in all but 2, with showers rather than tub. Not as nice as the *Douglas* but still clean, pleasant and professional. Rooms 5 and 6 are the best. **C** *Shaughnessy Village*, 1125 W 12th Av, T7365511. 240 rooms with 1 or 2 beds, the former being tiny. Bathrooms, balconies and TVs are diminutive, but rooms high up on the building's north side compensate with unbeatable views over the city. Lots of facilities such as sauna, small pool, jacuzzi, gym and common room, but the place is vast and very impersonal.

Airport
■ *on map page 58*

AL-A *Fairmont Vancouver Airport*, T2075200, www.fairmont.com Situated right in the main airport building, with large, soundproof rooms and facilities such as pool, hot tub, and spa. **B** *Delta Vancouver Airport*, 3500 Cessna Dr, T2781241, www.deltavancouverairport.com The nicest place to stay close to the airport, thanks to a riverside location by dozens of scenic little boats, with a pub (the *Elephant and Castle*) housed in a small pagoda on the water. Outdoor pool, exercise room, restaurant. **B** *Holiday Inn Express*, 9351 Bridgeport Rd, T4654329, www.hi-express.bc.ca About the best value of a clutch of mid-price places close to the airport. **C** *Fraser Arms Hotel*, 1450 Marine Dr, T2612499. Motel-style budget option on the highway near airport.

Long stay
To find an apartment, look in the classified section of the Vancouver Sun

E *Simon Fraser University*, McTaggart-Cowan Hall, Burnaby, T2914503, www.sfu.ca May-Aug only. Single and twin rooms with bath, common room and kitchen. **B-D** *UBC*, 5961 Student Union Blvd, T8221000, www.ubcconferences.com May-Aug only. Variety of options from basic 1-bed rooms with shared bath, kitchen, to fully equipped suites.

Camping
Campsites are a poor option, far from town, and often they only take RVs

With so many great hostels so well located in town, there seems little point in camping, especially as none of the campgrounds are pleasant compared to the many beautiful sites around BC. Only 3 are anywhere near town. **E-F** *Burnaby Caribou RV Park*, 8765 Cariboo Pl, T4201722. One of the better and closer options. Lots of facilities including heated indoor pool, hot tub, exercise room, games room. About 16 km from

Downtown. Bus No 101 and close to the useful 99 route. **E-F** *Capilano RV Park*, 295 Tomahawk Av, near Lion's Gate Bridge on North Shore, T9874722. Unattractive but about the best located. Facilities include full hook-ups, pool, jacuzzi, playground and games room. **E-F** *Richmond RV Park*, 6200 River Rd, T2707878. Quiet but unattractive. About 13 km from Downtown but close to airport. Bus No 411 or 401.

Further out, mostly in the southern suburbs, the following would only suit people wanting to stop on their way to or from the US border. **E** *Parkcanada RV Park & Tenting*, 4799 Hwy 17, Delta, T9435811. Handy for the Tsawwassen ferry but 27 km from Downtown. Hook-ups, tent sites, pool, showers. Bus No 640 from Ladner Exchange. **E-F** *Dogwood Campgrounds of BC*, 15151-112 Av, Surrey, 25 km from Downtown, T5835585, www.dogwoodcampground.com Huge site with hook-ups, tent-sites and pool. **E-F** *Peace Arch RV Park*, 14601 40th Av, T5947009, www.peacearchrvpark.com Large campground about 28 km out. Hook-ups, tent sites, pool, games room. **F** *Hazelmere RV Campground*, 18843 8th Av, White Rock, T5831167, www.hazelmere.ca Large, park-like setting some 35 km from town. Heated pool, hot tub, fitness room, games room. **F** *Parklander RV Park*, 16311 8th Av (Marine Dr E), White Rock, T5313711. Small, pleasant, wooded park near beach, about 35 km from town.

Eating

First-class international cuisine can be found here, especially Italian, French, Greek and East Indian, while the city's large Oriental population makes for a staggering number of cheap Chinese, Vietnamese and sushi joints. A current trend is for so-called 'fusion food', with many top chefs creating their own imaginative menus. Vancouver's Pacific Rim or West Coast cuisine involves lots of seafood, combining European techniques with Asian influences, and an emphasis on healthy eating and subtle flavours.

Vancouver has more restaurants per capita than any other Canadian city

Expensive *Bacchus*, 845 Hornby in the *Wedgewood Hotel*, T6085319. The interior is plush, with a piano, fireplace and cigar room thrown in. Food is classic French with a very good reputation. Weekend brunches afternoon tea and cocktail hour are popular specialities. Reservation recommended. *C Restaurant*, 1600 Howe, on False Creek, T6811164. Some of the best seafood you'll find anywhere, a broad range of it, prepared in exciting new ways. Great wine list includes many *sakes*. Large, open and airy interior with views that are even better from the more intimate upstairs balcony. Recommended. ***Diva at the Met***, 645 Howe, T6027788. A contender for the best in town, the food here is classic nouveau French, prepared with flair and creativity. Decor is bright and elegant, sophisticated but not stuffy. Main courses feature one of every type of fish and meat. Taster menu is your choice of 3 downsized main courses (entrées) for $60. Or try the cheese taster menu. Extensive wine list, many offered by the glass. *Il Giardino di Umberto*, 1382 Hornby, T6692422. Tuscan cuisine. Wonderful romantic interior with sloping ceilings, terracotta walls, bright tasteful art, lots of plants and racks of wine. Several rooms of differing sizes and a tiled, enclosed garden patio that must be the nicest in town. Extensive wine list. *Joe Forte's Oyster House*, 777 Thurlow, T6691940. Named after a popular historical Vancouverite (see box), this beautifully opulent room is fitted out with brass banisters and trimmings, wrought iron, marble columns, high ceilings, and huge mirrors, and dominated by a large horse-shoe bar. Great selection of beers, and a wine list that has been winning major prizes for the last 10 years. Live piano music every night. Seafood is its speciality, with a broad choice of oysters. Roof garden with smoking lounge and fireplace. *Le Crocodile*, 909 Burrard, T6694298. French-influenced cuisine whose sophistication lies in its simplicity. The ambience is upscale bistro, the prices reasonable for food of this calibre. *Piccolo Mondo*, 850 Thurlow, T6881633. Italian food that foregoes the pizza and pasta in favour of fish and meat. Small menu with refreshingly simple dishes, great wine list, and decor that is refreshingly simple and elegant.

Downtown
● *on map page 62*

Restaurants on Burrard and east are listed here, those on Thurlow and west are listed under the West End

Vancouver

▶ **Joe Forte**

Born in the Caribbean as Joe Seraphin, this lifeguard and swimming instructor arrived accidentally from England in 1885, bound for Victoria, but stayed anyway. He worked in the Bodega Saloon *and set up home above English Bay Beachhouse in a squatter's shack. It was partly by teaching people to swim and saving lives that he became one of the city's early heroes, but also because he was the scourge of hoodlums, even being given the rank of Special Constable. When he died in 1923, he was seen off by the city's longest ever funeral cortege.*

Mid-range *The Elbow Room*, 560 Davie, T6853628. Popular breakfast spot, famous for its large portions and the abuse regularly dished out to customers who fail to polish off their plates. *Kitto Japanese House*, 833 Granville, T6876622. Reliable central spot for sushi. *La Bodega Tapa Bar*, 1277 Howe, T6848814. Long-standing favourite with a quiet, romantic atmosphere, good sangria and food that is consistently rated as the town's best Spanish.

Cheap *Kam's Place*, 1043 Davie. Singaporean cuisine that's inspired rave reviews despite the cafeteria-style setting. *Olympia*, 820 Thurlow. Often voted best fish and chips in town. Mainly take-out with limited seating.

Seriously Cheap *Homer St Café*, 892 Homer, T6872228. Basic cheap breakfast spot overflowing with genuine character. *Fritz*, 718 Davie, T6840811. Large portions of fries enlivened by a choice of a dozen different dips. Open until 0300 Fri and Sat.

West End
● *on map, page 70*

The West End's large and lively population breathes constant life into the city's most competitive culinary district, with Robson, Denman and Davie representing the finest streets for restaurant window-shopping anywhere. **Expensive** *Brass Monkey*, 1072 Denman, T6857626. Extravagantly idiosyncratic and lavish decor, featuring a glittery bar, wrought-iron chairs, and plush velvet drapes. The menu is surprisingly understated, only hinting at the complex and delicious dishes that have torn many a local away from their former favourites. The great Martinis, wine list, and affable host all contribute to a memorable experience. *Café de Paris*, 751 Denman, T6871418. Perfectly captures the look of a French bistro, simple but classic and elegant. Food is various meats (rabbit, calf's liver, beef tartare, etc) expertly prepared in classic French ways. Nice bar. *CinCin*, upstairs at 1154 Robson, T6887338. Maybe the best Italian food in town. Mediterranean decor is warm and romantic, sophisticated and comfortable, with balcony seating for those summer evenings. Many awards, mostly for its wine list. *Delilah's*, 1789 Comox, T6873424. The atmosphere here is louche: tongue-in-cheek decadent with lots of red, velvet and gold gilt. Crowded and noisy, good for people-watching and famed for its Martinis. Food is variable but can be first-class. $24 for 2 courses, $33.50 for 4. *Le Gavroche*, 1616 Alberni, T6853924. Classic French cuisine served in an old house whose many small rooms make for an intimate, romantic atmosphere. *Liliget Feast House*, 1724 Davie, T6817044. First Nations' specialities served in a beautiful cellar space featuring cedar columns and tables, West Coast art, and seating designed by Arthur Erickson. Authentic regional dishes are cooked on alderwood grill. The platter for 2 with salmon, caribou, fiddleheads is the obvious choice. *Raincity Grill*, 1193 Denman, T6857337. *The* place to go for top-notch West Coast cuisine. Ingredients are fresh, locally produced, organic when possible, and used with subtlety and panache. The decor is equally modern, elegant and understated while the wine list focuses on BC's finest. *The Teahouse*, Stanley Park at Ferguson Point, T6693281. More genuinely classy than the *Fishhouse*, this too feels like a summer house, but far more bright and breezy, with lots of plants, and big windows offering fabulous views of English Bay. The menu is more cosmopolitan: Pacific Rim lobster ravioli, Peking duck, salmon tournedos.

Mid-range *Capers*, 1675 Robson. Vegetarian food, deli and bakery using fresh organic food. *Da Pasta Bar*, 1232 Robson, T8991288. Dark and intimate interior with big paintings. Portions are large, and at lunchtime all pastas are $7, wine and beer $4. *Gyoza King*, 1508 Robson, T6698278. Dark, atmospheric and very popular spot for small, tapa-style, Japanese dishes and sake. *Just One Thai Bistro*, 1103 Denman, T6858989. One of the more consistently praised Thai options in town. *Kafe Europa*, 735 Denman. Cosy, rustic-style Hungarian deli serving large portions of classic flavourful dishes at very reasonable prices. Schnitzel and strudel are specialities. *Tanpopo*, 1122 Denman, T6817777. About the best of the mid-range sushi houses, and certainly *the* choice for all-you-can-eat. *Tapastree*, 1829 Robson, T6064680. Large, casual but elegant space filled out with tasteful art, with a patio in front. Broad menu of wonderful tapas, maybe the best in town, at around $10 each. Open kitchen and bar. *A Taste of India*, 1282 Robson. Good reasonably priced authentic food in a cosy atmosphere.

Cheap *Hon's Wun-Tun House*, 1339 Robson, T6850871. Incredibly huge and bustling, very popular. Same menu as in Chinatown, same cheap prices. Huge servings of authentic Szechuan food prepared in an open kitchen. *Indica*, 1795 Pendrell, T6093530. Small, simple interior contrasting with the complex flavours of malai kofta or malabar shrimp curry. A lamb curry is just $9.50 including rice and naan. *Café Luxy*, 1235 Davie, T6695899. Broad range of homemade pasta dishes served with caesar salad and garlic bread for about $11. *Stepho's Greek Taverna*, 1124 Davie. Not much to look at, but rated some of the best Greek food in town, with generous portions and prices. Queues are the norm, even before it opens. *Hamburger Mary's*, 1202 Davie, T6871293. Diner-style joint serving big gourmet burgers till 0200 or later.

Expensive *Blue Water Café and Raw Bar*, 1095 Hamilton, T6888078. Upmarket but casual, very spacious interior, featuring brick walls, big wooden columns, leather chairs and couches, soft lighting and jazzy music. Open kitchen serves mainly seafood and steak. Large selection of wines and beers. *Cioppino's Mediterranean Grill and Enoteca*, 1133 Hamilton, T6887466. First-class Italian cuisine in 2 neighbouring rooms, one strictly formal, the other slightly more casual, both very stylish. *La Terrazza*, 1088 Cambie, T8994449. Italian cuisine done West Coast style, focusing on game and fish, using fresh ingredients like mixed organic greens and wild mushrooms. Tiles and murals dominate the modern, Mediterranean setting.

Yaletown
● *on map, page 62*

Mid-range *Simply Thai*, 1211 Hamilton, T6420123. Owned by the Thai chef, whose food is highly recommended. Interior is bright, with pale pastel walls, cream leather couches, graceful curved wood lines and simple brick and concrete floor. Considering such style and the well-heeled clientele it attracts, the prices are surprisingly reasonable. *Rodney's Oyster House*, 1228 Hamilton, T6090080. Classic converted warehouse space with brick walls and huge squared wooden beams. Downstairs is casual with stools at the bar, upstairs a little smarter. Clientele is slightly older but the ambience is lively and crowded. Focusing on oysters, mussels and chowder the food is excellent, and there's a good selection of wine and beer.

Cheap *Urban Monks*, 328 Nelson, T6691311. Vegan 'Zen' cuisine. Many options, all healthy. Suitably simple but tasteful decor.

Expensive *Borgo Antico*, 321 Water, T6838376. Spacious and classy, with a number of very attractive rooms. Upstairs has big arched windows with views of the North shore. Sister to *Il Giardino Umberto* (see page 87), not quite as superlative, but in a better location. *Water Street Café*, 300 Water, T6892832. Elegant, classy room with massive windows and outdoor seating. Mainly pasta, with some steak and seafood.

Gastown
● *on map, page 62*

Mid-range *Incendio Pizzereia*, 103 Columbia, T6888694. Also at 2118 Burrard next to the *Fifth Avenue Cinema*. Wooden tables in a colourful and casually smart room. Wood-oven pizzas.

Vancouver

Chinatown
The choice is intimidating, but it's hard to go wrong; food tends to be authentic Szechuan and servings are large

Mid-range *Buddhist Vegetarian Restaurant*, 137 E Pender. As well as regular vegetarian fare, they do a fine job of replicating meat-based dishes. No MSG, lots of fungi.

Cheap *Hon's Wun-Tun House*, 268 Keefer, T6880871. The obvious choice, having for some time scooped up most awards for best Chinese, best restaurant under $10, etc. Cafeteria-style decor, huge menu. *Kam's*, 509 Main, T6695488. Equally reliable, but smaller, with a more authentic feel. For a snack try one of the numerous bakeries for a curry beef, BBQ pork or honey bun; they quickly become addictive.

Granville Island
● *on map, page 70*

Mid-range *Cat's Meow*, 1540 Old Bridge St, T6472287. Burgers, pizzas, nice appetizers, good selection of beer and other drinks. Funky interior with leather tablecloths and comfy leather armchairs. *The Sand Bar*, 1535 Johnson St. Beautiful renovated warehouse with high ceilings, industrial metal trimmings and vast windows looking out over False Creek. Heated roof patio. Tapas and seafood, wood-grilled burgers and pizza. Fine selection of ales and wines.

Cheap The *Public Market* has countless excellent, cheap fast-food stalls selling all kinds of international cuisine. Outdoor seating by the water.

Kitsilano
● *on map, page 72*

Expensive *Bishop's*, 2549 W 4th Av, T7382025. Often voted the city's best all-round restaurant. Food made with 100% organic produce, most of it grown locally. Menu changes weekly. *Lumière*, 2551 W Broadway, T7398185. Often cited as Vancouver's finest restaurant. The interior is elegant, almost intimidatingly stylish and modern. There is no à la carte, just tasting menus from $80-120 without wine, apparently worth every penny. Bistro bar next door has tapas-style dishes at $12 a shot. *Maurya*, 1643 W Broadway, T7420622. Innovative West Coast versions of classic Indian dishes in surroundings that are spacious and exquisitely classy. The chef will create a menu for you for $22 per person. Reservations recommended. *Pastis*, 2153 W 4th Av, T7315020. French Nouvelle Cuisine, with a small, ever-changing menu using the freshest fish and meats. Taster menu is $65. Another of Vancouver's key players, with decor too casual to match the prices.

Mid-range *Annapurna*, 1812 W 4th Av. Original vegetarian Indian dishes, best of a few in the area. *Arirang House*, 2211 Cambie. Sit on the floor and enjoy a Korean BBQ: like a fondue with assorted meat and seafood. Also a variety of veggie dishes. Karaoke in the back. *Capers*, 2285 W 4th Av, T7396676. Deli-style vegetarian food in a large health food grocery store. Fresh baking, delicious cakes, salads, lots of hot and cold dishes sold by weight, organic when possible. Fresh juices, large outdoor seating area. *The Eatery*, 3431 W Broadway, T7385298. Trendy, very popular spot for Japanese-Western fusion food. Recommended. *Greens and Gourmet*, 2681 W Broadway. A vegetarian refuge with a calming plant-filled interior. Lots of delicious salads and assorted hot dishes all at $1.50 per 100 g. *The Naam*, 2724 W 4th Av, T7387151. The city's oldest vegetarian restaurant, good from breakfast to dinner, with generous portions. Simple interior and heated atrium-style patio. Open 24 hrs, with live music every night from 1900-2200, jazz/folk/world, etc. Licensed with beers on tap and wine by the glass or bottle at very reasonable prices. Lots of desserts. *Nyala*, 2930 W 4th Av, T7317899. Tasty Ethiopian food, mostly curries and stews, much of it vegetarian, served on very large platters with no forks. Dinner only. Veg buffet on Sun, Mon and Wed for $11. Beer on tap. Very reasonable prices. *Sophie's Cosmic Café*, 2095 4th Av, T7326810. A Kitsilano institution, now becoming too popular for its own good, with long queues for weekend brunches. Eccentric, diner-style decor and large portions. *Tangerine*, 1685 Yew, T7394677. Eclectic and upmarket food at moderate prices. Small and trendy locale close to Kits Beach, very popular with locals.

West Broadway
● *on map, page 76*

Expensive *Tojo's*, 777 W Broadway, T8728050. Hands-down the best (and most expensive) sushi restaurant in Western Canada with the freshest fish, best sake and most beautiful presentation. *Vij's*, 1480 11th Av, T7366664. The only Indian restaurant

Vancouver

that is regularly cited as one of the city's best overall eateries, with skilful, innovative variations on old favourites. No reservations so queues are common.

Mid-range *Afghan Horsemen*, 445 W Broadway, T8735923. Intimate, exotic decor, featuring lots of plants and ethnic art, and the chance to sit on the floor on rugs. Extremely popular and highly regarded. *Banana Leaf Malaysian Cuisine*, 820 W Broadway, T7316333. Beautiful decor with traditional works of art hung on bright yellow walls, and lots of plants. Wonderfully tasty food, including many veggie and seafood options. Recommended.

Cheap *Habibi's*, 1128 W Broadway, T7327487. Vegetarian Lebanese food, consisting of lots of small tapas-style dishes. Smart, pleasant interior, nice atmosphere, beer on tap. *Lan's Vietnamese*, 1471 W Broadway. Great food, lots of it, and cheap. *Sha-Lin Noodle House*, 548 W Broadway. Handmade noodles, bright lights, busy. *Kalamata Greek Taverna*, 478 W Broadway, T8727050. Some of the finest authentic Greek home-cooking in the city.

Expensive *The Cannery*, 2205 Commissioner, T2549606. Former cannery with rustic decor, two fireplaces, ocean views and a romantic atmosphere. Recommended for its creative seafood dishes, with the best selection of fish in the city and one of the finest wine lists.

Mid-range *Bukowski's Bistro*, 1447 Commercial, T2534770. An atmosphere worthy of the name, and large portions of food that never disappoints. Lively bar at the back, live jazz Mon, Thu and Sat, poetry readings and lectures other nights. Open till 0100 most nights. *Café Deux Soleils*, 2096 Commercial. Large vegetarian dishes, especially popular for breakfast. Friendly, rather alternative space with a play area for kids, and frequent live music. *Havana*, 1212 Commercial, T2539119. Good for breakfast through to dinner and tapas, but most notable for its lively atmosphere and heated patio, one of the best places to watch the world go by. Interesting decor features graffiti scratched into the walls and black and white photos of Cuba. *Latin Quarter*, 1305 Commercial, T2511144. Tapas, paella and sangria in a crowded, party atmosphere with frequent live music. *Pink Pearl*, 1132 E Hastings (Commercial Dr), T2534316. Dim sum here is an experience to savour: sit down and choose from the trollies that drift by laden with goodies. Also noted for its seafood.

Cheap *Sweet Cherubim*, 1105 Commercial. Health-food grocery store with a café attached that has wonderful baking and samosas, juices, smoothies and great value dishes that are vegetarian, organic and often vegan. Full dinner for $9. *Thai Away Home*, 1736 Commercial. Also at 1206 Davie (West End), and 3315 Cambie. Cheap but great Thai food in a very casual atmosphere. **Seriously cheap** *Baghdad Café*, 1018 Commercial. *Shawarmas* and *falafel* dishes, cushions on the floor or in the window.

Main Street
● *on map, page 76*

Mid-range *Locus Café*, 4121 Main, T7084121. Dark and brooding interior, with red and black walls and some whacky art. Almost too popular, especially with the young, alternative crowd. Equally good for food or a drink, with a few good beers on tap. Menu is mainly predictable, with a few surprises like ostrich and paella, portions are large. *Monsoon*, 2526 Main, T8794001. Full of colour and character, this trendy favourite specializes in gourmet Asian fusion cuisine at reasonable prices. Appetizers like masala fries with banana ketchup for $4. Mains include a 5-spice duck leg comfit with fancy trimmings for $15. *Slickity Jim's Chat 'n' Chew*, 2513 Main, T8736760. 0800-1700. Small, popular place packed with weird and wonderful artefacts, an unbeatable choice for breakfast. *The Whip*, 209 E 6th Av (Main St), T8744687. Funky little downbeat and arty café/pub with art scattered around. Salads, pan-seared yellow fin tuna with chipotle BBQ sauce sandwich, curries and pastas, and some great, cheapish beers on tap. Look for the old Tetley sign outside. Brunch 1000-1600 weekends, otherwise 1600-0030.

Commercial Drive & around
See map, page 58

Vancouver

Cheap The Punjabi Market has a number of cheap restaurants specializing in all-you-can-eat buffets. *India Sweet and Restaurant*, 6505 Main, is vegetarian only, with lots of choices, including a small salad bar. This is the largest, most popular and westernized option, with the bonus of beer on tap. *Sagar*, 6560 Main. Veg and non-veg buffet, but more famous for its *dosas*, a kind of rice crêpe from southern India, filled with the likes of lamb vindaloo or the traditional potato curry. *Zeenaz Restaurant*, 6460 Main. The best bet for meat-eaters, and the owner is a character.

Other South Vancouver areas
● *on maps, pages 76 & 58*

Expensive *Seasons in the Park*, Queen Elizabeth Park, T8748008. One of the most romantic, high-class choices in town, with a sumptuous interior and exquisite views. Fresh seafood and steak, good appetizers and brunch.

Mid-range *The Amorous Oyster*, 3236 Oak, T7325916. Cute Parisian-style bistro with very reasonably priced seafood dishes such as Cajun Seafood Wellington and baked oysters. *Tomato Fresh Food Café*, 3305 Cambie. Wonderfully colourful and spacious with friendly service and a good reputation for its fresh and eclectic menu. Good for breakfast and dinner, with lots of veggie options.

Cheap *On Lok*, 2010 E Hastings, T2533656. Enormous portions of reliably tasty Chinese food.

North Shore
● *on map, page 58*

Expensive *The Beach House*, 150 25th St, T9221414. At Dundarave Pier, West Van. Mainly seafood in a spacious, summery building with huge windows looking out onto English Bay. *Beach Side Café*, 1362 Marine Dr, West Van, T9251945. Award-winning fine-dining worth going out of one's way for. One of the best decks in town, with views across to Stanley Park and Kitsilano. *Hiwus Feasthouse*, Blue Grouse Lake, Grouse Mtn, T9840661. May-Oct, evenings only. Traditional cedar longhouse on an attractive lake. Nightly show costs $65 per person and includes native story-telling and legends, dancing, singing and a full dinner of Pacific Northwest Native cuisine. Reservations essential by 1630 the previous day. *The Observatory*, Main Building, Grouse Mtn, T9840661. Fancy restaurant serving fine West Coast cuisine with magnificent views (reservations necessary and free gondola ride included).

Mid-range *The Eiffel Café*, 4390 Gallant Av, Deep Cove, T9292373. French fusion creations in bright, elegant surroundings. Best of a few choices in the area. *Moustache Café*, 1265 Marine Dr, T9878461. Also at 2526 Main, T8794001. A casually stylish house-like setting, with eclectic, Mediterranean-influenced cuisine often cited as the North Shore's finest. *Raglan's Bistro*, 15 Lonsdale Av, T9888203. Small and elegant with a nice menu of Mediterranean dishes. Handily located next to the quay and market.

Cheap *Moodyville's*, 101 Lonsdale Av. Casual but stylish café with all-day breakfast for $5. *The Raven*, 1052 Deep Cove Rd. Superb neighbourhood pub with enormous portions of superior pub-style food.

Steveston
See map, page 58

Expensive *Shady Island Seafood Bar and Grill*, 3800 Bayview, T2756587. Most stylish of the numerous fish and chip places by the water serving all manner of seafood and steak. Spacious pub-like space, beer on tap, outside seating. **Mid-range** *Delgado's*, 3711 Bayview, T2755188. The village's best restaurant, but with limited seaviews. Beautiful, very Mediterranean interior, with lots of plants and a garden patio. Main courses (entrées) include paella, cedar-plank salmon, grilled steak with roquefort and rustic lamb shank. Broad range of tapas at $5-10. **Cheap** *Pajos*, T2040767, down on the wharf with limited seating but arguably the best fish and chips in town. *PJ's Grill* on Bayview has Oyster or halibut burgers to go.

Cafés

During one Vancouver performance, Bette Midler remarked: "I've never seen so much coffee in all my life. The whole town is on a caffeine jag, and still nothing gets done any faster". People here do take their coffee pretty seriously, so you never have very far to go to get a decent cup of Joe. Those below are just the cream, so to speak.

As everywhere, *Starbucks* are trying to take over the coffee scene like weeds in a flower garden. *Blenz* are equally ubiquitous but serve a reliable cup of coffee. The one at Granville/Davie is open 24 hrs. *Death by Chocolate*, specialists in yummy hip-swelling desserts, have many outlets, meaning you're never far from the next sugar fix. *The Bread Garden* is a perennial favourite for baking goods, breakfast and coffee. The one at 1040 Denman is open 24 hrs.

Chains

Downtown *Café Ami*, 885 W Georgia in the *HSBC* building, T6880103. Easily the most pleasant spot for a coffee Downtown. *The Blunt Bros*, 317 W Hastings, T6825868. Calling itself 'a respectable joint', this is the main bastion of attempts to sell Vancouver as the new Amsterdam. Smoking is permitted and large amounts of paraphernalia sold, but there's no booze. The interior is spacious, with lots of couches for vegging out. Live music, mainly acoustic, Wed-Sat. *The Amsterdam Café*, a couple of doors down at 305 W Hastings is the same sort of deal. **West End** *Benny's Bagels*, 1780 Davie, T6857600. Good coffee and a patio with unbeatable views of English Bay. *Bojangles Café*, 785 Denman, T6873622. One of the best coffee houses in town, a neighbourhood institution. *Meiriches Coffee and Tea House*, 1244 Davie. Another fine neighbourhood coffee shop.

    Gastown *Blake's*, 221 Carrall, T8993354. Exceptional downbeat and tasteful coffee house with good music, brick walls, beer on tap and a small cheap menu. *Cafe Dolcino*, 12 Powell St, T8015118. Perfectly situated on Maple Leaf Sq, with a couple of tables outside to take in the attractive scene. *Gastown Café*, 101 W Cordova. Cosy little spot with armchairs and antiques. **Chinatown** *Mr Coffee*, 39 E Pender. Cute little café. **Yaletown** *Don't Show the Elephant*, 1207 Hamilton. Bright and trendy tea salon/gallery with a kind of Oriental/futuristic feel that might be too self-consciously arty for some tastes, but gets top marks for originality. Open till late.

Downtown peninsula
● *on map, page 62*

Kitsilano *Benny's*, 2505 W Broadway. A wonderful arty, trendy and quirky atmosphere with great music. Good for coffee, bagels and melts. *Calhoun's*, 3035 W Broadway, T7377062. Huge and lively coffee shop with a slightly rustic feel. Great coffee, juices, breakfasts and baking. Open 24 hrs. *Epicurean Café*, 1898 W 1st Av, T7315370. Small, quietly stylish neighbourhood secret with some outdoor seating. Some of the best *java* in town, plus breakfast, panini, gelati, etc. *Terra Breads*, 2380 W 4th Av, T7361838. Baking to die for: breads, croissants, muffins, cakes and sandwiches to eat in or take away, and good coffee too. Recommended.

    Granville Island *Granville Island Coffee House*, T6810177. Cosy little spot away from the hustle and bustle on the boardwalk behind the *Sand Bar*. **South Main** This is a serious stronghold of the coffee-culture. *Cuppa Joe*, 189 E Broadway/Main. Ordinary looking, but has the best coffee in the area. *Lugz Coffee House*, 2525 Main, T8736766. Comfy, downbeat atmosphere with couches and outdoor seating. Some food and smoothies. *Soma Coffee House*, 2528 Main, T8731750. Minimalist, arty interior attracting a more trendy clientele. Lots of magazines to browse or buy, and some nice snacks. *Sweet Revenge Patisserie*, 4160 Main, T8797933. French-style salon with silk antique wallpaper, lace and china. Lots of fancy teas and decadent desserts, all made with natural ingredients. Open 1900-0100. **Commercial** *La Casa Gelato*, Venables/Glen. Tucked away in an unlikely spot is Vancouver's finest ice-cream emporium, with 198 flavours to choose from and servers who are pleased to let you taste and try before you

South of False Creek
● *on maps, pages 70 & 72*

Vancouver

buy. *Turk's Coffee Exchange*, 1276 Commercial. Arguably the best coffee in town, in a small but elegant interior. Great people-watching in the outdoor seating area.

North Shore   *Artisan Bakeshop*, 127 Lonsdale Av. Organic breads. *West of Java*, 1st St E/Lonsdale Av. Small and comfy coffee shop.

Bars

See also Clubs,
page 96

A tour of
Vancouver's bistros
and tapas bars
is an excellent way
to explore the city

Vancouver has a disappointing dearth of decent pubs. Many otherwise great bars ruin their own atmosphere with multiple TV screens that are impossible to ignore and always seem to be showing ice-hockey. Others mysteriously fail to stock any of the excellent microbrewed beers for which Vancouver has become renowned. But the biggest problem has been a set of outdated licensing laws that made pub status considerably more expensive than the restaurant-with-food alternative, and often impossible to acquire at all. Other silly laws included a ban on dancing without a special (unobtainable) licence. Such draconian measures, which led to Vancouver's reputation as 'the city that fun forgot', were thankfully overturned in April 2002, but we're still awaiting the much needed renaissance in bar culture. Now you won't be forced to eat something, and can merrily drink until 0400

One positive side-effect of the old rules was the burgeoning bistro and tapas culture. A whole panoply of funky, atmospheric little bars appeared, that serve tasty little dishes as well as drinks. They are listed here or in the restaurant section depending on where the emphasis lies.

Downtown
● *on map, page 62*

Bin 941, 943 Davie, T6831246. Small and intimate bistro with quirky decor, a lively atmosphere, and inspirational tapas. *DV8*, 515 Davie, T6824388. Dark, funky, rather louche bar, with interesting, progressive music and art displays. Belongs in a more hip and savvie city like San Francisco or Amsterdam. Popular with a trendy, alternative crowd. DJs play some very modern sounds till 0300, 0400 at weekends. *The Lennox*, 800 Granville/Robson, T4080881. Standard pub with some outstanding but overpriced beers. Located right on Downtown's busiest corner, the small patio is an ideal spot for watching the city rush by. *Lucy Mae Brown*, 862 Richards, T8999199. Genuinely stylish favourite with the young and trendy crowd. Downstairs is a hip and modern Martini bar playing trip-hop-style music. Upstairs is an expensive, reservation-only restaurant with a Pacific Rim menu whose strongest point is its starters.

Morrissey Pub, 1227 Granville. Big, dark and stylish with a river-stone fireplace and lots of dark wood and leather. Many beers on tap, and some decent cheap food. One of the better classy options. *Nelson Café*, 655 Nelson, T6332666. Small, cosy and unpretentious, with a wood floor and brick walls. Good for a quiet pint, brunch and burgers. Open till 0300 Fri and Sat. *The Railway Club*, 579 Dunsmuir, T6811625. Long-standing, down-to-earth upstairs bar, cosy and atmospheric with lots of wood, knick-knacks and intimate corners. Varied live music every night, sometimes with cover. Free movies Sun at 1800. *The Sugar Refinery*, upstairs at 1113 Granville, T6832004. Refreshingly quirky little place that feels like someone's living room. No two tables or chairs the same, all sorts of visual oddities scattered around, including the menu. Good beers on tap, live alternative music almost every night.

Gastown
● *on map, page 62*

Alibi Room, 157 Alexander, T6233383. Owned and frequented by movie people, this is a seductively hip and happening hot spot. As well as atmosphere, drinks and well-chosen, modern music, their small menu is as exciting and innovative as they come, at surprisingly reasonable prices. Try the pan-seared tandoori gnocchi, or for a snack the yucca and yam chips with chipotle mayo. *The Cambie*, 300 Cambie St, T6846466. A favourite for those who like their boozers gritty, down-to-earth and friendly. A huge, smokey space with the most crowded summer patio in town. Big selection of cheap beer and food, pool tables. *Honey Lounge*, 455 Abbott St, T6857777. Hip and dark bar, big and open, with impossibly comfortable couches smothered in huge velvet cushions, and a good Martini list. Loud, up-beat, conversation-killing music makes for a club-like atmosphere without the dancing. Open late. *Milk*, next door, is a trendy gay-bar, and *Lotus* downstairs is one of the city's best clubs.

   The Irish Heather, 217 Carrall St, T6889779. Bistro and Irish house. An upmarket version of the kind of genuine Irish pub that has spawned so many wannabe clones of late. Fine selection of ales includes the best Guinness in town. Tasteful, intimate interior with a glass conservatory at the back. Frequent live Celtic music, and a menu featuring fancy reworkings of Irish staples. *Steamworks Brewing Co*, 375 Water St. Huge brewpub comprising a number of differing spaces. Downstairs has a large open restaurant with a fairly industrial feel, and a more intimate corner with leather armchairs by the fire. The bar upstairs is more comfy and less pretentious. Food is predictable, but the beer is very good.

Section (3), 1039 Mainland St, T6842777. Decor is arty, very modern and interesting. High, silver booths, hardwood floor, weird art and artefacts, wrought-iron stools at the curved bar. This and the funky music attract a more hip and savvie crowd than the usual Yaletown yuppies. Heated patio. Food covers many bases: calamari, yammi fries, baked brie, salads, pastas, etc. *Soho*, 1144 Homer, T6881180. Stylish, unpretentious pub kitted out in brick and wood, with simple, rustic tables. Beer, billiards, food, tea and coffee. *Subeez Cafe*, 891 Homer, T6876107. Vast, open warehouse-style space with very high ceilings and huge concrete pillars. Dim lighting and weird art, including big screens showing silent black and white films. Music is equally odd, making for a strange and compelling atmosphere. Large selection of good draught beers and non-alcoholic drinks. Some overpriced food, including breakfast, but better for drinks. *Yaletown Brewing Co*, 1111 Mainland. Huge space, usually packed and boisterous. Decent beers brewed on premises.

Yaletown
● *on maps, pages 62 & 72*

Backstage Lounge, 1585 Johnson, T6871354, in the *Arts Club*. Great airy and down-to-earth spot with a lively patio, decent food, and live music almost every night. *Bridge's Pub*, next door to the Public Market. With its big windows, patio and views, this is another good spot for a pint, but eat elsewhere. *Dockside Brewing Co*, 1253 Johnston St in the *Granville Island Hotel*, T6857070. A hidden gem away from the hordes, with comfy leather armchairs and fine in-house beers. Menu is mid-range with wood-oven pizza and seafood.

Granville Island

Bimini's Tap House, 2010 W 4th Av. Large English-style pub with a good selection of beers and food, only spoilt by the unnecessary TV screens. More cosy seating upstairs or by the fire. *Jeremiah's*, 3681 W 4th. Unpretentious neighbourhood boozer. *King's Head*, 1618 Yew St, T7386966. Cosy neighbourhood pub with a classic English feel. Lots of wood and an upstairs balcony area offering intimate nooks and crannies. Frequent live acoustic-style music. *Truffles Bistro*, 1943 Cornwall, T7330162. Interesting little bistro with comfy couches and nice, gentle music. Tapas-style dishes and decadent hot chocolate. Open 1700-0100 or 0200. *Bin 942*, 1521 W Broadway, T7349421. Thin room stuffed with weird and wonderful pieces of art. Trendy and lively, with modern but mellow dance music. Reasonable beer selection, and an incredible menu of involved, delicious tapas. Open 1700-0200. *The Fringe Cafe*, 3124 W Broadway. Tiny downbeat bar with a bohemian attitude. *Lou's Grill and Bistro*, 3357 W Broadway, T7369872. Largish trendy bar/restaurant with terracotta walls, interesting art and a patio. Dim lighting, jazzy music, and a great selection of beer on tap, with some of the cheapest Guinness around.

Kitsilano & Broadway
● *on map, page 72*

Vancouver

Commercial/
Main Street
● *on maps,*
pages 76 & 58

The Main, 4210 Main. Simple, open decor, with wood floors and tables and sheltered outdoor seating. Greek food, live music most nights, and a friendly, lively vibe. *Public Lounge*, 3289 Main. 1700-0000, till 0100 weekends. Casual, downbeat bar with a mainly young and bohemian clintele. Small but interesting cheap menu and some well chosen (and cheap) microbrewed beers. *WaaZuBee Cafe*, 1622 Commercial, T2535299. Large, comfortable space, dark, atmospheric and arty, playing loud upbeat music. Good selection of beers and good food served in large portions. Best place for a drink on the Drive.

North Shore
● *on map, page 58*

The Raven, 1052 Deep Cove Rd, T9293834. Spacious, English-style neighbourhood pub with the best selection of draft beers in town, including 19 microbrews, and 6 imports. Lots of malt whiskies also. And the food comes in mammoth portions. Live music once or twice a week. Understandably popular. *The Rusty Gull*, 175 E 1st St, T9885585. Lively neighbourhood pub with good ales on tap, food and frequent live music. Magical views from the patio of the city with shipyards and derelict warehouses in the foreground. *Ya Yas*, at Horseshoe Bay. Technically a restaurant specializing in seafood, but more notable as the only place where you can sample the exquisite Granville Island Oyster Ale.

Clubs

Vancouver is not as fun a town for clubbing as it should be (see page 94), but for the short-term visitor, there are more than enough spots to check out. Those listed here tend to host DJs spinning radically different music every night, so generalizations are almost impossible. Most charge a cover of $5-10, and drinks can be on the pricey side. For an overview of the scene, look out for the quarterly magazine *Nitelife*. For more specific night-to-night details consult the indispensable *Georgia Straight* or the useful site **www.clubvibes.com**

Balthazar, 1215 Bidwell, West End, T6898822. Spacious restaurant and lounge that stays open and busy till late with 2 separate rooms where DJs spin progressive house and more mainstream sounds. *Bar None*, 1222 Hamilton St, T6897000. This favourite of the Yaletown yuppie set combines a loungey atmosphere with DJ theme nights and sometimes live music. *Crush*, 1180 Granville, T6840355. Calling itself a 'Champagne Lounge', this plush spot aims for an older, wealthier clientele. Music is lounge, R&B, jazz and soul. Queues. Tends to close earlier than most. *Drink Nite Club*, 398 Richards, T6871307. With its big dance floor, pumping music system and video screens, the varied music nights here are popular with a fairly young party crowd. *Element Sound Lounge*, 801 Georgia St, T6690806. Fancy club aimed at the upmarket Martini set. Top DJs play funk, techno, house, etc. *Ginger 62*, 1219 Granville, T6885494. Trendy spot for the young and beautiful to show off their outfits and moves. *The Lotus*, 455 Abbot St. Happening, unpretentious little club with low ceilings attracting a young, friendly, energetic crowd that keeps dancing till late. House music most nights. *Luv-A-Fair*, 1275 Seymour, T6853288. Massive club with varied music, often alternative, retro, disco, or theme-based. *Mesaluna*, 1926 W Broadway, T7335862. Latin club that's a lot of fun for dancing. Live Salsa Big Band Fri and Sat nights.

Plaza Club, 881 Granville St, T6460064. One of the classiest of the DJ-led party-atmosphere dance hot-spots, with one of the best sound and lighting systems. Very popular on Sats. *Purple Onion*, 15 Water St, T6029442, www.purpleonion.com 2 fairly intimate rooms: usually one has a DJ playing dance tunes and the other has a live band. Mixed, generally unpretentious crowd. *Shine*, 364 Water St, Gastown, T4084321. Smart, colourful and intimate club with varied DJ-led music, attracting a 20-30 crowd that's a bit more well-heeled than usual. One to dress up for. *Sonar*, 66 Water St, Gastown, T6836695. Nice basement space with brick walls and wood floors. One big area for bands/dancing and another for lounging. Music varies nightly from house to hip-hop and reggae. *Urban Well*, 888 Nelson, Downtown, T6386070. Also 1516 Yew St, Kitsilano, T7377770 (see under Comedy). Lounge/restaurant with DJs playing anything from jazz to house. *Voda*, 783 Homer, T6843003. Stylish, elegant interior aimed at an older, more upmarket clientele. Music could be soul, funk R&B or Latin. *Wett Bar*, 1320 Richards, T6627707. Huge, cavernous dance club with high ceilings, projection screens, a vast dance floor, and thumping music attracting a young raver or alternative crowd.

Entertainment

The first place to look for all weekly listings is the *Georgia Strait* available free on most major streets, in cafés, venues, etc. Tickets for most events are available through *Ticketmaster*, T2804444. Half-price same-day tickets for many events are available at the *Tickets Tonight* booth in the Visitor Information Centre, or online at www.ticketstonight.ca

Apart from the major galleries mentioned in the Sights section, Vancouver has a wealth of smaller spaces, usually highlighting the work of contemporary, local artists. Look also under Art in the Shopping section for commercial galleries, which are usually just as or even more interesting. **Granville Island** is the main focus for these, and also houses the *Charles H Scott Gallery* in the Emily Carr Institute, which always has interesting, sometimes controversial displays, with entrance by donation. The adjacent *Concourse Gallery* has frequent displays of student work. There are a few worthwhile artist-run galleries in Gastown, such as *Artspeak Gallery*, at 233 Carrall St, and *Vancouver Access Artist Run Centre*, 206 Carrall St.

Art galleries
Arts Hotline: T6842787, www.AllianceForArts. com, weekly events calendar and pages of information on the arts in Vancouver

Elsewhere, the *Grunt Gallery*, 116-350 E 2nd Av, and *Or Gallery*, 208 Smithe, usually have interesting displays. *Western Front*, 303 E 8th Av, tends to exhibit video and performance art. There is an active art scene on the **North Shore**. For details pick up a copy of *ae (arts eXposed)*, an annual arts magazine with full listings. *Presentation House Gallery*, 333 Chesterfield Av, is one of Vancouver's oldest galleries, housed in a 1902 building, with a good reputation for its photography and media arts exhibitions. *Seymour Art Gallery*, 4360 Gallant Av, houses interesting and often provocative exhibitions. *Ferry Building Gallery*, 1414 Argyle Av, on the Ambleside Waterfront, and *Silk Purse Arts Centre*, 1570 Argyle Av, concentrate on works by residents of the community. Both are free.

The best 2 cinemas in town are *Hollywood*, 3123 W Broadway, T7383211, www.hollywoodtheatre.ca, and the *Ridge Theatre*, 3131 Arbutus St/16th Av, T7386311, www.RidgeTheatre.com Both screen well chosen double bills for $5, usually the best of those just off the first-run circuit, or less well known but consistently worthwhile rep choices. Shows tend to change weekly at the former, every 2-3 days at the latter. Built in 1950, the *Ridge* is a delightful building, and the last to still offer a glassed-in 'crying room' for parents with babies or noisy children. *Pacific Cinematheque*, 1131 Howe St, T6883456, www.cinematheque.bc.ca is the main venue for rep, independent, art-house, foreign or just plain off-the-wall films. Shows change nightly. $9.25, $9.75/double bill, including membership fee. Also has a first-class film-reference library. *Blinding Light*, 36 Powell St, T8783366. Microtheatre in the back of a café showing very serious, alternative films and documentaries. Sun afternoon cartoons are free. *Fifth Avenue Cinemas*, 2110 Burrard, T2222991, gets most of the more mainstream international films, and has a good screen on which to see them. *Denman Place Discount Cinema*, 1737 Comox, T6832201, shows double bills for $5 on a reasonable screen.

Cinemas

For quality of reproduction, the *Alcan Omnimax* at 1455 Quebec St in *Science World*, T4437443, has a wrap-around screen and sound that gives it the edge even over the *Imax* at *Canada Place*, T6824629, www.imax.com/vancouver At least 7 shows per day from noon. 40-min documentary films $10.50, $8.50 concessions, feature films $12,

$10 concessions. Regular, well-placed cinemas include: *Granville Cineplex Odeon Cinemas*, 855 Granville St, T6844000. The best Downtown location but small screens; *Tinseltown*, 88 W Pender, T8060799. One of the best and most reasonably priced; *Van East*, 2290 Commercial Dr, T2511313, www.vaneast.com Tends to show the best of the first-run films.

Comedy venues

New Revue Stage, 1601 Johnston St, Granville Island, T7387013. Host of *Vancouver TheatreSports League*, 6 times world champions of comedy improvization. Wed-Thu 1930, Fri-Sat 2000, 2200 and 2345. $10-15. *The Gastown Comedy Store*, 19 Water, T6821727. Stand-up and improvization.

Urban Well, see Clubs, above, for details. Two large neighbourhood venues for stand-up comedy, as well as food, dancing or Martinis. *Yuk Yuk's*, 750 Pacific Blvd, Downtown, T6875233. The city's premier venue for stand-up comedy.

Gay & lesbian

The West End is the most gay-friendly part of town, especially Davie St

Pick up a copy of XtraWest to find out what's going on

The Dufferin, 900 Seymour, T6834251. Entertainment nightly, such as drag shows and strippers. *The Fountainhead*, 1025 Davie St, T6872222. Gay-friendly neighbourhood pub, with a heated and covered patio. *The Global Beat*, 1249 Howe St, T6892444. Casual lounge and billiards bar. *Milk Bar*, 455 Abbott, T685777. Stylish gay bar, with the gay-friendly *Lotus* club below. *Numbers Cabaret*, 1042 Davie, T6854077. Heaving nightclub with entertainment and dancing. Very cruisy, attracting an older denim/leather crowd. *The Oasis Pub*, 1240 Thurlow St, T6861724. Gay-friendly upmarket piano bar. *The Odyssey*, 1251 Howe St, T6895256. The main surviving gay club with high-energy dance music and entertainment nightly. *The Pump Jack*, 1167 Davie, T6853417. Leather bar.

Live music

Avant garde *The Western Front*, 303 E 8th Av, T8769343. Specializes in contemporary, sometimes avant garde music, from jazz to electronic to world. *The Sugar Refinery*, upstairs at 1113 Granville, T3311184. Alternative, avant garde, jazz or generally off-the-wall acts every night in a quirky setting.

Blues *The Yale Hotel*, 1300 Granville, T6819253. Divey bar that's the city's premier blues venue.

Classical *The Orpheum* (see below) is home to the Vancouver Symphony Orchestra and hosts most major classical events. *Queen Elizabeth Theatre* (see below) often plays host to opera and ballet. The *Chan Centre for the Performing Arts*, 6265 Cresent Rd, T8222697. Mostly dedicated to classical performances, this UBC venue has three stages in one complex, the main hall being one of the city's finest.

Folk *The Wise Hall*, 1882 Adanac, T7363022, www.roguefolk.bc.ca Nice neighbourhood venue that's the main focus for the *Rogue Folk Club*. *Vancouver East Cultural Centre*, 1895 Venables St, T2549578. A converted church and intimate space popular for chamber music, dance, folk, etc. *Fairview Pub*, 888 W Broadway, T8721262. English-style boozer with folk music almost nightly (often Celtic).

Jazz Vancouver's jazz scene is not as lively as the tourist bumf would have you believe. Many restaurants advertise live jazz, but it tends to be pretty awful or blues. For more details try the *Jazz Hotline*, T8725200, www.VancouverJazz.com *The Jazz Cellar*, 3611 W Broadway, T7381959, is the principal jazz venue in town, with local or visiting musicians most nights. *Norman Rothstein Theatre*, 950 W 41st, is an agreeable little hall that usually hosts jazz acts. *Hot Jazz Club*, 2120 Main, T8734131. Trad jazz on Tue, Sat and Sun, often big-band. Oldest jazz club in the city, as reflected in the rundown, Legion Hall decor. *Bukowski's Bistro*, 1447 Commercial Dr, T2534770. Live jazz Mon, Thu and Sat. *Ouisi Bistro*, 3014 Granville, T7327550. Creole restaurant with a jazz attitude and live bands 2-3 times weekly. *Rossini's Italian Restaurant*, 162 Water St, Gastown, T4081300, and 1525 Yew St, Kitsilano, T7378080. Live jazz nightly for diners. *O'Doul's*, 1300 Robson by the *Listel Hotel*, T6611400, is an upmarket, expensive restaurant with jazz nightly. See also *Avant garde*, above.

Latin *Kino Café*, 3456 Cambie, T8751988. Live music every night, usually flamenco or salsa. No cover for diners. Reasonable food, good beers. *Mesaluna*, 1926 W Broadway, T7335862. Live Salsa Big Band Fri and Sat nights.

Large venues As anywhere, when the big-name acts come to Vancouver they tend to play one of the high-capacity venues. *GM Place*, 800 Griffiths Way, T8997889, is where Floyd or the Stones would probably play. *Pacific Coliseum Concert Bowl*, PNE Grounds in Hastings Park, west of Hwy 1, T2804444. Where Britney Spears plays when she comes to town. The best and most popular venues for successful mid-range acts are the *Commodore Ballroom*, 868 Granville St, T7394550. A wonderful old venue with a 1,000-seat capacity and a massive dance-floor built on rubber tyres; and the *Orpheum Theatre*, 884 Granville St, T6653050. Probably the best venue in town (but no dancing allowed). When it was built as a part of the vaudeville circuit in 1927, this 2,800-seat venue was the largest theatre in Canada. The elegant Spanish Baroque-style interior with its arches, tiered columns and marble mouldings was almost converted into a cinematic multiplex before the city intervened. *Queen Elizabeth Theatre*, Hamilton/Georgia, T2999000. 1960s Modernist building with almost 3,000 seats. Hosts major rock and pop acts, as well as opera, ballet and musicals. *Vogue Theatre*, see Theatre, also receives big names, as well as a lot of tribute bands.

Smaller venues *Anza Club*, 3 W 8th Av, T8762178. Antipodean hang-out, rather basic but with cheap beer and frequent live music. *Backstage Lounge*, Arts Club, Granville Island. Small acts like jazz, folk, etc. *Bar None*, 1222 Hamilton, Yaletown, T6897000. Anything from rock or jazz bands to DJs. *Brickyard*, 315 Carrall, Gastown, T6853922. Smoky, rather sleazy venue for varied bands. *The Cobalt*, 917 Main, T6852825. Punk, metal and hardcore. *Croatian Cultural Centre*, 3250 Commercial Dr. Various acts. *The Piccadilly Pub*, 620 W Pender, T6823221. Thin, dark, smoky and packed. Live music most nights. *The Railway Club*, 579 Dunsmuir. Intimate venue for a variety of acts, but with poor sightlines. *Richard's on Richards*, 1036 Richards, T6876794. Attracts some of the best local and visiting acts and is a great venue to catch them: small and atmospheric with a brick wall as a backdrop behind the band, a balcony above for views, and arguably the best sound, lighting and sightlines in town.

Restaurants with regular live music include: *Café Deux Soleils*, 2096 Commercial, T2541195; *El Cocal*, 1037 Commercial, T4315451. Latin food in a laid-back, plant-laden environment and frequent live music such as reggae, blues, folk; *Latin Quarter*, 1305 Commercial, T2511144. Often Latin-based; *The Main*, 4210 Main St, varied, mostly local, rock/pop alternative acts, appealing to a fairly young audience; a great venue with hardwood floors, high ceilings and minimal decor; *The Naam*, 2724 W 4th Av, T7387151. Live music every night from 1900-2200, usually acoustic and worth checking out: jazz/folk/world, etc. Certain **churches** also host regular music, such as the *Holy Rosary Cathedral* at Dunsmuir/Richards, *Christ Church Cathedral* at 690 Burrard St, and *St Andrew's-Wesley Church*, 1012 Burrard.

See also Bars and Clubs

General Motors (GM) Place, 800 Griffiths Way, T8997889, is the 20,000-seat home of the Vancouver *Canucks*, T8994610, www.canucks.com, ice-hockey team and the Vancouver *Grizzlies* NBA Basketball team. The former generate the most local passion, and in season every bar in town seems to be perpetually showing their televized games. In 1995 they got the city in a lather by coming within a goal of winning the coveted Stanley Cup, and in 2002 they scraped into the play-offs by winning 11 straight games only to lose the next 3. *BC Place Stadium*, 777 Pacific Blvd, T4443663, the giant domed 60,000-seat stadium, is home to the *BC Lions*, T5837747, www.bclions.com who play Canadian Football (a little different from the American version) Jun-Nov. The *Giants* play Junior Hockey at the Colliseum, $12-16. The *Canadians* play baseball at the Nat Bailey Stadium in Queen Elizabeth Park from Jun-Sept. *Hastings Park Raceway* has been hosting thoroughbred horse racing since 1889.

Spectator sports

Theatre & performing arts

Most tickets must be bought through *Ticketmaster*, T2804444. The main season for concerts, opera, ballet etc is Oct-Apr, but a number of festivals run continual shows through the summer (see Festivals). As well as an active theatre world, Vancouver has achieved much recognition for its dance scene. The two main foci for theatre are Granville Island and the 'Entertainment District' of Downtown (see Sights).

Arts Club Granville Island Stage, 1585 Johnston St, T6871644. Small venue for casual theatre such as musical comedies. *Centennial Theatre*, 2300 Lonsdale Av, North Van, T9844484. Large and long-running venue. *Centre in Vancouver for the Performing Arts*, 777 Homer St, T6020616. Opposite the *Main Library*, and designed by the same architect, this state-of-the-art theatre, formerly the Ford Centre, is Vancouver's main Broadway-type venue for large-scale and popular theatre, dance and musicals. *Firehall Arts Centre*, 280 E Cordova, T6890926, www.firehallartscentre.ca An operating firehall from 1906-75, the building now provides a small, intimate setting for quality dance and theatre. *Jericho Arts Centre*, 1675 Discovery, beside the *HI hostel*. *Metro Theatre*, 1370 SW Marine Dr, T2667191. Crowd-pleaser works. *Pacific Theatre*, 1440 W 12th Av, T2734659. Small but talented company presenting serious plays. *Performance Works*, 1218 Cartwright St, Granville Is, T6890926. Small-scale contemporary works of a generally high standard. *Performing Arts Theatre*, 2055 Purcell Way, North Van in Capilano College. *Presentation House Theatre* 333 Chesterfield Av, North Van, T9903474. Contemporary theatre and performance art in a 1902 school building.

Stanley Theatre, 2750 Granville/12th Av, T6871644. An elegantly restored 1931 movie house, now an *Arts Club* venue for drama, comedy or musicals. *Vancouver East Cultural Centre* 1895 Venables, near Commercial Dr, T2549578. Affectionately known as 'the Cultch', this converted Methodist Church is one of the best performance spaces in the city, thanks to great acoustics and sightlines, and an intimate 350-seat capacity. It hosts a range of events, including theatre, music and dance, with an emphasis on the modern and sometimes controversial. *Vancouver Playhouse*, Hamilton/Georgia, T2999000 for info, T6653050 for tickets. Fairly intimate venue for serious theatre, including many modern Canadian works. *Vogue Theatre*, 918 Granville, T2804444. 1941 art deco-style building that has remained much the same, right down to the neon sign. Light-hearted pieces such as comedies and musicals. *Waterfront Theatre*, 1410 Cartwright St, Granville Is, T6851731. Serious theatre.

Festivals

Vancouver hosts as many major festivals as you would expect of a large city. Most of them take place in summer, when everyone takes to the beaches and parks to enjoy music and theatre in the sun. The year kicks off on **1 Jan** with the *Polar Bear Swim*, T6653424. Every year since 1819 on English Bay Beach, lunatic locals have proven themselves by starting the New Year with an icy dip. Watch if you can *bear* it. In early **Feb**, the 5-day *Vancouver International Boat Show*, T2941313, www.sportsmensshows.com, is held at BC Place. It's the largest and oldest boat show in Western Canada. Later that month the *Chinese New Year Celebrations*, T6623207, www.vancouver.about.com, last 15 days with parades, live music, craft demonstrations and storytelling, mostly at the Dr Sun Yat-Sen Classical Chinese Garden. The *Vancouver Storytelling Festival* is the main event in **Mar**. Celebrating its 25th year at the end of **Apr** 2003 is the week-long *International Wine Festival*, T8733311, www.playhousewinefest.com 40 events focused on the Vancouver Playhouse involve 150 wineries from 15 countries. Prices range from $55 for wine-tasting to $110 for a lecture and food/wine tasting at the city's top restaurants.

Things start to warm up in early **May** when Granville Island hosts the annual *Bluegrass Festival*, T6665784. Then comes the *Cloverdale Rodeo*, T5769461, www.CloverdaleRodeo.com, the second biggest of its kind in the west after the Calgary Stampede, attracting cowboys from all over the continent. Towards the end of the month the *International Children's Festival*, T7085655, www.youngarts.ca, involves a host of events to delight the youngsters in Vanier Park. *Bard on the Beach Skakespeare Festival*, T7390559, www.bardonthebeach.org, starts in **mid-Jun** and runs for 3 months. At the end of **Jun** is *Alcan Dragon Boat Festival*, T6882382, www.canadadragonboat.com, a weekend of racing and cultural activities on False Creek. At the same time it's the major *International Jazz Festival*, T8725200, www.jazzvancouver.com, 10 days of big and small acts on 40 stages around town, plus a free 2-day New Orleans-style street festival in Gastown.

Jul sees a host of events. The month kicks off with the 10-day *Dancing on the Edge Festival*, T6890691, www.mcsquared.com/edge, at the *Firehall Arts Centre*, Canada's largest showcase of independent choreographers from across Canada and the US. The following all start mid-month: *Vancouver Folk Music Festival*, T6029798, www.thefestival.bc.ca, 3 days of music and storytelling across the city; *Theatre Under the Stars*, T6870714, www.tuts.bc.ca, held in Stanley Park's Malkin Bowl, running for a month from mid-Jul. *Vancouver International Comedy Festival*, T6830883, www.comedyfest.com, 2 weeks of laughter on Granville Island and elsewhere. *Early Music Festival*, T7321610, www.earlymusic.bc.ca 18 days in the UBC Recital Hall. *Chamber Music Festival*, T6020363, www.vanrecital.com, 12 days of musical talent in Vanier Park's Crofton Schoolhouse. *Caribbean Days Festival*, T5152400, www.caribbeandaysfestival.com Music, limbo, food, dance and arts in Waterfront Park, North Shore.

Celebration of Light, T7384304, is an international fireworks competition held over 2 weeks from late-Jul to early-Aug. Each country puts on an hour-long show set to music. The fireworks are set off from a barge on English Bay. *Harbour Cruises* run firework cruises with dinner included, T6887246. The most popular places for watching are the West End beaches, the best spot is probably Vanier park. The first weekend of **Aug** the year's major gay and lesbian event, *Gay Pride Parade*, T6870955, www.gayvancouver.com, is a massive party for all who want to join in the spirit. A parade moves down Denman to Beach Av and on to the main party zone, Sunset Beach on English Bay. At the same time is the *Out on Screen Queer Film Festival*, www.outonscreen.com Also on this weekend is the *Powell Street Festival*, T7399388, with dance, music, theatre, and food vendors livening up Oppenheimer Park in 'Japan town'. *Abbotsford International Air Show*, T8528511, held on the second weekend of **Aug**, is the second largest air show in North America. State of the art aircraft from around the world compete and perform. After the success of the wonderful 2002 *Richmond Tall Ships Festival*, T1877-2470777, www.richmondtallships.ca, there are plans to hold it every 3 years, the next one being 2005. From **late Aug-early Sep**, the *PNE Fair* at the Pacific National Exhibition, T2532311, includes live entertainment, exhibits, livestock and the Playland Amusement Park with some 40 fairground rides. Take Bus No 4, 10 or 16 north from Granville.

Things gear down in **Sep**, but during the first weekend the *Molson Indy* car race, T2804639, www.molsonindy.com, goes right through town. The *Vancouver Fringe Festival*, T2570350, www.vancouverfringe.com, runs for 10 days in **mid-late Sep**, with 100 international companies giving 500 shows in indoor and outdoor venues. And about 300 films from 50 countries are shown at 17 theatres over the course of 17 days for the *Vancouver International Film Festival*, T6850260, www.viff.org The main event in **Oct** is the *International Writers (and Readers) Festival*, T6816330, www.writersfest.bc.ca, when 40 events are held over 5 days at 4 venues around Granville Island. At the start of **Nov** is the *Aboriginal Film and Video Festival*, T8710173, and at the end of Nov is the *East Side Culture Crawl*, www.culturecrawl.bc.ca, involving 190 artists in 20 buildings with maps available at the Strathcona Community Centre, 601 Keefer Street, T2154495. In **Dec** the VanDusen gardens are illuminated with 20,000 lights and there are seasonal displays for the *Festival of Lights*, T8789274, www.vandusengarden.org

Shopping

Antiques & junk Many antique, junk and consignment stores are clustered on stretches of Main St south of 7th Av, particularly from 16-20 and 26-28 Avs. Most of these are seriously overpriced. There are also many on Richards between Hastings and Pender. The best venue for bargain-hunting is the weekend *Flea Market* on Main St in the block south of Terminal Av.

Arts & crafts The best place for art-seeking is **Granville Island**. Cartwright St contains some of the key galleries. *Federation Gallery* at No 1241 is operated by members of the Federation of Canadian Artists; *Gallery of BC Ceramics* at No 1359, T6695645, is run by members of the Potters Guild of BC, with a large selection of top-notch pottery that changes monthly; *Crafthouse Gallery* at No 1386, T6877270, has a great collection of quality work including pottery, textiles and jewellery. The *Net Loft* opposite the *Public Market* houses many fine stores including: *Circle Craft*, T6698021, which showcases well-chosen pieces of unique craftsmanship; *Edie Hats*; *Maiwa Handprints* for fabric art and hand-printed fabrics; and *Mesa* for Latin-tinged folk art. At nearby *Studio Glass* you can watch the artists blowing glass. Railspur Alley is a nucleus for small and unique artist studios. If all this inspires you, *Opus* on Johnston St is an excellent, very large artist supply store.

Gastown has some interesting galleries, including *Industrial Artifacts* at 49 Powell St. A stunning collection of furniture and art, ingeniously fashioned from reclaimed pieces of old industrial machinery. Almost everything they have is painfully desirable. **South Granville St** is the best place to pick up works by established artists. *The Art Emporium* at No 2928 has been open since 1897, selling big-name domestic and international artists, from the famous Group of Seven to Picasso. *Monte Clark Gallery* at No 2339 specializes in avant-garde paintings, prints and photography.

Elsewhere are: *Buschlen-Mowatt Fine Arts*, 111-1445 W. Georgia St, T6821234. Upmarket gallery representing a large number of successful artists, Canadian and international. *Contemporary Art Gallery*, 555 Nelson. Exactly that. *Gift Horse Gallery*, 1826 Lonsdale Av, North Shore. Showcases the work of over 150 BC artists, many local, in a variety of media. *Helen Pitt Gallery*, 882 Homer St. Specializes in alternative, experimental works by up-and-coming artists that tend to be on the gritty and raw side. *Rendez-vous Art Gallery*, 671 Howe St, T6877466. Stylish, high-end space with a wide range of work from many key contemporary artists. Anything from landscapes to a big collection of Inuit pieces. *Robert Held Art Gallery*, 2130 Pine St. Exhibition dedicated to the work of the man known as the father of the art glass movement in Canada.

First Nations arts and crafts The best place to start looking for native art is on Water St in **Gastown**. Galleries here include: *First Nations Creative Gallery and Artist Co-operative* at No 20, T6029464. Owned and operated by aboriginal artists, presenting contemporary, experimental works as well as the usual more traditional stuff. Prices can be more reasonable than elsewhere. *Hill's Native Art*, No 165, T6854249. 3 floors of Northwest Coast arts and crafts, including some spectacular pieces. *Inuit Gallery*, No 345, T6887323, www.Inuit.com North America's leading Inuit Art Gallery, with very beautiful modern and traditional sculpture and prints. *Spirit Wrestler Gallery*, No 8, T6698813. Works by major artists of various First Nations, including some very high-class pieces of sculpture.

Other galleries include: *Aboriginal Arts*, 1044 Granville. *Coastal Peoples Fine Art Gallery*, 1024 Mainland St, Yaletown. A very broad collection of all kinds of First Nations arts and crafts. *Eagle Spirit Gallery*, 1803 Maritime Mews, Granville Island. Beautiful but expensive Northwest Coast Native art and carvings. *Khot-la-cha Coast Salish Handicrafts*, 270 Whonoak St, Capilano Reserve, T9873339. *Marion Scott Gallery*, 481 Howe St, T6851934. Good collection of new and old Inuit art, including prints, carvings and jewellery. *The Raven and the Bear*, 1528 Duranleau St, Granville Island. West Coast art aimed at the tourist market and a little kitschy as a result.

ABC Book and Comic Emporium, 1247 Granville. Row upon row of very cheap used **Books**
books in a central location. *Banyen Books and Sound*, 3608 W 4th, T7327912. Huge
selection, mainly new and non-fiction, with a focus on alternative lifestyles. *Barbara-Jo's
Books to Cook*, 1128 Mainland, Yaletown. *Book Warehouse*, 632 W Broadway/550
Granville/2388 W 4th/1181 Davie. New discount books. *Does Your Mother Know?*, 2139
W 4th Av. Magazine store with a giant selection, including some foreign papers. *Duthie
Books*, 2239 W 4th Av, T7325344. Big selection of new books that makes a nicer alterna-
tive to the ubiquitous *Chapters*. *Granville Book Co*, 850 Granville St. Large selection of
interesting books and magazines, great for browsing and open till midnight.

 Hermit Books, 2509 W Broadway. Excellent selection of used religion, philosophy,
psychology, etc. *Little Sister's Book and Art Emporium*, 1238 Davie. Gay and lesbian
bookstore where you can get a free copy of the *Gay and Lesbian Business Association
Directory*, www.glba.org. *Macleod's Books*, 455 W Pender, T6817654. Intimidatingly
large selection of varied used books. *Magpie Magazine Gallery*, 1319 Commercial Dr.
Oscar's Art Books, 1533 W Broadway. *Pulp Fiction Books*, 2418 Main. Dizzying quantities of used books. *Sophia's Books*, 492 W Hastings. Multilingual, art and cinema books.
Spartacus Books, upstairs at 311 W Hastings. Large selection of serious fringe non-fic-
tion, dealing with such matters as politics, ecology and sexuality. There are big, comfy
armchairs in which to sit and browse. *Tanglewood Books*, 2709 Granville St and 2932
W Broadway. Great selection of used non-fiction. *The Great Canadian News Co*, 1092
Robson, T6880609. Huge collection of magazines and foreign newspapers.

Most of the fashion and shoe chains, such as *Benetton*, *French Connection* and *The* **Clothes &**
Gap are found on Vancouver's undisputed retail Mecca Robson St, mainly between **accessories**
Burrard and Jervis. The nearby *Pacific Centre Mall*, at Georgia and Howe is the other
main hot-spot. Granville Street is a good area for off-the-wall new and used clothing
and footwear shops, such as *The Underground* at No 840, and *John Fluevog* at No 837.
Nearby on this street, *The Bay* is forever having sales where bargains can often be
found. The more expensive, exclusive designer labels such as *Chanel* at No 900 and
Versace at No 757 are found on W Hastings. For clothes that are less expensive but
maybe more original than those on Robson, 4th Av west of Burrard in Kitsilano is a
good bet. *Pharsyde* at 2100 4th Av, T7396630, stocks hip, casual clothing and shoes for
men and women. *Lulu Lemon*, 2113 4th Av, T7326111, sells unique items designed for
sports and yoga, but is equally popular for fashion. *Object Design Gallery* at 2072 4th
Av, T6830047, is one of the city's most distinctive jewellers, selling mostly silver items,
all handcrafted by local artists and very reasonably priced.

 The best area for funky **used and retro clothing** is Gastown around W Cordova St.
Deluxe Junk Co, at No 310, has an excellent (but pricey) selection. Round the corner,
Cabbages and Kinx at 315 W Hastings sells mainly new funky clothes and accessories
as well as smoking paraphernalia. Elsewhere, *Legends* at Main/32nd is one of the
better consignment stores.

 Erotica A couple of blocks southwest of Robson, Granville St starts to turn seedy. Just
before the bridge is Vancouver's small red light district, replete with XXX book stores and
peep shows. One block over on Seymour are the live goods. One interesting, long-standing shop is *Mac's Leather* at 1043 Granville St. Leather, PVC, S&M paraphernalia, piercing.

The best place for food shopping is the **Granville Island Public Market**, T6666477a **Food & drink**
mouth-watering high-end food hall and produce market open daily in summer 0900-
1800. **Lonsdale Quay Market**, T9856261, where the SeaBus arrives at the North Shore, is
a good second choice, open 0900-1830, till 2100 Fri. **Chinatown** is a great place to
browse, especially the open-air **night market** at 200 Keefer St and E Pender, 1830-2300,
Fri-Sun, Jun-Sep. *British Home*, Moncton St/No 1 Rd, Steveston, is a deli full of British
favourites like home-made pies, Hobnobs, Devon cream, and Twiglets. *Choices Market*,

1202 Richards, Yaletown. Huge grocery store with healthy options. *European Delicatessen*, 1220 Davie. Huge samosas, cabbage rolls, *spanokopitas*, sandwiches with your choice of meat or cheese. Limited seating. *Herbal Republic*, 2680 W Broadway. The place to go for tea. *Hidemi Japanese Confectionary*, 409 W Hastings. Japanese snacks. *Liquor Store*, 5555 Cambie St/39th Av. One of the biggest booze outlets in the country. *Minerva's*, 3207 W Broadway. Greek grocery store with lots of great cheeses, etc. Also has a few tables and some meals like roast lamb and *dolmades*. Good coffee. *Parthenon Supermaket*, 3066 W Broadway. Greek deli. *Tonina's Deli and Cafe*, 4125 Main. Great Mediterranean deli with a few seats. *Uprising Breads Bakery*, 1697 Venables off Commercial. Non-wheat organic breads made from spelt, etc. *Urban Fare*, 177 Davie, Yaletown. The hippest of supermarkets. You can even sit down for a glass of wine.

Gifts   For touristy souvenirs head to Water St in Gastown. For more unusual ideas check out the speciality shops on W 4th, such as *Kaya Kaya*, at No 2039, which carries Japanese porcelain and Chinese silk. *Obsessions*, at 595 Howe or 1124 Denman, has a wide range of gift ideas, while the *Vancouver Art Gallery Shop* has lots of inspiringly beautiful items. For something more off the wall, *Salmagundi West*, 321 W Cordova, T6814648, is a really fun shop, packed with eccentric oddities, toys and tit-bits. *The Postcard Place* in the Net Loft, Granville Island, has the city's best selection. See also Arts and crafts above.

Kids   *Kid's Market*, 1496 Cartwright St, Granville Island, T6898447, contains 25 stores just for children: many of the toys and clothes here are one-offs, educational and locally handmade. *The Games People*, 157 Water St. *It's all Fun and Games*, 1308 Commercial. *Kidsbooks*, 3038 W. Broadway. *Lil 'Putian's fashions for kids*, 2029 W 4th Av. *The Toybox*, 3002 W Broadway, T7384322. *Toys 'R' Us*, 1154 W Broadway.

Music   *A&B Sound*, 556 Seymour St, T6875837. Best deals on new music, large selection, listen before you buy. *Black Swan*, 3209 W Broadway,T7342828. New and used CDs and records of all kinds, including some harder to find stuff. Intelligent selection and knowledgeable staff. *Charlie's*, 819 Granville, T6882500. Biggest selection of cheap used CD's. *Highlife Records*, 1317 Commercial Dr. World music. *HMV* Robson/Bute. *La Bamba Records*, 937 Commercial Dr. Latin music. *The Magic Flute*, 2203 W 4th Av. Classical, jazz, world, mostly new. *Scrape Records*, 17 W Broadway. New and used heavy metal. *Zulu*, 1972 W 4th Av, T7383232. Big selection of new and used music of all kinds, with an emphasis on modern or alternative sounds.

Sports   The biggest of such stores are grouped together around W Broadway and Cambie. *Mountain Equipment Co-op*, 130 W Broadway, T8727858, has the broadest and best selection, and often the best deals, though you have to buy a $5 membership first. *3 Vets*, nearby at 2200 Yukon/6th Av, is also huge and all-inclusive. *The Backpackers Shop* at 183 W Broadway is run by HI, and useful for packs, related equipment, rentals and repairs. *Coast Mountain Sports* at 2201 W 4th is the other biggest and best all-round supplier. This is also the area for ski and snowboard stores, such as *Pacific Boarder* at 1793 W 4th Av, T7347245. For general supplies Downtown there's *Sport Mart* at 735 Thurlow, T6832433. For a great selection of used equipment head for *Sports Junkies* at 600 W 6th Av. Or try *Cheapskates* at 3644 W 16th, 3228 Dunbar or 3496 Dunbar.

Photography   *ABC Photocolour*, 1618 W 4th Av, are good for professional developing. *Dunne & Rundle*, 891 Granville, and *Lens & Shutter*, 2912 W Broadway, are also recommended for developing and carry a good variety of film and equipment (including used). For quick, cheap developing try *London Drugs* which has branches at 70 Granville, 1187 Robson and 1650 Davie.

The Geological Survey of Canada, 605 Robson/Seymour. A fine collection of maps and books. *International Travel Maps and Guides*, 552 Seymour and 530 W Broadway. Better for maps than books. *The Travel Bug*, 2667 W 4th Av. Books, accessories and maps. *Wanderlust*, 1929 W 4th Av. Best selection of travel books in town.

Travel books & maps

Sport and special interest

George C Reifel Migratory Bird Sanctuary, Westham Island, Richmond, T9466980, is a 360-ha sanctuary in the Fraser River which hosts thousands of birds on their way from Mexico to Alaska. There's a good viewing tower close to the parking lot. Shore birds start arriving in mid-August, followed by mallard and pintail ducks. Numbers rise during Sep and Oct, and peak in early Nov, when about 20,000 snow geese noisily arrive. Many birds remain all winter. Nesting occurs in Apr and May.

Bird-watching

Granville Island has plenty of operators. Check the *Charter Information Centre* by the Maritime Market, and *Granville Island Boat Rentals*, behind *Bridges Restaurant*, T6826287. *Bites-on Salmon Charters*, 200-1128 Hornby, T18776882483, www.bites-on.com *Deep Cove North Shore Marina and Rentals*, 2890 Panorama, T9291251. Boat, kayak, canoe and watersport rentals. $22.50-32.75 per hr depending on size, less for 3 hrs and mid-week, $119-$159 per day. *Jericho Sailing Centre*, at Jericho Beach, T2244177, www.jsca.bc.ca Sailing, windsurfing, kayaking and rowing lessons and rentals. *Sewell's Sea Safari*, 6695 Nelson Av, Horseshoe Bay, T9213474. Fishing guides, boat rentals. *Stanley Park Boat Rentals*, 1601 Bayshore, T6826257.

Boating/ fishing

Cliffhanger Indoor Rock Climbing Centre, T8742400. 750 sq m to climb over with views of the North Shore Mountains. For the best local climbing go to Squamish.

Climbing

There are some excellent golf courses around Vancouver, the best being situated outside the city. These include: *Meadow Gardens*, in Pitt Meadows to the east, T4655474. Constructed by Les Furber and aimed at experienced players; *Morgan Creek*, T5314653, the par-73 home to BC's CPGA, set in a naturally attractive landscape; *Northview*, in Surrey, T5740324. 2 courses designed by Arnold Palmer that include a 14-ha wildlife refuge; *Westwood Plateau*, in Coquitlam, T9454007. Famed for its spectacular natural features and mountain setting. Closer to town are: *McCleery*, T2578191, and *Fraserview*, T2576921, both on Southwest Marine Drive and open year round; and the *University Club*, T2241818 at UBC.

Golf

Hiking in the Coast Mountains on the North Shore is prime, a real boon for Vancouver's inhabitants. Those listed here are the pick of the bunch, ordered geographically from west to east. Even better trails are found further north around Squamish, Whistler and Garibaldi Provincial Park.

Hiking

    The Lions (15 km round trip, 1,525 m elevation gain. Trailhead: at Lions Bay on Hwy 99, turn east onto Oceanview Rd then left onto Cross Creek Rd, right onto Centre Rd, left onto Bayview Rd, left onto Mountain Dr, left onto Sunset Dr and park at the gate) This is a steep hike, but the views are great from the base of the Lions, especially if you can scramble down to the gap between them. Climbers can often be seen attempting the difficult ascent up the West Lion.

    Mount Gardner (16 km round trip, 750 m elevation gain. Trailhead: take the ferry from Horseshoe bay to Bowen Island) Directions are complicated so ask at the information centre or consult *Don't Waste Your Time in the BC Coast Mountains*. This is a fairly demanding but highly rewarding hike that is possible almost year round. Be sure to catch an early ferry to allow plenty of time. Panoramic views from the top are spectacular, taking in the Sunshine Coast, Gambier Island and Howe Sound, the Coast

Mountains, Vancouver and the Fraser Valley, Vancouver Island and the Georgia Strait, even Mt Baker in Washington.

Hollyburn Mountain (8 km round trip, 405 m elevation gain. Trailhead: by the ski area map next to the parking lot in Cypress Provincial Park) This is one of the finest and easiest trails on the North Shore. Panoramic views from the top include the city, Vancouver Island, the Lions, Mt Baker, and several other lofty mountains. Better still, you walk through probably the finest stand of ancient, giant cedar, fir and hemlock within reach of the city. It is also snow-free earlier and later than most, usually from mid-Jun to mid-Nov.

Mount Strachan (10 km round trip, 534 m elevation gain. Trailhead: as above) Another first-rate hike, this route follows the Howe Sound Crest Trail for a while before heading through Strachan Meadows then steeply up the edge of a gorge, alongside precipitous cliffs and through a beautiful stretch of old-growth forest. The north summit offers the best views, which take in Howe Sound, the Lions and Crown Mountain. This trail is rarely free of snow before mid-Jul. The **Howe Sound Crest trail** is a 30-km marathon from Cypress to Hwy 99 with an elevation gain of 1,185 m. It's a tough ordeal whose many trees tend to block most of the views that might otherwise justify the effort.

Brothers and Lawson Creeks (10-km loop, 437 m elevation gain. Trailhead: From Hwy 1 or Marine Dr take Taylor Way north. Turn left onto Highland Dr and continue until you can turn left onto Eyremount Dr. Park where this road intersects Millstream Rd) Walk west on gated road and look for signs for Brothers Creek Forest Heritage Walk. This short, undemanding hike takes in a gorge and some cascades, but is best recommended for the ease with which you can see some really big cedars in their natural environment.

Grouse Grind (5 km round trip, 854 m elevation gain. Trailhead: signed from the parking lot beneath Grouse Mountain gondola) Though in excellent condition this is a punishingly tough, steep trail, with few views to reward the effort. Treated as a workout it is worth doing, but don't let its fame and popularity fool you into thinking it might be a good hike. You can take the gondola back down for $5.

Coliseum Mountain (24.5 km round trip, 1,239 m elevation gain. Trailhead: follow Lynn Valley Rd to its very end into Lynn Headwaters Regional Park. This horribly steep and demanding trail is only for those who want to test themselves and get away from the crowds. It could be done as a day-hike, but makes much more sense as a backpack trip so that you can claim the reward of camping on this flat mountaintop, enjoying the sight of the city lights below. Day-time panoramas take in numerous mountains, including Mt Baker, the city, Georgia Strait and Vancouver Island. Of the shorter hikes the best are probably the *Lynn Loop* and *Headwaters* trails.

Mount Seymour (9 km round trip, 440 m elevation gain. Trailhead: Mount Seymour Provincial Park parking lot) Providing one of the easiest routes to astonishing summit panoramas, this trail is understandably very popular. But it is certainly no push-over. The route can be confusing, and is dangerously exposed to bad weather. Views from the top are some of the most extensive around, taking in the city and Fraser Valley, Vancouver Island and the Gulf Islands, and a whole bunch of lofty peaks. The route is rarely snow-free before Aug.

Elsay Lake (20 km round trip, 885 m elevation gain. Trailhead: as above) Covering much of the same terrain as the above, this is a far more rugged and difficult hike, its rewards not necessarily equal to the extra effort.

Golden Ears Mountain (24 km return, elevation gain 1,500 m. Trailhead: 11 km into Golden Ears Provincial Park, see page 78, fork left towards the West Canyon Trail and proceed 0.5 km) This impossibly demanding trail requires stamina, perseverance, and preferably some experience. It's just possible as a day-hike, but far better as a 2-day trek. For a 10.5-km day-hike, turn around at Alder Flats. The going beyond here gets tougher still, but far more rewarding, with a number of breathtaking peaks seen up close. Things get even more spectacular at Panorama Ridge. Plan to overnight here or at Alder Flats, then summit and descend on day two. Without mountaineering experience, the very peak of Golden Ears may be unsafe to attempt. **Lower Falls Trail** (5.4-km return) is the best of this park's shorter trails, and is very popular. Halfway to the 10-m falls is a beach area. Just beyond are some of the best views in the park.

The best local kayaking is up **Indian Arm**, reached from Deep Cove. This 30-km fjord **Kayaking** reaches deep into the Coast Mountains, passing old-growth forest and waterfalls, with ample chance to view wildlife. All the same, it still doesn't compare with some of the paddling available from Vancouver Island, such as in **Clayoquot Sound**, **Nootka Sound** or the **Broken Island Group**. The second best local starting point is Bowen Island, from where the 8 Paisley Islands can be visited as a day trip. **English Bay** and **False Creek** offer mellow paddling in the heart of the city. For rapids, head for the **Capilano** and **Seymour Rivers**.

    Bowen Island Sea Kayaking, T9479266, www.bowenislandkayaking.com Rentals and guided trips. Full-day lesson $99. 3-hr tour $49. Rentals $30 per 3 hrs, $50 per day. Tue 2 for 1 rental special. They also rent mountain bikes. *Deep Cove Canoe and Kayak*, T9292268, www.deepcovekayak.com *Ecomarine Ocean Kayak Centre*, Granville Island, T6897575, www.ecomarine.com Rentals. *Jericho Sailing Centre* (see Boating). Lessons $55. Drop-in $28 per 2 hrs, $48 per day. *Ocean West Expeditions*, 1750 Beach Av, T6885770, www.ocean-west.com *Takaya Tours*, 3093 Ghum-Lye Dr, North Van, T9047410, www.takayatours.com Tours of Indian Arm from Deep Cove with First Nations guides. 5 hrs per $75, full moon tours, 3 hrs per $40.

There is a lot of first-class, hard-core mountain biking around Vancouver, not for the **Mountain** inexperienced. The three main areas, each with multiple tough trails, are **Cypress**, **Sey-** **biking** **mour** and **Fromme** mountains. Trail maps of these areas ($6 each), along with some *Note that by law you* much-needed advice, are available at bike shops. See also *Mountain Biking BC* by Steve *must wear a helmet* Dunn. Seymour is probably the least difficult of these, but **Burnaby Mountain** and **Fisherman Trail** are more appropriate rides for intermediates/beginners. For more detailed professional information or tours contact Johnny Smoke at *Bush Pilot Biking*, T9857886, www.bushpilotbiking.com

    The best store Downtown is *Simon's Bike Shop* at 608 Robson, T602118. Rentals are $19 per day, $69 per week. $55 per day for a hard core mountain bike. In Deep Cove, there's *Deep Cove Bikes*, 4310 Gallant Av, T9291918. May-Sep only. $30 per day for basic mountain bike, $50 (and a big deposit) for a serious bike. Also on the North Shore is *John Henry* at 400 Brooksbank Av, one of the best all-round bike stores in town. The pick of the bunch near Stanley Park is *Spokes Bicycle Rentals*,1798 W Georgia St, T6885141, with road bikes, tandems, child trailers, baby joggers, etc. Regular bike $3.75 per hr, $15 per day; mountain bike $42 per 6 hrs. Also guided bike tours. *Bayshore* at 745 Denman, T6882453, rent rollerblades and strollers. The greatest concentration of bike stores is on W 4th Av or Broadway, with places such as the *Bike Cellar* at 1856 W 4th, T7387167.

The *Yellow Pages* is full of luxury yacht cruises. For something a little more authentic, go **Sailing** for *Cooper's Boating Centre*, 1620 Duranleau St, T6874110, www.cooperboating.com or just shop around in this part of Granville Island. *Deep Cove Yacht Club*, 4420 Gallant Av, North Van, T9291009, offer basic and intermediate cruising standard keelboat courses. Basic is $350 ($100 for boat-owners); intermediate is $600 ($300).

Cross-country Hollyburn Ridge in **Cypress Provincial Park**, www.cypress moun- **Skiing** tain.com, has 19 km of track-set trails including 7 km lit up at night, $15, T9220825. **Grouse Mountain** has 5.3 km of trails, lit at night. *Sigge's Sport Villa*, 2077 W 4th Av, T7318818, has the biggest selection of cross-country equipment, plus lessons and rentals. They run shuttles to Lost Lake in Whistler on Sat and Manning Park on Sun.

Vancouver

Skiing **Downhill** Cypress Mountain, T9265612, www.cypressmountain.com is geared towards more advanced skiers, with the largest vertical drop and terrain that divides up as 23% beginner, 37% intermediate, 40% expert. 5 chair lifts lead to 34 runs on 2 mountains, with night skiing on all runs. There is also a snowboard park with half-pipe, and 10 km of snowshoeing trails. A SnowPlay area has tubing and tobogganing. All rentals are available, and lessons are given for skiing and boarding. There is a café and a lounge. A ski pass is $42. The hill is open daily 0900-2230. **Grouse Mountain**, T9809311, www.grousemountain.com has easy access, tremendous views, night-skiing, and the best facilities. Day pass is $35, $25 youth, $19 seniors, $15 children. For night-skiing, 1600-2200, it is $26, $20 youth, $17 seniors, $12 children. For a 5-day pass, $139, $109 youth, $79 seniors, $49 children. A high-speed gondola takes you to the base then other lifts fan out from there. Take SeaBus to North Van then No 236 or No 232 straight to the lift. Also ice skating, snow shoeing, and cross country skiing. **Mount Seymour**, T9862261, www.MountSeymour.com is good for beginners and snowboarders, with 3 snowboard parks. Open 0930-2200 weekdays, 0830-2200 weekends. Day pass $29, $24 seniors, $14 children, with reduced rates from 1300 and 1600. Book of 5 tickets $119, $59 children. Ski rental $26, $15 concessions; snowboard rental $37, $31 concessions; package of lesson, lift ticket and rental is $61, $45 concessions. Snowshoeing $17-20 including rentals. The Snow Tube Park is a glorified toboggan hill with a tow back up. $11 for 2 hours, including the tube. Shuttle bus from Lonsdale Quay $7 ($5 concessions) return, $4 ($3 concessions) one-way. T7187771 for schedule. *Kenny's Fun Club* at 1833 Anderson St near Granville Island, T7384888, rents snowboards for $29 per day.

Scuba diving There is a great deal of quality scuba diving close to Vancouver. Whytecliffe Park at the western tip of the North Shore, Cates Park in Deep Cove, and Porteau Cove on Hwy 99 are all renowned underwater reserves, and the waters around Vancouver Island have been named the second best place to dive in the world by the Jacques Cousteau Society. *Diving Locker*, 2745 W 4th Av, T7362681, www.kochersdiving.com PADI diving instructors for 30 years. Beginner's course is $270 all inclusive. A wide range of advanced courses available, as well as 2- and 3-day dive trips from $400, *Sunday Safari* day-trips for $100 including all the gear, and equipment rental ($50 per day for the works). *BC Dive Adventures* 228 W Esplanade, North Van, T9832232, www.bcdive.com and *Rowand's Reef Dive Team* 1512 Duranleau St, Granville Is, T6693483, www.rowandsreef.com also come recommended for courses, trips and rentals. For used equipment try *Water Sport Exchange*, 3291 W Broadway, T7343667.

Swimming The 2 best swimming spots in town are the large open-air pool at Kits Beach (see page 72) and the professional-sized heated saltwater pool in the *Vancouver Aquatic Centre* at 1050 Beach Av, T6653424. The latter also contains a fitness centre.

Tennis Vancouver has over 180 free public tennis courts operated on a first-come, first-serve basis with a 30-min time limit if there are people waiting. The most popular and numerous are in Stanley, Queen Elizabeth and Kitsilano Beach Parks.

Yoga *Bikram's*, 203-2112 W Broadway, T7304553; *City Yoga*, upstairs at 2100 W 4th, T7305522, www.cityyoga.net *Wandering Yogi*, 1707 Grant/Commercial, T2511915, www.wanderingyogi.com

Tour operators and travel agents

Adventure tours *Bigfoot Adventure Tours*, T7779905, www.bigfoottours.com, 2-10 day tours around BC aimed at young, independent travellers/backpackers and departing from hostels. The 10-day 'Moose Run' tour does a loop via Whistler, the Rockies and Kelowna,

$380+tax. *Brewster Motorcoach Tours*, T18006611152, www.brewster.ca 2-7 tours around BC depart daily. *Explore BC Adventure Tours*, 1524 Duranleau St, Granville Island, T6891805, www.explore-bc.com A variety of tours including Grouse Mountain, nature walks, riverboat tours, rafting, flightseeing, etc. *Lotus Land Tours*, T6844922, www.lotuslandtours.com Broad range of activity-based tours including eagle-watching, snow-shoeing, whale-watching, river-rafting, sea-kayaking, hikes, etc. See also under Sports, above.

Champagne Cruises, T6888072, www.champagnecruises.com Sunset Cruise $25. **Boat tours** Dinner cruise from 1730-2030. *Danny's Rainbow Charters*, foot of 2nd Av, Steveston. 30-min narrated harbour tours. *False Creek Ferries*, see Getting around, also run tours for $8, $6 concessions, $4 children. *Harbour Cruises*, north tip of Denman St, T6329697, www.boatcruises.com All kinds of tours, including Sunset Dinner Cruises, Indian Arm Luncheon Cruise, and Vancouver Harbour Tour. *Sewell's Sea Safari*, 6695 Nelson Av, Horseshoe Bay, T9213474. Zodiac tour, 2½-hr tours $55, $25 concessions, with a chance of spotting seals and eagles. See also Boating, page 105.

Travel agents *Flight Centre*, T6069000 or T1888-9675331 have about 17 branches, including 1232 Davie, 909 Denman, 2194 W 4th, 1050 W Georgia, 655 W Pender, 610 Robson; *Travel Cuts* are at 567 Seymour St, T6592830, 120 W Broadway, T6592887, and Granville Island, T6592820. *Hagen's* at 204-1789 Davie, T2572088, is a reliable choice. For adventure travel there's *Fresh Tracks*, 1847 W 4th, T7377880.

Architecture Institute of BC, 100-440 Cambie St, T6638588, www.aibc.bc.ca 6 different **Tours of town** guided architectural tours running from Jun-Aug, Wed-Sun: Gastown, Chinatown, Downtown, West End, False Creek North/Yaletown. Tours start at 1330, $5 per person. *Vancouver Trolley*, T8015515, www.vancouvertrolley.com Trolley-bus. 2-hr tours with 23 stops start in Gastown, 0900-1430. Or get on and off as you wish. $24, $12 concessions for a day ticket. *Vancouver Sightseeing Tours*, T6855546, www.vancouver sight seeingtours.com Tours of the North Shore, Downtown or Whistler in a 10-person A/C van. *Walkabout Historic Vancouver*, 6038 Imperial St, T7200006. Walking tour with costumed guides recounting stories and folklore. *The X-tour*, T6092770, www.x-tour.com Visit sites used in filming the *X-Files*. Price starts at $99, with a maximum of 7 people.

Transport

TransLink, T5210400, www.translink.bc.ca, operate an inadequate network of city **Local** buses, a fast and generally efficient elevated rail system called the **SkyTrain**, and a pas- *See also Ins and outs,* senger ferry between Waterfront SkyTrain Station and North Vancouver's Lonsdale *page 54* Quay called the **SeaBus**. Tickets bought on any of these are valid for any number of journeys in any direction on all three within a 90-min period. The system is divided into 3 fare zones, with zone 1 covering almost everything of interest. Fares are $2 for 1 zone, $3 for 2 and $4 for 3. Concession fares are $1.50 for 1 zone, $2 for 2 and $3 for 3. Zone 2 and 3 tickets are $2 after 1830, at weekends and on holidays. A day pass is $8 ($6 seniors). There is also a transit service for the handicapped called **HandyDART** (see Directory, page 112, for more details). Information on all services, including maps and timetables for individual lines, is available at the Information Centre, public libraries, and SkyTrain ticket booths. A map covering all routes in the city exists and has been available at the Information Centre for $1.50, though these days they never seem to have copies. Ask anyway. Almost as useful is the booklet *Discover Vancouver on Transit*.

Bus Vancouver's bus system is rather poor and not geared towards visitors. The exact fare is dropped into a machine which never gives change. If you have bought a ticket in the last 90 mins (time of purchase is on the ticket), feed it into the machine,

Vancouver

which will give it back. The service, which is split between diesel buses and electric trollies, is being consistently cut back with fewer buses on all but the busiest routes and none at all after about 0030. Very few bus stops, and no vehicles, carry any information. Thankfully most routes run through Granville St Downtown.

The **SkyTrain** is a much better and faster service, but with only a few really useful stops: **Waterfront** in the old Canadian Pacific station next to Canada Place; **Burrard** at Burrard/Dunsmuir; **Granville**, beneath *The Bay* on Granville St; **Science World-Main St**; and **Broadway** at the Broadway/Commercial junction. Ticket machines give change. The **West Coast Express**, www.westcoastexpress.com is a weekday only commuter service that links Downtown with the eastern suburbs ($8 one-way) and is of little interest to visitors.

SeaBus ferries leave every 15 mins and take 12 mins to make the gorgeous journey across Burrard Inlet. They are wheelchair accessible and can carry bikes. On False Creek, the *Aquabus* runs from the south end of Hornby St to Science World, stopping at the Arts Club on Granville Island, the end of Davie St in Yaletown, and behind *Monk McQueens* at Stamp's Landing. Each stop is $2-3 depending on length. *False Creek Ferries* run from the Maritime Museum in Vanier Park to Science World, stopping at the Aquatic Centre on Beach Av, Granville Island Public Market, Stamp's Landing, and BC Place. From $2-5 one-way. 40-min tours are $8, $5 concessions.

Bike Vancouver is as tough as most cities for cyclists, but attempts have been made to encourage and facilitate this mode of transport, such as a network of bike-ways parallel to major transit routes. The brochure *Cycling in Vancouver*, available from the Information Centre or good bike stores, includes a map of these routes and other useful information for the cyclist. An increasing number of buses are now equipped with bike racks.

Taxis are well regulated and compare favourably with public transport prices. After midnight they become about the only way to get around. The main companies are *Black Top/Checker Cabs*, T1800-4941111, T6812181, and *Yellow Cab Co*, T6811111.

Long distance
www.yvr.ca is a useful resource for finding flights

Air Vancouver International Airport (YVR), T2077077, www.yvr.ca, is located on Sea Island in the mouth of the Fraser River, 13 km from Downtown, adjacent to Richmond.

Over 40 carriers service Vancouver, operating 17 international and 22 US-scheduled routes. Direct flights from **London Heathrow** are with *Air Canada*, *British Airways* and *Air Transat*, who are usually the cheapest; from **Amsterdam** with *KLM*; from **Frankfurt** with *Lufthansa*. Many other European airports connect with Vancouver via US cities such as **Denver, Houston** and **Chicago**. There are frequent flights from **LA, San Francisco, Seattle** and **Las Vegas**. *Air Canada* and *Qantas* fly from **Sydney**, Australia. All departing passengers have to purchase an Air Improvement Fee ticket, which is $5 for BC/Yukon, $10 for North America, $15 elsewhere. They can be bought from machines or airport booths and must be presented at security.

All transport to Downtown leaves from right outside the international terminal, except the city bus. This leaves from the Domestic terminal (follow signs), involves a transfer onto the useful Bus No 98B, and takes about 45 mins. The *Airporter shuttle* bus, T9468866, leaves every 15 mins from 0630-0010, heading to the major Downtown hotels, Canada Place, and the bus station. Tickets ($12 one-way, $18 return) from the infocentre, *Airporter* office or on the bus. A combined *Airporter/Greyhound* service to Whistler costs $33 one-way. Pacific run a service directly from the airport to Victoria (see below). **Taxis** operate around the clock, charging $25-$30 for the 25-min trip Downtown. *Limojet Gold Express*, T2731331, charge $40 for up to 8 passengers. All the major car-rental agencies such as *Avis*, *Budget*, *Hertz*, and *Thrifty* are located on the ground floor of the indoor parking lot.

Air Canada, *West Coast Air* and *Pacific Coastal* all have several daily flights for around $80 one-way to **Victoria**. **Floatplanes** and helicopters run by *West Coast Air*,

T6066888; *Helijet International*, T1800-6654354; *Harbour Air*, T6881277; and *Baxter Aviation*, T6836525, fly to **Victoria**'s Inner Harbour from Downtown, by Canada Place. The cost is about $100, saving at least an hour of bus time.

Bus Buses and trains all leave from the VIA Rail Pacific Central Station, 1150 Station St, in a grim but handy part of town near the Main/Terminal intersection and the Science World SkyTrain Station. *Greyhound*, T1800-6618747, www.greyhound.ca, have connections to most Canadian towns and to Seattle (see below). The following prices are one-way for adult/concession/child and times are approximate. There are 5 daily buses to **Banff** (11 hrs, $106/$95/$53), 5 to **Calgary** (15-17 hrs, $125/$113/$63), 2 to **Jasper** (11 hrs, $106/$95/$53), 5 to **Kamloops** (5 hrs, $51/$46/$26), 6 to **Kelowna** (6 hrs, $56/$51/$28), 8 to **Nanaimo** (2¾ hrs, $12.25/$11/$6, including the ferry), 3 to **Prince George** (12½ hrs, $104/$94/$52), 4 to **Toronto** (70 hrs, $332/$299/$166), 7 to **Whistler** (2½ hrs, $21/$19/$10) and 8 to Nanaimo from the Downtown bus station, (2¾ hrs$12.25/$11/$6 including the ferry) there is no need to catch a city bus to Horseshoe Bay. Look out for specials such as the 'Go Anywhere' fares, as little as $119 one-way or $189 return to anywhere in Canada if booked 14 days in advance.

Pacific Coach Lines, T1800-6611725, www.pacificcoach.com, operate at least 14 buses per day in summer, almost hourly, to **Victoria** from the bus station or airport. $29 ($20 concessions, $14.50 child) one-way including ferry, a little more from the airport. There are a few choices to **Whistler**. The *Snow Shuttle*, T7779905, leaves 3 times daily from all Vancouver hostels. $27 one-way/$49 return with hostel membership or student card. The *Snowbus*, T7365228, www.snowbus.ca, costs $42, sometimes as low as $29 return (currently closed but may reopen soon). A combined *Airporter/Greyhound* ticket from the airport is $33 one-way with frequent departures, while the *Perimeter Whistler Express*, T2665386, picks up at the airport and major hotels and charges $55 ($43 concessions) one-way. *Malaspina Coach Line*, T1877-2278287, runs 2 buses daily to **Powell River** on the Sunshine Coast (6 hrs).

To/from USA *Greyhound*, T1800-2312222, run 6 daily buses between **Seattle** and Vancouver, a 3½-4½-hr trip is $22 ($40 return). The *Quickshuttle*, T9404428, www.quickshuttle.com, also connects Vancouver with Downtown **Seattle**. 8 services leave daily from the *Holiday Inn* at 1110 Howe St, Downtown, stopping at the airport, with an express service from Canada Place Fri-Mon. The journey takes 3 hrs 45 mins, at $39 ($70 return) for adults, $27 ($49 return) for students, and $21 ($38 return) for children.

Ferry *BC Ferries* run from Tsawwassan, about 30 km south of Vancouver, to **Victoria**, the **Southern Gulf Islands** and **Nanaimo**. To get Downtown from here take bus No 404 and transfer to No 98 at Airport Junction ($4). The crossing to Victoria takes 95 mins and runs roughly 0700-2100. Horseshoe Bay, some 15 km northwest of the city on Hwy 99, is a far nicer terminal, and much more convenient for **Nanaimo**, as well as **Bowen Island** and the **Sunshine Coast**. To get Downtown take buses No 250 or No 257 ($3). The crossing to Nanaimo takes 95 mins and runs every 2 hrs or so from 0630-2100, with more in summer. A new, passenger-only, high-speed ferry operated by *Harbour Lynx*, T7534443, will take you from the waterfront *SeaBus* terminal to **Nanaimo** in 75 mins. From there *Tofino Bus Lines*, T1866-9863466, run minibuses to **Tofino**.

Train Like buses, trains leave from the VIA Rail Pacific Central Station, 1150 Station St, see above. *VIA Rail*'s *The Canadian*, T1800-5618630, www.viarail.ca, connects Vancouver and **Toronto** via **Kamloops**, **Jasper**, **Edmonton**, **Saskatoon**, **Winnipeg** and **Sudbury Junction**. It runs 3 times per week each way, leaving Vancouver on Fri, Sun and Tue. The entire journey takes 3 days and costs from $425 one-way to an astronomical $1,660 per adult in a double room. *Amtrak*, T1800-8727245, www.amtrak.com, run daily trains to **Seattle**.

Road The TransCanada (Hwy 1) runs east right across Canada, connecting Vancouver with **Banff**, **Calgary**, **Regina**, **Winnipeg** and **Toronto**. **Seattle** is 3 hrs south, **Whistler** 2 hrs north. If you want to explore Canada, or just BC, properly you are advised to have your own transport, since many of the best sights are not reached by public transport. In summer, a car and a tent are all you need. All the major rental agencies have offices Downtown. *Avis*, T6062869; *Budget*, T6687000; *Hertz*, T6064711; and *Thrifty*, T6061666, have a one-way service, meaning you can rent a car in Vancouver and drop it off elsewhere. Prices start at about $40 per day, $200 per week, $800 per month plus tax and insurance. Another option would be to rent something you could sleep in. A mini-van from *Rent-a-wreck*, T6880001, works out at about $590 per week all-inclusive. **RVs** are the expensive but luxurious choice. The following offer one-way rentals, often just to Calgary: *Candan*, T5303645, www.candan.com *Cruise Canada*, T9465775, www.cruisecanada.com *Go West*, T9875288, www.go-west.com *Westcoast Mountain Campers*, T2790550, www.wcmcampers.com Prices start at about $145 per day for a small unit, $193 per day for a 24-footer, plus tax and insurance. For long-term travellers, it would work out cheaper to buy a vehicle then re-sell it at the end of your trip. Bargains can be found in Vancouver. The classified section of the *Vancouver Sun* is a good place to start looking.

Directory

Airlines *Air Canada*, 1030 W Georgia, T1888-2472262; *Air Transat*, T1877-8726728; *American*, T1800-4337300; *British Airways*, T18002479297; *Continental*, T1800-2310856; *KLM*, T1800-3615073; *Lufthansa*, T1800-5635954; *Qantas*, T1800-2274500; *Westjet*, T1800-5385696.

Banks Finding an ATM in Vancouver is never a problem. The main Canadian banks are clustered in a few blocks around Burrard and Georgia. *CIBC*, 400 Burrard; *HSBC*, 885 W Georgia; *National Bank of Canada*, 555 Burrard; *Royal Bank*, 1025 W Georgia; *Scotiabank*, 650 W Georgia; *TD Bank*, 701 W Georgia. **Currency exchange**: *Benny Lee*, 619 W Hastings; *Citizens Bank of Canada*, 815 W Hastings; *Custom House*, 375 Water St; *Inter Currency*, 609 W Hastings; *Money Mart* have branches all over the city, including 1281 Howe, 498 W Broadway, 1895 Commercial, 199 W Hastings, and 24-hr at 345 E Broadway and 1195 Davie; *Moneywise*, 819 Davie; *Thomas Cook Foreign Exchange*, 130-999 Canada Place.

Communications **Internet**: *Cyberia*, 1284 Robson. Open 24 hrs, $4 per hr or $20 per 10 hrs; *Cyber Space*, 1451 Robson. *Dakoda's*, 1602 Yew St, Kitsilano; *Soapy's*, 141-757 W Hastings; *Westend Bay*, 1168 Denman. $10 per 5 hrs. *Library computer lab*, $2.50 per 30 mins. **Post**: The main Post Office with General Delivery (Poste Restante) is at 395 W Georgia. Others are at 595 Burrard St, 523 Main, 732 Davie. Letters can be posted at most pharmacies/chemists. **Press**: *Xtra West* is a gay and lesbian newsletter available around the West End.

Consulates **Australia**, 1225-888 Dunsmuir, T6841177; **Belgium**, 570-688 W Hastings, T6846838; **Denmark**, 755-777 Hornby, T6845171; **Germany**, 704-999 Canada Place, T6848377; **Italy**, 1100-510 W Hastings, T6847288; **Japan**, 900-1177 W Hastings, T6845868; **Netherlands**, 473 Howe, T6846448; **New Zealand**, 1200-888 Dunsmuir, T6847388; **Norway**, 200 Burrard, T6827977; **Sweden**, 1100-1188 W Georgia, T6835838; **Switzerland**, 790-999 Canada Place, T6842231; **UK**, 800-1111 Melville, T6834421; **United States**, 1075-1095 W Pender, T6854311, 24-hr visa information for US citizens, T1900-4512778.

Cultural centres *Vancouver Francophone Cultural Centre*, 1551 W 7th Av, T7369806. *Gay and Lesbian Centre*, 1170 Bute St, T6845307, programs/services, T6846869 helpline. Discussion groups, library, clinics, etc.

With more than 14,000 sidewalk ramps, Vancouver claims to be one of the most wheel- **Disabled**
chair accessible cities in the world. Half of the buses and all but the Granville St SkyTrain **access &**
station are wheelchair accessible, and the HandyDART is a bus service designed for **facilities**
wheelchair users. It mainly runs 0630-1900 weekdays, and can be booked at T4302692. *For more information,*
For information call T4302892. Vancouver Airport was designed to be friendly to those *see page 23*
with hearing, visual and mobility difficulties. For accessible taxis call *Vancouver Taxi* at
T2555111. To rent a lift-equipped van call the BC Paraplegic Association, T3243611. *Grey-*
hound have lift-equipped services to **Kelowna**, **Calgary** (via **Banff**) and **Prince George**,
and the *Pacific* service to **Victoria** is also accessible. For a list of hotels with wheel-in
showers contact *We're Accessible* at T7312197. **Drug info** T6609382.

Abbott, 404 Abbott, near Chinatown; *Broadway*, 3071 W Broadway; *Kitsilano Laun-* **Laundry**
dromat, 2208 W 4th Av; *Maquina Loca*, 1910 Commercial; *Swan's*, 1352 Burrard.

The magnificent **Vancouver Public Library** (see page 61) is at 350 W Georgia. Useful **Libraries**
branches are at 2425 MacDonald (Kitsilano), 370 E Broadway; 870 Denman (West End).

Hospitals: **Vancouver General**, 855 W 12th St, T8754111. **St Paul's** 1081 Burrard, **Medical**
T6822344. **Walk-in Clinics**: *Broadway and Burrard*, 1816 W Broadway, T7361888. Open **services**
0900-2100. *Care-Point Medical Centres*, T8781000, www.CarePoint.bc.ca, are open
0900-2100, till 1800 weekends at: 1623 Commercial, 1125 Davie, 1175 Denman; *Health*
Care, 2590 Commercial, T8711535; *Khatsahlano*, 2689 W Broadway, T7319187.
0900-2045; *Medicentre*, Bentall Centre, 1055 Dunsmuir, T6838138. **Pharmacies**: *London*
Drugs has branches at 70 Granville, 1187 Robson and 1650 Davie (24-hr); *Shoppers Drug*
Mart has branches at the Pacific Centre at 700 Georgia, and 1020 Denman. Also handy
are *Gastown Pharmacy*, 288 Carrall; *Kripps Pharmacy*, 994 Granville; *Pharmasave*, 1160
Burrard. **Dentists**: *Association of Dental Surgeons of BC*, T7367202. *Acute Medical Den-*
tal Centre, 2561 Commercial, T8770664 (24-hr). Walk-in clinic. **Alternative**: *Chinatown*
Centre, 165-288 E Georgia, T6053382. Walk-in clinic with acupuncture and traditional
Chinese medicine. *Integral Chinese Therapy Centre*, 105-1956 W Broadway, T7328968.
Travel clinics: 1030 W Georgia, T6815656; 601 W Broadway, T7369244.

Emergencies: T911. **Police**: 916 Granville, T7172920; 1122 Bute/Davie, T7172924; 200 **Useful**
Burrard, T7172916; 870 Denman, T8996250; 219 Abbott, T7172929. **Fire and Rescue**: 1090 **addresses**
Haro (Downtown), T6656007; 199 Main, T6656002; 1001 Nicola (West End), T6656006.
24-hr Crisis Centre, T8723311. **Pharmacies**: *London Drugs* on Davie and *Shoppers Drug*
Mart on Denman. Both 24hrs. **Women** Women's Resources Centre, T4828585; YWCA
Women's Information Centre, T8955790; Rape Crisis Centre, T2556344.

The Sunshine Coast

It is said that Highway 101 begins in Mexico City, or even somewhere in South Phone code: 604
America. Its northernmost leg, the only major strip of road on the Canadian main- Colour map 1,
land's Pacific Coast, is known rather optimistically as the Sunshine Coast. Getting grid B/C3
there entails a ferry from Vancouver's Horseshoe Bay to Langdale. About 10 min-
utes' drive away is the pretty harbour town of Gibsons Landing, a worthwhile day's
excursion from the city. Whether the rewards offered by continuing match the effort
(including another ferry) and expense is unsure. The towns have little appeal, good
beaches are in short supply, and the road delivers disappointingly few of the admit-
tedly wonderful ocean views. For divers, boaters and kayakers, however, the whole
coast is a playground, and there's plenty of good hiking and canoeing inland.
Powell River is the main service centre, but not a place to linger.

Ins and outs

Road travel from Vancouver to the Sunshine Coast involves 2 ferries. The first, from Horseshoe Bay to Langley leaves every 2 hrs or so, 0720-2115 (0620-2020 on the way back). The second is from Earl's Cove to Saltery Bay, also every 2 hours, 0630-2210 (0540-2115 on the return). $9 per person, $27.75 per vehicle for a return from Horseshoe Bay to Langley or a one-way to Saltery Bay. 4 ferries also arrive daily in Powell River from Comox/Courtenay on Vancouver Island, $7.50, $32.50 with vehicle, 95 mins. *Malaspina Coach Lines*, 4675 Ontario Street, T4855030, run 2 buses daily from Vancouver to Powell River, leaving 0830 and 1830, returning 0830 and 1430.

Air *Pacific Coastal*, T4822107, have up to 6 flights daily in summer from Vancouver to Powell River, $129 return, $99 one-way, less with 10 days' notice.

Gibsons Landing

Gibsons itself is a mediocre little town, but the quarter clustered around the harbour, known as Gibsons Landing, is probably the prettiest community on the Sunshine Coast. Dear to many Canadians as the setting for the long-running TV series *The Beachcombers*, it has much to offer tourists, with lots of worthwhile shops, art galleries and restaurants gathered around the **Visitor Information Centre** at 668 Sunnycrest Road, T8862325, www.gibsonschamber.com **Molly's Lane** is a boardwalk with various speciality shops, including *Cycle Fix*, where bikes can be rented; the **Maritime Museum**, with paraphanalia from the *Beachcombers*; and *Sunshine Kayaking*, T8869760, for rentals and tours.

From nearby **Langdale** there is a passenger ferry to **Keats Island** which has tent camping at *Plumper Cove Marine Park*.

Sleeping There are some nice, if pricey, sleeping options, many of them huddled around the picturesque harbour. **A** *Bonniebrook Lodge B&B*, 1532 Ocean Beach Esplanade, T8862887, www.bonniebrook.com 7 suites with their own jacuzzi, fireplace and sundeck, steps from the beach. Complimentary breakfast in their expensive but highly regarded restaurant (see below). Tenting and RV sites on the water, with showers (**F**). **C** *Caprice B&B*, 1111 Gower Pt Rd, T8864270. 3 lovely en suite rooms, pool, hot tub, patio, ocean views. **C** *Lookout B&B*, 318 Shoal Lookout, T8861655. 2 en suite rooms in a West Coast-style home. Balcony with great views. The best **motel** option is **C** *Ritz Inn*, close to the harbour at 505 Gower Pt Rd, T8863343.

The quaint little community of **Roberts Creek** may be worth a diversion. **E** *Moon Cradle Hostel*, at 1057 Roberts Creek Rd, T8854216, is a great budget option, with handcrafted cedar beds and a sauna. Price includes breakfast at the *Gumboot Garden Café*, next door, a mid-range restaurant serving delicious whole foods. **Camping** *Roberts Creek Provincial Park* on the highway has 25 primitive sites for camping in a beautiful old-growth forest with some walking trails. The day use area of the park, 1.5 km south, also has a beach.

Eating **Expensive** *Chez Philippe* at the *Bonniebrook* is the most luxurious place to eat. Close to the Information Centre are: **mid-range** *Leo's Mediterranean Tapas and Grill*, fine Greek dishes and Ouzo specials, and *Howl At the Moon*, upmarket Mexican cuisine, a deck with ocean views, and good breakfasts. **Cheap** *Gramma's Pub*, on the boardwalk, has good pub food, including a very cheap dinner special. Deck with wonderful views. *The Flying Cow* is great for coffee, fresh baking and sandwiches. At the end of the jetty you can buy fresh local seafood.

Sechelt Peninsula

The town of **Sechelt** sits on a narrow spit of land between the ocean and a long inlet that almost makes this peninsula an island. The usual services are here, but little else of interest apart from a large, popular and very nice campground at **Porpoise Bay Provincial Park**, 4 km north up Sechelt Inlet Road. Many hiking and biking trails criss-cross the peninsula, including the 33-km **Suncoaster Trail**, whose foothills offer incredible views and patches of old-growth forest. The shoreline has some pleasant bays and beaches, of which **Sargeant Bay** is maybe the most scenic, but few places to stay or camp.

Just before the second ferry crossing at Earl's Cove, a right turn leads to the pleasant village of **Egmont**, and **Skookumchuck Narrows Provincial Park**. Here the force of the tidal waters rushing to or from the ocean through a narrow section of the elongated inlet has resulted in a dramatic section of rapids which kayakers and seals love to surf. The spectacle of this phenomenon is not as impressive as the beautiful 4-km trail that leads to it, passing by a good, friendly bakery, and a forest of giant second-growth trees.

Sleeping & eating **AL-B** *Lord Jim's Resort Hotel*, about 16 km beyond Sechelt on Secret Cove, T8857038, www.lordjims.com is conveniently self contained, with a fine strip of private beach, cabins with kitchens, kayak and bike rentals, a licensed restaurant, playground, outdoor pool and so on. **F** *Porpoise Bay Provincial Park*, 4 km north up Sechelt Inlet Rd, T8983678. 84 private and treed sites, showers, and a large sandy beach. In **Egmont** the *Backeddy Pub* has good food and great views.

Powell River

Phone code: 604
Population, 14,000

The original Powell River, now known as the Historic Townsite, was one of the country's first planned towns, built mostly between 1911 and 1930 according to 'Garden City' precepts, whose novel aim was to provide even the lowliest workers with a house, garden, porch, and access to greenery. The streets originally fanned out like the spokes of a wheel whose centre was the mill, moving from the industrial to the commercial to the residential, all of it surrounded by a belt of greenery. The **Townsite Heritage Society** at 2865 Ash Avenue, T4833901, provides enthusiastic information, and a pamphlet outlining the self-guided tour that takes in 12 heritage sites, including the **Dwight Hall**, and **Patricia Theatre**, the longest-running cinema in North America.

Situated 31 km north of Saltery Bay, Powell River is the Sunshine Coast's most prominent town, with the majority of its facilities and the best **Visitor Information Centre** at 4690 Marine Avenue, T4854701, www.discoverpowellriver.com A useful base for many outdoor pursuits, particularly diving, it is nevertheless an unattractive, sprawling place dominated by the giant pulp-mill – to which it owes its existence – whose smoke and smell travel miles ahead to greet the approaching visitor. Ironically, the only area of interest is that immediately around the mill, some 3 km north of today's centre. Buses from Vancouver terminate here, and Westview ferry terminal has departures to Comox on Vancouver Island, opening up the possibility of a nice circuit back to Vancouver via Nanaimo or Victoria.

Sleeping **C** *Fiddlehead Farm*, 20 km by boat from Powell Lake, T4833018 (radio phone, let ring at least 10 times), F4853832. Homestead 32-acre farm with 6 rooms, sauna, and common area. Accessible from Sunshine Coast Trail, or 20-min boat-trip, $20 return. Phone to arrange. Ample trails and lakes in area. Price includes all meals plus use of canoes.

C-D *Adventure B&B*, 7439 Nootka St, almost 2 km S of Westgate ferry, T4857097. 2 comfortable rooms with lofts in a grand, cottage-style wooden house surrounded by gardens. Sunroom and sauna. **C-D** *Beach Gardens Resort*, 7074 Westminster Av, just south on the ocean, T4856267, bgardens@prcn.org Large, pleasant rooms with big windows, balconies and views.

D-E *Marine Inn*, 4429 Marine Av, T4854242. Fairly nice rooms, very convenient location close to Westgate ferry. **D-E** *The Old Courthouse Inn and Hostel*, 6243 Walnut St, Historic Townsite, T4834000. Heritage Tudor-style building. Dorms and private rooms with en suite baths. Old furniture and a homey feel. Right next to the mill.

Camping **F** *Haywire Bay Regional Park*, 5776 Marine Av, 7 km N on Powell Lake via Manson Av, T4831097. 42 sites, some with lake access. Playground, beaches, showers, hiking trails. **F** *Saltery Bay Provincial Park*, Mermaid Cove, just north of ferry. Attractive and private sites in a beautiful forest, 200 m from beach. Divers can see a 3-m underwater mermaid made of bronze. **F** *Willingdon Beach Municipal Campground*, 4845 Marine Dr, T4852242. Not very private campsites on beach, park, playground, showers, laundry. Closest to town. There are plenty of **forestry campsites** scattered around, many of them on the shores of lakes, such as Khartoum, Nanton, Lois or Dodd.

Eating **Mid-range** *La Casita*, 4578 Marine Av, T4857720. Funky blue adobe joint with authentic, reasonably priced Mexican food. *Chiang Mai*, 4463 Marine Av, T4850883. Very good Thai food, but poor ambiance. *Rocky Mountain Pizza and Bakery Company*, 4471 Marine Av. *The Shinglemill*, on Powell Lake, north of town. Nicely located pub rated for its restaurant, which specializes in seafood. **Cheap** *Jitterbug Café*, 4643 Marine Av. Central spot for coffee and baking. *Ljund Café and Bakery*, across from *Old Courthouse Inn*. *Starving Artist*, 4722 Marine Av. A delightfully cluttered hang-out spot with an arty, eccentric ambiance, and the best Italian coffee ever. Good wholesome food, such as homemade pittas stuffed with Mediterranean fillings.

Festivals **Mar** is the time to visit. It kicks off with the 10-day *Festival of the Performing Arts*, T4855575, and winds up with the annual 2-day *Jazz Festival*, T4859633.

Sports
For information on outdoor pursuits, www.roughlife.com

Canoeing and kayaking Powell Forest Canoe Route is an excellent 5-day trip travelling through 12 lakes with a choice of 20 forestry campgrounds and a few B&Bs along the way. Open Apr-Nov. Roughly 8-km canoeing, 10-km portage along good trails. Start at Lois Lake, 7 km down logging roads from a clearly marked turning 10 km past Saltery Bay. For kayak rentals, gear and drop-off/pick-up, there's *Powell River Sea Kayak*, T4832160, www.prcn.org/kayak, who also run all manner of tours around Malaspina Peninsula, Desolation Sound and beyond, ranging from a $39 sampler to 7 days for $1,999.

Diving Like Vancouver Island to the west, this area has some of the best diving in the world. For equipment rentals, charters, instruction and information, contact *Don's Dive Shop*, 6789 Wharf St, T4856969.

Hiking and biking The Sunshine Coast Trail stretches from Saltery Bay to the tip of the Malaspina Peninsula north of Lund, a total of 178 km. Pioneered by volunteer enthusiasts as a means of connecting the region's remaining sections of old-growth forest, this hike is still young and quite unknown, but destined to become a classic. Incorporating shorelines, lakes and panoramas, it's accessed from several points along the highway, skirting close to campsites, B&Bs and hotels, and connecting with the canoe route below. Look out for a number of interesting wooden bridges crossing creeks. For details contact the Information Centre or www.sunshinecoast-trail.com There are dozens of other hikes inland, covering all levels. A good but easy hike, with **wheelchair access**, is around Inland Lake. Bikes can be rented at *Taw's Cycle and Sports*, 4597 Marine Av, T4852555.

Buses terminate at the *Coast Hotel*, also stopping at Westview Ferry. *Powell River Transit* **Transport** *System*, T4854287, connects the airport with Downtown. Bus No 1 runs every hr on the hr from the Mall, inland on Alberni, to the Townsite and Powell Lake. Ferry to **Comox** leaves daily at 0800, 1200, 1715, 2045. Leaves Comox at 0620, 1000, 1515, 1915.

Bank *Royal Bank*, 7035 Barnet St, T4855968. **Communications** Internet: *Public* **Directory** *Library*, 4411 Michigan Av. **Canada Post**: 4812 Joyce Av, T4855552. **Laundry** *Atwater Market and Launderette*, 4454 Willingdon Av, across from Westgate Ferry. **Medical services** *Powell River General Hospital*, 5000 Joyce Av, T4853211.

The ravages of logging have lessened the popularity of this quiet island. Even **Texada** in the height of summer, long strips of deserted beach can be found. From **Island** Mount Pocahontas (532 m) there are stunning views of the Coast Mountains, Vancouver Island, and the Georgia Strait. During the prohibition, Texada apparently had the largest moonshine still north of San Fransisco.

Sleeping and eating **D** *The Retreat Motel*, Gillies Bay, T4867360. **F** *Shelter Point Regional Park*, Gillies Bay, T4867228, has oceanside or nicely treed private sites and showers. **Mid-range** *Texada Island Inn* is one of the few places to eat, with burgers, pastas and a patio.

Transport Ferries leave Powell River roughly every 2 hrs (0700-2100) for Blubber Bay on Texada Island, returning between 0645-2010. Return fare $5, $12 with a car.

Highway 101 ends 23 km north of Powell River at the village and marina of **Lund &** Lund, the closest inhabited point to Desolation Sound Marine Park. The larg- **Desolation** est water-access park in BC, with 5,666 ha of high land, and 2,570 ha of shore- **Sound** line and water, this is a kayaker's paradise, with countless places to dock and **Marine Park** spend the night. As well as paddling, there is ample fishing, hiking, and first-class scuba diving, famous for the size of the wolf eel and giant octopus. Petroglyphs can be seen at Walsh Cove.

   Savary Island, an 8-km long crescent-shaped clay ridge is about as remote as the accessible islands get. The north shore is one long white and grey sand beach, whose calm, shallow water is the warmest in the Pacific Northwest. There is a restaurant, art galleries, public campgrounds, bike rentals at the general store, and kayak rentals (T4833223).

Sleeping **AL-B** *Desolation Resort*, Malaspina Rd, to right just before Lund, T4833592, *Though little more* www.desolationresort.com Beautiful, luxurious chalets and apartments, all wood decor, *than a marina, Lund* fully equipped, with private decks overlooking the Okeover Inlet. 2-hr cruises to Marine *has some superb* Park for $48, rental of kayaks and canoes. Recommended. **B** *The Lund Hotel*, T4140474, *places to stay and eat* www.lundhotel.com A pretty hotel on the marina, built in 1889. Average rooms, restaurant, pub, giftshop, laundry, hot tub, grocery store. **F** *Okeover Arm Provincial Park*, end of Malaspina Rd, T8983678. 28 very nice but basic treed sites close to a rocky beach with oysters, mussels, and clams. Open year round. **F** *Y-Knot*, off Malaspina Rd, has primitive camping on terraced, fairly private sites. Rental of boats, canoes, and kayaks. There is a **forestry campsite** 2 km south of Lund, before Malaspina Rd.

Eating Expensive *Laughing Oyster*, just beyond Okeover Arm Park, T4839775. Exquisite West Coast food from a romantic patio with striking views of the inlet. Open from 1630. **Cheap** *Lund Market and Café*, a trailer to the left on the way into Lund. Good organic coffee, homemade bread, good value breakfasts and tasty organic beer. Internet access. *Nancy's Bakery* on the wharf has coffee, baking, and outside seating.

Vancouver

Sport and special interest For **kayak** rental and **diving** go to *Good Diving and Kayaking*, T4833223, behind the *Lund Hotel*.

Tour and tour operators For around $300 per group of up to 10, you can get there by chartered boat with *Ragged Island Charters*, T4839173, www.coastandmountains.bc.ca, or *Pristine Charters*, T4834541, pristine@prcn.org

Transport *Lund Water Taxi*, T4839749, runs to **Savary Island**, $7.50 one-way (subject to change).

Vancouver Island

Introducing Vancouver Island

The largest island on the west coast of North America,
Vancouver Island is dissected lengthwise by a central mountain
range. Most of the island's inhabitants live in communities along
The **East Coast**, which, sheltered from the Pacific and basking in a
rainshadow, has the mildest climate in Canada.

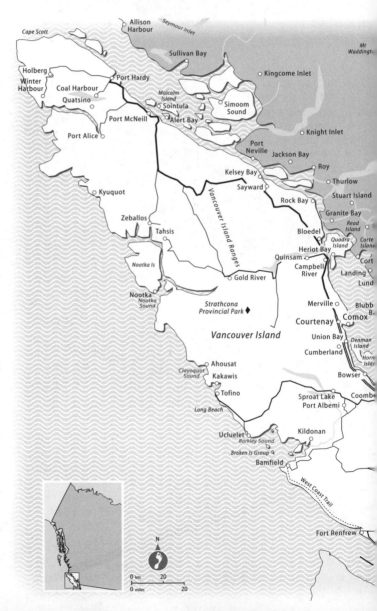

Cape Scott

Allison
Harbour

Seymour Inlet

Sullivan Bay

Mt
Waddingto

Kingcome Inlet

Holberg
Winter
Harbour
Quatsino

Coal Harbour

Port Hardy

Malcolm
Island

Sointula

Simoom
Sound

Port McNeill

Alert Bay

Knight Inlet

Port Alice

Port
Neville

Jackson Bay

Kelsey Bay

Roy

Kyuquot

Sayward

Thurlow

Rock Bay

Stuart Island

Vancouver Island Ranges

Granite Bay

Zeballos

Read
Island

Tahsis

Bloedel

Quadra
Island

Corte
Island

Nootka Is

Heriot Bay

Cort

Quinsam

Nootka
Nootka
Sound

Gold River

Campbell
River

Landing

Lund

Strathcona
Provincial Park ◆

Merville

Blubb
B.

Courtenay

Comox

Vancouver Island

Union Bay

Denman
Island

Cumberland

Horn
Islan

Ahousat

Clayoquot
Sound

Kakawis

Bowser

Tofino

Long Beach

Sproat Lake
Port Albemi

Coomb

Kildonan

Ucluelet

Barkley Sound

Broken Is Group

Bamfield

West Coast Trail

Fort Renfrew

N

0 km   20

0 miles   20

In a picturesque natural harbour, the very 'English' town of **Victoria**, known as the City of Gardens, is the provincial capital. The pretty sandy bays and villages to the north are overshadowed by the highway, so for some real tranquility it's best to head to one of the **Gulf Islands**, laid-back, friendly refuges for artists and eccentrics, with plenty of walks, viewpoints and beaches. Halfway up the coast, the pleasant town of Courtenay offers access to skiing at **Mount Washington** and hiking in **Strathcona Provincial Park**. Further north still, there is little but increasing wilderness and the chance to see orcas. Beyond the island's salmon capital of Campbell River most people are bound for the **Inside Passage** ferry from Port Hardy to Prince Rupert, or the remote Cape Scott trail.

Lashed by the Pacific Ocean the wild and rain-soaked **West Coast** is home to some of the world's biggest and oldest trees. The **Pacific Rim National Park** contains the ever-popular **West Coast Trail**, the kayaker's paradise of Barkley and Clayoquot Sounds, and the endless surf-beaten sands of **Long Beach**. The seaside village of **Tofino** is fun and picturesque, while further up the coast, Gold River is the gateway to wild and pristine **Nootka Sound**, another magnet for kayakers and cavers.

Vancouver Island

Things to do on Vancouver Island

- Combine a whale-watching tour from Tofino with a visit to Hot Springs Cove.
- Hike the East Sooke Trail, then dine at the famous *Sooke Harbour House*.
- Take a kayak trip round Clayoquot Sound or the Broken Islands Group.
- Have a drink in Victoria's *Swan's Pub* and admire its fine collection of First Nations art.
- Cruise down Alberni Inlet on the *MV Lady Rose*, or sail the Inside Passage to Prince Rupert.
- Stay at *Hollyhock Retreat Centre* and go oyster picking on Cortes Island.
- Camp at Salt Spring Island's Ruckle Provincial Park and watch the boats go by.

South Island

The southern section of Vancouver Island is easily the most densely populated, containing as it does the two biggest towns, Victoria and Nanaimo, which have a virtual monopoly on transport from the mainland. **Victoria**, the capital of British Columbia, is also arguably the province's most attractive town, with a first-class museum, plenty of excellent restaurants and bars, and countless flower-filled gardens. **Sooke** to the west is a worthwhile excursion, if only for its restaurants and the East Sooke Trail. Beyond, the rugged and practically uninhabited coast passes through **Juan de Fuca Provincial Park** and the Marine Trail en route to **Port Renfrew**, southern terminus of the **West Coast Trail**.

The Malahat Highway heading north from Victoria is fast and busy, offering few chances of escape, and little of interest other than the quaint town of **Chemainus** with its famous murals drawn by local artists. Despite a small but interesting Downtown, **Nanaimo** is probably best avoided. Far better value are the **Southern Gulf Islands**, with their laid-back, artistic spirit, and ample opportunities for hiking, biking, kayaking, swimming, fishing, and relaxing. At Parksville, beyond Nanaimo, the road splits: two highways head north and a third strikes west through the mediocre town of Port Alberni to the West Coast's **Pacific Rim National Park**.

Victoria

Phone code: 250
Colour map 1, grid C3
Population: 74,125
or 334,577 for
Greater Victoria

British Columbia's capital is the most charming and atmospheric town in Western Canada. Hemmed in on three sides by water, Victoria huddles around a picturesque boat-filled harbour, and lures visitors with its pleasant ocean walks, constantly fresh air and whale-watching. A liberal scattering of gardens, parks and flowers add to the natural beauty of the location. There's also a first-class museum, and a far better selection of restaurants and bars than you could reasonably expect of a town this size.

With the highest number of British-born residents in Canada, there's a degree of authenticity to Victoria's pervasive Englishness, but it's greatly exaggerated to attract American tourists, with many phoney sights best avoided. Certainly it might make an unwise first stop for anyone fresh off a plane from the UK, but after experiencing the soulless strip-malls and Legoland functionality of most Canadian towns, the grandeur of Victoria's architecture and its sense of history come as quite a relief.

Ins and outs

Although it's not on the way to anywhere else, Victoria is well served by public trans- **Getting there**
port and can be easily reached by air, bus, ferry or train. **Victoria International Airport** *For transport details,*
is 20 km north of Downtown on Hwy 17. An Airport Shuttle Bus leaves from Arrivals *see page 135*
and stops at the major Downtown hotels. Otherwise, a taxi should charge around $35
for the ride into town. The **bus terminal** is Downtown, at 700 Douglas St.

The **BC Ferry** terminal is in Swartz Bay, 40 km away at the north end of Saanich Peninsula. Bus No 76 leaves frequently for Douglas St. There is also a **bike trail** into Victoria.
American Ferries provide services to Victoria's Inner Harbour.

Victoria is connected by **train** with Courtenay to the north, and most communities
along the way.

Victoria's Downtown is so condensed that most of the major sites can easily be visited **Getting**
on **foot**, and orientation is simple. A comprehensive **bus** service operates throughout **around**
the city. Most services run from the corner of Douglas and Yates till roughly midnight.
There are numerous bike lanes, including one to Swartz Bay ferry terminal. **Driving** in
Victoria is confusing, with one-way streets and straight-ahead-only signs apparently
designed to frustrate outsiders (especially on Douglas). Parking is also a major problem, and the wardens are brutal.

Arriving by car, you will enter on Douglas St, a sleazy thoroughfare inhabited by Victoria's alarming number of street-dwellers, most of them kids. The Downtown core is
to the west, between Douglas and Wharf St, which follows the harbour. Between the
two is Government St, the main drag, which connects Downtown with the Inner Harbour and continues south past the Parliament Buildings and through a genteel residential neighbourhood to the ocean and the Beacon Hill area. Downtown's northern
boundary is Fisgard St, the nucleus of a small Chinatown. East of Douglas, the inter-
est-level quickly declines, but so do the prices.

Protected from the harsh winds of the Pacific by Washington's Olympic Peninsula, Vic- **Best time**
toria boasts the mildest climate in Canada, which means it can be enjoyed any time of **to visit**
year. Jan is the coldest month, with an average temperature of 6.5°C. Spring begins as
early as late Feb, and is arguably the most beautiful season, when the cherry trees are
in bloom. There is a holiday atmosphere throughout the summer, when Victoria's
many gardens erupt into colour, hanging baskets adorn the lamp-posts, thousands of
tourists mill around the Inner Harbour, and some kind of festival is usually underway.
Autumn begins in late Sep, when the gardens take on a fresh set of colours and many
of the tourists disappear.

The **Travel Information Centre** is at 812 Wharf St on the Inner Harbour, T9532033, **Tourist**
www.tourismvictoria.com Open 0830-1830 in summer, 0900-1700 in winter. For more **information**
general enquiries try the **Tourism Association of Vancouver Island**, T7543500.

History

The Victoria area was originally inhabited by Salish natives, particularly the
Lekwammen, whose main occupation was salmon fishing. Captain George
Vancouver was greatly impressed by the natural harbour, landscapes and climate, and James Douglas, who in 1842 came looking for a new local headquarters for the Hudson's Bay Company (HBC), declared the whole area a
'perfect Eden'. The local indigenous population helped him build a fort,
which they named Fort Camouson after a local native landmark, though this
was soon to change to Fort Victoria after the British Queen. First natives

attracted by the fur trade, then Brits brought over to settle the land on company farms, poured into the area, quickly making it the busiest harbour on the West Coast north of San Francisco. In 1846, when the US-Canadian border was fixed at the 49th parallel, the HBC's Pacific Northwest headquarters were moved north to Fort Victoria, which expanded still further throughout the 1850s as a supplies centre and stop-off point for prospectors on their way to the mainland gold-fields. Such expansion saw the arrival of immigrant groups, such as the Chinese, who established the biggest Chinatown in the west. The inevitable shanty town also grew, with the usual complement of brothels and bars, but the military and bureaucrats soon arrived to stamp their Victorian values on the burgeoning population, and when the Gold Rush ended they stayed on.

Meanwhile, in 1849, Britain sought to protect its interests by declaring Vancouver Island a crown colony, and merged it in 1866 with the mainland to form British Columbia. The harbour was used as an important base for the Royal Navy's Pacific fleet, a role it still fulfils today for the Canadian Navy. It soon became clear to British Columbia that future self-determination depended on joining the United States or the Dominion of Canada, an unpromising distance to the east. When Ottawa promised to build a railroad to link east and west, BC chose to join Canada, with Victoria as its provincial capital. The promise was only half kept though, since Vancouver was chosen as the western rail terminus, thus depriving Victoria of any hope of developing as an industrial base. When, in 1908, the Canadian Pacific Railway (CPR) built the *Empress Hotel*, it seemed to seal Victoria's fate as a town which would depend on tourism and bureaucracy rather than industry. Victoria became a firm favourite among the well-to-do European cruise-ship brigade at the start

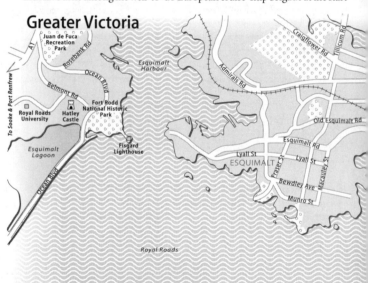

Greater Victoria

Detail map
A Downtown
Victoria, page 127

N

0 metres 500
0 yards 500

■ **Sleeping**
1 Craigmyle B&B Inn
2 Daffodil Inn

3 Palace on Dallas B&B
4 Spinnaker's

● **Bars & clubs**
1 Cambie

of the last century. Today 30% of the population works in tourism and the service industry, and roughly another 20% are retirees, attracted, like Captain Vancouver and James Douglas, by the location and climate.

Inner Harbour

A multitude of assorted craft, from kayaks and ferries, to yachts and floatplanes, ply the waters where passenger steamships once unloaded their genteel cargo. The wide open space and undeniable grandeur of the surrounding architecture conspire to create a magical atmosphere, especially in summer, when the harbour walkway throngs with art peddlers, buskers and tourists. The view landwards is entirely dominated by Victoria's grandest constructions: the Empress Hotel and the lavishly illuminated Parliament Buildings.

All but a few of Victoria's sights are easily reached on foot

Empress Hotel

Occupying as it does most of the Government Street block facing the Inner Harbour, the Empress Hotel is second in prominence and importance only to the Parliament Buildings. Designed by Francis Rattenbury, the architect responsible for almost all of the main buildings around the harbour, it was erected in 1908 and retains the opulence of the Victorian era splendidly. While you may not want to splurge on a room, a self-guided tour is recommended. Wear 'smart casual' dress, and explore the many lounges, lobbies and dining halls, all dripping with colonial excess. Maybe have a drink beneath the Tiffany-glass dome of the *Crystal Lounge*, or join the staggering number who partake in the ritual of high tea in the *Tea Lounge*. ■ *T3848111*.

Beside the *Empress*, at 649 Humboldt Street, **Miniature World** features tiny reconstructions of various themes such as the *World of Charles Dickens*, *Space*

Vancouver Island

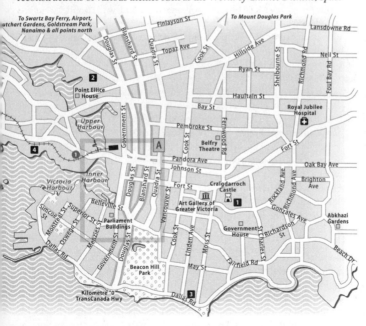

See also map on page 127

2201 or *Fantasyland*. The highlight is the scale model of the coast-to-coast Canadian Pacific Railway. ■ *Summer 0900-2100, autumn and spring 0900-1900, winter 0900-1700. $9, $8 concessions. T3859731, www.miniature world.com* Behind the *Empress*, at 713 Douglas Street, are the **Crystal Gardens**, which contain yet another Rattenbury design. The glassed-in conservatory, built in 1925, was modelled on London's ill-fated Crystal Palace. The tropical gardens contain 65 different endangered creatures including monkeys the size of a finger. There's also a popular tea room. ■ *Summer 0830-2000, rest of the year 1000-1630. $8, $4 concessions. T3811213.*

Royal British Columbia Museum

This is the best introduction to the province

Vancouver Island

Housed in a modest building to the south of the *Empress*, the top-notch Royal British Columbia Museum ranks as one of Canada's finest. Of the four permanent exhibitions, a perennial favourite is the **Open Ocean** exhibit, a 30-minute adventure that uses dark tunnels, lifts, films and state-of-the-art audiovisual wizardry to take you on a submarine ride through the wonders and mysteries of the sea. Visitors are admitted in groups of 10, so take a time-coded ticket and head on to the **Natural History Gallery**, where a series of extremely realistic dioramas evoke BC's many varied and extraordinary landscapes. Set within brilliantly recreated environments, the animals are so expertly stuffed that you half expect them to move. Particularly popular is a life-sized example of the woolly mammoths that roamed these lands until 13,000 years ago.

The **First Peoples Gallery** uses works of art, wooden masks, carvings, ancient artefacts, original documents, films, and audiovisual displays to recount the full, tragic history of British Columbia's aboriginal population. The journey through time continues with an exploration of the white man's world in the **Modern History Gallery**, which contains as much information on the province's social history as anyone could want, with countless artefacts and displays on the gold-rush and early pioneers, plus a recreation of turn-of-the-century Victoria, complete with cobblestone streets, buildings and alleys, and a movie-house that shows silent films. There's even a piece of Captain Vancouver's 1792 ship as it would have looked.

■ *Nov-Apr 0900-1700, May-Oct 1000-1700. $10, $7 concessions. 675 Belleville St, corner of Government St, T3567226, www.royalbcmuseum.bc.ca* Located at the Museum is the **National Geographic Imax Theatre**. ■ *Shows change hourly from 0900-2000, $9.75, $6.50 concessions; double bill $15, $11.75 concessions. Show and museum, $16.75, $12.25 concessions. T4804887, www.imax victoria.com*

Behind the museum on Elliot Street is **Thunderbird Park**, where a small collection of modern totem poles complements the First Nations Gallery within. A carving-shed offers the chance to see native masters at work. Next door, at 10 Elliot Street, is **Helmcken House**, the oldest surviving house in BC. Built in 1852 for a pioneer physician, it contains an unusually intact set of frightening 19th-century medical implements, as well as lots of other Victoriana. ■ *May-Oct 1000-1700, shorter hours the rest of the year. $5, $3 concessions.*

Parliament Buildings & around

Built in 1897, the very British-looking Parliament Buildings, also designed by Rattenbury, set the tone for the whole town, especially at night when they are atmospherically illuminated by 3,333 tiny lightbulbs.. The interior can be visited on a free guided tour, but despite the anecdotes and efforts of the guides, and a few historical artefacts (such as the dagger that killed Captain Cook), it's really not as impressive as the outside. The front lawn and garden is a popular place for tourists to hang out. ■ *Daily 0830-1700. 501 Belleville St, T3873046.*

In front of the Parliament Buildings is a brace of attractions suitable for kids. The **Royal London Wax Museum**, designed by the prolific Rattenbury, is in the same vein as London's famous Madame Tussaud's, and just as inexplicably popular. Kids particularly love the Chamber of Horrors. ■ *Daily 1000-1900 (1700 in winter). $7.50, $6.50 seniors, $5 students, $3.50 children. 470 Belleville St, T3884461, www.waxworld.com* Jutting out into the harbour, the **Pacific**

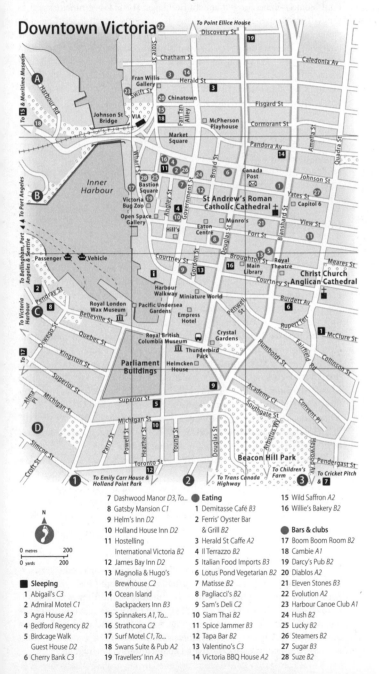

Downtown Victoria

Vancouver Island

N	7 Dashwood Manor *D3, To...*	● **Eating**	15 Wild Saffron *A2*
0 metres 200	8 Gatsby Mansion *C1*	1 Demitasse Café *B3*	16 Willie's Bakery *B2*
0 yards 200	9 Helm's Inn *D2*	2 Ferris' Oyster Bar	
	10 Holland House Inn *D2*	& Grill *B2*	● **Bars & clubs**
■ **Sleeping**	11 Hostelling	3 Herald St Caffe *A2*	17 Boom Boom Room *B2*
1 Abigail's *C3*	International Victoria *B2*	4 Il Terrazzo *B2*	18 Cambie *A1*
2 Admiral Motel *C1*	12 James Bay Inn *D2*	5 Italian Food Imports *B3*	19 Darcy's Pub *B2*
3 Agra House *A2*	13 Magnolia & Hugo's	6 Lotus Pond Vegetarian *B2*	20 Diablos *A2*
4 Bedford Regency *B2*	Brewhouse *C2*	7 Matisse *B2*	21 Eleven Stones *B3*
5 Birdcage Walk	14 Ocean Island	8 Pagliacci's *B2*	22 Evolution *A2*
Guest House *D2*	Backpackers Inn *B3*	9 Sam's Deli *C2*	23 Harbour Canoe Club *A1*
6 Cherry Bank *C3*	15 Spinnakers *A1, To...*	10 Siam Thai *B2*	24 Hush *B2*
	16 Strathcona *C2*	11 Spice Jammer *B3*	25 Lucky *B2*
	17 Surf Motel *C1, To...*	12 Tapa Bar *B2*	26 Steamers *B2*
	18 Swans Suite & Pub *A2*	13 Valentino's *C3*	27 Sugar *B3*
	19 Travellers' Inn *A3*	14 Victoria BBQ House *A2*	28 Suze *B2*

Undersea Gardens is a giant underwater aquarium full of octopuses, eels, salmon and other kinds of fish. ■ *Daily 1000-1900 (1700 in winter). $7.50, $3.50 concessions. 490 Belleville St, T3825717, www.pacificunderseagardens.com*

Emily Carr House
Four blocks behind the Parliament Buildings, at 207 Government Street, is Emily Carr House. Built in 1864, this is where the much-loved Canadian painter and writer (see page 456) was born and where she lived most of her twilight years surrounded by all sorts of animals. Her paintings are important historically as well as artistically because she made a visual record of the coastal native villages of her time. There is a gift shop and a small art gallery showing the work of other local artists. ■ *May-Oct 1000-1700, Feb-Mar 1200-1600. $5.35, $4.28 concessions. T3835843, www.emilycarr.com*

Point Ellice House
A third significant historic house, situated north of Downtown at 2616 Pleasant Street on Upper Harbour, is best reached by catching a Harbour Ferry from opposite the *Empress*. Point Ellice House is a well-restored Victorian residence full of original furnishings, with the added bonus of a lovely garden. Afternoon tea is served until 1600. ■ *Summer 1200-1700. $5, $3 concessions. T3806506. Bus No 14 or the Harbour Ferry.*

Downtown

This is Victoria's oldest quarter, and if you look up above the tacky gift shops on Government Street with their nasty ground-floor façades, you'll discover some fine brick and stone buildings. Check out, for example, the art nouveau-style tobacconists at No 1116. There are always good buskers along here, but for the first-class restaurants and bars that are the area's real attraction, wander down adjacent streets like Yates.

Bastion Square, site of the original Fort Victoria, is pleasant enough, but there's little to see except the handsome former provincial courthouse, which today houses the **Maritime Museum**. Several exhibition spaces here contain myriad artefacts from the Pacific Northwest's maritime history, highlight of which is the *Tillikum*, the dug-out canoe in which Captain John Voss made his three-year attempt to circumnavigate the globe in 1901. ■ *0930-1630 , $6, $2 concessions. 28 Bastion Sq, T3854222, www.mmbc.bc.ca* Nearby at 1107 Wharf Street is **Victoria Bug Zoo**, an off-beat but strangely compelling collection of weird and wonderful insects from around the world. Fascinating and educational. ■ *Summer 0930-2100 daily, rest of year Mon-Sat 0930-1730, Sun 1100-1730. $6, $5 concessions, $4 children. T3842847, www.bugzoo.bc.ca*

Concentrated around Fisgard Street and the absurdly named Gate of Harmonious Interest is the oldest **Chinatown** in Canada. Eating is the main event here. Fan Tan Alley, former red-light district and apparently the narrowest street in Canada, has some nice little shops to explore.

East of Douglas
Possessing no more charm than the average Canadian town, the area east of Douglas is only worth exploring in search of cheaper shops and eateries. A notable exception is a brace of particularly handsome old churches. **St Andrew's Roman Catholic Cathedral** at Blanshard and View was designed in 1892, inspired by the medieval cathedrals of Europe. It's a colourful building, combining brick, granite, limestone, wood, glass and gold, with a most imposing spire. **Christ Church Anglican Cathedral** at 912 Vancouver Street is a massive grey stone structure with two big towers and a huge arch.

Outskirts

If you spend more than a day in Victoria, you could follow Douglas Street south to the ocean and the beautiful Beacon Hill Park. Here you will see the results of Victoria's wonderful climate. Winding paths lead through all manner of different trees, from mighty old-growth giants to ornamental deciduous species, past duck ponds, swans and roaming peacocks, and between gardens where tens of thousands of flowers are lovingly tended and arranged. There are also some excellent free tennis courts, lawn bowling, a soccer field and a cricket pitch as well as a **Petting Zoo** for children. ■ *Mid-Mar to mid-Oct. Donation.* From here it is a lovely stroll along the ocean, with many good viewpoints and trails down to the rock pools. Those with a vehicle or bike should follow the coast east along Dallas Road, taking the scenic routes and admiring the grand houses, maybe as far as the genteel community of **Oak Bay**. ■ *24 hrs daily. Free. Getting there: bus No 5 or No 11.*

Beacon Hill Park & the coast
Orcas can sometimes be seen from the ocean-front along Dallas Road

If Beacon Hill has whet your appetite, Victoria has many more resplendent gardens to admire. It would be hard to justify the hype or the price of the Butchart Gardens, but the 20 ha here, comprising Japanese, rose, Italian, and sunken gardens, are certainly very beautiful in any season, even at night when they are spectacularly illuminated. Stunning firework displays set to music take place on Saturday evenings in July and August at no extra cost, and there's often live music and puppet shows. There's a gift shop, restaurant, coffee shop and a dining room serving the ubiquitous high tea. ■ *Summer 0900-2230 daily, earlier in winter. You can stay until 1 hr after gate closes. $18 ($14 off-season), $7 concessions, $2 children. T6525256, www.butchartgardens.com Getting there: follow red signs west on to Keating Rd from Hwy 17, 20 km north of Victoria, 20 km south of ferry. Central Saanich bus No 75 from Douglas St, or Laidlaw bus (see Transport, page 135).*

Butchart & Butterfly Gardens

While this far out, you can also take in the nearby **Butterfly Gardens**, an indoor conservatory predictably packed with colourful 'critters' that flutter by. ■ *Mar-Sep 0900-1700. $8.75, $7.75 seniors, $5 children. 1461 Benvenuto Rd, 3 mins before Butchart Gardens, T6523822, www.butterflygardens.com*

An alternative to the above is the **Abkhazi Gardens**, a gorgeous property created by Prince and Princess Abkhazi in the 1940s, and recently saved from housing developers through a purchase by the Land Conservancy. The upper garden affords great views of Victoria and the Juan de Fuca Strait. ■ *Mar-Oct, Wed-Fri and Sun 1300-1600. Suggested donation $8, $4.50 concessions. 1964 Fairfield Rd. T4798053, www.conservancy.bc.ca Getting there: Bus No 7 from town.*

A few sights are clustered together in an area called Rockland, east of Downtown up Fort Street. None quite justifies the distance on its own, but together they could provide a decent morning's diversion. The **Art Gallery of Greater Victoria** has an extensive and varied permanent collection, including a massive store of Japanese art, and quite a few less distinguished works by Emily Carr (see page 456). Pieces are constantly rotated and are supported by visiting exhibitions. ■ *Mon-Wed and Sat 1000-1700, Thu 1000-2100, Sun 1300-1700, $5, $3 concessions, under 12s free. 1040 Moss St, east of Downtown off Fort St, T3844101, www.aggv.bc.ca Getting there: bus No 11, 22 or 14, from Downtown.*

Rockland

Vancouver Island

A short walk away, **Craigdarroch Castle** was built in 1887-89 by Robert Dunsmuir, a Scottish mining expert who was drafted in to help exploit the black seams, and ended up discovering the most productive coal mine in North America, becoming BC's first millionaire in the process. Thanks to a shrewd business sense and utter lack of scruples, his net worth when he died – a mere six months before the castle's completion – was $20 million. The rooms are exquisitely decorated, with magnificent stained glass, immaculate Victorian furnishings and ornaments, and a few oddities like a 3-D picture made of human hair. Be sure to linger over the first few rooms, as these are the best. ■ *Summer 0900-1900, winter 1000-1630. $10, $5.50 concessions, $2.50 children. 1050 Joan Crescent, off Fort St. T5925323. Getting there: bus No 11 or 14.*

While in the area you might also want to take a stroll around the 6 ha of ornamental gardens at **Government House**, where the British Royal Family stays when visiting. ■ *Dawn till dusk. Free. 1401 Rockland Av, T3872080. Getting there: bus No 1.*

Excursions

Mount Douglas, a 10-ha park overlooking the Haro Strait and Washington's San Juan Islands, has hiking trails leading up to a viewpoint, and there's also a decent beach. ■ *Cordova Bay Rd, 9 km north. Getting there: bus No 28 from Downtown.*

Built in 1909 for James Dunsmuir, son of Robert (see above), **Hatley Castle** is a worthwhile excursion for those enchanted by Craigdarroch Castle. It's situated on the campus of Royal Roads University, 8 km west of town off the Sooke Rd (Highway 14), and is surrounded by a pretty park containing 65 ha of gardens. ■ *Getting there: bus No 50 to Western Exchange then No 39, 52 or 61, or Galloping Goose Trail by bike.* There is also a YWCA and YMCA here.

Fort Rodd National Historic Park, 12 km northwest in Colwood, is a tranquil 45-ha park that contains some historic military installations and the popular, very pretty **Fisgard Lighthouse**. Overlooking Esquimalt Harbour from the end of a causeway made out of scrap cars, this is the oldest lighthouse on the Pacific, having been in continuous operation since 1860. ■ *1000-1730. Fort Rodd Hill Rd, T4785849. Getting there: bus No 50 then transfer to No 39 at the Western Exchange.*

Thetis Lake Park, 10 km west on Highway 1, is the best local spot for freshwater swimming, but can get very busy. It also has the closest campground to town. ■ *Getting there: bus No 50 then transfer to No 58 at the Canwest Mall, or Galloping Goose Trail by bike.*

Goldstream Provincial Park, 19 km north of Victoria on Highway 1, is a vast park with a number of short trails and a campground. The day use area is at the junction of Finlayson Arm Road. The **Freeman King Visitors' Centre** and interpretive centre is accessed from the picnic area. Open daily in summer, with natural and human history displays, slide shows, films, and guided walks. From mid-October to December the chum, coho and chinook salmon can be seen entering the Goldstream River after their journey to the ocean. Several short walks lead to waterfalls or abandoned gold mines. There's a viewpoint at the top of **Mount Finlayson** (419 m). The trail starts on the Finlayson Arm Road. The longest walk is the **Prospectors' Trail**, starting at the same place. ■ *Getting there: bus No 50 from town, transfer to No 58 at the Canwest Mall.*

Essentials

The Inner Harbour is lined with mostly expensive hotels, while the residential area to its south and the oceanfront roads beyond are full of pretty B&Bs. Most of the cheap motels are predictably scattered along the roads into town. Reservations can be made through the Information Centre at T1800-6633883.

Sleeping
■ *on maps,*
pages 124 & 127

Victoria has a good range of accommodation options, and for once the choice stretches beyond chain hotels and motels

Downtown LL-L *The Fairmont Empress*, 721 Government St, T3848111, www.fairmont.com If you want to feel like royalty and expense is no issue, this is the place. As well as several restaurants and tea rooms, there is a health club and spa. **L** *The Magnolia*, 623 Courtenay St, T3810999, www.magnoliahotel.com Another plush option with classic decor and its own spa. Some rooms have harbour views. Continental breakfast included. **L-A** *Spinnakers*, 308 Catherine St, T3842739. 9 beautiful big rooms in a heritage home with en suite baths and private entrance. Breakfast included. **L-A** *Swans Suite Hotel*, 506 Pandora Av, T3613310, www.swanshotel.com Huge, very stylish suites built of brick and wood with high ceilings and lots of great art. Excellent value. Highly recommended. Superb pub and restaurant downstairs.

　　C *Agra House*, 679 Herald St, T3801099. Plain but decent rooms in a handy, central location by the tiny *Taj Mahal* restaurant. **C** *Bedford Regency*, 1140 Government St, T3846835. Smallish rooms in a fancy-looking building. Cheaper units are good value. **C** *Strathcona Hotel*, 919 Douglas St, T3837137. Standard rooms but good value, and a great location. **C** *Travellers' Inn*, 8 locations, the most convenient being 1961 Douglas St, T9531000 and 1850 Douglas St, T3811000. Rooms are pretty standard and not the amazing deal they would have you believe, but at least you're guaranteed to get one. Free shuttle from ferries.

　　D *Daffodil Inn*, 680 Garbally Rd, T3868351. Probably the best of the super-cheap motels. Fairly close to town, big rooms, kitchenettes, dated decor. **E** *Hostelling International Victoria*, 516 Yates St, T3853232, victoria@hihostels.bc.ca Quiet, professional hostel in a nice big building with high ceilings. Very convenient location Downtown. Private rooms $4 extra, laundry, big kitchen, common room, lockers, etc. **E** *Ocean Island Backpackers Inn*, 791 Pandora Av, T3851788, www.oceanisland.com More rough and ready, geared to young travellers, with pub crawls arranged, etc. Fairly central location. Shared common room, café and kitchen. Dorms and private rooms.

South of Inner Harbour LL-L *The Gatsby Mansion*, 309 Belleville St, T3889191, www.bellevillepark.com Big, fancy Victorian house on the harbour. Martini lounge, restaurant, breakfast, canopy beds, etc. **LL-B** *Dashwood Manor*, 1 Cook St, T3855517, www.dashwoodmanor.com A broad variety of elegant Victorian rooms, some with balcony, jacuzzi or ocean views. Breakfast and evening cheese and wine. All rooms have en suite baths and kitchens, cheaper ones being very good value. **L** *Abigail's Hotel*, 906 McClure St, T3885363, www.abigailshotel.com Small but very posh, 5-star English-style establishment in a heritage Tudor-style building. Breakfast included. **L-A** *Holland House Inn*, 595 Michigan St, T3846644. 17 B&B rooms with balconies, some with fireplace and 4-poster bed. Full breakfast.

　　B *Birdcage Walk Guest House*, 505 Government St, T3890804. En suite rooms with kitchens in a heritage home. Good location. Breakfast included. **B** *Helm's Inn*, 600 Douglas St, T3855767, www.helmsinn.com Good location and price. Reasonable rooms. Continental breakfast. **B** *James Bay Inn*, 270 Government St, T3847151. Rather plain rooms in a historic building. **B** *Surf Motel*, 290 Dallas Rd, T3863309. Old fashioned but right on the ocean. **B-C** *Admiral Motel*, 257 Belleville St, T3886267, www.admiral.bc.ca Most reasonably priced on the Inner Harbour. Breakfast included.

　　C *Cherry Bank Hotel*, 825 Burdett Av, T3855380. Quirky, eccentric warren of a place. Comfy rooms, some with shared bath. Full breakfast included. **C** *Craigmyle B&B Inn*,

1037 Craigdarroch Rd, next to the castle, T5955411. Pleasant B&B in Rockland. 17 units, all with private bath. Full breakfast. **C** *Palace on Dallas B&B*, 1482 Dallas Rd, T3619551. One of the few right on the ocean. Shared bath.

Camping All campgrounds are some distance from town. **F** *Goldstream Provincial Park*, Sooke Lake Rd at southern end of the park, 19 km north on Hwy 1, T3874363. 150 decent sites among the trees. **F** *Island View Beach RV/Tent Park*, Homathko Rd, T6520548, in Saanich, handy for the Butchart Gardens. Beach, showers. **F** *McDonald Provincial Park*, McDonald Park Rd off Hwy 17 near Swartz Bay, T3912300. 49 nice sites, very convenient for late ferry in or early ferry out. **F** *Sidney Spit Provincial Marine Park*, T4741336. Take a ferry from Sidney at the end of Beacon Av (the main drag), $10.75 return for the ferry, leaves on the hour every hour. Great swimming, white sand beaches, bird-watchers' paradise, tent camping. No campfires or biking. **F** *Thetis Lake*, 1938 W Park Lane, T4783845. Closest to town (10 km). Showers, laundry, beach, good swimming.

Eating
● *on maps,*
pages 124 & 127

Expensive *Herald St Caffe*, 546 Herald St, T3811441. Long-established favourite with locals. Creative gourmet food using fresh local ingredients in pleasantly busy, unpretentious surroundings. Great wine list. *Restaurant Matisse*, 512 Yates St, T4800883. High-class French cuisine in elegant, romantic surroundings. From 1730 Wed-Sun. *Wild Saffron*, 1605 Store St, T3613150. Small but mouth-watering menu, combining West Coast and French cuisines. Simple but classy decor with lots of local art. Extensive wine list. Dinner only.

Mid-range *Ferris' Oyster Bar and Grill*, 536 Yates St, T3601824. Small and incredibly popular, with a great atmosphere, excellent food that concentrates on seafood, and reasonable prices. Highly recommended. Try their baked oyster platter. *Il Terrazzo*, 555 Johnson St, T3610028, www.ilterrazzo.com Authentic Italian food cooked in a wood oven. Huge menu and romantic atmosphere. *Lotus Pond Vegetarian*, 617 Johnson St, T3809293. One of many Chinese restaurants, but 100% vegan. *Pagliacci's*, 1011 Broad St, T3861662. Dark interior with a musical theme and frequent live music. Very intimate and usually packed. Italian food, wine, and great cheese-cake. *Re-bar*, 50 Bastion Sq, T3602401. Funky, colourful and popular old favourite, serving a small menu of mainly vegetarian international dishes, such as curry, enchiladas, potstickers and lots of salads. There's also a fresh juice bar. *Siam Thai Restaurant*, 512 Fort St, T3839911. Stylish brick and wood interior, broad menu with surprisingly moderate prices. *Spice Jammer*, 852 Fort St, T4801055. The best of a few places for East Indian food. *Spinnakers Brewpub*, 308 Catherine St, across the Johnson St Bridge or take the harbour ferry, T3862739. The menu in this exceptional pub is predictable with the likes of wood-oven pizza and burgers, but exceptional because the freshest local ingredients are used, and everything's prepared from scratch. Great breakfast option, excellent beer. Very popular, reservation recommended. *The Tapas Bar*, 620 Trounce Alley, T3830013. A broad selection of mouth-watering tapas served in a colourful Mediterranean ambience featuring lots of art. Pleasant outdoor seating away from the traffic. Popular and recommended. *Willie's Bakery*, 537 Johnson St, T3818414. Great baking and creative breakfasts for those who take the day's first meal seriously. Wonderful garden patio and organic coffee.

Cheap For cheaper food of all descriptions, walk a block east of Douglas to Blanshard. Or there are a predictably large number of Chinese restaurants around Fisgard St, most offering good value lunch options. *Italian Food Imports*, 1114 Blanshard. Great deli with cheap sandwiches to go. *Sam's Deli*, 805 Government St, is the best option for takeaway food. Big sandwiches. *Valentino's*, 762 Broughton St. A tiny place with great, cheap breakfasts and homemade pasta. *Victoria BBQ House*, 1714 Government St. Excellent, fresh Chinese buns and BBQ pork by the pound.

Bean Around the World, 533 Fisgard St. Good but expensive coffee. *Demitasse Cafe*, **Cafés**
1320 Blanshard. Best coffee in town, good lunch menu. *Torrefazione Italia Inc*, 1234
Government St, T9207203. Great coffee, and a nice place to hang out, with magazines
and papers to browse.

The Cambie, 856 Esquimalt Rd in the *Esquimalt Inn*. Unpretentious pub, typical of the **Bars**
chain. Good value beer and food. Varied entertainment. *Darcy's Pub*, 1127 Wharf St.
Classic pub with an attractive interior. Lots of space and a good selection of beer, much
of it locally brewed. *Harbour Canoe Club*, 450 Swift St, T3611940. Wonderful reclaimed
industrial warehouse with big wooden beams. Huge patio in the summer overlooking
the ocean, live music at weekends, and a moderate menu. *Hugo's Brewhouse*, at the
Magnolia Hotel, 625 Courtney St, T9204844. Dark, somewhat industrial interior, very
hip and popular. Clientele and mood changes throughout the day, turning into a
thumping nightclub at 2200 playing mainly house music. *Lucky Bar*, 517 Yates St,
T3825825. see Live music, below. *Spinnakers Brewpub*, see Eating, above. *Steamers*,
570 Yates St. Popular student hang-out. The place to go shoot some pool. *Suze*, 515
Yates St, T3832829. Very hip, dark and funky Martini bar with some outdoor seating.
Small creative menu with international influence. *Swans Pub*, 506 Pandora Av,
T3613310. A magnificent establishment. Best of the brewpubs with a great selection of
quality ales, a roomy yet cosy atmosphere, and above all one of the best collections of
West Coast aboriginal art you'll see anywhere.

Cinema *Capitol 6*, 805 Yates St and Blanshard, T3846811. **Entertainment**
Box office for any
event, T3866121

Clubs Visit www.clubvibes.com for a full run-down. *Boom Boom Room*, 1208 Wharf
St. Young, party atmosphere. *Diablos*, 1601 Store St. Varied music. Hip hop on Sat is a
popular favourite. *Eleven Stones*, 751 View St. Posh and elegant club, attracting a
trendy, beautiful crowd. *Evolution*, 502 Discovery St, T3883000. The only place for
alternative sounds. Small, energetic, unpretentious venue for hard-edged and alternative music. Drink specials most nights. *Hugo's*, see Bars, above. *Hush*, 1325 Government St, T3850566. Gay-friendly club, small and friendly. Gets some top DJs playing
mostly house. *Sugar*, 858 Yates St, T9209950. Probably the best club in town. Open
Thu-Sat, but you'll have to queue. Varied music, good lights and lasers.

Galleries *Open Space*, 510 Fort St. Non-commercial gallery exhibiting local artists.
Fran Willis Gallery, 200-1619 Store St. Some wonderful, whimsical local art.

Live Music *Royal Theatre*, 805 Broughton St, T3866121. With over 1,400 seats, this
attractive 1913 heritage building is Victoria's major music venue, hosting the Symphony Orchestra, Pacific Opera, major plays, dance, and most big visiting names of all
genres. *Lucky Bar*, 517 Yates, T3825825. Trendy, wacky little bar with live music nightly,
usually very good and packed to the gills.

Theatre *Belfry Theatre*, 1291 Gladstone, T3856815, www.belfry.bc.ca *McPherson*
Playhouse, 3 Centennial Square, Government/Victoria, T3866121. Open since 1914, a
delightful venue for films, dance, music and a gallery showing local visual art.

*JazzFest International,*T3884233, www.vicjazz.bc.ca, is a 10-day event at the end of **Festivals**
Jun, with jazz, blues and world beat occupying 12 stages around town. *FolkFest* in Jul,
www.icavictoria.or/folkfest, T3884728, occupies the Inner Harbour and Market Square
with 9 days of performing arts, wonderful food, arts and crafts, fireworks, and a 3
night-long world beat rave. Also in Jul for one weekend is the *Rootsfest Music Festival*
at Royal Roads University, 2005 Sooke Rd, T3863655, www.rootsfest.com The *Victoria*

Vancouver Island

Shakespeare Festival has performances throughout **Jul** and **Aug** at the Heritage Theatre, St Ann's Academy, 835 Humboldt St, T3600234, www.islandnet.com/~tinconnu, $14, $12 seniors, $10 children. The *Victoria Fringe Theatre Festival*, T3832664, www.victoriafringe.com, in **Aug** is the event for which Victoria is most famous, with countless venues staging all manner of shows from noon to midnight for 11 days. $5 for membership, $8 for indoor shows.

Shopping Downtown is the place for shopping, with most of the key chain and fashion stores found in the *Eaton Centre*, a whole block between Government and Douglas, Fort and View, and *Mayfair Shopping Centre*, between Douglas, Blanshard and Finlayson. Fort St between Douglas and Linden is known as **Antique Row**. Arguably Canada's most gorgeous **book store** is *Munro's* at 1108 Government St, T3822464. The 7½-m coffered ceiling, stained-glass windows, wall-hangings and well-chosen art create an environment perfect for browsing. **Johnson St** is the place for used books and CD's. *Renaissance Books* at 579 has a good if pricey selection. **Pandora** is the best bet for more off-beat and funky **clothes**. For **First Nations art and crafts**, head straight to *Hill's Native Art* at 1008 Government St, T3853911, whose wide selection of masks, carvings and jewellery are the real thing rather than the usual mass-produced rubbish. For gift ideas, try **Market Square**, on Store between Johnson and Pandora. This very attractive brick building and courtyard is a lovely place to stroll, though most of the stores tend to be bland or tacky. Government St has the monopoly on **souvenirs**, but they tend to be horribly touristy. *Sports Traders*, 508 Victoria St, has a giant selection of used **sporting equipment**. *The Wine Barrel*, 644 Broughton St, carries only BC **wines**, as well as a wealth of information on them.

Sports The Outdoor Recreation map ($6.50) published by Davenport is well worth picking up. It covers biking, hiking, kayaking and camping for south/central Vancouver Island. To rent just about anything, including skis, bikes, camping equipment, kayaks and surfboards go to *Sports Rent*, 611 Discovery St, T3857368. Victoria is famous for its **biking**, with the **Galloping Goose** among other trails, and several off-road mountain bike areas. For trail information, call T5984556, www.cyclingvictoria.com Pick up a map at bike stores ($3). For rentals there's *Cycle Victoria Rentals*, 950 Wharf, T3852453; *Fort Street Cycle*, 1025 Fort St, T3846665; *Chain Chain Chain*, 1410 Broad St, T3851739. **Diving** can be arranged through *Ogden Point Dive Centre*, 199 Dallas Rd, T3809119, www.divevictoria.com For fishing contact *Adam's Fishing Charters*, 19 Lotus St, T3702326. Close to town are some highly scenic **golf** courses. *Olympic View* , at 643 Latoria Rd, T4743673, has 18 holes, 12 lakes and 2 waterfalls; *Cordova Bay*, T6584444, has 18 holes overlooking the ocean and Gulf Islands. *Harbour Rentals*, 450 Swift St, below the *Harbour Canoe Club*, rents **kayaks**, **canoes** or **rowing boats** for exploring the Inner Harbour and Gorge Harbour. *Ocean River Sports*, T3613536, is a more serious kayak rental and tour operation. **Swimming** *Crystal Pool*, 2275 Quadra St, T3610732.

Tour operators **Bus and carriage** *Enchanted Tours*, T4753396, run tours up to 5½ hrs in a small a/c bus. *Gray Line*, 700 Douglas, T3886539, and *Royal Blue Line*, Belleville St, in front of the Coho ferry terminal, T3602249, www.royalbluelinetours.com, both use double-deckers imported from England for their narrated tours of town. A few companies offer horse and carriage tours: *Black Beauty Carriage Tours*, 180 Goward Rd, T3611220; *Tally Ho Horse Drawn Tours*, Menzies/Belleview, T3835067, and *Victoria Carriage Tours*, 251, Superior St, T3832207.

Cycle *Cycle Treks*, T3862277, 450 Swift St, run cycle tours of Victoria, the Gulf Islands and Vancouver Island.

Diving *Ogden Point Diving Centre*, T3809119, 199 Dallas Rd. Tours, sales, rentals, boat charters.

Ferry *Victoria Harbour Ferry*, 4530 Markham St, T7080201, run regular 45-min narrated harbour tours for $12, $6 concessions, and 50-min narrated gorge tours for $14, $7 concessions.

Garden *Victorian Garden Tours*, 2-145 Niagara St, T3802797, www.victoriagarden tours.com, run narrated tours of private and public gardens in a 6-person van.

Ghost *Ghostly Walks*, 634 Battery St, T3846698, depart 1930 nightly from the Information Centre.

Sport and adventure *Island Adventure Tours*, 1032 Oliphant St, T8127103, offer hiking, kayaking and cultural tours with a First Nations perspective. Also along the inner harbour are *Eagle Wing*, T3919337, and *Springtide*, T8836722, www.springtidecharters.com, who run biking, sailing and hiking tours, including a half-day cycling tour of the city for $65. For canoe and kayak tours, try *Vancouver Island Canoe and Kayak Centre*, 575 Pembroke, T3619365. *Nature Calls Eco-tours*, 12 Falstaff Place, T1877-3614453, also organize hiking trips.

Train *Pacific Wilderness Railway*, 450 Pandora St at the *Via Rail* station, T3818600, www.pacificwildernessrailway.com, run a 2¼-hr round-trip to the top of the **Malahat Mountain** in a vintage mid-20th-century railcar, with trestles, tunnels and views of Mt Baker. Leaves daily in summer at 0900, 1200, and 1500 ($29).

Walking tours *Architectural Institute of BC*, T1800-6670753, www.aibc.ca, run guided walking tours of Victoria with an architectural slant. There are 5 tours, 2 of which are available on any given day. They run Tue-Sat, Jul-Aug, leaving at 1130 and 1430 from the Community Arts Council Office, G6, 1001 Douglas St. They last 1½-2 hrs, $5. *Victoria's Best Walking Tours*, T4797610, 715 Eastridge Place, is another option.

Whale watching There are at least 10 whale-watching operators on the Inner Harbour alone. They all offer similar deals and trips last for 3 hrs, the real decision being whether you want to go in a zodiac, hard-shell, sail boat or cruise ship. Two possibilities are *Great Pacific Adventures*, T3862277, 811 Wharf St, and *Naturally Salty Excursions*, T3829599, 950 Wharf.

Local Bike: There are numerous bike lanes, including one to Swartz Bay ferry termi- **Transport** nal. The 60-km **Galloping Goose Trail** starts in View Royal, stretching to Sooke and beyond. Buses are bike equipped, and a very good bike map can be bought at any bike store for $3.

Bus: *BC Transit* operate a comprehensive bus service throughout the city. Single-fare tickets cost $1.75 ($1.10 concessions) or $2.50 ($1.75 concessions) for 2 zones. If taking more than 1 bus in the same direction, ask for a transfer at no extra charge. A sheet of 10 tickets costs $15 ($10 concessions). A day pass is $5.50 ($4 concessions). The low-floor buses are wheelchair accessible, but only from designated stops. To find out which, call T7277811. For general information, T3826161. *Laidlaw*(see below) run 9 daily buses to the Butchart and Butterfly Gardens.

Long-distance Air: Victoria International Airport, T9205611, www.victoriaair-port.com, is 20 km north of Downtown on Hwy 17. The Airport Shuttle Bus, T3862525, $13, leaves from Arrivals every 30 mins from 0700-2100, stopping at the major Downtown hotels. Otherwise you can try *AAA Airport Taxi*, T7278366, or *Empress Taxi*, T3812222, which should charge around $35 for the ride into town. *Air Canada*, *West Coast Air* and *Pacific Coastal* (see Directory, below, for telephone numbers) all have several daily flights for around $80 one-way from **Vancouver**. *Harbour Air Seaplanes*, T5375525, www.harbour-air.com, have regular flights daily from Vancouver, $93 one-way. This takes you from Downtown Vancouver (by Canada Place) to Victoria's Inner Harbour, saving at least an hour of bus time. It can be considerably cheaper to fly to **Nanaimo**, 113 km to the north.

Vancouver Island

Vancouver Island

Bus: *Laidlaw Coach Lines*, T1800-3180818, www.grayline.ca, run 6 daily buses north to Nanaimo, from where 2 services run to Tofino and 5 to Campbell River. Fares follow a zone system, at $2.75 per zone. To **Nanaimo** is 7 zones, to **Campbell River** is 16. *Pacific Coach Lines*, T6628074, operate a service to **Vancouver**, leaving Victoria bus station daily every 2 hrs 0600-1800; leaving Vancouver bus station and airport every 2 hrs 0545-1945. $27 one-way.

Ferry: The **BC Ferry** terminal, T3863431, www.bcferries.com, is in Swartz Bay, 40 km away at the north end of Saanich Peninsula. Services run to Tsawwassen (for **Vancouver**) and the **Southern Gulf Islands**. Bus No 70 leaves frequently for Douglas St ($2.50). There is also a **bike trail** into town. Ferries between Swartz Bay and Tsawwassen leave every other hour, 0700-2100 or hourly at peak times. $9.50 single, $34 with vehicle. Several daily ferries run from Brentwood Bay on the Saanich Penin-sula to **Mill Bay** across the inlet, $4.25, $15.25 with vehicle. **From the US** *MV Coho*, T3862202, from Port Angeles to the Inner Harbour, US$8, $30 with vehicle; *Victoria Clipper*, T3828100, from Seattle to the Inner Harbour, US$75; *Washington State Ferries*, T3811551, Anacortes (San Juan Island) to Sidney, US$11, $29.75 with vehicle.

Train: The *Via Rail* station, T1800-5618630, www.viarail.ca, is at 450 Pandora, right on the ocean front. The *Malahat* service leaves daily at 0815, more often in summer, running as far north as **Courtenay** with several stops on the way including **Chemainus** and **Nanaimo**, and on-off privileges. $41 one-way, $54 return with 7 days' notice.

Directory   **Airline offices** *Air Canada*, T3609074. *West Coast Air*, T3884521 *Pacific Coastal*, T6556411. **Communications** Internet: *Peacock Billiards/Cyber Cafe*, 834 Johnson St, open until late; or library. **Canada Post**: 714 Yates, T9531352. **Gay and lesbian** Vic-toria has an active but discreet gay scene. Best information resource is www.gayvictoria.com **Laundry** *The Laundry*, 1769 Fort St. *Maytag Homestyle Laundry*, 1309 Cook St. **Library** *Greater Victoria Public Library*, 735 Broughton St. **Medical services** *Royal Jubilee Hospital*, 1900 Fort St, T3708000; *Mayfair Walk-In Clinic*, 3147 Douglas St, T3839898; *East-West Health Centre*, 626 Courtenay St, T3844350. **Useful addresses** Police, T911 emergency, T9957654 otherwise. **Ambu-lance**, T7272400.

Victoria to Port Renfrew

Sooke

Phone code: 250
Colour map 1, grid C3   A short 30-km hop west from Victoria, easily reached by City Bus No 61 or the Galloping Goose bicycle trail, Sooke distinguishes itself from most Vancou-ver Island villages in three clear ways: it has an artist's community to challenge anything on the Gulf Islands; the best collection of first-class, good-value B&Bs anywhere; and a few excellent restaurants. Many visitors drive out from Victoria for the food alone. For a full list of artist's studios pick up the *Art Map* from the **Visitor Information Centre**. They also have extensive pictures of local accommodation. ■ *Summer 0900-1800 daily, winter Tue-Sun 0900-1700, closed Mon. 2070 Phillips Rd, T6426351, www.sooke.org*

Excursions   On a warm summer day, you'd be mad not to pay a visit to **Sooke Potholes Park**, north of town at the end of Sooke River Road. It's a magical spot with natural swimming pools carved out of rock, and mellow waterfalls that have caves hidden behind them. Above is a partially built 'castle', an abandoned project turned folly, with some interesting architectural features such as giant wooden beams. Fun to explore, it also offers some fine views.

East of Sooke, Gillespie Road leads south from Highway 14 to a peninsula that contains the wonderful and surprisingly underused **East Sooke Regional Park**, a little pocket of wilderness packed full of hiking trails and viewpoints. The **Coast Trail** is an excellent one-day hike that stretches 10 km between trailheads at Pike Road and Aylard Farm. With jagged cliffs, windswept bluffs and beautiful, unspoilt rainforest, this trail is in good condition and compares favourably with the Juan de Fuca trail (see below). Allow at least six hours. Beechey Head is a favourite spot for spotting turkey vultures or watching the annual hawk migration at the end of September.

Sleeping

Most B&Bs are luxurious, with big rooms, wooden furniture, high ceilings and views. Best value is **B** *Olympus Resort*, fairly central at 3018 Menzer Rd, T6426310, www.sookeresort.com 4 rooms with double beds. Right on the ocean with hot tub on a deck. The cheap option is **D** *Heron House*, 1994 Kaltasin Rd, T6423366. **E** *Pacific Trails Hostel*, 8959 West Coast Rd, T6427007, www.pacifictrailshostel.com Dorm and private rooms, kitchen, laundry, kayaking, surfing and whale-watching tours. **Camping F** *Sooke River Flats Campsite*, beside the Visitor Information Centre. Basic but handy.

Eating

Expensive *Sooke Harbour House*, 1528 Whiffen Spit Rd, T6423421, www.sookeharbourhouse.com A popular outing for Victorians, and frequently voted one of the best restaurants in BC. Casually classy with ocean views, a sophisticated menu that changes daily, and a great wine list. The emphasis is on fresh seafood, with herbs and vegetables from their own garden. They also have some excessively opulent and very expensive lodging.

Mid-range *Cove Point*, Hwy 14 east of town, T6426671. The only reasonable place to eat that's on the water. Seafood and steak. *Mom's*, unmissable in the very centre of town. The epitome of a diner with grouchy waitresses, booths, cheap breakfast, the whole bit. A local institution. *17 Mile Pub*, 9 km east on the highway. English-style pub in a historic building, with a good selection of beer and food. **Cheap** *The Fish Trap*, on the highway in town, beside the *PetroCan*. The choice place for fish and chips.

West of Sooke

Between Sooke and Port Renfrew the highway never strays far from the coast, which is dotted with a string of deserted, surf-beaten beaches looking out over the Juan de Fuca Strait that separates Vancouver Island from Washington.

Sleeping and eating AL-B *Point No Point*, 23 km west of Sooke, has decent cabins and suites on a long private beach, and a well-regarded restaurant (mid-range) serving lunch, English tea and dinner. **Jordan River**, 36 km west of Sooke, has a free but basic campground right on the water, and *Shakies*, a seriously cheap take-out burger shack with picnic tables overlooking the ocean. Breakfast, fish and chips, shrimp and oysters. **Camping F** *French Beach Provincial Park*, 20 km west of Sooke, has a nice campground with wooded sites and a mile-long sand and gravel beach.

Juan de Fuca Provincial Park

Colour map 1, grid C3

Just to the west, the trail and sand of **China Beach** mark the beginning of the provincial park, which protects several long sandy beaches and a strip of coastal rainforest, all of it connected by the **Juan de Fuca Marine Trail**. This 47-km wilderness route opened in 1995 to provide an alternative to the over-burdened West Coast Trail. A guidebook to the trail is available from the Sooke Information Centre ($13). Unlike the West Coast Trail, there is no fee or registration programme, nor do you have to walk the whole thing. Four trailheads along the highway provide access: from east to west, China Beach, Sombrio Beach, Parkinson Creek and Botanical Beach. **Mystic Beach**, just west of China Beach, has a 45-minute hike through rainforest and over a suspension bridge to good sand, a waterfall and some shallow caves. **Sombrio Beach** is the best point for surfing while **Botanical Beach** is a great place for exploring tidal pools.

Camping Wilderness camping is allowed at **Mystic**, **Bear**, **China** and **Sombrio** beaches, or in the forest at **Little Kuitche Creek** and **Payzant Creek**. The fee of $5 per person per night is payable at trailheads. Vehicle camping is available at all trailheads but Botanical Beach. More information from *BC Parks*, T3912300, who publish a useful leaflet/map (free). Be aware that wood ticks exist in this region, most prevalent between Mar and Jun.

Transport The *Juan de Fuca Trail Shuttle Bus*, T4778700, runs from Victoria, stopping at Sooke and every trailhead. Daily at 0650 from the bus station at 700 Douglas St. Return leaves Port Renfrew at 1615. $30-35 one-way. Shuttles between trailheads charge $15, flag them down. Reservations are recommended.

Port Renfrew There's little reason to visit this logging and fishing village other than to start or finish the Juan de Fuca Trail (see above) at Botannical Beach 6 km to the south, or the **West Coast Trail** (see page 166). This starts across a narrow inlet at Gordon River, which also has an **Information Centre**. As well as the Juan de Fuca Trail Shuttle Bus (see above) there is also a service to Bamfield at 0900 ($50), for hikers who need to get back to their vehicles. The village has little of interest except Canada's tallest Douglas fir tree (73.5 m). There's a general store with limited camping gear, plus a pub and a couple of basic restaurants. Stock up on supplies in Victoria. Many forestry recreation sites, plus a few campgrounds, are dotted along a network of logging roads to the north. Ask at the Gordon River Information Centre. Logging roads also lead north to Cowichan Lake, a rough route that may appeal to those who have come from Victoria and don't want to retrace their steps.

Sleeping C *Arbutus Beach Lodge*, 5 Queesto Dr, T6475458. B&B with 5 en suite rooms and hot tub. C *Trailhead Resort*, Parkinson Rd, T6475468. Large rooms with kitchens, sauna, deck, and walk-in tent camping for $5 per person. E *Port Renfrew RV Park and Marina*, Gordon River Rd, north end, T4783674. Large campground, with separate tenting area across bridge.

Carmanah Walbran Provincial Park Along with those in Clayoquot Sound around Tofino, the trees in this park to the west of Port Renfrew are among the world's tallest, with some spruce reaching 97 m. There was an uproar when logging companies tried to chop them down. The park is accessible to vehicles via logging roads from Cowichan Lake.

Cowichan Valley

Phone code: 250
Colour map 1, grid C3

It's easy to get lost; pick up a Cowichan Tourism Association map in Mill Bay or Victoria

Driving north from Victoria to Nanaimo, the main chance of respite from the busy highway, besides a walk in Goldstream Provincial Park, is provided by the broad Cowichan Valley. Winding country roads weave through the fertile landscape, leading to pretty little villages such as Cowichan Bay, and to a number of wineries. Duncan is the region's main town, and renowned for its large collection of totem poles. Lake Cowichan to the west offers good fishing, water sports and several cheap campgrounds, but the area's attractions are overrated. Far more appealing is Chemainus, a charming if touristy village, famous for its murals by local artists.

If a tour of wineries appeals, the greatest concentration on Vancouver Island is around Cobble Hill (though the wine cannot compare with that produced in the Okanagan). Don't be tempted to check out nearby Shawnigan Lake. The village is pleasant, but the lake itself is entirely surrounded by holiday homes belonging to wealthy Victorians. A better detour is east of the highway down Cherry Point Road. At No 840 is *Cherry Point Winery* where you can stop in for a tasting at any time. The perfect complement is *Abbott's Choice Fine Cheeses* at 1282, T7150563, with a number of different cheeses from goat to Camembert.

Cobble Hill

Cherry Point Road eventually gets you to Cowichan Bay, the prettiest of many coastal villages, where all the buildings along the water are built on stilts. The best time to visit is the first weekend in August, during the second largest regatta on Canada's West Coast. Otherwise there's not much to do, though you could take a sailing trip.

Cowichan Bay

Sleeping and eating The obvious place to stay is the reasonable **C** *Wessex Inn*, 1846 Cowichan Bay Rd, T7484214. Nice rooms with kitchenette, balcony and sea view. For eating, *Bluenose*, situated on the waterfront, is half expensive fancy seafood restaurant and half cheap diner. The *Masthead Restaurant* is a casual mid-range seafood joint with great views.

Sports *Great Northwestern Adventure Co*, T7487374, www.great-northwestern.com for sailing trips.

The epithet 'City of Totems' gives away the only real reason for stopping in Duncan. There are about 80 poles, mostly Downtown or along the highway. Pick up a map from the helpful **Visitor Information Centre**, next to *Overwaitea* on the highway, T7464636, www.duncancc.bc.ca A walking tour leaves from in front of the train station on Canada Avenue. ■ *Summer Tue-Sat 1000 and 1600. Free.* To find out more about the history and meaning of the totems, pick up *The Totem Walk of Duncan* ($5).

Duncan

Just to the south of town, at the **Quw'utsun Cultural Centre**, there's a collection of traditional buildings, but not much else to justify the entrance fee other than a mixed-media presentation that runs on the half hour. ■ *1000-1700. $10, $6 concessions.* About 1 km north on the highway, and similarly overpriced is the **BC Forest Discovery Centre**, a 40-ha site full of forestry artefacts, where you can learn everything about forests from the people who chop them down. ■ *$8. A narrow-gauge steam train takes people round from 1000-1730 in Jul and Aug.*

One of the best wineries in this area is **Vigneti Zanatta**, who also have a beautiful, very popular but expensive restaurant with excellent lunches and dinners, and a lovely garden patio. ■ *Mar-Dec Wed-Sun. 5039 Marshall Rd, Glenora, T7482338.* Glenora is also where the Cowichan River Trail starts (see below). If you're around in September, take in the **Festival of Wines**. ■ *$40 includes tasting, shuttle bus from Duncan and lunch, www.islandwineries.ca*

For nearby wineries pick up a map from the Information Centre

Sleeping, eating and entertainment B *Fairburn Farm Country Manor*, 3310 Jackson Rd, T7464637, www.fairburnfarm.bc.ca, is a 19th-century manor-house on 52 ha, with lots of animals and trails. 7 en suite rooms, library, lounge and patio. **A-B** *North Haven*, 1747 Herd Rd, T7464783, is a 1914 heritage home full of antiques with a parlour, library and 3 lovely en suite rooms. The best place for food is the mid-range *Arbutus*, 195 Kenneth St. For something lighter, there's *Island Bagel Company Bakery* on Station St. For coffee and nightly entertainment head for *Coffee on the Moon*, 1st St.

There are plenty of motels, mostly on the highway, and a couple of fine B&Bs

Vancouver Island

Cowichan Lake
Just north of Duncan, Highway 18 follows Cowichan River to this major lake and town of the same name. Both river and lake are well known for fishing, almost the sole draw of an area that has been decimated by logging and brags about having the most 'productive' forest in Canada. Among other minor attractions signed from the highway, **Cowichan River Provincial Park** contains **Skutz Falls** where salmon can be seen climbing the fish ladders. This is also one end of the **Cowichan River Footpath**, a 20-km trail that connects with Glenora just outside Duncan. The lake itself is pretty and warm, lined with cheap campgrounds (see below), though access is on a rough, active logging road of the kind best avoided.

At the western edge of the lake, **Nitinat** gives access to the halfway point of the **West Coast Trail** (see page 166), reached by the *West Coast Trail Shuttle Bus*, T4778700, from Port Renfrew or Bamfield. Rough logging roads from Nitinat also provide the only road access to the giant trees of Carmanah Walbran Provincial Park (see page 138). **Nitinat Lake** is a top windsurfing destination.

There's little to the town of Lake Cowichan, though it has all facilities for those who wish to stay

Sleeping C *Lake Cowichan Lodge*, 201 Cowichan Lake Rd, T7496717. The obvious choice, with reasonable kitchen suites. E *River's Edge Hikers Hostel*, 160 Cowichan Lake Rd, T7017616. A decent budget option. **Camping** At least 5 basic forestry-run campgrounds are scattered along the logging road that circles the lake, including F *Pine Point*, just beyond Youbou, which has some nice sites on the north shore. F *Gordon Bay Provincial Park*, 14 km south on South Shore Rd, is particularly popular thanks to its fine sandy beach. Hot showers and flush toilets. F *Cowichan River Provincial Park* has sites at *Skutz Falls* (see above) and a better campground on Riverbottom Rd, also signed from the highway.

Chemainus
Phone code: 250
Colour map 1, grid C3
Despite its banal hype and excessive popularity, Chemainus is the best reason to stop between Victoria and Nanaimo. It is essentially one big outdoor art gallery, famous for the 33 very good murals that depict the history of the town and area. The first was commissioned in 1983 as a brave attempt to attract tourism after the local sawmill went belly-up and threatened to sink the town with it. The ploy worked, with tourists, murals and artisans continuing to arrive long after the mill ironically reopened. Such success owes much to the fact that Chemainus is a charming little village in its own right. You can pick up a useful mural map for $1 at the friendly **Visitor Information Centre**, ■ *0900-1630 daily, closed weekends in winter. 9796 Willow St, T2463944, www.chemainus.bc.ca* Just outside, you can take a 45-minute **horsedrawn carriage** tour of town ($7).

A few murals are in the old, lower part of town, which is reminiscent of a traditional British village, quaint and sedate, but a little too twee for its own good. This is especially true of the many B&Bs, all full of doilies and frilly lace or adorned on the outside with fake turrets and the like. It's worth a wander, though, if only for the restaurants (see below). The ferry to **Thetis Island** leaves from here, though there's nothing to see there except a few hiking trails. The heart of the new town is Willow Street, with some nice gift shops such as *The Pottery Store*, with work by local artisans. Chemainus Road heads south from here through a number of small seaside villages including **Crofton**, terminus for the ferry to Salt Spring Island (see page 148). A nice place here for a pint and a meal is the *The Brass Bell Pub*. To the north of Chemainus, **Ladysmith** is also touted as a pretty heritage town, and it does have some fairly nice buildings, but frankly the hype is much ado about nothing.

As it leaves town, Chemainus Rd passes a string of old renovated mill houses, and the best places to stay. **C** *Olde Mill House*, 9712 Chemainus Rd, T4160049, www.oldemillhouse.ca 3 very nice, cosy rooms with great beds and en suite baths. Ask for the one with TV and its own private garden and deck. Almost next door is the eccentric *Old House of Many Colours*, for cheap but good homestyle food, all day breakfast, soups, bagels and coffee. **E** *Chemainus Hostel*, 9694 Chemainus Rd, T2462809, with standard dorms, kitchen, and bike rentals. **D** *Horseshoe Bay Inn*, 9567 Chemainus Rd, T4160411, is the best place for a drink, and has some surprisingly nice, good value rooms, some with clawfoot tub and king-size bed. **Camping F** *Bald Eagle Campground*, T2469457. A decent campground on a river 5 km south of town.

Mid-range *Hummingbird Tea House*, next door, T2462290, is similarly attractive if not so highly regarded locally. *The Waterford*, 9875 Maple St, T2461046. Crêpes for lunch, varied menu for dinner, good portions, pleasant interior and a lovely garden patio. The *Willow Street Café*, 9749 Willow St, is the best spot for a break in the new town, with coffee and snacks in a beautiful big house, and a nice patio.

Sleeping & eating
The best places to eat are in the old town

Nanaimo

More central than Victoria 113 km to the south, Vancouver Island's number two city has grown in importance as its main transport hub and service centre. Rapid expansion has sadly resulted in an endless and appalling fringe of malls, megastores and billboards that inspires most potential visitors to run away and bypass Nanaimo altogether. It comes as a surprise then that swaddled by this outer growth of crass and ugly urban sprawl is a small Downtown with a sense of history and a genuine, if slightly seedy, character. The warren of twisty streets around Church Street and Commercial Street is conveniently close to the ferry and train, and is packed with decent pubs, authentic diners, used book and music stores and art galleries. It's also adjacent to the scenic harbour, with the first real views of the mainland Coast Mountains for those heading north. There are some nice beaches and sea walks, as well as the usual watersports. It's not a place worth going out of your way for, but if circumstances demand a stay, it could be made worthwhile.

*Phone code: 250
Colour map 1, grid C3
Population: 73,000*

Vancouver Island

Ins and outs

Nanaimo-Collishaw **airport** is 15 km south of the city on Hwy 19. A shuttle bus runs regularly to Downtown. Seaplanes arrive at the Seaplane Terminal behind the Bastion. There are 5 separate ferry terminals in Nanaimo. Those from **Horseshoe Bay** arrive at **Departure Bay**, 2 km north of Downtown (Bus No 2 or *Seaporter* shuttle). Those from **Tsawwassen** arrive at the more inconvenient **Duke Point** to the south of town. *Seaporter* shuttle buses run Downtown. *Via Rail* run one **train** daily each way between **Victoria** and **Courtenay**. The station is on Selby St, walking distance from Downtown. The **bus** terminal is also a short walk from Downtown at Comox/Terminal, with regular services north, south and west with *Laidlaw*, and from Vancouver with *Greyhound*.

Getting there
For Transport details, see page 145

Nanaimo's Downtown is very small and easily explored on foot. City buses meet Downtown at Harbour Park Mall and go as far north as Qualicum Beach.

Getting around

The Tourist Information Centre is well-stocked but inconveniently situated far from Downtown at 2290 Bowen Rd. From Hwy 1, turn west onto Comox Road then follow signs. Jun-Sep 0800-1900 daily, winter Mon-Fri 0900-1700, Sat 1000-1600. T7561016, www.tourismnanaimo.com

Tourist information

Vancouver Island

History

Five bands of Salish natives originally occupied the area they called *Sney-ne-mous*, 'meeting place'. In 1852 they made the mistake of showing samples of the black rock that existed locally in staggering proportions to agents from Hudson's Bay Company (HBC) of all people. The white man then came in droves to exploit one of the greatest coal mines of all times, and a few of them became millionaires; notably Robert Dunsmuir (see page 130). Now that the mines are closed, the town depends on forestry, six deep-water docks, a busy port, and deep-sea fishing.

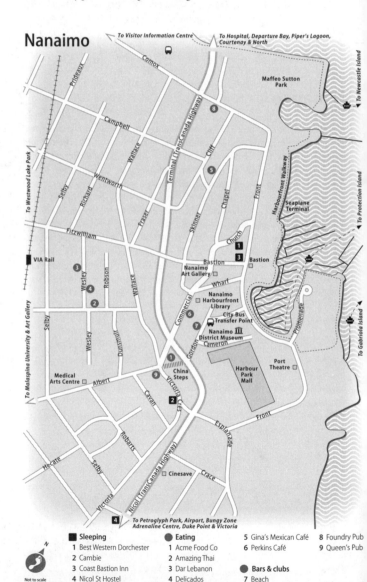

Nanaimo

■ Sleeping	● Eating	5 Gina's Mexican Café	8 Foundry Pub
1 Best Western Dorchester	1 Acme Food Co	6 Perkins Café	9 Queen's Pub
2 Cambie	2 Amazing Thai		
3 Coast Bastion Inn	3 Dar Lebanon	● Bars & clubs	
4 Nicol St Hostel	4 Delicados	7 Beach	

Not to scale

Sights

Nanaimo's sense of history is largely upheld by the centrally located **Bastion**, a squat, wood-plank building which is the oldest of its kind in the west. Constructed by the HBC a year after their 'discovery' of coal, its purpose was to keep the natives under control while their land got plundered. Sometimes the whole population of white folk hid out here till a period of unrest abated. In summer, a small **museum of HBC memorabilia** is open, and a ceremonial cannon fires at noon Monday-Saturday to the accompaniment of Scottish bagpipes and Highland dancing. ■ *Jun-Aug 1000-1700. By donation. 63 Front St.*

The nearby **Nanaimo District Museum**'s rather predictable reproductions of native dioramas, the old Chinatown, and a coal mine fall flat after the Royal BC Museum in Victoria. Its best feature, which can be seen for free, is the collection of petroglyph copies on the lawn at the back. Far more satisfying than the originals in the Petroglyph Park (see below). ■ *Daily 0900-1700, closed Sun and Mon in winter. $2, $0.75 concessions. 100 Cameron Rd, T7531821.* Also close by, and more worthwhile, is the **Nanaimo Art Gallery**, which showcases work by over 40 West Coast artists. ■ *Mon-Sat 1030-1730. By donation. 150 Commercial St, T7412214. There is another at Malaspina College, 900 5th St, T7558790.*

Petroglyph Park is a shoddy affair situated 3 km south on Highway 1. Traffic noise and signs of vandalism exacerbate the poor presentation of these sadly eroded works. There are castings of the originals, but fewer than at the museum (see above). Further south, and far more popular, is the **Bungee Zone Adrenaline Centre**, the first legal bungee jumping location in North America, and still one of the best and most professional. Jump 43 m from a bridge ($95), or go for one of the alternatives: a zip line ($50) or a giant swing that reaches speeds of up to 140 km per hour ($50). ■ *35 Nanaimo River Rd, T7167874, www.bungyzone.com For a pick-up from the Nanaimo ferry, call T1800-6687771. Camping and restaurant on site.*

Walks

Piper's Lagoon on Hammond Bay Road makes for a romantic evening stroll through Garry oaks along a rocky and grassy spit with mountain views. More conveniently central is the **Harbourfront walkway** which heads north for 4 km from the Departure Bay ferry, offering views and fresh air, plus cafés, restaurants and gift shops. **Westwood Lake Park** to the west of town is a wilder, less busy area with a 5½-km loop trail and good swimming.

Excursions

Newcastle Island

For trips to Gabriola Island, see page 155

Free of cars and inhabitants, the entirety of Newcastle Island has been designated a Provincial Park, with 18 km of maintained trails, including a 7½-km walk around the island. The highlight is **Saysetsen Village**, deserted by the Coast Salish in 1849, can be visited, but there's little to see. However, the park is currently administered by the local native band, who plan to develop this and other cultural sights over the next few years. Ask at the restored Pavilion Building, which provides food, equipment rentals and information. For good views head to the lookout at **Nares Point** on the island's northwest tip. There is also an excellent campground (see below). ■ *Getting there: ferries, T3912300, www.scenicferries.com, leave May-Sep only, every hour on the hour 1000-1900 from Maffeo-Sutton Park behind the Civic Centre. $5 one-way, bikes $2. The crossing takes 10 mins.*

Protection Island Protection Island is residential and far less interesting, but it does have (apparently) Canada's only floating pub, the *Dinghy Dock*. ■ *Getting there: ferries, T7538244, leave regularly from the Boat Basin behind the Harbour Park Mall. The crossing takes 10 mins.*

Essentials

Sleeping
■ *on map, page 142*

The best options for comfort and location are 2 chain hotels: **B** *Best Western Dorchester*, 70 Church St, T7546835. Rooms and suites with views. Restaurant. **B** *Coast Bastion Inn*, 11 Bastion St, T7536601. Ocean views, sauna, exercise room, restaurant and lounge.

The best mid-range options in town are all **B&Bs**: **B** *Long Lake B&B*, 240 Ferntree Pl, T7585010, www.lodgingnanaimo.com 3 en suite rooms with private entrance. Private beach on the lake close to town. Canoes. **C** *Pepper Muffin Country Inn*, 3718 Jingle Pot Rd, T7560473, www.peppermuffin.com 3 en suite rooms with private entrance in a farm setting. 10-min drive from town but will pick up from ferry. Lounge, decks, library, hot tub. **D** *Beach Estates Inn*, 800 Beach Dr, T7533597. Pleasant rooms with shared bath. Breakfast included. Short walk to Departure Bay Ferry. The **motels** in town are pretty standard, but the following are cheap and handy for the Departure Bay ferry: **D** *Bluebird Motel*, 995 Terminal Av, T7534151. **D** *Buccaneer Inn*, 1577 Stewart Av, T7531246. **D** *Departure Bay Motel*, 2011 Estevan Rd, Island Hwy N, T7542161.

There are 2 excellent hostels in town: **E** *The Cambie*, 63 Victoria Cres, T7545323. Single-sex dorms and some private en suite rooms. Small common kitchen and sitting area, great café and pub downstairs. Price includes breakfast and admission to weekend gigs. **E** *Nicol St Hostel*, 65 Nicol St, T7531188, www.nanaimohostel.com A first-class hostel with a variety of rooms, private or dorms, and tent sites (**F**), including all hostel amenities. Laundry, kitchen, common rooms, free internet, views, discounts for local businesses. **E** *Cosmic Cow*, 1922 Wilkinson Rd, T7547150. Inconvenient for Downtown but close to Duke Point ferry. Will pick up from bus or ferry if pre-arranged. Very nice rooms with twin beds in a farm setting. Bike rentals, laundry, internet, breakfast included.

Camping Apart from *Nicol St Hostel*, which has the most convenient tent sites (see above), the best spot is **F** *Newcastle Island Provincial Park*, T3912300. May-Sep only. 18 walk-in sites, first-come first-served. Showers and flush toilets. **F** *Living Forest Oceanside*, just before Duke Point at the end of Maki Rd, T7551755. Some sites with ocean views, showers. Buses on the highway, 500 m walk away.

Eating
● *on map, page 142*

Expensive *Mahle House*, Cedar/Hemer Rd, T7223621. Gourmet cuisine in a house setting. Ever-changing menu features venison, crab, and lamb, with emphasis on the sauce.

Mid-range *Acme Food Co*, 14 Commercial St, T7530042. Stylish with antique wood tables, brick walls, and high ceilings. International menu with a West Coast accent. Sushi bar in the back. Live music. *Amazing Thai*, 486 Franklyn St, T7547818. Authentic and very reasonable. *Bluenose Chowder House*, 1340 Stewart Av, T7546611. Best bet for seafood. Nice patio. *Dar Lebanon*, 347 Wesley St, T7559150. Delicious Middle-Eastern food served in an elegant Victorian house. Outdoor patio seating by a fountain. *Gina's Mexican Cafe*, 47 Skinner St, T7535411. Authentic Mexican food in suitably colourful surroundings.

Cheap *Delicados*, 358 Wesley St. Cheap Mexican, good salads. There are a couple of cheap and seedy diners on Church/Commercial St, but better is **Seriously cheap** *The Cambie*, 63 Victoria St. Bakery/café has excellent cakes and pastries, burger and pint for $5, cheap breakfast. The best place for **coffee** is the *Perkins Café* at 234 Commercial St.

Bars & clubs *The Cambie*, 63 Victoria St. Cheap, spit-and-sawdust boozer with live music on weekends ($3 cover). *Foundry Pub*, 125 Comox Rd, is a standard but decent pub. *Queen's Pub*,

34 Victoria Cres. Dark and slightly dingy, perfect for the nightly live music. *Longwood Brew Pub*, Turner Rd/Island Hwy to the north. Bad location but a nice pub. The 2 main nightclubs are: *The Beach*, 37 Gordon St; *Club Voodoo*, 1 Terminal Av.

Entertainment

Cinema *Avalon*, 6631 N Island Hwy, T3905021; *Cinesave*, Nicol St near Harbour Park. Cheap movies, not quite the latest releases; *Galaxy*, 4750 Rutherford Rd, T7298000. **Theatre** *Port Theatre*, 125 Front St, T7544555, www.porttheatre.nisa.com Outside Victoria, this is probably the best venue for plays and the performing arts. *Malaspina University College Theatre*, T7588522, also a venue for theatre and music (Bus No 15).

Festivals

Nanaimo Festival, late **May**-early **Jun** involves all manner of cultural events in and around the beautiful Malaspina College at 900 5th St. On the 3rd weekend of **Jul** is the 4-day *Marine Festival*, featuring music, fireworks on the harbour, and the famed World Championship Bathtub Race, when hopefuls compete for the coveted silver plunger trophy. The *Cadillac Van Isle 360° Yacht Race*, www.vanisle360.nisa.com, is a 2-week, 580-nautical mile race that begins and ends in Nanaimo. It happens every 2 years around **mid-Jun**, next in 2003.

Shopping

Arts and crafts *Hill's Native Art*, 76 Bastion St. Large selection of top-notch West Coast carvings and jewellery, as well as some Inuit art. *Artisans' Studio*, 70 Bastion St. Local artists' co-op. **Books** *Bygone Books*, 99 Commercial St. The best of many used book stores on this street, with a great selection including lots of Canadian fiction and non-fiction. **Maps** *Nanaimo Maps & Charts*, 8 Church St. A giant collection of nautical and topo maps. **Music** *Fascinating Rhythm*, 174 Commercial St. One of the best new and used CD stores in the West. Huge selection.

Sports

Several places around Nanaimo are recommended for **diving**, such as the sunken *HMCS Saskatchewan*, an artificial reef teeming with marine life. For information contact the *Nanaimo Diving Association*, 2290 Bowen Rd, T7292675, www.divebritishcolumbia.com For lessons, charters and guided dives, contact *Ocean Explorers Diving*, 1956 Zorki Rd, T7532055, www.oceanexplorersdiving.com The many little islands off the coast – with resident sealife such as octopus, seals and otters – also help make this a prime location for **sailing** and **kayaking**. *Seadog Kayaking & Sailing*, T4685778, www.seadog.bc.ca, provide lessons, tours and rentals for both. Skippered sailing charter is $70 per 2 hrs, $290 overnight. *The Kayak Shack*, T7533234, also arrange tours and lessons. For **bike** rentals go to *Chain Reaction*, 12 Lois Lane. *Nanaimo Leisure and Aquatic Centre*, 741 3rd St, has a good pool, plus sauna, hot tub and exercise room.

Transport

Local City buses: T3904531, www.rdn.ca.ca, all meet Downtown at Harbour Park Mall and go as far north as Qualicum Beach. **Taxis**: *AC Taxi*, T7531231. *Budget Car Rentals*, 17 Terminal Av, T7547368.

Long distance Air: Nanaimo-Collishaw airport, T2454191, 15 km south of the city on Hwy 19, has several flights daily from **Vancouver**. The *Nanaimo Airporter* shuttle bus, T7582133, runs frequently to town. *Harbour Air Seaplanes*, T5375525, operate regular flights from Vancouver Harbour to the Seaplane Terminal behind the Bastion. $49 one-way, 15 mins. Daily flights from Vancouver with *Canadian Western Airlines*, T2339292, are $90 one-way; *Air Canada*, T2457123, $80 one-way.

    Bus: The bus station is at 1 Terminal Av, walking distance from Downtown. *Laidlaw Coach Lines*, T7534371, www.grayline.ca, run 7 buses daily to **Victoria** ($22), 2 west to **Port Alberni** and **Tofino** (0830 and 1230), 5 north to **Campbell River**, of which the 0830 continues to **Port Hardy** and 4 to **Departure Bay**. *Greyhound*, T1800-2312222, www.greyhound.ca, run 8 daily buses to **Vancouver**, 2½ hrs.

Vancouver Island

Ferry: There are 5 ferry terminals in Nanaimo. *BC Ferries*, T1888-2233779, www.bc ferries.com operate the following services: to Vancouver's **Horseshoe Bay** from Departure Bay, 2 km north of Downtown. Every 2 hrs 0630-2100, $9.50 one-way, $43 with vehicle, crossing time 95 mins; to Vancouver's less convenient **Tsawwassen** from Duke Point, 12 km south. Every 2½ hrs 0515-2245, prices as above, crossing time 2 hrs; to **Gabriola Island** from Nanaimo Harbour behind the Harbour Park Mall Downtown. Roughly hourly 0615-2255, $5.25, $18.75 with vehicle, crossing time 20 mins. *Nanaimo Seaporter* shuttle bus, T7532118, connect the 3 terminals with Downtown, charging $15 to Duke Point, $6.50 to Departure Bay for 1 or 2 people. A new, passenger-only, high- speed ferry operated by *Harbour Lynx*, T7534443, takes you from Vancouver's waterfront *SeaBus* terminal to Nanaimo. Smaller ferries leave from behind the Bastion for **Protection Island**, and from Maffeo-Sutton Park to the north for **Newcastle Island** (see page 143).

Rail: *VIA Rail*, T1800-5618630, www.viarail.ca, run 1 train daily each to **Victoria** and **Courtenay**, more on weekends in the summer, $21 either way.

Directory **Communications** Internet: at library. **Canada Post**: Harbour Park Mall. **Laundry** *Boat Basin Laundry*, Harbour Park Mall. **Library** *Nanaimo Harbourfront Library*, 90 Commercial St. **Medical services** *Nanaimo General Hospital*, 1200 Dufferin Cres, T7542141. *Medical Arts Centre*, 350 Albert St, T7533431. **Useful addresses** Police, 303 Prideaux St, T7542345.

Beyond Just south of Parksville, some 30 km north of Nanaimo, a major parting of
Nanaimo roads occurs. The older and more scenic Coast Highway, 19A, winds its way through town then north via a series of bays and sleepy seaside villages. The Inland Island Highway 19 bypasses all of this and, with a dearth of scenic interest, caters to those whose just want to get north. Highway 4 branches immediately west from the latter towards Port Alberni, Tofino and the Pacific Rim National Park, passing a few diversions on the way.

Southern Gulf Islands

The clustered nature of the Southern Gulf Islands makes for excellent island-hopping, but their proximity to Vancouver and Victoria mean they are much busier than their northern cousins, especially at the peak of summer, when accommodation can get very tight.

Southern Gulf Islands

Strait of Georgia

Protection Island
Newcastle Island
Gabriola Island
Gabriola Village
Malaspina Gallery
Gabriola Museum
Departure Bay
Duke Point
Nanaimo

To Tsawwassen
Drumbed Provincial Park
Valdes Island
Dionisio Point Provincial Park
Bodega Ridge
Galiano Island
Montague Harbour Provincial Marine Park
St Mary Island
Thetis Island
Kuper Island
Stuart
Vesuvius Bay
Ganges
Long Harbour
Channel
Salt Spring Island
Mt Maxwell Provincial Park
Ladysmith
Chemainus
Crofton

Not to scale

■ **Sleeping**
1 Bedwell Harbour Island

The Gulf Islands

The Strait of Georgia between Vancouver Island and the mainland is dotted with an archipelago of islands of varying sizes. While each has its own inexpressible flavour, their common geographical location and relative isolation – two sometimes three steps removed from the mainland – have given the Gulf Islands a distinctive character which lends some validity to wild generalizations.

Time here moves at a pace that, by comparison, makes even Vancouver Island seem hectic and uptight. This laid-back spirit has attracted a rare mixture of bohemians, hippies, eccentrics, draft-dodgers, pot-growers and an inordinate number of writers and artists, including a few celebrities. To meet some local characters, just hang out for a while in one of the colourful pubs or cafés. Together with arts and crafts, there is an emphasis on health and whole foods, spirituality and healing, with an abundance of galleries and studios, spas

and retreats, and weekend markets stocked with organic local produce.

The islands provide a much better vantage point than Vancouver Island to appreciate the beauty of the Georgia Strait: the awesome Coast Mountains rising steeply behind forested islands and convoluted coastlines. Each seems to have at least one good hike leading up to a great viewpoint and usually there are bald eagles in residence. The mild climate here has coated the islands with lush vegetation that includes all kinds of trees, wild flowers and berry bushes. Even the beaches tend to be better and less crowded than the main island, and marine life is as prevalent as elsewhere on the West Coast. You can often gather the abundant oysters, clams and mussels freely, but beware the deadly red tide. Call T604-6662828 for information, or ask the locals. Note that throughout the islands the lack of drinking water remains a perennial problem.

Ins and outs

The Vancouver-Victoria ferry passes right through the middle of the islands, most of which are accessed by ferry from Tsawwassen (**Vancouver**), Swartz Bay (**Victoria**), as well as each other. The exception is Gabriola, a short hop from Nanaimo. *BC Ferry* schedules can be confusing and are subject to change, so phone ahead to check. Prices given are for 1 foot passenger/1 car and driver. If driving, reservations are a must in the summer. For information and reservations: T1888-7245223, www.bcferries. com *Seair*, T18004473247, operate scheduled flights from **Vancouver** to Ganges on Saltspring, around $70 one-way.

Getting there

The ultimate way to explore the islands, and the whole West Coast for that matter, is by **sailing-boat**, whole fleets of which tour the region throughout the long temperate season. Much more feasible for most people is the **kayak**, which allows even more freedom, and access to parts other travellers cannot reach. Failing that, **cycling** is a great way to get around. Traffic is comparatively light, and generally one windy road covers each island. They tend to be a bit hilly, though, so a certain fitness level is required, but it only costs

Getting around

$2 to take bikes on the ferry. Few of the islands have bus services, so **hitchhiking** is a way of life. If a car doesn't stop for you, it's usually a tourist.

Tourist information

Drinking water is scarce on the islands

Most beds on the islands are in B&Bs. In summer the islands are extremely busy, so accommodation can be difficult to find and reservations are recommended. Try the free service provided by ***Canadian Gulf Islands Reservations***, T1888-5392930, www.gulfislandreservations.com Some of the most scenic campgrounds in Western Canada are to be found on the islands. Combine this with the transport situation, and those on a tight budget can, for once in Canada, do very well. Check the *Gulf Islander* (available on the islands or ferry), www.gulfislands.net, to find out what's on.

Salt Spring Island

Phone code: 250
Colour map 1,
grid C4
Population: 10,000

Salt Spring is the busiest, biggest and most populated of the Gulf Islands, and the only one with a village that could be considered a town, the oddly named **Ganges**. There are more eating and drinking options here than elsewhere, and more chance of finding walk-in accommodation at any time of year. The pay-off is the loss of tranquility and quaintness, though these are easily found in other parts of this sheep-dotted island. The small but eager to please **Visitor Information Centre**, at 121 Lower Ganges Road, T5375252, is by the shopping centre car park. ■ *0900-1600 all year*. Also visit www.saltspringtoday.bc.ca

At the south end of the island, 9 km east of Fulford Harbour at the end of Beaver Point Road, is **Ruckle Provincial Park**, the largest and one of the nicest on the Gulf Islands. Trails here incorporate forest, 7 km of shoreline, farmland and historic buildings. There's a good chance of spotting marine life and birds, but the park's outstanding feature is its campground (see Sleeping, below). For some truly awe-inspiring views, head to the top of **Mount Maxwell Provincial Park**. There are some trails through big old trees, but the temptation is just to sit down and gawp. It's also a good place to experience the full power of the winds that can whistle down the strait. ■ *Getting there: just south of Ganges take Cranberry Rd west to Mt Maxwell Rd, then climb stiffly for 8 km.* Longer, more remote hikes lead up Mount Tuam and Mount Bruce, west of Fulford Bay. Swimming is good at **Vesuvius Bay**, or at **St Mary Lake** (north of Ganges) and **Cusheon Lake** (south) for fresh water.

Sleeping
■ *on map,*
page 149

Apart from a couple of standard motels, Salt Spring's beds are mostly in B&Bs, of which there are over 100. Check at the above websites or the Information Centre, which has a picture book to help you choose and will take reservations. St Mary Lake is surrounded by 'resorts', usually offering second-rate cabins.

A *Quarrystone House*, 1340 Sunset Dr, 6 km from Vesuvius Bay, T5375980, www.quarrystone.com 4 en suite rooms with ocean views, balconies, private entrance, hot tub. **A-B** *Green Acres Lakeside Cottage Resort*, 241 Langs Rd, T5372585, www.ultranatural.com One of the better options at St Mary Lake. **A-B** *Salt Spring Lodge*, 641 Fulford-Ganges Rd, T5379522, www.saltspringlodge.com 2 very attractive and spacious suites that could sleep 6, with kitchenettes and ocean views, plus one smaller double. **B** *Anchor Point B&B*, 150 Beddis Rd, 1 km south of Ganges, T5380110, www.anchorpointbb.com 3 well-appointed en suite rooms, with lounge, library, balcony and hot tub. Will pick up at ferry.

C *Beachcomber Motel*, 770 Vesuvius Bay Rd, T5375415. Standard but good value. Some rooms have ocean view, some have kitchenette. **C-D** *Wisteria Guest House*, 268 Park Dr, 10-min walk from Ganges, T5375899. 6 rooms with shared bath and lounge. Breakfast included. **D-E** *Salt Spring Island HI Hostel*, 640 Cusheon Lake Rd, T5374149.

Vancouver Island

Salt Spring Island

Ganges

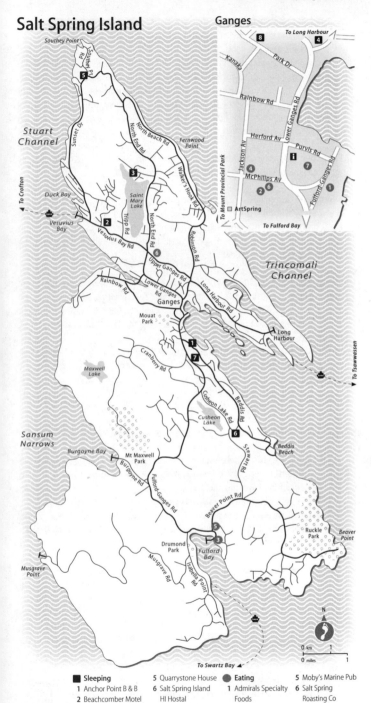

Vancouver Island

■ Sleeping
1 Anchor Point B & B
2 Beachcomber Motel
3 Green Acres Lakeside Cottage Resort
4 Harbour House

5 Quarrystone House
6 Salt Spring Island HI Hostal
7 Salt Spring Lodge
8 Wisteria Guest House

● Eating
1 Admirals Specialty Foods
2 Barb's Buns
3 Fulford Inn
4 House Piccolo

5 Moby's Marine Pub
6 Salt Spring Roasting Co
7 Tree House Café

Situated on 4 forested hectares, within walking distance of beaches and the lake, this very popular and friendly hostel has dorms and private rooms in a cedar lodge, plus 3 tepees and 2 small but delightful (and heavily booked) treehouses. Shared kitchen and living room. Bike and scooter hire. Open Mar-Oct. Getting there is the only problem.

Camping F *Ruckle Provincial Park*, 9 km east of Fulford Harbour at the end of Beaver Point Rd, T3912300. The 8 spots for RVs are nothing special, but those with a tent can walk in and claim one of the 70 sites dotted along the shore with exquisite views of Swanson Channel and many a passing sailing boat or ferry. One of the best camping experiences in Western Canada.

Eating

To meet some of the local characters, just hang out for a while in one of the colourful pubs or cafés

Expensive *House Piccolo Restaurant*, 108 Hereford Av, Ganges, T5381844. Highly regarded gourmet cuisine in casual but smart surroundings.

Mid-range *Fulford Inn*, at Fulford Harbour. Nice pub with rooftop patio overlooking ocean. *Moby's Marine Pub*, 124 Upper Ganges Rd, T5375559. A fine pub, popular with locals, and one of the more reliable bets for food. Try the teriyaki salmon burger. Also apparently the only place to experience locally brewed Gulf Island Brewery beers on tap. The Porter beer is excellent.

Cheap *Admirals Specialty Foods*, 146 Fulford-Ganges Rd, in town. Mostly sushi to go. *Bonnie's Buns*, off McPhillips Av, Ganges. Popular bakery with pizza, pastries and all sorts of delicious baking. *Tree House Café*, 106 Purvis Lane, Ganges, T5375379. Tiny but hugely likeable establishment with baking and coffee, outdoor seating, and live music most nights.

The island must be full of **coffee** junkies given the inordinate number of places selling decent java. The explanation is no doubt the quality of the beans roasted by the *Salt Spring Roasting Co*, T6532385, who also run two cafés: a nice local hang-out in Fulford Harbour with a patio, and the meeting-place of choice in *Ganges* at 109 McPhillips Av, with some decent baking and snacks, and good art on the walls.

Festivals *Festival of the Arts*, T5374167, in Jul is a month-long orgy of what the Gulf Islands do best.

Sports *Island Escapades*, 163 Fulford-Ganges Rd, T5372537, www.islandescapades.com Highly respected company for sailing, kayaking, hiking and climbing; rentals, lessons and tours. *Saltspring Kayaking*, 2923 Fulford-Ganges Rd, T6534222. Rentals of kayaks and bikes, tours and lessons. *Sea Otter Kayaking*, 149 Lower Ganges Rd, T5375678, www.seaotterkayaking.com Rentals and 3 tours a day. All have good reputations. **Frisbee golf** is popular at Mouat Provincial Park just opposite Ganges. **Scuba diving** is popular off the coast of Ruckle Provincial Park.

Shopping **Art stores and studios** are all over Ganges and most offer the chance to meet the artist. Ask at the Information Centre for a full list. From Jun-Sep, *Art Craft*, held in Ganges' Mahon Hall, provides a great opportunity to see (and buy) the work of some 200 or so Gulf Island artists. *Coastal Currents Gallery* on Hereford Av has an exceptionally tasteful selection of arts, crafts and gifts well arranged in a big house. *Vortex Gallery*, Grace Point Sq, www.vortexgallery.com, shows the work of local artists that have made a name for themselves in the international art world. Although this is a commercial gallery, and therefore free, the prices are so elevated that nobody expects visitors to do much more than browse. For local crafts and organic produce, cheeses and conserves, music and food, head for the excellent **Saturday Market**, 0830-1530 Apr-Oct in Centennial Park, Ganges, www.saltspringmarket.com For **books**, *Sabine's Fine Used Books* in the town centre has the best selection.

Air *Harbour Air Seaplanes* T5375525, www.harbourair.com have regular daily flights **Transport** from **Vancouver**, $65 one-way.

Ferry 3 ferries arrive at different harbours on Salt Spring. Swartz Bay (**Victoria**) ferries arrive at **Fulford Bay**, $6 return ($25.25 with car); Tsawwassen (**Vancouver**) ferries arrive at **Long Harbour**, $9 one-way to the island ($44.50 with car), or $5 one-way returning to the mainland, ($23.25 with car). **Vesuvius Bay** receives several sailings daily from **Crofton** in the Cowichan Valley, $6 return ($25.25 with car). *Gulf Island Water Taxi*, T5372510, runs to **Galiano**, **Mayne** and the **Penders** Wed and Sat Jul and Aug, Sat in Jun. $20 return. They will transport your kayak for $5.

Road Ganges is at the northern end of the island, some 15 km along the main Fulford-Ganges Rd from Fulford Bay, about 6 km from the other harbours. There is no public transport, but hitchhiking is easy. **Bikes** are the best way to get around. Rentals from the *Hostel* (also scooters) or *Saltspring Kayaking* (see above). Otherwise try *Silver Shadow Taxi*, T5373030.

Cultural centre *ArtSpring*, 100 Jackson, T5372102, www.artspring.ca The island's **Directory** main venue for music and performing arts. **Laundry** *Mrs Clean*, Gasoline Alley behind the *Petrocan* in Ganges. **Medical services** *Lady Minto Gulf Islands Hospitals*, 135 Crofton Rd, T5385545. *Galiano Health Care Centre*, T5393230. Provides health care on 4 'outer islands'. Walk-in Thu 0700-1045. *Skin Sensations*, 2102 Grace Point Rd, T5378807. Spa, reiki, reflexology, massage.

Galiano Island

Despite its popularity and proximity to Victoria and Vancouver, Galiano is *Phone code: 250* still nicely undeveloped, the closest thing even to a village being the ferry ter- *Colour map 1, grid C4* minal of **Sturdies Bay**. There are plenty of walks through old-growth forest, much of it protected by the assiduous efforts of locals. There are no banks or cash machines, so bring sufficient cash. Nor is there a tourist office, just a booth with ads and leaflets. Pick up the all-important map here or on the ferry. **Galiano Island Visitor's Association** can be reached at T5392233, www.galianoisland.com

The long, skinny finger of Galiano sits in the Georgia Strait pointing westwards away from Sturdies Bay in the east. Sturdies Bay Road connects fairly soon with Porlier Pass Road, which runs the length of the island. Alternatively, just after the ferry, a left turn down Burrill takes you along Bluff Road and through **Bluffs Park**, a beautiful chunk of old-growth forest. Shortly thereafter, a left fork leads to Active Pass Drive, and the trailhead for ascending **Mount Galiano**, a satisfying hike leading to views of the Olympic Mountains, Navy Channel and, on a clear day, all of the southern Gulf Islands. Take the right fork instead, then a left down Montague Road, which connects eventually back with Porlier Pass Road, just before **Montague Harbour Provincial Marine Park**. There are three white shell beaches here, a café and store, cracking sunsets and a great campground. A 3-km shoreline trail runs around Gray Peninsula. Two-thirds of the way along the island, Cottage Way gives access to **Bodega Ridge**, a 3-km walk with views all the way. **Dionisio Point Provincial Park** at the west end has camping but marine access only, with many rare flowers and fine views. You can dive there with *Galiano Diving*, T5393109, www.gulfislands.com, who also operate a water taxi.

AL *Galiano Inn*, 134 Madrona Dr, T5393388, www.galianoinn.com One of the nicest **Sleeping** lodges on the islands. Sumptuous decor with lots of space, fireplace, down duvets. ◼ *on map,* Breakfast in their restaurant (see below) provided. **A** *Bellhouse Inn*, 29 Farmhouse Rd, *page 152*

T1800-9707464, www.bellhouseinn.com Historic farmhouse on the ocean near the ferry. 3 romantic en suite rooms with balconies and great views. **B** *Driftwood Village Resort*, 205 Bluff Rd E, T5395457, www.driftwoodcottages.com Good location near ocean, nice setting, very varied cottages. Ferry pick-up. **C** *Bodega Resort*, 120 Monastee Rd, at west end of island, T5392677. Log cottages that sleep up to 6. Spacious, comfy and excellent value. Beautiful expansive grounds full of fruit trees and stone carvings. Good views, horseback riding available. **C** *High Bluffs Guest House*, 170 Bluff Rd, T5395779. 3 en suite rooms, sauna, hot tub, lounge, breakfast. Ferry pick-up. **Camping F** *Montague Harbour Provincial Park*, T3912300. Wonderful walk-in sites overlooking ocean, and some nice vehicle sites. Trails and beaches. Reservation crucial in summer.

Eating   **Expensive** *Atrevida*, at *Galiano Inn*, 134 Madrona Dr, T5393388. Delicious West Coast food in a gorgeous location with ocean views. *La Bérengerie Restaurant*, Montague Rd close to the park, T5395392. 4-course French meal $27.50, reservations required. Attractive and popular open-air café in summer (mid-range). Also 3 rooms to rent (**C**). **Mid-range** *Hummingbird Pub*, 47 Sturdies Bay Rd. Cosy pub with decent food. The best place to meet locals. **Cheap** *Max & Moritz Spicy Island Food House*, by the ferry landing. Take-out German and Indonesian food.

Sports   **Diving** *Galiano Diving*, T5393109, www.gulfislands.com, arrange diving and also operate a water taxi. **Kayak** rental and tours from *Galiano Island Sea Kayaking*, 637 Southwind Dr, T1888-5392930, www.seakayak.ca *Sporades Tours Inc*, T5392278. Sightseeing on a fishing vessel. Captain has 40 years' experience.

Transport   **Bus** *Go Galiano Island Shuttle*, T5390202, is a taxi and bus service with some scheduled routes. Their buses run hourly, 1000-2300 daily Jul-Aug, 1700-2300 Fri and Sat, Jun and Sep ($3), with 'pub runs' from Sturdies Bay to the *Hummingbird Pub* from 1730-2230 ($2). **Ferry** from **Tsawwassen** once daily in the morning, $9 ($44.50 with vehicle), from **Saltspring** via Pender and Mayne once daily in mid-afternoon, $9 ($30 with vehicle). *Gulf Islands Water Taxi*, T5372510, connects with Salt Spring (see above). **Taxis** run 0600-midnight Jul-Sep ($3 + $1.25 per km). *Galiano Bicycle Rental*, 36 Burrill Rd, Sturdies Bay, T5399906. *Galiano Boat Rentals*, Montague Harbour, T5399828.

Pender Islands   North and South Pender, connected by a one-lane wooden bridge, are even sleepier than most, with little to do but swim and walk. The ferry terminal of

Galiano Island

Dionisio Point Provincial Park
Porlier Pass
Strait of Georgia
Pebble Beach
Spanish Hills
Bodega Beach Dr
Cook Rd
2 Monastee Rd
Spotlight Cove
Bodega Ridge
Vineyard Way
McCoskrie Rd
Lovers' Leap View Point
Retreat Cove
Retreat Cove Rd
Trincomali Channel

N
0 km   1
0 mile   1

■ **Sleeping**
1 Bellhouse Inn
2 Bodega Resort

3 Driftwood Village Resort
4 Galiano Inn & Atrevida

5 High Bluffs Guest House
6 Montague Harbour Provincial Park

Otter Bay has a summer-only **Information Centre**, 232 Otter Bay Road, T6296541, and a marina where you can rent bikes. But the closest thing to a community is a small shopping plaza halfway down the north island on Bedwell Harbour Road. For swimming there's Hamilton Beach on the north island, or Mortimer Spit just south of the bridge. For fresh water, head for Magic or Roe Lakes. Hiking trails to Mount Norman and Beaumont Marine Park begin just over the bridge. The former is recommended for views. Horse riding is available at *Brackett Cove Farm*, T6293306.

Sleeping and eating LL-B *Bedwell Harbour Island*, South Pender, T6293212, www.bedwell-harbour.com From condos or cabins to just plain rooms, all with fire-places. Restaurant and *Marine Bar and Bistro* serving Gulf Island Microbrews. Great views from balcony. **AL** *Alice's Shangrila*, 5909 Pirate's Rd, T6293433 www.alicesoceanfrontbnb.com Big house with 511 sq m of wrap-around balcony and 360° views from a cliff top. 3 en suite rooms with private hot tub and TV. **C** *Inn on Pender Island*, 4709 Canal Rd, T6293353. Standard. Just south of the plaza, next to **F** *Prior Centennial Provincial Park*, T3912300. 17 basic sites in a nice treed setting. *Pistou Grill* in the Plaza, has fair (mid-range) bistro food in a comfy environment with outdoor seating.

Transport BC Ferries from **Salt Spring** arrive twice daily during the week, once on Sat, $3, ($10 with car); those from **Tsawwassen** via Galiano and Mayne arrive daily, $18 ($56.50 with car).

Reached only from Galiano (daily, $3, $10 with a vehicle), Mayne, **Mayne Island** www.mayneislandchamber.ca, is a delightfully sleepy place. Just down the road from the ferry terminal at Village Bay is the main community of **Miner's Bay**, named in the mid-19th century when Mayne was the key Gulf Island stopover during the Fraser River Gold Rush. Several heritage buildings here include the Springwater Lodge (1890), the small museum (1890) and St Mary Magdalene Church (1898). The closest thing to a town, this is the place to rent kayaks, bikes and diving equipment. Try *Kayak and Canoe Rentals*, 359 Maple Drive. The beaches at Bennet or Campbell Bays are good for swimming and basking. The best hike is the steep 45-minute ascent in Mount Parke Regional Park. The trail starts at Montrose Road near the Fernhill Centre, and leads to thumping views of Plumper Sound to the south.

Vancouver Island

● **Eating**
1 Hummingbird Pub
2 La Bérengerie

3 Max & Moritz Spicy
Island Food House

Sleeping and eating LL-A *Oceanwood Country Inn*, 630 Dinner Bay Rd, T5395074, www.oceanwood.com Comfy yet stylish rooms on the ocean, many with private decks. Outdoor hot tub, sauna, bikes. Breakfast included in their expensive restaurant, which is open for dinner daily 1800-2300, and is certainly the best place to eat. **B-D** *Blue Vista Resort*, 563 Arbutus Dr, T5392463. Modern cottages close to beach. Ferry pick-up, bike rental. **E** *Springwater Lodge*, 400 Georgina Pt Rd, T5395521. Old and worn, but cheap and handy. Other than a splurge at *Oceanwood*, Miner's Bay has a few choices for eating. *Mayne Inn*, for fish and chips and breakfast; *Miner's Bay Café* for breakfast and sandwiches, and the *Manna Bakery Café* for coffee, pastries and baking.

Transport For transport there's only *MIDAS Taxi*, T5393132. To charter a **sailing boat** call *Island Charters*, T5395040.

Saturna Island Even more remote, and a little bigger than Mayne and the Penders, Saturna makes for good exploring, and has some of the best sand beaches in the Gulf Islands, notably at **Winter Cove Marine Park** at the northwest tip. Good, warm swimming is also possible at **Russell Reef** on the north shore. In summer the best whale-watching is at **East Point Park**, which also has a beach, good views and a lighthouse. A fine hike is to the 497-m summit of **Mount Warburton Pike**, from where there are commanding panoramas. There's also a good trail at **Brown Ridge** in the southwest. The small community of Saturna Point has a general store with post office and the summer-only **Information Centre**, www.saturnatourism.bc.ca

Gabriola Island

■ Sleeping
1 Gabriola Campground
2 Haven By the Sea

3 Hummingbird Lodge B & B
4 Sunset B & B
5 Surf Lodge & Sunset Lounge

● Eating
1 Silva Bay Pub
2 White Hart Pub

Sleeping A *Saturna Lodge and Vineyard*, 130 Payne Rd, overlooking Boot Cove, near ferry, T5392254. 7 beautiful rooms with private balcony and hot tub. Expensive fine dining restaurant with a great BC wine list. Tours and tasting at the only winery on the Gulf Islands. **B** *Lyall Harbour B&B*, 121 East Point Rd, close to ferry, T5395577. 3 en suite rooms with high ceilings and private decks, in an attractive home. Full breakfast in solarium dining room. Good value. **B-C** *East Point Resort*, East Point Rd, T5392975. 6 cottages with kitchens and bath. On the beach close to Lighthouse Park. Boat rentals. There are no campgrounds on the island, and not much choice for eating beyond a pizza joint and pub. **C-D** *Breezy Bay B&B*, 131 Payne Rd, T5395957. 1890s home on a 50-acre farm. Orchards, gardens, forest, beach. **C-D** *Sandy Bay B&B*, 449 East Point Rd, T5392641. En suite waterfront rooms. Private beach.

Transport Ferries: daily from **Swartz Bay**, $6.25 return ($21.50 with car), non-stop on weekdays, and from **Mayne**, $3 ($10 with car), arrive at Boot Cove. **Kayaks** can be rented from *Saturna Sea Kayaking*, nearby at 121 Boot Cove Rd, T5395553. On the island, the only transport is a **taxi**, the *Saturna Island Shuttle*, T5395359.

Gabriola Island

Gabriola is one of the quickest Gulf Islands to get to, and one of the most worth-while. Straight ahead from the ferry on North Road is the Village Centre, hub of local activity, which contains the summer-only **Information Centre**, T2479332, www.gabriolaisland.org, a couple of nice cafés and some of the island's 40-odd galleries. On Thanksgiving weekend in October there is a **Gallery Tour**, when studios are open to the public for three days. The website above also describes walking and driving tours. The other main annual event is the annual *Salmon BBQ* in August. The Farmer's Market, near the village on Saturday and Wednesday, is a good place for local organic produce and crafts.

Phone code: 250
Colour map 1,
grid C3

Wonderful rock formations can be seen from the approaching ferry, and at various parks throughout the island. Best of these is the highly pho-togenic **Malaspina Gallery**, a collec-tion of beautiful wave-shaped stone sculptures carved by the sea. ■ *From the ferry, turn left onto Taylor Bay Rd and left again onto Malaspina Dr.* **Drumbed Provincial Park** at the southeast corner has good swimming and an easy, pleasant walk leading to the island's best views, with a chance to see otters and eagles. Many **petroglyphs** are scattered around the island. Most are inaccessible or very hard to find, but you can see some on South Road (behind the United Church). *Gabriola: Petroglyph Island,*

by M and T Bentley, is an invaluable resource for those keen to seek them out. A collection of decent reproductions decorates the garden of the small and otherwise not very interesting **Gabriola Museum**. ■ *Winter Sat and Sun, 1300-1600, longer hours in summer but dependent on funding. $2.*

Sleeping
■ *on map,*
page 154

B *Hummingbird Lodge B&B*, 1597 Starbuck Lane, T2479300. 3 en suite rooms in an attractive house near the beach. Private decks, hot tub, lounge, kitchenette. **B-C** *Sunset B&B*, 969 Berry Point Rd, T2472032. 2 comfortable en suite rooms in a romantic home by the sea. Ferry pick-up by arrangement. **C** *Surf Lodge & Sunset Lounge*, 885 Berry Point Rd, T2479231. Ocean-view, rooms in a log-cabin lodge. Great views from the lounge. **C-D** *Haven By the Sea*, 240 Davis Rd, T2479211. A centre for personal development courses, but open to casual guests. Cabins nicely located on the ocean, a bit faded but good value. Facilities include gym, sauna, outdoor hot tub and pool. Restaurant serves decent buffet-style meals at very good prices. **Camping F** *Gabriola Campground*, 595 Taylor Bay Rd, T2472079. 28 sites in a nice forest setting close to the water. Open Apr-Oct.

Eating

In the village centre is the cosy *Suzy's Restaurant* with some good daily specials. *Raspberry's* is a hip little licensed café with very good coffee and occasional live jazz. *Silva Bay Pub*, T2478662, is the nicest place for a drink, and also has very good food, a patio and pool table. *White Hart Pub*, directly off the ferry, is a decent pub with patio. Don't be scared to try the *Gabriola bar*, a combination of quality dark chocolate and garlic.

Entertainment

Gabriola Artworks, 575 North Rd, represents many of the 50-plus resident artists. *The Yew Tree Gallery*, 535 North Rd, T2477555, an art gallery with jazz or classical concerts.

Sports

High Test Dive Charters, T2479753. $140 per person per day, includes accommodation, meals, tanks, and dives. Gear rental extra.

Transport

Local: The easiest way to get around the island is by **bike** or **kayak**. Rent either at *Cycle and Kayak*, T2478277. **Hitching** works well too, or you can use *Gabriola Taxi*, T2470049.

Long distance   Air: *Pacific Spirit Airlines*, T2479992, run a float-plane from Vancouver Air Seaplane Terminal in Richmond to **Silva Bay** at Gabriola's eastern tip. $65 one-way for the 7-min flight. **Ferry**: *BC Ferries*, T1888-2233779, www.bcferries.com, run hourly 0615-2255 from **Nanaimo Harbour**. $5.25, ($18.75 with vehicle), crossing time 20 mins.

Pacific Rim National Park

There is an $8 per day entrance fee ($42 season pass) that applies throughout the national park

The 130-km stretch of coastline between Tofino and Port Renfrew must surely rank as Vancouver Island's greatest attraction. Fringed with dense rainforest and mountains, rocky bays and countless islands, this is a ruggedly beautiful and relatively unspoilt paradise. The Pacific Rim National Park that preserves this taste of wilderness is divided into three sections. The most popular and accessible part is **Long Beach**, a 20-km series of beaches lined with short trails through the lush rainforest. To the north and south are the park's two main bases, **Tofino** and **Ucluelet**, the former a strong candidate for BC's best seaside town. Just south of the latter is the **Broken Islands Group**, an archipelago of tiny islands in Barkley Sound, a paradise for kayakers, but virtually off-limits to everyone else. In the park's southern section, starting at the boardwalk village of **Bamfield**, is the **West Coast Trail**, one of the most challenging, rewarding and popular hikes in North America.

With an exceptionally high level of rainfall, and shorelines beaten by the relentlessly violent Pacific, the West Coast's long beaches are unlikely to attract those who simply want to lie in the sun, read a book, and take the occasional relaxing swim. This is more a place for doing things. The breakers are (by Canadian standards) great for surfing. In the off-season, storm-watching is an increasingly popular activity. The ruggedly romantic coastline invites you to take long walks, explore the tide-pools, or try beachcombing. The heavy precipitation is bad news for campers – who should be sure to have a decent tent or bring two tarps, one for underneath – but it's one of the best places to see some of the world's biggest trees.

The lack of human habitation is matched by an abundance of marine life. Whale-watching is a particularly big draw, with some 22,000 grey whales migrating through from mid-March to early April on their way from Baja California to Siberia. The beginning of the migration is celebrated for two weeks during the **Pacific Rim Whale Festival**, with various whale-related events throughout the park and in Tofino and Ucluelet. Books to enhance your appreciation of the park include the *Official Guidebook to Pacific Rim National Park Reserve* (MacFarlane et al, 1996); *The Pacific Rim Explorer*, by Bruce Obee; and *Island Paddling*, by MA Snowden.

Highway 4 from Parksville is a worthwhile drive in itself, offering the first real glimpses of Vancouver Island's forested interior. Before long, signs appear for **Englishman River Falls Provincial Park** to the south, where there's hiking, biking, fishing and a large, pleasant campground, as well as the falls. A little further, **Coombs** is a bizarre place with a tacky amusement park attitude. Keep going unless you want to see some goats on a roof, or get yourself a concrete garden ornament. **Little Qualicum Falls Provincial Park**, at Km 19, features more impressive falls, swimming holes, and a large but scenic campground. In summer there are always lots of cars parked at the adjacent **Cameron Lake**, which has a splendid beach.

Highway 4 to Port Alberni

Macmillan Park, opened by the eponymous logging giants, features **Cathedral Grove**, a tiny patch of old-growth spruce and cedar left behind almost as a sick joke to show tourists how the whole island once looked. A few points still exist around the island where the real thing can be seen, notably in Clayoquot Sound close to Tofino.

To the south, **Mount Arrowsmith** offers winter skiing and summer hiking, though not of the Mount Washington standard.

Port Alberni

The only reason to stay in this ugly, sprawling mill town is in order to catch the **MV Lady Rose**. This Scottish freighter started out delivering mail and supplies to isolated communities around Barkley Sound at the other end of Alberni Inlet, the island's longest fjord. But the journey has become so popular with passengers that a second boat has been added, the Norwegian **MV Frances Barkley**, and reservations are almost essential. This is a fantastic way to travel to Bamfield (for the West Coast Trail), Ucluelet or the Broken Islands Group. It can equally be treated as a cheap cruise, simply to enjoy the dramatic scenery and wildlife, though the boats were not built for comfort. See Transport for details of sailings. Boats leave from Harbour Quay, also coincidentally the nicest part of town. The **Visitor Information Centre** is on the Highway from Parksville at 2533 Redford Street, T7246535.

Phone code: 250
Colour map 1, grid C3

Vancouver Island

If you have time to kill, the best local diversion is the **McLean Mill National Historic Site**, Canada's only steam-operated mill and an interesting building. ■ *1000-1800. $6.50, $4.50 concessions. West of town at 5633 Smith Rd, T7231376, www.alberniherige.com* Staggeringly popular when first operated in 2001, an old **steam train** runs from Harbour Quay to the mill, a half-hour ride along the water with robberies staged by men on horseback. ■ *Thu-Mon, last train leaves Port Alberni at 1300. $20 return, $15 concessions, includes mill admission.* The mill can also be reached by hiking or biking the 20-km **Log Train Trail**, which starts at the Visitor Information Centre.

Sleeping

Many of the town's motels are on Redford St (Hwy 4a) from Parksville. Best of a mediocre bunch is **B-C** *Villager Lodge Alberni Inn*, 3805 Redford St, T7239405, www.alberni-inn.com River Rd on Hwy 4 west is a nicer area to stay, but less convenient for the *Lady Rose*. There are, however, public buses into town. **B** *Cedar Wood Lodge*, 5895 River Rd, T7246800. 8 very nice rooms with down duvets and fireplace. Breakfast included. **C** *Somass Motel*, 5279 River Rd, T7243236. Small and pleasant. **D** *Riverside Motel*, 5065 Roger St, T7249916. A little closer to town and nicely located. Simple rooms with shower only.

E *The Personal Touch Hostel*, about 5 blocks from Harbour Quay at 4908 Burde St, T7232484. Dorm rooms in a large house with kitchen, living room, laundry. Professional and friendly. **Camping** **F** *Dry Creek Campground*, 4th Av/Napier, not far from the Quay, is convenient and reasonable. **F** *Sproat Lake Provincial Park*, 13 km northwest off Hwy 4, has some nice sites on the north side. All the lakeside sites are RV pull-through types. This is a very popular place for fishing, warm swimming and water sports, with summer cottages crowding the shoreline. *Stamp River Provincial Park*, 14 km north on Hwy 4 to Beaver Creek Rd, T9544600. Small, forested campground. From late Aug to Dec, half a million salmon travel up the falls via ladders, an incredible sight.

Eating

Mid-range *Swale Rock Cafe*, 5328 Argyle St, is a reliable choice, with seafood, curry, burgers, etc. Down-to-earth, good portions. If willing to go further afield, the *Clam Bucket* on the other side of town, at 4479 Victoria Quay, is recommended by locals, with large portions of good seafood. **Cheap** *Blue Door Cafe*, 5415 Argyle St. The place for cheap breakfasts. Head down to the quay for coffee shops.

Sports

Alberni Outpost, 5161 River Rd, T7232212, for **kayak** rentals. *Ark Resort*, 11000 Great Central Lake Rd, T7232657, run excursions to Della Falls in Strathcona Park (see page 175). They also have some campsites (**F**).

Transport

The office for the *MV Lady Rose* and *MV Frances Barkley* is on Argyle St, T7238313, www.ladyrosemarine.com All sailings leave at 0800 from Harbour Quay just down the road. To **Bamfield**: Tue, Thu, and Sat year round, arriving at 1230, returning at 1330, $45 return. To **Ucluelet** and **Broken Islands** (Sechart): Jun-Sep, Mon, Wed, Fri, arriving in Sechart at 1100, returning at 1530, $40 return; arriving in Ucluelet at 1230, returning at 1400, $25 one-way. Additional sailings in the summer. The same company runs the unique *Sechart Lodge* in Sechart on Barkley Sound (see page 166). If the *Lady Rose* schedule doesn't work for you, try *Toquart Water Taxi*, T7207358. Toquart to Broken Islands, $35, Toquart to Lodge, $30, Sechart to Bamfield, $25, all one-way.

Long Beach

Phone code: 250
Colour map 1, grid C2

The 130-km rollercoaster ride from Port Alberni to Long Beach, with frequent great views of the wild, rocky landscape, provides a fitting introduction to the rugged West Coast. A left turn at the intersection with the Pacific Rim

Coastal rainforests

◀

Temperate Coastal Rainforests have existed some two million years, but are extremely rare, originally comprising just 0.2% of the earth's land surface. They are one of the most biologically productive ecosystems on earth, with a greater biomass per hectare than any other. Their estuaries, intertidal and subtidal zones have also supported some of the world's most diverse marine life, as well as some of the most complex human civilizations ever to emerge without the benefit of agriculture. Despite all that, they are among the least studied ecosystems on earth, and time is running out: about half of the original forests have already been cut down, including 95% of those that covered Washington, Oregon and California. Large tracts remain only in British Columbia, Alaska and Chile.

British Columbia still contains about a quarter of the world's remaining temperate rainforest, even though 53% has been axed. On Vancouver Island the figure is 74%, and though 13% of the island's area is protected by parks, only

5.7% of the temperate rainforest is protected. The single largest remaining tract is in Clayoquot Sound, 74% of whose productive ancient forests are still open to logging and, despite the protests of thousands of citizens, two companies still retain significant logging rights in the Sound. Interfor's plans for 2002-03 involves building 83 km of new logging roads in the area, and extracting 825,000 cu m of old-growth wood from 43 cut-blocks covering 1,860 ha. A Scientists' declaration has recently called for an end to large-scale clear-cut logging in this area. Even the government-appointed scientific panel recommended that]logging must not compromise the integrity of the ecosystem, that community values should be respected, and that watershed cutting should be restricted to 1% per year. For more information contact the David Suzuki Foundation, T7324228, www.davidsuzuki.org or The Friends of Clayoquot Sound, 331 Neill St, Tofino, T7254218, www.island.net~focs

Vancouver Island

Highway leads 8 km to Ucluelet. Most people turn right towards Tofino, 36 km away, soon entering Long Beach, the collective name for a 20-km stretch of forest-fringed bays and beaches. Almost immediately on the right is the **Parks Information Centre**. ■ *Mid-Jun to mid-Sep*. From here the highway runs parallel with the ocean, giving access to a number of beaches, and nine official trails, marked on the map and described below from east to west. Most of these are short and sweet.

The **Willowbrae Trail** (1) starts 2 km towards Ucluelet from the junction, and leads 1.4 km to Florencia Bay. The trail's origins go back to the time when pre-highway pioneers had to walk between Ucluelet and Tofino. On the way a left fork (2) leads to the tiny and quiet **Half Moon Bay**. Heading to Tofino, just past the Information Centre is the **Gold Mine Trail** (3), which follows an old prospectors' path to the long, scenic and relatively calm beach of **Florencia Bay**. A few kilometres further, Wickaninnish Road leads to the beach and centre of the same name, plus a few trails. First of these is the **Bog Trail** (6), an 800-m boardwalk loop through the stunted, twisted trees that grow in a peat moss environment. Totally level, it is the only wheelchair accessible trail. Continue for the **Wickaninnish Centre**, T7267706, situated at the eastern end of Long Beach itself. Wickaninnish was a powerful native chief, as borne out by his name, which means 'having no one in front of him in the canoe'. He gained much respect for his mediation between the White Man and native fur trappers. The centre has a restaurant, and is useful for

Beaches & trails

information when the Parks Office is closed. It also has films and exhibits on the natural and cultural history of the Pacific Rim. The rip-tides here are particularly dangerous, but it's a good safe spot for storm-watching, and there's a whale-watching telescope. From Wickaninnish, **South Beach Trail** (4), leads 750 m to a tiny pebble beach, branching left onto **Wickaninnish Trail** (5), which leads 5 km through rainforest to Florencia Bay.

Either side of the highway, 4 km further on, are the two 1-km loops through giant trees of the **Rainforest Trail** (7). Interpretive signs on Loop A explore forest life cycles, while those on Loop B look at forest structure and inhabitants. About 1 km further, a short road leads to the parking lot for **Combers Beach** (still part of Long Beach), and **Spruce Fringe Trail** (8), a 1½-km boardwalk loop that explores the tenacious nature of the Sitka spruce, which can withstand the harsh salt and wind of the ocean's edge, thereby providing a protective buffer behind which less resilient trees can grow. You start at the twisted and weather-beaten spruce, and retreat from the beach, watching the trees getting bigger and bigger. The next turning is to the excellent *Greenpoint Campground* (see page 162). A few kilometres further is the closest parking lot to the beach, with wheelchair access. At the western end of Long Beach is **Schooner Beach** reached by a 1-km trail (9). About 4 km towards Tofino, a short drive and walk lead up to **Radar Hill**, with panoramic views of Clayoquot Sound. Shortly thereafter, the peninsula narrows and you pass **Cox Bay**, and **Chesterman** and **Mackenzie** beaches just outside Tofino.

Tofino

Phone code: 250
Colour map 1, grid C2
Population: 1,286

For Excursions from Tofino, see page 164

The overwhelming popularity of this whaling-station turned surf town is partly due to its formidable location. Sitting at the end of a narrow peninsula in the middle of beautiful Clayoquot Sound (see box), surrounded on all sides by ocean and islands, it is also the closest base for exploring the endless shoreline of Long Beach. A handful of excursions lead to outstanding destinations like Hot Springs Cove, one of the finest remaining stands of giant old-growth trees on Meares Island, or an encounter with aboriginal culture on Flores Island. Other local activities include whale-watching, world-class sea-kayaking, the country's best surfing, hiking, bear-watching, beachcombing and storm-watching.

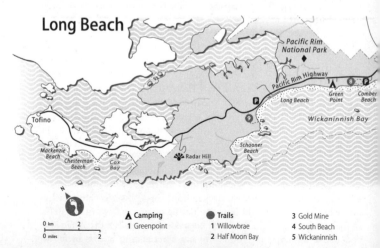

Long Beach

Pacific Rim National Park

Pacific Rim Highway

Green Point *Comber Beach*

Long Beach

Wickaninnish Bay

Tofino

Schooner Beach

Mackenzie Beach

Chesterman Beach

Cox Bay

Radar Hill

N

0 km   2
0 miles   2

Camping
1 Greenpoint

Trails
1 Willowbrae
2 Half Moon Bay

3 Gold Mine
4 South Beach
5 Wickaninnish

Despite being packed to the gills throughout the summer, Tofino itself just about manages to remain a scenic seaside village, and for most people the happy holiday resort atmosphere only adds to the experience. It has also led to a much a finer selection of restaurants, cafés, shops and accommodation than would normally be found in so small a town. If you want to avoid other tourists, however, think about going to Ucluelet instead. The busy **Visitor Information Centre** is at 121 3rd Street, T7253414, www.tofino-bc.com, is open from April to September. A Pacific Rim National Park Pass costs $8 a day, $42 season pass.

Eagle Aerie Gallery highlights the work of native artist Roy Henry Vickers. Whatever you think of his work, take a moment to admire the building itself, a longhouse replica with some beautiful carvings and a dug-out canoe. ■ *Summer 0900-2100, low season 0930-1730. 350 Campbell St.* The **Rainforest Interpretive Centre** gives a free introduction to this remarkable ecosystem. ■ *451 Main St, T7252560.* Just out of town towards Long Beach, the **Botanical Gardens** contain 5 ha of gardens, old-growth forest and shoreline. Hardly worth the entrance fee, given the abundance of free local beauty, but their restaurant is well regarded. ■ *0900-dark. $10, $2 concessions, valid for 3 days.*

Tofino's many B&Bs represent a much better deal than the few motels, which are overpriced. A multitude of resorts/lodges at Mackenzie and Chesterman beaches, on the way into town, offer anything from ugly old cabins to luxurious suites. **Chesterman**, 7 km out and connected by bike path to Tofino, is an ideal place to stay if you have a vehicle. It's quiet and directly on the beach. All prices go down considerably after Labour Day in Sep. In summer, reservations are essential pretty much everywhere.

The swankiest place around is the **LL** *Wickaninnish Inn*, Osprey Lane, Chesterman Beach, T7253100, www.wickinn.com The swankiest option. Rooms have natural, stylish decor with lots of wood, including handmade driftwood furniture. Balconies and floor-to-ceiling windows make the most of the ocean view. Lots of extras such as fireplaces, CD players, books, binoculars, oversized tubs and huge TV's. Their *Pointe Restaurant* is renowned. Full spa not included in price but ask about packages. **LL-B** *Middle Beach Lodge*, 400 Mackenzie Beach, 3 km south, T7252900, www.middlebeach.com One of the best of its kind. The timber lodge features hardwood floors, pine furnishings and stone fireplaces. Lodge rooms are quite plain but have decks with views. There are also some suites and luxurious ocean-front cabins. Continental breakfast included.

Sleeping
■ *on map,*
page 162

AL-A *Cable Cove Inn*, 201 Main St, T7254236, www.cablecoveinn.com Beautiful rooms, some with hot tub or fireplace. Beach access, views, decks. Breakfast included. **AL** *Pacific Sands Beach Resort*, 1421 Pacific Rim Hwy, Chesterman Beach, T7253322, www.pacificsands.com Ample lawns, hiking trails and its own stretch of manicured beach. 1- and 2-bedroomed suites with decks, kitchens and fireplaces, or 2-bedroom cottages with all mod cons.

B&Bs **B** *Brimar B&B*, 1375 Thornberg Cres, Chesterman Beach, T7253410, www.brimarbb.com 3 en suite rooms in a beachfront home. **B** *Gull Cottage*, 254 Lynn Rd, Chesterman Beach, T7253177, www.gullcottagetofino.com 3 en suite rooms in a Victorian home. Hot tub and

To Port Alberni ▶

Parks Information
Centre

Wickaninnish
Centre

Wickaninnish
Beach

Florencia
Bay

To Ucluelet ▲

6 Bog
7 Rainforest
8 Spruce Fringe
9 Schooner Cove

Vancouver Island

Vancouver Island

guest lounge. **B-C** *Red Crow Guest House*, 1084 Pacific Rim Hwy, close to *Botanical Gardens*, T7252275, www.tofinoredcrow.com 3 rooms in a waterfront home set in old-growth forest with views. Private baths, deck, trails, canoes. **C** *Hummingbird B&B*, 640 Mackenzie Beach Rd, 3 km south, T7252740, 3 rooms with private bath in a West Coast-style wooden home. **B** *Water's Edge*, 331 Tonquin Park Rd, T7251218, ironside@island.net A wonderful West Coast home with a common room offering the best views of all. Large en suite rooms, hot tub and staircase to tide pools. Breakfast included.

D *Dolphin Motel*, 1190 Pacific Rim Hwy, 3 km south, T7253377. Cheapest of the motels. Very basic but acceptable. **D** *Paddler's Inn*, 320 Main St, T7254222. Simple but pleasant rooms with views, shared baths and kitchen, breakfast included. **D** *Tofino Swell Lodge*, 341 Olsen Rd, T7253274. 7 en suite rooms on the water at the edge of town. Shared kitchen. **D-E** *Whalers On the Point Guesthouse*, 81 West St, T7253443, www.tofinohostel.com Spanking-new, *HI-affiliated hostel* with dorms and some private rooms. Very spacious with first-class facilities including kitchen, laundry, sauna, and a wonderful solarium sitting-room with harbour views. Discounts on tours and lessons. Reservation essential. Highly recommended.

Camping E *Bella Pacifica Campground*, 3 km south, T7253400. Access to Mackenzie Beach. Small sites, some on beach. Coin showers, laundry. **E** *Crystal Cove Beach Resort*, 3 km south, T7254213. OK sites if in a pinch. Also log cabins. **F** *Greenpoint Campground*, 19 km south. The only campsite in Long Beach, and

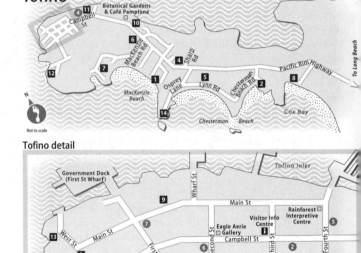

Sleeping
1 Bella Pacifica Campground
2 Brimar B&B
3 Cable Cove Inn
4 Dolphin Motel
5 Gull Cottage
6 Hummingbird B&B
7 Middle Beach Lodge
8 Pacific Sands Beach Resort
9 Paddler's Inn
10 Red Crow Guest House
11 Tofino Swell Lodge
12 Water's Edge
13 Whalers On the Point Guesthouse
14 Wickaninnish Inn & Pointe Restaurant

Eating
1 Alleyway Café/Costa Azul
2 Caffe Vincente
3 The Common Loaf Bake Shop
4 The Marine Pub
5 Raincoast Café
6 Schooner On Second
7 Surfside Pizza

easily the best one around. Small but private and densely treed sites, some overlooking the beach. Operates on a first-come first-served basis, and heavily over-burdened, so arrive early and get on the waiting list.

Expensive *Pointe Restaurant*, at the *Wickaninnish Inn*, (see Sleeping, above), T7253100. Excellent reputation for gourmet dining and spectacular panoramic ocean views. A 9-course meal with wine is $165. A drink in the lounge is more affordable and almost as gratifying. *Raincoast Café*, 4th/Campbell St, T7252215. Fast gaining a reputation as *the* place to eat. Cuisine is first-class Asian-West Coast fusion. Decor is stylishly minimalist, with an open kitchen. *Schooner On Second*, 331 Campbell St, T7253444. Generally considered the best place for gourmet seafood, but also has some fine salads. Romantic atmosphere.

Mid-range *Alleyway Café/Costa Azul*, 305 Campbell St, T7253105. Good breakfast option by day, great Mexican food in the evening. Airy, laid-back atmosphere and garden patio. *Café Pamplona*, T7251237, at the *Botanical Gardens*. Miniscule but mouthwatering menu that changes daily. Most ingredients come straight from their garden. *Surfside Pizza*, 120 1st St. Best pizza in town.

Cheap *The Common Loaf Bake Shop*, 180 1st St, T7253915. A local institution and meeting-place. Fresh baking, good coffee, and pizza. Bulletin board with useful info. *Caffe Vincente*, 441 Campbell St, T7252599. A more upscale café, with fancy sandwiches and cakes at moderate prices. Internet for $7 per hr. For those self-catering, note that fresh **crab** is widely available year round for about $10-15 each.

Eating
● *on map,*
page 162

Tofino is surprisingly lacking in good places for a drink. *On the Rocks Lounge*, T7253100, at the *Wickaninnish Inn* (see Sleeping, above), has the best views. *The Marine Pub* at the *Weigh West Resort*, 634 Campbell St, T7253277, is the best choice in town, with good views and a few choices on tap.

Bars

Wildside Booksellers and Espresso Bar, 320 Main St, has a well-chosen selection of new fiction and **books** relating to the area. *Storm Light Marine Station*, 316 Main St, is the place for **camping** and **sports gear**. There is a lot of fake and tacky **First Nations** 'art' around. For a better, more authentic selection head to *The Village Gallery*, 321 Main St, which sells some great wooden masks and paintings.

Shopping

Clayoquot Sound may well be the Coast's best overall location for **kayaking**. It's less crowded than the Broken Islands Group but more so than Nootka Sound, and the beauty of the scenery is almost unparallelled. Be careful though: the currents and waves here are dangerous, causing a few deaths every year. If in doubt, go with a professional. *Rainforest Kayak*, www.rainforestkayak.com, offer eco-friendly lessons and tours; *Remote Passages Sea Kayaking*, T7253330, www.remotepassages.com, offer day and evening paddles and will instruct beginners; *Tofino Sea Kayaking Co*, T7254222, www.tofino-kayaking.com, also do tours, and will rent to experienced kayakers. A resident Aussie may tell you that the **surfing** in the area is overrated, but it's about the best you'll find in Canada. A couple of places are recommended for gear, rentals, lessons and advice: *Storm Surf Shop*, 171 4th St, T7252155. Lessons $59 per day, rentals $25 per day; and *Live To Surf*, 1180 Pacific Rim Hwy, T7254464.

Sport
For bike rental, see
Transport below

Whale-watching is the number one activity hereabouts. For excellent value, combine it with a trip to Hot Springs Cove. There are many decent operators in town. To narrow them down decide if you want to go in an inflatable zodiac or a rigid-hull cruiser. The former tend to get thrown around a bit, making for an exciting and wet ride, the latter are a little calmer. 2 widely recommended companies with long-standing reputations are *Sea Trek Tours*, T7254412, www.seatrektours.bc.ca Whale-watching in a glass-bottomed

Tour operators

Vancouver Island

boat, $60 per 2 hrs. Hot Springs Cove/whale-watching, $85 per 6½ hrs. Bear-watching $60 per 2 hrs. Times vary according to tides, website updated daily; *Remote Passages*, T7253330, www.remotepassages.com   Emphasis on educational trips. Zodiacs only. Whales $60 per 2½ hrs, whales and hot springs, $89 per 6½ hrs. Sea kayaking $58 per 4 hrs, includes walk on Meares Island. *Ocean Outfitters*, T7254412, www.seatre ktours.bc.ca, and *Adventures Pacific*, T7252811, will both leave you for a day or two as part of the package and at no entra expense. For **fishing** try *Bruce's Smiley Seas Charters*, 380 Main, T7252557. *Tofino Airlines*, T7254222, www.tofinoair.ca, run tours, as well as scheduled and chartered flights.

Transport   **Local**   Everything in Tofino is close together, clustered around Campbell St and Main St. A bike is recommended for getting to the beaches. Bikes can be rented at *Fibre Options*, Campbell/4th, T7252192. *Rainforest Boatshuttle*, T7253793, and *Meares Island Big Tree Taxi*, T7267848, both charge about $20 return to **Meares Island**.

Long distance   Air: *Atleo River Air Service*, T7252205, atleoair@alberni.net, run a **float-plane** service from the International Airport Seaplane Terminals of **Vancouver** and **Victoria**, $350 one-way, $550 return.

Bus: Daily buses run to Tofino from Nanaimo, and there are connections with the ferry from Vancouver. *Laidlaw Coach Lines*, T1800-3180818, www.graylines.ca, operate 2 daily **buses** to Tofino via **Port Alberni**, leaving **Nanaimo** at 0840 and 1230.

Ferry:The 0630 ferry from Vancouver connects with the former, arriving in Tofino at 1250. These buses leave Victoria at 0540 and 0930. The eastbound service leaves daily at 1000 and stops in **Long Beach**.

Directory   **Communications Internet**: the hostel (Whalers On the Point Guesthouse) has internet access. *Caffe Vincente*, 441 Campbell St, charges $7 per hr. **Canada Post**: 1st/Campbell. **Hospital**   261 Neill St, T7253212. **Laundry**   *Bead Comber*, Campbell between 2nd and 3rd St. Laundry service only.

Excursions from Tofino

Meares Island   The lush rainforest of Meares Island, closest of the local big islands, is certainly a
See also Sports and   tempting sight from Tofino, just 15 minutes away by water-taxi. This is one of
Tour operators   the best places in Canada to go for a walk through giant ancient trees. On the 3-km loop of the **Big Cedar Trail** you'll gasp at trees that are more than 6 m across, and wonder why the logging companies are still doing their best to cut them down. A shorter boardwalk stroll leads to the 2,000 year-old **Hanging Garden Cedar**, the biggest tree in Clayoquot Sound at 18.3 m in circumference.

Vargas Island   Vargas Island, 5 km north of Tofino, a beautiful place with fine sand beaches.

Sleeping   C *Vargas Island Inn*, T7253309. A great place to stay. They deal mostly with kayak tour companies, which provide the best way of getting there.

Flores Island   Flores Island, 20 km away, is easily reached by water-taxi. The village of **Ahousat** is one of the best places to encounter First Nations people and culture. Their **Ahousat Wildside Heritage Trail** is a marvellous 11-km hike through rainforest and beaches to Mount Flores viewpoint. It's $20 to use unless staying at the *Hummingbird Hostel* in Ahousat (see below). From here, *Matlawaha Water Taxi* offers a cheap way to get to Hot Springs Cove, $30 return each, with a minimum of six people.

Sleeping and eating E *Hummingbird Hostel*, Ahousat, T6709679, www.humming-bird-hostel.com, has dorm beds and kitchen facilities. Across the way, the *General Store Café*, has good fish and chips.

The most popular excursion from Tofino, and understandably so, is the 37-km boat trip to Hot Springs Cove. The hour-long water-taxi ride costs about $60 return per person. At $85 per 6½ hrs, tours that combine the trip with whale-watching turn out to be much better value (see Tour operators above). From the cove jetty, a 2-km boardwalk leads through rainforest to the gloriously romantic springs. The waters emerge at 43°C (108°F), then cascade down to the sea through a series of ever-cooler pools. The crowds which take the edge off the experience in summer can only be avoided by staying overnight.

Hot Springs Cove

B *Hot Springs Lodge*, T6701106. A motel-style set-up with kitchenettes in the en suite rooms. Guests are advised to bring groceries. Situated across the water from the springs, they lend row boats at no extra charge. **A** *Innchanter*, T6701149, www.innchanter.com This 1920s arts-and-crafts-style coastal freighter, moored just off the dock, offers the Cove's most intimate and stylish accommodation. The 5 rooms are small but cute and full of character, with shared bath. The shared living room has a fireplace, sofas and a splendid library. The price includes breakfast and dinner, excellent food often involving locally caught seafood. Recommended. There is also the native-run **F** *Maquinna Campground*, T6701100, beautifully situated in a forest right on the ocean, next to the dock and close to the springs. There are no facilities other than drinking water, wood and firepits.

Ucluelet

Meaning 'people of the sheltered bay', Ucluelet is a major fishing port that has retained the feel of an ordinary village. For some this may make it preferable to the more tourist-oriented Tofino. Certainly there's just as good a chance of seeing whales, and Tofino's longest running operator, *Jamie's Whaling Station*, T7267444, also runs excursions here. This is also the place from which to get to Barkley Sound and the Broken Islands Group. The very helpful **Visitor Information Centre** can tell you more about B&Bs and the many operators for whale-watching, fishing, kayaking, etc. ■ *Mon-Fri 0900-1700. 100 Main St, T7264641, www.ucluletinfo.com.* At the south end of town, the **Wild Pacific Trail** is a very nice 2.7-km loop that passes a lighthouse, with views of Barkley Sound and sometimes whales. Amphitrite Point on this trail is one of the best locations for storm-watching.

Phone code: 250
Colour map 1, grid C2

LL-L *Tauca Lea By the Sea*, situated on a point out in the water at 1971 Harbour Cres, T7264625, www.taucalearesort.com Luxurious, fully equipped suites in a beautiful lodge with kitchen, fireplace and more. The expensive *Boat Basin* restaurant serves gourmet West Coast dishes in elegant surroundings with fantastic views. For a unique experience try the **AL-C** *Canadian Princess Resort*, 1943 Peninsula Rd, T7267771, www.obmg.com State rooms in an old steam ship, with bunk beds and shared bath, or nicer on-shore rooms with modern conveniences. Very popular. The resort's lounges are the best choices for a quiet drink. There are several decent motels along Peninsula Rd, best value being the **C** *Pacific Rim Motel*, at 1755, T7267728; the **C-D** *Peninsula Motor Inn* at 1648, T7267751; and the **C** *Thornton Motel* at 1861, T7267725.

Sleeping & eating

Mid-range For food locals go to *Matterson House*, at 1682 Peninsula Rd. Big servings of home-cooked food in a homey environment. In a similar vein is the licensed *Blueberries Cafe*, 1627 Peninsula Rd, which has a patio with views. **Cheap** *Smileys*, further west on the Peninsula Rd, is a favourite diner, good for fish and chips and breakfast.

Vancouver Island

Broken Islands Group

Colour map 1, grid C2

Only the highly experienced should even think about paddling here without a guide, of which there are many in Tofino, Ucluelet and Bamfield

The central block of the national park consists of an archipelago of over 100 islands scattered throughout Barkley Sound, a dream location for sea-kayakers who come here in droves despite the difficult access. Coastal wilderness doesn't get much more remote than this, so the scenery is spectacular, with plenty of undisturbed temperate rainforest, and a good chance of seeing marine wildlife, including major colonies of sealions. Archaeological digs have shown that native peoples also favoured the spot, with evidence of habitation on the islands dating back thousands of years.

These days the Broken Islands are well known among kayaking and scuba-diving circles, and can be shockingly overrun in summer, with campsites regularly overfull and the chance of being alone increasingly slim. Studies indicate that measures will be necessary to limit the numbers. The other problem is that the waters are notoriously treacherous. Submerged rocks, reefs, sea caves, exposed channels, plus extreme, unpredictable weather and freezing water, make this a very dangerous area.

Sleeping & eating

Camping is in designated areas only, for which there is a charge of $5 per person per night. There is very little drinking water available on the islands so take all you will need. The only place to stay is at the **D** (**B** with meals) *Sechart Lodge*, T7238313, operated by Alberni Marine Transport who run the *Lady Rose*. Simple rooms with shared bath. This gloriously remote 1905 whaling station makes a great base from which to explore the region. Kayaks and canoes are rented for $35 per day, and for $30-45 they will transport you and your boat where you wish.

Transport

For those who can go it alone, the best way to arrive is aboard the ***MV Lady Rose*** from Port Alberni or Bamfield (see page 167). Otherwise you have to charter a boat or plane, or drive to the launching area at **Toquart Bay**. Turn off Hwy 4 12 km northeast of the Tofino junction, then it's 16 km on a rough logging road. You'll need the appropriate charts, 3670 and 3671, available locally or from *Canadian Hydrographic Service*, 9860 West Saanich Rd, Sidney, T3636358.

West Coast Trail

Colour map 1, grid C2/3

At least 66 ships at the bottom of the ocean bear witness to the treacherous nature of a strip of coast known as the 'graveyard of the Pacific'. Following the sinking of the *SS Valencia* in 1906, the decision was taken to convert an old 1890 telegraph trail between Port Renfrew and Bamfield into an escape route for survivors of shipwrecks, since this stretch of coast is practically uninhabited, covered in the densest forest, and subject to appallingly heavy rainfall. From the 1960s, BC's trailblazing hiker community began to rediscover the opportunity to experience some of the most pristine and spectacular wilderness imaginable. Today it is recognized as one of North America's greatest hikes, and quotas are in operation to limit numbers.

The trail runs 75 km from **Pachena Bay**, 5 km south of Bamfield, to **Gordon River**, a ferry ride from Port Renfrew. It takes an average of 6-7 days, and is a commitment not to be entered into lightly. This challenging obstacle course could easily degenerate into a nightmare for those ill-equipped or lacking in fitness. Over 60 hikers have to be evacuated each year, usually with strained knees and ankles. As the official blurb puts it: "You must be self-sufficient, prepared for foul weather, slippery terrain, creek fording, long days and heavy packs. You must be prepared to wait out storms and high water on

Vancouver Island

creek crossings". If in doubt, it is possible to hike half of the trail, beginning at **Nitinat Lake**. Naturally, full camping equipment, plenty of food, good rain gear and boots, and a proper map and tide table are essential. Camping on the beach above the tide line is recommended. Small driftwood campfires are allowed on the beach only, but take a small stove and fuel for cooking. Avoid shellfish, which could be poisonous.

The trail is open 1 May-30 Sep, and heavily booked, especially in Jul and Aug. Quotas **Trail** limit numbers to 60 starters per day, 26 each from Pachena Bay and Gordon River, and **information** 8 from Nitinat Lake. Of these, 6 each from Pachena Bay and Gordon River are available on a first-come first-served basis. Get on the waiting-list at the trailhead, and be prepared to hang around for a few days. **Reservations**, taken 1-3 months before your starting date, beginning 1 Mar. T3871642 (or T1800-6636000 within Canada and USA). Be sure to register at the trailhead by noon on your allotted day, or your spot may be taken. Before starting it is required to take a 1½-hr orientation session, held daily at 0930, 1200, 1330, and 1530 at the trailhead **Information Centres**. Pachena Bay, T7283234, and Gordon River, T6475434, both open daily 0900-1800. For year-round information, the **Park Administration** office is in Ucluelet, T7267721, www.parkscan.harbour.com/pacrim

The trail user fee is an unnegotiable $70. There are 2 ferries during the hike, at Gordon River and Nitinat Narrows, $12.50 each, payable when registering. In addition, those starting at Nitinat Lake have to take a water taxi costing $25. There is no bank or ATM at either Bamfield or Port Renfrew. *West Coast Trail Shuttle Bus*, T4778700, runs daily from Victoria and Nanaimo and between trailheads. Service to Nitinat is not daily. Reservations are recommended. See under Port Renfrew and Bamfield for more details. If all this seems too complicated, crowded or expensive, or if you just plain can't get a place, consider doing the **Juan de Fuca Trail** instead (see page 137).

Bamfield is a tiny town on the edge of Barkley Sound, at the mouth of the **Bamfield** Alberni Inlet. Unless arriving on the oft-vaunted *MV Lady Rose*, access is on a horrible 100-km logging road from Port Alberni. Nobody would bother were it not for Pachena Bay, 5 km away, the northern terminus of the formidable **West Coast Trail** (see above). Having come so far, however, it's well worth having a look round. The main part of town is a somewhat drab, no-nonsense service centre for the forestry industry, but on the other side of a narrow inlet, accessible only by water taxi, T7209246, is a boardwalk village the very unlikelihood of whose location has kept it much more authentic than certain others further north. Here a community of artists has taken root. Wandering along boardwalks from studio to studio is a delightful way to spend an afternoon. There is a café and a lovely deck where the ferry docks. **Brady's Beach**, a 20-minute walk away, is a fine and popular place to catch some rays: long, sandy, and a little bit wild. Bamfield is also a good starting point for kayaking the **Broken Islands Group**. Contact *Broken Island Adventures*, T7283500 for diving and kayaking, or *Rendezvous Dive Ventures Ltd*, T7209306.

B *Bamfield Lodge*, on the boardwalk side, will pick up, T7283419, **Sleeping** www.bamfieldlodge.com Cabins with kitchen. **AL-B** *Woods End Landing Cottages*, 380 Lombard St, T7283383, www.woodsend.travel.bc.ca Fully equipped, 2-bedroom cottages with private decks. Situated on the water amidst secluded gardens. Use of rowing boat, and kayak rentals. **C** *Bamfield Trails Motel*, at the dock on the town side, T7283231. Standard motel, but good food at the pub. At the end of the West Coast Trail is the wonderful, native-run **F** *Pachena Bay Campground*, T7281287. Right on a very fine beach, a perfect place to relax before or after the hike. Reservations essential.

Transport   The ultimate way to arrive is with the *MV Lady Rose* from Port Alberni, T7238313. Passenger only, 0800 Jul-Sep Tue and Thu-Sun, rest of the year Tue and Thu only. The journey is a delight in itself, and you avoid the dreaded road. If driving, be careful and carry at least one good spare tyre. The *West Coast Trail Shuttle Bus*, T7233341, www.trailbus.com leaves daily from 700 Douglas St, **Victoria** at 0650 stopping in **Nanaimo** and **Port Alberni** ($55 one-way). Another leaves **Gordon River** and **Port Renfrew** at 0900 ($50), for hikers who need to get back to their vehicles. Both go to town and **Pachena Bay**, leaving again at 1300.

Central Island

North of dreary Parksville, the Coast Highway offers increasingly striking views of the island-dotted coastline and mainland Coast Mountains as it passes through a series of small villages and bays which are pretty enough but not especially worth lingering over. **Courtenay**, a pleasant town in its own right, gives access to **Mount Washington Ski Hill** and the western, more elevated section of **Strathcona Provincial Park**. The latter is one of Vancouver Island's highlights, offering some first-class hiking among its highest peaks. The bulk of the park is reached from uninspiring **Campbell River** on Highway 28, one of the few to cross over to the untamed West Coast. At road's end is small and remote **Gold River**, gateway to the largely undiscovered wilderness of **Nootka Sound**, a kayaker's paradise that can be easily and cheaply toured aboard the *MV Uchuck III*. As further south, a visit to at least one of the **Gulf Islands** is highly recommended, particularly **Hornby** or **Cortes** which, two steps removed from the main island, are more relaxed yet brimming with character.

Parksville   As drab a town as you could hope to see, Parksville's main drag is the Coast Highway, lined with malls and fast-food joints. There's little reason to stop unless you happen to pass through in July during **Sandfest**, which attracts thousands of visitors for the World Sandcastle Competition. About 3 km to the south, however, is one of the coast's finest beaches at **Rathtrevor Beach Provincial Park**. The tide goes out almost 1 km here, making the 2-km strip of sand ideal for beachcombing and picking over oysters. At high tide the fairly shallow water is as warm as the sea gets in Canada. Be warned that in summer the beach is insanely crowded and reservations are essential for the campground. The **Visitor Information Centre** is at 1275 Island Highway East, T2483613, www.chamber.parksville.bc.ca The stretch of coast north to **Qualicum Bay** is a great bird-watching zone.

A whole clutch of   **Sleeping L-B** *Tigh-Na-Mara*, 1095 Island Hwy, T2482072, www.tigh-na-mara.
resorts surround   com Classy log cabins, heated pool, kitchens. Restaurant. **D** *Arbutus Grove Motel*,
the park   1182 Island Hwy, T2486422. Standard but close to the beach, the most reasonable of the overpriced motels. **D** *Riverbend Resort*, 924 Island Hwy, T2483134. Best value, due to its poor location across the highway. Fully equipped cabins set amongst trees.
Camping T9544600, 200-odd sites, of which 25 are walk-in. Reservations are essential in summer.

Eating *Red Pepper Grill*, 193 Memorial Av, T2482364. Set in a casually stylish house Downtown, with very reasonable prices for seafood, steak, and some Mexican dishes.

Tour operators *Pacific Rainforest Adventure Tours*, T2483667, www.rainforest nature hikes.com, is a local company specializing in hiking tours through old-growth forests.

While the Inland Highway charges relentlessly northwards to Courtenay, the Coast Highway passes through a number of small communities, most possessing a few accommodation choices, the odd eatery, and a bit of beach. The first of these is tiny **French Creek** from where a passenger-only ferry leaves three times daily in summer, a couple times per week in winter, for Lasqueti Island. New levels of remoteness are attained here. With no electricity and very few cars, it's a perfect retreat from civilization.

Lasqueti Island

Sleeping and eating C *Old Bakery B&B*, T3338890. A beautiful place to stay. Self-contained wood cabin 2 mins' walk from the ferry. The island also has a pub and a Mexican restaurant.

Biggest of the seaside villages, Qualicum Beach tries to attract visitors by advertising its high number of artists and writers. Find out more at the **Visitor Information Centre**, 2711 West Island Highway, T7529532, but for a touch of the bohemian a trip to the Gulf Islands is a safer bet. This is best treated as a decent place to stop for bite to eat on the waterfront.

Qualicum Beach

Sleeping There are many standard motels to choose from, plus a couple of more unusual options. **B** *Qualicum College Inn*, 427 College Rd, just off the highway, T7529262. A Tudor-style ex-college with a striking, authentically historic interior and a big garden. Rooms have a fireplace and/or balcony. Restaurant and lounge. **D** *Captain's Inn*, 2795 Island Hwy, T7526743. Beachfront motel with some character and a large patio. **D** *St Andrew's Lodge*, 3319 Island Hwy, T7526652. Old fashioned and rather odd. Cottages with kitchen are good value, but spartan and cold.

Eating Mid-range Of several seafood restaurants, *The Beach House*, 2775 W Island Hwy, is probably the best. The menu is eclectic and of a high calibre, the interior stylish, with an inviting patio. *Fish Tales Café*, 3336 W Island Hwy, serves fish and chips in a Tudor-style house.

About 15 km north of Qualicum Beach, a gravel road leads 12 km to Horne Lake, where a set of caves can be explored either alone or on one of several tours lasting from 1½ to seven hours. For details, call T7578687, www.horne lake.com The lake has some first-class rock-climbing. Horne Lake Amphitheatre is one of the toughest climbs of its kind in the country. There is a campground (**F**). Further north, huge piles of oyster shells define **Fanny Bay** as one of the world's most prolific suppliers of the fabled aphrodisiac.

Horne Lake

Sleeping and transport D *Seahaven B&B*, 6660 South Island Hwy, T3351550, www.seahaven.org The main incentive to stay here would be the proximity to Buckley Bay and the several daily ferries to Denman Island ($4.75 return, $16.50 with car, 10 mins).

This mellow island is another magnet for all kinds of artists, who can be seen displaying and performing at the annual **Festival of the Arts** in early August. **Denman Village**, walking distance from the ferry, is the island's focal point, with bikes and scooters for rent at the local store, but no Information Centre or cash machines. **Fillongley Provincial Park**, 4 km away on the opposite (east) side has a long pebble shoreline with great beachcombing, plus large stands of old-growth cedars and Douglas firs, views of the Coast Range, and a

Denman Island

number of trails, one of which is wheelchair-accessible. **Boyle Point Provincial Park** at the south end also has trails through giant trees and great views, and there's a good chance of seeing eagles and sea lions. Off the northwestern tip, only accessible by water, is **Sandy Island Provincial Park**, where camping is allowed. *Denman Island Sea Kayaks* (see below), will help you get there.

Sleeping There are plenty of B&Bs scattered around, most found at www.denmanisland.com A few are right in or near the village and ferry, including **C** *Hawthorn House*, 3375 Kirk Rd, T3350905. 3 en suite rooms in a 1904 heritage home with hot tub, views and garden. **D-E** *Denman Island Guest House*, 3806 Denman Rd, T3352688. Lovely wooden home with 5 private rooms, dorms and the bizarre 'tree sphere', a completely round room in a tree. **Camping F** *Fillongley Provincial Park*, T9544600, has 10 drive-in campsites on the beach.

Eating The bistro and drive-through café at *Denman Island Guest House* (see above) is the best bet for food. In the village are *Denman Café and General Store*, with vegetarian food, burgers, and coffee; and *Denman Bakery and Pizzeria* with fresh baking daily.

Sport *Denman Island Sea Kayaks*, T3352052.

Hornby Island From Gravelly Bay in the southeast of Denman, several daily ferries make the 10-minute journey to Hornby. From the dock at Shingle Spit, a single road (Central Road), leads most of the way round the island. One small hub of activity is near a bakery roughly 4 km away, but the island's main centre is on the east side, clustered around the **Ringside Market** and the *Co-op*. This health-conscious grocery store doubles as a post office and liquor outlet. Close by is an ATM machine, bike rentals, and the **Information and booking**

Denman & Hornby Islands

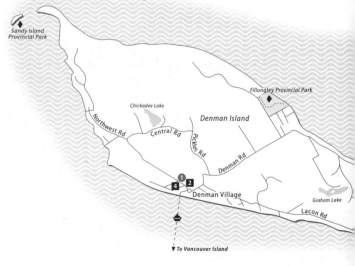

Sleeping
1 A Tidal Treasure B&B
2 Denman Island Guest House
3 Good Morning B&B
4 Hawthorn House
5 Hornby Island Resort, Wheelhouse Restaurant & Thatch Pub

Not to scale

centre, T3350506, www.hornbyisland.com for free B&B reservations and information. Within walking distance is **Tribune Bay Provincial Park**, with a beautiful long sandy beach, bike rentals, and camping. St John's Road, north of the *Co-op*, leads down the island's southeastern spit to **Helliwell Bay Provincial Park**, where a gorgeous 5-km circular walk takes in some amazing bluffs with great views and nesting eagles. Apart from the Performing Arts Festival and The Bike Race (see Festivals, below), another summer draw is scuba-diving and the rare prospect of seeing 6-gilled sharks. There's a diving base, marina and accommodation at **Ford's Cove**, though equipment has to be rented on Vancouver Island.

Sleeping   A-B *A Tidal Treasure*, T3353006. One of the island's best B&Bs. 3 very pleasant, light-filled rooms, with en suite baths and balcony. **C** *Good Morning B&B*, T3351094, has 3 more moderate rooms with shared bath. For motel-style rooms and cottages on a sandy beach, there's **C** *Hornby Island Resort*, 4305 Shingle Spit Rd, T3350136. **F** *Tribune Bay Campsite*, T3352359, has 120 drive-in sites, some with hook-ups. **F** *Bradsdadsland Campsite*, about 3 km from the ferry on Central Rd, T3350757, has a friendly, family atmosphere and good sunsets.   ■ *on map*

Eating   *Wheelhouse Restaurant*, in *Hornby Island Resort* (see above), is the best bet for food, with nightly BBQ and buffet. *Jan's Café*, beside the *Co-op*, is the clear choice for breakfast and coffee. For a pint and food, head for the *Thatch Pub* by the ferry dock, which has a lovely deck and Fri night jazz.   ● *on map*

Festivals   Though smaller than Denman, and two steps removed from the main island, there is generally more happening here, especially in summer when various festivals draw hordes of visitors. A perfect time to visit is in **Aug** during the week-long

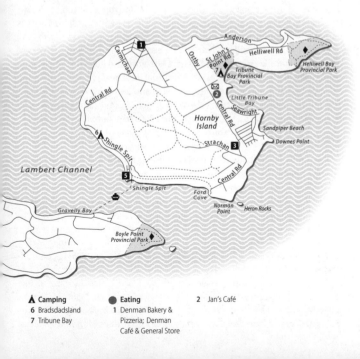

⚑ Camping
  6 Bradsdadsland
  7 Tribune Bay

● Eating
  1 Denman Bakery & Pizzeria; Denman Café & General Store

  2 Jan's Café

Vancouver Island

Hornby Island Performing Arts Festival, T3352734. *The Bike Race* in Sep, www.thebikerace.com, is a huge, out-of-control event, with music, free camping, food, and plenty of lunatic mountain bikers. To see what draws them, check out some of the excellent trails in the Stachan Valley.

Sports *Hornby Bike Shop*, by the *Co-op*, T3350444. Map and rentals (as well as internet access). For **kayak** lessons, rentals and tours, contact *Hornby Ocean Kayaks*, T3352726.

Transport From Gravelly Bay in the southeast of **Denman**, several daily ferries, at sporadic times, make the 10-min journey to Hornby, the last one at 1750. $4.75 return, $16.50 with car.

Courtenay and the Comox Valley

Phone code: 250
Colour map 1,
grid B/C3
Population: 18,420

Of the three sister towns clustered within the farming landscape of the Comox Valley, Courtenay is certainly prominent. While its outskirts are characteristically ugly, the small Downtown is probably the nicest on the island after Victoria and Tofino. A clutch of decent shops, restaurants, cafés and galleries make this a much better place to stop than Campbell River to the north, and it's the obvious base from which to explore the **Forbidden Plateau** section of Strathcona Park, or to go skiing at nearby Mount Washington (see below). The helpful **Visitor Information Centre** is at 2040 Cliffe Avenue, T3343234, www.tourism-comox-valley.bc.ca

The outskirts of town merge seamlessly with the more genteel **Comox**, pleasantly situated on Comox Harbour, and home to a significant airport and Canadian naval base, a marina, a few decent pubs, and a handful of attractions. The trio is completed by **Cumberland**, the rough-and-ready former site of a massive coal mine, now trying to attract visitors to a museum highlighting those dusty days. Since the best of the island is close by and further south, it's worth considering the ferry from Courtenay to Powell River on the Sunshine Coast as part of a nice loop back to Vancouver (see Transport, below).

Fossils from an 80-million-year-old sea bed at nearby **Puntledge River** are on display at the **Courtenay and District Museum and Palaeontology Centre**, along with dinosaur replicas, and the usual local history fare. Fossil tours, twice daily in July and August (less in spring and autumn), include a lecture and tour of the museum and a drive to the site to find (and keep) fossils. ■ *Tue-Sat 1000-1700 except in winter, Sun 1200-1600 summer, closed in winter. $3, $2.50 concessions. Tours $15, $7.50 concessions. Reservation recommended. 207 4th St, T3340686, www.courtenaymuseum.ca*

The 3.6 ha of landscaped grounds at **Filberg Lodge and Park** (see Festivals) are open to the public. ■ *$1. Park 0800-dusk year round; lodge Jun-Aug 1100-1700 daily, May and Sep weekends only. 61 Filberg Rd, Comox, T3392715.* In April and May, the town fills up with trumpeter swans, whose biggest habitat in North America, maintained by *Ducks Unlimited*, is right in town. The **Riverside Walkway** beside the estuary makes for a pleasant stroll.

Sleeping **AL-A** *Kingfisher Oceanside Resort*, 4330 Island Hwy S, 7 km south, T3381323. Luxurious beachfront suites with balconies and fireplaces, and oceanview rooms. Hot tub, pool, sauna, fitness room, spa, expensive restaurant, and lounge. Nicest of a large selection of B&Bs is **C** *Greystone Manor*, 4014 Haas Rd, 2 km south, T3381422. 3 rooms with private bath in a waterfront heritage home surrounded by beautiful flower gardens. **C-D** *Copes' Islander B&B*, 1484 Wilkinson Rd, T3391038. Beach, private entrance, views, close to ferry.

D *Estuary House B&B*, 2810 Comox Rd, T8900130. En suite rooms, good value. There are numerous motels strung along Cliffe Av on the way Downtown, such as **D** *Sleepy Hollow Inn*, at 1190, T3344476. Standard rooms, kitchen extra. **E** *Courtenay Riverside Hostel*, 1380 Cliffe Av, T3341938. Handily situated in a big old house Downtown. Friendly and helpful. Lockers, laundry, kitchen, internet. **E** *Comox Lake Hostel*, 4787 Lake Trail Rd, 6 km west, T3381914. On the way to Forbidden Plateau and Comox Lake, so good for instant access to the great outdoors. Will pick up at bus or train in Courtenay, otherwise very difficult to get to. Tent sites, private rooms, kitchen, laundry. **Camping** 22 km north at **F** *Miracle Beach Provincial Park*, 1812 Miracle Beach Dr, exit Hwy 19 at Hamm Rd, T3372400. 200 sites close to a large, sandy beach. Showers. Very popular in summer. **Saratoga Beach**, nearby in Black Creek, also has a long sandy beach stuffed with 'resorts': tightly packed cabins on the beach, all overpriced in the **B-C** range.

Expensive *Fitzgerald's Bistro*, 932 Fitz Av. Sophisticated fine dining in a cosy, intimate setting. *The Old House*,1760 Riverside Lane, T3385406. A long-standing favourite with locals. Sumptuous and atmospheric wooden house, full of romantic nooks and crannies, fireplaces, gables, and a nice patio. Menu is seafood and steak with an international touch. If not hungry, at least go for a drink. **Mid-range** *Atlas Café*, 250 6th St, T3389838. Vegetarian global food, great salads and coffee, curries and wraps. The locals' favourite. *Thai Village*, 2104 Cliffe Av, T3343812. Quaint and authentic. *Tita's Mexican Restaurant*, 536 6th St, T3348033. Authentic dishes in colourful surroundings. **Cheap** *Bar None Café*, 244 4th St. Excellent coffee and fresh baking, vegetarian food, good breakfast. The best place for a pint is in Comox at the *Edge Marine Pub*, 1805 Beaufort Av. Deck onto the ocean, bistro with good food.

Eating

Sid Williams Theatre, 442 Cliffe Av, T3382420. Music, dance, live theatre.

Entertainment

On the first weekend in **Aug** the massive *Filberg Festival* takes over Filberg Lodge and Park, 61 Filberg Rd in Comox. 4 days of the best arts and crafts in BC, with great food and music. $8 entry, T3349242, www.filbergfestival.com *Vancouver Island Music Festival* in mid-**Jul** involves 3 days of Canadian and World music at various venues around town.

Festivals

Mountain biking is very big in the area, with 50 km of trails around Cumberland, and more at Mt Washington. Try Seal Bay Park for an easy scenic ride. Several races and mountain bike festivals are held each year. For rentals and trail information go to *Dodge City Cycles*, 1st and Perinth in Cumberland; or *Simon's Cycles Ltd*, 1841 Comox Av in Comox. For **hiking** see Strathcona Provincial Park, page 175. For downhill and nordic **skiing** at Mt Washington see below. For sports equipment and rentals try *Ski, Surf and Kayak Shop*, 333 5th St, T3388844, or *Mountain Meadows*, 368 5th St.

Sports

Wheelies Mountain Adventures, T3383070. Bike tours. *Comox District Mountaineering Club*, T3362101. Glacier tours. *Comox Valley Kayaks*, T3342628, www.comox valleykayaks.com Lessons and rentals. *Tree Island Kayaking*, T3390580. Rentals and tours. *Pacific Pro Dive*, T3386829, www.scubashark.com

Tour operators

Local Taxi: *United Cabs*, T3397955.

Transport

Long distance Air: Comox Valley Airport receives daily flights from **Vancouver** with *Pacific Coastal* (from $200 return), and from **Calgary** with *West Jet* (from $300 return).
   Bus: The station is Downtown at 9-2663 Kilpatrick Av. *Laidlaw Coach Lines*, T334-2475, www.grayline.ca, have 4 buses to and from **Victoria** daily. Local buses are operated by *Comox Valley Transit System*, T3395453. Bus No 11 runs to the ferry and airport, stopping at 4th Av/Cliffe, where many other routes converge. $1.25. No service on Sun.

Vancouver Island

▶ **Hippies and red-necks**

Canada social distinctions, rather than being related to a deeply entrenched sense of class, tend to be of a more subtle and ideological nature. Those at the extreme ends of the spectrum would refer to each other as 'red-necks' and 'hippies'; most people are somewhere in between but definitely leaning in one direction or the other. As in so many spheres of Canadian life, what defines these people is their relationship to the land, and specifically to the issue of logging. Extreme hippies, or 'tree-huggers', are against cutting down trees per se, regarding this as an immoral act that only the heartless could condone. An incorrigible red-neck, on the other hand, has failed to evolve beyond the attitude prevalent a couple of centuries ago, believing that the earth is man's to plunder, that it is our right, even our destiny, to subjugate the planet to our will and take from it what we can. The red-necks will argue as if they honestly believed that the forestry industry, and by extension the West's whole economy, could not survive without the demise of all that standing lumber.

The sad thing from an outsider's point of view is how the antagonism of these two extremes prevents either from being able to see the middle ground. Yes, BC's economy depends on the forestry industry. No, that doesn't justify cutting down 1,000-year-old trees because they're worth more; logging in watersheds, thus depriving people of clean water; or razing huge swaths of land rather than logging selectively in such a way that the forest can regenerate.

Ferry: *BC Ferries*, T1888-2233779, www.bcferries.com, run 4 daily sailings from Little River, 13 km north of Comox to **Powell River** on the Sunshine Coast, $7.50, ($32.50 with vehicle), 95 mins.

Train: *Via Rail*, T1800-5618630, www.viarail.ca, currently runs 1 train daily from **Victoria**, $31 one-way. 0830 from Victoria, 1330 from **Courtenay**. The station is on McPhee Av, a short walk from Downtown.

Directory **Communications** Internet: at the library, or *Cardero Coffee & Tea Co*, 208 5th St. **Canada Post**: 1812 Comox Av, Comox. **Laundry** *Maytag Home Style Laundry*, 2401 Cliff Av. **Library** 410 Cliffe Av. **Medical services** *St Joseph's General Hospital*, 2137 Comox Av, T3392242.

Mount Washington Ski Area Situated 25 km northwest of Comox, and mostly easily reached on the Inland Island Highway, this medium-sized hill receives a lot of powder, an average of almost 9 m annually. Canada's first six-person chairlift is currently being constructed as part of an expansion programme that should considerably raise the hill's profile. Small, unintimidating and with superb ocean views, it's a great one for beginners and intermediates. Eight lifts lead to 50 alpine runs (25% beginner, 40% intermediate, 35% expert). There are also 55 km of track-set cross-country trails, and 20 km of snowshoeing trails. You could also try **snow-tubing**. ■ *A day-pass is $45 for alpine, $17 for cross-country. Some trails are lit up for night-skiing, Fri and Sat 1630-2100.*

From the end of June to early October the gondola opens at 1000 for biking and hiking, with arresting views of Comox Glacier, the Coast Mountains, and the Georgia Strait ($9.81, $14.73 with lunch). Bikes can be rented here, but it's cheaper in town. Favourite downhills include the steep and scary **Monster Mile**, and **Discovery Road**. There's also a free nine-hole disc golf course (frisbee rental $3.50) and horse riding for $30 per hour. Open in the summer is a pub/restaurant, a coffee bar and on Sundays the arts and crafts **Mountain Market**.

Sleeping Accommodation at the resort is generally expensive, except for the new **D-E** *Mount Washington Guest House*, T8988141, www.mtwashingtonhostel.com Shared, double or family rooms in a chalet. Shared kitchen and lounge, deck with hot tub, skiing right outside the back door. Otherwise package deals offer the best value. Try **Central Reservations**, T3381386, www.mtwashington.bc.ca, or *Peak Accommodations*, T8973851, www.peakaccom.com

Strathcona Provincial Park

Established in 1911, this is BC's oldest park and it contains the lion's share of *Colour map 1, grid B2* Vancouver Island's most elevated peaks, including its highest point, **Golden Hinde** (2,200 m). It also provides one of the few chances to sample the beauty of the island's gloriously undeveloped interior. Hiking is the main activity, with most trails clustered in two areas. The Forbidden Plateau region is accessed from Courtenay, with trailheads at Paradise Meadows, right next to Mount Washington Ski Area (see above), and Forbidden Plateau Ski Area, 19 km west of Courtenay. The Buttle Lake area (see below) is reached via Highway 28 from Campbell River. The more remote southern section of the park, including the famous Della Falls (see below), is accessed, with difficulty, from Port Alberni. Pick up a free blue *BC Parks* map and information, from the Visitor Information Centres in Courtenay or Campbell River. National Topographic Series maps, scale 1:50,000 are -92 F/11 Forbidden Plateau, and -92 F/12 Buttle Lake.

Jutting out from the park's eastern flank the high altitude of the Forbidden **Forbidden** Plateau means that hikers barely have to climb to reach alpine scenery and **Plateau** views. **Paradise Meadows** trailhead, 1½ km from Mount Washington Road down Nordic Lodge Road, 35 km from Courtenay, gives the easiest access to this formidable zone. A 4-km hike, with minimal elevation gain, leads to **Kwai Lake**, an excellent base with a backcountry campground and a network of trails radiating out like spokes in all directions.

The Forbidden Plateau (**Wood Mountain**) trailhead is 19 km from Courtenay, adjacent to a former ski area. In 2001 this was closed after acts of vandalism had tainted the area and the trails were falling into disrepair. This trailhead is also further removed from the nucleus of trails around Kwai Lake, which is 15 km away via the **Plateau Trail**. For long-distance hikers this is no bad thing, and a couple of longer hikes begin here: **Mount Becher** trail is a 9-km round-trip with 580-m elevation gain, and excellent views of the Comox Valley, Georgia Strait and Coast Mountains. **Douglas** and **McKenzie** lakes, 9 km away, are good for fishing.

Buttle Lake Road heads south from Highway 28, 47 km west of Campbell **Buttle Lake** River, and follows the edge of this long, skinny strip of water into the very heart of the park. It's a fantastic drive, offering hiking options of all lengths. The **Park Visitor Centre** is at the junction. The *Campbell River Airporter*, T2863000, $40 for two, will drop people here or at the lodge (see below).

Lupin Falls, near the north end, **Karst Creek**, two-thirds down, **Myra Falls**, at the bottom, and **Lady Falls**, off Highway 28, are all short and easy walks leading, usually through lush rainforest, to gorgeous waterfalls.

Most of the longer hikes start at the lake's south end. **Flower Ridge**, at 29.6 km, is a steep and rough 14-km round trip (extendable to 24 km), gaining 1,250 m elevation up to an open alpine ridge. **Bedwell Lake** (with complicated access, see *BC Parks* map) is a 12-km hike with 600-m gain, also leading to good mountain views and a campground on the lake. Accessible only by boat from the Auger Point day-use area is the **Marble Meadows** trail, 13 km return, 1,250 m gain. Many different peaks can be reached from here, and the Golden Hinde is visible. From Highway 28 at the western edge of the park, the **Crest Mountain** trail, 10 km return with 1,250-m gain, gives quick access to the alpine scenery and views. South-facing, it's a good choice early in the season.

Della Falls Many people, lured by photos, want to hike to Della Falls, the tallest in North America. Locals opine that the reward is not worth the effort. Access is from Port Alberni (not Buttle Lake). A boat must be taken across Great Central Lake, then the hike is 32 km return with little elevation gain and a couple of unbridged creeks to cross. The best way to go is with *Ark Resort*. For details see Port Alberni, page 157.

Sleeping & eating Just before the Buttle Lake junction, outside the park boundary, is the superlative **A-D** *Strathcona Park Lodge*, T2863122, www.strathcona.bc.ca There are very nice rooms in the lodge, as well as modern but simple cabins of all sizes. You don't have to be a guest to partake of the healthy, all-you-can-eat buffet meals at reasonable prices. This well-established centre is an excellent place to receive proper training and guidance if you are interested in outdoor pursuits but lack the confidence or know-how to go it alone. All manner of rentals, lessons and tours are offered by friendly, enthusiastic staff. All-inclusive holiday packages, including meals and unlimited use of kayaks and canoes, run from $129 per person.

Camping There are 2 vehicle-accessible campgrounds on Buttle Lake Rd, **F** *Buttle Lake* at the north end and **F** *Ralph River* at the south end. Both have spacious and private sites on the lake, outhouses but no showers. Free after 30 Sep. Backcountry camping, including use of designated areas such as Kwai Lake, is $5 per person per night, self-registration, cash only. Many are accessible by boat only. For Forbidden Plateau day-hikers, accommodation is available at Mt Washington Ski Area (see above) or Courtenay.

Campbell River

Phone code: 250
Colour map 1,
grid B2/3
Population: 30,500

Those approaching Vancouver Island's third largest town from the north are greeted by a sawmill of horrendous proportions, then a maze of malls. Along the Coast Highway from the south is a neverending strip of seafront houses and hotels. So Downtown, draped nicely around the water, comes as a relief, but there's still no good reason to stop unless you're there to fish. The oft-seen epithet 'Salmon capital of the world' is for once well-justified, and in winter there's plenty of halibut too to keep the industry rolling. Those not of the hook and line inclination can go snorkelling and see the red giants up close (see Tour operators, below).

Campbell River Museum has exhibits on pioneers, fishing and First Nations, and an unusual multimedia presentation of a mystical journey beneath the sea from a native perspective. ■ *Summer Mon-Sat 1000-1700, Sun 1200-1700; winter Tue-Sat 1200-1700. $5, $3.75 concessions. 470 Island Hwy, T2873103, www.crmuseum.bc.ca* **Wei Wai Kum House of Treasures**, also on the highway at the Discovery Harbour Shopping Centre, sells and exhibits First Nations arts and crafts in a building modelled on a West Coast 'Big House'. Inside is **Gilda's Box of Treasures Theatre**, a venue for performances by aboriginal dancers, drummers and singers, and salmon feasts. ■ *Shows summer only Tue-Sat 1600, Sat 1300. $20, $10 concessions. T2877310.*

At 182 m long, 46 m of it jutting out over the ocean, **Discovery Pier** is a popular and easy place to fish ($2). It's open 24 hours, and lit up at night.

Remember that you'll need a Sport Fishing licence to go after them ($108 for non-residents). **Quinsam Salmon Hatchery** is the place to learn more about the local obsession. The salmon spawning run peaks between July and September. ■ *0800-1600. Free. 5 km west on Hwy 28.*

Otherwise, the best advice is to catch a ferry to the lovely, laid-back Discovery Islands of Quadra and Cortes, or head west on Highway 28 for 48 km to *Strathcona Park Lodge* (see above) where there's some great accommodation, good food, and everything for the outdoors enthusiast. For a taste of wild and remote beauty, keep going west to Gold River and the as yet unspoilt Nootka Sound (see page 180). The **Visitor Information Centre** and **Art Gallery** are at 1235 Shoppers Row (Ocean Highway) ■ *Mon-Sat 0900-1900 summer, Mon-Fri 0900-1700 winter. Gallery Tue-Sat 1200-1700, free. T2874636, www.campbellrivertourism.com*

AL *Painter's Lodge*, 1625 MacDonald Rd, T2861102, www.obmg.com The nicest option by far. A variety of luxurious rooms with ocean or garden views, pool, hot tub, tennis courts, gift shop, restaurant and pub. Free water shuttle to their *April Point Lodge*, T2852222, on Quadra Island.

   C *Haig-Brown House*, 2250 Campbell River Rd, T2866646, www.oberoon. ark.com/kdbhbh Best of the few B&Bs. 3 rooms with shared bath in a heritage house with very large garden on the river. **C** *Hotel Bachmair*, 492 S Island Hwy, T9232848, bachmair@oberon.ark.com Not too central, but best value of many hotels to the south. Rooms have balconies, with kitchens available in the nicer ones. **C** *Rustic Motel*, 2140 N Island Hwy, T2866295, www.rusticmotel.com Decent, recently renovated rooms, $10 extra for kitchen. Amenities such as laundry, sauna, hot tub and dry room included, as well as breakfast. **D** *Town Centre Inn*, 1500 Dogwood St, T2878866. Standard Downtown option. Breakfast included. The cheaper motels sprawl along the S Island Hwy, such as the average **D** *Big Rock* at 1020, T9234211.

   Those **camping** have some better choices. **F** *Elk Falls Provincial Park*, 2 km west on Hwy 28, T9564600. 122 very nice sites on the Quinsam River, as well as trails and the dramatic 24-m falls. It's also a very popular fishing spot. The smaller *Loveland Bay Provincial Park*, T9564600, is more of a trip, but very quiet as a result. Follow signs from Hwy 28, then 15 km on a gravel road. *Morton Lake Provincial Park*, T9564600, is even smaller and more remote and has sites on the lake. Head north on the Island Hwy to Menzies Bay, then take a logging road west for 20 km. Sites sit between 2 lakes.

Expensive *Harbour Grill*, 1334 Island Hwy, T2874143. Seafood and French cuisine. **Mid-range** *Baan Thai Restaurant*, 1090B Shoppers Row, T2864853. Extensive and authentic menu, rooftop patio. *Eat Well Market*, 581 11th Av. Snacky vegetarian food, lunch and early dinner only. *Spice Island*, 2269 S Island Hwy. Dinner only, closed Sun and Mon. Very tasty Thai, Vietnamese, Indonesian or Chinese food. **Cheap** *Tomeli's Fish'n'Chip Bistro*, 151 Dogwood St. Fresh fish, 2 for 1 on Tue and Wed. *The Uptown Ideal Café*, below *Baan Thai*. Good central choice for a cheap breakfast.

Cinema *Capri Cineplex*, 100-489 Dogwood St S, T2873233; *Galaxy*, 250 10th Av, T2861744. **Theatre** *Tidemark Theatre*, 1220 Shoppers Row, T2877415. Distinctive peppermint-pink venue for live theatre and music, with art displays in the lobby.

Campbell River Kayaks, 1620 Petersen Rd, T287228

Aboriginal Journeys, T8501101, www.aboriginaljourneys.com Whale- and bear-watching tours with some native history and culture thrown in. *Eagle Eye Adventures*, T2860809, eagleeye@connected.bc.ca Conscientious whale- and bear-watching trips.

Sleeping
Though smaller, Courtenay, a mere 44 km to the south, has a much better selection of restaurants and accommodation

Eating

Entertainment

Sport

Tour operators

Vancouver Island

Paradise Found Adventure Tour Co, 165-1160 Shellbourne Dr, T9230848, www.paradisefound.bc.ca Spend 3-4 hrs snorkelling beside the migrating and spawning salmon, early Jul-late Oct. Also climbing, hiking, whale-watching, caving, snowshoeing, or snorkelling with colonies of sealions at Mitlenach Island.

Transport *BC Ferries*, T1888-2233779, www.bcferries.com, operate a regular service to Quadra Island, with another from there to Cortes. *Campbell River Airporter*, T2863000, run a service to Strathcona Park on request, $40 for 2. *Laidlaw*, T3854411, www.grayline.ca, run 5 **buses** per day to and from Nanaimo, $19.25, and Victoria, $44. 1 daily bus continues north to Port Hardy, $49.

Directory **Communications** Canada Post: 1251 Shoppers Row. **Laundry** *Campbell River Laundry*, 1231 Shoppers Row. **Library** 1240 Shoppers Row. **Medical services** *Campbell River Hospital*, 375 2nd Av, T2877111.

Discovery Islands

Phone code: 250
Colour map 1,
grid B3

At the northern end of the Georgia Strait is an incredibly convoluted clustering of large and tiny islands through which are threaded numerous narrow channels and inlets. One can only imagine the difficulty with which Captain George Vancouver would have negotiated, let alone charted, this maze. The landscapes here are even more dramatic than usual, best enjoyed from Quadra and Cortes, the only Discovery Islands that are easy to access. All these closely huddled, virtually uninhabited islands, along with the proximity of Desolation Sound Marine Park (see page 117) on the other side of the strait, makes this an exciting playground for sailors and kayakers. A good source of information is www.discoveryislands.ca

Quadra Island
Phone code: 250
Colour map 1, grid B3

Quadra is the biggest of the key Gulf Islands, and one of the most populated. The main hub is **Quathiaski Cove**, which hosts most stores and a popular Saturday Farmer's Market. A short drive or hitch across the island is the nicer village of **Heriot Bay**, which has a summer-only **Visitor Information Booth**, T2852724, www.quadraisland.ca, an adjacent *Credit Union*, and bike/kayak rentals. Neither is as good a place for soaking up the Gulf Island vibe as similar centres on Cortes, Hornby or Gabriola, though the usual plethora of galleries and studios is easily found.

The island's main attraction for visitors is the native village of **Cape Mudge** that sits at its southern tip. Construction here of the outstanding **Kwagiulth Museum**, was a major condition of the return in the 1980s of numerous items that the government confiscated in 1922 as part of an attempt to wipe out the powerful Potlatch ceremony (see page 457). The result is one of the country's finest collections of masks, costumes, and other Potlatch artefacts. Native guides give tours explaining the history and significance of the items. There's also an interesting collection of vintage photos. The museum is currently closed for renovation and is due to reopen in 2004. ■ *1000-1630 Mon-Sat, Jun-Sep 1200-1630 Sun. T2853733.* The adjacent **Carving and Artist Centre** exhibits a number of old totem poles, and craftsmen can be seen creating new works. A walk from here leads to a 100-year-old lighthouse, and a beach with over 50 petroglyphs. The attractive *Tsa-Kwa-Luten Lodge* (see Sleeping) set in a 445-ha forest, recalls the village's original Kwak'wala name, meaning 'gathering place'. ■ *1000-1630 Mon-Sat, Jun-Sep1200-1630 Sun.*

The vast bulk of the island is north of the two main communities, barely inhabited, and criss-crossed with some very fine hiking and biking trails. The most popular hike is up **Chinese Mountains**, with splendid panoramas at the top. Nearby **Morte Lake** is also a worthwhile destination. The trail to **Nugedzi Lake** is a steady climb through old-growth forest also leading to excellent views. For mountain biking, Mount Seymour has most of the best descents, with some 400-m drops. For swimming and mainly rocky beaches head for **Village Bay Park** or **Rebecca Spit Provincial Park**; the latter also makes a nice stroll.

Sleeping and eating L *April Point Resort*, T2852222, www.aprilpoint.com Affiliated to *Painter's Lodge* in Campbell River, with a free shuttle from there (see page 177). Beautiful spacious rooms, restaurant with ocean views from wrap-around balcony, sushi bar. Kayak, bike and scooter rental. **B** *Tsa-Kwa-Luten Lodge*, 1 Lighthouse Rd, Cape Mudge, T2852042, www.capemudgeresort.bc.ca Beautiful wooden-beam building based on a traditional West Coast 'Big House'. Ocean views from high bluffs surrounded by forest. Lodge rooms and 2-4-bedroom cabins with kitchen. Sauna, jacuzzi, all manner of guided tours and activities, including native cultural events. **C** *Heriot Bay Inn*, T2853322, www.heriotbayinn.com Rooms with private bath, or cottages, plus 60 campsites (**F**) with showers. Kayak, bike and canoe rentals, pub and restaurant. Price includes breakfast.

   E *Wilby Inn*, 129 Joyce Rd, 6 km from Quathiaski ferry, T2852573, call for directions or pick-up ($5 per party). Beautiful and peaceful waterfront hostel on an old 28-ha farm. Rooms with shared bath. Big kitchen and living room. Plenty of hiking and trails. **E** *Travellers' Rural Retreat*, 10-15 mins' drive from Heriot Bay ferry on a logging road, T2852477 for directions. Small and extremely remote guesthouse right on the water. Favoured by artists or those seeking a place for some silence. **Camping** The only place to camp is the *Heriot Bay Inn* (above). In Quathiaski Cove is *Waco Taco*, a great, authentic Mexican restaurant.

Sports Cycling Trail maps, information and rentals are available at *Island Cycle* in Heriot Bay, T2853627. There are also maps on-line at www.discoveryislands.ca For **kayak** tours and rentals, contact *Coast Mountain Expeditions*, T2870635, www.coastmountainexpeditions.com *Coastal Spirits Sea Kayaking*, T2852895, or *Spirit of the West Kayak Adventures*, T2852121, www.kayakingtours.com *Island Dreams Adventures*, T2852751, run sea **canoe** tours. *Discovery Charters*, T2853146, will take you **whale-watching** or **hiking**.

Transport Ferry *BC Ferries*, T1888-2233779, www.bcferries.com, leave Campbell River every hr on the half hr, arriving at Quathiaski Cove on **Quadra**, $4.75 return ($16.75 with car), 45 mins. 6 ferries daily leave from Heriot Bay on the other (east) side of the island, arriving at Whaletown on **Cortes**, $5.75 ($20.25 with car), 45 mins. There is no public transport here, but hitching is easy. For **bike** rentals and tours there's *Island Cycle* in Heriot Bay, T2853627.

In many ways, Cortes (www.cortesisland.com) is *the* quintessential Gulf Island. As with Hornby (see page 169), being two steps removed from the main island exaggerates the spirit of the people, who are very laid-back and friendly. The **Arts Festival** in mid-July is a good time to meet them. **Manson's Landing**, some 15 km from the ferry landing at Whaletown, is the community's main focus, with a café, cash point (ATM), post office, launderette and free store.

Cortes Island
Phone code: 250
Colour map 1, grid B3

   Manson's Landing Provincial Park has one of the better sand beaches around, and a warm freshwater lagoon for swimming, with the chance to legally pick some of the clams and oysters that are all over the island. The adjacent **Hague Lake Provincial Park** is good for hiking. **Smelt Bay Provincial Park**, 25 km south of the ferry, has camping and a nice beach walk to **Sutil**

Vancouver Island

Point. At Cortes Bay is the bizarre folly of **Wolf Bluff Castle**, an eccentric, five-storey structure, including a dungeon and three turrets. The island's most famous feature is the popular **Hollyhock Retreat Centre** where you can follow courses on yoga and meditation, or simply enjoy the relaxing grounds, great vegetarian food and decent accommodation.

Sleeping B *Hollyhock*, T9356576, www.hollyhock.bc.ca This peaceful and beautiful retreat offers lots of options, which can include all meals, as well as meditation, yoga, hot tub, kayak and sailing trips, and mind and body workshops. The food is gourmet vegetarian with an excellent reputation. Reservations recommended. **C** *Cortes Island Motel*, close to Manson's Landing, T9356363. Standard but convenient. **D** *Blue Heron B&B*, 20 km from Whaletown ferry, T9356584 for directions. 4 rooms, en suite or shared bath, right on the ocean. **D** *Gorge Harbour Marina Resort*, 5 km from ferry on Hunt Rd, T9356433. Standard rooms, 46-site campground (**F**) with hook-ups for RVs, scooter, boat and kayak rentals. A far nicer campground for tents is at **F** *Smelt Bay Provincial Park*, see above, T9544600.

Eating Mid-range *Cortes Café*, in Manson's Landing, is the place of choice for most locals, with good food using locally grown ingredients, coffee, smoothies, and a popular summer deck. For something more upmarket the *Old Floathouse* at the *Gorge Harbour* (above) is recommended.

Transport *The Cortes Connection*, T9356911, runs to and from the *Greyhound* depot in Campbell River, $12, $8 concessions, plus $5.75 for ferry. They also cover scheduled routes on the island: one end to the other is $7, $3 concessions. To **Quadra** is $9, $4.50 concessions, plus $5.75 for ferry. 6 ferries daily leave from Heriot Bay on the other (east) side of **Quadra**, arriving at Whaletown on **Cortes**, $5.75 ($20.25 with car), 45 mins. *Gorge Harbour Marina Resort* (see above) rents out scooters and kayaks.

Gold River and Nootka Sound

Colour map 1, grid B2 Nootka Sound is touted as the 'Birthplace of BC', for it was here at Yuquot in 1778 that Captain James Cook made his first West Coast landing. When he asked the Mowachaht people the name of their land, they thought he wanted directions around a smaller island, and replied 'Nutka, itchme' (Go around that way). Mistaking it for a place name, Cook dubbed the region Nootka, a name that was eventually extended to the people themselves. So warm was the welcome he received from Chief Maquinna, that he nicknamed the place 'Friendly Cove', and quickly entered into a burgeoning trade in sea otter fur that made Yuquot the busiest port north of Mexico for several years.

Today this wild and undeveloped portion of Vancouver Island's Northwest Coast is attracting a new breed of adventurer. It is quickly being discovered by BC's in-the-know outdoor fraternity, who come to sea-kayak around its hundreds of small islands, surf the Pacific breakers, dive to the reefs and walls where gill shark roam, fish, explore the numerous local cave systems, rock climb, or hike a section of the West Coast that is guaranteed to be crowd-free. If all that sounds too hard-core, a delightful way to see this rugged strip of coast is aboard the *MV Uchuck III* which, similar to the *MV Lady Rose* out of Port Alberni, has become a popular way to take a cheap cruise (see Transport).

Gold River Access is from Gold River, a beautiful 91-km drive from Campbell River on Highway 28. There's little to the town itself, which was utterly dominated by logging until the pulpmill closed in 1998. Since then the people have increasingly looked towards tourism for their survival, slowly developing the infrastructure to meet and encourage interest in the region. There's a summer-only **Visitor Information Centre** at Highway 28 and Scout Lake Road, T2832418, www.village.goldriver.bc.ca In June, Gold River hosts the **Burning Boot Festival**, culminating in the **Great Walk**, a 70-km trek on gravel roads, considered the toughest walk in North America. It ends at **Tahsis**, an even smaller, more remote community at the end of a long inlet leading from Nootka Sound. Canada's best caving can be undertaken nearby. There is a summer-only **Visitor Information** booth at Rugged Mountain Road, T9346667. Even further removed, **Zeballos** and **Yuquot** are tiny communities accessible only with the *MV Uchuck III*, and are perfectly placed for kayakers to push further into pristine territory. For Zeballos information, call the Village Office, T7614229.

Gold River C *Ridgeview Motor Inn*, 395 Donner Court, T2832277. Reasonable rooms, views over the village. D *Peppercorn Trail Motel*, 100 Muchalat Dr, T2832443. Pretty basic. Also has 75 campsites with showers (**F**). D *Shadowlands B&B*, 580 Dogwood Dr, T2832513. 3 fairly large and decent rooms, some with private bath.

    Tahsis D *Tahsis Motel*, Head Bay Rd, T9346318. Basic rooms. Pub and restaurant.

    Zeballos C *Mason's Motor Lodge*, 203 Pandora Av, T7614044, www.masons lodge.zeballos.bc.ca Views, decks, some kitchenettes, tours arranged. C *Zeballos Inlet Lodge*, 167 Maquinna Av, T7614294. 5 fairly large rooms with private baths and TVs. Continental breakfast included. Laundry, covered patio with BBQ.

    Yuquot (Friendly Cove): **D-F** *Yuquot Cabins and Campground*, T2832054. Fairly basic accommodation on a Native Reserve.

Sleeping & eating

Caving Tahsis is the prime spot for caving, with networks like the **Thanksgiving Cave System**, **Wyameer Park Caves**, and many others appropriate for professionals only. **Quatsino Cave** is the deepest cave in North America. **Upana Caves Recreation Area**, 17 km northwest of Gold River on the road to Tahsis, has a group of caves with 15 entries and 450 m of passages, which can be self guided. Details and a useful map can be found at www.village.goldriver.bc.ca **Little Huson Cave Regional Park** near Zeballos contains several easily accessed caves. For more details contact the *BC Speleological Federation*, T2832283.

    Climbing and hiking Climbing is excellent at **Crest Creek Crags** on Hwy 28, 15 km east of Gold River, with 100 or more routes. See www.village.goldriver.bc.ca for a map. A 35-km three-day **hike** runs along the rocky shorelines of **Nootka Island**, passing old First Nations sites. Access is by float plane or the *MV Uchuck III*.

    Kayaking Nootka Sound cannot compare to Clayoquot Sound for scenery, but is just as outstanding for kayaking, and far less crowded. The best spots are **Nuchatlitz Inlet** and **Marine Provincial Park** to the west of Tahsis, and **Catala Island Provincial Marine Park**, still further west. The former offers the best chance of spotting sea otters. **Gold River** has three different stretches popular with experienced whitewater kayakers, including a famous section known as the **Big Drop**.

    Surfing There is great surfing at **Bajo**. Surfers in the know apparently get taken out by Clay Hunting of *Tatchu Adventures*, in Tahsis, T1888-8952011, www.tatchuadventures.com, who also organizes kayaking and hiking trips with an emphasis on healthy living, organic foods, etc.

Sports

Unfortunately there is no public transport to **Gold River**. You can either rent a car or try your luck with hitching. A rough but scenic logging road leads 70 km northwest to **Tahsis**. The ultimate way to travel in these parts is aboard the 100-passenger *MV Uchuck III*, a 1942 US minesweeper. Reservations are required and the schedules are

Transport

always changing, so call T2832325 or check out the informative www.mvuchuck.com Possibilities include round-trips to Tahsis, day-cruises to Friendly Cove, an overnighter at the yet-more-remote Zeballos (via Tahsis), or a 2-day cruise round Yuquot Sound. By prior arrangement they can 'wet-launch' you in your kayak anywhere along the route ($13 extra, $18 for canoes or double kayaks). Rough one-way prices are: **Yuquot** $40, **Tahsis** $28, **Zeballos** $40. If their schedule doesn't jive with yours, try *Maxi's Water Taxi*, T2832282. *Air Nootka*, T2832255, www.airnootka.com, run scheduled, chartered and flightseeing trips, but they don't fly *to* Gold River from anywhere useful.

North Island

North of Campbell River, the solitary highway heads inland through increasingly wild, uninhabited scenery. Countless rivers and small lakes might interest the fisherman, otherwise there's little to stop for, though Schoen Lake Provincial Park might interest campers in search of tranquillity. The coast is regained at Port McNeill, an ugly mill town from where ferries head to the interesting native community of **Alert Bay** and the tiny village of **Sointula**, which has a fascinating history. Just south of Port McNeill, a logging road leads to **Telegraph Cove**, formerly the ultimate boardwalk village, now turned into a heritage resort. Picturesque but phoney, it is still one of the world's top spots for seeing orcas.

Most travellers who venture into this northern section will be heading to **Port Hardy** in order to catch the **Inside Passage** ferry to **Prince Rupert** or the **Discovery Coast Passage** ferry to **Bella Coola**. These long, scenic journeys are a wonderful way of travelling to the north. Also accessed from Port Hardy is **Cape Scott Provincial Park**, as rugged and remote a place to hike as anyone could hope for, and notoriously wet.

Telegraph Cove
Many tourists journey down 11 km of windy logging road (8 km south of Port McNeill), or pay the $35 for a taxi, to see this tiny picturesque boardwalk village. The wooden houses on stilts are quaint enough and have been lovingly restored, complete with plaques telling their story. You can even rent one (see below). Sadly this is no longer a real village, the only current inhabitants being staff of the company who now own the whole site. Further recent development has only served to render the poor village more unattractive, touristy and inauthentic. If you want to see a real boardwalk town, go to Bamfield (see page 167).

The best reason to come here is to see orca (killer whales)

Johnstone Strait, and particularly the ecological reserve 20 km away at **Robson Bight**, is one of the most reliable places in the world to see resident pods of orca, who like to rub themselves on the gravel beaches. The best time is mid- to late June.

Sleeping For an inflated price you can stay in one of the boardwalk houses of **L-C** *Telegraph Cove Resort*, T9283131, www.telegraphcoveresort.com A long way down a private road 4 km before the Telegraph Cove cut-off is **B** *Hidden Cove Lodge*, T9563916, www.hiddencovelodge.com Smallish but nice en suite rooms in a classic wooden West Coast building. Breakfast included, kayaks rented, tours arranged. **Camping** There is a campground (**F**) set in a beautiful forest above the village, with slightly crowded sites, showers, and ocean access.

Eating On the boardwalk is the very attractive and expensive *Killer Whale Café*, with steak and seafood, and the mid-range *Old Saltery Pub*, whose beautiful wood interior and fireplace create a cosy atmosphere for a pint and some pub food.

Tour operators *Stubbs Island Charters*, T9283185, www.stubbs-island.com, at the end of the boardwalk, are the oldest whale-watching company in BC, and very popular, so book ahead. They charge $65 for 3½ hours.

Alert Bay and Sointula

Port McNeill is an ugly mill town best avoided, but it does give ferry access to two interesting island settlements. With its high population of aboriginal Namgis, Alert Bay, on Malcolm Island, is one of the best places in BC to learn about native culture past and present. Nearby Sointula, on Cormorant Island, also has an interesting history, having been the site of a Finnish community's attempts to establish their own Utopia.

Phone code: 250
Colour map 1, grid B2

Everything in Alert Bay is close and easy to find. If in doubt, the **Visitor Information Centre** is at 116 Fir Street, T9745024, www.alertbay.com To the left when disembarking from the ferry is the **U'mista Cultural Centre**, which contains a large selection of wooden masks and other Potlach items (see page 457) confiscated by the government and now slowly being returned. ■ *Mon-Fri 0900-1700. By donation. T9745403.* Supposedly the tallest totem pole in the world, 52.7 m, is up the road, as are the **Namgis Burial Grounds** which contain many more poles, though respect demands that these be viewed from the road. The **Big House** is an impressive building, with traditional dance performances for the public in summer. ■ *Jul-Aug 1300 Wed-Sat.* **Robson Bight Ecological Reserve**, a 30-minute boat ride away, is a great place to see orca rubbing their bellies on the gravel. The pods arrive in mid June and stay until mid October. **Broughton Archipelago** across the Queen Charlotte Strait is the place to go for kayaking and diving. *Cedar Sticks Paddling Co*, T9742404, arrange rentals and tours.

The most compelling thing about Sointula is its history. Finnish for 'harmony', the community started out in 1900 as an attempt by a group of Finnish coal miners from Nanaimo to start their own Utopia, led by the charismatic guru Matti Kurrika. The group dissipated in 1904 but much of the population today is descended from those who remained; Finnish is still spoken, and everyone has a sauna. Orcas can be seen from the 10 km of ocean trails at **Bere Point Regional Park**, which also has camping. A speciality of the island is sea-foam green rugs made of fishing nets.

Alert Bay D *Orca Inn*, 291 Fir St, T9745322. Basic hotel rooms with ocean views, restaurant and pub, walking distance from ferry. E *Sunspirit Guest House*, 549 Fir St, 2 km from ferry, T9742026. Very nice, cosy hostel. **Camping** F *Alert Bay Camping*, Alder Rd, T9745213. 23 sites, some with hook-ups.

Sleeping

Sointula C *Ocean Bliss B&B and Cottage*, 1st/Rupert, T9736121, www.oceanbliss.com 1 room with private bath and balcony, and a rustic cedar cottage that could sleep 4, with kitchen and shower. D *Sea 4 Miles Cottages*, 145 Kaleva Rd, 2 km from ferry, T9736486. 2 fully equipped 2-bedroom cottages right on the ocean.

Alert Bay For a cultural native tour in a giant sea canoe, along with traditional food and storytelling, contact *Waas Eco-Cultural Adventures*, T9748400. *Seasmoke Whale Watching*, T9745225, www.seaorca.com, run tours in a whale-friendly sailboat, $70 for 5 hours, including Devonshire tea.

Tour operators

Vancouver Island

Transport   **Ferry** Alternate ferries from Port McNeill run to Alert Bay on **Cormorant Island**, and Sointula on **Malcolm Island**. There are several daily sailings to each, but no direct transport between the islands. Both are $5.50 return, $18.25 with vehicle. There is no transport on the islands, but **bikes** can be rented on Alert Bay at *Adam's Cycles*, Fir St.

Port Hardy

Phone code: 250
Colour map 1, grid B1
Population: 5,283

For ferry details,
see page 185

Vancouver Island's northernmost community, 230 km from Campbell River, is a long way to go for what is essentially just another rather dull fishing village. But there are three good reasons why many people find themselves passing through. For most it is to embark on one of the spectacular ferry journeys up the coast: the **Inside Passage** to Prince Rupert, or the **Discovery Coast Passage** to wild and remote Bella Coola. These routes could be built into any number of excellent circuits, or just enjoyed as a cheap cruise. They both lead through rugged and pristine stretches of wilderness coast, dissected by long fjords, dotted with tiny islands and lined with steep mountains, waterfalls and untouched rainforest. There's always a good chance of seeing whales, dolphins, sea lions and eagles. The ferry dock is at **Bear Cove**, 10 km away on the other side of Hardy Bay. For more adventurous travellers, Port Hardy is the last chance to stock up on provisions for a trip to **Cape Scott Provincial Park**, as rugged and weather-beaten a place as anyone could hope to visit, with some hiking trails not for the faint of heart (see below). Finally, this is one of the very best locations on Vancouver Island for scuba diving, with fantastic visibility and a good chance of seeing dolphins and wolf eels. The best times for diving are spring and autumn.

Most of the town is on Market Street, including the **Visitor Information** at No 7250, T9497622, www.ph-chamber.bc.ca, and a tiny **museum**. ■ *Tue-Sat 1200-1700. $1 donation.* Otherwise, there is little reason to venture Downtown. On the way in from the south, Hardy Bay Road shoots off to the right, a far nicer place to stay, with the two best hotels, restaurants and bars around, nicely situated on a marina. Further southeast, near the airport, **Fort Rupert** has the long **Stories Beach**, and the trailhead for the **Tex Lyon Trail** which goes to **Dillon Point** along the shoreline (nine hours return). While there, check out the **First Nations Copper Maker Gallery** to see traditional artisans at work. ■ *Mon-Sat 0900-1700. 114 Copper Way, Fort Rupert, T9498491, www.calvinhunt.com* **Coal Harbour** to the southwest is a historic whaling station.

Sleeping & eating   Due mainly to the Inside Passage ferries, Port Hardy is a busy place, so in summer it pays to have a reservation, especially if catching the day ferry from Prince Rupert, which gets in at 2230. **B** *Glen Lyon Inn*, 6435 Hardy Bay Rd, T9497115, info@glenlyoninn.com Decent rooms with balconies and views. The mid-range restaurant/pub is probably the best bet for food, very popular with locals. **B** *Quarterdeck Inn*, 6555 Hardy Bay Rd, T9020455, www.quarterdeckresort.net Best option, with luxurious, spacious rooms and hot tub. Price includes breakfast. The restaurant/pub here is also good. More attractive than the *Glen Lyon* next door, but less popular.

C *Oceanview B&B*, 7735 Cedar Pl, T9498302, oceanvue@island.net 3 en suite rooms with views. Will pick up from ferry. **C** *Pioneer Inn*, 4965 Byng Rd, T9497271, pioneer@island.net Take the turn towards Coal Harbour, then onto Byng Rd. Quiet, big rooms, $10 extra for kitchenette, restaurant. Best value Downtown is the **C-D** *Seagate Hotel*, 8600 Granville St, T9496348, www.seagatehotel.com Good rooms with big windows, priced according to views. Some with balconies, kitchenette extra.

Camping F *Quatse River Regional Park and Campground*, 8400 Byng Rd, T9492395. Very nice sites among trees. Quiet, showers, laundry. All proceeds go to the salmon enhancement programme. Vehicle storag. **F** *Wildwoods Campsite*, signed from road 2 km from ferry, T9496753. Closest to harbour, consequently a bit crowded, but fairly private, with showers and laundry, and vehicle parking for foot passengers. There are a few cheap eating options Downtown, none particularly nice. *Captain Hardy's* has a bit of character, along with cheap breakfasts, fish and chips, and burgers.

There are excellent opportunities for outdoor pursuits around Port Hardy, and a whole host of operators keen to take you scuba diving, whale-watching, kayaking, fishing or hiking. A good place to start is at *Outdoor Experience*, 7145 Market St, T9020440, www.island.net/charters, a booking agent which represents most of them. Or else go to *Catala Charters*, 6170 Hardy Bay Rd, T9497560, www.catalacharters.net A reliable operation, recommended by locals, who do just about everything, including diving and water taxis to Cape Scott. For **kayak** rentals and tours try *North Island Kayak*, T9497707, www.island.net/nikayak, or *Odyssey Kayaking Ltd*, T9020565, www.odysseykayaking.com

Sports

Air Flights from **Vancouver** ($176 one-way) and **Bella Coola** with *Pacific Coastal Airlines*, T2738666, www.pacific-coastal.com

Transport

Bus *Laidlaw Coach Lines*, T3854411, www.grayline.ca, operate 1 daily bus to/from **Nanaimo** (0830) and **Campbell River** (1215), leaving Port Hardy at 0900 (0945 Sat), and stopping at the ferry when there is a sailing.

Ferry The 2 popular northbound services are run by *BC Ferries*, T3863779 or T1888-2233779, www.bcferries.com The **Inside Passage** goes to **Prince Rupert**. In summer, services run every other day, leaving both termini at 0730, arriving at 2230. $99 one-way, $49.50 concessions (plus $233 for a car). The rest of the year ferries make stops and take longer, leaving Port Hardy mainly on Sat at 1800 (meaning most of the journey is in the dark), and leaving Prince Rupert mainly on Fri at 1100. Shoulder season $70, $35 concessions (plus $165 for a car), low season $52, $26 concessions (plus $124 for a car).

Cabins are available, $50 for the day, $100 for the night, more expensive with shower. Kayak/canoe $17.50, bike $6.50. The **Discovery Coast Passage** to **Bella Coola** only runs in summer. Direct ferries take 13 hrs, but most stop at McLoughlin Bay (Bella Bella), Namu, Shearwater, Klemtu, and Ocean Falls, all utterly remote and ideal for experienced and adventurous sea-kayakers. Services leave Bella Coola on Mon (direct), and Fri at 0800, Wed at 0730; Port Hardy on Tue and Thu (direct) at 0930, and Sat at 1130. $103, $51 concessions, (plus $205 for a car). Kayak/canoe $13, bike $6.50.

To access the park drive 67 km from Port Hardy on gravel logging roads past the small town of **Holberg** to the Cape Scott/San Josef Bay trailhead at the southeast corner of the park. Situated at the northwestern tip of this rainy island, Cape Scott Provincial Park brings new levels of meaning to words like rugged, wet and wild. Due to the remoteness and consistently appalling weather, a long hike here is not to be undertaken lightly. The plus side is that the constant rain makes for incredibly lush and beautiful forest. There are 23 km of white sand beaches in the park, so in the unlikely event of good weather you'll probably get one all to yourself. Grey whales, orcas, seals and otters are frequently seen from the lonely shores, but the creatures you'll see most, in good weather or bad, are mosquitoes and other blood-sucking bugs.

Cape Scott Provincial Park
Insect repellent is as essential as rubber boots

Vancouver Island

The biggest hiking challenge is the tough 48-km return trip to **Cape Scott**, located at the end of a narrow spit that does a very convincing impression of the end of the world. Before embarking on such an ordeal, be sure to pick up the blue *BC Parks* map and get thoroughly briefed at the Port Hardy **Visitor Information Centre** (see above), or visit the very useful website www.capescottpark.ca Maps can usually also be found at various information shelters. For those with less experience and/or ambition there are some fine shorter trails. The San Josef Bay Trail is the most accessible, a 5-km return hike to some sandy beaches. The best, most impressive beach is **Nels Bight**, a six-hour hike one-way. On a clear day climb to the top of **Mount St Patrick** for fantastic views. The trail then continues to **Sea Otter Cove**, a 10-km, five-hour hike one-way.

Sleeping There is only wilderness walk-in **camping** in the park, in designated sites or where you please. Locals recommend the beach, which is best for drainage, but check tidal charts at the information shelters first. Nightly user fee is $5 per person, pay at the trailhead or someone will be around to collect.

Transport **Bus** service from Port Hardy, *Sites to Sea Charters*, T9497773. **Water taxi**, *Catala Charters*, T9497560, www.catalacharters.net

Southern Interior BC

Introducing Southern Interior BC

British Columbia's Southern Interior is criss-crossed with towering mountain ranges, broad river valleys, and long skinny lakes. In a couple of days you could drive through the snow-clad peaks and glaciers of the **Coast Mountains**; the arid, semi-desert hills of the **Okanagan**, covered in orchards and vineyards; the heavily forested slopes, rocky bluffs and pristine lakes of the **West Kootenays**, punctuated by the glaciated peaks of the **Columbia Mountains**; the arid moonscape and muted colours of the **Thompson Valley**; and the sheer cliff walls of the **Fraser Canyon**.

All the outdoor pursuits you could want are here too, including several fine, relatively uncrowded ski resorts. Each area has its own appeal. The Sea-to-Sky Highway is the obvious magnet for outdoor fans, with some of Canada's best hiking, skiing, climbing and biking. If you just want to lie on a beach or tour a few wineries, head for the Okanagan, whose balmy climate has made it a top holiday destination. Many of Western Canada's most charming and atmospheric small towns are former mining communities concentrated in the West Kootenays.

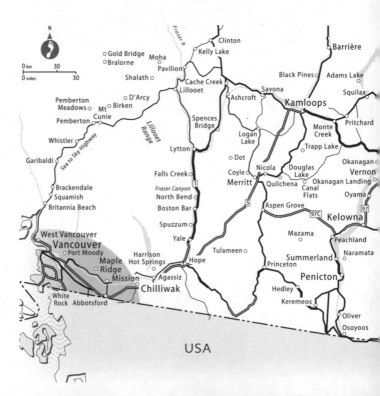

Heading east from Vancouver, the scenic **Sea to Sky Highway** (Highway 99) climbs into the Coast Mountains and past the famous ski resort of Whistler. Eventually it connects with the striking arid landscapes of the Thompson Valley near Cache Creek, where it picks up the TransCanada. The second half of this road is steep, windy and prone to closure in winter.

If you're in a hurry, take the **TransCanada** (Highway 1) from Vancouver. At Hope it suddenly shoots north through the tunnels and along the sheer cliff faces of the torrential Fraser Canyon. It too leads to Cache Creek, following the Thompson Valley to Kamloops, then on towards the Rocky Mountains.

The high-speed **Coquihalla Highway** (Highway 5) runs directly from Hope to Kamloops. It misses the Fraser Canyon and Thompson Valley, but is rarely subject to closure.

Another alternative is the rather dull **Crowsnest Highway** (Highway 3) that runs parallel with the US border. The advantage is that it gives access to the hot, dry Okanagan and the pristine, forested mountains of the West Kootenays.

Southern Interior BC

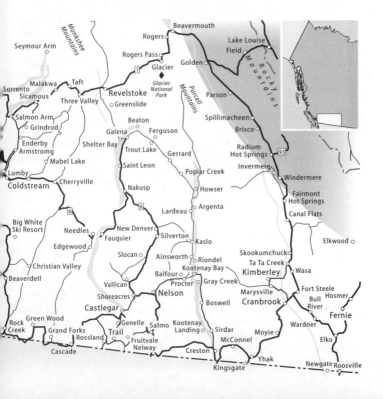

Things to do in Southern Interior BC

- Hike up the Stawamus Chief in Squamish then have a pint or meal at the *Howe Sound Brewing Company*.
- Float down the river at Brackendale and see the world's largest congregation of bald eagles.
- Indulge in a wine-tasting tour of the Okanagan, preferably around sleepy Naramata.
- Ski or board at several small but excellent hills such as Rossland's Red Mountain, Nelson's Whitewater or Fernie.
- Witness one of the world's greatest salmon migrations on Adams River in the Shuswap.

Sea to Sky Highway

The Sea to Sky Highway is the popular name for Highway 99, which follows Howe Sound north from Vancouver's Horseshoe Bay to the rock-climbing, wind-surfing and bald eagle capital of **Squamish**, before heading upwards through the gloriously scenic Coast Mountains to **Garibaldi Provincial Park** and the world famous ski centre of **Whistler**. All kinds of outdoor activities are at their best along this road, including many first-class hikes (for the cream, see boxes on page 192 and page 196). Understandably, this is an incredibly busy stretch of road, earmarked to be widened and overhauled if Whistler succeeds in its bid for the 2010 Winter Olympics. The traffic gets lighter beyond Whistler, the road higher and windier, but the scenery is consistently inspiring as you head to the small communities of **Pemberton** and **Lillooet**. Though you might not make it that far in winter, the road finally intersects with Highway 97 near Cache Creek, where you can get onto the TransCanada. As the opening leg of a journey east, this drive is hard to beat.

Britannia Beach   The opening stretch of highway is dramatic indeed, as the twisting road clings tenaciously to sheer cliffs, with views of Howe Sound and mountains on both sides swinging abruptly into view. It also contains no less than 10 important **scuba diving** sites renowned for oversized sealife that includes wolf eels and giant octopuses. **Whytecliff Park** at Horseshoe Bay is a famous marine reserve, and **Porteau Cove Provincial Park**, at 37 km, is the Lower Mainland's most popular diving destination, with warm, shallow water and a series of artificial reefs created by sunken shipwrecks, including a Second World War minesweeper. There's a rocky beach here and a rather unattractive campground (**F**).

The first clear destination is the **Mining Museum** at Britannia Beach, 11 km south of Squamish. This was once the largest copper mine in the British Empire, with a population of 60,000, an output of 1.3 billion pounds of copper in 70 years, and a reputation for polluting the surrounding waters. Housed in the run-down but striking 'Concentrator', justly labelled an icon, the museum is full of relics, photos and still-working machinery. Various demonstrations such as gold-panning are part of the tour, but the highlight is the train-ride through an old mine tunnel. ■ *May-mid-Oct, 0900-1630. $9.50, 7.50 concessions. T6888735, www.bcmuseumofmining.org*

Eating *Britannia House Restaurant and Tea Room*, open till 1700, is a heritage house with views and a great breakfast menu.

Murrin Provincial Park, 2 km further north, marks the beginning of hiking and climbing country, with rock-faces suitable for novices. A hike to the **Giuseppe Garibaldi Lookout** gives a taste of the amazing views to come. **Shannon Falls** is the next obvious stop, an impressive 335-m waterfall visible from the road but well worth the five-minute leg-stretch to see up close. From here or the campground (**F**) 1 km down the road, you can watch climbers grappling with the sheer granite walls of the sublime **Stawamus Chief**, Canada's number one rock-climbing venue (see below).

Murrin Provincial Park

Squamish

Despite its extraordinary mountain-ringed location, Squamish is not much to look at, and with a couple of notable exceptions its facilities are very poor. Yet it's a magnet for outdoor enthusiasts, with the best rock-climbing and windsurfing in Canada, excellent hiking and mountain biking, and plenty of fishing and kayaking.

Phone code: 604
Colour map 1, grid C4
Population: 16,000

Above all, Squamish is famous for its climbing, with some 200,000 hopefuls coming from around the world to take on the 95-million-year-old **Stawamus Chief**, the second biggest granite monolith on Earth, and an awesome spectacle towering over the Squamish sprawl. Those same massive rock walls that are so good to climb also act as a funnel, channelling the Howe Sound's perpetually strong ocean winds straight into town. Meaning 'Mother of the wind' in Coast Salish, Squamish has come to be recognized as the country's windsurfing capital.

A third local claim to fame is held by **Brackendale**, 10 km to the north, which has counted more **bald eagles** than anywhere else in the world. Attracted by the spawning salmon, an estimated 10,000 of these magnificent birds stop by every winter, and are now protected by the creation of the 550-ha **Brackendale Eagles Provincial Park**. The best places to see them and get more information are the *Brackendale Art Gallery* on Government Road, north of Depot Road, T8983333, www.brackendaleartgallery.com, and the *Sunwolf Outdoor Centre* at 70002 Squamish Valley Road, 4 km off Highway 99, T8981537, www.sunwolf.net

If you want something to see rather than do, the choice is limited to the **West Coast Railway Heritage Park** at 39645 Government Road. It's chock full of vintage railway paraphernalia including carriages, 50 locomotives and a restored Executive Business Car. A 3-km miniature steamtrain ride takes visitors around the park. ■ *1000-1700. $6, $5 concessions. T8989336, www.wcra.org* The **Visitor Information Centre** is at 37950 Cleveland Avenue. ■ *Summer Mon-Sat 0900-1800, winter Mon-Fri 0900-1700. T8929244, www.squamishchamber.bc.ca*

Squhomish Natives came to the Squamish Valley to hunt and fish, getting their first glimpse of white men in 1792, when Captain Vancouver arrived to trade. The settlers that eventually followed lived on cattle raising and agriculture. Around 1912 some real-estate promoters decided a more 'civilized' name than Squamish was needed, and chose the inspiring title Newport. Local people never liked this, so a few years later the railway invited school children to select a new name and win a $500 prize. The winning selection was... Squamish.

History

▶ ## Hikes around Squamish

From south to north some of the best are: **Stawamus Chief** (6, 9 or 11 km round trip, 612 m elevation gain. Trailhead: Shannon Falls Provincial Park, or 1.2 km further north) The mighty chief is not just for climbers. It makes a great, not too difficult hike, and is snow-free as early as March and as late as November. With fantastic views and the proximity to Vancouver thrown in, it's no surprise that this is one of the busiest hikes around. Most people make for the first (south) of the three summits, so try heading for the second or third, or even hike to them all. Descending is more fun via the second summit than the East trail.

Lake Lovely Water (10 km round trip, 1,128 m elevation gain. Trailhead: 10.6 km north of town turn west onto Squamish Valley Road. Turn left onto a dirt road at Km 6 and park by the BC Hydro right of way at Km 2) You need to canoe across the river, or arrange a ferry (roughly $20 per person) with Kodiak Adventures, T8983356. This is a very tough, demanding hike on a wickedly steep and narrow trail. However, the aptly named destination, set in a dramatic mountain cirque, is possibly the most spectacular lake in the Coast Mountains. Consider packing a tent and spending an extra day or two exploring. Even better, book a place in the Alpine Club of Canada hut, T6872711. If you do and there are no members around, you could use one of their two rowing-boats to check out the views from the middle of the lake. Lambda Lake makes a worthwhile half-day side trip.

High Falls Creek (12 km round trip, 640 m elevation gain. Trailhead: Take Squamish Valley Road as above. At Km 24.2 stay right on Squamish River Road. Park at Km 3.1 and look for sign 100 m further on the right.) As well as falls and gorges, this sometimes steep route offers views of the Tantalus Range. Continue up to the logging road and descend it in a loop. The views make up for any lack of trail aesthetics.

Sleeping
Squamish has a very poor selection of accommodation

B *Howe Sound Inn and Brewing Company*, 37801 Cleveland Av, T8922603, www.howesound.com Beautiful wooden building, stylish rooms, sauna, climbing wall, view of the Stawamus Chief, great pub and restaurant. **C** *Sunwolf Outdoor Centre*, 70002 Squamish Valley Rd in Brackendale, 4 km off Hwy 99, T8981537, www.sunwolf.net 10 riverside cabins, located at the meeting of Cheakamus and Cheekeye Rivers. Eagle-watching, whitewater rafting, and kayaking. On-site café. **D** *Garibaldi Budget Inn*, 38012 3rd Av, T8925204. About the best bet for cheap motel-style rooms. Those with kitchen are worth the extra. **D-E** *Squamish Hostel*, on the highway at the entrance to town, T8929240. Brand new, large hostel with accommodation in 4-6 bed dorms or private rooms with en suite bath. Facilities include a lounge with fireplace, a large kitchen and dining room, TV room showing films, a games room, laundry, lockers and storage, a balcony with views of the Chief, internet access, BBQ and a bouldering cave.

Camping F *District of Squamish Public Campground*, 1 km north. Ugly but very close to town and cheap. **F** *Klahanie Campground*, 5 mins south, opposite Shannon Falls, T8923435. Fairly private sites with plenty of trees, showers, and a restaurant. **F** *Stawamus Chief Provincial Park*, 5 mins south, T8983678. 45 walk-in sites and 15 ugly parking lot sites. No fires. Handy for hikers and climbers. **F** *Alice Lake Provincial Park*, 13 km north on Hwy 99, T8983678. 108 wooded, private sites, none of them very close to the beach. Pretty lake with fishing and swimming, showers, big grassy area.

Eating

Expensive *Furry Creek Golf and Country Club*, 20 km south, T8962224. Great appetizers and brunch on Sun. **Mid-range** *Red Heather Grill*, at *Howe Sound Inn*, 37081 Cleveland Av, T8922603. Menu with creative West Coast food, salads and pizzas. The restaurant and pub have tasteful decor and lively ambience, with a patio offering views of the Stawamus Chief. Highly recommended. *Wigan Pier*, behind the *Best Western*, off Hwy 99 to the north. Highly rated English-style food like fish and chips or steak and kidney pie, and a good selection of English beer. *Indian Hut*, 38040 Cleveland Av. Decent spicy offerings. **Cheap** *Rainforest Grill 'n' Go*, 38054 2nd Av. Organic coffee and beer, sandwiches, healthy food. Also a few hostel-style rooms (**E**). *Sunflower Bakery Café*, 38086 Cleveland Av. Good coffee and freshly baked goods.

Festivals Towards the end of **Jun** is the *Test of Metal Mountain Bike Race*, T8985195, www.testofmetal.com This is one of the most exciting and prestigious mountain bike events in the world. The annual *Squamish Days Logger Sports*, T8929244, www.squamishdays.org, in **mid-Aug**, is the biggest chainsaw bonanza in Canada. Competitions, races, beef barbecue, gospel singing, a parade and hoedown; a real slice of life. Incorporating the official Eagle Count, the *Brackendale Winter Eagles Festival* will enjoy its 18th year in **Jan** 2004. Contact the Brackendale Art Gallery (see page 191) for details.

Sports **Climbing** Almost 300 routes traverse the 625-m face of the **Stawamus Chief**, including the University Wall, considered Canada's most difficult climb. But the Chief is only one of many climbing venues around Squamish. **Smoke Bluffs**, for instance, also has over 300 routes of all levels. The most up-to-date book is *Squamish New Climbs* by Kevin McLane. A very handy on-line climbing guide is **www.squamishrock.com** *Vertical Reality Sports Store*, 38154 2nd Av, is a good source of information and also rents equipment. For instruction, contact Chris Lawrence, T8923141.

Mountain biking There are countless trails around Squamish, suitable for all levels up to the most extreme. The majority are concentrated in the **Smoke Bluffs** and **Crumpit Woods** area east of town, or around **Alice Lake** and the **Garibaldi Highlands** further north. The free *99 North* magazine contains some useful maps. Ask also at *Tantalus Bike Shop*, 40446 Government Rd/Hwy 99, who rent bikes.

Wind-surfing and kayaking A popular spot for wind-surfing and whitewater kayaking, is **Squamish Spit**, just past the Railway Heritage Park about 3 km from town. It's maintained by the *Squamish Windsurfing Society*, T9269463, who charge a small fee. On a good day, this makes for a great spectator sport. For kayak rentals there's *Sea to Sky Ocean Sports*, 37819 2nd Av ($30 per 4 hrs). *Valhalla Pure Outfitters*, in Squamish Station, is the best place for **camping** gear, outdoor clothing and climbing equipment.

Tour operators *Canadian Outback Adventure Co*, T1800-5658735. Eagle-watching river-rafting trips with transport from Vancouver or Whistler. *EcoMountain Tours*, T1800-9254453, www. ecomountaintours.com Anything from half-day to 9-day hiking tours with an emphasis on nature and aboriginal culture. *Glacier Air Tours*, T6830209, www.pacificspirit tours.com Glacier flightseeing trips.

Transport **Bus** Squamish bus station is inconveniently situated at Garibaldi Highlands, 1 km north on Hwy 99. *Greyhound*, T1800-6618747, www.whistlerbus.com, run 6 daily buses each from **Vancouver** and **Whistler**, and 4 from **Pemberton**, all but one of which fortunately stop Downtown. The 0800 and the 1300 *Perimeter* buses from **Vancouver Airport** stop in Squamish.

Drivers should fill up their tanks here, as prices go up 10¢ per litre in Whistler

Train and boat From early May to late Sep, *BC Rail*'s steam train the *Royal Hudson* runs to Squamish. The round trip costs $48, $41 seniors, $12.75 children. For an extra $21.50, one leg can be done on board the *MV Brittania*. The train departs North Vancouver at 1000, arrives 1200, and departs Squamish at 1400. The boat departs Vancouver Harbour at 0930, arrives 1230, and departs Squamish at 1330. T9845246 for reservations.

Directory **Communications** Canada Post: Cleveland Av/Victoria St. **Laundry** *Cascade Laundry*, 38921 Progress Way. **Medical services** *Squamish Medical Clinic*, 37979 Cleveland Av, T8923535.

Southern Interior BC

Garibaldi Provincial Park

For hikes in the park, see box, page 196

Once you get beyond the sprawl emanating from Squamish, the journey to Whistler is a delight, giving an idea of the incredible scenery contained within Garibaldi Provincial Park to the east. This is the nearest thing to a wilderness park you'll find within such easy reach of a major city and two prime sporting centres. Too popular for some people's taste, it still offers spine-tingling scenery

Garibaldi Provincial Park

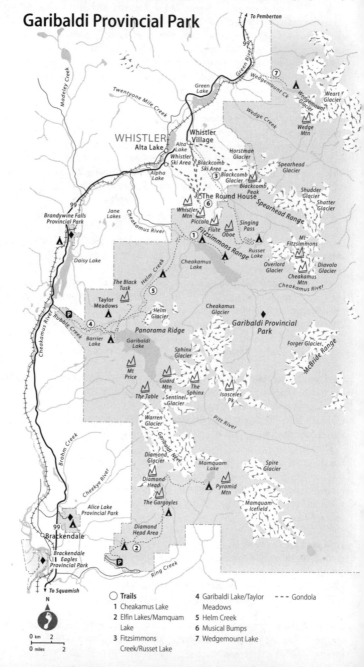

⭕ Trails
1 Cheakamus Lake
2 Elfin Lakes/Mamquam Lake
3 Fitzsimmons Creek/Russet Lake
4 Garibaldi Lake/Taylor Meadows
5 Helm Creek
6 Musical Bumps
7 Wedgemount Lake

- - - Gondola

packed full of pristine lakes, rumbustious rivers, alpine meadows, soaring peaks, and huge glaciers. The hiking here is some of the best to be found outside the Rockies, and the trails are clearly signed and well maintained. For more details pick up the blue *BC Parks* map, or call them at T8933678. Walk-in campsites are primitive and tend to be self-registration, so take some cash.

Whistler

Whistler is the largest ski area in North America and is consistently voted the continent's number one ski resort by many respected publications. The terrain is vast, the facilities state-of-the-art, and the management bend over backwards to make sure the visitor's every need is anticipated. Other winter sports include endless cross-country ski trails, backcountry skiing, heli-skiing, dog-sledding, horse-drawn sleigh rides, snowmobiling, snowshoeing, and many more exotic possibilities. With Garibaldi Provincial Park right next door, this is also a hiking haven in summer, when just about every kind of outdoor pursuit is available.

Phone code: 604
Colour map 1, grid B4
Population: 7,348
Altitude: 640 m

If you're looking for cheap, down-to-earth fun on the snow, head to the Kootenays or Okanagan instead

As a result of its year-round attractions, Whistler is steadily becoming the domain of the wealthy and prices for everything, especially real estate, have risen astronomically in recent years. The atmosphere can be terribly posey and elitist, all designer ski labels and fancy sun-glasses. Young jocks are the second pre-dominant social group, and with so many of them getting pumped-up on the slopes all day and drunk in the evening, the atmosphere can get a little boister-ous, and single women may attract more attention than they would want.

The purpose-built townsite centres on Whistler Village, where the ski lifts are, with Village North and Upper Village within walking distance. A toy-town maze of fancy hotels, bars, restaurants and sport stores, the resort's unreal, Legoland appearance could attract or repel depending on your taste and state of mind. The decision to keep all traffic out of the centre, leaving pedestrians to stroll around at leisure, reinforces the impression of being in a holiday-camp, and the perpetual party atmosphere is helped along by several major seasonal festivals, with smaller events almost every weekend. On the outskirts are a few satellite suburbs, such as Function Junction and Creekside to the south, Alpine Meadows and Emerald Estates to the north, all of them connected by local bus service, and containing much of the more affordable accommodation.

Maybe because most visitors arrange everything they need through their hotel, the small **Tourist Information Centre** on Highway 99 at Lake Placid Rd, T9325528, www.mywhistler.com, is pretty useless. A bit better is the **Activity and Information Centre**, in the Conference Centre at the Whistler Way end of the Village. For skiing information T9323434, www.whis-tler-blackcomb.com A wealth of information, including maps, can be gleaned from the seasonal publications *Whistler Journal* and *99 North*, www.99north.com, both free and distributed around town. The widely avail-able *Whistler Survival Guide* is useful for anyone planning to live or work here.

Whistler Village is little more than a big hotel and condo complex. The luxury choices are endless, though most substitute comfort for character. Booking during the peak season and Canadian or US holidays is essential. Those just turning up are best advised to call **Central Reservations**, T6645625, F9385758, who know what is available in each price range, and also offer ski/accommodation packages that can work out the cheap-est option. They do not deal with B&Bs, which as usual represent the most pleasant mid-range choice. It's a challenge to find a bed for less than $120. The few hostels catering to budget travellers fill up very quickly, so reservations are highly recom-mended. Rates are greatly reduced in the summer months, and double at Christmas.

Sleeping
■ *on map, page 198*

There are no real addresses for the hotels in Whistler and they are located mainly in the satellite suburbs

▶ ## Hikes around Garibaldi Provincial Park and Whistler

Elfin Lakes/Mamquam Lake (22 km or 44 km, 915 m or 1,555 m elevation gain. Trailhead: 3.1 km north of Squamish look for the Diamond Head sign, turn east – right – onto Mamquam Rd, and continue 15 km) This trail leads quickly to outstanding views of the mighty snowcapped Tantalus Range, so it's no surprise that it gets irritatingly overcrowded at weekends. The walk to Elfin Lakes is along an ugly road also open to cyclists. In winter it becomes a popular nordic skiing route. If possible leave much of the crowd behind by continuing to Mamquam Lake. The campground here is in a wonderful setting (though you're unlikely to reach it on day 1), and views from the ridge above are exceptional. The Elfin Lakes campground can be very busy. There is also a rudimentary overnight shelter with 34 bunk beds and a stove (a fee is collected). A number of side-trips fan out from here, the best leading to Little Diamond Head: take the Saddle trail to the Gargoyles then ascend an extra 170 vertical metres.

Garibaldi Lake/Taylor Meadows (35 km round trip – at the most – 2,450 m elevation gain. Trailhead: Rubble Creek. 38 km north of Squamish, or 20 km south of Whistler, turn east at the Black Tusk sign and proceed 2.6 km) This is one of the most rewarding areas for hiking in the park, with many options available for making your own itinerary. Garibaldi Lake is huge, vividly coloured with glacial flour, and surrounded by sights like Guard Mountain and the Sphinx Glacier. You can camp here or at the broad, flower-strewn Taylor Meadows a few kilometres away. Both are wonderful locations, but don't expect to be alone (remember to bring cash for camping fees). Be sure to do at least one side trip. The most highly recommended is Panorama Ridge, which affords expansive views of ice and peaks, including Mt Garibaldi and the Warren Glacier. The second obvious option is the distinctive volcanic peak known as the Black Tusk. The trail passes through expansive wildflower meadows and leads to awesome views, but the summit requires some serious scrambling.

Brandywine Meadows (13.6 km round trip, 600 m elevation gain. Trailhead: 15 km south of Whistler, 44 km north of Squamish, turn west onto Brandywine Forestry Rd. Park on left at Km 4.4 km – if your vehicle can make it this far) This is a popular, first-class hike to an alpine bowl full of wildflower meadows and set beneath towering cliffs. Early August is best for the flower show.

Cheakamus Lake (6.4 km return, 12.8 km with a loop of the lake, elevation gain negligible. Trailhead: 7.7 km south of Whistler, 51.3 km north of Squamish, turn east onto a logging road and continue 7.5 km to the road's end) This is an easy enough hike for anyone, and negotiable from early June to late October. The trail leads through patches of old-growth forest, and the big, beautiful turquoise lake itself is surrounded by ice-covered peaks that soar 1,600 m over its shoreline. Bikes are allowed as far as the lake, where there is a campsite for those who wish to spend a bit of time at this gorgeous spot. The trout fishing is excellent.

Helm Creek (16 km round trip, 717 m elevation gain. Trailhead: as above) This is an alternative route into the Garibaldi Lake area, and the two hikes combine very well to make a 24 km one-way trip (though this requires a shuttle or hitching). Coming from the Helm Creek end is a longer and steeper route but consequently far less crowded, and the campground at the creek

LL *Canadian Pacific Château Whistler Resort*, 4599 Château Blvd, at the base of Blackcomb Mountain, T9388000, www.chateauwhistlerresort.com As grandiose as they come, with every imaginable luxury, this is the ultimate in ski resort opulence. **AL** *Listel Hotel*, 4121 Village Green, T9321133, www.listelhotel.com One of the more attractive expensive hotels, with an outdoor heated pool, saunas and jacuzzi. *Riverside Resort*, is smaller and much nicer than the more popular ones mentioned above. Day hiking from there to Garibaldi Lake is a recommended option.

Musical Bumps (19 km round trip to Singing Pass, 727 m elevation gain) This is the nickname for Piccolo, Flute and Oboe Summits. You can go as far as you wish (or time allows) on this ridge-walk. Access is from the gondola, which takes you up 1,136 m, meaning almost anyone can enjoy the type of views usually only attained after hours of work. It's just a short ascent to the ridge, then the heart-stoppingly gorgeous views over a 360° panorama of peaks and glaciers are continuous. Cheakamus Lake and Glacier and Mount Davidson are the highlights, along with vast alpine meadows. To attain bonus vistas of Brandywine Mountain, the glacier-clad Tantalus Range and the Pemberton Icefield, climb up Whistler Mountain first and descend on the Burnt Stew trail rather than reaching the Musical Bumps via Harmony Lakes. Catch the earliest gondola possible (probably 1000). Reaching Flute summit and returning in time for the last gondola should be possible, but getting to Oboe summit and back is tricky. Ideally, make it a 22 km one-way trip over the Bumps to Singing Pass then out via Fitzsimmons Creek Valley, though this means hitching or arranging a shuttle (see below). Take plenty of water as the ridge is dry.

Blackcomb Peak (9 km round trip, 355 m elevation gain) From Whistler Village parking lot take the Fitzsimmons trail and watch for the chairlift icon. Take the chairlift up 1,174 m to Rendezvous Lodge. Again, this makes it easy to reach dizzying vistas. Almost immediately the Cheakamus and Overlord Glaciers are visible, and soon you're strolling through fields of heather

and wild flowers. Ascend on the Overlord Summit trail to Decker Tarn, then descend on the Outback trail, making a nice loop. Scrambling higher from the tarn will lead to even better views.

Fitzsimmons Creek/Russet Lake (19 km round trip, 945 m elevation gain) Trailhead: From Blackcomb Way follow signs to Singing Pass Trailhead, 5 km up a dirt road. This hike can be done one-way as a second leg of the Musical Bumps trail above. Or if you object to paying for the gondola, take this free route into the alpine. The path climbs at a reasonable grade, and takes you through some gorgeous flower meadows, with views that include the stunning Cheakamus Lake. From an easily attained ridge just above the dramatic setting of Russet Lake a dizzying, almost unparalleled array of ice is visible, including the Cheakamus and Overlord Glaciers and the Pemberton Icefield.

Cougar Mountain Cedar Grove (5 km round trip, 150 m elevation gain. Trailhead: 5 km north of Whistler turn west onto a dirt road signed Cougar Mountain Ancient Cedar Trail) Proceed 5 km. This is less a hike as an experience. The short walk is nothing special, but the ancient cedars at the end are impressive and humbling.

Wedgemount Lake (14 km, 1,160 m elevation gain. Trailhead: 11.8 km north of Whistler, 20.6 km south of Pemberton, turn east at the – Garibaldi – Wedgemount Lake sign and proceed 1.9 km up Wedge Creek Forestry Road) This steep, demanding climb leads to a beautiful lake in Garibaldi Provincial Park, passing a 300 m waterfall on the way. Take warm clothes as it tends to be chilly by the lake.

For further details you could refer to Kath and Craig Copeland's Don't waste your time in the BC Coast Mountains.

Southern Interior BC

8018 Mons Rd, T9055533, www.whistlercamping.com, about 1.5 km from the village of Blackcomb Way, attractive, fully equipped log cabins with kitchen, VCR, and small patios (see under Camping, below). A *Cedar Springs B&B*, 8106 Cedar Springs Rd, Alpine Meadows, 4 km north of the village, T9388007, www.whistlerbb.com 8 attractive and very varied rooms, all decorated in wood. Communal lounge, buffet breakfast,

Whistler

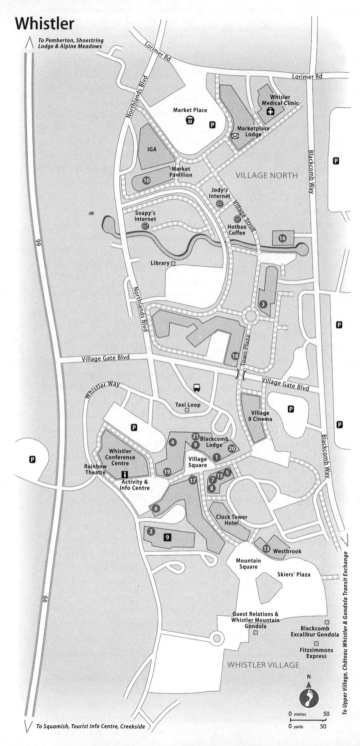

To Pemberton, Shoestring
Lodge & Alpine Meadows

Lorimer Rd

Lorimer Rd

Northlands Blvd

Whistler
Medical Clinic

Market Place
M

P

Marketplace
Lodge

IGA

Market
Pavillion

VILLAGE NORTH

Blackcomb Way

P

10

Jody's
Internet
@

Soapy's
Internet
@

Village Stroll

@
Hotbox
Coffee

16

Library

3

99

Village Gate Blvd

Town Plaza

P

18

Village Gate Blvd

Whistler Way

Taxi Loop

Village
8 Cinema

P

P

P

Whistler
Conference
Centre

P

4

21
9

Blackcomb
Lodge

20

Rainbow
Theatre

i
Activity &
Info Centre

19

Village Square

1

17

7
15
5

8

6

Clock Tower
Hotel

2

9

13

Westbrook

Mountain
Square

Skiers' Plaza

Blackcomb Way

To Upper Village, Château Whistler & Gondola Transit Exchange

Guest Relations &
Whistler Mountain
Gondola

Blackcomb
Excalibur Gondola

Fitzsimmons
Express

WHISTLER VILLAGE

N

0 metres   50
0 yards   50

99

To Squamish, Tourist Info Centre, Creekside

Orientation

To Pemberton
Emerald Estates
Green Lake
Alpine Meadows
99
Meadow Park Recreation Centre
6
4
Nicklaus North Golf Course
11
Château Whistler Golf Course
Upper Village
12
Lost Lake
7 **5**
Village North
Alta Vista
Whistler Golf Course
99
8
3
Whistler Village
10
Alta Lake
11
99
N
Nita Lake
Alpha Lake
14 **i**
1
13 **12**
Whistler Creekside
To 2
0 km 1
0 mile 1

■ Sleeping
1 Backpackers Hostel & Whistler Resort & Club
2 Brandywine Falls, Function Junction & Squamish
3 Château Whistler Resort & Mallard Bar
4 Cedar Springs B&B
5 Edelweiss Pension
6 Edgewater Lodge
7 Haus Heidi Pension B&B
8 HI Whistler
9 Listel
10 Renoir's Winter Garden B&B
11 Riverside R V Resort
12 Shoestring Lodge, Gaitor's Bar & Grill & the Boot Pub
13 South Side Lodge Hostel

● Eating
1 Araxi Ristorante
2 Bearfoot Bistro
3 Caramba!
4 Gone Bakery & Soup Co
5 Ingrid's Village Café
6 Kypriake Norte
7 La Bocca
8 La Brasserie des Artistes
9 Moguls Coffee Bean
10 Pasta Lupino
11 Rim Rock Cafe
12 South Side Deli
13 Sushi Village
14 Uli's Flipside

● Bars & clubs
15 Amsterdam Café & Maxx Fish
16 Brewhouse Restaurant & Pub
17 Citta's
18 Garfinkel's
19 Moe Joe's
20 Savage Beagle
21 Tommy Africa's
□ - - - Gondola

afternoon tea, free bus to the hill. **A** *Edgewater Lodge*, 8841 Hwy 99, Meadow Pk, own transport a must, T9320688, www.edgewater-lodge.com Beautiful and quiet, with patios onto Green Lake, and restaurant. **A** *Renoir's Winter Garden B&B*, 3137 Tyrol Cr, T938-0546. 5 en suite rooms, hot tub, views.

B *Edelweiss Pension*, 7162 Nancy Greene Dr, Village North, T9323641. 8 en suite rooms. Whirlpool, sauna, bus pick-up. Great value. **B** *Haus Heidi Pension B&B*, 7115 Nesters Rd, T9323113, www.hausheidi.com 8 en suite rooms, views, sauna and hot tub. **B** *Whistler Resort and Club*, 2129 Lake Placid Rd, Creekside, T9322343, www.Rainbow Retreats.com Oldest hotel in town. Hot tub, canoes and bikes. **C-E** *The Shoestring Lodge*, 7124 Nancy Greene Dr, Village North, T9323338. New. 4-person dorms or private rooms, each with ensuite bathroom. Close to town, with pub and restaurant (see below)

E *Backpackers Hostel*, 2124 Lake Placid Rd, Creekside, T9321177. 20 dorm beds, shared kitchen. 5-min walk to the ski lifts. **E** *HI Whistler*, 5678 Alta Lake Rd, opposite side of lake, T9325492. Nice budget option. Clean and quiet. 1 private room and 32 dorm beds. Canoes and bikes available, sauna and internet. 5 buses into town per day. Reservations essential. **E** *South Side Lodge Hostel*, Creekside, 6 km south, T932- 3644, www. snowboardwhistler.com 24 beds in 4-bed dorms rented by the week only in winter ($240 per week). Mainly for snowboarders. Kitchen, useful info. **Camping E** *Riverside RV Resort*, 8018 Mons Rd, T9055533, www.whistlercamping.com Situated on 16 ha by a creek about 1.5 km from the village off Blackcomb Way, this is about the only real choice for campers, and open all year. Fairly private sights for tents, full service for RVs. Facilities include hot showers, BBQ, laundry, games room, café, grocery store, volleyball and putting. They rent bikes, skis and other gear, arrange tours, and provide free shuttles to the gondolas. **F** *Brandywine Falls*, 10 km south on Hwy 99. There are **forestry** campgrounds further out at Calcheak and Alexander Falls.

Southern Interior BC

Eating
● on map, page 198

Most of Whistler's restaurants and bars are in or around Village Square

Expensive *Araxi Ristorante and Pub*, in the Square, T9324540. With an excellent menu, this is widely considered the best in town. *Bearfoot Bistro*, 4121 Village Green, T9323433. Sumptuous surroundings. Taster menus are $85 for 3 courses. Wine bistro has à la carte menu featuring lots of game. *Rim Rock Cafe*, Whistler Creekside, south on Hwy 99, T9325565. A local favourite. Very comfortable and attractive interior, crab and lobster on the menu. *Sushi Village*, in the *Westbrook*, T9323330. Top-notch sushi.

Mid-range *Caramba!*, 4314 Main St, Village North, T9381879. Incredibly popular, with a lively atmosphere and Mediterranean food such as calamari or wood-oven piz-zas. *La Bocca*, Village Square, T9322112. Eclectic West Coast fusion cuisine that is almost expensive. Funky colourful interior with a nice bar. *La Brasserie des Artistes*, next door, T9323569, has a more laid-back atmosphere, lower prices, and a great breakfast menu. *Gaitor's Bar and Grill*, at the *Shoestring Lodge*, see Sleeping, above, T9385777. Down-to-earth spot for Mexican food. *Kypriake Norte*, opposite the *Listel*, see Sleeping, above, T9320600. Possibly the best Greek/Mediterranean food in town, with great specials and reasonable prices. Laid back and friendly ambience. *Pasta Lupino*, Market pavilion, Village North, T9050400. Home-made pasta dishes in a casual bistro style setting. *Uli's Flipside*, Creekside, T9351107. Open and colourful interior with good art. Menu covers anything from paella to perogies, with $10 specials from 1500-1700. Huge portions. Good Martinis. Check out their brand new tapas bar *Casa*, in St Andrews House, Whistler Village. **Cheap** *Ingrid's Village Café*, just off the Square, T9327000. Cheap breakfasts and lunches, homemade bread and yummy sandwiches. Very popular. *South Side Deli* at Creekside serves a big breakfast.

Cafés
Gone Bakery and Soup Co, behind *Armchair Books*, next to the Liquor Store. Warm, cosy and down-to-earth. A great spot for coffee, baking, soups, salads and some meals. *Moguls Coffee Bean* in the *Blackcomb Lodge* is also good for coffee.

Bars & clubs
There are plenty of busy pubs around the village, most offering live music every weekend in the winter. For weekly listings pick up a free copy of *This Week*. *Amsterdam Café* on the Square, T9328334, is the most pleasantly atmospheric little place, mostly living up to its name. *Boot Pub*, in the *Shoestring Lodge*, see above, T9323338, is where the locals tend to hang out. It's more down-to-earth and tends to get some decent bands. *Brewhouse Restaurant and Pub*, by Blackcomb Way in Village North, T9052739, has a decent selection of microbrews and a great patio for people-watching. *Citta's* on the Square is about the only place with a pool table. *Garfinkel's*, just north of the footbridge, has the biggest stage in town, so gets a lot of the biggest acts. For a quiet Martini try the swanky *Mallard Bar* in the *Château*, T9388000. *Maxx Fish*, below the *Amsterdam*, T9321904, is probably the best nightclub, with DJs mainly playing house, hip hop and funk. *Moe Joe's* in the Square, is a small but fun spot playing funky dance tunes. Nearby, the *Savage Beagle* has a laid-back lounge and dining room upstairs and a heaving dance-floor below. *Tommy Africa's*, T9326090, attracts a younger crowd with hip-hop style sounds.

Entertainment
Cinema *Rainbow Theatre*, 4010 Whistler Way, T9322422. A brand-new 8-screen cinemaplex is about to open close to Village Square beneath the Mongolie Grill. *Village 8 Cinema*, T9325833. A brand new 8-screen multiplex.

Festivals
In early **Dec**, the annual *Whistler Film Festival*, T9383200, www.whistlerfilmfestival.com, gets everyone in the mood with a showing of mountain films as well as other Canadian independent productions. Throughout the winter Whistler plays host to a stream of ski and snowboard competitions, including the *Snowscene*, in **mid-Dec**, T7877770, www.snowscene.ca, which features the FIS Snowboard World Cup; *Big Mountain Experience* in **early-mid Jan**, which has the Freeskiers Championships; the *Peak to Valley Slalom Race* in early **Feb**, T9052034; the *Canadian Alpine Championships* in **mid-Mar**; and

the *International Juvenile Ski Races* in early **Apr**. On the third week of that month is the biggest annual winter sports event in North America, the *Telus World Ski and Snowboard Festival*, www.livelarge.ca This huge 10-day party features free outdoor concerts, the world snowboarding championship, and downhill ski freestyle events. Smaller events take place almost continually throughout the winter, including *Altitude*, www.outontheslopes.com, in early *Feb*, a week-long gay pride event. In summer the spirit is kept alive with a number of mountain bike competitions and various smaller events. The best place to fin out exactly what's going on is: Whistler-Blackcomb, T9323434, www.whistler-blackcomb.com

Skiing Between them, the two mountains of Whistler and Blackcomb offer skiers over **Sports** 2.800 ha of terrain, featuring 12 bowls, 3 glaciers and 200 marked trails. With the system of 33 state-of-the-art lifts being constantly upgraded, time spent queuing up is kept to a minimum. Customer service is incredibly attentive (a man at the lodge's front door, for instance, will offer you a tissue to wipe your nose). Facilities on the two hills include at least 12 restaurants, some of them huge, with microwaves if you want to heat up your packed-lunch. All sell similar food, but for a more upmarket experience there's *Christine's*, T9387437, in the *Rendezvous* on Blackcomb. Reservations necessary.

Whistler and Blackcomb Mountains each have their own characters and devotees. **Whistler** is traditionally more laid back and suitable for beginners and intermediates, and has a Family Zone at the *Emerald Express*. The breakdown of terrain for the two hills is very similar (see chart page 46), with 55% intermediate. **Blackcomb** is the one that breaks most of the records, boasting for example the 2 longest lift-serviced vertical falls in North America. Its Terrain Park is a favourite with snowboarders and serious experts. For the latter there is also an Expert Park, which you can only enter with a helmet and a special endorsement on your pass.

For beginners these big mountains can be intimidating, so a lesson is recommended, especially as *Whistler's Ski School*, reputed to be one of the best in North America. Prices are about $93 per day, $499 per day with a private instructor. For intermediates to become familiar with the terrain there are free tours run by the *Mountain Hosts* daily at 1000 and 1300 (phone for details). Basic avalanche awareness courses are also available. Equipment can be rented from stores, hotels or on the mountain. *Affinity Sports* have a number of branches including the Village Square, the *Pinnacle Hotel*, the *Clocktower*, and the *Blackcomb Lodge*. It is worth spending a little extra on high-performance gear.

On a fresh powder day the *Fresh Tracks Breakfast* is highly recommended. Tickets, $20 on top of the regular lift pass, can be reserved or bought at the lift. Turn up at 0700; you are taken up to the *Roundhouse* for a decent buffet breakfast then let out onto the fresh snow at 0800, a good 50 mins before the regular crowds arrive.

The *Whistler Express*, *Fitzsimmons Express* and *Blackcomb Excalibur* gondolas all leave from the south side of the Village. The *Wizard Express* and *Magic Chair* lifts both head up to Blackcomb form the Upper Village. A day pass for all lifts is $65/32/free for 6 years and under. You can ski between the hills for a taste of both. The hills are open daily 0830-1500, from mid-late Nov depending on conditions. Blackcomb closes in Apr, Whistler continues till early Jun. For info, weather, snow and lift reports T9323434, www.whistler-blackcomb.com

Cross-country skiing is best at Lost Lake, with 32 km of trails which are lit up at night, $10, T9050071, www.crosscountryconnection.bc.ca The *Valley Trail* runs all over, linking the Village, Lost Lake, Alta Lake, Alpha Lake and beyond. There are also some good trails at the *Château Whistler* and *Nicklaus North* Golf Courses. Acres of **backcountry skiing** surround Whistler, much of them in Garibaldi Provincial Park, but this is only for those with experience or a guide. **Heli-skiing** starts at about $629 per day. 2-hour **dog-sledding** tours of the Soo Valley cost $125 per person for 2.5 hrs and leave 4 times daily. **Horse-drawn sleigh rides** leave hourly from 1700-2000 and cost $45 per person. **Snowmobile** tours for all levels start at $89 per 2 hrs for a double. **Snowshoeing** is possible just about anywhere. Tours start at $49 per 2 hrs. **Winter fishing** starts at $139 per person for ½ a day. **Helicopter sight-seeing** tours start at $149 per person for 20 mins. See Tour operators below for any of these activities.

For hiking, see box page 196 **Summer sports** Not long after Whistler Mountain closes in June, the Seventh Heaven Chair starts running up to the 43-ha Horstman Glacier on Blackcomb for summer **skiing**. Largely used by professionals and free-style clinics, there is also space for casual skiers ($39 day-pass). **Mountain bikers** can carry their steeds on the lift up to *Whistler Mountain Bike Zone*, open May-Sep, which consists of 100 km of single-track trails. For rentals try *Mountain Riders* in the Village, or *Whistler Bike Company*, 4050 Whistler Way. Even those not wanting to hike (see above) should consider ascending in the gondola for magnificent views of Black Tusk, Cheakamus Glacier and Cheakamus Lake.

There is **climbing** in Nordic Estates between the Village and Creekside (there is a gondola at Creekside). *The Great Wall Climbing Centre*, T9057625, have 2 walls, one indoors at the *Westbrook Hotel*, another outside at the base of Blackcomb Mountain. They also arrange 4-hr tours in Jul and Aug, $79 per person. Within walking distance of the Village, Lost Lake has 30 km of **hiking/biking** trails. **Fishing** for trout and **swimming** are popular here and at a number of other nearby lakes. Alta Lake is good for **windsurfing**. For indoor swimming head to *Meadow Park Rec Centre*, 6 km north on Hwy 99, T9357529, which also has an exercise room, skating rink, sauna and hot tub. Tour operators (see below) will take you **hiking**, **horse riding**, float- or whitewater **rafting**, **jet-boating**, **fishing**, **bear-viewing**, even on a 4x4 **hummer** tour. Finally, Whistler has a growing reputation as a **golf** Mecca, with many new and challenging courses designed by the likes of Jack Nicklaus and Arnold Palmer.

Shopping The *Market Place* in Village North contains the most useful selection of shops of all kinds, including an *IGA* supermarket. In the Village, the grocery store, liquor store and *Armchair Books*, are conveniently grouped together under one roof close to the square.

Tour operators *Whistler Valley Adventure Centre*, T9386392, www.whistleradventure.com, and *Cougar Mountain*, 36-4314 Main St, T9324086, www.cougarmountain.ca, can set you up with just about anything. *Whistler Cross Country Ski Centre*, T9327711, www.whistlernordiccentre.com, run guided hikes ($99pp per day) and cross-country skiing. *Whistler Alpine Guides Bureau*, T9383228, www.whistlerguides.com, arrange tours and instruction for skiing, snowboarding, ice climbing and mountaineering. *Whistler River Adventures* at the gondola, T9323532, organize river-rafting, $60 per 2 hrs.

Transport **Local** Whistler's efficient local transit system, *The Wave*, T9324020, www.whistler.com/transit, links the many satellite suburbs, with all routes converging on Village Gate Boulevard. The free *Village Shuttle* runs around the village and to the gondola all day.

Long distance Bus Whistler's bus station is at 4338 Main St, T9325031, www.whistlerbus.com *Greyhound*, T1800-6618747, run 7 daily buses from **Vancouver**, $21 one-way. Their non-stop *Ski Express* leaves at 0630 arriving at the Village 0830. *Bigfoot's Snow Shuttle*, T7779905, runs 3 times daily from all Vancouver hostels, $27 one way, $49 return. If it's running, the *Snowbus*, T7365228, www.snowbus.ca, is the cheapest at $42 return, possibly less. A combined *Airporter/Greyhound* ticket from the airport is $33 one-way with frequent departures. *Perimeter Whistler Express*, T2665386, picks up at the airport and major hotels and charges $55, $43 one-way.

Train *BC Rail*'s *Cariboo Prospector* has sadly been taken out of service.

Car   Drivers are advised to leave their car in Vancouver. The road to Whistler is over-crowded, everything in the village is within walking distance, and parking costs about $10 per night. *Avis Rent-a-car* is in the *Holiday Inn* at 4295 Blackcomb Way, T6855546.

Banks   *North Shore Credit Union* is next to the footbridge across Village Gate Blvd; *Royal Bank* is at the west end of the village on Whistler Way; *TD Bank* and *Thomas Cook* are found in Market Place, Village North. **Communications**   Canada Post: Market Place. Internet: *Hotbox Coffee and Internet*, Town Plaza, Village North; *Jody's Internet Services*, Village Stroll, Village North; *Soapy's Internet Station, Alpenglow Building, Village North.* **Laundry**   *Dual Mountain Cleaners, Market Place, Village North.* **Library**   by the car park off Main St, Village North. **Medical services**   *Whistler Medical Clinic*, 4380 Lorimer Rd/Blackcomb Way, T9324911; *Dental Group*, Market Place, T9323677. **Photography**   *Whistler One Hour Film Processing*, close to the Village Square. **Useful addresses**   Police: Village Gate Blvd/Blackcomb Way, T9322020; **Fire**: T9322020.

Directory

Pemberton

Beyond Whistler, the views open out as the highway approaches the steeper, more dramatic mountains to the north. Many people choose to stay in Pemberton and commute the half-hour to Whistler. Certainly the village is calmer and more picturesque, utterly free of the tourism-gone-mad that has blighted its popular sister to the south. And though there is little to Pemberton itself, the surrounding area is rich in possibilities for hiking, biking and fishing. There are also two fine hot springs within striking distance. The summer-only **Visitor Information Centre** is at 7374 Highway 99 on the way into town, T8946175, www.pemberton.net

Phone code: 604
Colour map 1,
grid B4
Population: 855
Altitude: 213 m

Just east of Pemberton a rough road strikes north from the wonderfully scenic Mount Currie, passing through D'Arcy and eventually making its own tortuous way to Lillooet. At Devine, a gravel road heads 18 km west to **Birkenhead Lake Provincial Park**, a remote destination with 85 primitive campsites for those seeking utter tranquillity. There's a good chance of spotting mountain goats, moose and blue herons, and the 3.5-km lakeshore trail is pleasant enough. More impressive for those in the area is **Place Creek Falls**, a 3-km return hike. At 21.4 km from Mount Currie take the dirt road right and proceed roughly 2 km.

Hikes

Accessible from Highway 99 are a number of more highly recommended hikes. One of the most rewarding, but longest and most difficult to access, is the **Stein Divide** (28.6 km, 1,265 m elevation gain. Trailhead: 10.3 km north of Mount Currie turn southeast onto the In Shuk-ch Forestry Road. At Km 16.6 turn left onto Lizzie Creek Branch Road. Most vehicles will want you to stop at Km 8 and walk). The trail through this region is extremely tough and demanding, but the reward is the solitude of unspoilt alpine wilderness with a frequent smattering of lakes, mountains and glaciers. Highlights are the views from Tabletop Mountain, and the eerily beautiful colour of Tundra Lake.

About 30 km north of Pemberton, 69 km south of Lillooet is Joffre Lakes Recreation Area and the excellent **Joffre Lakes trail** (11 km, 370 m elevation gain). This relatively easy hike leads to 3 gorgeous teal lakes set in exquisite mountain scenery. The first lake would be a worthy reward for hours of hiking, but is reached after a mere 5 minutes. So whatever your fitness, don't drive by without stopping to hike at least this far. The only downside is the trail's understandable popularity.

Southern Interior BC

Rohr Lake/Marriott Basin trail (9 or 16 km, 430 m elevation gain. Trailhead: 3.7 km north from the above, then 1 km down Cayoosh Creek Forestry Road) Though fairly short, this considerably less busy trail is tough, narrow, steep and sometimes obscure, so suitable only for experienced hikers. The reward is solitude, a pristine meadow and an amethyst lake set beneath the lofty Mount Rohr.

Cerise Creek trail (8 km round trip, 305 m elevation gain. Trailhead: 12.5 km north of Joffre Lakes, then 6 km southwest on Cerise Creek Main Forestry Road) This short, fairly easy hike leads to a moraine offering great views of the Anniversary and Matier Glaciers and the peaks to which they cling.

Hot springs This is one of the best regions for hot springs, though they're characteristically hard to reach. **Meagre Creek Hot Springs** is the largest and one of the best in BC although it is generally inaccessible except between May and October. Even then seek advice before setting out. Follow Lillooet River logging road 64 km northwest of Pemberton. Due to former abuses, a caretaker has been employed to look after the spring, and a $5 fee is charged. **Skookumchuck Hot Springs** is free, and also one of BC's best. Follow Highway 99 east to Mount Currie, then take a very rough forestry road south along Lillooet River, passing on the way various deserted homesteads and two native graveyards. The 54 km drive takes about 1½ hours. Watch for small metal numbers attached to tree stumps by the road. The springs are between 22 and 21, close to Hydro tower 682. Less visited than the above, nude bathing is much more likely.

Sleeping & eating There are a couple of standard motels/hotels in town, but much better are the many B&Bs, ranging from **L-D**, a few of them clustered around Pemberton Meadows Rd. **B** *Log House B&B*, 1357 Elmwood Dr, follow signs in town, T8946000, www.loghouse inn.com 7 nice rooms in a beautiful log home with private shower-only, a deck with good views, and hot tub. **B** *Pemberton Valley Vineyard and Inn*, 1427 Collins Rd, just off Pemberton Meadows Rd, T8945857, www.whistlerwine.com 7 large, light and airy rooms (3 in winter), surrounded by a vineyard. En suite claw-foot tubs, deck with mountain views, hot tub, vegetarian breakfast. **F** *Nairn Falls Provincial Park*, 3 km south of Pemberton, T8983678. 94 okay sites, plus hiking, fishing, and a 1.5-km walk to the falls.

For meaty food, *The Outpost*, 1392 Portage Rd, is reasonable. But *the* place to go overall is *Pony Espresso*, 1426 Portage Rd, T9381926. Good for coffee, breakfast and melts, it also has a menu of tasty pastas, salads and pizzas for dinner. A popular hang-out for locals, with good beer on tap, a deck on the roof and outdoor seating. For something special the *Wicked Wheel Pizza Co*, 2021 Portage Rd, Mount Currie, on the way to Lillooet, T8946622, is recommended. Worth the short drive from town.

Sports For **bike** rentals and information, try *High Line Cycles*, 1392 Portage Rd. *Pemberton Soaring Centre*, Airport Rd, T8945727 will take you **gliding**.

Lillooet
Phone code: 250
Colour map 1, grid B5
Population: 2,058
Altitude: 239 m

The journey to Lillooet is much more of a commitment than the easy jaunt to Pemberton, but well worth the effort. The road narrows down and becomes more tortuous, with brake-destroying steep sections, narrow wooden bridges, multiple evidence of land-slides, and ever more breathtaking mountain views. At Lillooet, Highway 99 meets the **Fraser River Valley**. As if in anticipation, the scenery changes about 20 km south of town with the arrival of a series of eye-catching boney rock faces, followed by an incredible downhill section, then the sudden appearance of **Seton Lake**, its water a striking milky aquamarine. This is a popular spot to fish for sturgeon.

After all this raw splendour, the town itself comes as a predictable disappointment. The setting is spectacular, but this tawdry meeting-place of highways and railway is dusty and unattractive. The only reason to come this far is the journey, especially, until recently when the service was discontinued, aboard *BC Rail*'s *Cariboo Prospector*, one of the best railway trips in Canada, and sadly missed. Should you choose to stop, all the bare necessities are found close together on Main Street, including the **Information Centre** at No 790, T2564308, April to October.

Beyond Lillooet the scenery becomes even more extraordinary. The vast canyon, its cliffs dropping an impossible distance down to the Fraser River below, leads towards the harsh weather systems of the Cariboo and the Thompson Valley, both typified by vast, desert-dry landscapes in shades of yellow, red and ochre, dotted with lonely scraps of scrubby vegetation. Highway 99 intercepts Highway 97 just north of Cache Creek, from where the TransCanada heads east to Kamloops and beyond. Alternatively, Highway 12 follows the Fraser River south from Lillooet, picking up the TransCanada at Lytton and continuing south to Hope, from where you could head back to Vancouver to complete a very scenic loop.

Sleeping and eating   Of the town's motels **C** *4 Pines*, 108 8th Av, T2564247, at least has big rooms and baths. It's worth paying the extra for newer rooms which have kitchenettes, a bonus since there's nowhere decent to eat in town. **E** *Reynolds Hotel* on Main St, T2564202, is surprisingly nice for the price, with big bathrooms, mountain views, and bags of character. **Camping** *BC Hydro*, to compensate for the building of the local dam, have provided a free campground (**F**) with fairly nice sites on the creek to the south of town. Further south there is a spate of equally reasonable forestry campgrounds just off the highway. The Greek restaurant *Dino's* on Main St is probably the best place for food.

TransCanada Highway

The TransCanada Highway is one of the world's longest roads, stretching from Victoria in the West to St John's, Newfoundland at Canada's easternmost extremity. It remains Highway 1 as far as the Manitoba/Ontario border, and for most of this distance is paralleled to the north by Western Canada's other great highway, the Yellowhead (Highway 16). Joining just west of Winnipeg, their dual courses are easily picked out on a map. The TransCanada links Vancouver with Kamloops, Banff, Calgary and Regina, while the Yellowhead runs from Prince Rupert through Prince George, Jasper, Edmonton and Saskatoon.

In BC, Highway 1 is mostly a beautiful drive, running through some very varied landscapes: the steep walls and thrashing water of the Fraser Canyon; the arid vistas of the Thompson Valley; weirdly-shaped expanses of water in the Shuswap; and increasingly sublime mountain scenery as it cuts through the Columbia Mountains. It is also the most direct route to the Rockies, which is where most visitors understandably want to go.

The string of sprawling suburbs that line the TransCanada as it follows the Fraser River east from Vancouver barely lets up until you clear Chilliwack, some 120 km from Downtown. Even then, the fast and busy dual carriageway leaves little chance to enjoy the scenery until beyond Hope. The first real diversion is north to Harrison Hot Springs, especially worthwhile in September, when international sculptors create giant, intricate works of art at the

Harrison Hot Springs
Phone code: 604
Colour map 1, grid C5
Population: 1,060

annual **Sandcastle Festival**, or in July when the annual **Festival of the Arts**, T7920025, www.ucfv.bc.ca brings the town alive with flamenco, jazz and folk music, theatre, and visual art.

Since 1926, this pretty little town on the shore of the large Harrison Lake has been dominated by the luxurious *Harrison Hot Springs Resort* (see below).

Non-guests can take the waters in the public pool down the road, but it is ugly and over-priced ($7). Thermal aficionados could make a day-trip to the superb natural hot springs at **Clear Creek**. Follow a very rough logging road (four wheel drive recommended) along the east shore of Harrison Lake for 53 km, veering right onto the barely driveable Clear Creek Road (marked by blue painted rock). Continue for 1.5 km, then walk 10 km (less with a four wheel drive) to four tubs that are maintained by locals. Camping allowed. Ask for more precise directions at the **Visitor Information Centre** at 499 Hot Springs Road, T7963425, www.harrison.ca A great 10.5-km walk from this centre goes to **Campbell Lake**, with wilderness camping on the lake. Much more of the same is to found along the rough Morrison Valley Road from Harrison Mills to the west.

Sleeping and eating **AL** *Harrison Hot Springs Resort*, 100 Esplanade Av, T7962244, www.harrisonresort.com With 3 outdoor pools of varied temperatures, a new indoor spa, masseurs, restaurants, and a comfortable lounge area, this is a popular place to be pampered. The rooms have balconies and lake or pool views, and the *Copper Room* has live music nightly for dinner/dancing. A short drive up the east side of the lake is the impossibly romantic **AL-A** *Little House on the Lake B&B*, 6305 Rockwell Dr, T7962186, www.littlehouseonthelake.com There are several mediocre motels on Esplanade including the **C** *Harrison Village Motel*, 280 Esplanade Av, T7962616.

Camping About 7 km beyond the *Little House on the Lake B&B* is *Sasquatch Provincial Park*, T8242300, with 3 lakeside campgrounds, the nicest being **Hicks Lake**, with sandy beaches and hiking trails.

For a pint and food there's the wooden *Old Settler Pub* at 222 Cedar Av. *La Côte D'Azur*, 310 Hot Springs Rd, T7968422, has fantastic and expensive French cuisine, but smallish portions.

Transport *Greyhound* from Vancouver to **Chilliwack** ($13), then a public bus via Agassiz ($3). If driving, take Highway 1 to the Highway 9 east of Chilliwack, or the mellower Highway 7 to Hot Springs Rd.

Hope

Phone code: 604
Colour map 1, grid C5
Population: 7,032

Hope's claim to fame as the 'Chainsaw Carving Capital' tells you all you need to know, though the carvings by Pete Ryan are very impressive and worth a look. Most of them are in the town park, but the nicest are at *Manning Park Resort* (see page 220). In truth, most people pass through, or usually by, Hope on their way somewhere else, for it sits at a major meeting of ways. Most necessities are on the highway, here called Water Street, including the Greyhound Station, and the **Visitor Information Centre** at No 919, T8692021, www.hopechamber.bc.ca

There's some good hiking and biking around, including the **Othello Quintette Tunnels**, a 90-m deep solid granite wall that was blasted through in 1911 as part of the Kettle Valley Railway (see page 233). A loop around Kettle Valley Road and Othello Road offers plunging views of the Coquihalla Canyon Gorge and the river below. A shorter but steeper hike is the 2 km **Mount Hope Lookout Trail** from the TransCanada/Old Hope-Princeton Way junction, which affords views of the Fraser Valley.

Sleeping and eating   Hope's motels are legion, most of them clustered on Water St or Old Hope-Princeton Way. On the latter is the most comfortable option in town, **C** *Quality Inn*, at 350, T8699951. Spacious, full kitchen, pool, hot tub and sauna. On the former is the good value **D** *Inn Towne Motel*, at 510, T8697276. Reasonable rooms, plus a pool, jacuzzi and sauna. **Camping   F** *Coquihalla Campsite*, on Kawkawa Lake Rd, T8697119, is large and lovely, with very private sites in a heavily forested spot by the river. *Silver Lake Provincial Park*, 6 km southeast via Silver Skagit Rd, T8242300, is a nice, quiet spot with 25 sites and swimming.

For food, try the **mid-range** *Kibo*, 267 King St, off Water St. A tiny, atmospheric restaurant with an equally small menu of tasty Japanese cuisine. The licensed *Skinny's Grille*, west on Flood Hope Rd on the way to Silver Creek, offers good meat-based fodder, and live music on Sat nights.

Fraser Canyon

Between Hope and Lytton, the mighty Fraser River's massive volume of water is forced through a narrow channel between the sheer rock faces of the Cascade and Coast Mountains. For the longest time it was believed that the canyon was unpassable, and indeed it feels like a miracle of engineering and sheer audacity that the nation's major highway *and* railway pass through it. By either means, the journey is breathtaking. The road by turn clings to high narrow ledges scraped and blasted out of steep cliff faces, disappears into a multitude of tunnels, or hugs the banks of the churning river. A whole different challenge was to prevent these transport routes from upsetting the annual migration of salmon, since this river is host to one of the world's greatest salmon runs, with millions of the huge fish fighting their way over a series of natural and man-made obstacles to their spawning grounds further north. Both the Fraser and Thompson rivers are also renowned for their formidable river rafting.

Along the way you can find out the history of Simon Fraser (see page 443), one of the greatest early explorers of North America, who was seeking a route to the Pacific, and followed this river along its whole 1,300-km course thinking it was the Columbia. The hellish canyon section, driven today in a couple of hours, cost him 35 days of hard labour to cross. More willing visitors were the prospectors who flocked to the area when gold was struck near Yale in 1858, BC's first major **Gold Rush**. Gold panning still takes place throughout the vast network of interlaced creeks and rivers. The best places to try your hand are, from south to north, the mouth of the Coquihalla River in Hope, Emory Creek, Waterfront Park in Yale, various creeks in Spuzzum, and the panning reserve in Lytton.

The area around tiny Yale, 25 km north of Hope, is the prettiest part of the drive, surrounded by sheer cliffs. It's hard to believe, but during the Fraser Valley Gold Rush, this sleepy village of less than 200 became one of North America's largest cities, with a population of over 20,000. You can find out all about it at the small **Yale Museum**, situated on the highway, here called Douglas Street. ■ *Jun-Sep 0900-1800. By donation. T8632324.* The best places to get a good look at the fantastic surrounding scenery are **Spirit Caves**, a steep one-hour hike away, and **Mount Linky**, a two-hour hike.

Phone code: 250
Colour map 1,
grid C5

Yale
There's no Information Centre, so try asking for directions at the museum

Sleeping and eating   There's nowhere in town to eat, but if you want to stay, try the **C-D** *Historic Teague B&B*, a 19th-century house with 3 rooms right on the river. The **D** *Fort Yale Motel* at the north end, T8632216, has spacious bright rooms with good views. **Camping**   Campers should stay at the lovely **F** *Emory Creek Provincial Park*,

Southern Interior BC

10 km south, T604-8513000.

Hell's Gate & beyond The river reaches its awesome crescendo at Hell's Gate, so-named because in 1808 Simon Fraser called it 'A place where no human should venture, for surely these are the gates of Hell'. Here the mighty Fraser is forced through a gorge 38 m wide and 180 m deep. The thrashing water reaches a depth of 60 m, and thunders through with imponderable power. For $11, $7 concessions, the much-touted Hell's Gate Airtram gondola carries people across the canyon for up-close views of the spectacle, a very short journey made by up to 2,500 people a day. On the other side is a series of displays on salmon and the measures taken to help them complete their migration in the face of so many man-made obstacles. There's also a restaurant where you can eat them filleted for a reasonable $15. Free canyon views can be had 8 km south at **Alexander Bridge Provincial Park**.

As the highway heads north, the scenery remains spectacular, slowly taking on the dry, Wild West characteristics of the Thompson Valley, which the road follows from Lytton. There's little to the remaining towns, except as bases for some of the province's best river-rafting. At the junction of the Fraser and Nahatlatch River, just north of **Boston Bar**, are adrenaline-charged rapids with silly names like Meatgrinder, Twisted Sister, and Lose Yer Lunch. Further north, between Spences Bridge and Lytton, the rafting on the Thompson River is excellent, with rapids sporting such titles as The Frog, Devil's Kitchen, The Cauldron, and The Jaws of Death. For a more relaxed run, the best is Yale to Hope on the Fraser River.

Sports *Fraser River Raft Expeditions*, on the river side at the south end of Yale, T8632336, www.fraserraft.com is a small, friendly company offering 1 to 8-day rafting tours anywhere in the valley starting at $105 a day. *Kumsheen Raft Adventures*, T1800-6636667, www.kumsheen.com are the most professional operation around, with every type of trip on all the local rivers, and gear rental. All-in packages involve a stay at their beautiful Adventure Resort, 5 km north of Lytton, which has deluxe cabin tents, a campground, restaurant, fabulous pool and spa, trails, etc. *Skihist Provincial Park*, T604-8513000, is 1 km away. 56 decent sites, some with dramatic views of the Thompson Valley, and hiking trails on part of the historic Cariboo Wagon Rd.

Cache Creek Situated at the major crossroads of Highway 97 and Highway 1, Cache Creek sees a lot of traffic, but has retained the feel of a backwater town from the 1950s. The surrounding scenery is absolutely breathtaking, an arid, rocky moonscape of vast wrinkled mounds in shades of yellow and red, practically vegetation-free. The 'Painted Bluffs' between Savona and Ashcroft offer the best example of these colourful rock formations. Anomalous volcanic activity has resulted in much semi-precious stone, including jade, that attracts rock hounds. Buses arrive daily from all directions.

Sleeping and eating The nicest place to stay and eat is the new **C-D** *Bear's Claw Lodge*, Hwy 97 north, T4579705. Comfortable rooms, spacious guest lounge in the fetching log-built lodge. A good alternative is **C** *Bonaparte Bend Winery*, just north of town on Hwy 97, T4576667. B&B with 3 rooms, private bath, use of kitchen and laundry. Best to reserve. Bistro open for light lunches in very pleasant surroundings. Wine-tasting summer 1000-1800, rest of the year 1000-1600. Of the many motels, none has much to recommend it, but the **E** *Sundowner*, 1085 Hwy 1, T4576216, is at least very cheap.

Kamloops

The sublime Thompson Valley landscape that hypnotizes drivers between Cache Creek and Kamloops provides an incongruously magnificent setting for this bland city. Endless hills of near-desert scorched earth, barely able to sustain the odd lonesome pine, fill the horizons with their subtle hues and weird shapes. It is an unlikely location for the second largest city in BC's interior, but a chance meeting of valleys has made this an important transport hub ever since the days when the canoe was the vehicle of choice; in fact, the Shuswap name Cumloops means 'meeting of the waters'.

Phone code: 250
Colour map 1, grid B6
Population: 77,281
Altitude: 345 m

Today the meeting is of the Canadian Pacific and Candian National railways, and two major highways connecting Vancouver, the Rockies and all points east, the Okanagan to the south, and the north via Prince George. In short, it's a tough place to avoid, but there's scant reason to stop.

Getting there & around
For Transport details, see page 211

    Kamloops **airport**, 6 km northwest of town on Tranquille Rd, receives internal flights only. **Trains** run from **Vancouver** and **Calgary**, while *Greyhound* **buses** operate daily to **Vancouver**, **Calgary**, **Prince George** and **Kelowna**. For drivers, Highway 5 north is confusingly referred to as the Yellowhead. Local buses converge at the Thompson Park Mall, Downtown on Lansdowne.

The **Visitor Information Centre**, T3743377, www.adventurekamloops.com is badly placed on the TransCanada West, at junction 368 with Highway 5A to Princeton.

Tourist information

History

Kamloops missed out altogether on the Gold Rush excitement just to the west. The city was settled by more down to earth pioneers, who recognized its great potential for ranching. Among them was a determined group of 'Overlanders', who battled their way over the Rockies to form Fort Kamloops in 1862. A number of heritage buildings remain, including the Old Court House that now contains the Hostel. Heritage Walking Tour maps, available at the museum and Information Centre, take you on a self-guided walk.

Sights

Downtown Kamloops has little to offer except the lovely **Riverside Park** with rose gardens, walks along the river, and live music every night at 1900 in July and August. Nearby at 207 Seymour/5th Avenue, **Kamloops Museum and Archives** chronicles the growth of this ranching town, with displays on the fur trade, Gold Rush and railway, plus 10,000 archive photos, and a collection of historic artefacts and stuffed animals. ■ *Tue-Sat 0930-1630, by donation, T828-3576.* Kamloops is home to the **Bear Brewing Co**, purveyor of the *Black Bear* ale, one of BC's finest. ■ *Tours are available at 965 McGill Pl, T8512543.*

    Five minutes north on Highway 5, **Secwepemc Museum and Heritage Park** is an interesting place to learn more about the Secwepemc, or Shuswap, whose culture thrived here for thousands of years. A full-size replica of a 2,000-year old village contains traditional pit houses showing various phases and styles of construction. Archaeological artefacts complement more modern photos. There's also an interpreted trail, and gardens with traditional plants. Guided tours available. ■ *Mon-Fri 0830-2000, Sat and Sun 1000-1800. $6, $4 concessions. T8289801.*

▶ **David Thompson**

The hunt to follow the Columbia River all the way to the Pacific consumed many an explorer. David Thompson, described as "the greatest land geographer who ever lived", nevertheless came across the water's mountain source twice, and both times took a wrong turn. In 1811 he finally succeeded, only to find that the Americans
had beaten him by a few weeks. Thompson ended up dying poor and unknown, despite founding a series of important trading posts along BC's winding rivers. He is also the first recorded Canadian to spot a UFO, having described a 'large blob' flying through the air in Manitoba, 1792.

If you want to explore the surroundings, a two-hour walk starting 4 km west on Tranquille Road leads to the **Hoodoos**, tall sandstone sculptures carved by wind and water. Or go hunting for semi-precious stones and **fossils** with a guided geological tour (see Tour operators below), and see remains from the last ice age when the vast Lake Thompson covered much of the area.

Essentials

Sleeping There are 4 main areas for accommodation. The most upmarket are on **Rogers Way** near the junction of Hwys 1 and 5A, off Pacific Way. The best is the fairly classy **B** *Four Points Sheraton* at 1175, T3744144, www.fourpoints.com Big rooms, pool, hot tub, sauna, nice lounge and restaurant. **Columbia St**, the main access road into town has most of the mid-range options. **D** *Econo Lodge*, at 775, T3728235, has very nice rooms with large beds, new furnishings and carpet, and balcony. Ask for a room with a view. **D** *Sagebrush* at 660, T3723151, also has nice big rooms plus sauna and hot tub. **East on Highway 1** are the cheap, sleazy motels, not worth the small saving. The exception is **D** *Country View Motor Inn*, just off the highway at 176 Comazzetto Rd, T3747222. Big rooms with fridge.

Downtown is the best place to be. **C** *The Plaza*, 405 Victoria St, T3778075, is a 1926 building whose rooms are small but newly renovated and full of character. **D** *Scott's Inn*, 11th/Columbia, T3728221. Ask for a room in the 'Bambi' section. Nice and big with kitchen. **E** *Joyce's B&B*, 49 W Nicola St, T3741417, has 3 rooms with shared bath, laundry, and a nice garden. **E** *Old Courthouse HI Hostel*, 7 West Seymour St/1st Av, T8287991. Large heritage building with lots of character and space, though the dorms are a bit confined. Kitchen and common areas. Dining room still has the jury seating and judge's podium. **E** *Rafter 'G' Hotel*, 569 Seymour St, T6614602. A bit creepy with bullet-proof glass at the front desk, but cheap. Rooms have private bathrooms and TV.

Camping The only site in town is the **F** *Silver Sage Tent and Trailer Park*, 771 E Athabasca, T8282077. A grassy parking lot. **F** *Knutsford RV Park*, 6 km out of town in Knutsford, T8282077, is a bit better. **F** *Paul Lake Provincial Park*, 17 km east off Hwy 5 N, T8523000, is a nice secluded spot on a lovely lake, with good fishing and a steep hike to the top of Gibraltar for views. **F** *Lac Le Jeune PP*, 37 km south off Hwy 5, T8523000, has sites on the lake and fishing. **F** *Juniper Beach PP*, 45 km west on Hwy 1, T8523000, is a bit crowded, and the juniper trees are disappointing.

Eating **Expensive** Voted best overall by locals for 6 years is *Chapters Viewpoint*, 610 W Columbia St, at the *Panorama Inn*, T3743224. Big menu with wide price-range. Good salads, steak and seafood, fantastic views and outdoor seating.

Mid-range *Amsterdam*, 428 Victoria St. Open for breakfast and lunch until 1500. Omelettes and pancakes in a great old brick building. *Hot House Bistro*, 438 Victoria St. Vegetarian cuisine with a laid-back South American atmosphere, and international food from Mexica to India. *Taj Mahal*, 775 Columbia St, T3141149. Good, authentic

Indian food. *Warunee's Thai Restaurant*, 413 Tranquille Rd on the north shore, T5547080. Excellent Thai food and friendly service.

Cheap *Bagel Street Café*, 428 Victoria St. *Barbeque Kitchen*, 273 Tranquille Rd. Best of the many 'authentic' Chinese joints. Try the garlic dumplings. **Seriously cheap** *Fratelli Foods*, 223 Victoria St. $3 wraps to go. The best **coffee** is at *The Grind*, 476 Victoria St. Good wraps, and a friendly place to meet locals and pick up info.

Cactus Jack's Saloon, 417 Seymour St, for line dancing and hootin' it up. *The Cell*, 124 Victoria St, is where the youngsters go for some bump and grind. *Elements Café*, 229 Victoria St, T3721341. Live jazz and mid-price food. *Jukebox Jive*, 355 Landsowne, for the boogie woogie. There's live music at *The Plaza*, 405 Victoria St. — **Bars & clubs**

Art *Kamloops Art Gallery*, 465 Victoria St, by the library, www.galleries.bc.ca/kamloops Large collection of quality works by inspiring artists. One of the picks of town. Tue-Sat, $3. **Cinema** *Cineplex Odeon*, 612 Victoria St, and at the Aberdeen Mall; *Halston Drive-In Theatre*, 277 Halston Conn Rd; *Paramount Twin*, 503 Victoria St. **Theatre** *Sagebrush Theatre*, 821 Munro; *Western Canada Theatre Co*, 1025 Lorne St. — **Entertainment** *For information and tickets, call Kamloops Live! on T3745483*

The best reason to visit is the annual *Kamloops Pow Wow*, T8289700, on the third weekend in **Aug** at the Special Events Facility. Everyone is welcome, and it's the best way to get an authentic taste of contemporary aboriginal culture. Brightly clad dancers from over 30 different bands across Canada and Northern US perform to the rhythms of drumming and singing. One of the best Pow Wows in the country. — **Festivals**

Second Glance, 246 Victoria St, has an extensive selection of used **books**. Local interest, philosophy, and Canadian fiction. — **Shopping**

There's lots of good **mountain biking** locally, and it's a great way to explore the weird landscapes. The best places are Sun Peaks and Lac Dubois. *Full Boar Bike Store*, 310 Victoria and at Sun Peaks, provide rentals and info. There are 11 **golf** courses around Kamloops, including *Rivershore*, T5734211, and *The Dunes*, T5793300. The area is also famous for its **trout fishing**, with over 200 nearby lakes. Among the closest and best are Paul Lake, 23 km northeast, and Lac Le Jeune, 35 km south. — **Sport**

Rocky Mountaineer Railtours, T1800-6657245. The *Red Leaf Tour* is a 1-night, 2-day train ride from Vancouver to Jasper or Banff, with a night in Kamloops. $540 includes all meals. Longer tours continue to Calgary. *Kamloops Geological-Paleontology Tours*, 1075 Calmar Pl, T5542401, run guided tours in the mountains looking for crystals, fossils and minerals. $60 per day. — **Tour operators**

Local Bus: *BC Transit* bus No 1 (Tranquille) goes to the North Shore, airport and city park; bus No 3 (Crosstown) runs round town to the youth hostel and *Greyhound* depot. **Taxi**: *Kami Cabs*, T5541377, or *Yellow Cabs*, T3743333. — **Transport**

Long distance Air: The airport is 6 km northwest of town on Tranquille Rd. The *Airport Shuttle*, T3144803, runs to Downtown, $8-10. *Air Canada*, T1888-2472262, fly daily to **Vancouver** and **Calgary**; **Central Mountain Air**, T1888-8658585, fly daily to **Kelowna** and **Prince George**.

Bus: The *Greyhound* station is at 725 Notredame Dr, T3741212, with 5 daily buses to **Vancouver**, $50; 4 to **Calgary**, $85; 3 to **Prince George**, $71; and 3 to **Kelowna**, $25.

Train: *Via Rail*, T1800-5618630, www.viarail.ca, run west to **Vancouver** on Thu, Sat and Mon, $65; to **Jasper**, **Edmonton**, **Saskatoon**, **Winnipeg** and **Toronto** on Wed, Sat and Mon.

Southern Interior BC

Directory   **Communications** Canada Post: 301 Seymour St. **Internet**: free upstairs at the library Tue-Thu 1400-1600, Fri-Sat 1000-1200. **Laundry** *McCleaners Laundromats*, 437 Seymour. **Library** 465 Victoria St. A nice modern, airy place. **Medical** Royal Inland Hospital, 311 Columbia, T3745111.

Sun Peaks   This cute little ski village 45 minutes northeast from Kamloops is one of the
Ski Resort   interior's nicest. Six lifts service 80 runs on 970 ha of terrain mostly suitable for beginner/intermediates. More cash is currently being invested to open another lift and 200 more hectares. There are also 50 km of groomed cross-country trails. In summer the lift stays open for mountain biking (rentals on site) and hiking. There is also swimming, fishing, canoeing, and a golf course.

Sleeping and eating The village has 15 cafés and restaurants, and several lodges, including **B** *Sun Peaks Lodge*, T5787878. Balconies, spa, breakfast included. The budget option is **E** *Sun Peaks Hostel*, T7636024. Free pancake breakfast, kitchen, common room, internet, ski in/ski out, canoes. Phone them for transportation from Kamloops. For information call Guest Services, T5787842, or Activities, T5785542.

Transport Follow Hwy 5 north for 19 km to Heffley Creek, then right for 31 km at the Sun Peaks sign. There is a shuttle bus from Kamloops airport, $27 one way, T3778481. Note that the local First Nations band sometimes block the road because they oppose plans for further development, claiming the land to be theirs.

The Shuswap

Colour map 2,   East of Kamloops, the startlingly arid vistas of the Thompson Valley soon give
grid B1   way to duller scenery and then an abundance of water. The strangely shaped Shuswap Lake, with four long arms and a host of satellite lakes, provides 1,130 km of shoreline, beaches and temperate waterways to explore. Of the many provincial parks hereabouts, at least nine are marine parks accessible only by boat, the most popular and dramatic being **Cinnemousun Narrows** where the four arms meet. The classic way to see the lake is in a houseboat rented by the week in Sicamous (T8362220), though this is expensive, and only feasible with a group. The alternative is to rent a canoe and take a tent.

Like the Okanagan, the Shuswap has become a second home for Albertans and northern BCers 'getting away' on their summer holidays. Much of the accommodation is rented out by the week, and many campgrounds are constantly full. The further you get from the highway, the smaller the hordes, but it is debatable whether the rewards justify the effort.

The North   Heading east on the TransCanada, the north shore is reached via a bridge
Shore   from **Squilax**, home to the excellent *Caboose Hostel* (see below). Apart from houseboats, the Shuswap, and particularly **Adams River**, is famous for salmon. The best place to see them is in **Roderick Haig-Brown Provincial Park**, 5 km north from Squilax. The water turns brilliant red each October, but particularly every fourth year (2002, 2006, etc) when 1.5 million salmon return. The park has trails with viewing platforms on both sides of the river: the lower one is easy, the upper trail is more of a hike, winding for 18 km through a canyon. To raft this river, contact *Adams River Rafting*, 3993 Squilax-Anglemont Rd, Scotch Creek, T9552447 ($44 for a 2½-hour trip). From here, the paved road continues north to **Adams Lake** and continues, providing a short cut to Barrière on Highway 5, en route to Wells Gray.

The road gets rougher and less crowded the further east you go towards remote **Seymour Arm**, where some of the region's many petroglyphs are to be found, along with good camping at **Silver Beach Provincial Park**.

Sleeping and eating E *Caboose Hostel*, Squilax, T2752977, www.hihostels.bc.ca The main building is a historic General Store on the lake, and the dorm beds are in old cabooses (railway cars), each with its own kitchen and bathroom. There is kayaking, bat-watching, bike rentals, pet llamas, an authentic sweat lodge, plus cross-country skiing and ice-skating in winter. The proprietor is very knowledgeable about local lore and activities. Phone ahead to arrange pick-up from the *Greyhound* which stops nearby four times daily.

Camping F *Bush Creek Provincial Park*, Adams Lake, 5.5 km up a rough logging road. One of the nicest, most peaceful and scenic places to camp in the area. East of Squilax at **Scotch Creek**, F *Shuswap Lake Provincial Park*, 1210 McGill Rd, T8513000, has 270 nicely wooded, private and well-equipped sites, as well as a large beach. Should this be full, a likely event in summer, there are dozens of private campsites scattered along the shore, all cramped and rather unpleasant. There are plenty of B&Bs, however, and public beaches. Further east there's good camping at F *Silver Beach Provincial Park*, T8513000.

Between the lake's two biggest arms, minor roads peel off to remote campgrounds that promise a rare chance of privacy. The best hopes are **White Lake Provincial Park**, 8 km east between the arms, and **Herald Provincial Park**, 12 km along the north shore of the lower arm, with a sandy beach and an easy trail to Margaret Falls. In **Sorrento**, *Crannog Ales*, 2 km west on Elson Road, T6756849, is an organic brewery with tours and tastings.

South to Salmon Arm

Sleeping and eating B-C *Trickle Inn*, T8331890, in **Tappen**. B&B, with 5 rooms in a Victorian heritage home, and a very posh restaurant where mouth-watering 4-course meals are $50 a head including wine.

The rapid and unsightly expansion of the Shuswap's main resort town reflects the area's growing status. It's a thoroughly dull place, not worth stopping for except in late-August when the superb three-day **Roots and Blues Festival** livens things up with acts performing on six stages, T8334096, www.roots andblues.ca ($100 at gate, $30-40 per day). Camping is available. For three weeks in summer, the excellent 30 year-old **Caravan Farm Theatre** stages daily outdoor shows at Knob Hill, east of Enderby to the south. For 10 days before New Year's Eve they also put on a touring play which involves a sleigh ride to different sets dispersed through the forest (T5468533 for details). Otherwise, the town's best diversion is a 9-km boardwalk trail along the lake in Waterfront Park, starting at the **Visitor Information Centre**, 751 Marine Park Drive (follow signs), T8322230, www.sachamber.bc.ca Between May and September you're likely to see one of the 250 pairs of endangered western grebe performing their extraordinary mating dance. Rock-climbing is big at nearby **Haines Creek**. Pick up the very informative *Trail Guide* at the Information Centre.

Salmon Arm

Sleeping Most motels are clustered on the TransCanada, a convenient one being C *Best Western Villager Motor Inn*, across from the bus depot at 61-10th St, T8329793. D *Margaret's B&B*, 224 Kault Hill Rd, T8040171, has 3 rooms in a lovely log home with fabulous views of the lake from a private patio. **Camping** There's a well-equipped E *KOA* campground at the junction of Hwys 1 and 97B, T8326489, with laundry, showers and a pool. **Eating** *Mino's*, 720 22nd St, has good Greek fare. The *Rio Grande* on Hudson

The Information Centre has details about the many B&Bs

Southern Interior BC

Downtown has reasonable Mexican food. *Hazbeanz* on Alexander St is the place for coffee. You can sample the excellent *Crannog* stout at the *Hideaway Pub*.

Transport Salmon Arm receives 4 **buses** daily from **Kamloops** or **Kelowna**, $18, and several from **Vancouver**, $60.

Sicamous Though smaller and prettier than Salmon Arm, there's still little reason to stop in Sicamous, 31 km to the east, unless you're interested in hiring a house boat. If so, all the companies are clustered together on the marina, so you can shop around and see what you're getting. The **Visitor Information Centre** is at 110 Finlayson Street, T8363313, www.sicamouschamber.bc.com Ask for directions to the stunning historical suspension bridge at Malakwa, 17 km to the east.

Sleeping and eating C *Sicamous Inn*, on Highway 1 east of Highway 97A, T8364117, has reasonable rooms and hot tub. **D** *Alpiner Motel*, in town on Hwy 1, T8362290, is the best value. Cabins with large beds and kitchenette, and some very cheap tenting sites. **D** *The Artist's House*, 20 Bruhn Rd, 1 km west, T8363537, is a colourful, antique-filled B&B with views. **D** *Cedars Motel*, 1210 Paradise, T8363175, is a pleasant wood-finished place. *Moose Mulligans* at the *Super 8 Motel* on the marina has good pub food and draft beer.

Tour operators *Bluewater Houseboat Rentals*, T8362255, is as good as any. Best value is the four-day midweek rate of $945 for up to 8, with kitchen. *Sicamous Water Tours and Charters*, T8364318, do 2-hour tours with narrative and petroglyph-viewing, $80 per four people. They also act as a water taxi for $80 per hr. *Get Wet Rentals Ltd*, 1130 Riverside Av, rents all water toys including jet-skis for $250 per day and canoes for $40 per day.

Revelstoke

Phone code: 250
Colour map 2, grid B2
Population: 8,500
Altitude: 455 m

Around Revelstoke the scenery takes a dramatic upswing as the highway enters the lofty Columbia Mountains with increasingly frequent glimpses of the majestic Rockies beyond. Besides its splendid location, this is a friendly, attractive town with a laid-back attitude and lots of heritage buildings sporting turrets and wrap-around balconies. A self-guided tour brochure that takes you round 60 of them is available from the two **Visitor Information Centres**: year-round at 204 Campbell Avenue, T8375345, www.revelstokecc.bc.ca, summer-only at corner of Highways 1 and 23 North, T8373522. Naturally, outdoor pursuits hereabouts are abundant and top-notch (see Sports). Those coming from the Rockies might want to take Highway 23 south and the Galena Bay ferry to access the Kootenays as an alternative to the TransCanada.

Revelstoke Railway Museum is worthwhile for railway buffs. Highlights include an entire passenger car, a locomotive and an interactive Diesel Simulator. ■ *Jun-Jul 0900-2000 daily, Apr-May and Aug-Oct 0900-1700 Mon-Sat, winter 1300-1500. $6, $3 concessions. Victoria Rd, opposite the bears, T8376060, www.railwaymuseum.com*

Mount Revelstoke National Park Smallest of the great national parks, Mount Revelstoke was founded in 1914 to protect the particularly steep Clachnacudainn Range of the Columbia Mountains. The main access is on Summit Road, north of the TransCanada as it goes through town. The park's longer trails are from the top, most popular being the **Miller Lake** trail, 12 km round trip. The **Meadows in the Sky** trail is a 1-km loop that takes in some of the fabulous wildflower-covered alpine meadows, at their most vibrant in July and August. A couple of other short trails are accessed straight from the highway to the east. The **Giant Cedars**

trail is a 1-km boardwalk loop through some mighty ancient forest, while the equally easy **Skunk Cabbage Boardwalk** gives a taste of wetland temperate forest. See also Sports below.

Canyon Hot Springs, just east of the park, is a swimming-pool type affair with camping (**F**). ■ *May-Sep 0900-2100. $6.50. T8372420.*

A *Mulvehill Creek Wilderness Inn B&B*, 4200 Highway 23, 19 km south towards Shelter Bay ferry, T8378649. 8 rooms with en suite bath in peaceful setting on Arrow Lakes. Canoes, hot tub, library, billiards, etc. **B** *The Regent Inn*, 112 1st St, T8372107, www.regentinn.com Large, luxurious rooms with big beds and baths. Sauna and hot tub. **C** *Four Seasons Manor B&B*, 815 Mackenzie Av, T8372616. 5 en suite rooms in a stately 1905 heritage home full of antiques. Friendly, helpful owners. **C** *Wintergreen Inn B&B*, 312 Kootenay St, T8373369. 10 very nice 'theme' rooms with en suite baths, deck, and recreation room in a quiet spot close to Downtown. **D** *Monashee Lodge*, 1601 3rd St W, T8376778, www.monasheelodge.com Quiet motel with hot tub, light breakfast included. **E** *Revelstoke Traveller's Hostel and Guest House*, 400 2nd St, T8374050, www.hostels.bc.ca One of *the* great hostels. 76 beds in clean, bright, wood-finished dorms of up to 4, or couple's rooms at no extra charge. 6 kitchens, common room, free internet. Unbeatable ski package, $18.50 including room and lift ticket. Also the best standby rate for cat-skiing, $175 per day. Reservations recommended.

Camping F *Lamplighter Campground*, Nixon Rd, 0.5 km on Highway 23 S, T8373385, is the closest to Downtown. Modern, fairly nice sites. Shower, laundry, playground. **F** *Williamson Lake Campground*, 818 Williamson Lake Rd, 5 km south on 4th St/Airport Way. Ideal for families, on a small, warm lake away from highway. Playground, canoe and rowboat rentals, showers, laundry. **F** *Blanket Creek Provincial Park*, Highway 23 S, halfway to Shelter Bay ferry, T8253500. 64 sites on Arrow Lakes by Sutherland Falls. **F** *Martha Creek Provincial Park*, 20 km north on Hwy 23. Not the nicest of campgrounds, but a wonderful location on Lake Revelstoke, with good swimming, and a nice 7-km hike up to alpine lakes through old-growth cedar and hemlock.

Sleeping

Eating

Expensive *112 Restaurant*, in the *Regent Inn*, 112 1st Av, T8372107. Best choice for fine dining. **Mid-range** *Frisbee Ridge Teriyaki*, 201 1st St, T8375449. Japanese and Korean cuisine, a local favourite. *Manning's Restaurant*, 302 Mackenzie Av, T8373200. The best Chinese option. *The Three Bears Bistro*, 114 Mackenzie Av. Mainly lunch, home-made bread and pastries, good coffee. **Cheap** *Woolsey Creek*, 212 Mackenzie Av. Couches, art on walls, small international menu. The best coffee, as well as sporting gear, is at *Burtz Outdoor Equipment and Café*, 217 Mackenzie Av.

Bars & clubs

Big Eddy Inn, 2108 Big Eddy Rd, is the best pub in town, with decent food. *The Pub* in the *Regent Inn* is non-smoking and more sophisticated. **Nightclub** *The Rock Pit*, 312 1st St.

Entertainment

Cinema *The Roxy*, Mackenzie Av, just off Victoria Rd.

Festivals

Blues Festival, T8375500, 3rd weekend in *Jun*. *Mountain Arts Festival*, T8375345, in *Sep* features 3 days of events including street performers.

Sports

Summer For **climbing** head to the Lauretta Slabs, 15 min east in the National Park. Park on the north side of Hwy 1, then walk 7 mins up a narrow trail to the large boulder. Most **hiking** takes place in Mt Revelstoke National Park (see above). A 10-km trail up Mt Revelstoke starts behind the Railway Museum. A splendid but out-of-the-way hike is the **Keystone and Standard Basins** trail (14.6/22 km, elevation gain 400/608 m. Trailhead: Drive Hwy 23 50 km north along the east shore of Lake Revelstoke). Turn right onto Keystone Creek Forestry Rd and proceed 16.3 km. The hiking is remote and lonely with grand views of the Columbia Range. At 11 km is the free *Standard Cabin*. There's some great **mountain biking** in the area too. Get a trail map from the Information Centre, or ask at *High Country Cycle and Sports*, 188 MacKenzie Av.

Winter   The local **ski hill** is **Powder Springs**, 4 km south of town, T1800-9914455, www.catpowder.com   Very small and low-profile, with only one lift, it's practically free if you're staying at the hostel. Otherwise a lift pass is $28. Most locals go **backcountry** skiing across the river on the 'Five Fingers' of Mt McPherson, visible from town. This is the best, most convenient spot, with northern exposure insuring good snow conditions. For **cross-country** trails in the McPherson area, contact *Nordic Connection*, T8376168. **Cat-skiing** is huge here too, with bookings taken 1 year in advance (see Tour operators, below). The 10-km trail to Mt Revelstoke (see above) can be **snow-shoed** in winter. For all winter sport rentals, got to *Freespirit Sports*, 203 1st St W.

Tour operators   *Alpine Adventure Company*, T8375417, www.raamountainguides.com Ski touring, rock climbing, heli-trekking and more. *Cat Powder*, 1601 3rd St W, T8375151, www.catpowder.com Best rates are standby, otherwise book 1 year ahead for $525 per day. *Canadian Mountain Holidays*, T8379344, www.cmhski.com, service one of the biggest helicopter skiing areas in the world, with 14,000 sq km of terrain.

Transport   The *Greyhound* Station, T8375874, is on Fraser Dr just off Hwy 1. 5 **buses** daily to **Vancouver**, $60, and 4 to **Calgary** via **Banff**, $58.

Directory   **Communications** **Internet**: at *Revelstoke Traveller's Hostel* (see Sleeping, above), free for guests. **Canada Post**: 301 3rd St. **Laundry** *Family Laundry*, 1st St. **Medical services** *Queen Victoria Hospital*, 1200 Newlands Rd.

Glacier National Park

Colour map 2, grid B2   With the major parks of the Rockies so close, not many people stop to admire this chunk of the Selkirk Mountains, yet the peaks here are just as lofty and impressive, and even more snow laden. As its name suggests, Glacier National Park's defining feature is the 422 fields of permanent ice that cloak an incredible 14% of its area year-round. Whereas most of the world's glaciers are rapidly retreating, the largest one here, Illecillewaet Neve, is still growing, and some 70 new glaciers have recently been identified forming on the melted remains of their predecessors. As you might expect, the weather that fuels this ice-factory is wet and frequently abysmal.

The park's most appreciative visitors are professional climbers, and in-the-know skiers. **Rogers Pass** is recognized as one of the best backcountry skiing areas in the world, with some 1,349 sq km of skiable terrain featuring descents of up to 1,500 m. For all but the most experienced, a professional guide is essential. Avalanches here are very common, and a group of accompanied school children were tragically killed here in early 2003. For daily updated information about snow conditions phone *Backcountry Report*, T8376867. Hikes in the park (see below) tend to be short and striking. Unfortunately, you're never very far from the highway, which is frequently in earshot. *Footloose in the Columbias* is a useful hiking guide to Glacier and Revelstoke National Parks. The extensive **Nakimu Caves** system can be explored on guided tours only. Ask at the very helpful **Visitor Information Centre**, 1 km west of Rogers Pass. June to September 0900-2100, rest of the year 0900-1700. T8376274. As well as trail maps and information they have a number of impressive and entertaining hi-tech displays, and run guided walks in the summer.

History

Like so many of the mountain parks, Glacier was put on the map by the arrival of the Canadian Pacific Railway, which was routed through Rogers Pass (1,327 m) in 1885. The CPR built one of its grand hotels and established some hiking trails, with park status following a year later. Climbers were drawn to the area almost immediately. Due to an endless struggle with avalanches, a tunnel was blasted beneath the pass in 1916, quickly spelling the end of the hotel. Fresh life was brought by the building of the TransCanada Highway in 1962, which is kept open thanks to the world's most extensive avalanche-control system.

Hiking

Glacier Crest (10.4 km return; elevation gain 1,005 m. Trailhead: turn into Illecillewaet Campground and proceed just over 1 km to car park) This glorious trail takes you up the ridge between the park's two major glacier-bearing valleys, Illecillewaet and Asulkan, with ample views of both. You start in an old-growth forest, follow a burbling stream, ascend a steep canyon wall into a land of icy peaks, and top out at a viewpoint offering dramatic 360° views. The last stretch is dangerous if wet, so do not attempt after recent rain.

    Perley Rock (11.4 km return, 1,162 m gain. Trailhead: as above) This steep and challenging trail would be a torment without the well-built switchbacks. The Illecillewaet Glacier is again on full display, along with the polished bedrock beneath its receding tongue. The higher you go, the better the views get, and on the way back they're even better.

Glacier National Park

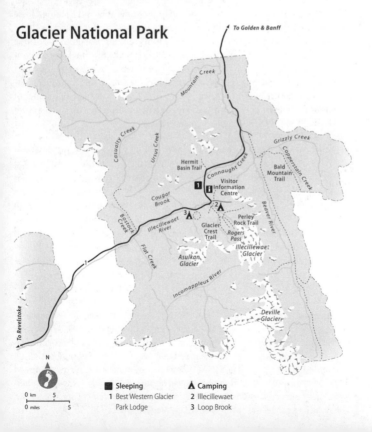

Sleeping
1 Best Western Glacier Park Lodge

Camping
2 Illecillewaet
3 Loop Brook

0 km 5
0 miles 5

Hermit Basin (5.6 km return, 770 m gain. Trailhead: 1.4 km northeast of Rogers Pass Information Centre) Even steeper than the above, but well maintained, this grunt leads to a tiny alpine shelf with great views of the peaks and glaciers on the park's south side. There are four tent pads for overnight stays.

Bald Mountain (35.2 km return, 1,354 m gain, 3 days. Trailhead: 11 km northeast of Rogers Pass – or 11.5 km south of northeast park entrance – turn onto Beaver Valley-Copperstain Road. Go left after 1.2 km and proceed 200 m) This long and little-used trail slogs through old-growth forest for most of the first day, but then rewards you with an 8-km-long ridge covered in wildflower meadows (prime grizzly bear habitat). The scenery is gob-smacking, with the glacier-supporting massif in full view across the valley.

Sleeping
■ *on map,*
page 217

The only beds in the park are at **B** *Best Western Glacier Park Lodge* right on Rogers Pass, T8372126, www.glacierparklodgecanada.com Heated outdoor pool, 24-hr café and service station. Otherwise, there are a number of lodges on the way to Golden. **Camping F** *Illecillewaet Campground* is 3.7 km east of Rogers Pass. In the park are backcountry campsites and cabins. For the Wheeler Hut and Asulkan Cabin reserve at T403-6783200; for the Glacier Circle Cabin and Sapphire Col Hut, T8377500. You can also camp southeast of the park boundary where no fees or restrictions are in place.

Golden

Phone code 250
Colour map 2,
grid B2
Population 4,107
Altitude 790 m

Golden's location could hardly be more fortuitous: halfway between Glacier and Yoho national parks at the junction of the Columbia and Kicking Horse rivers, with the Selkirk and Purcell ranges to the west, and the Rockies to the east. Predictably the town fails to live up to its setting, though the appalling stretch of services on the highway bear no relation to the tiny but fairly pleasant centre down below. With the arrival of what promises to be one of BC's greatest ski hills, Golden has big changes ahead. Naturally enough, this is another magnet for adventure enthusiasts, with plenty of hiking, biking and all manner of outdoor activities. The year-round **Visitor Information Centre** is at 500 10th Avenue, T3447125, www.goldenchamber.bc.ca

Sleeping
Golden's mountain setting has led to a proliferation of log-built lodges, mainly west of the TransCanada, helicopter fly-in. **B-D** *Goldenwood Lodge*, 14 km west, then 6 km east on Blaeberry School Rd, T3447685, www.goldenwoodlodge.com Lodge rooms, cabins and teepees. Vegetarian food, canoe and bike rentals. **C** *HG Parson House B&B*, 815 12th St, T3445001, is a good choice, with 3 rooms in a heritage home. **C** *Mary's Motel*, 603 8th Av, T3447111, is a good, if overpriced stand-by, with 2 pools, sauna, hot tub and 81 rooms. **E** *Kicking Horse Hostel*, 518 Station Av, take Hwy 95 exit off Hwy 1 then first left before the overpass, T3445071. Dorms, kitchen, sauna, camping. **Camping F** *Whispering Spruce Campground*, 1430 Golden View Rd, off Highway 1 E, T3446680. 135 sites. Far better is the campground at **F** *Waitabit Creek*, 23 km to the west. Turn north onto Donald Rd for 0.5 km then left down Big Bend Rd for 2 km. On the river with views.

Eating
Expensive *Eagle's Eye View*, T1866-7545425. The highest restaurant in Canada, at the top of the ski hill by way of the gondola (free with reservation). Fine dining and even finer views from a timberframe building with masses of glass and a stone fireplace. Prices are more reasonable than you would expect. *Cedar House*, about 4.5 km south at 735 Hefti Rd, T3444679. Casual Pacific Rim-style fine dining in a quiet, forested area with a lovely patio. **Mid-range** *Kicking Horse Grill*, 1105 9th St, T3442330. International fusion cuisine. **Cheap** *Jenny's Java Express and Internet Café*, 420 9th Av, has the best coffee. The pub of choice is the *Mad Trapper*, at 1203 9th St.

Mount Seven is considered Canada's premier **hang-gliding** site, hosting the annual
Western Canadian Hang Gliding Championships and the Canadian National Paragliding
Championships in Aug. **Ice climbing** is big here with 60 different routes in the area. For
used climbing equipment and rentals go to *Higher Plateau*, 804 Park Dr. For **mountain
bike** rentals, sales and service, and to find out about local trails, head to *Selkirk Source for
Sports*, 504 9th Av, T3442966. Between May and Sep, the aquamarine 'untamed' Kicking
Horse River provides class III and IV rapids for exciting **river rafting** and **kayaking**. Gentler trips explore the unique wetlands of the Columbia River. There are 14 km of
cross-country **skiing** trails at Dawn Mountain, T3447144. For downhill skiing see below.

Sports

Alpenglow Aviation Inc, 210 Fisher Rd, T3447117. $98 per hr for flight-seeing, of the
Bugaboos for example. *Golden Mountain Adventures*, Highway 1, T3444650,
www.adventurerockies.com Cater to all needs: rafting, biking, hang-gliding, snow-
mobiling, bird-watching, skiing, etc. *Rocky Mountain Rafting Co*, on Highway 1 next to
the *A&W*, T3446979, www.rockymountainadventure.com *Wet'n'wild*, 1509
Lafontaine Rd, T3446546. Rafting on the Kicking Horse or kayak tours on the Columbia.

Tour operators

Bus The *Greyhound* station is at 1402 Highway 1 W, T3446172, with 4 buses daily from
Calgary, $39, 5 from **Vancouver** via Vernon, $90, and 1 from **Invermere**, $13.

Transport

The first major BC ski resort to get development approval since Blackcomb 25
years ago, Kicking Horse is set to shake things up in the ski world. Expansion is
still underway, but with 1,620 ha of skiable terrain, a verticle rise of 1,245 m, and
a pair of alpine bowls reached in just 12 minutes by the state-of-the-art
eight-person Golden Eagle Express Gondola, it is certainly up there with the
likes of Whistler and Lake Louise. The difference is that here you'll enjoy the
powder without the crowds. Architect Oberto Oberti has designed the terrain
with skiers, not posers, in mind, seeking to emulate the kind of skiing you get in
the Alps 'where long, enclosed lifts go to the highest peak and then everyone
spreads out into the wide-open space'. Until further development, however,
this is not the best place for the amateur skier.

**Kicking Horse
Mountain
Resort**

Essentials The resort is 13 km from Golden, across the river off Highway 95. A day pass
is $40. *Mount Seven Taxi*, T3445237, run a shuttle from town in winter and summer. The
gondola stays open May-October, 1000-2100 ($18/7), to take diners up to the restaurant
(free with reservations). There is currently no accommodation on the hill, but it's part of
the plan. For more information T1888-7061117, www.kickinghorseresort.com

Highway 3: the border towns

Zig-zagging its way eastwards, never far from the US border, Highway 3 is
about the least exciting way to cross BC. There are highlights, but they cannot
compare with the finest of the province's outstanding scenery, and some long
stretches are just plain boring. A considerable advantage of this route, however, is that it offers the chance to detour into the wonderful Okanagan or
West Kootenay regions, which the TransCanada by-passes completely.

Manning Provincial Park

At the eastern end of the park, the Ultra Fuels gas station has cheaper fuel than Princeton, and authentic East Indian food

Even with the TransCanada heading north at Hope, the road remains busy and unpleasant until the Coquihalla also branches off, leaving Highway 3 to narrow down and begin a fairly steep ascent into the towering Cascade Mountains. At last the scenery can be enjoyed, as the winding highway follows the Skagit then the Similkameen River through a vast area of wilderness occupied by Manning Provincial Park and the bordering Skagit Valley Park and Cascade Recreation Area, with no communities to speak of until Princeton, 126 km away. This area is liable to have snow most of the year, and in winter is excellent for cross-country skiing, with some 130 km of ungroomed backcountry trails, a small ski hill, and 30 km of groomed trails, $14, T8408822. For general information call T8408836.

Most of the hiking trails, which range from 0.5 km to 30 km, begin in and around the park's only accommodation, the *Manning Park Resort*. Of other good trails, with access from Lightning Lake (see below), the best is the 7½-hour return hike to the east peak of **Frosty Mountain**, the park's highest point. The steep climb is rewarded by a ridge walk with fantastic views.

Sleeping and eating B *Manning Park Resort*, T8408822, www.manning parkresort.com, is worth checking out just for the artfully crafted chainsaw carvings inside and out, after which the rooms and cabins fall rather flat. There's a café, restaurant and lounge to warm up in, plus bike, ski, canoe and kayak rental. **Camping** Of the park's 4 campgrounds, the most convenient is at F *Lightning Lake*, 5 km from here, with 88 sites, canoeing, and access to more trails.

Princeton

Phone code: 250
Colour map 1, grid C5
Population: 3,036

After the long townless stretch from Hope, most people who stop in charmless Princeton are too tired to drive somewhere more interesting. Anglers are drawn by the 48 trout-fishing lakes within 60 km, most with basic campsites, 15 of them clustered together about 37 km north on Highway 5A. Between April and July, there are also good local runs for kayaking, canoeing and rafting. The town's highlight is a good **museum** with a very large fossil collection and much information about trainrobber Bill Miner, 'the gentleman bandit', who never took the ladies' jewellery. ■ *Hours vary, generally Tue-Sat 1000-1800, Sun-Mon 1100-1500. By donation. 167 Vermilion, T2957588.* The **Visitor Information Centre** is at 195 Bridge Street, T2953103, www.town.princeton.bc.ca

Highway 5A connects Princeton with Kamloops via Merritt. The so-called **Princeton Castle**, an unfinished 90 year-old cement plant that has crumbled to resemble a castle, is an unusual diversion 3 km down this road.

Sleeping and eating There are quite a few above-average motels here, best of which are the D *Evergreen*, 1 km east on Highway 3, T2957179, and the D *Princeton*, 156 Bridge St, T2956906, whose big rooms have a personal touch. **Camping** Campers should hang on for the 17 nice sites at F *Bromley Rock Provincial Park*, 21 km east of Princeton, T4946500. Best bet for food is the **mid-range** *Apple Tree Restaurant* in an old house on Vermilion Av, close to the *Greyhound* depot.

Hedley

East of Princeton, the landscapes tend increasingly toward the arid, rolling hills of the Okanagan, perfect for wine and fruit cultivation, and the stretch east to Osoyoos is one of the most scenic sections of this highway. The tiny village of Hedley was once one of the most important gold-mining towns in BC. The **museum**, which doubles as a **Visitor Information Centre**, has photos, artefacts, and lots of information about the many interesting remains and historic buildings around town, including a self-guided tour. Borrow their binoculars to see from the porch the remains of **Mascot Mine**, set amongst dramatic swirls of rock. Declared a National Heritage Site in 1993, the mine's cause has been taken up by the Upper Similkameen Native Band, who are attempting to restore its buildings and create what is destined to be an important tourist attraction. ■ *Summer 0900-1700 daily, rest of the year Thu-Mon. By donation. 712 Daly St, signed from highway, T2928422.*

Sleeping and eating C *Colonial Inn B&B*, Colonial Rd, T2928131, is a historic house with 5 nice rooms. **C** *Gold House B&B*, at 644 Colonial Rd, T2928418, www.thegoldhouse.com has 4 rooms (some sharing a bath) in the mine's former office and storage room built in 1904, with a wrap-around balcony and nice views. Behind here are the scenic remains of a crushing plant known as the Stamp Mill. **E** *Whistle Stop*, just west on Hwy 3, has amazing-value cabins, old fashioned but quaint and homey, with kitchenettes. **Camping F** *Stemwinder Provincial Park*, also just west, T4946500, has 27 nicely wooded and fairly private campsites on the river. *The Gold Dust Pub*, off the highway east of town, is the best bet for food and drink.

From the highway, 3 km west of Keremeos, Ashnola River Road leads over a historic red covered bridge, and follows this pretty waterway 23 km to the Lakeview trailhead. This is the most direct of three routes into the spectacular 33200-ha Cathedral Provincial Park. It is a steep six- or seven-hour hike (or $65 ride, see below), with 1,300 m elevation gain in 16 km. From the near desert of the Okanagan, the landscape changes to lush cedar and Douglas fir, then to pine, spruce, balsam fir and larch, finally climbing above the tree line to gain magnificent uninterrupted panoramas of the Cascade Mountains. It is well worth the grunt, for this is paradise, with seven beautiful alpine lakes within easy walking distance, their stunning turquoise waters emphasized by the surrounding sharp granite peaks. The trout fishing is excellent, and there's a good chance of seeing mountain goats, bighorn sheep and marmots.

Cathedral Provincial Park

Around **Quiniscoe Lake** are the main wilderness campground, a Ranger Station, and a private lodge. From here a network of trails leads to the other lakes and much more. **Ladyslipper Lake**, the furthest and prettiest, is a mere 2.5 km away. Beyond are a number of strange rock formations that can all be seen on a 10-km round trip. The **Devil's Woodpile** is a series of upright jointed basalt columns. **Stone City** is a bizarre moonscape of eroded quartz monoliths. The **Giant Cleft** is a massive split in the granite mountain face. **Quiniscoe** and **Pyramid** mountains can both be reached via **Glacier Lake**, each a 7-km round trip. A day's hike away is a wilderness campground at the **Haystack Lakes**. There is also a four-day hike to **Manning Park**.

Sleeping and eating LL-AL *Cathedral Lakes Lodge*, T4921606, www.cathe-dral-lakes-lodge.com, where rooms are $100-175 per person including all-you-can-eat buffet meals, hot tub, and canoes. Open Jun-mid-Oct, reservations required. Campers may purchase meals at the lodge. A jeep ride to the top is $65 per person, free if you get a room. **Camping** As well as **Quiniscoe Lake**, there are campsites at the Lakeview trailhead, at **Buckhorn** 2 km further down Ashnola River Road (vehicle accessible), and at **Lake of the Woods**. Visitors should be prepared to rough it.

Keremeos is set in the most stunning stretch of Highway 3, a full-blown Okanagan landscape, surrounded by orchards, and especially beautiful when the trees are in blossom. Justifiably dubbed the 'fruit stand capital of BC' the selection, quality and prices are exceptional even by local standards. There is good golfing in the area, mountain biking at nearby Cawston, and the

Keremeos

Phone code: 250
Colour map 1, grid C6
Population: 1,167
Altitude: 413 m

extraordinarily scenic **Cathedral Lakes Provincial Park**, but the major attraction in town is the **Keremeos Grist Mill and Gardens**. First built in 1877 to supply pioneers with gold fever travelling the Dewdney trail, this mill has been lovingly restored as a very popular 'living museum'. Everything still functions as it did over a century ago: ancient strains of wheat grown on the premises are ground by the water-powered mill and baked into bread which is sold in the café. People in costume do the work and give tours of the operation. ■ *Mid-May to mid-Oct 0930-1700. $5 including tours at 1030, 1200, 1330, 1500 and 1630. 2 km north on Hwy 3A.*

Sleeping and eating The best place to stay is **C** *Login B&B*, on Hwy 3 W, T4992781. A log house with pleasant rooms and views. For food try the *Pasta Trading Post*, 629 7th Av, T4992933. Antique-store turned restaurant, specializing in steak and seafood, with a garden patio, and a couple of B&B-style rooms (**C**).

Towards Osoyoos Highway 3A cuts across from Keremeos to the main Okanagan Valley road (Highway 97) and gives access to **Apex Ski Resort** (see Penticton), but it's worth staying on Highway 3 for the views around Osoyoos 46 km further east. The road climbs for a good 30 km before reaching the striking, highly photogenic **Spotted Lake** 11 km west of Osoyoos. The water's high levels of epsom salts, calcium and magnesium result in large, almost circular blotches, which change colour dramatically according to weather conditions. Mud from the lake was used by natives to alleviate aches and pains, and was believed to heal the spirit, bringing youth and wisdom. Warring enemies met here in peace to soothe battle wounds. For commanding views of the Okanagan Valley head 20 km up Kabau Forestry Road, just west of here, to the 1-km **Mount Kabau Lookout Trail**. The Tuculnuit Trail, a 4-km loop, offers different views.

The major resort town of Osoyoos (see page 228), is excessively popular thanks to its exceptionally warm, dry climate, proximity to the US border, and fabulous location at the end of the long, broad Okanagan Valley. Osoyoos Lake, which the town and highway bisect, is one of a chain of lakes heading north, lined with orchards and vineyards. There are great sweeping views from the highway on both sides of town as it switchbacks its way down to the valley floor.

East of Osoyoos the highway runs through the aptly named Boundary Country, the scenery slowly shifting between the extremes of the barren Okanagan and the green, densely forested mountains of the Kootenays, and not as compelling as either. There are certainly some fascinating rocky landscapes, but by BC's standards it's a boring drive, with few reasons to stop. At **Rock Creek**, the junction with Highway 33 to Kelowna, is the decent *Prospector Pub*, with good food, large servings, and a patio on the creek. On the highway just west of tiny **Midway** is the **Kettle River Museum**, which celebrates the Kettle Valley Railway (see box page 233). ■ *$2, T4492614*, Extensive leftover tracks now act as a hiking trail which passes through here.

Greenwood Greenwood is a quaint little town whose Wild West appearance is still more natural than contrived. It's a good place to shop for antiques and collectibles, and there are plenty of heritage buildings. Pick up a Frontier Walking Tour map at the **Visitor Information Centre**, 214 Copper Road South, T4456355, www.greenwoodheritage.bc.ca, or just stroll around reading the interesting anecdotes on the front of each old building. Check out the City Hall, worth entering for its stained glass, or the Fire Station opposite. *The Windsor Hotel* has the longest-running saloon in BC, brimming over with character. The *Copper Eagle Cappucino and Bakery* has classy wood and copper decor.

Sleeping D *Evening Star*, Hwy 3 east of town, T4456733, is one of many standard motels. **D** *The Forshaw House B&B*, across from City Hall at the end of Deadwood St, T4452208, is a heritage building whose small rooms have private or shared bath. Bike rentals. **F** *Boundary Creek Provincial Park*, 2 km west on Highway 3, T4946500, has 18 nice sites, and trout fishing. **Camping F** *Jewel Lake Provincial Park*, 12 km off Hwy 3 1 km to the east, has 26 forested primitive sites on the lake.

At the junction of Highway 3 and Phoenix Road, 19.5 km west of Grand Forks **Grand Forks** is the **Phoenix Interpretive Forest**, a 22-km drive through historical sights including a Doukhobor Village and an old cemetery. Granby Road at the east end of town takes you to some nice swimming spots on the river, access to the further reaches of **Gladstone Provincial Park** and, after 100 km (45 km of which is paved) to the very remote **Granby Provincial Park**, with countless opportunities for wilderness camping and hiking. Otherwise there's little of note except a great Farmer's Market on Tuesday and Friday mornings. Ask for details at the **Visitor Information Centre**, on the highway at 37362 5th Street. Weekdays 0830-1615, T4422833, www.boundary.bc.ca

Sleeping and eating The best place for eating and sleeping is the **B** *Golden Heights Estate Inn*, to the east at 7342 Bluff St, T1888-9335339, www.goldenheights.com This c1895 mansion has been recently renovated into a charming guesthouse whose 4 rooms have private bath, antiques and wool carpets. Hot tub and steam room, 4-course breakfast included. Its expensive *Rattlesnake Mountain Restaurant* has a gourmet menu including local organic produce and stuffed trout, and a BC wine list. The atmosphere is romantic with warm, cosy decor. Otherwise, the best motels are the **D** *Imperial*, 7389 Riverside Dr, T4428236, and **D** *Motel 99*, 7424 Donaldson Dr, T4428501.

Many Doukhobor descendants live in and around Grand Forks (see page 226). If you want to try some of their traditional food, the most reliable option is the *Chef's Garden*, Hwy 3 W, T4420257. The *Station Pub*, 7654 Donaldson Dr, T4425855, has a nice atmosphere with good beer on tap and a reasonable restaurant upstairs. *Kocomo's Coffee House*, 7361 2nd St, T4420500, is good for its borscht, home-baking, and patio garden.

Despite its wonderful location, this small town fails to live up to its tourism **Christina Lake** potential. There are few facilities and lake access is poor. Fortunately, over half of the lake is contained within **Gladstone Provincial Park**, easily accessed via the Texas-Alpine turn-off, 5 km north on the highway. Turn onto Alpine Road and carry on to the end for the campground (see below). A very satisfying hiking and biking trail begins here, hugging the lake to its northern tip. A right fork then continues deep into the park, the left leading to more private wilderness campsites, one close by on Christina Lake, another on Xenia Lake further to the west. You could also hire a canoe and cross the main lake to one of the remote wilderness campgrounds on the west shore. If entering town from the west, look for a road south that leads to the Kettle River and a big waterfall.

Sleeping and eating There are few decent options in town. **B** *Sunflower Inn B&B*, Alpine Rd 159, T4476201, suninn@sunshinecable.com, has the best beds. 3 rooms with shared bath, private beach, canoes. The standard **D** *Parklane Motel*, 31 Kingsley Rd, T4479385, is at least away from the highway. *Moon Beans*, Johnson Rd next door to *Wild Ways*, has good coffee and internet access. **Camping F**, at the end of Alpine Rd, T4946500, is a well-equipped but over-popular campground.

Sports For canoe rentals and information, bikes and general outdoor gear, head to *Wild Ways* on Johnson Rd off the highway.

Rossland

Phone code: 250
Colour map 2, grid C1
Population: 3,768
Altitude: 1,038 m

Beyond Christina Lake, you're well and truly in Kootenay country, and the winding mountain road has some striking moments as it climbs steadily towards **Poulson Pass**. First-class groomed and track-set cross-country skiing trails (for which a small fee is requested) are reached via a few car parks signed from the highway, or from **Nancy Greene Provincial Park** next door. Here you can ski around a lovely lake that also has a beach for summer swimming and fishing. The park marks the junction with Highway 3B, which leads 20 km south to Rossland. On the way are some more fine, ungroomed (and free) Nordic ski trails at Nancy Greene Summit.

All this makes a fitting introduction to Rossland, one of the great unsung skiing centres, and 'Mountain bike capital of Canada'. Most people who live here are obsessed with one or both of these activities, so the atmosphere is saturated with an outdoor mentality. In winter the population doubles as the town fills up with predominantly Australian ski-bums. Besides being young, lively, friendly and given over in winter to a party atmosphere, this is also an exceptionally picturesque little town with wide, impossibly steep streets, mountains all around, and views above the clouds. For information, go to the **Chamber of Commerce** at 2185 Columbia Avenue, T3625666; or the **Visitor Information Centre** at the museum (see below).

Many facilities, including the *Greyhound* depot, are in **Trail**, a much bigger town 11 km away on Highway 22. Utterly dominated by the *Cominco* zinc and lead-smelting complex (the local hockey team are known as the 'Smoke Eaters'), Trail is an ugly place best avoided.

In the 1890s Rossland was a booming gold-mining town, with 7,000 people, 42 saloons and four local newspapers. The **Rossland Museum** (which doubles up as the Information Centre) has information about that era. Their interesting tours take you through a spooky (and chilly) turn-of-the-20th-century mine filled with old equipment. ■ *Mid-May to mid-Sep, 0900-1700, tours 0930-1530. $8, $5 seniors, $3 children including tour. Junction Hwys 22 and 3B, T3627722, www.rossland.com*

Sleeping **AL-D** *Rams Head Inn*, Red Mtn Rd, just before ski hill, T3629577, www.rams head.bc.ca By far the best option. Beautiful but homey rooms, common room with big stone fireplace, sauna, outdoor hot tub with view, games room, breakfast included. Prices go right down in summer. **B** *Uplander Hotel*, 1919 Columbia Av, T3627375. Convenient Downtown choice, but with a noisy bar downstairs. **C** *Angela's Place B&B*, 1520 Spokane St, T3627790. 6 rooms with private entrances, hot tub, fireplace, garden, creek running through property. **C** *Red Mountain Village*, at the base of the hill, 3 km north on Hwy 3B, T3629000. Condos, motel rooms, cabins and RV spaces. Old fashioned decor. **D** *Swiss Alps Inn*, 1199 Hwys 3B/22, T3627364. Hot tub, restaurant. **E** *Mountain Shadow Hostel*, 2125 Columbia Av, T3627160. Dorms and private rooms, common room and kitchen, internet access, not very clean. **Camping** **F** *Rossland Lions Park*, Red Mtn Rd, 1 km north on Highway 3B. 18 sites, some with hook-ups. Summer only.

Eating **Mid-range** *Mountain Gypsy Café*, 2167 Washington St, T3623342. Delicious gourmet dishes, lots of daily specials, exquisite presentation as well as taste. Friendly, laid-back atmosphere. A firm favourite with locals, so reservations recommended. *Sunshine Café*, 2116 Columbia St, T3627630, 0730-1500 only. Good for breakfast and pannini. *The Uplander Hotel*, 1919 Columbia Av, T3627275, has a restaurant and a lounge (non-smoking). It has its own mid-range menu with sandwiches and pastas, or choose from the expensive restaurant menu with creative appetizers and salads, steaks, etc. For **coffee**, there's the **Alpine Grind Coffee House**, 2207 Columbia Av, T3622280, with a deck, views and liquor licence, or the *Goldrush Café*, 2063 Washington St, T3625333, a bakery with sourdough bread, a decent bookstore, and internet access.

The Flying Steamshovel Inn, Washington/2nd Av, T3627373. More of a daytime pub **Bars** than the *Uplander*, and a nicer space. Small, intimate and very light, with pool table, good selection of beer on tap, drink specials and good pub food. *The Powder Keg Pub*, in the *Uplander*, 1919 Columbia Av. The most happening spot with frequent live music, and pool tables. Smoky and often packed. *Rock Cut Neighborhood Pub*, 3052 Highway 3B, across from ski hill, T3625814. Patio with great view, pub food, non smoking.

Red Mountain Ski Hill, 3 km west on Hwy 3B, T3627669, www.ski-red.com, is open **Sports** Nov-Apr. A day pass is $42. It's a great hill for experts, with 45% black diamond runs, and lots of tree-skiing. The vertical gain is an impressive 880 m, but a relatively low elevation can cause problems when the weather is uncooperative. The Paradise area is good for beginners, and very pretty with lots of views and sun. For **cross-country** skiing there are the **Black Jack** trails across from Red Mountain, T3629000, $7 day pass. See also Nancy Greene and Poulson Summits above. Rentals available at the hill, or at *Powder Hound*, 2040 Columbia Av, who also rent bikes. **Buses** to the hill leave the *Uplander Hotel* at 0845, returning at 1550. Hitching is also fairly easy.

There are several good hiking and skiing trails right from town, but Rossland is especially famous for its **mountain biking**, with over 100 km of trails. Ask at *The Sacred Ride*, 2123 Columbia Av, T3625688, for information and rentals. **Old Glory** is a great 8-hr return **hike** to 360° views of surrounding mountain ranges. Trailhead is 11 km north of town on Highway 3B. The best place for **swimming** is *Trail Aquatic and Leisure Centre*, 1875 Columbia Av in Trail, T3686484. New, unchlorinated pool, sauna, hot tub, fitness room, and the best facilities for a long way.

Books *Goldrush Books and Espresso*, 2063 Columbia Av. **Food** *Red Mountain Mar-* **Shopping** *ket*, 2104 Columbia Av. Healthy food and fresh vegetables.

Bus The *Greyhound* station is in **Trail** at 1355 Bay Av, T3688400. Local buses between **Transport** Rossland and Trail leave every 1½ hrs from Cedar/Spokane in Trail, from Jubilee/St Paul in Rossland. Since *Greyhounds* tend to pass through at ungodly hours, you might need a **taxi**. *Champion Cabs*, T3643344, charge about $15.

Communications Canada Post: 2090 Columbia Av. **Internet**: *Goldrush Café*, see **Directory** above. **Laundry** Beside the *Goldrush*. **Medical services** *Trail Regional Hospital*, 1200 Hospital Bench, Trail, T3683311.

Despite a potentially beautiful location at the junction of the Kootenay and **Castlegar** Columbia Rivers, Castlegar is a hopelessly drab place. Right on Highway 3A is the area's only airport, T3655151, known locally as 'Cancelgar' due to the tendency of fogs to interrupt services. Opposite is the **Kootenay Gallery of Art History and Science**, which has regional, national and international exhibitions usually of a high standard, that change every five or seven weeks. Decent gift shop. ■ *Mar-Dec 1000-1700 Wed-Sat, 1200-1700 Sun. $2, under 12s free. T3653337.* Also worthwhile is the interesting **Doukhobour Village Museum**. ■ *May-Sep 1000-1800, $4, $2 concessions. T3656622.* The only sensible thing to do now that Highway 3 has become so tedious again is to take Highway 3A to Nelson and the West Kootenays, a nice tour which could land you on the TransCanada at Revelstoke.

▶ ## Spirit wrestlers

The Doukhobors originated as a peasant group in southern Russia who rejected church liturgy, believing that God dwells in each man and not in a church. They also rejected secular governments and preached pacifism. The name Doukhobors, meaning 'spirit-wrestlers', was first applied by a Russian Orthodox archbishop who implied that they wrestled against the Holy Spirit.

Persecuted in Russia, the group emigrated to Canada in 1898-99. In this they were assisted by British and American Quakers, and novelist Leo Tolstoy, whose ideals greatly coincided with their own. More than 7,400 originally settled as a community in what was to become Saskatchewan. Initially, they were allowed to live communally and register for individual homesteads, and they received concessions regarding education and military service. But when, in 1905, they refused to swear an oath of allegiance, their homestead entries were cancelled, and most of them followed their leader Peter Verigin to southern British Columbia. Of the 30,000 or so descendants of the original Doukhobor settlers that remain, about half are still active in the culture, maintaining their religious customs, Russian language and pacifism. Many of them live in the Kootenay Boundary district between the Slocan Valley and Grand Forks, where hard work and agriculture have helped them to thrive.

Sleeping There are plenty of places to stay here including the **C** *Days Inn*, 651 18th St, T3652700, and the **D** *Twin Rivers Motel*, 1485 Columbia Av, T3656900, but with Nelson and Rossland so close, why bother? **Camping** It's worth making a detour 19 km west off Highway 3A (through Robson) to **F** *Syringa Provincial Park*, T8253500, with 60 very nice, private sites on the shore of the Lower Arrow Lake. **Eating** The place to eat is the expensive but first-class *Gabes*, at 1432 Columbia Av, T3656028. You can get a good cup of java at *Common Grounds*, handily placed at 692 18th St.

Salmo If you missed it before, another chance to head to Nelson comes at tiny Salmo, a cute little town that's held on to a pioneer feel. If driving on, check your fuel and brace yourself for a steady 50 km climb. If coming the other way, be sure to have good brakes. At 1,774 m, **Kootenay Pass** is the highest in British Columbia, and often covered with snow. Impatient locals head there for some excellent backcountry skiing while awaiting the powder lower down. It's a pretty enough drive, but the views don't really arrive until the top, where there's a beautiful lake and a number of inviting hiking trails.

Sleeping If stopping try the **D** *Reno Motel*, 123 Railway Av, T3579937. Good value suites with bathtubs. **Camping** There's a **F** city campground just around the corner.

Creston

Phone code: 250
Colour map 2, grid C2
Population: 5,000
Altitude: 611 m

After a long descent, the highway enters a wide, flat valley, created by the flood plain of the Kootenay River. The resultant rich soils have helped Creston to survive on the back of its fruit at times when the rest of the Kootenays were hit hard by the closure of silver and copper mines. Fruits of all kinds are still grown here and are available from June to October. The marshes around the river have also been a favourite with birds, and today the **Creston Valley Wildlife and Interpretive Centre** protects 7,000 ha, home to 265 bird species. As well as watching stations and the displays at the centre, there are hiking and biking trails, canoeing, and a 150 sq-m mural. ■ *24 hrs daily. Interpretive Centre end Apr to mid-Oct. 11 km west of Creston on Hwy 3, T4026908, www.cwildlife.bc.ca*

Downtown Creston has a rather odd feeling to it, maybe because it seems as if it really belongs in Alberta. The area is well known for its golf courses and the good fishing in Duck Lake. **The Stone House Museum** has a replica Kutenai canoe that apparently proves the migration of people from Russia over the Bering Strait. ■ *May-Sep 1000-1530. $2. 219 Devon St, T4289262.* The **Tourist Information Centre** is at 1711 Canyon Street, T4284342, www.crestonbc.com From here Highway 3A heads north along the east shore of Kootenay Lake, then on to Nelson via what was until recently the longest free ferry ride in North America (see page 247). Highway 3 continues east to the large, horrible town of Cranbrook, then on through the pleasant ski-town of Fernie to the Alberta border at the Crowsnest Pass. All this is covered in the East Kootenays section, see page 258.

Sleeping & eating

C *Cranberry Manor B&B*, 330 NW Boulevard, T4289520. The nicest place to stay. Comfortable top floor of a heritage home with kitchen and living room. **D** *City Centre Motel*, 220-15 Av, T4282257, and **D** *Downtowner Motor Inn*, 1218 Canyon St, T4282238, are central but standard, though the latter has a sauna and whirlpool. **Camping F** *Little Joe's Campground*, 5 km east on Highway 3, T4282954. 20 wooded and private sites beside a creek. Showers and hook-ups. *Monro's*, 1403 Canyon St, T4287222, is a reasonable mid-range place for food, with pasta, chicken, ribs, and salad bar. *Annette's Delicatessen*, 1127 Canyon St. The best place for coffee, lunches and baking. Open roughly 0900-1700.

Okanagan Valley

The region surrounding the long, north-south Okanagan Valley and its string of skinny lakes has a very rare ecosystem. Sitting in the rain shadow of the Cascade and Coast Mountains, it receives less rain and more sun than anywhere else in the country, becoming increasingly dry and arid towards the south, where Osoyoos contains Canada's only living desert, complete with cacti, rattlesnakes and scorpions. The colours are no less striking for being subdued, and the barren hills and rocky bluffs possess an awe-inspiring quality, a strange beauty that only benefits from its sharp contrast with the forested greenery typical of southern BC.

Such a climate is ideal for vineyards and orchards, making the Okanagan the province's number one producer of fruit and wine, the latter gaining an ever-stronger international reputation. While an orchard tour is recommended, a trip around some wineries is essential. There are dozens scattered throughout the valley offering tours and generous free tastings, with many also operating decent bistros.

Retirees also find the climate conducive, and for some time now have been moving here en masse, leading to a proliferation of hospices, homes, golf courses and evangelical-style churches. More recently, the combination of sun, warm water and ample stretches of lakefront has caused the whole region to become one big summer holiday resort. Families from the prairies make an annual pilgrimage to its heaving beaches. Retired RVers from the United States arrive in droves, reducing local traffic to a choked crawl. Youngsters from all over come to party, get a tan and indulge in noisy watersports. Such excesses can be avoided, however, and as ever those who thrive on outdoor pursuits will find plenty on offer, including three major ski-hills.

Best time to visit

The best times to visit the Okanagan are spring and autumn, not just to avoid the excessive summer crowds, but to catch blossom and harvest times. The former runs from roughly mid-Apr to mid-May, the latter continues as late as the end of Oct. Coinciding nicely with these periods are the region's big wine festivals, which engulf the whole valley. The **Spring Wine Festival** in early May is a major event, but much bigger and older is the **Fall Wine Festival** in late Sep/early Oct, which is entering its 23rd year. About 90,000 people attend over 100 events at various locations, including dinners, parades, and grape stomps. For information on both festivals, T8616654, www.owfs.com   A much newer event is the **Ice-wine Festival** held mid-late Jan.

Wine

With the exception of some of the more southern vineyards, the Okanagan's growing season is too short for red wines. As well as many German-style whites and some decent Chardonnays, the region's reputation is built on its Pinot Noirs, sparkling whites, and increasingly on its prize-winning ice wines. Made from grapes harvested at -8°C and pressed while still frozen, this sweet, strong wine, expensive to produce and buy, is made on an annual basis only in Canada.

Wineries are clearly marked from the highway. The areas with the greatest concentration, and therefore most suitable for a tour, are Kelowna, Naramata, and the 'golden mile' in Oliver. Ask at *Penticton's Wine Centre* (see page 229) or Kelowna's Wine Museum (see page 235) for more details. A couple of useful websites are **www.winesnw.com/okanagan2.html** and **www.bcwine.com/wineries**

Osoyoos

Phone code: 250
Colour map 1, grid C6
Population: 4,135
Altitude: 277 m

From either direction, Highway 3 has to descend rapidly via a series of steep switchbacks to get down to Osoyoos. Views from the top highlight the town's superb position on, and even in the middle of Osoyoos Lake. This is the southernmost of a string of lakes contained within the long, broad Okanagan Valley, which can be seen winding its way endlessly to the north. Highway 97 follows it through a weird desert landscape of barren scrub-covered hills. This is the driest part of the Okanagan, with Canada's lowest rainfall and some of its highest temperatures. The desert here is the real thing, complete with rattlesnakes, lizards and cacti, though as a living ecosystem it has been almost entirely lost to an endless parade of highly successful orchards and wineries. The climate's ability to support even exotic fruits like pomegranates has prompted a half-hearted Mediterranean theme in Osoyoos.

Despite all this, the town itself is extremely ugly, especially the nasty motel strip that follows Highway 3 across the lake. This doesn't seem to deter the hordes who come in summer to sunbathe on the beaches and swim in some of the country's warmest (but sadly polluted) water, which averages 24° C in summer. The **Tourist Information Centre** is at 9202 Highway 97, T4957142, www.osoyooschamber.bc.ca

For excursions to the Spotted Lake and Mount Kabau Lookout trail, see page 222

Before irrigation became the norm, most of this land was occupied by Canada's only living desert, an extension of the Great Basin Desert in the US, and part of the Sonoran Desert ecosystem that runs right down into Mexico. The **Desert Centre** aims to protect the small, fragile pocket that remains, supporting over 100 rare plants, and over 300 rare invertebrates, including about two dozen that were previously unknown and are found nowhere else in the world. Fauna include the Great Basin Spadefoot Toad, Western Rattlesnake, and Tiger Salamander. The dominant flora are antelope-brush and wild sage. There is over a mile of boardwalk from which to observe the desert's features, but these are often so subtle that only the genuine enthusiasm of the guides brings the experience to life. Tours run every hour on the hour, the first and last offering the best chance of seeing animals. Night tours are offered once a month in summer. Many special tours are run, such as a birding tour at 0630 on Wednesdays. ■ *Mid-Apr to mid-Oct. $6, $3 concessions. Just north of town, off Hwy 97 to Oliver, T4952470, www.desert.org*

Sleeping *In summer accommodation is greatly overpriced and fills up quickly*

The cheaper motels, mostly along the strip on Hwy 3, are still sporting 70s decor and brown carpets. **B** *Inkameep Point Lodge Guesthouse*, 2 km north on Hwy 97, T4956353. 4 semi-detached cottages and lodge rooms with kitchens. Right on the lake with private beach and pier for windsurfing and sailing. Canoes rented. Breakfast included. Reservations required. **C** *Avalon Motel*, 9106 Main St, T4956334. Small suites with kitchenettes and decks. New rooms are worth the extra. **C** *Spanish Fiesta/Falcon Motels*, 7104/6 Main St, T4956833/7544. Small reasonable rooms with kitchenettes, right on the lake with own stretch of beach. Swimming pool and jacuzzi. **C** *Villa Blanca B&B*, 23640 Deerfoot Rd, 10 km east on Hwy 3, T4955334. 3 rooms with gorgeous views from hilltop. Private bath, breakfast included. **C** *The White Horse B&B*, 8000 Highway 3 W, T4952887. Great location just out of town. 3 rooms with private bath, patio, views.

E-F *Brook Vale Holiday Resort*, 1219 Lakeshore Dr, T4957514. The last of many RV parks along this road, also with simple cabanas, bedding not supplied. **Camping F** *Haynes Point Provincial Park*, follow Highway 97 S, then look for signs, T4946500. Beautifully located on a sand spit reaching out into the lake. Showers, flush toilets, sites a bit too closely packed. The busiest provincial campground in BC, so reservation essential. **E-F** *Inkaneep Campground*, turn off Hwy 3 on east side of town, T4957279. Pretty location on the beach with many weeping willows. Not very private sites. Showers, laundry, boat rentals.

Eating *Considering its summer popularity, there is a dearth of decent places to eat in Osoyoos*

Mid-range *The Burrowing Owl Pub*, 7603 Spartan, T4953274, is the best bet, with great if predictable food, and lots of it. Good beer on tap, pool table. *Campo Marina*, 7506 Main St, T4957650. Italian cuisine. Opens 1700 Tue-Sun. **Cheap** *Osoyoos Burger House*, 6910 Main St, T4957686. Best spot for breakfast. For coffee go to *Beans Desert Bistro*, 8323 Main St, which also does breakfast. Another decent pub is the *Ridge Brewing Co*, junction Hwys 3 and 97. Brews its own beers (good stout). Pub food.

Sport

Osoyoos Golf and Country Club, 12300 Golf Course Dr, T4953355.

Transport

Bus The *Greyhound* stop is at 6015 Lakeshore Dr, T4957252, with 3 daily buses to Vancouver ($60), 2 to **Kelowna** ($20), and 3 to **Calgary** ($90).

Directory

Communications Internet: free at Information Centre or library. **Canada Post:** Spartan Dr/78th St. **Library** Main St. **Medical services** The nearest hospital is in Oliver, 20 km to the north.

Penticton

Phone code: 250
Colour map 1, grid C6
Population: 33,000
Altitude: 344 m

The rather ordinary town of Penticton mutates every summer into a hectic, throbbing beach-fest, attracting both families and a younger crowd who come to party and show off their tans. The big attraction is sun: Penticton gets more of it, and less rain, than most of the continent's more famous resorts, and temperatures regularly exceed 35°C, sometimes reaching up to 45°C. Sandwiched between two lakes, the town also has plenty of sand and water to go round. The **Visitor Information Centre**, 888 Westminster Avenue West, T4934055, www.penticton.org, is open 0800-2000 daily in summer, otherwise 0900-1700 Monday-Friday, 1100-1700 Saturday and Sunday. There's also an information booth five minutes south on Highway 97, open 0900-1700 weekends, daily in July and August.

Those bored of the beach scene will find plenty of sporting activities, including the popular 'tubing' experience. A tour of the wineries is another good option. The **Wine Centre** has extremely informative and knowledgeable staff who will help you find the ones that most appeal. They also stock a broad range of Okanagan wines and do daily tastings. ■ *888 Westminster Av West, in the Visitor Information Centre, T4902006.*

History Some geologists claim that the eastern shore of Okanagan Lake is the edge of the older North American land mass, and that the lake is a water-filled chasm, created when the newer volcanic land from the west was pushed into it by the shifting of the Pacific plate. This would explain the belief that almost every type of rock in the world can be found within 40 miles of Penticton. In the early 1900s gold was discovered beneath the lake, but the cost of extracting it proved too expensive.

Beaches Most of the action happens on **Okanagan Beach** around the *Lakeshore Resort*. All manner of gear can be rented here for water-skiing, jet-skiing, ski-mobiling , sailing, windsurfing, para-sailing, paddle-boating, etc. The beaches around **Skaha Lake** to the south are more family oriented. If nude beaches are more your style, the local one is at **3 Mile**, towards Naramata.

Sights For boat enthusiasts, the **SS Sicamous**, on the beach at 1099 Lakeshore Drive, is a fully restored and decked out 1914 paddlesteamer. For railway buffs the highlight is a working model of the Kettle Valley Railway (see page 233). ■ *Summer 0900-2100, rest of year 0900-1700. $4, $1 concessions. T4920403.* The usual small-town stuff can be found at the **Penticton Museum**, in the library at 785 Main Street, T4902451.

Excursions **Apex Ski Resort**, 33 km west of Penticton, is dwarfed by Kelowna's Big White and even Vernon's Silver Star, but its smallness is its strong point. **Nickel Plate Nordic Centre** 6 km away, has excellent cross-country skiing, with 30 km of groomed and trackset trails and 20 km of backcountry trails. There are some nice but expensive lodges to stay at, a hostel in the works, and an RV parking lot (**F**). The *Gunbarrel Saloon and Restaurant* is a very popular no-smoking spot for grub and pints. Equipment rentals and lessons are available at the hill. ■ *Nov-Apr. Day pass is $42. T2928222.* The *Magic Ski Bus* from Cherry Lane Mall or *Tim Hortons* runs up at weekends and holidays.

Vaseux Lake Provincial Park, 15 km south, is renowned for its bird-watching, bighorn sheep and rattlesnakes. Bird-watchers should check out *Rave* at 27a Front Street, Penticton.

Sleeping Penticton has a lot of hotels and motels, although most are fairly dreary. **AL** *Penticton*
Finding a room *Lakeside Resort*, 21 Lakeshore Dr, T4938221, www.rpbhotels.com The luxury option in
shouldn't be a the best possible location, with pool, hot tub, balconies, bar, casino, and a first-class res-
problem except taurant. **A-B** *Sandman Hotel*, 939 Burnaby Av W, T4937151, www.sandman.ca Stan-
during the Ironman dard mid-range choice, reliable and well located. Kitchenettes, pool and hot tub.
Triathlon in August
    C *Crown Motel*, 950 Lakeshore Dr, T4924092, www.crownmotel@penticton.com Best value of the many motels rubbing shoulders opposite the main beach. Reasonable-sized rooms with small patios and BBQs, and a heated outdoor pool. **C** *Log Cabin Motel*, 3287 Skaha Lake Rd, T4923155, www.logcabinmotel@penticton.com Not the most convenient location, but one of the only motels in town with any character. Heated outdoor

pool, playground. Large variety of rooms, good for families. **C** *Riordan House B&B*, 689 Winnipeg St, T4935997. 3 rooms decorated with antiques in a beautiful 1912 heritage house not far from Downtown and the beach.

E *Penticton HI Hostel*, 464 Ellis St, T4923992, www.hihostels.bc.ca Friendly, well-run hostel in a Downtown building full of character. Dorms and private rooms with shared bath, kitchen, TV lounge, laundry, lockers, BBQ. Good for information. The following campgrounds are all **F**, (**E** for hook-ups): *Banbury Green RV Park*, 5 km south on Hwy 97, T4975221. A pleasant, wooded site right on the lake, below an orchard. *Camp-Along Resort*, 6 km south on Hwy 97, T4975584, www.campalong.com In an apricot orchard with a pool and good views of, but no direct access to Skaha Lake. *Wright's Beach Camp*, 4071 Skaha Lake Rd, T4927120. Quite ugly and cramped despite trees and beach, but still about the best of the many in town around Skaha Lake.

Expensive *Magnum's* at the *Lakeside Resort* (see above) has an excellent reputation for fine dining in luxurious surroundings, with attentive service and prices that are surprisingly reasonable. **Mid-range** *Lost Moose Lodge*, 7 km east on Carmi Rd, then 3 km on Beaverdell Rd, T4900526. It's quite a trek, but locals recommend heading out to this lovely, quiet spot for their widely renowned barbecue. Reservations necessary. They also have rooms (**D**), and campsites (**F**). *Theo's*, 687 Main St, T4924019, www.eatsquid.com A local institution. Vast and very popular, yet intimate and personal. Big portions of tasty, authentic Greek cuisine. An extensive wine list, good service, and a patio for summer dining. *Salty's Beach House*, 1000 Lakeshore Dr, T4935001. An eccentric, extremely popular spot, appropriately resembling a beach shack, serving tasty seafood specialities from Mexico to Thailand. More pricey than you'd expect.

Cheap *Elite*, 340 Main St. An authentic diner, worth visiting for the atmosphere alone: horseshoe booths and decor that looks as if it hasn't changed since the place opened in 1927. Cheap breakfasts and other predictable favourites such as grilled cheese sandwiches. *Lee's Delights*, 139 Westminster Av W. A small sit-down or takeaway joint serving various oriental cuisines: Chinese, Thai, sushi. All delicious and very reasonably priced. See also *Il Vecchio* under Shopping. Easily the best place in town for coffee is the arty and atmospheric *Green Beanz Café*, 218 Martin St.

In summer Penticton is a very lively town, and it doesn't take long to find where the action is. The crowd's loyalties depend on variables like happy hours, drinks specials, favoured DJs, and live music, but most evenings begin at the *Barking Parrot Lounge* in the *Lakeside Resort*. Sophisticated but laid-back, it's the nicest place for a drink and understandably a long-term favourite. *Blue Mule Country Club*, 218 Martin St, T4931819. Open till 0200 Wed-Sat. A club usually specializing in country music. *The Element*, 535 Main St, T4931023, and *Nite Moves*, 333 Main St, T4931222, are both rather typical small-town clubs, mainly attracting a younger crowd.

Art *Art Gallery of the South Okanagan*, 199 Front St, T4932928. An attractive space, intelligently managed, with a good little gift shop. Tue-Sat 1000-1700. $2, Tue free. **Cinema** *Pen Mar*, 361 Martin St, T4925974.

As well as taking part in the *Spring and Fall Wine Festivals* (see page 228), Penticton hosts a massive *Peach Festival* in early Aug, T4934055. Maybe the most entertaining event of the year is the *Beach Blanket Film Festival* in Jul, when various movies are shown through the evening on Okanagan Beach. The last weekend of Aug is the busiest in Penticton's calendar, with every room in town reserved months ahead. The *Ironman Triathlon* is taken very seriously, requiring 4,000 volunteers to run, and attracting 1,000 iron men from over 30 countries.

Eating

Bars & clubs

Entertainment

Festivals

Southern Interior BC

Shopping **Books** *The Bookshop*, 238-242 Main St. An excellent used book store, arguably one of the best in the country for its breadth and organization of stock, and knowledgeable staff. Over the road is a shop selling new books. There is a string of **craft and gift** stores along the cute but disappointingly short Front St, which is trying very hard to bring a bit of colour and culture to Downtown. The Art Gallery also has a nice gift shop. **Food** *Il Vecchio*, behind the bus station on Robinson is a well-stocked Mediterranean deli making exquisite sandwiches to order.

Sports **Hiking and biking** The surrounding area is rich in possibilities for outdoor pursuits. The most challenging section of the Kettle Valley Railway trail is north of Penticton, climbing 900 m through 2 tunnels and past Chute Lake on the way to the Myra Canyon on the edge of Kelowna. It's a superb route for hiking or biking. Access is where the rail crosses Naramata Rd, or right from this road to the top of Arawana or Smethurst roads. *The Bike Barn*, 300 Westminster Av W, has everything a cyclist could desire including trail information and rental for $25 per day. **Campbell Mountain** and **Ellis Ridge Canyon** are also recommended for hiking, while **Munson Mountain**, of volcanic origin, is a nice walk and the obvious place for views. **Rock-climbing** Skaha Bluffs has world-class rock-climbing, with 260 climbs and 400 bolted routes. Learn how to do it with *Skaha Rock Adventures*, T4931765. **Skiing** Carmi Rd runs east to the Carmi cross-country ski trails. **Apex Ski Hill** (see above) is within striking distance for downhill skiing. In town, a cycling/walking path has been made along the 8 km River Channel that connects the two lakes. Or you can float down it in a giant inner-tube with *Coyote Cruises*, 215 Riverside Dr, T4922115, Jun-Sep 0900-1630, $10 including transport back.

Tour operators *Bacchus Tours*, T8099133, will take you around some of the neighbouring wineries. You drink, they drive. *Vista Treks*, T4965220, run 3-hour bike tours of the Kettle Valley Railway for $25 (+$15 bike rental). Ask if they're doing their Sep 40-km wine walk from Kelowna to Osoyoos.

Transport **Bus** Penticton is an important bus junction. The *Greyhound* station is just off Main at Nanaimo/Ellis, with 7 buses daily (5 on Sat) to **Vancouver** ($54), 3 to **Calgary** ($90), and 4 to **Kamloops** ($34). *Handy Dart* buses, T4925814, run regularly from Downtown to Skaha Lake and Naramata.

Directory **Banks** The banks cluster around Main/Nanaimo. **Communications** Internet: There are many internet cafés around town, such as *The Mousepad Café*, 320 Martin St, and *Net Werx*, 151 Front St. **Canada Post** is in *Plaza Card and Gifts*, 1301 Main St.

Naramata For those who understandably love the Okanagan's climate, scenery, orchards and vineyards, but feel that its towns are all a little crass and over-crowded, the answer is Naramata. This sleepy little village is about 16 km north of Penticton on the east side of Okanagan Lake, away from the highway, the only drawback being the lack of a decent public beach. Surrounded by vineyards, this is the perfect place for a winery tour, which energetic visitors could even manage on foot. The following are open from spring to autumn for drop-in tastings and lunch in their patio bistros. **Hillside Estate**, 1350 Naramata Road, T4936274 (hourly tours and lunch from 1100-1700); **Lake Breeze**, 930 Sammet Road, T4965659; **Red Rooster**, 910 Debeck Road, T4964041 (some of the valley's finest reds).

Sleeping and eating The place to stay is the newly renovated **A** *Naramata Heritage Inn and Spa*, T4966808, www.naramatahotel.com 12 lovely rooms in a very attractive building, breakfast included. It also contains the recommended *Rock Oven Dining Room*,

Kettle Valley Railway ◀

When silver was struck in the Kootenays, the Canadian Pacific Railway was too far north to help exploit the finds. The north-south valleys made access much easier from across the border, and as the Americans increasingly gained control of the situation, fears grew that the US would end up annexing southeast BC. The result was the Kettle Valley Railway (KVR), 'the most expensive railroad ever built' due to the meandering, virtually impenetrable terrain it conquered with tools no greater than hand-picks and shovels. Completed in 1916, thanks to the skill and tenacity of Chief Engineer Andrew McCulloch, this outstanding accomplishment was perpetually plagued by heavy snow and avalanches in winter, then washouts and rock-slides

in spring. Like most of Canada's great rail lines it was eventually killed by the modern obsession with roads, the last train running in 1989.

Today some 600 km of the KVR are suitable for hiking and biking, and much of it will form part of the TransCanada Trail. The best sections are between Penticton and Kelowna, especially Myra Canyon Tressles just outside the latter. Also worthy of note are the exceptional Othello Tunnels just outside Hope. For more information, visit the KVR Museum in Midway, or www.members.home.net/kettlevalley Books include B Sanford's McCulloch's Wonder *and D & S Langford's* Steel Rails and Iron Men *and* Cycling the KVR. *For up-to-date trail information, try www.planet.eon.net/~dan/kvr*

Southern Interior BC

and the *Cobblestone Wine* Bar, which has occasional live music. **D** *The Village Motel*, 244 Robinson Av, T4965535, is a very pleasant, friendly place. Almost opposite, **D** *BC Motel*, 365 Robinson Av, T4965482, is another decent option. Highly recommended for food is *Robinson Road Bistro*, 340 Robinson Av, T 4965500. Great, varied menu, very nice atmosphere and decor. Seating outside, and live music at weekends.

The road from Penticton to Kelowna is a windy, attractive drive. Summerland houses the **Kettle Valley Railway Steam Train**, the only section of the line still being used, though it's a child-oriented attraction rather than a form of transport (it covers just 10 km in two hours). From late May to early October the train leaves Prairie Valley Station (take Prairie Valley Road from the Highway) at 1030 and 1330 on Saturday, Sunday and Monday, and also on Thursday and Friday from July to September. ■ *$12, $8.50 concessions. T49 8422, www.kettlevalleyrail.org* Also worth a visit are the **Summerland Ornamental Gardens**, a 6.5-ha spread of colour overlooking orchards, wineries, a gorge and the lake. ■ *$2 donation. 4200 Hwy 97 S, T4946385.*

Summerland

Sleeping Campers can stay at **F** *Okanagan Lake Provincial Park*, 11 km north on the Highway, over 40 km from Kelowna, T4946500. North and south sites have different characters, but both are on the lake. In the 1950s thousands of non-native trees were planted here, such as Russian olive, Chinese elm, and Lombardy poplar. Fairly private sites, showers.

Eating and wineries A couple of nearby wineries are recommended. *Sumac Ridge*, Hwy 97, T4940451, are experts in sparkling wines, and run the *Cellar Door Bistro*, the only one in the valley offering dinner. Summer from 1200 for lunch (daily), from 1730 for dinner (closed Mon). Tours: daily on the hour 1000-1600 in summer. Tasting: 0900-1700, to 1900 summer. Near **Peachland** is *Hainle*, 5355 Trepanier Bench Rd, T7672525. Organic wine. Their *Amphora Bistro* is recommended for lunch, Apr-Oct Thu-Sun. Tasting: Tue-Sun 1000-1700 summer.

For Kelowna wineries, see page 238

Kelowna

Phone code: 250
Colour map 1, grid C6
Population: 96,288
Altitude: 344 m

The Okanagan's biggest and most central town, Kelowna offers more recreational and cultural possibilities than its neighbours, but also more of the brash commercialism and crowds that so detract from the region's natural charms. However you arrive, first impressions are unfavourable; Kelowna has become a willing victim of the worst kind of crass urban sprawl. Strips of malls, megastores, and nasty motels line the major thoroughfares, while the surrounding grid of parallel streets seems an endless parade of retirement homes, housing estates and evangelical-style churches, devoid of character or landmarks.

Trapped inside this distressing example of irresponsible development, however, is the remnant of a smaller, earlier, much nicer town. Centred on the pretty lakefront **City Park** is the Okanagan's most pleasant Downtown area, decorated in summer with hanging baskets of flowers. To the north is the interesting and expanding **Cultural District**. And beyond the urban grid is a green belt of orchards, vineyards, and golf courses, with plenty of decent walks including the outstanding **Myra Canyon** section of the Kettle Valley Railway.

Ins and outs

Getting there
For Transport details, see page 240

Kelowna's international **airport**, is situated 10 km north on Hwy 97, with flights from Seattle as well as major Canadian cities. A regular shuttle runs Downtown, as does a city bus (with a change at Orchard Park). The *Greyhound* station is at Orchard Park Mall, 2366 Leckie Rd, off Hwy 97, about 5 km from Downtown, with daily **buses** from all directions. Local buses No 3, 7 and 19 run into town.

Getting around

Kelowna's Downtown is small enough to explore on foot, but some of the more worthwhile attractions require transport. A network of local buses operates from a depot Downtown on Queensway between Ellis and Pandosy. Driving is frustrating and best kept to a minimum. Cycling is not recommended.

Hwy 97 follows the north-south orientation of Okanagan Lake up its west side from Penticton, with scenic views all the way until the ugly suburb of Westbank marks the beginning of Kelowna's outer sprawl. Eventually the highway crosses the lake on Canada's longest floating bridge, landing in the heart of Downtown. Changing its name to Harvey Av, it heads due east through town as Kelowna's main thoroughfare, before eventually turning north towards the airport and Vernon. On the way out, Hwy 33 branches east to the Big White Ski Resort and Hwy 3. Downtown is comprised of a few blocks by the lake north of Harvey, centred on Bernard Av. Pandosy St, becoming Lakeshore Rd, heads south from Harvey, following the contour of the lake.

Tourist information

Tourism Kelowna is handily located at 544 Harvey Av, T8611515, www.kelownachamber.org Summer Mon-Fri 0800-1800, Sat-Sun 0900-1800; winter Mon-Fri 0800-1700, Sat-Sun 1000-1500.

Sights

The Okanagan success story began here in 1859 when the French priest Father Pandosy established a mission and planted a couple of apple trees. So well did they grow that the first orchards were planted in 1890. The **Father Pandosy Mission**, with eight hand-hewn log buildings, four dating back to the original settlement, is open to visitors. ■ *Apr-Oct. 3685 Benvoulin Rd.* The small centre that formed to service surrounding farms and orchards first began to grow in earnest when its wonderful climate and location caught the attention of the retirement community, who came to dominate the city for decades and attempted to prevent the building of a university because they didn't want their town being overrun with young people. The untrammelled expansion that led to today's ugly sprawl largely began after the building of the Coquihalla Highway in 1986.

Downtown & the Cultural District

Particularly in summer, Kelowna's Downtown is a pleasant place for a stroll. Most of the shops and restaurants cluster around Bernard Avenue, which heads west to meet the lake close to three of the city's landmarks: a white sculpture called *The Sails*, a model of the legendary lake monster, Ogopogo, and the 1948 paddlewheeler, the *MV Fintry Queen*. To the south is **City Park**, a big green area fronted by a beach, perfect for lazing around and enjoying the stunning views across the lake, with frequent events and live music in summer.

North of Bernard, a waterfront walkway leads past the yachts and sailboats in the **marina** to an interesting area roughly bounded by Water and Ellis Streets and Queensway and Cawston Avenues, which has become known as the Cultural District. The tranquil **Kasagai Japanese Garden** behind City Hall is a pleasant place to escape the city noise. Just beyond is a district whose many large old buildings, former warehouses mostly, are either being reclaimed by worthy artistic causes or replaced by modern municipal constructions that conform to the cultural theme. Within a few blocks are the new and impressive **library**, the main sports and music venue, Skyreach Place, a brand new **Community Arts Centre**, plus several museums, theatres, gift stores, and a clutch of commercial and public art galleries. The *Grower's Supply Building* on Cawston Avenue has been transformed into the **Rotary Centre for the Arts**, a place where the you can watch works of art in the making. There's a theatre available to local performing groups, as well as eight resident artists and a potter, whose studios can be visited to see them and buy their wares. You can also go to the art gallery, commercial gallery and bistro. ■ *0800-2300. Free, except for theatre. T7175304, www.rotarycentreforthearts.com*

For always excellent, mostly Canadian, exhibits, head for the **Kelowna Art Gallery**. ■ *Tue-Sat 1000-1700 (to 2100 Thu), Sun 1300-1700. By donation. 1315 Water St, T7622226.* The **Art Ark Gallery** is the best of the private galleries, with some exceptionally beautiful items. ■ *135-1295 Cannery Lane, T8625080, www.theark.com* The **BC Orchard Industry Museum**, T7630433, and **Wine Museum**, T8680441, are situated together in the restored brick Laurel Packinghouse, built in 1917. The former has displays on the history of the fruit business and a model railway. The latter is the best place to find out about local wines and which wineries to visit. ■ *Entry by donation. 1304 Ellis.* **Kelowna Museum** has the usual municipal collection. ■ *470 Queensway, T7632417.*

Beaches

Considering the length of its lakefront, Kelowna has a disappointing dearth of decent beach-space, and certainly cannot compete with Penticton. Apart from **City Park**, whose beach is fairly long but narrow, the town's most popular beaches are south along Lakeshore Road, via Pandosy Street. **Gyro Beach**, popular with youngsters and posers, is where you're most likely to hire water-skis, jet-skis and other water toys. **Rotary Beach** is popular with windsurfers. Both are small and crowded. For something more private, look out for the public beach access signs scattered along Lakeshore Road, which lead to tiny patches between the private beaches that have snapped up most of the sand. At the very end of this road is a small nude beach. Most locals avoid swimming in the lake, which they know to be extremely polluted.

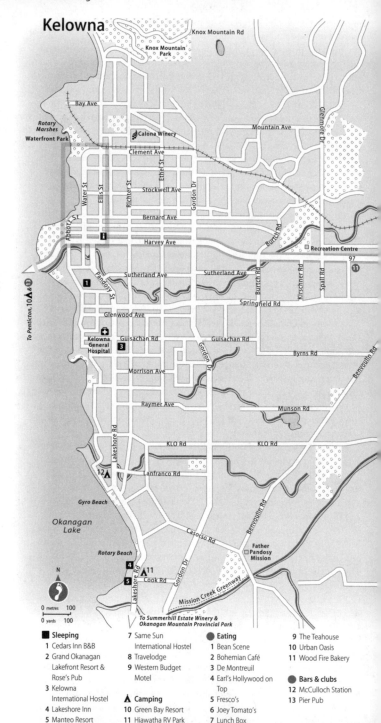

Kelowna

Southern Interior BC

Sleeping
1 Cedars Inn B&B
2 Grand Okanagan Lakefront Resort & Rose's Pub
3 Kelowna International Hostel
4 Lakeshore Inn
5 Manteo Resort
6 Royal Anne
7 Same Sun International Hostel
8 Travelodge
9 Western Budget Motel

Camping
10 Green Bay Resort
11 Hiawatha RV Park
12 Willow Creek

Eating
1 Bean Scene
2 Bohemian Café
3 De Montreuil
4 Earl's Hollywood on Top
5 Fresco's
6 Joey Tomato's
7 Lunch Box
8 Mon Thong
9 The Teahouse
10 Urban Oasis
11 Wood Fire Bakery

Bars & clubs
12 McCulloch Station
13 Pier Pub

Downtown Kelowna

The **Lakeside Promenade** continues uninterrupted from City Park north to **Waterfront Park**, an area of lagoons, beaches, trails and lawns, and an outdoor stage that is the main focus for live music and events in summer. Further north at the end of Ellis Street, are the **Rotary Marshes**, a good place for bird-watching, and the 235-ha **Knox Mountain Park**, with a trail that climbs high up to yield unbeatable views of the town, lake, floating bridge and valley.

At the other end of town, via Pandosy/Lakeshore or Gordon Drive, the **Mission Creek Greenway** is a lovely 18-km pathway that follows the course of the lake's main artery right through the site of Father Pandosy's original mission. It's totally flat, suitable for wheelchairs. Far more difficult to reach, but the most recommended hike/bike in the area is the **Myra Canyon Trestles** section of the Kettle Valley Railway. This 12-km trail takes you through tunnels and over bridges, affording views that are truly magnificent. Take KLO to McCulloch Road; about 2 km after the pavement ends, take Myra Forest Service Road to the right and climb about 8 km uphill. A perfect afternoon would combine this with a meal at the *Teahouse*, a tour of their orchards, and a pint in the *McCulloch Station Pub*. The Kettle Valley Railway continues all the way to Naramata/Penticton via Chute Lake, where you can fish for rainbow trout, and stay in a tent (**F**) or rustic cabin (**D**) at *Chute Lake Resort*, T4933535.

At the very end of Lakeshore Drive is the 10,500-ha **Okanagan Mountain Provincial Park**, whose many trails lead through landscapes ranging from semi-arid hillsides to sub-alpine forests. One of the best is the **Mountain Goat** trail which climbs through a granite obstacle course to Divide Lake. The **High Rim** trail is a 50-km wilderness route from Kelowna to Vernon, offering tasters of the Okanagan's many diverse landscapes.

Hiking & biking

Southern Interior BC

Ogopogo

A model on Kelowna's waterfront next to The Sails *depicts the undulating form of the Okanagan's favourite celebrity. This snakelike cousin of the Loch Ness Monster was known for hundreds of years by natives, who called it* N'ha-a-itk, *and carried chickens to toss from their canoes as sacrificial offerings. Ogopogo inspired such fear that in 1926 the government had to assure locals that a new ferry would be fitted with monster-repelling devices. Sightings are still extremely frequent, and with a depth of 300 m in places, there's little doubt that the lake could harbour some undiscovered prehistoric creature(s). With a $2 mn reward offered for proof of the beast's existence, Ogopogo generates as much fervour as its Scottish relative.*

Wineries
See also
Summerland,
page 233

Kelowna *Calona*, 1125 Richter St, T7629144, is BC's oldest winery, and the most central in Kelowna. Tours: 1100, 1300, 1500 and 1700 in summer, 1400 winter. Tasting: 1000-1900 summer, 1000-1700 winter. *Summerhill Estate*, 4870 Chute Lake Rd, T7648000. Possibly the most interesting and progressive organic winery, where bottles are aged in a giant pyramid. There's a settler's cabin to visit, and the *Veranda Bistro* serves lunch daily 1100-1400. Tours: daily on the hour, 1300-1600. Tasting: 1000-1800. **Westbank** *Mission Hill*, 1730 Mission Hill, T7687611. Newly expanded to include a bell tower that rings on the hour and overlooks the whole valley, and a classic arched barrel room. Tours: hourly 0900-1700 in summer, less otherwise. Tasting: 0900-1900 summer, 0900-1700 winter. *Quail's Gate*, 3303 Boucherie Rd, T7694451. Good selection of wines sampled in a turn-of-the-century storehouse. The *Old Vines Patio* serves lunches catered by *De Montreuil*. Tours: daily on the hour 1100-1600 summer, less otherwise. Tasting: 0900-1900 summer, or less.

Sleeping
■ on map,
page 236

Kelowna has plenty of beds, though the mid-range choices and campgrounds are somewhat lacking. Best of all are its 2 excellent hostels. **LL-AL** *Manteo Resort*, 3766 Lakeshore Rd, T8601031, www.manteo.com The fanciest place in town, with suites and 2- or 3-bedroom villas. Waterfront restaurant and patio, pools, hot tubs, saunas, spa, gym, tennis courts, private beach, boat rentals. **L-A** *Grand Okanagan Lakefront Resort*, 1310 Water St, T7634500, www.grandokanagan.com A giant place with all the facilities in a great location. **A** *Lakeshore Inn*, 3756 Lakeshore Rd, T7634717, www.LakeshoreInn.com Comfortable, pleasant rooms on the lake, with a private stretch of sand next to Rotary Beach. Swimming pool and kitchenettes.

B *Royal Anne Hotel*, 348 Bernard Av, T7632277, www.royalannehotel.com Big rooms with balconies (best on 2nd floor) and views, in a handy location. Exercise room and saunas. **B** *Cedars Inn B&B*, 278 Beach Av, T7631208. A 1906 heritage home with private baths, stone fireplace, bikes, close to beach and wineries. **B-C** *Travelodge*, 1627 Abbott St, T7637771, www.travelodge.com Nothing special, but the perfect location across from City Park.

Harvey Av (Hwy 97 N),
a particularly ugly part
of town, is the street
for cheapish motels

D *Western Budget Motel*, 2679 Harvey Av, T7632484, is just about the cheapest motel option. **E** *Kelowna International Hostel*, 2343 Pandosy St, T7636024, www.kelowna-hostel.bc.ca Well located close to Downtown and the beach, this clean, friendly and helpful little hostel has dorms and private rooms with shared bath. Kitchen, lounge, laundry, internet, free pick-up from the bus station, even a free coffee and pancake breakfast. **E** *Same Sun International Hostel*, 245 Harvey Av, T76 9814, www.samesun.com This vast new Downtown building has 30 private rooms and 100 dorms with top facilities including kitchen, common room, lockers, laundry, etc.

Camping The only 2 campgrounds right in town, both on Lakeshore Rd, are crowded and often fully booked. **E** *Hiawatha RV Park* at 3787 Lakeshore Rd, T8614837, is open Mar-Oct, with heated pool and hot tub. **F** *Willow Creek Family Campground*, 3316

Southern Interior BC

Lakeshore Rd, T7626302, is open year round and has its own beach. Many more are located in Westbank, across the floating bridge, all of them off Boucherie Rd, itself off Hwy 97. Best of these is **E** *Green Bay Resort*, 1375 Green Bay Rd, T7685543, which has a heated pool, hot tub, games room, sand beach, playground and showers. Best of all, but even further from town, are the 2 **F provincial parks** to the north on the west shore. Cross the bridge and follow signs. Open Apr-Oct, T4946500, and extremely busy. *Bear Creek*, at Km 9, has 122 sites on the lake, with showers. **F** *Fintry*, at Km 32, has 100 sites amidst big trees on the lake. See also **F** *Okanagan Lake Provincial Park*, page 233.

Expensive *De Montreuil*, 368 Bernard Av, T8605508. Thoughtfully prepared and pre-sented European haute cuisine in colourful, artistic surroundings. Not cheap and not for the ravenous. More affordable lunch specials. *Fresco's*, 1560 Water St, T8688805. Exquisite fine dining prepared by a top chef. *The Teahouse*, 3002 Dunster Rd, via KLO and east, T7129404. Far from Downtown and hard to find, set in an orchard with a patio and views. Sister of *De Montreuil*, who will give directions. Similar culinary approach, but a better all-round experience. **Mid-range** *Earl's Hollywood on Top*, 211 Bernard Av, opposite City Park, T7633121. Usual *Earl's* fare (see page 40), in very comfortable surroundings with great views. *Joey Tomato's*, 2475 Highway 97 N, T8608999. Good, varied menu and a very popular summer patio. *Mon Thong*, 1530 Water St, T7638600. Very good authentic Thai cuisine, but smallish portions.
    Cheap *Bohemian Café*, 363 Bernard Av. Attractive and popular Downtown pur-veyor of good breakfasts and coffee. *Lunch Box*, 509 Bernard Av. Famous for their sand-wiches, especially the Montreal smoked meat. Outdoor sitting. *Wood Fire Bakery*, 2041 Harvey Av. Excellent, healthy and cheap baked goods, breakfasts and lunches.

Bean Scene, 274 Bernard Av. Casual and agreeably downbeat. Good coffee, bad food. Outside seating close to the beach. *Urban Oasis*, 1567 Pandosy St. Smart, trendy coffee spot with a good selection of juices, teas, magazines, and light healthy food.

McCulloch Station, McCulloch Rd/KLO. A nice, big, old-fashioned type of pub. *Pier Pub*, last turning on the right before you hit the floating bridge coming from the west. Nice waterside location and patio. Busy, noisy and smoky. Good food, often involving great lobster/crab/steak deals. *Rose's Pub*, part of the giant *Grand Hotel* complex on Water St, has an attractive patio overlooking the lake and marina, perfect for summer drinking.

Art *Alternator Gallery*, 273 Bernard Av, T8682298. Contemporary works mostly by local artists. *Geert Maas Sculpture Gardens and Gallery*, 250 Reynolds Rd via Hwy 97 N and Sexsmith Rd, May-Oct Mon-Sat. Bronze sculptures and other works by this well known and respected artist. See also under Sights. **Cinema** *Paramount Theatre*, 261 Bernard Av. The only surviving one-screen wonder. *Orchard Plaza 5*, 1890 Cooper Rd. One of the cineplexes. **Music** *Okanagan Symphony*, T7637544, various venues. *Skyreach Place* on Water St, T9790888, is the major arena for big-name concerts and sporting events. **Theatre** *Sunshine Theatre*, 1304 Ellis St, T7634025.

Kelowna is the natural main focus of the *Spring* and *Fall Wine Festivals* (see page 228). The *BC Orchard Industry Museum* also hosts the smaller *Cherry Fair* in mid-Jul and *Apple Fair* in mid-Oct. In mid-May is the 2-day *Black Mountain Rodeo*. The 3-day *Kelowna Regatta* takes over the marina and City Park in mid-Jul, and features the popular *Mardi Gras Street Festival*. The *International Dragon Boat Festival* is a 3-day event in Sep.

Books *Mosaic Books*, 411 Bernard Av. Lots of new books and a coffee shop in which to inspect them. *Ted's Paperbacks and Comics*, 269 Leon Av. The best selection of used books. **Gifts** A whole strip on Ellis St, north of Bernard.

Eating
● *on map,*
page 236

See also under
Wineries, page 238,
for a selection of
bistros, usually with
great views but only
offering lunch

Cafés

Bars

Entertainment

Festivals

Shopping

Southern Interior BC

Southern Interior BC *(side margin)*

Sports *Sparky's* in the Grand, 1310 Water St, T8622469, rent anything a person could possibly
For hiking and biking, want, from power-boats to baseball gloves. *Sports Rent*, 3000 Pandosy St, T8615699,
see page 237 rent bikes, skis and all manner of water toys. Of the many **golf** courses around Kelowna,
the best are *Harvest Golf Club*, 2725 KLO, T8623177, where you play through orchards
with lake views; *Gallagher's Canyon*, 4320 Gallagher's Drive W, T8614240, whose narrow
fairways run harrowingly close to a steep ravine; and the *Okanagan Golf Club*, 3200 Via
Centrale, T7655955, which has 2 championship courses. For **swimming** and a work-out,
the *Recreation Centre* is at 1800 Parkinson Way (Highway 97/Spall), T8603938. *Speed
Zone* at 911 Stremel Rd off Hwy 97, T7651434, has intense grand prix **go-carting**.

Tour operators *Monashee Adventure Tours*, T7629253, www.vtours.com/monashee Tours of the
Kettle Valley Railway, agri-tours, peddle and paddle tours. Apr-Oct. *Okanagan Valley
Wine Train*, 991 Richter St, T1888-6748725. 7-hr BC wine tasting trip aboard a restored
Super Continental passenger train. Jun-Oct, Wed-Sat 1600, Sun 0900. *Okanagan Wine
Country Tours*, 1789 Harvey, T8689463. Daily, year-round. Half-day tours visit 3 or 4
local wineries, day-trips to Osoyoos. *Winds and Rivers Escapes*, T5493722. Winery
tours by canoe, May-Oct.

Transport **Local** *BC Transit*, T8608121, www.kelownatransit.com, operate a network of local
buses from a depot Downtown on Queensway between Ellis and Pandosy.

Long distance Kelowna **airport** is 10 km north on Hwy 97. Daily flights from **Vancouver**, **Victoria**, **Calgary** and **Edmonton** with *West Jet*, from **Calgary** and **Vancouver** with
Air Canada Regional, and from **Seattle** with *Horizon Air*. The *Airporter* shuttle,
T7650182, runs regularly to Downtown. City bus No 8 runs to Orchard Park. The *Greyhound* station is at Orchard Park Mall, 2366 Leckie Rd, off Hwy 97, T8603835, www.grey-
hound.ca 6 daily **buses** to Vancouver ($55), 3 to **Calgary** ($80), 4 to **Edmonton** ($120),
3 to **Kamloops** ($25), 3 to **Prince George** ($92), and 9 to **Vernon** ($10).

Directory **Airline offices** *Air BC/Air Canada*, T8618441; *WestJet*, T4915600; *Horizon Air*,
T1800-5479308. **Communications** Internet: the only cyber-café in town is *Mind
Grind*, 1340 Water St. **Canada Post**: In *Hallmark* or *Kelowna Stationers* on Bernard.
Laundry *Village Laundry 2000*, 2-1551 Sutherland Av. **Library** 1380 Ellis St. Very
impressive, funky new building. **Medical services** *Kelowna General Hospital*, 2268
Pandosy St, T8624222. Walk-in clinics at 515 Harvey Av, 605 KLO, 1990 Cooper Av.

Big White Ski Resort

Phone code: 250 Big White is BC's second largest ski resort with 890 ha of skiable terrain and an
Colour map 2, grid C1 average of 750 cm of powder per year. Of its 105 runs, an unequalled 52% are
for experienced skiers only. Perks include three snowboard parks, night ski-
ing, a high-speed gondola, and North America's largest Tube Park ($12 for
two hours, $10 concessions). The village is bigger than most, with extensive
facilities, but it's also unattractive and difficult to navigate. The only other
drawback is the frequently bad weather, with 'Clarence' the cloud prone to
make an appearance at any time. The hill is open late November-April,
T7653101, www.bigwhite.com It's a 55-minute drive from Kelowna, 21 km
southeast on Highway 33 then 25 km east on Big White Road. The resort
operates a shuttle from Downtown.

Sleeping Big White can sleep an impressive 8,900 people, mostly in lodges that are all very similar and quite expensive. To find out about ski packages, often the best deal, T7658888.
There are 2 good hostels. **E** *Bumps*, on the left on the road to the upper village,

T1888-5956411, is the more intimate choice. Dorms and double rooms with private bath. Common room, internet, lockers, laundry. **E** *Same Sun Ski-In Hostel*, in the *Alpine Centre* at the top of the mountain, T1877-5621783, www.samesun.com Dorms and private doubles, hot tubs, internet, laundry, kitchen, free pancake breakfast. If staying at their hostel in Kelowna, there's a shuttle bus for $5.

There are plenty of eating and drinking spots. The mid-range *Raakel's* in *Dos Hofbrauhaus*, T7655611, has great food and dancing. **Snowshoe Sam's** is the most popular pub, with good food upstairs. *Loose Moose* in the *Happy Valley Lodge* is the place for cocktails. **Eating**

A shuttle runs from the airport, daily 0330-2330, $60 return, also picking up at the *Greyhound* station, T1800-6632772 to reserve. The *Gameboy* bus, T7653101, mostly for kids, picks up at various downtown spots around 0700 Fri-Sun and throughout the Christmas and spring breaks, returning at 1630. **Transport**

Vernon

If moving north from Kelowna, Highway 97 is a pleasant enough drive, half of it right alongside Wood and Kalamalka Lakes, but for a real taste of the Okanagan, away from the hustle and bustle, it is highly recommended you take the much slower road along the west bank of Okanagan Lake by crossing the floating bridge, then following signs to Bear and Fintry Provincial Parks. If you do this, it is tempting to bypass Vernon altogether. Oldest of the Okanagan towns, it is also the least interesting. Its two local beaches, **Kal Beach** on Kalamalka Lake and **Kin Beach** on Okanagan Lake, are decent enough, but quite small and far removed from town. With the highway going straight through its middle, the small Downtown is blighted by an excess of traffic, and not even the plethora of murals painted in 2000 can liven things up. The town's museum is at 3009 32nd St, next to the ugly clock tower.

Phone code: 250
Colour map 2,
grid B1
Population: 23,514
Altitude: 416 m

It must be significant that, apart from a first-class hostel, all the things worth noting here are far from town. **Ellison Lake Provincial Park** has some of the least spoilt beaches around Okanagan Lake, and much more besides. **Silver Star Mountain Resort** is one of the province's most charming ski hills. The **Okanagan Highlands** east of Oyama offer a wealth of wilderness hiking and camping around small trout-filled lakes. And 12 km north on Highway 97 is the **O'Keefe Ranch**, a popular 20-ha site with original buildings and furnishings from1867, as well as animals, a restaurant, and a decent gift shop. ■ *May-Oct 0900-1700. $6.50, $4.50 concessions. T5427868, www.okeeferanch.bc.ca* For more details on any of these, ask at the **Visitor Information Centre**, south of town at 701 Highway 97, T5421415, www.vernontourism.com An additional summer-only Information Centre is north at 6326 Highway 97, T5452959.

B *Best Western*, 3914 32nd St, T5453385. The best place to stay, thanks to a surprisingly beautiful, tropical courtyard garden with a pool and restaurant, and a genuine creek running through the middle. $10 extra for a room with balcony facing this delight. **D** *The Globe Motel*, 3900 33rd St, T5422327. 1 block over from the gaggle of cheap motels strung along Hwy 97 (32nd St) and so less noisy. Quite big, reasonable rooms. **D** *Schell Motel*, 2810 35th St, T5451351. Good value rooms with kitchenettes. Outdoor heated pool and hot tub. Close to Downtown. **E** *Lodged Inn HI Hostel*, 3201 Pleasant Valley Rd, T5493742, www.windsrivers.bc.ca Huge and beautiful 1894 home surrounded by gardens and trees. Fantastic interior with hardwood floors, a library, lounge, meeting room and kitchen. Dorms and private rooms. Activities arranged. Highly recommended. **Sleeping**

Camping F *Dutch's Tent and Trailer Court*, 15408 Kalamalka Lake Rd, T5451023. Reasonable setting, conveniently close to the lake and Kal Beach. Open year round. **F** *Ellison Provincial Park*, 16 km southwest on Okanagan Lake, T4946500. Take 25th Av west from Downtown and keep going straight. 71 private, wooded sites in a gorgeous park with hiking trails, great beaches, a playground and playing field, and even an underwater park for snorkelling and diving.

Eating **Expensive** *The Eclectic Med*, 3117 32nd St, T5584646. Lives up to its name. The menu is impressively broad and varied, the decor simple, tasteful, and quite romantic. A little over-priced though. **Mid-range** *Merona's*, 2905 29th St, T2604257. Intimidatingly large portions of good Greek food and cheap beer in surroundings nicer than the exterior suggests. **Cheap** *J-don*, 2900 30th Av. Cafeteria-style Japanese joint. Cheap, fast and popular. *Woodfire Bakery*, 2806 32nd St. Great baking and home-cooked meals until 2100. Very reasonable prices.

Cafés *Bean Scene*, 2923 30th Av. Casual Downtown spot for good coffee. *Portillo*, 2706 30th Av. Comfortable and attractive coffee shop slightly out of the centre. Good snacks and cakes. Nice views from patio. *Sir Winston's*, 2705 32nd St. Pleasant English-style pub close to Polson Park.

Entertainment **Art gallery** 31st St/31st Av. **Cinema** *Towne Theatre*, 2910 30th Av.

Shopping **Books** *The Book Nook*, 2908 30th Av. Used books. **Camping equipment** *Surplus Herbie's*, 34th St/31st Av.

Transport The *Greyhound* Station is at 30th St/31st Av, with 8 buses daily from **Kelowna** ($10), 3 from **Kamloops** ($19), and 4 from **Salmon Arm** ($12). *Vernon Regional Transit System*, 4210 24th Av, T5457221.

Directory **Communications** Canada Post: 3101 32nd Av/31st St. **Medical services** *Vernon Jubilee Hospital*, 2101 32nd St, T5452211.

Silver Star Mountain Resort Silver Star is smaller and much prettier than Big White, its buildings all painted bright, cheerful colours, the people relaxed and friendly. Skiing here (November-April) is good for beginners and intermediates, with 583 ha of terrain, over 100 runs, and a snowboard park. There's also 100 km of cross-country ski trails in the area ($12). In summer (June-September) the hill stays open for great biking and hiking. There is an **Information kiosk** in the village centre, T5586092, and a free shuttle bus around the resort. A lift pass costs $48 per day. From Highway 97 North, turn right onto Silver Star Road, then continue 22 km. For more information call T5420224, www.silverstarmtn.com

Sleeping and eating Of the village's 8 resident hotels the best deal is **A-B** *Silver Lode Inn* on the upper side, T5495105, www.silverlode.com Hot tub and nice rooms. Otherwise there is the **E** *Same Sun Hostel*, the uppermost building, T5458933, www.samesun.com Dorms and private doubles with shared bath. Kitchen, common room, hot tub, and a free pancake breakfast. $5 for a shuttle from the *Kelowna Same Sun Hostel*. There is also an RV parking lot (**E**). As usual, package deals are a good bet. Contact **Central Reservations** at T5586083. There are several eating places. The fancy option is the expensive dining room in the *Silver Lode Inn*. *Putnam Station Inn* is good for drinks and pub food. *Bugaboo's Bakery Café* is the place for snacks.

West Kootenays

Flanked on all sides by the Purcell, Selkirk and Monashee mountain ranges, the West Kootenays is a ruggedly beautiful region whose charm has no doubt been preserved by the fact that it is not on the way to anywhere. Its mostly small communities, with Nelson as their focal point, are scattered along the north-south valleys of the major Arrow and Kootenay Lakes, and the smaller but equally stunning Slocan Lake/River. Tortuous roads, with destinations of no great importance, follow winding courses through landscapes that possess a certain primordial quality. Green rounded hills rise up behind vast lakes, dotted with rocky bluffs, shrouded by snow or mist.

Getting around the West Kootenays is almost impossible without your own vehicle

It was the mountains, and the many ores they contain, which attracted the first white settlers to this region. The legacy of that mining boom is a handful of interesting ghost towns such as Sandon, as well as a large number of pretty little towns like Nelson, Kaslo, New Denver and Rossland, which possess a degree of character rarely found in Western Canada. Today a different kind of seeker is lured by the majesty of the mountain scenery. Outdoor enthusiasts come to enjoy skiing, mountain biking and hiking of a calibre to match anything in North America, with a fraction of the crowds drawn to the Rockies or Whistler. There's even the added bonus of a few good, accessible hot springs.

An atmosphere comparable to the laid-back spirit of the Gulf Islands also brings those seeking an alternative to the rat race. There is a genuine interest in spirituality, the arts, healthy living and organic farming (as well as less legal crops), with a proliferation of artisans, musicians and healers. It is this spirit, often over-simplified as 'neo-hippy', that adds colour to the Kootenays, though it clearly exists in opposition to the traditional logging communities, whose way of life is now in serious peril.

Nelson

Beautifully situated on Kootenay Lake in a natural amphitheatre of rolling hills, Nelson is the obvious centre of the West Kootenays and arguably the most interesting small town in BC. The focal point for hundreds of small communities scattered through the surrounding valleys, it caters to a large population without having to house or employ it, thus combining the positive facilities of a large town with the charm and friendliness of a small one. In particular, Nelson has an unexpected range of quality restaurants, live music venues, cafés and craft stores. Benefiting from the creativity as well as sheer quantity of the many satellite villages, it is one of the greatest small-arts towns on the continent. In summer the numerous artists and artisans present **Artwalk**, T3522402, a tour around their galleries and workshops.

Phone code: 250
Colour map 2, grid C2
Population: 10,000
Altitude: 516 m

Other aspects of local colour are crystallized here. The long-haired and dreadlocked abound, hanging out around the *Kootenay Co-op* and *Oso Negro*, playing drums and guitars. Outdoor enthusiasts have built and maintained a network of trails famous in mountain-bike circles, and Nelson acts as the centre of an area equally revered for its backcountry skiing. In an attempt to counter such youthful energies local conservatives have implemented some surprisingly patrician laws: no dogs allowed Downtown, no busking, no groups, no hacky-sack (a popular game played by kids). And whose idea was it to line the lakefront with a mall, a *Walmart*, the *Prestige Lakeside Resort* and the garbage dump?

Southern Interior BC

Otherwise town planning has been intelligent, deliberately retaining an overall appearance that has barely changed in the last 100 years, with over 350 well looked after **heritage buildings**. Everything of interest is within walking distance, most of it on Baker Street, where even the most pedestrian of businesses tends to be housed in a distinctive, historic building. The **Visitor Information Centre** at 225 Hall Street, T3523433, www.discovernelson.com, can supply a *Heritage Walking Tour* pamphlet which takes in the major sights. Among the best are the **Courthouse**, **City Hall**, the **Heritage Inn** and the old **Railway Station**. The historic tramway **Streetcar 23** runs along the waterfront by the mall. ■ *Summer 1200-1800. $2, $1 concessions.*

The development of Nelson was due to the discovery nearby of copper and silver ore. Incorporated in 1896 with a population of 3,000, it had its own hydrogenerating station, street cars, sewer system, and police force. Transport by road, rail and water helped keep the town alive when the mines went bust. Those interested in the mining history should talk to the curator

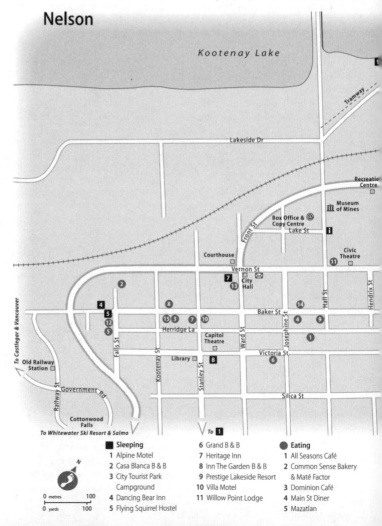

Nelson

Kootenay Lake

Sleeping
1 Alpine Motel
2 Casa Blanca B & B
3 City Tourist Park Campground
4 Dancing Bear Inn
5 Flying Squirrel Hostel
6 Grand B & B
7 Heritage Inn
8 Inn The Garden B & B
9 Prestige Lakeside Resort
10 Villa Motel
11 Willow Point Lodge

Eating
1 All Seasons Café
2 Common Sense Bakery & Maté Factor
3 Dominion Café
4 Main St Diner
5 Mazatlan

of the free **Museum of Mines** next to the Information Centre. ■ *0900-1700. Free*. For accounts of the town's general history, visit the small **Nelson Museum**. This is standard small-town stuff, with a sometimes interesting gallery downstairs, and an extensive photograph and archive collection available. ■ *Summer Mon-Sat 1300-1800, winter 1300-1600. $2, $1 concessions. 402 Anderson St, T3529813.*

B *Prestige Lakeside Resort*, 701 Lakeside Dr, T3527222, www.PrestigeInn.com Nelson's luxury option, with all the associated facilities, and lakeview rooms for a few dollars more. Good value. **C** *Casa Blanca B&B*, 724 2nd St, T3544431. 3 rooms in an elegant, wood-finished Art Deco home in a quiet area overlooking the lake. Gardens, guest living room. **C** *The Grand B&B*, 1413 Front St, T5055005. 2 comfortable en suite rooms in a heritage house with antique furnishings, fireplaces, jacuzzi, and decks. **C** *Heritage Inn*, 422 Vernon St, T3525331, www.heritageinn.org The best mid-range hotel in town. Rooms have lots of space, antique furniture, feather duvets, and a very comfortable atmosphere. Breakfast included. Lounge, pub and restaurant downstairs. **C** *Inn the Garden B&B*, 408 Victoria St, T3523226, www.innthegarden.com 6 rooms plus a 3-bedroom guesthouse in a Victorian home, 1 block from Baker St. **C** *Willow Point Lodge*, 2211 Taylor Dr, 6.5 km north on Hwy 3A, T8259411. 4 en suite rooms and 2 honeymoon suites, garden and hot tub.

D *Alpine Motel*, 1120 Hall Mines Rd, T3525501. Small rooms but convenient for Downtown and the Salmo Hwy. **D** *Villa Motel*, 665 Highway 3A, directly over the orange bridge, T3525515. Standard rooms, but good views and a decent indoor pool and hot tub. **E** *The Dancing Bear Inn*, 171 Baker St, T3527573, www.dancingbearinn.com A superior hostel, clean and comfortable. 2-bed dorms and private rooms with nice shared bathrooms. Use of kitchen, lounge area, laundry, storage and lockers. **E** *The Flying Squirrel Hostel*, 198 Baker St, T3527285, www.flyingsquirrelhostel.com Colourful and friendly, more hostel-like, but the dorms and rooms have private bathrooms. Kitchen and common area, laundry, lockers, and internet. **Camping F** *City Tourist Park Campground*, High St, T3527618. Small and not very private, but wooded and handy. Showers and laundry. **F** *Kokanee Creek Provincial Park*, 20 km east on Hwy 3A, T8253500. Trees, sandy beaches, hiking trails.

Sleeping
■ *on map*

B&Bs are plentiful and the most pleasant option, but usually need to be booked ahead. Check at the Information Centre for a long list

Southern Interior BC

6	Oso Negro
7	Outer Clove
8	Rice Bowl
9	Sidewinders
10	Stanley's on Baker & Boomtown Emporium

● **Bars & clubs**
11	Civic
12	Fluid Lounge
13	Mike's Place
14	Queen's
15	Royal Blues

Eating

● *on map, page 244*

The turnover of restaurants in Nelson is amazing; these are mostly long-lasting favourites

Expensive *All Seasons Café*, 620 Herridge Lane, T3520101. Generally considered the best in town. Beautifully prepared and presented cuisine, though servings are a bit small and tables a little cramped. Impressive selection of wines and malt whiskies. *Fiddlers Green*, 2710 Lower 6 Mile Rd, 10 km east on Hwy 3A, T8254466. Fine dining in a romantic setting. **Mid-range** *Cafe Danube*, 415 Hall St, T3540566. A small European-style café full of art, curios and tasteful kitsch. Crepes are the speciality, especially chicken paprika and beef goulash, along with a few more expensive dishes. Extensive, well-chosen wine and beer selection. *Mazatlan*, 198 Baker St, T3521388. Unmistakably authentic Mexican favourites in bright, attractive surroundings. Very lively and popular. Strong, huge margaritas. *Outer Clove*, 536 Stanley St, T3541667. Everything on the menu, even the ice cream, revolves around garlic. Especially good for lunches. **Cheap** *Main St Diner*, 616 Baker St, T3544848. The best place to go for burgers, fish and chips, etc. Good portions and prices, fine beers on tap, and a summer patio. *Stanley's on Baker*, 401 Baker St, T3544458. Particularly recommended for breakfast, but their lunch specials are often the best deal in town. Impeccable service.

Cafés

Common Sense Bakery and Maté Factor, 202 Vernon, T3520325. Situated on an almost hidden staircase between Baker and Vernon streets, this relaxing little healthy bakery and café has the feel of a tree house. A lovely spot, especially on a hot day. Delicious cakes and cookies, salads and wraps. *Dominion Café*, 334 Baker St. New York-style coffee shop with an elegant wooden interior and attractive patio. Great sandwiches. *Oso Negro*, Victoria/Josephine. Famous company that roasts its own coffee. Try the *Prince of Darkness*. Seating outside but not in, usually crowded. *Sidewinders*, 696 Baker St. Conveniently located, a comfortable space and good coffee.

Bars & clubs

Fluid Lounge, 198 Baker St, T3544823. A great little basement club with a no-smoking policy. The recently renovated funky interior shows off the work of some local artisans. Friendly, unpretentious atmosphere, plush armchairs, quality Nelson beers, and a good range of Martinis. Well-chosen live bands or DJs most nights, anything from jazz to house to kids' shows, usually with a funky edge. Cover charge varies. *Civic*, 705 Vernon St, T3525121. The interior here is less attractive, but it also gets some good bands. The beer and cover are cheaper, you can smoke if you want, and there's a deck outside. The *Heritage Inn* has 2 bars. *The Library* is the nicest place for a quiet drink, and also has good food. *Mike's Place* is the key boozer in town, its 3 levels are usually packed solid and hazy with smoke. Nelson Brewery beers on tap, reasonable pub food, big screens for sports fans, and 3 pool tables. Royal Blues (currently known as the *Star Juno Town Pub*), 330 Baker St, T3522449. Another venue, decent in its own way, more like a pub but also focusing on live music, which has traditionally been of a bluesy nature. New patio on Baker St.

Entertainment

Cinema *Civic Theatre*, 104-719 Vernon St. Often has more interesting films on Thu night. **Theatre** *The Capitol*, 421 Victoria St. Opened in 1927, considered at the time one of the finest on the continent.

Festivals

During the annual *Streetfest*, T3521831, in **Jul**, local and international performers of all kinds provide all-day entertainment along Baker St, passing the hat round in true busker style. The standard is generally excellent, the atmosphere wonderful. In **mid-Jul** it's the *Starbelly Jam* on the East Shore, a 2-day world/folk/roots affair with major and minor acts. Close to Salmo, the annual *Shambhala* takes place in **mid-Aug**. This is a massive and increasingly popular rave, with several different, very imaginatively conceived stages/dance areas dotted around in the forest. About the best of its kind, with non-stop music for 3 days. Call T3527623, www.farmboyparties.com

Books *Oliver's Books*, 398 Baker St. Best new selection. *Pack Rat Annie's*, 411 Kootenay **Shopping** St. Wide range of used books, as well as new and used CDs, and a good café/restaurant. *Copper Mountain*, 602 Josephine. A fine collection of non-fiction, especially of a meta-physical nature. **Camping equipment** *Valhalla Pure Outfitters*, 626 Baker St. *Snowpack Outdoor Experience*, 333 Baker St, is a *Patagonia* outlet. **Crafts and gifts** *The Craft Connection*, 441 Baker St. An impressive collection of work by many local artisans. *Indigo Road*, 327 Baker St, is the other essential stop for quality gift ideas. *Holy Smoke Culture Shop*, up a flight of stairs from the east end of Baker St. A local institution, selling quality pot-related regalia. **Food** *Kootenay Co-op*, 295 Baker St. The best place for healthy, organic local produce (and people-watching). *The Rising Sun French Artisan Bakery*, 281 Herridge Lane, behind the *Bank of Montreal*, has caused quite a stir among locals with the quality of its breads. *The Tree of Life Market* is held on Sat in Cottonwood Falls Park, near the old railway station. Locally grown produce. **Photography** *Vogue*, 565 Baker St. Helpful. **Sports** *Boomtown Emporium*, 104-402 Baker St. The only place for used equipment. *Gerick Cycle and Sports*, 702 Baker St. *Kootenay Experience*, 306 Victoria St, for skiing equipment. *The Sacred Ride*, 213 Baker St, for mountain-bike and snowboard equipment. *Village Ski Hut*, 357 Baker St.

Climbing *Gravity Climbing Club*, 513 Victoria St, T3526125. Information, equipment **Sport** and an indoor climbing wall. Nelson is a **mountain biking** Mecca with dozens of trails maintained and regularly used by keen locals. Ask at *The Sacred Ride*, 213 Baker St, for details. Vancouver-based *TourBC*, T1877-6062453, www.tour-bc.net run 7-day bike tours around the Kootenays. With an average snowfall of 1,300 cm, **Whitewater Ski Resort**, T3544944, www.skiwhitewater.com, is famous for its powder and backcountry skiing. The terrain is for fairly advanced skiers, with lots of tree skiing. A discounted lift price is available if just going up once to ski the 'bowls' and tour around. There is no accommodation but the lodge has a very good restaurant, a pub, and ski rentals. A lift pass costs $37. Head south on Hwy 6 for 15 km to the steep Whitewater Ski Rd. For information visit the office upstairs at 513 Victoria St. The **swimming** pool in the *Recreation Centre* on Vernon St is not one of the best examples.

The *Greyhound* station, T3523939, www.greyhound.ca, is in the lakeside mall. 2 daily **Transport** buses go west to **Kelowna** for connections to **Vancouver**, and **Kamloops**, and east to **Cranbrook** for connections to **Banff**, **Calgary** and beyond. All **local transit** routes converge at the junction of Baker St and Ward St. For information T3528201. A single weekly shuttle goes to **Kaslo**, 1 to **Nakusp**, and a few daily to the **Slocan Valley**. See those places for more details. *Go Wild Tours*, T3521164, www.gwt.com, run tours of the Kootenays.

Communications Internet: *Box Office & Copy Centre*, 622 Front St ($2 per 15 min). **Can- Directory** ada Post: 514 Vernon St. **Laundry** *Plaza*, 616 Front St. **Library** 602 Stanley St. **Medical services** *Kootenay Lake Regional Hospital*, 3 View St, T3523111. Dentist: Dr RD Clarke, 110 Baker St. Pharmacy: *Pharmasave Drugs*, 685 Baker St. **Useful add-resses** Police: 606 Stanley St, T3543919; **Fire**: 919 Ward St, T3523103; **Ambulance**: T3522112.

From Nelson, Highway 3A follows a minor arm of Kootenay Lake towards **Balfour** Kaslo (an hour's drive), meeting the lake proper at Balfour, which is little more than a landing stage for the ferry to Kootenay Bay on the East Shore. The 9-km crossing takes 40 minutes, leaving every 50 minutes in summer, otherwise every two hours. Until recently it was the longest free ferry ride in the world. From here, Highway 3A continues south to Creston (see page 257).

Sleeping D *Cedars' Lakeshore Inn*, beside the ferry, T2294777, has 4 large rooms with kitchens.

Ainsworth Hot Springs From Balfour, it is Highway 31 that continues north, shortly coming to Ainsworth Hot Springs. The first village to be settled in the West Kootenays, in 1887, it now has fewer than 100 residents. Situated in the Kootenay Arc, an area rich in minerals, it also became the site of the area's first commercial hot springs. Today's resort features a horseshoe-shaped cave, the site of a mining shaft that had to be abandoned when miners struck the hot water. There is also a swimming pool with slightly cooler water, and an icy-cold dipping-pool. ■ *1000-2130 for the public. $7, $11 day-pass.* The pools are open from 0830, and free for guests at the resort.

Sleeping and eating **B** *Ainsworth Hot Springs Resort*, T2294212, www.hot naturally.com, has decent rooms and a fairly expensive restaurant overlooking the pools. Their weekly Indian buffet is excellent. **D** *Ainsworth Motel*, on Hwy 31, T2294711, is a nice alternative, with lake views and kitchenettes.

Kaslo

Phone code: 250
Colour map 2,
grid C2
Population: 1,063
Altitude: 536 m

With an idyllic setting on Kootenay Lake, surrounded by provincial parks and some of the highest mountains in the province, Kaslo is the quintessential small Kootenay town. So pretty, in fact, that surely only its remoteness has protected the charming atmosphere of its wooden houses and friendly, laid-back inhabitants from rampant tourism. A perfect base from which to explore the great outdoors, there's little to do in town, but the lake offers fishing, boating and waterskiing, and the views never disappoint. The summer-only **Visitor Information Centre** is at 324 Front Street beside the *SS Moyie*, T3532525, www.klhs.ca.ca

Like so many of its neighbours, this formerly sawmill-driven town boomed with the discovery in 1893 of silver. Originally called Kane's Landing, it was the region's first incorporated city with 27 saloons (now it has two pubs). It survived the bust when the ore ran out thanks to agriculture, steamships that serviced the mining industry and, one suspects, the determination of inhabitants not to leave so idyllic a spot.

SS Moyie The *SS Moyie*, built in 1890, is the oldest surviving paddlesteamer in North America. Able to operate in extremely shallow waters, such vessels were vital for the economy of the Kootenays, carrying men, provisions and ore to and from the mines before the advent of roads. In later days their cargo consisted of pleasure-cruisers. Retired in 1957, the *Moyie* was bought by the Village of Kaslo from the Canadian Pacific Railway for $1. Now she is a designated National Historic Site and BC landmark, complete with artefacts, models and some eerie sound effects. ■ *Mid-May to mid-Oct 0900-1700. $5, $2 concessions. 324 Front St, T3537323, www.klhs.bc.ca*

Sleeping On Kootenay Lake to the north along Hwy 31 are a number of cabins and camping (**F**) spots, including **C** *Lakewood Inn*, 6 km north on Hwy 31, T3532395, www.lakewoodinn.com Cabins of varied age and size on Kootenay Lake among trees and gardens. Kitchenettes and patio, use of sauna, marina and beach. Steep access. **D** *Beachcomber's Resort and Marina*, 551 Rainbow Dr, at the Marina on other side of bay, reached by Highway 31, T3537777. Rooms for up to 6 people, with kitchenettes, decks, views and BBQ, most with showers not tubs. **D** *Kaslo Motel*, 330 D Av, T3532431, www.kaslomotel.com Standard but handy. Ask for one of the refurbished rooms.

E *Kootenay Lake Backpackers Hostel*, 232 Av B, T3537427, klhostel@pop.kin.bc.ca Dorms and 4 private rooms with shared baths, kitchen, living room and sauna. Friendly and homely. Bikes, canoes and kayaks for rent, and internet access for $2.50 per hr. The owner is knowledgeable about local hiking, biking and skiing trails. **Camping** F *Municiple Campground*, close to *SS Moyie* on Front St. Shower. F *Mirror Lake Campground*, 5 km south on Hwy 31. Not particularly attractive, but a nice location with a beach. Good for kids. Showers, boat rentals. 5 mins drive further south are the very attractive **Fletcher Falls**, where a Forestry Site has free wilderness camping.

Expensive *The Rosewood Café*, 213 5th St, T3537673. House setting, BBQ on patio in summers, gourmet dishes including seafood. **Mid-price** *The Crooked Café/Meteor Pizza*, 4th/Front St. Homemade pizzas, wraps, sandwiches, etc. Good *Oso Negro* coffee. Licensed with summer patio (one of the only places to drink in town). *The Treehouse*, 419 Front St, T3532955. A variety of good value, home-cooking-style food. Popular meeting place for locals. Open 0700-2000. **Cheap** *Silver Spoon Bakery*, 301 Front St. Good coffee and sandwiches, fresh bread, croissants and breakfasts, in a summer house-style room. The **pub** in town is horrible. Try the *Fisherman's Tale Pub*, 551 Rainbow Dr, across the bay on the Marina (take Hwy 31). Outdoor seating with a great view.

Eating

Langham Cultural Society, Av A, opposite the Post Office, T3532661. Arts centre with consistently fine displays for such a small town, and a host of historic photos and artefacts upstairs, documenting such things as the local Second World War Japanese internment camps.

Entertainment

The whole town bursts with life during the *Kaslo Jazz Fest*, T3537538, kaslojazz@netidea.com, in early **Aug**. This fabulous event attracts good acts to play on a floating stage on Kootenay Lake.

Festivals

Kaslo is the best base from which to head off **hiking** in Kokanee Glacier Provincial Park. Take Hwy 31A, 6.4 km northwest, then a poor road 24 km along Keen Creek to the parking spot (4WD advised). This gets you closest to the glacier and the heart of the park (see page 251). For a shorter walk to 360° panoramas of lake and mountain ranges, do the 2-km loop to Buchanan Lookout. From here, a further 2.5-km hike leads to even better views. Follow Hwy 31A west for 9.2 km then take the rough Buchanan Forest Service Road to the right for 11 km. An extreme **mountain bike** trail heads straight down 1,220 m from here. There are also 2 launch sites for the Kaslo **hang-gliding** club.
Kaslo is also gateway to arguably the best **backcountry skiing** in BC. Cat-skiing and heli-skiing packages, about the only way to get to it, are expensive enough to put off all but the most wealthy or dedicated. For the best advice on this and other outdoor pursuits, talk to Leni at the *Outdoor Adventure Centre*, 331 Front St, T3537349, www.discoverycanada.ca She also rents **kayaks**. Another source of information is www.kootenayexperience.com and the owner of the hostel is helpful.

Sports

Kaslo is difficult to reach without your own transport. A single shuttle for **Nelson** leaves Wed morning, returning in the afternoon.

Transport

Communications Canada Post: Av A. **Medical services** The nearest hospitals are in **Nelson** or **New Denver**, but both have only limited facilities.

Directory

Highway 31 to Galena Bay

This beautifully scenic drive follows the west bank of Kootenay Lake from Kaslo to Galena Bay, where a free ferry crosses Upper Arrow Lake to connect with the TransCanada at Revelstoke. This is way off the beaten track, with no public transport, very few services, and a 99-km section of rough dirt road to

Colour map 2, grid B2

negotiate. Still it's mostly quite flat, ideal for adventurous bikers or those who revel in the remote. The paved section up to Howser would make a nice excursion from Kaslo, passing scattered no-nonsense farming communities that have retained a frontier homesteader feel. There's first-class hiking in the Purcell Wilderness Provincial Park across the lake (see below).

Beyond Howser the road deteriorates, with some steep and rough sections along Trout Lake. At its northern end, a worthwhile diversion for those heading from Revelstoke to Nakusp, sits the quaint and quirky village of **Trout Lake**. Containing as it does some of the loftier accessible parts of the Selkirk Mountains, this area, especially scenic **Ferguson** close-by, is a favourite with snowmobilers and backcountry skiers, also offering good fishing and gold-panning. At **Galena Bay**, Highway 23 heads north to Revelstoke (via the ferry), or south to Nakusp, passing a number of hot springs.

Purcell Wilderness Provincial Park
About 35 km from Kaslo, between Kootenay and Duncan Lakes, a bridge crosses Duncan River to the east bank and the vast expanse of Purcell Wilderness Provincial Park. A right turn then leads to the small communities of Argenta and Johnson's Landing. Beyond the latter, the **Fry Creek Canyon** trail is a fairly easy, thoroughly rewarding 10-19 km return hike, taking four to seven hours. The canyon walls rise vertically over 1 km from the creek waters, an awesome spectacle. From Argenta, the **Earl Grey Pass** (or **Hamill Creek**) trail is a tough but rewarding 61-km, three-to-five-day one-way trek along the route by which Chief Kinbasket of the Shuswap Natives led his people to their present home near Invermere. Though the path is distinct, it is full of obstacles and very demanding, so consult a hiking guide and local information before attempting it. You're not likely to see another soul, and the stands of ancient giant cedars are magnificent. It's worth doing the one-hour scramble up Slate Peak north of the pass for 360° views that rival anything in the Rocky or Coast mountains.

From Duncan River Bridge, continue straight for the trailheads of three more highly recommended hikes. Ask in Kaslo or consult a hiking guide for exact directions. **Monica Meadows** is an easy 8-km round-trip, about five hours, with 579 m elevation gain. This beautiful alpine meadow, surrounded by glacier-clad mountains, is full of bright flowers at the height of summer. Access is difficult and a four-wheel drive is needed. Easier to reach, and preferable for views is the more challenging **Jumbo Pass** trail, 8.4 km, six to seven hours with 686 m elevation gain. The view from the pass is stunning. There's a hut for overnight stays, T3424200 for reservations. Access is also easy to the **Macbeth Icefield** trail which usually takes nine or 10 hours, with 874 m elevation gain, but the final section could add an extra 3.6 km to the 12 km round-trip. This is harder still, though the views of the dual waterfalls cascading down from the glacier surrounded by a sea of ice are worthy rewards.

Sleeping & eating
The first stretch of road is thick with cabins, B&Bs, and campgrounds, including 2 sites in **Kootenay Lake Provincial Park**: **F** *Lost Ledge,* at Km 25, has 12 sites on the lake with calm, privacy and a large beach; **F** *Davis Creek,* at 28 km, has 12 even more private and primitive sites, but a rockier beach and no drinking water. **Meadow Creek**, at 40 km has *Drifters Pub and Restaurant* with cheap (**E**) but unpleasant (mainly single) rooms. Just north is the very nice **C** *White Grizzly Lodge*, 110 Duncan Dam Haul Rd, T3664306, www.whitegrizzly.com A log house with stone fireplace, hot tub, breakfast included. Other meals available. Hiking and cat-skiing tours arranged. **Howser**, 8 km on, has a pretty forested campsite on Duncan Lake with drive-in and walk-in sites, and a big sandy beach. In **Trout Lake** the **E** *Windsor Hotel*, T3692244, with restaurant, is a wonderful, eccentric establishment that looks just as it must have when built in 1892.

Highway 31A and Sandon

From Kaslo, a more agreeable option than the slog north to Galena Bay is to follow Highway 31A to New Denver in the Slocan Valley. Clinging to the side of the lovely, fast-flowing Kaslo River as it picks its way through the steep cliffs of the Selkirk Mountains past a series of charming little lakes, this is one of the most scenic routes in the Kootenays.

About halfway down is the abandoned mining townsite of Retallack and the **Retallack** *Retallack Ski Resort*, T2267784, www.retallack.com, one of the best and easiest bases for that world-famous backcountry skiing. *Powder* magazine has said: "Featuring some of the steepest tree skiing in BC's southern interior, the peaks, ridges, and bowls around Retallack draw drool from skiers on the cat ride up, and make them downright giddy on the ski down." There are nearly 5,000 ha to play on with an average of 600 m runs, and a staggering 10 m of snow per year. The cost is $450 per day including accommodation in the picturesque lodge, guided cat-skiing, and all meals. Skiing alone costs $300 a day, with a standby rate of $200. There is also some exceptional summer hiking nearby in **Goat Range Provincial Park**. Access is possible but tricky unless staying at the lodge ($110 including breakfast). The challenging 14.6-km round-trip to **Mount Brennan** (seven to 10 hours, 1,463 m elevation gain) is a favourite. The trail starts 5 km from Retallack, leading through the upper cirque of Lyle Creek Basin. From here the exceptional views give a taste of the mouth-watering panorama from the top, which takes in glaciers and icefields, and the countless peaks of a few ranges, including the Rockies. Another favourite is the moderate **Whitewater Canyon** trail, a 13.5-km round-trip starting 2.7 km from Retallack, taking eight to nine hours, with 893 m gain.

Further down the highway, a signed gravel road leads 13 km to the quintes- **Sandon** sential mining ghost-town of Sandon. At its peak, Sandon had electricity (before Vancouver), an opera house and a red-light district, 24 hotels and 23 saloons. After a fire and two floods, there is little left to evoke that heady history, but the location and dilapidated remains are worth the diversion, especially since some excellent hikes begin here. It's hard to beat **Idaho Peak** for ease and stunning views: a steep but manageable gravel road leads 18 km to a car park, then it is just a 1.4-km walk to the Forestry Lookout at the summit, and exquisite vistas. Alternatively, the **K&S Railway/Galena** trail combines views of the Valhalla Range with a pleasant forest hike and a history lesson that follows on nicely from a visit to Sandon. The summer-only **Information Centre** there can provide a leaflet which talks you through the glory-days of 'Silvery Slocan' along the 14.5-km trail (one-way) which passes old mine works and numerous artefacts on its way to New Denver (via Three Forks) along the old ore-carrying railway line. If you parked in Sandon, you have little choice but to hitch back.

Established in 1922, this 32,000-ha park is one of BC's oldest. Radiating out **Kokanee** from the eponymous glacier and **Mount Cond**, which at 2,775 m is the park's **Glacier** highest peak, are a number of creeks whose deep valleys provide the park's **Provincial Park** access routes. Out of the drainage patterns has evolved a complete network of trails (120 km of it well maintained), most of them originally built to service the small mines whose remains are still visible. There are three glaciers, over 30 alpine and sub-alpine lakes, and endless forested valleys to admire. Fauna most likely to be seen include black and grizzly bears, mountain goats, marmots, pikas and ground squirrels. Of three cabins, the most famous is the historic **Slocan Chief Cabin**, full up in winter, first-come first-served in summer. Many trails start here, including the easy and popular one-hour hikes to **Smuggler Ridge** and **Kokanee Glacier**. Pick up a blue *BC Parks* map, available at information centres, and consult a good hiking guide. For more information, call T8254421.

Park information The following entry points are all well signed:

Keen Creek Turn south off Hwy 31A, 6.4 km northwest of Kaslo. This 24-km rough road requires 4WD in all but peak conditions, but gives deepest entry into the park. Many trails lead from the car park at Joker Millsite, including a 4.8-km, 3-hr hike to the **Slocan Chief**, or one of similar length to **Joker Lakes**.

Kokanee Creek Turn north off Hwy 3A, 19.2 km east of Nelson. This easier 15.2-km road leads to a car park at Gibson Lake. There is a short loop round the lake. The 8.8-km, 4.5-hr hike to the **Slocan Chief** passes 4 major lakes and gives easy access to extreme wilderness conditions. The **Glory Basin Circuit** is a moderate 24-km hike taking in most of the park's key sights. Possible in 10 hrs, but better as a 2-day trip camping at Kaslo Lake.

Enterprise Creek Turn east off Hwy 6, 14.4 km north of Slocan. Parking area at 16 km. Trails lead to **Tanal Lake**, 6.4 km, 3 hrs; and **Slocan Chief**, 10.4 km, 5 hrs.

Woodbury Creek Turn west off Hwy 31, 6.4 km north of Ainsworth. Parking area is at 13.2 km. 2 cabins are accessible, each about 4 hrs' walk: **Woodbury Hut** is a moderate 8-km hike. **Silver Spray** is shorter but harder. Above it is an old mine site and some very well preserved relics.

Lemon Creek Turn east off Hwy 6 at Lemon Creek, 14.4 km south of Slocan. Park off the road at a signed trailhead after 16 km. A varied hike of 9.6 km, 5 hrs, not all of it well marked, leads to the beautiful **Sapphire Lakes**.

Slocan Valley

Colour map 2, grid C2 Running north to Nakusp from a point midway between Castlegar and Nelson on Highway 3A, this eastern section of Highway 6 remains one of the more deeply buried jewels in the undiscovered treasure chest of the Kootenays. Clinging to the course of the enchanting Slocan River/Lake, sandwiched between Valhalla Provincial Park to the west and Kokanee Glacier Provincial Park to the east, this winding road weaves between undulating green hills, rugged bluffs and fast-flowing icy creeks. The scenery has a pristine quality, even by local standards. The distinctive Kootenay spirit is also particularly strong, with an inordinate number of healers, artists and musicians. Many people fall in love with the valley and never leave. Passers-by would be surprised how many people live in the warren of properties hidden in the woods and on the back roads. The communities offer no obvious entertainment besides the great outdoors and the warmth of the locals.

North to Slocan City Probably the best place to meet the locals is in **Winlaw**, the first stop of any significance driving north, and in many ways the heart of the valley, though there appears to be nothing to it but a gas station, restaurant, and a cluster of funky shops. Even more ephemeral is **Lemon Creek**, though it has one of the best places to stay and eat, and offers access to the Kokanee Glacier. On a clear day, staggering views of the Valhallas appear on the stretch to Slocan City where the winding river turns into a lake. This would be a lovely spot but for the (apparently doomed) mill that dominates what is basically a logging town. Across the easily located bridge is **Slocan Lake** trail. An 8-km, four-hour walk, with fine views not quite ruined by the mill, leads to Evans Creek and the

Valhalla Retreat and Tipi Lodge, T3653226, also accessible by canoe from Slocan (see Sports). From here the **Cahill/Beatrice Lake** trail offers relatively easy access (12 km, six hours) to the rugged Valhalla Provincial Park (see page 255), where there is wilderness camping.

Above Slocan, the road climbs fairly steeply away from the lake towards a fine viewpoint. The following stretch of road is particularly interesting, clinging to cliff faces, taking hairpin curves, crossing rickety wooden bridges, and losing sight of the lake until a bend is turned and it suddenly fills the whole panorama. Before long, another viewpoint offers the chance to stop and take it all in. Almost 3 km north of here, a steep dirt road winds down through a gravel pit and ends. Well-trodden paths then lead down to **Bannock Point**, a beautiful, clothing-optional beach, great for swimming, diving and wilderness camping. Soon enough, the highway leads back down to the lake and a brace of picturesque old mining towns just a few kilometres apart, settled when silver and lead were found in nearby Idaho Mountain. The first, Silverton, is just a string of buildings along the highway, one of them a **museum** with displays of old mining equipment spread across its lawn. There is also a surprising number are **artists' galleries** and studios. | **Silverton**

The second town, New Denver, shares many qualities with Kaslo. This pretty little lakeside town with its quaint wooden houses still resembles the mining boomtown it once was. Almost everything of interest is located on 6th Avenue, which leads to **Greer Park**, with a shady picnic area and lakeside walk. The summer-only **Visitor Information Centre** is at 101 Eldorado Avenue, T3582719, www.slocanlake.com **Valhalla Nature Centre**, at 307 6th Avenue, has information and trail maps of Valhalla and White Grizzly Provincial Parks for $4. Visit the **Silvery Slocan Museum** to learn all about the town's mining history. ■ *Summer 0930-1600, $2. 1202 6th Av, T3582201.* Alternatively, you can hike along the old mining railway to Sandon, with historical details supplied along the way (see page 251). | **New Denver**

Another slice of local history is explored at the **Nikkei Internment Memorial Centre**. In early 1942, in the wake of the Japanese bombing of Pearl Harbour, Japanese-Canadians, most of them living in Vancouver, were dispossessed of their belongings and herded into internment camps. This interesting museum is housed in one such camp, and contains a lovely formal Japanese garden. ■ *May-Sep, 0900-1700. $4, $3 seniors, $2 children. 306 Josephine St, T3587288.* One famous inmate of another camp at Lemon Creek was David Suzuki, the well-respected biologist and environmentalist. There's a small Japanese garden here, and another, the **Kohan Reflection Garden**, on 1st Avenue.

From New Denver the highway continues 47 km north to Nakusp. After 5.6 km, turn east and drive 26 km along the East Wilson Creek Forestry Road, with its fine views, to reach the trailhead for the **Alps Alturas** trail into the remote **Goat Range Provincial Park**. This moderate 5.6-km round-trip, five to six hours, 579-m elevation gain, gives quick access to subalpine meadows, ending at a glaciated lake basin with views across the Selkirks to the Monashee range.

Arranged south to north. **Slocan Park** B *Beach Front Luxury Resort*, T2267772. Handily situated on the highway but also right on the river, with its own beach. 1 room and 1 suite, both with kitchen and en suite bath. Suite has its own patio. **Winlaw** Throughout BC, but particularly in the Kootenays, there is much enthusiasm for 2 forms of architecture: timberframe and straw-bale houses. They don't come much better than C *Arica Gardens B&B*, 6307 Youngs Rd, T2267688, www.aricagardens.com This exquisite | **Sleeping** building comes close to most people's dream home. 2 spacious, luxurious rooms are a steal at this price. Knowledgeable hosts can also arrange a whole manner of activities to help you get the most out of the area. Recommended. **D** *Karibu Park Cottages and Campground*, 5730 Cedar Creek Rd, off Hwy 6, T2267306. Cabins sleeping up to 6, with kitchens, TV and VCR. Dated decor. Also nice wooded camping sites (**F**), with coin-op showers. **D** *Slocan Valley B&B*, 6351 Slocan River Rd, T2267276. 1 en suite room and a suite, kitchen, indoor pool, hot tub, use of canoe, bikes, etc.

Lemon Creek C *Lemon Creek Lodge*, 7680 Kennedy Rd, T3552403, www.lemon creeklodge.com Lodge rooms with shared bath, or fully equipped cabins that are great value, especially for families. Sauna. Price includes breakfast. Good restaurant (see below). Campsites (**F**) lacking in privacy. **Slocan D** *Three Maples B&B*, 710 Arthur St, T3552586. 2 reasonable rooms. **D-E** *Little Slocan Lodge*, T1-800-505-6788, www.littles locanlodge.com 6.5 km from Slocan. Follow directions to Valhalla Provincial Park (see page 255), or phone for details and possible pick-up. Occupying 100 beautiful ha on the very edge of Valhalla Provincial Park, this brand new hostel is just what the valley needed. From here you can go hiking, climbing, mountain biking, canoeing or skiing. Incorporating straw-bale and timber-frame elements, the character building contains dorms, private and family rooms, 2 common rooms, kitchen, a licensed café, lockers, laundry and a great deck. **F** *Springer Creek Campground*, 1020 Giffin Rd, T3552226, May-Sep. 25 sites in wooded area, some with hook-ups. Showers. Information.

Silverton AL-B *Silverton Resort*, 15 Lake Av, T3587157. 6 fully equipped, attractive log cottages of differing sizes on lake. Canoe, kayak and boat rentals. **C** *Mistaya Country Inn B&B*, 10 km south of Silverton, signed from highway, T3587787, www.mistayaresort@netidea.com Nice rooms with shared bath in a very remote spot. Hot tub. Horse-riding trips offered ($35 per 2 hrs, $65 per ½ day with lunch). Stay in a tepee (**E**). **C** *William Hunter Cabins*, 303 Lake Av, T3582844. 6 gorgeous handcrafted log cabins on the lake, with kitchenettes and decks. Canoe rental. **F** *Municipal Campground*, on lake at Leadville/Turner. Primitive wooded location with a beach and boat dock. **New Denver C** *Sweet Dreams Guesthouse*, 702 Eldorado Av, T3582415. 5 rooms in a beautiful heritage house near the lake, with reservations-only restaurant. Kayak rentals. Breakfast included. **D** *Valhalla Inn*, 509 Slocan Av (Hwy 6), T3582228. Standard hotel rooms, though with glacier views. The more expensive ones are much nicer. Pub and standard restaurant downstairs. **F** *Municipal Campground*, south side of village, T3582316. Right on beach, but pretty dingy. **F** *Rosebery Provincial Park*, 6 km north, T8253500, May-Sep. 33 very nice, private sites on the banks of a creek.

Eating Winlaw *Hungry Wolf Café*, 5709 Hwy 6. Mainly standard fare, with breakfasts, popular brunch at weekends, and a good selection of vegetarian food (try the spinach salad). **Lemon Creek** *Lemon Creek Lodge*, see above. Best option for miles around. **New Denver** *The Apple Tree Sandwich Shop*, 210 6th Av. Creative and varied sandwich menu, good coffee, outdoor seating in garden. Open till 1600. *Panini*, 306 6th St. A bright and comfortable spot, offering the town's best coffee, breakfast and lunches. Also one of the few places selling wine and beer. *The Wild Rose Mexican Restaurant* in Rosebery, 5 mins north of New Denver, T3587744, is recommended for fine Mexican food. Open daily 1700-2100 in summer.

Festivals Between **Jul** and mid-**Aug**, the small communities around New Denver host *Slocan Lake Art Walk*, with maps available from information centres. The tiny village of Hills, just beyond New Denver, hosts a celebrated 1-day *Garlic Festival* on the second Sun in **Sep**.

Shopping **Arts and crafts** can be bought directly from the artisans in Silverton. **Books** *Jennie's Book Garden*, Winlaw. Small shop packed with an eye-opening, intelligently selected range of desirable fiction and non-fiction. *Earth Spirit*, almost next door, specializes in metaphysical books and artefacts, and New Age music. **Clothing** *Valhalla Pure Outfitters*, 101 Eldorado/6th Av, New Denver. Outdoor clothing, equipment and information. First of the famous chain.

Canoeing on Slocan River is mostly leisurely but there are some rapids around Lemon Creek. Most people put in at the **Winlaw bridge** and take out at **South Slocan**. Ask around or contact *Wild Ways*, T3598181, 1286 Hwy 6, for rentals, lessons and guided tours. Canoes and **kayaks** can also be rented from *Smiling Otter*, at 8846 Slocan West Rd, Slocan City, T3552373, who give tours and lessons. A fun way to see the river is by floating down it in an inner tube. These can be rented ($5 per day) from the *Race Track* gas station in Slocan Park, the first village north of the Hwy 3A junction. There are some good cliff faces for **rock climbing** just past the mill in Slocan. For **hiking**, see Kokanee Glacier and Valhalla provincial parks, and above. There are **ski trails** around Winlaw Regional Park, along the banks of the river, or on the old railway track. **Golf** *Valley View Golf Course* is at 6937 Hwy 6, just north of Winlaw, T2267241.

Sports

It is almost essential to have a vehicle. 3-4 minibuses per day run between **Slocan City** and **Nelson**, with 4 others between Nelson and **Passmore** at the southern end of the valley. The schedules are complex, so call T3528201 for details. A ticket is $1.50-3 on a zone system. Buses from **Nakusp** (see page 255) pass through Tue and Thu, and can be flagged down. Otherwise, hitchhiking is a way of life.

Transport

Communications Canada Post: Winlaw Minimart; 219 6th Av, New Denver. **Medical services** *Slocan Community Hospital*, 401 Galena St, New Denver, T3587911.

Directory

This 49,000-ha park was designated in 1983 after years of campaigning and protest on the part of locals who sought to protect such an extraordinary area from the whims of logging companies. It is easy to see how the jagged, snow-capped peaks here inspired association with the dwelling place of the Nordic pantheon. There is much here to satisfy professional adventurers and climbers, but from June to October beginners can also gain easy access to areas of extreme wilderness. The routes leading in are long and confusing, so seek more complete instructions before heading out. The most popular hike is to **Gwillim Lakes** via Drinnon Pass. Signed access from Highway 6 is at Passmore, south of Winlaw, or Slocan City. From the former turn left at Km 25.3, from the latter turn right at Km 20.3, onto Hoder Creek Forestry Road. Follow for 18.8 km and turn right for the last rough 2.4 km. The 11.6-km round-trip, with 701 m elevation gain, is fairly easy and could be accomplished as a 10-hour hike. It is tempting to stay at the lovely meadow campground, giving time to explore **Lucifer Pass**, a further 3 km, three-hour hike with a scramble at the end, and even better views. **Mulvey Basin** is most people's second choice. From Slocan, follow signs down the Little Slocan Lakes Forestry Road for 10.9 km, then turn right onto Banock Burn and follow for 12.9 km. This 9.7-km round-trip (five or six hours, 765 m elevation gain) is more difficult, but the rewards are incredible glacial sculptures and world-class mountaineering.

Valhalla Provincial Park

Nakusp

Attractive enough in its lakeside setting, Nakusp cannot rival some of the other Kootenay towns for picturesque qualities. What it does have, however, is hot springs, making this a worthwhile stopover for those heading from the Okanagan or Nelson to the TransCanada Highway (see Transport page 256). This area is also one of the best places in BC for wild mushrooms. In town, the

Phone code: 250
Colour map 2, grid C2
Population: 1,813
Altitude: 450 m

biggest attraction is the lake itself, easily admired from a pleasant **promenade** which also takes in a small but pretty **Japanese Garden**. Almost everything of any importance is found on or near the main street, Broadway, including the small **Visitor Information Centre** at 92 6th Avenue, T2654234, www.nakusphotsprings.com, which is disguised as a paddlesteamer, with the inevitable small-town **museum** next door. **Summit Lake Ski Area**, 20 km south, has been operating for 36 years. It doesn't try to compete with the likes of Whitewater, but is cheaper, geared towards families, and ideal for beginners. ■ *Wed, Fri, Sat and Sun, 1000-1530, night skiing Wed and Fri, 1800-2100.*

Sleeping On Hwy 6 heading west, the lake is lined with cabins, 'resorts' and campgrounds, a quiet and scenic choice if you have your own transport. At Km 3 is **C** *Arrow Lake Chalets*, T2654889, www.arrowlakechalets.kootenays.com 5 fully equipped chalets. At Km 2.5 is **C** *O'Brien's*, T2654575, www.obriens.kootenays.com 3 fully equipped, hand-crafted log cabins. On the way to the springs is **D** *Huckleberry Inn*, 1050 Hot Springs Rd, T2654544, Huckinn@aolcom 4 comfortable theme rooms decorated with tasteful kitsch. Good value, but showers not tubs. **D** *Kuskanax Lodge*, 515 Broadway, T2653618, kuskanax@cmhinc.com A heli-skiing base, sometimes fully occupied, otherwise the best option in town, with a good restaurant and bar. **D-E** *Selkirk Inn*, 210 6th Av W, T2653666. Standard rooms but spacious and clean. Sauna.

Camping F *Nakusp Village Campground*, 381 8th St northwest, has wooded sites in a quiet part of town with fire-pits and showers. Better still is **F** *McDonald Creek Provincial Park*, 10 km west on Highway 6, T8253500, Apr-Oct, with 38 wooded and private sites close to the beach. No showers or hook-ups. **F** *Summit Lake Provincial Park*, 13 km south on Hwy 6, T8253500, May-Sep. 35 sites with toilets and water taps but no hook-ups (there's a private RV park next door). With fine views of the Selkirk Mountains, good fishing, common sightings of mountain goats and an agreeable climate, this is a very popular spot. At the end of summer, thousands of migrating toads flood from the lake.

Eating **Mid-range** *Kuskanax Lodge Restaurant* (see above) serves burgers/pastas, etc, but also some more exciting main courses, very well cooked, presented and served. Menu also available in the lounge, a nicer environment with a good selection of beers on tap. *Wylie's Pub*, T2654944, and *Picardo's*, T2653331, share a location, 401 Broadway, and a menu, which concentrates on southern favourites like ribs, and lot of appetizers. The pub, favoured by a younger crowd, is a preferable location if only for the fish-tank. **Cheap** The best bet for breakfast is the *Broadway Deli Bistro*, 408 Broadway. *The Hut Drive Inn* on Broadway, is a local institution for cheap takeaway fast food and ice cream. The best coffee in town is poured at *What's Brewing on Broadway*, 420 Broadway.

Transport **Bus** *Nakusp Transit*, T2653674, provides local services and runs to **Nelson** Tue and Thu at 0830, returning at 1445. *Arrow Lakes Bus Lines*, T3587109, run to **Vernon** at 0720 Mon, Wed and Fri, returning at 1520.

By **car** it is 49 km north to the free **ferry** at Galena Bay, and a further 49 km to Revelstoke and the TransCanada Highway. Ferries from Galena Bay to **Shelter Bay** leave hourly from 0530-0030; hourly from Shelter Bay 0500-midnight. Hwy 6 heads west from Nakusp towards **Vernon** and the **Okanagan**, via the free ferry at Fauquier. This leaves every ½ hr 0500-2200. The 135-km road to Vernon is a lonely, windy drive with few buildings or services, and lots of deer on the road at night.

Halycon Hot Springs The hot springs around Nakusp have been used by native peoples for centuries. In 1897 the first private sanitarium brought the healing waters to westerners and enjoyed tremendous success until it burnt down in 1955. It was totally rebuilt in 1997, and opened as Halcyon Hot Springs, the nicest private resort in the Kootenays, with some of the most therapeutic water in North America, sulphur-free and lithium-rich, a treat for body and mind. The three pools, hot (42° C), warm (35° C) and cold (13°C), overlook the Arrows Lake. ■ *0800-2200. $6 for a dip, $4 concessions, $9 day pass, $6 concessions. Located 34 km north on Hwy 23, T2653554, www.halcyon-hotsprings.com*

Sleeping Options include attractive but small 1-room cabins with a double futon and bunk beds, and shared outdoor baths. **C-D**, including swim passes. Better value are the chalets **A**, with kitchenettes, living-room, and all mod cons. There are unattractive RV and tent sites (**F**), the latter overlooking the lake. Facilities include day-care facilities, horse and jet-skis rentals, horse riding and snowmobile tours, and plans for kayak rental.

From the outskirts of Nakusp, a scenic 12-km road leads to the Nakusp Hot Springs, cheaper and closer than Halcyon, but not as appealing. Here a simple, round, outdoor swimming pool is divided in two, with respective temperatures of 100°C and 107°C in winter, slightly cooler in summer. ■ *Summer 0930-2200, winter 1000-2130. 92-6th Av NW, T2654528. Dip: $6, $5 concessions, day pass: $8.50, $7.50 concessions; $2 Mon. A bus leaves from the Senior's Lodge in town at 1000 Mon, and from Overwaitea at 1100 Wed.* **Nakusp Hot Springs**

Sleeping Chalets with kitchenettes and TV are a bit shabby, but a good deal at **D**, including passes. The campsite (**F**) is unpleasant.

There are a few smaller, undeveloped and free hot springs reached by logging roads about 24 km north on Highway 23. Most locals prefer them to the commercial operations. Saint Leon and Halfway are most people's favourites, the former situated amidst giant old-growth trees. Nudity is common at both. Neither is easy to find. Ask around for directions. **Saint Leon & Halfway**

East Shore

The easiest route between Nelson and Creston is via Salmo. But for those with no need to hurry, the route via the ferry at Balfour (see page 247) is infinitely more enjoyable. Highway 3A hugs the lake tightly on its way from Kootenay Bay to Creston, meandering slowly through wonderfully dramatic scenery, and passing a series of sleepy villages, collectively known as the East Shore, that offer few reasons to stop. As so often in the Kootenays, the journey is an end in itself. For one weekend in mid-July, the pace quickens dramatically for the splendid **Starbelly Jam** global music festival. *Colour map 2, grid C2*

At **Kootenay Bay**, a right turn from the ferry takes you in five minutes to **Pilot Bay Provincial Park**, open year round with free camping, swimming, fishing, and extensive trails leading to more remote wilderness campsites. Just off the highway, towards Riondel, is the highly respected yoga study and retreat centre, *Yasodhara Ashram*, T2279224, www.yasodhara.org Beds here are $70 per person including meals. The nearby retreat centre, *Tara Shanti*, T2279616, is a little cheaper at $95 for two including breakfast.

There's a nice artisan scene 5 km further at Crawford Bay, with a blacksmith at *Kootenay Forge*, a glass blower at *Breathless Glass* and an old-fashioned broom maker at *North Woven Broom*, all encouraging you to watch them at work. An **Information Centre** is just off the highway, T2279267, June-September. **Crawford Bay**

Southern Interior BC

Sleeping and eating   For a touch of style, try **B** *Wedgwood Manor*, 16002 Crawford Creek Rd, T2279233. An exquisite heritage house built for Wedgwood's daughter, full of antiques, and set on 20 ha with numerous trails. **D** *Kokanee Chalets*, T2279292, has standard motel rooms, and campsites (**F**) with shower, hot tub and hook-ups. The *CCR Pub* is a good place for a drink and cheap food, whilst the *Abracajava Café*, Apr-Oct Thu-Sun, has healthy food and good coffee.   *Kokanee Springs*, T2279226, is a world-class **golf** course with a restaurant.

Gray Creek & Boswell   There's not much at Gray Creek, except for a few beaches and the old-style **General Store** on Chainsaw Av, famous for selling just about everything. The pick of accommodation on the East Shore is further south at Boswell. The nearby **Glass House**, constructed entirely from 500,000 embalming fluid bottles assiduously collected from colleagues by a retired mortician, is a truly fascinating oddity, all the more so as it was built as a home, not a tourist attraction. ■ *May-Oct. $5. T2238372.*

Sleeping   **F** *Lockhart Creek Provincial Park*, 13 km south of Gray Creek, T8253500, Apr-Oct, has 13 basic but wooded and private campsites, with a beach and trail. **B** *Kootenay Lake Lodge*, Boswell, T2238181, www.kootenaylakelokge.com   has 7 spacious rooms in a beautiful log house, with antique furniture, balconies and views. Breakfast and use of canoe, row-boat and bikes included. **F** *Kootenay Kampsites*, 1 km south (May-Oct), with reasonable wooded sites, hook-ups and showers, is the last campsite before Creston 39 km further on.

East Kootenays

This vaguely defined region consists of the mainly uninteresting towns between Golden and Cranbrook on Highway 95, and east of the latter on Highway 3. Following the **Columbia River Valley** along one section of the Rockie Mountain Trench, North America's longest valley, Highway 95 is flanked by the Purcell Range to the west and the Rockies to the east, with continual views of white-capped peaks. Fed from the lake of the same name, the Columbia River continues to Revelstoke, north of which it turns abruptly and plunges south to the States, where it swings west and empties into the Pacific at Astoria, Oregon. On the way through BC it has been dammed in many places, becoming a series of lakes, notably the **Arrow Lakes**.

Despite the scenery, a number of fabulous and underused parks, and a proliferation of thermal waters, this is a boring road to drive. There are few towns, and most are deadly dull or horribly commercial. Only **Invermere** offers anything like the spirit more readily encountered in the West Kootenays. Campers will find a dearth of sites. Unless you haplessly find yourself in the dismal town of Cranbrook, or are going climbing in the **Bugaboos**, there is no good reason to choose this route. The highlights along this stretch of Highway 3 are **Fort Steele Heritage Town**, one of the best examples of the 'living museum' genre, and **Fernie**, a delightful little town with one of BC's best and least overrun ski hills.

Transport   The Hwy 3 section of the East Kootenays is served by 2 daily *Greyhound* buses running between Kelowna and Fort McLeod, Alberta, with connections to Vancouver and Calgary. The Columbia Valley is served by 1 daily bus between Cranbrook and Golden.

Reached by a good 47-km gravel road from Brisco, 27 km north of Radium, **Bugaboo** Bugaboo Provincial Park is famous in rock-climbing circles for its spectacular **Provincial Park** granite spires. Though the long access is off-putting, a couple of good trails allow hikers to enjoy the park's rugged beauty and extensive glaciers. **Bugaboo Spires** trail (10 km return, 660 m elevation gain. Trailhead: parking lot at Km 43.3) leads to the base of the spires and *Conrad Kain Hut*, which sleeps 40 people and is equipped with propane stoves. Exploring beyond is recommended. **Cobalt Lake** trail (17.4 km return, 930 m elevation gain. Same trailhead) involves a lot of hard work before mind-expanding views take over. A shorter trail (10 km return) leads from *Bugaboo Lodge*, which is operated by Canadian Mountain Holidays, T7627100. Pick up a blue *BC Parks* map at any local information centre, or call them at T4224200. Climbers should get the Nat Topo Map 82K/10 and/or 82K/15, and might enjoy *Bugaboo Rock: A Climber's Guide* by R Green and J Benson.

Heading south from Golden (see page 218), the first community of any size is **Radium Hot** Radium Hot Springs, whose spa, within the **Kootenay National Park**, is the **Springs** most commercial and least pleasant in the region. Essentially a thermally heated swimming pool, it is overcrowded in summer with up to 4,000 people a day. Having said this, since the ticket price includes the admission charge to the national park, there seems little reason for those entering the park not to stop for a quick soak. The only western access to this wonderful park, the town of Radium, is a nasty example of rampant tourism, little more than a string of cheesy motels, which tend to be full throughout the summer, even though Invermere, just 13 km south, is a far more attractive place to stay. The only thing to see in Radium is the **Thousand Faces Sculpture Gallery**, a collection of chainsaw carvings with legends and stories built into them, the artist himself a curiosity. ■ *$1. Hwy 93/Madsen Rd.* The extremely busy **Visitor Information Centre** is on the highway at 7556 Main Street East, T3479331, T1800-3479704, www.rhs.bc.ca

Sleeping and eating The best places to stay are up on a hill adjacent to the park entrance, with wonderful views and a healthy distance from town. **B** *Chalet Europe*, 5063 Madsen Rd, T3479306 www.chaleteurope.com Balconies, telescope, sauna, jacuzzi, small games room. **C** *Rocky Mountain Springs Lodge*, 5067 Madsen Rd, T3479548. Big rooms with balcony, breakfast included. Also the best food in town, featuring sushi and some German specialities. The nicest in town is **B** *Village Country Inn*, 7557 Canyon Av, T3479392, www.villagecountryinn.bc.ca Rooms have big beds and VCRs.

D *Pinewood*, 4870 Stanley St, T3479529, is the nicest of the endless motels in town. Spacious, kitchenettes, nestled in spruce trees. **E-F** *Misty River B&B and HI Hostel*, Hwy 93, the closest building to the park entrance, T3479912. A new HI hostel, with the usual facilities, some private rooms, and bike rentals. **Camping F** *Canyon RV Resort*, close to town on Sinclair Loop Rd, T3479564. Ask for a creekside site. **F** *Dry Gulch Provincial Park*, 5 km south, T4224200. A comparatively small and attractive site. For food, the expensive *Old Salzburg* has good German fare, plus seafood and steak.

Invermere

Situated away from the highway on Windermere Lake, Invermere has the laid-back character and charm of a West Kootenay town. Though there's little to do but fish or hang out by the lake in Kinsmen Park, a number of decent cafés, restaurants and shops on and around 7th Avenue make for a far more pleasant environment than any other town on this highway.

Phone code: 250
Colour map 2, grid C3
Population: 2,721
Altitude: 859 m

Southern Interior BC

Sleeping Decent places to stay are thin on the ground. **B** *Best Western*, 1310 7th Av, T3429246, is convenient and reliable but nothing special. **D** *Mountain View Lodge* 747 12th St, T3426618, is quiet and has kitchenettes. **D** *Primrose Manor B&B*, 1512 9th Av, T3429664. Best option. Pretty rooms with shared baths, and a suite that's worth the extra. **E** *Wandering Rogue Hostel*, 1010 12th St, T3423445. Friendly and cheap. Mainly dorms. For **camping**, the best sites are 7 km north at **F** *Dry Gulch Provincial Park*, T4223212.

Eating & shopping

The formidable Kicking Horse Coffee is roasted locally, so lovers of the bean can get a good cup almost anywhere

The local food situation is much more promising. **Expensive** *Strand's* 818 12th St, T3426344. Fancy international cuisine. Watch for early-bird specials. *Myrtles on Main*, 1321 7th Av, T3420281. Creative gourmet menu, nice cosy atmosphere. Recommended. **Mid-range** *Blue Dog Café*, 7th Av, T3423814. Wholesome vegetarian food. Great coffee. Not open till 1000. **Cheap** *Quality Bakery*, 7th Av. Wood-oven baking and coffee. *Café on 12th St*, behind the *Blue Dog*, has coffee and internet. Attached is *The Book Cellar*, with new and good-value used books. Nearby are *Mustard Seed Market*, a juice bar with organic produce, and *Village Arts*, a craft store that profiles local artists.

Sports *Panorama Ski Resort*, T3426941, www.panoramaresort.com 20 km west on Panorama Drive, has an impressive 1,200-m vertical drop, and some of the longest ski runs in the province. Features pricey lodging, bars and restaurants, including the great *Toby Creek Dining Room*. Lift passes are $49. *RK Heli-Ski Panorama*, T3423889, 2,000 sq km of backcountry terrain for prime powder skiing. Just past the resort is one of the few access points for the **Purcell Wilderness Provincial Park** and the 61-km **Earl Grey Pass** trail to Argenta (see page 250). *Columbia Rafting Adventures*, T1877- 7067238, www.columbiarafting.com, arrange trips on the Columbia and Kicking Horse rivers.

Fairmont Hot Springs Fairmont began life 100 years ago as a stage coach stop. When the thermal waters were discovered, the stop became a popular one. These days, there's nothing to the town but the spa, a commercial swimming-pool style affair but nicer than Radium. ■ *Open to the public 0800-2200. $6.50.* Golf is big here, with 12 courses within a 30-minute drive of Fairmont, not including a plague of mini-golfs. Local natives, whose ancestors were conned out of the land, have built some free baths, very nice and infinitely more intimate. Follow the path to the left just before the RV registration. A small stone building contains three pools crafted out of cement, clean and private, big enough for one. There's another outside, carved into the rocks. Below the resort at the bottom of a waterfall is a lovely tepid natural pool, surrounded by multicoloured rocks. It's free and hardly used. Better still are the free Lussier Springs (see below).

Sleeping **A** *Fairmont Hot Springs Resort*, T3456311, www.fairmonthotsprings.com, is comfortable and includes use of springs, but is overpriced all the same. The resort also runs an RV Park (**E-F**), but tents are mysteriously not allowed.

Canal Flats Provincial Park Just south of Fairmont are the **Dutch Creek Hoodoos**, a set of wierd sandstone formations that rise 122 m beside the highway. A little further, **Columbia Lake** starts to entice the motorist with expanses of pretty, aquamarine water, but the only way to get down to it is at the Canal Flats Provincial Park. With no beach or camping, there's little to justify the diversion, though the breezes are good for windsurfing. The only interesting thing about Canal Flats itself is the story behind the name. The canal was built by Adolphe Baillie-Grohman in an ambitious attempt to drain 20,000 ha of land in the Creston area 240 km to the west, while opening up a north-south navigational system from Golden to Montana. Only two boats ever made it through this dramatic failure, the second ripping out the locks as it went. A year later the Canadian Pacific Railway shut it down.

Sleeping F *Dutch Creek RV Resort*, near the Dutch Creek Hoodoos, T3456558, has nicely spaced sites surrounded by trees. Showers, laundry and swimming pond.

Just beyond, a rough road leads 17 km east to **Whiteswan Lake Provincial Park**. Well signed at the park's entrance are the wonderful, and free, Lussier Hot Springs. This small natural pool has a nice setting right next to a creek, and water as hot as anyone could want. Nudity is prohibited, but locals probably ignore that. The park also has plenty of camping and hiking opportunities. Another 30 km along the road is the **Top of the World Provincial Park**, one of the most remote regions of all, with five wilderness campgrounds, a number of short trails, and good fishing in **Fish Lake**.

Lussier Hot Springs

Kimberley

South of Skookumchuck the highway splits in two, both branches leading to Cranbrook. The eastern route – far more direct for those heading east on Highway 3 – graciously avoids the dreaded Cranbrook, and passes through Fort Steele Heritage Town (see below). The longer western route traverses BC's highest town, Kimberley, touted as the 'Bavarian City of the Rockies' in a surprisingly successful attempt to attract tourists following the closure of the massive lead and zinc mines that once provided most local income. The whole affair is almost unbearably kitsch, but after so many drab, functional little towns, this quirky little place is at least fun and original. Its main square – sorry, *Bavarian Plazl* – is a pleasant enough pedestrian area, with shops, cafés and restaurants.

Phone code: 250
Colour map 2, grid C3
Population: 6,900
Altitude: 1,113 m

B *House Alpenglow*, above town at 3 Alpenglow Ct off Dewdney Rd, T4270273. A friendly B&B with 3 pleasant wood-finished rooms and hot tub. **D** *North Star Motel*, 2 km north on Hwy 95 A, T4275633. Big, clean rooms. In town, Chef Bernard (see below), on top of his cooking prowess, manages a number of rooms, all very nicely priced in the **E** range. **E** *Mozart House Inn and Restaurant*, 130 Spokane St, T4277671, similarly has a bunch of small but acceptable rooms with en suite shower. **E** *Same Sun Hostel*, 275 Spokane St, above the *Ozone Pub*, see below, T4277191. Dorms and private rooms with kitchen, common room and laundry. **F** *Happy Hans Campground and RV Park*, 10 km from the centre, 2.6 km up St Mary's River Rd, T4272929. Riverside setting, showers.

Sleeping
Stiff competition keeps down accommodation prices in town

Predictably enough, most food in town is German. Some of the most authentic is to be found at the **expensive** *Old Bauernhaus Restaurant*, 280 Norton Av, off Dewdney Rd, T4275133. This extraordinary 350-year old house was dismantled in the Alps and shipped to Kimberley, where it was reassembled in 1989. *Chef Bernard*, 170 Spokane St, in the *platzl*, T4274820, prepares award-winning German/Canadian fusion food, including famous fondus. **Cheap** *The Snowdrift Café*, 110 Spokane St, in the *platzl*, has good coffee, and great vegetarian food, including big sandwiches with homemade bread. It's also licensed. What **nightlife** there is happens at *Ozone Pub*, 275 Spokane St.

Eating

Fort Steele Heritage Town

This reconstructed late 19th-century town is one of the best of its kind outside Barkerville in the Cariboo, and gains much from the surrounding mountainous scenery. It began life in the 1860s as Galbraith's Landing, a ferry and provisions stop for gold prospectors on their way to Wildhorse Creek, 6 km to the east. The prosperous town began to die following a piece of corrupt political wrangling that diverted the railway to the less suitable settlement of Cranbrook.

Colour map 2, grid C3

Southern Interior BC

Reconstruction began in 1961, and today there are over 50 buildings, some original, some replicas and some brought in from elsewhere. The overall effect is a convincing step back in time. All the requisite shops and services are represented, with costumed staff acting out their role, while also filling in historic details and anecdotes. The blacksmith shoes horses, the candy shop and bakery sell wares that are made on the spot, the restaurant with its wood-fired brick oven serves meals. There's a working printer, a tinsmith shop, general store, farm animals, street dramas, and live shows in an old-time music hall. You can even get taken round in a steam train or horse-drawn wagon. ■ *Jul-Sep 0930-1800. $8.50, $7.25 senior, $5 13-18 year-olds, $2.25 children, $19.25 family. May-Jun and Oct slightly cheaper. Nov-Apr closed, although you can wander around the grounds free of charge.* **Steam train**, *Jul-Sep only, hourly 1130-1730, $5, $3 concessions. Live 1890s variety shows in the* **Wild Horse Theatre**, *Jul-Sep, 1400 and 2000, $6, $3 concessions. An all-inclusive pass for train, theatre, horse-drawn wagon tour, and admission for 2 days is $18, $8.50 concessions. 9851 Hwy 93/95, 16 km northeast of Cranbrook, T4176000, www.fortsteele.bc.ca*

Sleeping **C** *Wild Horse Farm*, T4266000, has 3 attractive rooms. **Camping F** *Fort Steele Original Campground*, 2 km south, T4265117. 60 quiet wooded sites, heated pool and showers, hook-ups for RVs. **F** *Fort Steele Resort and RV Park*, T4894268. 200 sites right by the town, heated pool, showers, hook-ups. **Transport** No public transport. *Star Taxi*, T4263888, charge about $25 one way, from Cranbrook.

Cranbrook

Phone code: 250
Colour map 2, grid C3
Population: 18,476
Altitude: 921 m

The Columbia Valley and Highway 95 meet Highway 3 at Cranbrook, an important junction but a thoroughly ugly town with no obvious redeeming features. The expansion of the **airport** to receive international flights will further boost its importance in the region, and increase the chances that the unsuspecting traveller might get stuck here. If so, the small **Downtown** is certainly a better place to be than the dismal highway, here called Cranbrook Street.

Sleeping **C** *Mount Baker Heritage Hotel*, Downtown at 1017 Baker St, T4893433. Clean, reno-
& eating vated rooms, but small. Some have jacuzzi tubs. **D** *Town and Country Hotel*, 600 Cranbrook St, T4266683. On the highway, but the best value, with very big rooms. **D-E** *Lazy Bear Lodge*, 621 Cranbrook St, T4266086. The standard cheap motel. For food, *Midorak*, at 1013 Baker St, T4894808, is the nicest mid-range option, with Korean dishes and sushi. *The Cottage*, on 9th Av, is popular with locals. Perogies, burgers, sandwiches, and cheap breakfasts. *Kootenay Roasting Company*, 821 Baker St, serves great coffee and fresh baking.

Transport **Air** *Air Canada Regional*, T1888-2472262, is currently the only company servicing the airport, with regular scheduled flights to **Calgary** and **Vancouver**, but this is due to change. **Bus** The *Greyhound* station is tucked away behind the *McDonalds* on Cranbrook St, with 2 daily buses to **Vancouver** ($100) via Kelowna, 3 to **Calgary** via **Banff** ($53), 3 to **Prince George** ($160), and 1 to **Golden** ($28).

Fernie

Phone code: 250
Colour map 2, grid C3
Population: 5,000
Altitude: 1,010 m

East of Cranbrook, increasingly exciting views of the Rockies loom into view. Surrounded by the soaring, jagged mountains of the Lizard Range, Fernie is the only town that does the setting justice. Recent expansion of its excellent ski hill has resulted in a fair amount of 'development', meaning hotels strung along the highway. Luckily the pretty little **Downtown** has been almost entirely spared. Most buildings here were constructed in brick or stone after a fire in 1908 wiped out the whole town in 90 minutes. A historical walking tour highlights these heritage buildings, many of which are clustered around 6th Street and 4th Avenue. A map is available at the **Visitor Information Centre**, Highway 3/Dicken Road, daily 0900-1700, T4234655, www.FernieTourism.com

Until quite recently Fernie's copious challenging runs and plentiful powder were a fairly well-kept secret, along the lines of Red Mountain in Rossland. A mere 7 km from town, connected by a convenient shuttle bus, it's still a great choice for those who know their skiing and would rather stay in a real town, with good restaurants and bars and excellent cheap accommodation, rather than a purpose-built resort like Whistler. A ski pass is $56. For general information, call T4234655, www.skifernie.com For details on ski packages call *Fernie Destinations Central Reservations Office*, T4239207.

Fernie Alpine Resort

B *Park Place Lodge*, 742 Hwy 3, T4236871, www.parkplacelodge.com Very nice, spacious and stylish rooms, some with balconies or kitchenettes. Indoor pool, hot tub and sauna. Pub and bistro. **C** *Little Witch Log Inn*, 141 Commerce Rd, beside the Information Centre, T4234696. 6 large, wood-finished rooms with comfy beds. **D** *Barbara Lynn's B&B*, just off the highway close to town, T4236027. 10 small rooms, hot tub, mainly shared baths. **D** *Three Sisters Motel*, 441 Hwy 3, T4234438. Cheapest motel, an option only if unable to stay at a hostel or B&B.

Sleeping

E *SameSun International Lodge*, Hwy 3, T4234492, www.samesun.com One of the finest hostels you will ever see. Beautiful, spacious building with dorms and nice private rooms with en suite baths, plus all facilities including a games room, hot tub, sauna, even a piano. **E** *Raging Elk Hostel* 892 6th Av, T4236811, www.ragingelk.com Another great hostel, with dorms, semi-private and private rooms, and a sauna. **Camping F** *Mount Fernie Provincial Park*, 2 km west on Park Rd, T4224200. 40 nice sites, wooded and private.

Expensive *Lizard Creek Lodge*, Fernie Alpine Resort, T4232057, www.lizardcreek.com This restaurant has a dress code of 'smart casual' and a menu to match. French leanings. Seafood, buffalo, duck, poached pear with a white chocolate mousse. More affordable is *The Old Elevator*, 291 1st Av, T4237115. Steaks, pastas, creative sauces. Tapas in the lounge. **Mid-range** *The Curry Bowl*, Hwy 3 W Indian, Japanese, Vietnamese and Thai food. Closed Mon. **Cheap** *Mug Shots Bistro*, 592 3rd Av. Good breakfast and coffee, fresh juices, used books, internet ($5 per hr).

Eating

Our Cappucino Corner, 2nd Av/5th St, also good for java. For locals and ski-bums, most drinking takes place at *The Pub Bar and Grill*, in the *Park Place Lodge*, see above. *The Grizzly Bar* is the apres ski bar at the resort. For dancing, locals head for *The Eldorado Lounge*, Downtown on 2nd Av, while *The Northern* 2 blocks down, is more for tourists.

Bars & clubs

The Arts Station, in an old train station on 1st Av, has an art gallery, theatre and restaurant. **Cinema** *Vogue Movie Theatre*, 321 2nd Av.

Entertainment

Powder, Peddle, Paddle Race marks the closure of the ski-hill in **Apr**. It's an excuse for a big party disguised as a fun variation on the triathlon. *The Gathering* in early **Aug** is a fun weekend event held at *Island Lake Lodge*, 10 km north, with music, visual arts, poetry, crafts, story-telling, etc. $60 per 3 days, $80 with camping, T4234395, www.fernietourism.com

Festivals

Sports As well as **skiing**, Fernie is well known to enthusiasts for **hiking**, **mountain biking** and **rock-climbing**, much of it in Mt Fernie Provincial Park, and **river-rafting** on the Elk River (see below). For rentals and information go to *Bike and Ski Base*, 442 2nd Av; or *The Quest Outdoor Sports Rentals*, 527 7th Av. *Function Junction* on 3rd Av has used sports equipment. *Fernie Aqua Centre* is across the railway tracks for **swimming**.

Tour operators *Canadian Powder Tours Chalet*, T4233019, www.skiaccommodation.com For a luxury experience in a lodge with gourmet meals, BC wines, hot tub, cat-skiing, and snowshoeing. *Cokato Llama Adventures*, T4233097, www.cokato-llama-adventure.com Llama touring. $70 per half day including lunch. *East Kootenay Snowmobile Tours*, T4233883. $123 per half day. *Fernie Wilderness Adventures*, T4236704, www.fernie adventures.com backcountry skiing, cat-skiing, hiking, fishing, lodge accommodation. *Fernie Fat Tire Adventures*, T1888-4237849, www.ferniefattire.com backcountry mountain bike tours in BC and the Rockies. *Mountain Pursuits*, T4236739, www.elkvalley.net/ mountainpursuits Year-round guided hiking, skiing, climbing, mountaineering.

Transport A shuttle to the ski hill leaves from several spots in town including the hostels. The *Greyhound* station is at 742 Hwy 3, T4236871, with 2 buses daily in each direction. *Dicken Bus Lines*, T4239244, www.thebigredbus.com, run a shuttle to Fernie from **Calgary** and **Cranbrook** airports.

Directory **Communications** Internet: *Mug Shots Bistro*, see Eating, above. **Canada Post**: 491 3rd Av. **Library** 492 3rd Av. **Medical services** *Rocky Mountain Health Centre*, 901 5th Av, T4234718.

Sparwood Despite the proximity of the Rockies, the road from Fernie to the Continental Divide at Crowsnest Pass (and beyond) has a dilapidated, depressed demeanour after years of mining. Tours of Canada's largest open-cast coal mine at Sparwood leave from the **Information Centre** at Highway 3/Aspen Drive. ■ *Jul and Aug Mon-Fri 1330.*

Elk River & Elk Lakes Provincial Park From here scenic Highway 43 follows the Elk River 35 km north to the attractively situated wilderness village of **Elkford**. A further 63 km of gravel road then leads to the headquarters and principal trailhead of Elk Lakes Provincial Park. Most of this remote park is above the treeline in the front ranges of the Rockies, with many peaks and glaciers, a host of colourful wild flowers in summer, and as good a chance of spotting wildlife as other humans. The main 7-8-km trail leads past Lower and Upper Elk Lakes, then follows a couple of creeks to the Petain Creek Waterfalls and Glacier, with views of the prominent Castelnau Hanging Glacier. There are wilderness campgrounds at Lower Elk Lake, halfway at Nivelle Creek, and at the falls. Other trails give access to **Peter Lougheed Provincial Park** to the north (see page 304) and **Height of the Rockies Provincial Park** to the west. There are no facilities, and those planning more than a rudimentary hike should get the Nat Topo Map 82J/11 (Kananaskis Lakes).

A second rough road leads 55 km east of Elkford to the equally stunning wilderness of **Mount Armstrong** (2,792 m). Before going anywhere, call in at Elkford's **Information Centre** at Highway 43/Michel Road, T8654362, where you can also get directions to the municipal **campground** (**F**) and the main local attraction, **Josephine Falls**.

Sleeping There are 2 pretty standard places to stay in town. **D** *Hi Rock Inn*, 2 Chauncey St, T8652226, and **E** *Elkford Motor Inn*, 808 Michel Rd, T8652211.

Northern British Columbia

Introducing Northern BC

North of the TransCanada Highway lies a vast underpopulated hinterland of almost unimaginable proportions. Big animals such as grizzly bears, moose, elk, and caribou still survive here in

significant numbers. Hunting is big business, and the rivers and shores are renowned for their fishing. Although the scenery lacks the diversity of the South, the landscapes along one section of the Cassiar Highway, and the glacier-lined road to **Stewart**, challenge even those along the Icefields Parkway. First Nations culture is much more alive here, particularly along the **Skeena River** and on **Haida Gwaii**, the 'Galapagos of the North'. In **Gwaii Haanas Park** you can tour abandoned ancient Haida villages. The **Cariboo-Chilcotin** is a Wild West ranching landscape rich in ghost towns and Gold Rush history, including **Barkerville**, the ultimate living museum. There are one-off oddities too, like the **Nisga'a Lava Bed Park**. Even the dull **Alaska Highway** (Highway 97) has the formidable **Liard Hot Springs**.

Highway 97 and **Highway 5** run north from Southern BC, the latter offering little besides access to the wonderful Wells Gray Provincial Park, and a jaw-dropping encounter with the Rockies' highest peak, **Mount Robson**. Both lead to the **Yellowhead** (Highway 16), and **Prince George**, the undisputed gateway to the North, and the pleasant fishing port of **Prince Rupert**. Just beyond Hazelton, the **Cassiar** (Highway 37) shoots north towards the Yukon and Alaska, a highly recommended trip.

Northern BC

> **Things to do in Northern BC**
>
> - Visit 'Ksan Historical Village and drive the *Hands of History* tour of First Nations villages.
> - Witness the dramatic lunar landscapes of Nisga'a Memorial Lava Bed Park.
> - Tour remote, abandoned Haida villages in Gwaii Haanas National Park.
> - Drive the scenic road to Stewart and see the astounding Bear Glacier.
> - Watch grizzly bears fish for salmon outside Hyder, Alaska.
> - Take a dip in the beautiful Liard hot springs.

The Cariboo

Phone code: 250
Colour map 1, grid A6

*The most obvious route to Prince George and the North runs through the middle of a vast plateau between the Coast and Cariboo Mountain Ranges. This is dry ranching country whose broad horizons are laden with endless pine forests and literally thousands of lakes. Apart from **anglers**, for whom this is a paradise, most people find that its scenic appeal runs thin fairly quickly, and without a single town of any interest, the monotony is only broken by constant reminders of the area's **gold-mining** past. The region's main towns are Williams Lake and Quesnel, but the only real attraction is **Barkerville**, an extensive reconstruction of that Gold Rush town. Nearby are **Bowron Lakes**, which have been voted one of the world's top ten canoeing destinations.*

Ins & outs   *Greyhound* buses operate between **Prince George** and **Cache Creek**, with connections to **Kamloops** and **Vancouver**. Sadly, however, the *Cariboo Prospector* train has been discontinued. For more information, go to **www.cariboo-net.com**

History   Major finds around Yale in the lower Fraser Valley encouraged prospectors to spread north, their path soon facilitated by the building of the Cariboo Wagon Road in 1861. Starting in Lillooet, this stagecoach route eventually led to Barkerville, where the ultimate lucky strike occurred in 1862, drawing some 100,000 hopefuls up the road by the end of the decade. Today's Cariboo Highway (Highway 97) follows most of that original route, passing former resting and provision stops with names like 100 Mile House, spelling out (incorrectly, as it turned out) the distances from Lillooet.

Clinton   Today's Cariboo Highway begins at Cache Creek (see page 208), whose dry bluffs and colourful rock formations set the right tone for the drive to come. Clinton, 40 km north, is one of the better places for anyone who would like to experience the cowboy lifestyle first-hand by staying on a working Guest Ranch (also known as Dude Ranches; T4592640 for information). A good map will show that a vast area west and north of here is covered with provincial parks and a network of dirt roads that connect isolated villages, ranches and remnants of mining communities. There are endless possibilities for exploring if you have a reliable vehicle and a passion for this kind of scenery and history.

100 Mile House   Just south of 100 Mile House, Highway 24 heads east, connecting with Highway 5 at **Little Fort**, 93 km north of Kamloops. This is known as the Interlakes Highway, highly renowned for its fishing, with over 100 well-stocked lakes of various sizes to choose from. 100 Mile House itself is a dull town, but has all necessary services. The **Visitor Information Centre** at 422 Highway 97

South, T3955353, www.tourism.100mile.com, can provide details about fishing, bird-watching at the **Marsh-Wildlife Sanctuary**, the 200 km of groomed Nordic skiing trails in the area, and the two-day canoe-trip that joins 12 small lakes in **Moose Valley Provincial Park**, some 30 km to the west. To the east a rough road via Canim Lake gives access to the western edge of **Wells Gray Provincial Park**.

Sleeping and eating The best of many places to stay in town is the **C** *Red Coach Inn*, 170 Hwy 97 N, T3952266. There's a **F** *Municipal RV Park* at 385 Birch Av, T3952434. Cheaper budget motels are north at **Lac La Hache**. 108 Mile, to the north, has the best lodging, at **B** *Hills Health and Guest Ranch*, T7915225, and the best food at the golf course.

This boring town has the area's most useful year-round **Visitor Information Centre** at 1148 Broadway St, T3925025, www.bcadventure.con/wlcc Otherwise it is best recommended for the excellent local mountain biking. Hiking is also good in the Williams Lake Valley, and there are a few decent local golf courses. Rafting trips are operated down the Farwell Canyon to the west, and whitewater kayaking is worth looking into. The **Williams Lake Stampede**, which was first held in 1919 and takes place on the weekend closest to 1 July, is one of the biggest and oldest of its kind in BC, with over 13,000 spectators for events like steer wrestling and chuck wagon racing (T3926585).

Williams Lake

Sleeping The nicest places to stay are **C** *Drummond Lodge and Motel*, 1 km S at 1405 Hwy 97, T3925334, with a nice setting, and lake views; and **D** *Rowat's Waterside B&B*, 1397 Borland Rd, T3927395. 4 rooms on the lake with lounge, decks, en suite baths and full breakfast. **Camping F** *Williams Lake Stampede Campground*, at 850 Mackenzie St, T3986718, is not as nice as **F** *Wildwood Campsite*, 13 km north on the highway, T9894711. Both have facilities for RVs.

Sports Mountain biking Ask at *Red Shreds Bike Store*, 95 1st Av, T3987873, www.redshreds.com

To the west, the extraordinary **Chilcotin Highway** (Highway 20) runs 456 km to Bella Coola (see page 272). If visiting Tweedsmuir Provincial Park, be sure to pick up the indispensible blue *BC Parks* map and/or the relevent Nat Topo map(s) in Williams Lake, as well as any supplies. To the east, a little circuit could be made along dirt roads to the small, pretty towns of **Likely** and **Horsefly**, both close to lakes and full of Gold Rush artefacts. The former in particular is the main base for exploring old mining sites and ghost towns such as **Bullion Pit** and **Quesnel Forks**. Likely also gives access to the major **Quesnel Lake**, which keen paddlers could follow east to the remote and beautiful **Cariboo Mountains Provincial Park**.

Around Williams Lake

   Xats'ull Heritage Village, T9892323, is situated on a plateau overlooking the Fraser River, 33 km north of Williams Lake in Soda Creek. The first of its kind in North America, it features pit houses, petroglyphs, a sweat lodge, tepees and native artefacts, and operates one- and 12-day cultural programmes where crafts and skills are taught, stories told, food and lodging provided, etc.

Sleeping Close to Likely are **D** *Neilsen's Lakeshore Cabins*, Cedar Creek Rd, T7902258, and **D-E** *Moreshead Lake Resort*, Likely Rd, T7902323, both with basic cabins and campsites.

Quesnel North of Williams Lake, the reappearance of the Fraser River breathes some fresh life into the scenery. But the forests in these parts have been horribly decimated, so it comes as no surprise that Quesnel is an ugly logging town. Gold Rush enthusiasts might enjoy the four-day **Billy Barker Days Festival** held the third week in July, and a visit to **Quesnel Museum and Archives**, the best museum in the Cariboo. ■ *Open year round. $2. 703 Carson Av, T9929580.* It's located in Le Bourdais Park along with the **Visitor Information Centre**, T9928716, www.city.quesnel.bc.ca Ask about the hoodoos in Pinnacle Provincial Park to the west, fly fishing and canoeing on the Blackwater River, and the 420-km **Mackenzie Heritage Trail** that ends near Bella Coola, one of the most demanding treks in Canada.

Barkerville

Colour map 1, grid A5 The main reason to stop anywhere in the Cariboo is **Barkerville Provincial Historic Park**, 82 km east of Quesnel. The most impressive monument to local history, it's also set in the refreshingly beautiful scenery of the Cariboo Mountains. Billy Barker struck it lucky here in 1862, and for the next 10 years Barkerville took its turn at being the biggest town north of San Francisco and west of Chicago.

Today it is the biggest and best of the many reconstructed Heritage Towns scattered around the country, with over 100 historic displays and demonstrations, and 125 restored buildings full of costumed, role-playing staff. The **Theatre Royal** features live vaudeville shows, and there are plenty of restaurants, including a Chinese one in the old **Chinatown**, and shops selling their wares. You can pan for gold, get photographed in period costume, tour the cemetery, and ride in a stage coach. ■ *May-Sep 0800-2000. $8, $2.25 concessions; $5 for stage coach ride; $9, $5 concessions for theatre; all-inclusive package $23.50, $13.75 concessions. There is no public transport from Quesnel apart from Gold Safari Tours, T9943302.*

Sleeping There are historic rooms right in the village at **A** *St George Hotel*, T9940008. 7 rooms in
& eating 1890s style, some with en suite, breakfast included; and **B-C** *Kelly House B&B*, T9943328. 3 rooms, shared or private bath, down duvets. **F** *Barkerville Provincial Park*, 3 km east, T3984414, has 168 sites in 3 campgrounds, but reservations are still recommended in summer. There are showers and hiking trails. In **Wells**, 8 km west, a charming, picturesque town that has attracted many artists, there is **B** *The Wells Hotel*, 2341 Pooley St, T9943427, a homely heritage inn with comfy rooms, a pub and a restaurant.

Bowron Lake Barkerville provides the easiest access to Bowron Lake Provincial Park, 24
Provincial Park km further east. This mountain wilderness, the top of a protected belt that runs north from Wells Gray Provincial Park, offers swimming, hiking, and camping, but is especially renowned as one of the ten best canoe routes in the world. The 116-km circuit of 11 lakes with eight portages takes a minimum of seven to 10 days.

Park essentials Access is limited, with reservations and a registration fee of $55 per person paid at the **Visitor Centre** in the campground, T4355622. For cabins, campsites, canoe rentals or full tours, contact the luxurious **AL-C** *Beckers Lodge Resort*, T9928864, www.beckers.bc.ca, or **D** *Bowron Lake Lodge*, T9922733, www.bowronlakelodge.com There is also a summer-only wooded campground (**F**, T3984414) with 25 sites, and a visitor centre. Again, *Gold Safari Tours*, T9943302, provide the only transport.

The Chilcotin

One of Canada's most unlikely roads, the Chilcotin Highway (Highway 20) — Colour map 1, grid A3
heads 456 km west from Williams Lake to Bella Coola, one of the last great wil-
derness settlements, whose only other access is by ferry from Port Hardy at the
northern tip of Vancouver Island. The first 350-km stretch passes through the
remote but flat, rather monotonous scenery of the Chilcotin Plateau. **Heckman**
Pass *(1,524 m) marks the end of the plateau and start of a 30-km section of nar-*
*row, winding, unpaved road, culminating in '***The Hill***', 10 extraordinary kilo-*
metres of steep, brake-grinding switchbacks with up to 18% grades. Before 1953,
a 60-km gap existed here, considered impassible by engineers and economically
unfeasible by bureaucrats. Finally, the locals built it themselves in a mere three
years, and named it the 'Freedom Road'. The major highlight along the way is the
exceptional **Tweedsmuir Provincial Park**, *BC's largest park, containing some*
of the most remote trails in the Coast Mountains.

There are no buses to or around the Chilcotin. Access is by **plane**, or **ferry** from **Port** — **Ins & outs**
Hardy, Vancouver Island (see page 185).

As in the Cariboo, those enflamed by this kind of country will find much to — **The Chilcotin**
explore on the back roads mostly to the south. **Bull Canyon Park**, 10 km west — **Plateau**
of Alexis Creek, is a good spot to admire the glacial blue water of the Chilcotin
River and some fine rock walls. A little further west, a rough road leads to
Nazko Lakes Provincial Park, where a 20-km canoe trip can be made
between six lakes with easy portages. At Chilanko Forks, a fair 12-km road
leads to scenic **Puntzi Lake**, with good fishing, visiting pelicans and trumpeter swans, and 360° views.

From **Tatla Lake**, helicopter companies such as *White Saddle Air*,
T4761182, whisk hardcore enthusiasts to the Coast Mountains' highest peak,
Mount Waddington (4,016 m), or its largest body of water, Chilko Lake. Also
Canada's highest major lake, Chilko is contained by the vast wilderness of
Ts'ylos Provincial Park, which can be reached via 60 km of rough roads. The
Chilko River's Lava Canyon is well known for its river rafting with a drop of
19 m/km over a 24-km stretch, including the infamous 'White Mile'. Contact
Hyak Wilderness Adventures, T1800-6637238, www.hyak.com

After the fishing, trail-riding and float-plane centres of Nimpo Lake and
Anahim Lake, the plateau finally crests at **Heckman Pass**, before descending
'the Hill' into Tweedsmuir Provincial Park.

Sleeping D *Puntzi Lake Resort*, T4811176, 1 of 5, has lakeside cabins and campsites,
canoe and boat rentals.

Tweedsmuir Provincial Park

British Columbia's largest park, Tweedsmuir contains 8,967 sq km of — Colour map 3, grid C4
breathtaking wilderness, spanning the full gamut of peaks, glaciers, wild- — Pick up the blue BC
flower meadows, waterfalls, forests and lakes, and is home to thriving popu- — Parks map/guide in
lations of black and grizzly bears, moose, caribou and mountain goats. — Williams Lake
Governor General Baron Tweedsmuir came here in 1937 and said 'I have
now travelled over most of Canada and have seen many wonderful things,
but I have seen nothing more beautiful…than the great park which BC has
done me the honour to call by my name'. On its eastern edge the plateau

Northern BC

gives way to the **Rainbow Range**, so named for the wonderful spectrum of reds, oranges, yellows and purples present in the fragmented layers of rock and eroded lava. The park's western boundary is marked by the giant granite peaks of the rugged Coast Mountains.

A number of hiking trails lead from the Rainbow Range trailhead, interconnecting to provide a variety of routes. The **Octopus Lake** trail is an easy 16-km hike (one-way) to a campsite. The **Crystal Lake** trail is a difficult 25-km hike with 1,000 m elevation gain, leading to the Mackenzie Valley close to the Rainbow Cabin. Both can be extended to a cabin and campsite at Tanya Lakes, 25 km further on. For guided horse-riding trips, contact David Dorsey Jr, Anahim Lake, T7423251.

On the highway, midway through the park at Atnarko River, is the main campsite, with water, toilets and wood. Nearby, an old tote road, suitable only for high-clearance vehicles, leads 13 km to the **Hunlen Falls/Turner Lake** trailhead. The spectacular Hunlen Falls is a major draw, plummeting 260 m and disappearing in a cloud of spray. But the trail there is a difficult 16.4-km hike with an elevation gain of 2,000 m. Just to the south is Turner Lake, starting point of an excellent 19-km canoe route whose chain of seven lakes is connected by easy portages, with six campsites and great fishing. Rentals are available at the lake. Further west is **Stuie**, the only village in the park. Nearby is the best of the park's short hikes, the two-hour **Burnt Bridge Loop**.

Sleeping and eating As well as the campgrounds mentioned above, **A-B** *Tweedsmuir Lodge*, Stuie, T9822402, www.tweedsmuirlodge.com, has rooms, chalets, hot tub, and dining by reservation.

Bella Coola

Phone code: 250
Colour map 1, grid A2

If you have the money to charter a plane for a flight-seeing tour, this would be the place to do it

From Tweedsmuir Park, Highway 20 leads through Bella Coola Valley, mythical home of the thunderbird, whose nest is formed by the bowl-shaped walls and peaks. Sitting at the end of a long, saltwater fjord, Bella Coola's chief asset is its stunning scenery. The town is surrounded by utter wilderness, home to some of the healthiest animal life in the country, including particularly large grizzlies. Rafting, kayaking or canoeing down the river are other great ways to appreciate the surroundings. Salmon fishing is also particularly good hereabouts.

Otherwise, there's little to do but watch the activity around the Marina or go for a hike, unless your visit coincides with the annual **rodeo** at the end of June, or the **Discovery Coast Music Festival** at the end of July. There's no Visitor Information Centre, but information can be obtained at T7995919, or www.centralcoastbc.com

History The Bella Coolas, or Nuxalk Natives, depended for thousands of years on the abundance of salmon in their rivers. Alexander Mackenzie (see box), who was helped to the ocean by them in 1793, named the place where they met 'Friendly Village' in honour of their hospitality. Today their descendants can still be seen catching and smoking fish in the age-old way. About half of today's non-aboriginal population can trace their heritage back to the first white settlers, a group of 120 Norwegians who were led here from Minnesota by Pastor Christian Saugstad in 1894, in order to found a Utopian society. Unlike many similar attempts, such as Sointula (see page 183), the hard-working Scandinavians managed to survive the challenge. Their story can be read at www.nordicfolks.com

Alexander Mackenzie

◀

Born in Scotland, one of a handful of intrepid North West Company explorers to open up Canada's great interior, Alexander Mackenzie became the first person to cross America, north of Mexico. It was his second attempt. The first time, he took a wrong turn and ended up travelling all the way to the Arctic Ocean along the waterway that now bears his name, which he called the 'River of

Disappointment'. Undaunted he set out again in 1793, relying on the skill of native guides and voyageurs. He followed the Peace River into the Rockies then battled his way across the mountains to the Pacific. After a close call with the fierce native Bella Bella, he retreated, having left on a large boulder Canada's most famous bit of graffiti: "Alexander Mackenzie, from Canada, by land, 22 July 1793".

Bella Coola Museum, on the highway, is mostly housed in a 19th-century **Sights** Norwegian school-house, and contains many settler relics, as well as aboriginal and Hudson's Bay Company artefacts. ■ *$2. T7995767*. In Hagensborg, 23 km east, there are more signs of the Norwegian past at the the **Sons of Norway Heritage House**, on the highway. ■ *$2.* The **Thorsen Creek Petroglyphs**, halfway between the towns, are a hundred or so aboriginal rock drawings. To visit these and other local First Nations sites with a guide, contact the local 'Goodwill Ambassador', Darren Edgar, at T7995715.

The Clayton Falls logging road, heading southwest from the Marina, leads to **Hiking** the 2.7 km **MGurr Lake** trail, a good place to view local fjords and the Coast Mountains. Further on, a trail leads to **Blue Jay Lake**, with a campground and a boardwalk trail around peat bogs, and on to **Gray Jay Lake**. A further drive leads to the **Big Cedar**, which at 4.6 m across, is one of BC's biggest trees. Directions are tricky: try the phone number or website above. From Hagensborg, Nusatsum Valley leads 25 km south to a trail and campsite at **Odegaard Falls**, and 34 km to the longer **Hammer Lake/Ape Lake** trail.

The fairly upmarket **C** *Bella Coola Valley Inn*, Mackenzie St, T7995316, is closer to the **Sleeping** ferry and has a restaurant, patio and pub. The most interesting choice by far is **& eating** **C** *Tallheo Cannery Inn*, 10 mins from the dock, boat transport provided, T9822344. 15 *There are few* rooms in a restored early-20th-century cannery village. Meals and canoe/kayak tours *lodgings in town* available. **C-D** *Bella Coola Motel*, Clayton St, T7995323, has reasonable rooms with kitchens and rental of scooters, bikes and canoes.

On the highway east, closer to the airport, is the standard **D** *Bay Motor Hotel*, at Km 14, T9822212, with a café, restaurant and pub, and the much nicer **C** *Brockton House*, at Km 16, T9822298, with large rooms, kitchens, one nice suite, a heated pool, and breakfast. Best of all is **D** *Sinclair House*, 10 km east of Hagensborg, T1888-8676668, a 3-room B&B with private bath, guest lounge, library, jacuzzi, and dinners by arrangement.

Camping F *Hagen Haven RV Park and Campground*, is 8 km out on the highway, T7995659. On a creek with showers, laundry and hook-ups. Nicer is **F** *Bailey Bridge Campsite*, off Hwy 20 on Salommpt Rd, Hagensborg, T9822342. Located on river with showers and 4 basic cabins with kitchenettes (**E**).

For food and coffee, there's the *Cozy Corner Café*, at Cliff St/Burke Av.

For **plane charters**, there's *Bella Coola Air*, T9822957, or *Sharp Wings*, T9822957. Floating **Tour operators** down the river with *Heritage River Rafting*, T7995603. For **sea-kayak** and **canoe** tours, try *Coyote Tours*, T7995136. For **fishing**, contact *Bella Coola Outfitting*, T9460640.

Northern BC

Transport **Air** The airport is in Hagensborg. *Pacific Coastal Airlines*, T9822225, have scheduled daily flights to **Vancouver**, and **Port Hardy** on Vancouver Island, and can be chartered. **Bus** There are currently no buses to Bella Coola, but ask in Williams Lake. **Ferry** *BC Ferries*, T3863779 or 1888-2233779, www.bcferries.com, operate the *Discovery Coast Passage* between **Port Hardy** and Bella Coola, with some services also stopping at the tiny coastal communities of **McLoughlin Bay** (Bella Bella), **Namu**, **Shearwater**, **Klemtu**, and **Ocean Falls**. Summer only, reservations essential. Schedules may change, but currently services leave Bella Coola on Mon (direct) and Fri at 0800, Wed at 0730; leave Port Hardy on Tue and Thu (direct) at 0930, and Sat at 1130. Direct ferries take 13 hrs. $103/$51 plus $205 for a car. Kayak/canoe $13, bike $6.50.

Kamloops to Prince George

*Sometimes confusingly called the South Yellowhead, Highway 5 is a longer route north than the Cariboo. Passing between the Cariboo and Rocky Mountains, its scenery is stimulating enough, but none of the towns on the way offer any interest beyond rudimentary accommodation and food. **Wells Gray Provincial Park**, however, is one of the most rewarding parks in BC, and relatively underused thanks to the proximity of the high-profile Rockies. That range's highest point, the perfectly proportioned **Mount Robson**, swings suddenly into view north of Valemount, and is so exquisitely framed by the highway heading north that almost every driver feels obliged to stop and take a photo. **Valemount** is a good base for the classic Mount Robson/Berg Lake hike (see page 338), with plenty of places to stay. Ask at the **Visitor Information Centre**, 99 Gorse St, T5664846, www.valemount-bc-org At Tête Jaune Cache, Highway 5 meets the Yellowhead proper, which heads east to Edmonton via **Jasper**, and northwest through duller scenery to Prince George.*

Ins & outs 2 daily *Greyhound* buses each way cover this route, as do 3 weekly *VIA Rail* trains on their way to Jasper.

Wells Gray Provincial Park

Phone code: 250
Colour map 2, grid A1

Situated in the Cariboo Mountains, The scenery in Wells Gray is extremely varied, including large lakes and river systems, some impressive waterfalls, extinct volcanos, lava beds, and mineral springs. Deer, caribou, moose and bears are frequently seen, there's good fishing in most of the lakes and rivers, and bird-watching at the abandoned Ray Farm. The south of the park has many alpine meadows, while the inaccessible north and east edges are lined with peaks and glaciers. As in the Rockies, summers can be quite wet, the driest month being April. While there are many first-class hiking and canoeing trails, you don't have to walk far to see some of the most impressive natural phenomena.

The park entrance is at Hemp Creek, 40 km from **Clearwater** on the mainly paved Clearwater Valley Road, with no public transport. At the junction with Highway 5 is the very helpful **Information Centre**, T6742646, which provides details on road, trail, campground and weather conditions, sells topographic maps, hands out free blue *BC Parks* maps, and has some displays on local human and natural history. They can also put you in touch with operators for horse riding, float planes, guided canoeing and whitewater rafting. On the way to the park is **Spahats Creek/Falls**, where the creek has carved a 122-m deep canyon through layers of lava. There's a campground here (**F**) and a viewpoint where you can admire the canyon and 61-m falls.

Beyond Hemp Creek, a side road leads to **Green Mountain Viewing Tower** and a chance to take in the full extent of the surrounding wilderness. Further along, the wide and powerful Murtle River crashes down **Dawson Falls**, which can be observed from various vantage points along a short trail. Where the road crosses the river, the **Devil's Punch Bowl** (or Mush Bowl) is the dramatic result of fierce water cutting its way through a narrow gorge. A little further on, a 10-km side road heads left to the most impressive sight of all, the 137-m **Helmcken Falls**.

The main road continues for 23 km, passing three more vehicle accessible campsites (all **F**) and the homestead remains of **Ray Farm** on the way to **Clearwater Lake**. Linked by a short portage to Azure Lake, this is ideal canoeing country, with a possible 102-km round-trip, fishing, and campsites all the way. Canoes can be rented from *Clearwater Lake Tours*, T6743052. A 2-km trail leads from Clearwater Lake campground to the **Dragon's Tongue** lava flow, while the 12-km **Chain Meadow Loop** takes you to numerous viewpoints.

From **Blue River**, some 90 km north of Clearwater, a narrow, winding 24-km gravel road leads to the large and beautiful **Murtle Lake** and more canoe routes. From the road's end it's a 2.5-km hike to the canoe launch, and a further 1.5 km to a campground on a sandy beach. All the other campsites and trails dotted around the lake are accessible by canoe only. **Mahood Lake** on the park's western boundary is reached on an 88-km road from **100 Mile House** (see page 268). There's a campground, trails to Canim and Deception Falls, and more good canoeing.

B *Helmcken Falls Lodge*, by the park entrance, T6743657, has decent rooms, dining, **Sleeping** trail rides and guided hiking and canoeing. **B** *Wells Gray Guest Ranch*, 9 km before the **& eating** entrance, T6742792. Log cabins with kitchens and shower. Restaurant. All the park's vehicle-accessible **campgrounds** fill up in summer, but can be reserved at T8513000. A small fee is charged for wilderness camping.

Otherwise, there are plenty of choices in **Clearwater**, including the upmarket **B** *Clearwater Lodge*, 331 Eden Rd, T6743080. Queen beds, kitchenettes, jacuzzi, pool, hot tub, sauna, restaurant. **D** *Jasper Way Inn*, 57 Old North Thompson Hwy E, T6743345. Good views over Dutch Lake, kitchens. **D** *Wells Gray Inn*, on the highway, T6742214, Not such a good location but comfortable and one of the few places to eat. There are also lots of choices for **camping**, but the most pleasant are west at **F** *North Thompson River Provincial Park*, T8513000, and east at **F** *Birch Island*, T6743991. **Blue River** also has lots of choices, including the comfortable, European-style **C** *Glacier Mountain Lodge*, 869 Shell Rd, T6732393, breakfast included; and the cheap but reasonable **D** *Blue River Motel*, Spruce St, T6738387.

Prince George

Situated at the crossroads of the only highways heading north, No 97 and No 16, Prince George is the most important service centre and transport hub for an incredibly vast region, and almost impossible to avoid for those heading that way. This is also the focus for some of the most heavily logged land in Canada, resulting in an ugly industrial town choked with mills, timber yards and processing plants. The best advice is to pick up supplies, then escape as quickly as possible. For a tour of the giant forestry operations, contact Tourism Prince George, whose two **Visitor Information Centres**, www.tourismpg.bc.ca, are at the junction of the highways, (summer only, 0900-2000, T5635493), and Downtown at 1198 Victoria Street and 15th Avenue (Monday-Saturday 0900-1600, longer in summer, T5623700).

Phone code: 250
Colour map3, grid C6
Population: 72,406
Altitude: 575 m

Northern BC

If you have a little time to kill, the best place to head is **Fort George Park**, on the Fraser River about ten minutes' walk southeast of Downtown. As well as a Miniature Railway, playground, waterpark and Native Cemetery, it contains the **Fraser-Fort George Regional Museum**, also known as Exploration Place. A number of heritage buildings from the city's foundation remain, along with artefacts and displays. ■ *Summer, daily 1000-1700, otherwise Wed-Sun. $9, $6 concessions. T5621612, www.theexplorationplace.com*

From here, the pleasant Heritage River Trail, an 8-km loop that connects a number of parks, follows the Fraser 2 km to **Cottonwood Island Nature Park**, which contains several interpretive trails and the **Railway and Forestry Museum**. A collection of steam engines, assorted railway relics and forestry artefacts are presented mostly in the open air. ■ *May-Oct, daily 0900-1700. $6, $5 seniors, $3 children. T5637351, www.pgrfm.bc.ca Take River Rd from 1st Av.*

There are also a couple of galleries worth a visit: the **Native Art Gallery**, has a good collection of quality local and national native works for sale. ■ *1600 3rd Av, T6147726.* **Two Rivers Gallery** has consistently impressive exhibitions. ■ *$4, $3 concessions, 725 Civic Plaza, T6147800.*

Sleeping
■ *on map, opposite*

Downtown A *Coast Inn*, 770 Brunswick St, T5630121. Restaurants, pool, sauna gym, lounge and pub. D *Credo Manor B&B*, 6872 O'Grady Rd, T9648142. Spacious, comfortable rooms, breakfast. D *Downtown Motel*, 650 Dominion, T5639241. About the nicest of the conveniently central budget options. D *Queensway Court Motel*, 1616 Queensway St, T5625068. One of many budget options. E *National Hostel*, 1201 1st Av, T5647010. Private rooms only. Shared bath, kitchen and common room. **Highway 97 south** D *Carmel Inn*, No1502, T5646339. Standard but reasonable. F *Fraser River RV Park*, T3304453. One of the better campgrounds, with wooded sites on the river, and showers. Off **Highway 97 north** are C *Esther's Inn*, 1151 Commercial Dr, off 10th Av, T5624131. Sauna, pool, hot tub, lounge, restaurant; C *Sandman Inn & Suites*, 1650 Central St, T5638131. Suites with kitchenette, sauna, pool. **Highway 16 west** D *Bon Voyage Motor Inn*, No 4222, T9642333. New rooms, restaurant. E *College Heights Motel*, 5 km from town, T9644708. Cheap and grotty. F *Blue Spruce RV Park*, 5 km west of highway junction on Kimball Rd, T8647272. Pool, laundry, showers, playground.

Eating & drinking
■ *on map, opposite*

The best upmarket option is the **expensive** *Da Moreno*, 1493 3rd Av, T5647922. 2 great **mid-range** options are: *Buffalo Brewing Co*, 611 Brunswick St. A funky, modern interior, lively atmosphere, lots of drink and food specials, good beer brewed on the premises, and a decent menu; *Foodteller*, 508 George St, T5620450. European and Canadian cuisine in an elegant interior with a stylish bar. Fancy but casual. For coffee, head for *Javva Mugga Mocha*, 304 George St.

Entertainment **Cinema** *Famous Players*, 172-1600 15th Av, T6123993. **Theatre** *Prince George Playhouse*, 2833 Recreation Place, T5638401.

Shopping **Camping supplies** *Centre City Surplus*, 1222 4th Av. A very impressive range of outdoors equipment/clothing.

Transport **Air** Prince George's airport, 4141 Airport Rd, T9632400, is 10 km east of town off Hwy 16 on the Old Cariboo Hwy, T9632400. The *Airporter* shuttle, T5632220, stops anywhere in town, $8, $2.50 concessions. *Emerald Taxi*, T5633333. There are at least 12 flights in and out per day, often cheaper than the bus. *WestJet*, T9638123, has 5 daily flights from **Calgary** and 2 from **Vancouver** via Kelowna. *Canadian Regional* has 7 daily flights from **Vancouver**. *Central Mountain Air*, T1888-2472262, 3 daily to **Dawson Creek**, and 1 to **Calgary** and **Smithers**. *Peace Air*,T5633060, to **Grande Prairie**, **Fort St John** and **Fort Nelson**.

Bus The *Greyhound* station is at 1566 12th Av, about 5 blocks from Downtown, T5645454, www.greyhound.ca Take No 3 or No 4 bus from Victoria St. 2 buses daily link with **Prince Rupert** ($95), 2 with **Jasper** ($50), 3 with **Vancouver** ($100), and 2 with **Terrace** ($75). For **Regional Transit** information, T5630011.

Train *VIA Rail*, T1800-5618630, www.viarail.ca, run 3 trains weekly to and from Jasper ($73) and **Prince Rupert** ($94), much cheaper if booked 7 days ahead. The station is Downtown on 1st Av (Hwy 16), reached by buses No 1 and No 3.

Airlines *Canadian Regional*, T18882472262. **Banks** *Scotiabank*, 390 Victoria; *TD   Directory Bank*, 299 Victoria. **Communications** Internet: *Isle Pierre Pie Co*, 409 George. **Laundry** *White Wash*, 1-231 George. **Library** 887 Dominion. **Medical services** *Prince George Regional Hospital*, 2000 15th Av, T5652000.

Prince George to Prince Rupert

This is a key route, connecting with the Cassiar Highway and Prince Rupert's ferries to Haida Gwaii, Alaska and Vancouver Island. But it's mostly a monotonous drive with little reason to stop before the Hazeltons, where a cluster of First Nations villages make for an interesting tour. Beyond here, the Yellowhead joins the powerful Skeena, BC's second biggest river, whose fantastic broad valley is flanked by wild mountain scenery. A recommended diversion from Terrace is up the Nass Valley to see the **Nisga'a Lava Bed Park**.

Between Fraser Lake and Houston, the highway runs through the Lakes Dis- **West to** trict with good fishing in over 300 wilderness lakes. There's prime **Smithers** bird-watching at the **Vanderhoof Bird Sanctuary**, located on the Pacific Flyway. Fort St James, 53 km north of here, gives onto a 300-km network of lakes and rivers ideal for canoeing. Its **National Historic Park** is a restored Hudson's Bay Company post staffed by costumed interpreters. Drivers should try

Northern BC

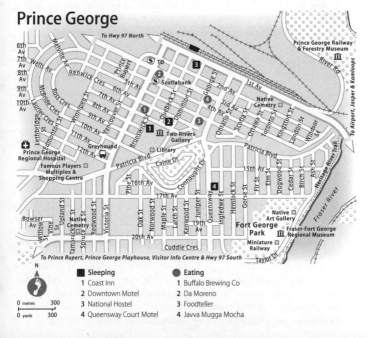

Prince George

Sleeping
1 Coast Inn
2 Downtown Motel
3 National Hostel
4 Queensway Court Motel

Eating
1 Buffalo Brewing Co
2 Da Moreno
3 Foodteller
4 Javva Mugga Mocha

0 metres 300
0 yards 300

to make it to **Telkwa**, 360 km west of Prince George, a pretty riverfront village full of heritage buildings, with a charming pioneer museum that provides *Walking Tour* brochures.

Sleeping C *Douglas Motel*, Hwy 16 W, T8465679. Nice log cabins with fireplaces, kitchens, and patios. River views, sauna. **F** *Tyhee Lake Provincial Park*, T8477320, has 59 nice forested sites, trails and a beach.

Smithers

Smithers, 10 km further on, is one of the most pleasant towns in Northern BC. There are plenty of hiking, biking and skiing opportunites in the area, many in the **Babine Mountains Recreation Area**, 15 km east, and at **Hudson Bay Mountain**. To do the first-class hike up the latter, ask for directions at the **Information Centre**, 1411 Court Street, T8475072. There are two options, a very steep 4-km route via **Glacier Gulch** with 927-m elevation gain, and the much gentler 9-km hike via **Crater Lake**, much of it through meadows, with 1,076 m gain. There are fossil beds to explore at **Driftwood Canyon Provincial Park**, 11 km northeast. The Babine and Bulkley Rivers are good for canoeing, kayaking or river rafting. Across from the Information Centre, the Central Park Building contains the **Bulkley Valley Museum**, T8475322, and the **Smithers Art Gallery**, T8473898, both worth a quick look.

Sleeping and eating B-C *Hudson Bay Lodge*, 3251 Hwy 16 E, T8474581, www.hblodge.com The best option, this attractive hotel also has a restaurant, pub and café. The cheapest option is the reasonable **E** *Florence Motel*, 4160 Hwy 16 W, T8472678. For wholesome food in a friendly atmosphere, try *Mountainside Café*, 3763 4th Av. For coffee, there's *Mountain Eagle Books and Cappuccino*, 3775 3rd Av.

The Hazeltons

The region around Old, New and South Hazelton has for 4,000 years been home to the Gitxsan Wet'suwet'an people, the most easterly of the West Coast First Nations. Like all Native American groups, their way of life was irrevocably disrupted by the white man's arrival, but a decision by the tribe's elders in the 1950s to preserve what remained of their legacy has made this one of the best places in Western Canada to encounter aboriginal culture. At the **Visitor Information Centre** on the highway in **New Hazelton**, T8426071, you can pick up a copy of the *Hands of History* self-guided driving circuit, which covers over 110 km of First Nations villages. Many have collections of both old and new totem poles, as well as traditionally significant sites. Among the most interesting are **Kispiox**, 13 km north, **Gitwangak** (Kitwanga), 43 km west at the junction with Highway 37, and **Gitanyow** (Kitwancool), 35 km north of there.

Old Hazelton, 8 km north of Highway 16 on a secondary road, is a nicely restored 19th-century sternwheeler terminus full of heritage buildings, including a **museum**. A pair of totems mark the entrance to the regional highlight, 'Ksan Historical Village.

'Ksan Historical Village & Museum

This 1970 reconstruction of a settlement that had stood on the site for centuries until 1870, was the main focus of attempts to resurrect the dying culture. The grounds contain seven colourful longhouses, many totems, an art gallery, a gift shop and a carving studio where skilled artists can be seen working on plaques, poles, masks and bowls. The museum contains a host of artefacts such as robes and headdresses, all collected from within a 50-km radius and still used in ceremonies. In July and August, the 'Ksan Performing Arts Group put on the celebrated *Breath of our Grandfathers*, a performance which explores the potlatch celebrations outlawed in 1884 (see page 457).

King of the fish

Anyone who doubts the salmon's status as lord of the fishy realm need only contemplate the mysterious life-span of this remarkable creature. All five species of Pacific salmon are born in gravel beds in streams. Laid in the autumn, their eggs are incubated through the winter by ice and snow up to several feet deep. In spring they emerge as inch-long fry, then spend up to a year or more in a nearby river or lake before heading downstream to the ocean. One early summer day, after about three to five years of greedy feeding and extensive growth, an unknown impulse compels them to return to their birthplace. For pink, chum and coho salmon this is generally a matter of a few hundred kilometres or less, but chinooks and sockeyes have to cover distances of up to 1,600 km, and do so at speeds of more than 50 km per day. While sockeye is the best species for eating, chinooks are especially sought by sport fishers: they live the longest and are also by far the heaviest salmon, weighing up to 54 kg. Little is know of the means by which these fish navigate such vast distances back to remote backwaters. Some scientists believe it's the result of a highly developed sense of smell, others put it down to an ability to work out direction from the stars. For weeks the salmon struggle upstream against natural and man-made obstacles, jumping up steep waterfalls and negotiating fierce rapids. What's more, the entire journey is undertaken without food. On the way, they change colour, the furthest voyagers turning from their normal blue-tinged silver to varying shades of red, even brilliant crimson. In some species the males mutate considerably, gaining a humped back and sharply hooked nose. Eventually, beaten and bruised, they reach the exact place of their birth and, after enacting the reproductive stage of the life cycle, promptly die.

The best places to see the salmon are on the Adams River in the Shuswap, the Campbell River on Vancouver Island, or around the Skeena River between Prince George and Prince Rupert in Northern BC.

■ *Summer 0900-1700. Giftshop and museum open year round. $2. Guided tours are conducted by native women, summer only ($6). T8425544, www.ksan.org*

Sleeping There are a couple of motels in **New Hazelton**, including **E** *Bulkley Valley Motel*, 4444 Hwy 16, T8426817. Otherwise you can stay at the pretty riverfront **F** *'Ksan Campground*, T8425297.

Tour operators For a guided tour, canoe rentals, or a drifting trip, contact *Skeena Eco-Expeditions*, T8425249.

With the entrance of the Skeena, a river capable of rising 5 m in a day and fluctuating 18 m between low and high tide, the scenery suddenly comes alive. The broad valley is framed within magnificent mountain peaks such as the photogenic Seven Sisters, which dominate the southern skyline west of Kitwanga. Terrace, the biggest town since Prince George, is another logging centre and almost as ugly and uninteresting. Its surroundings are quite the opposite, however, and should be experienced.

Terrace
Phone code: 250
Colour map 3, grid B3
Population: 13, 372,
Altitude: 67 m

Fishing for all kinds of salmon in the Skeena and its many tributaries is a major obsession hereabouts, and this is one of the best places to see the creeks turn red in spawning season (August-September). It's also a good region for thermal waters, such as the easily reached **Mount Layton Hot Springs**. ■ *Mon-Fri 1400-2200. Sat-Sun 1100-2200. $4.50, $2.50 concessions. 16 km south on Hwy 37 to Kitimat, T7982478.* They also have rooms (**C**). In winter, the fairly undeveloped **Shames Mountain**, 35 km away, T6388754, www.shames.8m.com, has good skiing with lots of powder. In autumn, this area is unparallelled for wild mushroom picking. The helpful **Visitor Information Centre** at 4511 Keith Avenue, T6352063, www.terrace tourism.bc.ca, can give advice on all the above, and provide a list of local hikes.

Sleeping and eating Many cheap motels line Hwy 16 W. Downtown is the upmarket **B-C** *Coast Inn of the West*, 4620 Lakelse Av, T6388141, www.coasthotels.com **D** *Costa-Lessa Motel*, 3867 Hwy 16 E, T6381885. The best-value budget choice. The best **campsites** are in provincial parks, **F** *Lakelse Lake*, 10 km south towards Kitimat, and **F** *Kleanza Creek*, 19 km east on Hwy 16. In town is the **F** *Ferry Island Campground*, follow signs from the highway, T6152951. By far the best place to eat is the excellent and moderately priced **Don Diegos**, 3212 Kalum St, T6352307, open till 2100, whose floating menu is more international than straight Mexican. Colourful, very popular, quite romantic, good portions. Sangria and a good wine list.

Nisga'a Memorial Lava Bed Park
Recently the Nisga'a made history as the first Native band to negotiate legal ownership of their traditional land in the Nass Valley

Just west of town, the Nisga'a Highway heads north to the pretty **Kitsumkalum Lake** and the remarkable Nisga'a Memorial Lava Bed Park, arguably the area's top attraction. In the mid-18th century the most recent of several volcanic eruptions wreaked havoc here, burying several villages and killing some 2,000 Nisga'a. The whole area is now a fascinatingly eery lunar landscape, with exquisite blue-green ponds and streams whose pristine quality of resurgent nature suggest a scene from a fairy tale. Many of the creeks hereabouts are good places to see salmon in season. Hiking to the **volcanic cone** is permissable only on guided tours from May to August. ■ *6 km round trip. $12, $5 concessions. T6332150.* The Park **Visitor Centre** and headquarters, T6389589, is in a striking longhouse at Vetter Creek, 26.5 km from the tour start. Pick up one of the self-guided auto tour brochures ($1.50). There's a simple but pretty campground (**F**). Ask about local B&Bs.

Prince Rupert

Phone code: 250
Colour map 3, grid B3
Population: 14,643
Altitude: 40 m

*Most travellers will be passing through Prince Rupert on their way somewhere else, but this picturesque fishing town, which enjoys a delightful location on Kaien Island at the mouth of the Skeena River, is worth a stop, especially when the sun is shining (though the euphemism 'City of Rainbows' gives a clue to how much it rains). The First Nations history, art and culture that are so integral to this region are highlighted in the excellent **museum**, while the whole town is liberally peppered with one of the largest collections of **totem poles** in the north, both Tsimshian and Haida. **Cow Town**, a pretty little harbour area dotted with gift shops and restaurants, is the place to relax. A large number of Chinese and Vietnamese descendants lend the town a cosmopolitan flavour that is unusual in the north. Plenty of worthwhile tours and excursions run from town to abandoned **native villages**, or to see **whales** or **grizzlies**. Sport fishing is a big draw for anyone who wants to go after some unusually large specimens.*

Ins & outs
For Transport details, see page 283

A **bus/ferry** service meets scheduled flights from Prince Rupert's airport, on Digby Island. *BC Ferries* operate the Inside Passage to **Port Hardy** on Vancouver Island and a regular service to Haida Gwaii. There are sailings to Skagway, Alaska. **Trains** run to **Jasper** with an overnight stop in **Prince George**, and there are daily buses to Prince George.

Tourist information
Visitor Information Centre, 215 Cow Bay Rd, T6241994, www.tourismprincerupert.com Summer Mon-Sat 0900-2000, Sun 0900-1700, winter Mon-Sat 0900-1700.

History

The Tsimshian Nation have inhabited this area for over 10,000 years, thriving on the excellent fishing. In fact, before the Europeans arrived, the harbour was one of the most densely populated areas north of Mexico. The modern city of Prince Rupert owes its existence to the vision of Charles Hays, president of the Grand Trunk Pacific Railway, who in 1909 chose the deep water harbour of Tuck Inlet as the site of BC's first planned city, the western terminus of Canada's second cross-country railroad, and an intended rival to the port of Vancouver. All of that ended abruptly when he returned from a financing trip to England aboard the Titanic. The start of the First World War and end of the rail era turned local fortunes to fishing, especially for salmon, halibut and herring and a number of cannery villages quickly sprang up along the coast. Today pulp and forestry are also important, and the city prospers from the huge volume of business it enjoys as the West Coast's only major port north of Vancouver.

Sights

Another major part of PrincPrince Rupert's major attraction is certainly the **Museum of Northern BC**, also known as Na Xbiisa Lagigyet, meaning 'Treasure Box of the Ancient Ones' in the Tsimshian language. The Great Hall illustrates the history and culture of the Northwest Coast back to the end of the last ice age, through exhibits and ancient artefacts. The Treasures Gallery showcases the superb artworks for which the local aboriginal peoples are famous, while the Hall of Nations examines the cultures of other First Nations. There are always decent temporary exhibits in the Monumental Gallery and Ruth Harvey Art Gallery, and the Gift Shop is stocked with locally made articles such as carved masks, silver Haida jewellery and books on art and culture. In summer there are daily tours of the museum at 1400, as well as the Heritage Walking Tour and Totem Pole Walking Tour around town, the Archaeological Harbour Tour and, three times per week, presentations of *The Prince Rupert Story*, a one-hour dramatization and slide show. They also provide brochures for a self-guided walking tour of town. One block away at Market Place is the **Carving Shed**, T6242421, where native artists can usually be seen at work. ■ *Summer Mon-Sat 0900-2000, Sun 0900-1700, winter Mon-Sat 0900-1700. $5, $1 concessions. 100 1st Av W, T6243207, www.museumofnorthernbc.com* The **Prince Rupert Archives**, with 20,000 historic photos, are at 100 1st Av E.e Rupert's past is the story of the railway, thoroughly explored in the **Kwinitsa Station Railway Museum**, which is housed in the original 1911 station. ■ *Jun-Aug 0900-1700. By donation. Bill Murray Way, T6245637.*

North Pacific Cannery and Fishing Village, 30 minutes away in Port Edward, is very popular. The cannery was operational from 1889-1981. Now the whole village has been restored and opened as a living museum with tours, exhibits and live performances. There's also *The Salmon House* restaurant, T6283273, a café, and a hostel in the old bunkhouse, **F** *The Waterfront Inn*, T6283538. ■ *May-Sep 0900-1800, several tours daily. $7.50, $5 concessions. T6283538, www.northpacific.org 3 buses daily from town.*

Excursions
See also Tour operators, below

    Mount Oldfield is a challenging 8.4-km return hike with good views; it's a continuation of the shorter Mount Oldfield Meadows boardwalk trail. Another 5-km hike leads through old-growth forest to **Butze Rapids** 6 km east of town.

Essentials

Sleeping
■ *on map*

Reservations are recommended in the peak season

Top of the line is the luxurious **A** *Crest Hotel*, 222 1st Av W, T6246771. Hot tub, gym, sauna, sundeck, restaurant and lounge. **C** *Andrée's B&B* , 315 4th Av E, T6243666, www.andreesbb.com Beautiful big rooms with hardwood floors and harbour views. **C** *Java Lodge* , 516 3rd Av, T6222833. 4 very nice large rooms right Downtown. TVs and free internet, deck, laundry, shared bath.

D *Aleeda Motel* 900 3rd Av W, T1888-4602023, www.aleedamotel.bc.ca Comfy and clean rooms, some with kitchenette. **D** *Eagle's Bluff B&B* , 201 Cow Bay Rd, in Cow Bay, T6274955, eaglebed@citytel.net 7 rooms with lots of character, mostly en suite. Located right on the harbour with great views. **D-C** *Inn on the Harbour*, 720 1st Av, T6249107. Slightly more stylish than most. Ask for room with harbour views.

E-F *Pioneer Hostel* 167 3rd Av E, T6242334, www.citytel.net/pioneer Close to town and Cow Bay. Basic, no frills hostel with scant kitchen facilities, dorms the best deal. **F** *Park Avenue Campground*, 1750 Park Av, T6245861. Big ugly parking lot but close to ferry. **F** *Prudhomme Lake Provincial Park*, 15 km east on Hwy 16, T7982277. Much nicer, with 24 wooded sites by the lake.

Eating
● *on map*

Prince Rupert has no shortage of restaurants, many of them Chinese or serving seafood

Expensive *The Waterfront* in the *Crest Hotel*, see above. Steak and seafood. **Mid-range** *Cow Bay Café*, 205 Cow Bay Rd, T6271212. Creative seafood dishes with an international edge. Menu changes daily. Casual café-style interior, overlooking harbour. Good wine list. Recommended and popular, so reserve. *A Japanese Sushi Story*, 34 Cow Bay Rd, T6274560. *Smile's*, 113 Cow Bay Rd, T6243072. c1934 diner-style steak/seafood joint with a good reputation. Deck overlooking marina. **Cheap** *Green Apple*, 301 McBride St. A local institution for cheap and tasty fish and chips. Self service, plastic cutlery. *Macey's*, 519 3rd Av. One of the countless Asian joints Downtown. The food is good, authentic and inexpensive. Vietnamese, Chinese and Thai, cheap breakfasts.

Cafés & bars *Cowpuccino's* 25 Cow Bay Rd. Funky, bohemian atmosphere, with good coffee and great fresh baking. *Javadotcup*, 516 3rd Av. Stylish, trendy and spacious with baking, speciality coffees and internet. The best bars are *Breaker's Pub*, 117 George Hills Way in Cow Bay. Huge windows and a patio with harbour views. *Prince Charles Lounge* in the *Crest Hotel* (see above). Comfy with a good choice of draft beers.

Entertainment *Famous Players Cinema*, 525 2nd Av W, T6246770. *Performing Arts Centre*, 1100 McBride St, T6277529. *Harbour Theatre*, 3rd Av W/9th St, T6276277.

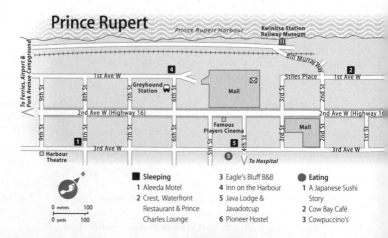

The *All Native Basketball Tournament*, T6278997, held in **Feb** will celebrate its 45th   **Festivals**
year in 2004. It's a massive event, attracting over 10,000 spectators to watch basketball
all day every day for at least a week. The *Islandman Triathlon*, T6244995, takes place in
early **Jun**. Later that month *Seafest*, T6249118, involves 4 days of various small events.

For **aboriginal art** go to the museum, see Sights, above. Cow Bay has several **gift**   **Shopping**
shops. All sorts of locally **smoked salmon** is available at *Dolly's Fish Market*, 7 Cow
Bay Rd, and fresh fish can usually be bought at the dock.

Farwest Sport and Cycle, 212 3rd Av W, rent **bikes** for $25 per day. **Hiking** maps are   **Sports**
available at the Information Centre. **Butze Rapids**, 6 km east of town, are reversing
tidal rapids, comparable to Skookumchuck Rapids on the Sunshine Coast, excellent
for whitewater **kayak** surfing, though the 4.5-6-m tides are for experienced kayakers
only. A long list of **fishing** charter companies is available from the Information Centre. All 5 species of salmon as well as halibut and lingcod are plentiful in local hot
spots such as **Chatham Sound** and **Work Channel**. The season for salmon is
May-Sep, peaking in Jul-Aug. Halibut is May-Sep. There's freshwater trout fishing in
the rivers from May-Oct, and steelhead Mar-Apr. For supplies, go to *Trayling's Tackle
Shop*, 635 2nd Av, T6249874.

Other than those offered by the museum, most tours involve wildlife viewing or a trip   **Tour**
to **Laxspa'aws (Pike Island)**, which contains 3 abandoned First Nations villages dating   **operators**
back as far as 1800 years. *Laxspa'aws Pike Island Tours*, T6283201,
www.pikeisland.ca, run 3.5-hr tours (including the 9-km boat ride), leaving daily
May-Sep at 1130, $45, $30 concessions. Tickets at the museum. **Whale-watching** is
big business here, with high concentrations of humpback whales to the north, as well
as grey whales and orcas. The best time is Aug-Oct, or May-Jul for orcas. Tours average
at $80 per person. **Khutzeymateen Bear Sanctuary**, the only protected grizzly habitat
in Canada, is 45 km to the northeast, and only accessed by water. The average tour is
6-8 hrs for $140-175. People get very excited about the possibility of seeing one of the
rare and elusive white **Kermode (Spirit) bears**. While the chances are slim, the best
place to catch a glimpse is at **Princess Royal Island** far to the south, the nucleus of their
known habitat. The best time is Sep-early Oct.

The following well-established companies offer all or most of the above, as well as
inexpensive harbour tours, so shop around. *Palmerville Lodge*, T6248243,
www.palmerville.bc.ca; *Seashore Charters*, T6245645, www.seashorecharter.
com; *West Coast Launch*, T6279166,
www.citytel.net/westwhales. Or do the
same things under your own steam with
Eco-Treks Kayak Adventures, 203 Cow Bay
Rd, T6248311, www.citytel.net/ ecotreks
Kayak tours from 3 hrs to 7 nights. Also lessons and rentals ($45/day). For **flight-see-
ing** tours contact *Inland Air Charters*,
T6242577, www.inlandair.bc.ca

Air Prince Rupert's airport is located on   **Transport**
Digby Island. A bus/ferry service, T6243355,
meets scheduled flights, $11 one-way to
Downtown. The return service leaves from
Rupert Square Mall. *Air Canada Jazz* fly
twice daily to Vancouver. *Hawk Air* is often
cheaper, especially for one-way.

Map labels:
Cow Bay
Cow Bay Rd
Visitor Info Centre
Museum of Northern BC
Prince Rupert Archives
Carving Shed
George Hills Way
Market Place
1ST AVE E
Cow Bay Rd
3rd Ave E
To Hwy 1 & Library

4 Green Apple
5 Macey's
6 Smile's

● Bars & clubs
7 Breaker's Pub

Northern BC

Bus Local buses are operated by *Prince Rupert Transit System*, 225 2nd Av W, T6243343. The *Greyhound* station is at 112 6th St, T6245090, www.greyhound.ca, with 2 daily buses to **Prince George**.

Ferry *BC Ferries* operate the **Inside Passage** to **Port Hardy** on Vancouver Island, and a regular service to **Haida Gwaii**, aka the Queen Charlotte Islands.. *Alaska Marine Highway*, T6271744, www.dot.state.ak.us/amhshome, have at least 4 weekly sailings most of the year to **Skagway**, Alaska, with daily sailings in peak season. They stop in some or all of: Keichikan, Wrangell, Petersburg, Sitka, Hyder, Stewart, Juneau, Haines and Hollis. **Local ferries** *Prince Rupert Water Taxi*, T6243337, run 4 times daily Mon-Fri from the Information Centre to the native village of **Metlakatla** across the harbour ($6). Local ferries go 3 times weekly to Port Simpson, T6245411, and twice weekly to Kincolith, half way up Portland Inlet, T6246116, 6½ hrs.

Train *VIA Rail*, T1800-5618630, www.viarail.ca, runs 3 weekly daylight-only trains to Jasper with an overnight stop in Prince George.

Directory   **Airlines** *Air Canada Jazz*, T1888-2472262; *Hawk Air*, T1866-4295247. **Communications** **Internet**: at the library and *Javadotcup*, 516 3rd Av W. **Canada Post**: 365-500 2nd Av W. **Laundry** *King Koin*, 745 2nd Av W. **Library** 101 6th Av W. **Medical services** *Hospital*, 1305 Summit, T6242171.

Haida Gwaii:
The Queen Charlotte Islands

Colour map 3, grid C1

For all island Essentials, see page 288

This 300-km long, horn-shaped archipelago roughly 150 km west of Prince Rupert consists of two big islands and the 200 or so islets that surround them. One of only two places in Western Canada to have avoided glaciation during the last ice age, Haida Gwaii harbours many species of flora and fauna not found anywhere else on earth, hence prompting associations with the Galapagos. The world's largest black bears live here, as well as its greatest populations of Peale's peregrine falcons and black-footed albatross. Marine life is equally abundant, making for excellent fishing and whale-watching. Fin, sperm, Right, humpback and grey whales migrate through, and resident pods of orca can be seen almost anywhere, even coming right up to the shores of Queen Charlotte City.

The natural beauty and diversity is only one reason why many of BC's experienced travellers would rate Haida Gwaii as a prime destination. A second is the ***Haida*** *themselves, who have thrived on these islands for over 10,000 years. Widely recognized as being one of the most sophisticated aboriginal peoples on the continent, they are consummate artists and craftsmen, whose works are sold all over Canada. Like few other spots in Canada, this still feels like native land. Or rather, it feels like nature's land, rugged and weather beaten even by West Coast standards, and scantly inhabited by a mere 6,000 predominantly aboriginal souls.*

Ins and outs

For Transport details see page 290

Ferries arrive at Skidegate on **Graham Island**, which contains almost all of the inhabitants in a few communities connected by a single paved road. **Queen Charlotte City** is the main base with the most useful **Information Centre**. Apart from the **museum** at Skidegate, this northern island's main attraction is **Naikoon Provincial Park**. South of the Skidegate Narrows, connected by ferry, is the long, tapering **Moresby Island**, whose name also embraces the myriad tiny islets that surround it. Barely populated, it is an almost inaccessible wilderness, the whole southern half of which is now protected as **Gwaii Haanas National Park**, whose abandoned Haida villages are one of the main highlights of the islands.

Haida Gwaii

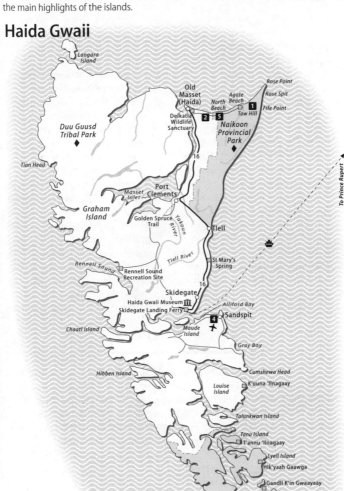

Sleeping	3 Gwaii Haanas Guest	5 Rapid Richie's Rustic
1 Agate Beach	House	Rentals
Campground	4 Moresby Island	
2 Alaska View Lodge	Guesthouse	

Northern BC

▶ ## The Haida

The art of the Haida, among the most revered of any indigenous group, is utterly distinctive: almost anyone would recognize their particular style of representing animals and mythical creatures, often in red and black. Indeed, their artworks and crafts were highly prized even before the coming of the white man, a fact that contributed to their success in trade with other tribes. Prolific carvers of totem poles, they also used the giant red cedars that once flourished on the islands to make huge dug-out canoes and beautiful, elaborate cedar-plank houses decorated with extensive carvings. For many people, one highlight of a visit to Haida Gwaii is the opportunity to buy some authentic Haida art. There are some beautiful masks and jewellery available, and delicate carvings in argillite, a black, slate-like rock only found on these islands and only carved by the Haida.

Almost inevitably, part of the Haida's sophistication expressed itself in warfare.

Their reputation as fearful warriors, their wont to raid and loot rival villages, combined with their unsurpassed sea-faring skills gained them the label 'Vikings of the Pacific Northwest'. More recently, they have proven themselves powerful negotiators in their dealings with logging companies and politicians, to the extent that Haida delegates have even travelled to Brazil in order to advise indigenous groups there. This is in spite of the fact that their population was decimated by smallpox and other epidemics brought by the first Europeans. Estimated at around 8,000 in 1835, their number had dropped to 588 by 1915. This tragedy forced them to abandon almost all of their villages, especially on the southern island, and today many of these can be visited on tours, their houses and totems slowly returning to the earth. Only one, Sgan Gwaii (Ninstints) at the southern tip of Moresby Island, has been preserved and declared a UNESCO World Heritage Site.

Climate   A fault line stretching from California to Alaska passes close to the west coast of Haida Gwaii, adding occasional earthquakes to the most wind- and tide-lashed coastline on the Pacific. A trip to this uninhabited side is recommended for the experience, which brings new meaning to the word rugged. Cape St James at the southern tip is the best place for storm-watching, with an average wind-speed of 34 km/hr. It is little wonder that the communities cling to the protected east coast with its fine beaches. The warm streams of the so-called Japanese Current keep temperatures surprisingly mild here, even in winter. Combined with the copious amounts of rain that perpetually shroud the islands, this has resulted in a lush covering of ancient rainforest.

Graham Island

Skidegate   Ferries arrive at Skidegate Landing. About 500 m east of the terminal at Qay'llnagaay is the **Haida Gwaii Museum**, a fine introduction to the human and natural history of the islands. There is much Haida art to see, including an excellent assortment of argillite carvings, and usually the *Loo Taas* (Wave Eater) cedar canoe designed by the latter-day Haida genius Bill Reid (see page 74). A platform here is a good place for spotting migrating whales. Skidegate village, a further 2 km east, has an **Arts Co-op** and **carving shed** where artists can be seen at work.

Queen Charlotte City   This picturesque fishing village 5 km west of the ferry has little going on, but is in an attractive location, and indispensible for making arrangements. The excellent **Visitor Information Centre** is at 3220 Wharf St, T5598316, www.qcinfo.com, May-September 1000-1900. Here you can pick up maps, brochures, and a permit to visit the abandoned villages on Moresby Island, and sign onto a tour, the only way to get there. The **Parks Canada Office**, for information on Gwaii Haanas National Park, is above the *City Centre Grocery Store*, T5598818, www.parkscan.harbour.com/gwaii Monday-Friday 0800-1630. The **Ministry of Forests** on 3rd Avenue, T5598447, can give information on the forestry campgrounds dotted around both islands. If planning to drive on the logging roads, first get up-to-date details from **McMillan Bloedel**, T5594224. One destination reached by such roads from Queen Charlotte City is **Rennell Sound Recreation Site**, about the best place to experience the wild West Coast, with wilderness campgrounds and paths through rainforest to sandy beaches.

Highway 16, the island's only paved road, runs north from Queen Charlotte City through Skidegate to Tl'ell, Port Clements and Masset. Halfway to Tl'ell a wooden carving marks the site of **St Mary's Spring**. According to legend, those who drink from here are destined to return.

Tl'ell and Port Clements

    Tl'ell itself is a tiny artist community, and home to the Naikoon Park HQ and interpretive centre (see below). Trails along the Tl'ell River lead to endless beaches and dunes, and the shipwreck of the *Pezuta* (two hours each way). At Port Clements, a small **museum** explores the pioneer history of the islands. A trail leads through temperate rainforest to the erstwhile site of the **Golden Spruce**, sadly chopped down by a crazed logger in 1997. A few kilometres further is the site of the partially carved **Haida Canoe**.

The island's most populated town, Masset is an ugly ex-military base with atrocious housing and limited accommodation. The summer-only **Information Centre** at 1455 Old Beach Road, T6263995, can point you towards the local attractions. To the north is **Delkatla Wildlife Sanctuary**, the best place for bird-watching on Haida Gwaii, with more than 140 species. **Old Masset**, or Haida, is 2 km west, with old and new totem poles, a small museum and some canoe and carving sheds. The Village Office on Eagle Road, T6263337, is the place to ask for permission to visit ancient village sites within **Duu Guusd Tribal Park** to the northwest.

Masset

From Masset, the road leads 26 km east past large trees and funky houses to the Naikoon Park trailhead at Tow Hill, a 130-m volcanic cliff with amazing rock formations created by lava flows. These are best appreciated at its base, reached by a 1-km trail, where a blowhole springs into action when the tide comes in, and sea creatures cling to the rocks. Two other beautiful paths lead to the top of Tow Hill. From here you can take in the full extent of **North Beach** which follows the whole strip of coast from Old Masset to Rose Spit. This is a good place to collect razor clams, scallops and crabs (a salt-water fishing licence is needed for the latter).

Naikoon Provincial Park & Tow Hill

    Just west of Tow Hill is **Agate Beach** with great camping, and beachcombing for Japanese glass fishing-floats and sake bottles as well as whalebones, agate and sea creatures. A 10-km hike from Tow Hill leads to **Rose Spit**, a sacred Haida site and ecological reserve at the northeast corner of Naikoon Park. This 12-km sand peninsula can be walked or biked on a 40-km loop. A longer two-day circuit involves taking the **Fife Point** trail from Tow Hill to the east side of the park, then walking around Rose Spit and back to Tow Hill. It's a good idea to get a tide chart before setting off.

Northern BC

Moresby Island

Colour map 3, grid C1/2 Ferries from Skidegate dock at **Alliford Bay**. The island's only village, **Sandspit**, is 15 km east and little more than an airport and an Information Centre, T6375362, May-September 0900-1800. South from here is **Gray Bay**, a large sandy beach with a great forestry campsite. A four-day trek leads south from here to Cumshewa Head, with beautiful beaches on the way.

Gwaii Haanas National Park Reserve Half of Moresby Island is protected from the logging companies by Gwaii Haanas National Park Reserve, which includes 1,600 km of coastline and 138 islands. There are no hiking trails, and entry is by boat or float plane only, involving a potentially expensive tour for all but experienced kayakers, who have endless scope for exploration and whale-watching.

Most visitors to the park are there to see the abandoned villages and over 500 important archaeological features that are evidence of 10,000 years of occupation. Today these are co-managed by the government and the Haida Nation. The five most culturally significant sites are manned by **Watchmen**, traditional guards sometimes seen on top of totem poles wearing distinctive tall hats. They live at the sites in the summer and are very liberal with information. **K'uuna 'Ilnagaay** (Skedans) on Louise Island, the easiest village to access, was painted by Emily Carr (see page 456) in 1907 before most of the buildings and totems returned to the earth. A trail meanders through the eerie but beautiful remains of the ancient village and cemetery. Look out for abandoned logging equipment now covered with moss.

T'annu 'Ilnagaay (Tanu) on T'anuu Island is a beautiful spot facing two beaches. **Hlk'yaah Gaawga** (Windy Bay) on the eastern shore of Lyell Island is where the Haida blocked the road in 1985, bringing an end to logging in South Moresby, hopefully forever. A longhouse where the Watchmen now live was built in commemoration. There are trails here through 1,000-year-old trees that are 70 m tall. Some have been 'culturally modified' to make dugout canoes, and holes can be seen where the quality of the wood was checked.

Gandll K'in Gwaayaay (Hot Spring Island) is a gorgeous place with a dozen hot pools. A bath house is provided for rinsing off before dipping in. **Sgang Gwaay** (Ninstits), off the west coast of Kunghit Island, is a UNESCO World Heritage Site and the only village that has been preserved. Facing the beach are over two dozen totem poles, a magnificent display of standing Haida mortuary poles in the world, despite the fact that many have been removed to museums.

Park information Before entering the park you must buy a **permit** and attend a 90-minute **orientation** session. These take place daily at 0800 and 1930 in summer. A limit is placed on the number of visitors to the sites. To make a **reservation** ($15 per person), call T3871642, or show up at the 0800 orientation session at the Queen Charlotte City Information Centre and hope for one of the 6 daily **standby** spots. For up to date requirements and information, contact the Queen Charlotte City or Sandspit Information Centres, or call the Watchmen on T5598225. Park fees are $10 per day, $10 per night, with a flat rate of $60 for 6-14 nights. **Camping** is allowed anywhere but cultural sites. The beach is best so that the water will erase any traces (check tide first).

Essentials

The Haida do not seem to be interested in exploiting tourism. Consequently, services like hotels and restaurants are few and not of a particularly high standard. This lack of commercialization is part of the charm of the islands.

Queen Charlotte City A-C *Gracie's Place*, 3113 3rd Av, T5594262. 5 units ranging **Sleeping**
from a 2-bedroom suite with kitchen and bathroom to a closet-like room. Antiques
and patio. Will pick up from airport. **C** *Sea Raven Motel & Restaurant*, 3301 3rd Av,
T5594423, www.searaven.com Regular motel room, balcony, good for breakfast.
D *Moonglow B&B*, 3611 Hwy 33, 5-min walk from town, T5598831. 2 spacious rooms
with breakfast and shared bath. Also tenting sites (**F**). **E** *Dorothy & Mike's Guesthouse*,
3127 2nd Av, T5598439. 8 rooms, some with full kitchen. Breakfast included. **D-E** *Pre-mier Creek Hostel and Lodging*, 3101 3rd Av, T5598415. Rooms in an eclectic 1908
building with a long balcony. Or 8 dorm beds, and a double room, in the adjacent hos-tel, with laundry and bike rentals.

   Tl'ell **D** *Riverside B&B*, Richardson Rd, T5574418. 4 spacious new rooms with bal-cony, private entrance and bath. **F** *Misty Meadows Campground*, 0.5 km north of Tl'ell in
Naikoon Park. 64 km of beach. No reservations. **Tow Hill Road** **C** *Alaska View Lodge*, No
12291, 11 km from Masset, T6263333, www.alaskaviewlodge.com 4 rooms on the
ocean with shared or private bath, balconies, and breakfast. **D** *Rapid Richie's Rustic
Rentals*, No 15900, 16 km from Masset, T6265472, www.beachcabins.com Sweet
cedar-shake cabins on the beach, with lots of windows facing the sea. Wood stove, cook-ing facilities, very comfy but no flush toilet (private outhouse). **F** *Agate Beach Camp-ground*, 26 km east of Massett near Tow Hill. On the beach.

   Moresby Island **C** *Gwaii Haanas Guest House*, Rose Harbour, T5598638,
www.gwaiihaanas.com Remote setting in the south of the park on Kunguit Island.
Rustic, with solar power and outhouses. 4 rooms, 3 meals a day included, organic and
fresh. Access is 1-hr float plane ride, $125-275 per person 1-way depending on length
of stay. Kayak rentals $95 per week for guests. **C** *Sandspit Inn Hotel*, 200 m from airport,
T6375334. Restaurant and pub. **D** *Moresby Island Guesthouse*, 385 Alliford Bay Rd, 1
km from airport, T6375300. 10 rooms with shared bath, breakfast, laundry, shared
kitchen, bike rentals.

Queen Charlotte City *Howler's Bistro and Pub*, centre of town, T5598602. Great **Eating**
views of ocean, good beer on tap, pool tables, regular menu of burgers, steaks, sea-food. *Hanging By A Fibre*, 3207 Wharf St. Coffee and art gallery. **Port Clements** *Myles
from Nowhere*. Coffee shop with some great books and crafts. **Tl'ell** *Tlell River House*,
on Bietush Rd, T5574211. Beautiful spot, outdoor seating, good food. *Dress For Less*, on
the highway. A funky spot with good coffee, used clothes, local news and great art.

Bike *Wings on Wheels* 7 nights including food and B&B accommodation for $1,500. **Tour operators**
Birding *Delkatla Bay Birding Tours*, Masset, T6265015. **Ecotours** *Haida Gwaii Eco-tours*, T1877-5598333, www.gwaiiecotours.com 1 or several-day ecologically friendly
tours by bike, canoe, kayak or on foot. **Kayak** *Butterfly Tours*, T604-7407018, www.but-terfly tours.bc.ca Licensed for tours in Gwaii Haanas, including visits to abandoned Haida
villages, 8-12-day trips in small groups. *Gabriola Cycle and Kayak*, T2478277. *Queen
Charlotte Adventures*, T5598990. Llama treks and kayaking. **Zodiac** tours *Moresby
Explorers*, T6372215. **Sailing** is a good way to see the abandoned villages. Some compa-nies have cabins for overnight trips. *Blue Water Adventures*, T5598207. *Anvil Cove
Charters*, T5598207. Also kayaking. For **Float Plane** charters, see Transport.

There are **gift shops**, studios and galleries all over Graham Island. The best are the **Shopping**
Co-op in Skidegate and *Haida Art & Jewellery*, 387 Eagle Av, Old Masset, T6265560.
Books *Bill Ellis Books*, 720 Hwy 33, Queen Charlotte City.

Kayaking is the obvious activity, with plenty of islands to explore, and a good chance **Sports**
of seeing whales (including orcas) sealions and otters. Experience – or a guide – is nec-essary. Stay away from the West Coast, and remember that sealions can be dangerous.

Northern BC

Peter McGee's *Kayak Routes of the Pacific North West* is recommended by *BC Parks*. Try *Moresby Explorers* for rentals, T6372215. **Hiking** Trails in Naikoon Park or from Gray Bay on Moresby, but not in Gwaii Haanas. Rennell Sound on the West Coast is a popular place for **Scuba diving**. **Bikes** can be rented at *Moresby Island Guest House* in Sandspit, T6375300; or *Premier Creek Lodging* in Queen Charlotte City, T5598415.

Transport   **Long distance**   **Air** The airport is in Sandspit, T6375660. *Air Canada Jazz*, T1888-2472262, has regular flights from Vancouver. *Montair*, T604-9466688, www.mon tair.com, has flights from Vancouver to Masset. Float planes from Prince Rupert are operated by *Harbour Air*, T5590052, and *South Moresby Air Charters*, T5594222. A **shuttle**, T1877-7474461, meets all *Air Canada* flights, $14 to Queen Charlotte City.

Ferry *BC Ferries*, T3863431, www.bcferries.com, operate a service from Prince Rupert to Skidegate (usually 6½ hrs). Reservations recommended. Summer: from Prince Rupert at 1100 Sun, Thu, Fri and Sat, 2100 Mon, 1300 Wed; from Skidegate 0730 Wed-Sat, 1100 Mon and Tue. $25, $12.50 concessions, plus $93 with car. Rest of year: from Prince Rupert at 2300 Sun and Mon, 1330 Thu; from Skidegate 0600 Sun and Mon, 2000 Thu. $19, $9.50 concessions plus $71 with car. Kayak/canoe $7, bike $6. Cabins available.

Local   Bus In summer 3 buses travel each way between Masset and Sandspit via Queen Charlotte City, stopping at the airport only on weekends at 0945. Fares range from $5-30 including ferry costs. **Car**: Other than the paved road from Queen Charlotte City to Masset, all driving is on logging roads, which require much care. Give way to logging trucks, and call *Weyerhauser* first to make sure the road isn't active, T5576810. **Car rentals**: *Budget*, T6375688, and *Thrifty*, T6372299 (Sandspit); *Rustic Rentals*, T5594641 (Skidegate). **Ferry**:The *BC Ferries* service between Skidegate (Graham Island) and Alliford Bay (Moresby Island), runs 12 times daily each way, $4.75return, $16.75 with vehicle. **Taxi**: *Bruce's Taxi* in Sandspit, T6375655; *Pete's Taxi* in Skidegate, T5598622. **Water taxi**: *SMC Water Taxi and Sea Bus*, T5598383; and *T&S Water Taxi*, T5598689 (Skidegate).

Directory   **Banks** ATMs and *Credit Unions* at Queen Charlotte City and Masset. **Communications** Internet: at libraries and Northwest Community Colleges in Queen Charlotte City and Masset. **Canada Post**: 117 3rd Av in Queen Charlotte City; 1633 Main St in Masset. **Laundry** City Centre Store in Queen Charlotte City. **Library** 138 Bay St in Queen Charlotte City; 2123 Collison in Masset. **Medical services** *Queen Charlotte Islands General Hospital*, 3209 3rd Av in Queen Charlotte City, T5594300; 1760 Hodges in Masset, T6264700.

Cassiar Highway

Joining the Yellowhead at Kitwanga and running to just west of Watson Lake in the Yukon, Highway 37 is one of the West's last great frontier roads, second only to the Dempster, further north, for providing the sense of adventure that made the now-tame Alaska Highway famous. If doing a circuit, it would be better to drive this road from north to south. The southern section, particularly between Meziadin Junction and Iskut, has some of the best scenery in BC, with the sharp peaks and vast glaciers of the Coast Mountains almost tapping on your windshield. The apotheosis comes with the mandatory 65 km side-trip to Stewart/Hyder, a road lined with icefields, waterfalls, and hanging glaciers, including the amazing **Bear Glacier**. *Just outside Hyder,* **Fish Creek** *is one of the best places to see salmon and the many bears that come to catch them. From Dease Lake further north, a trip back in time can be made to the remote, pretty village of* **Telegraph Creek**.

This windy, often narrow road is currently 85% pavement or sealcoat, perfectly man- **Ins & outs**
ageable for any kind of vehicle (though it's advisable to carry 2 good spare tyres). Yet
outside the peak season you're almost as likely to see a black bear as another driver.
There are few towns or services, and on either side of the road nothing but wilderness
for hundreds of kilometres. A full list of facilities is available from **Information Centres**
in Prince Rupert, Terrace and Meziadin Junction. For the first time on the way north, it is
important for drivers to fill up with petrol when they get the chance, especially as
prices rise quite steeply the further you go.

There is no public transport on this highway but *Seaport Limousine* runs a bus from
Terrace to Stewart (see page 292).

Two villages just north of the junction, **Gitwangak** (Kitwanga), and   **North to**
Gitanyow (Kitwancool), have some interesting old and new totem poles (see   **Meziadin**
page 278). If driving the highway in autumn, look out for *The Zoo*, about 70   **Junction**
km from Kitwanga. In season, this shanty town of makeshift tarpaulin huts
houses hundreds of mushroom-pickers, along with shops, restaurants and
even a bar. The whole unofficial industry that surrounds the harvesting of
wild and valuable Pine Mushrooms (*masutake*) is the closest modern equiva-
lent to the Gold Rush, with some people making a small fortune, others barely
scraping together the bus fare home, and everyone hoping to stumble upon
the motherlode. *The Zoo* could be seen as the Dawson City of its day, as raw
and authentic a slice of life as you could ever hope to encounter. Don't expect
anyone to tell you where the mushrooms are though.

Meziadin Junction, 90 km further on, has a pleasant lake and campsite (**F**,   **Bear Glacier**
T8477320), good fishing, and a small summer-only **Information Centre**.
From here, Highway 37A runs through 65 km of BC's most unmissable scenery
to Stewart and its Alaskan twin, Hyder. Those in a hurry should at least detour
28 km to the famous Bear Glacier, an eery blue sheet of ice that comes right
down to the road, glows in the dark, and cracks and groans like a living thing.

Stewart and Hyder

The ramshackle little town of Stewart, an odd sprawl of buildings that look only   **Stewart**
semi-permanent, is another slice of life. At the **Stewart Historical Museum** on   *Colour map 3, grid B3*
Columbia and 6th Avenue, you can learn all about the twists of fortune that
constitute the town's interesting history, including a spell as North America's
largest gold mine town. ■ *Summer 1100-1900. $3. T6362568.* To this day, many
locals feel that the town has unfulfilled potential, and consider all kinds of
schemes to make its fortune. A few film-makers have agreed, though, that Stewart's most reliable natural resource is its incredible setting at the heart of an
amphitheatre of mountains whose steep rocky peaks rise almost vertically from
the the Portland Canal, one of the world's longest fjords.

There's not much to do, but the summer-only **Visitor Information Centre** at 222 5th Av, T6369224, www.stewartcofc.bc.ca, can recommend some
local hikes, and provide pamphlets for the **Heritage Walking Tour** around
town, and the **Salmon Glacier Auto Tour**. The latter follows the Salmon
River through mining country in BC and Alaska to the massive **Salmon Glacier** and **Summit Lake**. In mid-summer, this entire lake drains under the glacier leaving behind a weird landscape of scattered icebergs.

On the other side of the fjord, Hyder draws a lot of tourists just by being such   **Hyder**
an easily accessed part of Alaska. A surprisingly popular ceremony has built   *Colour map 3, grid B3*

up here. It's almost compulsory to get 'Hyderized', which entails downing a shot of incredibly hard liquor in one of the town's two almost permanently open bars. A much more legitimate draw is the viewing platform at **Fish Creek**, about 7 km away, possibly the best and most reliable place to safely enjoy the awesome spectacle of grizzly and black bears. You will see grizzly mothers teaching their cubs to fish for salmon, and observe the different strategies these fascinating animals adopt according to their personalities.

Sleeping & eating **Stewart C** *King Edward Hotel and Motel*, Columbia/5th Av, T6362244. The obvious place to stay. Motel rooms are slightly nicer and $10 more. The hotel contains almost the only restaurant, pub and coffee shop in town, with fish and chips and king crab the specialities. Otherwise, there's the standard **D** *Alpine Motel* on Conway St, T6362445; and **D** *Kathi's B&B* on Brightwell St, T6362795. **F** *Rainey Creek Campground*, 8th Av, T6362537, is on a salmon stream at the edge of town, and the starting point for a few local trails. For food, the more popular choice with visitors is the *Bitter Creek Café*, with an eclectic menu and an outside deck. Most locals prefer the *King Edward*. There's also *Fong's Garden*, and *The Pizza Factory*.

Hyder has a couple of cheaper motels, the **D** *Grand View Inn*, T6369174, and **D** *Sea Alaska Inn*, T6369003. The latter also has a campsite, **F** *Camp Run-a-muck*, one of the town's 2 restaurants – the other being the *Border Café*, T6362379 – and one of its pubs – the other being the *Glacier Inn*.

Transport *Seaport Limousine*, T6362622, runs a bus from Terrace to Stewart, Mon-Fri, $32, $16 concessions one-way. Leaves Terrace at 1700, Stewart at 1000.

Bell II The 250-km drive north of Meziadin Junction is breathtaking, with some of the finest mountain views in Canada. Almost halfway is Bell II, home of *Last Frontier Heliskiing*, who offer first-class glacier and open-bowl skiing in the heavy snow of the Skeena Mountains, with runs up to 1,500 m. They also have a gas-pump, camping (**F**) and the *Bell II Lodge*.

Sleeping and eating **B** *Bell II Lodge*, T8818530, www.bell2lodge.com Very nice log cabins, a sauna, hot tub, games room, lounge, restaurant, and coffee shop. Ask about their package deals.

Iskut & around Iskut is little more than another gas-stop, but it enjoys a marvellous location between two major protected areas. **Spatzizi Plateau Wilderness Area** to the east is an important habitat for woodland caribou, moose, and mountain goats who dye themselves red by rolling around in iron oxide dust (*Spatzizi* means 'red goat' in the local Tahltan language). To the west is **Mount Edziza Provincial Park**, named after a 900,000 year-old volcano, whose 2,500-m-wide crater is only seen by very experienced climbers or float-plane passengers. Some 30 cinder cones in the park were caused by small eruptions about 1,300 years ago. Between these, a Provincial Recreation Area protects the **Stikine**, another of BC's great rivers, one section of which is justifiably known as the **Grand Canyon**. Theoretically, these wonders are accessible by horse trail, canoe or even on foot. In practice, however, it proves almost impossible to get to them without a float-plane or helicopter.

Sleeping and eating Iskut has more places to stay than most. **B-C** *Bear Paw Resort*, 8 km north, T/F2343005, bearpaw@mail.ocis.net, is a very handsome and well-run lodge with nice rooms, hot tub, sauna, and balconies with great views. Camping (**F**). Set meals available ($42 per person extra). Tailormade wilderness trips, $200 half-day,

$300 full-day: canoeing, mountaineering, skiing, etc (but not into the park). **C** *Red Goat Lodge*, T2343261, nicely located on a lake 2 km south. Rooms and cabins, camping (**F**), canoe and equipment rentals ($45 per day), llama trips (but not into the park).

Tour operators Float-plane and helicopter trips operate out of Tatogga Lake, 15 km south (*Harbour Air*, T1800-6894234), or Dease Lake, 83 km north (*Northern Lights Air*, T8474400). An easier option is to get on a tour with *The Bike, Hike & Paddle Touring Co.*, based 6 km south on Eddontenajon Lake, T2343456, www.bikehikepaddle.com, who run all-inclusive kayak, canoe hiking and biking trips from $100-$300 per day.

Dease Lake, 83 km north of Iskut, is a miserable little place, though it does **Dease Lake** have a small, useless Information booth, T7713900, and a *BC Parks* office, T7714591.

D *Northway Motor Inn*, T7715341, has nice, spacious rooms with kitchenette for $5 extra, and a reasonable restaurant. **F** *Lions Club Campground*, 8 km south, is nicely situated on the Tanzilla River.

West of here, an unlikely 113-km dirt road leads to Telegraph Creek, a much **Telegraph** more serious undertaking than the jaunt to Stewart, not suitable for RVs or **Creek** trailers. The first 75 km are rough and utterly boring until the road joins the Stikine River Canyon, where it abruptly enters an absurdly steep section of one-lane switchbacks with blind corners, grades of up to 20%, and speed limits of 10 km per hour. The dramatic scenery peaks just before the tiny native fishing village of **Tahtlan**, as the road follows a narrow ridge between two canyons, their walls diving straight down, the lava rock on both sides chiselled into weird and wonderful shapes.

Telegraph Creek may not appear to justify the effort, though it has hardly altered since the 19th century, when it functioned as a telegraph station and supply post for the gold-rush towns further north. That anyone can still eke out a living in so remote a location is a sobering lesson in itself. From here the Stikine can be paddled all the way to Alaska. Motor boat tours can be arranged and canoes rented at the **D** *Stikine River Song Lodge and Café*, T2353196, the town's only hotel, restaurant, and food store.

The highway north of Dease Lake is dotted with pretty little aquamarine lakes such as **Good Hope Lake**. Abundant quantities of high-grade jade are found in the metamorphic rock around here and sold at *Jade City*. The only accommodation on this deserted and scenically challenged stretch of road is for campers at **F** *Boya Lake Provincial Park*, 82 km from the Yukon border.

Alaska Highway in BC

*Every year, thousands of RVs make a pilgrimage up the Alaska Highway, pausing in **Dawson Creek** to get a picture by the **Mile Zero** cairn. Part of the attraction is the road's history. Following the Japanese invasion of the Aleutian Islands in the Second World War, and the threat thus posed to Alaska and the Pacific sea routes, a road north was deemed necessary. Favour fell to the 'Prairie Route', which fortuitously followed a chain of air bases known as the **Northwest Staging Route**. Some 20,000 mainly US soldiers worked through appalling conditions to complete the highway in October 1942, an incredible achievement that took a mere seven months. When it opened to the public in 1948, so many vehicles were defeated by its challenge that a further period of closure was declared.*

Northern BC

Ins & outs
For Transport details, see page 294

The Alsaka Highway still holds on to its reputation as being the first great frontier road into the frozen north, despite the fact that continual rebuilding and straightening have turned it into a well-paved, extremely easy drive, with accommodation, fuel and food possibilities at fairly regular intervals. In fact, the only real challenges left are the sheer distance and the boredom. On this first stretch to the Yukon there are no communities worth stopping for, and the landscapes only begin to get interesting towards the end, as the road enters the northern reaches of the Rocky Mountains. Finally, with the border practically in sight, your patience is rewarded by the incomparable Liard Hot Springs.

Prince George to Dawson Creek

The stretch of Highway 97 that runs north to connect Prince George with the start of the Alaska Highway at Dawson Creek is known as the John Hart Highway. The monotony of this 409-km journey is relieved only by occasional glimpses of the Rockies, building towards the scenic highlight of **Pine Pass** (933 m). Before that, only **Crooked River Provincial Park** at Km 70 is worth a mention for the long stretch of sandy beach on Bear Lake, and an adjacent campsite (**F** , T5656340). Campers should hold on for the **F** *Pine Valley Park Lodge*, a very attractive spot just below the pass.

Beyond, the road drops into the flat, semi-prairie landscapes of the Peace River district. There's not much to **Chetwynd**, apart from a few places to stay including the **D** *Stagecoach Inn*, 5413 S Access Rd, T7889666. A road runs 94 km south from here to **Tumbler Ridge**, whose Information Centre, T2424702, can give details about **Monkman Provincial Park**, 60 km further south on a gravel road. Most people visit to see the dramatic 60-m **Kinuseo Falls**, or to hike into the unspoiled splendour of the Northern Rockies along the 24-km **Monkman Lake** trail. There's a campground at the falls, and wilderness sites along the trail.

Dawson Creek
Colour map 4, grid B2

This is a dull town better avoided unless you're after that shot of the **Mile Zero** cairn. There's an **Information Centre**, T7829595, and small **museum** on the highway at 900 Alaska Avenue.

Sleeping and eating Lots of motels cater to those unable to avoid staying, top of the line being the **C** *Ramada*, 1748 Alaska Av, T7828595. **D** *Lodge Motor Inn*, 1317 Alaska Av, T7824837. About the cheapest, and handy for the *Greyhound* station. **Campers** should try to make it 28 km north to *Kiskatinaw Provincial Park*, 5 km down the Old Alaska Hwy at Farmington, T7873407, near a historic curved wooden bridge. Otherwise, best of a bad bunch in town is the *Mile '0' RV Park and Campground*, 2.5 km north, T7822580. By far the best place to eat is the *Alaska Café* on 10th St. Decent food and a good bar in a handsome old wooden building.

Transport *Greyhound* buses, 1201 Alaska Av, leave twice daily from **Prince George** to Dawson Creek ($55). From there buses leaves Mon, Wed and Fri for **Whitehorse** ($180) via Fort Nelson and Fort St John, and every day except Sun to **Fort Nelson**. Catch the midnight bus from Prince George in order to make the connection at Dawson Creek. From Whitehorse to Prince George buses leave Mon, Wed, and Fri.

Fort Nelson
Colour map 4, grid A2

The only two towns, as opposed to fleeting hamlets, on this stretch are Fort St John and Fort Nelson. The former arrives after just 75 km, too soon even for a pee-break. The latter is an essential fuel and food stop, especially for those brave souls heading up the Liard Trail to Yellowknife. (Watson Lake, the next major town on the Alaska Highway, is 520 km away.) The **Visitor Information Centre**, on the north side of town at 5315B 50th Avenue

Northern BC

South, T7746400, www.northernrockies.org, is open May-September 0800-2000 daily, with lots of information about the Yukon, Northwest Territories, and the Northern Rocky Mountain Park just to the west.

Sleeping and eating C *Woodlands Inn*, 3995 50th Av S, T7746669, www.woodlandsinn.bc.ca Nicest of the many places to stay in town. Good rooms, hot tub, laundry, restaurant and lounge. The best motel is **D** *The Almada Inn*, 5035 51st Av, T7742844, rcyre@pris.bc.ca New rooms, $10 more for kitchenette. Also reasonable is **D** *Bluebell Inn*, 4103 50th Av S, T7746961. Standard rooms with kitchenette, laundry and a restaurant. Nicest of all is **D** *Ardendale Wilderness Experiences*, 8 km out of town on the Old Alaska Hwy, T7742433. A log home with 3 en suite rooms, guest lounge, hot tub and horse riding. Breakfast included. **Campers** would do best to keep going or stay at *Andy Bailey Provincial Park* 28 km to the south, set on a river with a beach and fishing. Fee by donation. There is nowhere good to eat, though the *Shangri-La Canadian Chinese* at the north end of town is acceptable.

At Fort Nelson the highway changes direction, heading due west. After 75 km, eye-popping views to the south announce the return of the Rockies. Much of the visible wilderness is contained within the **Northern Rockies Mountains Park**, which borders another three parks, all of them part of a protected area the size of Ireland called the **Muskwa-Kechika Management Area**. Access is only by plane, canoe, or hiking in from Stone Mountain Provincial Park. There are many free backcountry campsites along the rivers. The most recommended hike into NRMP is the **MacDonald Creek/Wokkpash Loop**, a 70-km slog starting at the end of Churchill Mine Road, with great views of gorges and 30-m high hoodoos.

The Northern Rockies

Summit Lake Provincial Park is a pretty spot on the edge of the park, but its campground is devoid of privacy. The **Summit Peak** trail, opposite, is a fairly steep 5-8-km loop with great mountain views getting better the higher you go.

Sleeping and eating The best beds for miles around are yet further west at **B-D** *Northern Rockies Lodge*, T7763481, www.northern-rockies-lodge.com Very nice log-style lodge rooms, chalets or standard motel rooms. Good but expensive German restaurant. Open year-round. They also have fly-in cabins from $300 per person, photo safari tours, and float-plane tours from $79 to $490 for a trip to Virginia Falls in Nahanni National Park. There are 2 great campsites in the lovely **Muncho Lake Provincial Park**: **F** *Strawberry Flats*, and **F** *MacDonald*.

You'd have to be mad to travel the Alaska Highway and not visit the Liard Hot Springs, one of the best experiences Northern BC has to offer. A boardwalk leads over marshes through thick, lush vegetation, which, thanks to the higher temperature caused by the thermal waters, includes much flora that is utterly incongruous this far north, such as 14 types of orchid. Surrounded by this kind of greenery, the two pools have a timeless quality, since little has been done to 'improve' what nature has wrought. The first pool is bigger and more popular, with clear, shallow water whose temperature ranges from too hot at one end to tepid at the other. The second, smaller pool is 300 m further along the boardwalk in an even more natural setting, with warm, murky water of sufficient depth that you can swim around. Between the two is a hanging garden where wild flowers grow at the right time of year. The whole experience is magical and, unbelievably, free.

Liard Hot Springs Provincial Park
Colour map 6, grid C2

Northern BC

Sleeping and eating Nearby is the **D** *Liard Hot Springs Lodge*, T7767349. Very nice rooms in a log-cabin-style lodge, wooden decor, no TV, mid-range restaurant. There is a nice **F** *Campground*, T7873407, within walking distance of the springs and open year-round. Reservations are recommended.

Canadian Rockies

Introducing the Canadian Rockies

The Canadian Rockies are like the Egyptian Pyramids: it's hard to imagine why anyone would visit the country without seeing them. And even if you go feeling that the reality will never live up to all the hype, you come away agreeing that words cannot hope to do justice; the Rockies deserve their reputation as Canada's premier attraction and one of the natural wonders of

the world, taking their place alongside other great ranges like the Himalayas, Alps and Andes. A trip to the Rockies can be pretty much anything you want it to be. You can stay in luxury resorts, eat haute cuisine food, play golf on world-class courses and see heavenly scenery without even straying from your vehicle. Or you can hike for days in breathtaking mountain wilderness through fields of wild flowers beneath giant hanging glaciers, camping beside magnificent waterfalls and emerald lakes, without ever seeing any sign of life other than the occasional whistling marmot, soaring eagle and inquisitive sheep.

Hiking is the obvious activity in the parks and the best way to commune with the exceptional scenery. But just about every other major outdoor activity is pursued here too: canoeing, whitewater rafting, mountain biking, climbing, fishing, caving, skiing, skating, golf and soaking in hot springs. There are few conventional 'sights' or cultural features in the towns, with the very significant exception of the Banff Centre for the Arts, but you are constantly surrounded by Nature's ultimate masterpiece.

Canadian Rockies

> ## Things to do in the Canadian Rockies
>
> - Stay at the *Moraine Lake Lodge* and hike the Valley of the Ten Peaks.
> - Drive the incomparable Icefields Parkway and take an easy hike up to Wilcox Pass.
> - In winter, walk through the ice palaces of Maligne or Johnston Canyons.
> - Ride a horse into the Tonquin Valley.
> - Stay at Takakkaw Falls campground and walk the Iceline trail.

Ins and outs

Getting there
For transport details, see individual towns

Calgary has the closest major **airport**, a mere 128 km east of Banff. There are several shuttle services directly from the airport. *Greyhound* run daily **buses** between Vancouver, Banff and Calgary. **Edmonton** has the closest airport to Jasper, a distance of 362 km. There are 3 daily *Greyhounds* between them, plus 2 from Prince George and 3 from Vancouver. *Via Rail* operate 3 weekly **trains** to Jasper from Vancouver and Kamloops in the west, and Edmonton, Saskatoon and Winnipeg in the east. They also run 3 weekly services to Prince George.

Getting around

The best way to get around the Rockies is with your own vehicle or by bike (starting at Jasper is easier). Be aware that some people are prone to slam on their breaks in the middle of the road if they spot a sheep or deer. Drive defensively! *Greyhound* buses connect Banff with Lake Louise, Field and Jasper. The *Canadian Rockies Hostel Shuttle* leaves Banff daily at 1300, stopping at all hostels on the way to Lake Louise and Jasper. For other bus tours see page 318.

Tourist information

There are first-class **Visitor Centres/Parks Offices** in Banff, Lake Louise Village, Field (Yoho), and Jasper. Parks staff are excellent sources of information about hikes and all other park activities, and usually keep a small library of key hiking guides. They hand out very useful maps with trail descriptions and backcountry guides, and issue compulsory Wilderness Passes for backcountry camping. They also organize guided hikes and other activities, and operate a voluntary Safety Registration programme for those engaging in potentially hazardous activities.

Friends of the Parks sell an assortment of guide books and maps. The *DEMR* 1:50,000 topographic maps are expensive and tend to cover a limited area. The *Gem Trek* maps cover more terrain, so can be more useful. Most hikes are clearly marked, well-maintained and much trodden, so finding your way is rarely an issue. *Parks Canada* produce two 1:200,000 maps – one for Banff, Yoho and Kootenay; one for Jasper – which are recommended as an overview.

Visitor Centres keep track of local accommodation vacancies. If turning up without a reservation, their assistance can save a lot of time and hassle. They even have a courtesy phone. For a useful overview of all the parks, including maps that show the major trails, campgrounds and hostels, pick up *The Mountain Guide* from any Visitor Centre. Or visit www.parkscanada.gc.ca **Weather information** is available at T7622088.

Best time to visit

Summer is best for most people, specifically Jul and Aug, when the days are warm and long and the trails most likely to be dry. Naturally, this is also when the trails and towns are at their busiest, which can be horrifying if you've come to get away from it all. Spring and autumn are much calmer, and certain trails can be hiked as early as mid-May and as late as Oct. The majority, however, are snow-bound until Jul, and in autumn the weather can be dangerously unpredictable. Sep is a favourite month for many people, as all the larches turn a glorious gold. Even at the height of summer, the Rockies receive a lot of rain, especially on the west of the divide. You could have clear blue skies every day for a week, or just as easily endure three weeks of solid downpours. At high altitude anything can happen any time, and snow is *never* out of the question.

Winter The ski season generally runs from mid-Dec to the end of May, but conditions are best in Mar when days are warmer and longer and the powder is most plentiful.

Park fees

Banff and Jasper have booths on the main access roads collecting park fees. Day passes are $5, $2.50 concessions, valid for all the parks up to 1600 the following day. No fee is charged for through traffic. An annual pass costs $35, $18 concessions, valid for entry to all 11 national parks in Western Canada. If staying for a week or more, it is well worth getting one of these, as they also entitle you to discounts at a number of sights and for certain tours. You can buy a pass at information centres and some camp-grounds, or by credit card at T1800-7487275. Day passes can be bought at 24-hour automatic pass machines. Wilderness Passes for backcountry camping are $6 per person per night. An annual pass, good for unlimited wilderness camping in all Western Canada National Parks, is $42. You can trade 7 day-pass receipts for one of these. If you buy one, you still have to register every time you use a backcountry site.

Sleeping

The most convenient way to see the Rockies is with your own transport and a tent. There are **campgrounds** throughout the parks. Regular sites cannot be reserved, so turn up early. 'Guerilla camping' (finding a spot where you don't have to pay) is difficult. *Parks Canada* and the *Alpine Club of Canada* (HQ in Canmore) operate a number of backcountry **huts**. All Park-run campgrounds in Banff and Jasper National Parks operate on a first-come, first-served basis. Information at T7621550 and T8526177 respectively.

The second best strategy is to stay in **youth hostels**. The large ones in Banff and Lake Louise are excellent, and there are smaller, more basic hostels dotted around, often in convenient locations. Hostels in Banff National Park and Yoho can be reserved at T7621358; those in Jasper National Park at T8523215. **Hotels** charge a lot more, and are limited to the townsites of Banff, Jasper, Lake Louise and Field. Banff and Jasper offer the biggest choice, while Field has many good value **guesthouses**.

The Rockies

The Canadian Rockies stretch almost 1,500 km from the United States to the Yukon border. At the southern end, joined to the much bigger Glacier National Park in the United States, is **Waterton National Park**, which despite its smaller size contains scenery every bit as wonderful as the major parks further north. Beyond Jasper a series of wilderness and provincial parks such as Willmore and Kakwa, right up to the Northern Rockies at the top of BC, protect less famous and elevated, enticingly remote portions of the range, where those seeking solitude can still find it. Just to the west, **Glacier** and **Mount Revelstoke National Parks** and **Wells Gray Provincial Park** contain scenery that in many ways equals that of the Rockies but is actually in the Columbia Mountains.

For all that, the Canadian Rockies usually refers to a very distinct cluster of four national parks that together have been designated a UNESCO World Heritage Site: **Banff**, **Jasper**, **Kootenay** and **Yoho**. These are the parks covered in this section, along with the principal parks that are immediately adjacent: BC's **Mount Robson**, which contains the highest peak in the range and one of the best hikes; **Mount Assiniboine**, which protects the second most famous and photogenic of the range's peaks; and **Kananaskis Country**, which covers a large region of foothills to the south of Banff.

Colour map 2
grid A1-C4

Canadian Rockies

Of the big four contiguous national parks, Banff and Jasper are east of the Continental Divide in Alberta, and contain the overwhelming majority of the terrain. Kootenay and Yoho are on the other side of the divide in BC. Banff is far and away the most famous and crowded of the parks, and contains the greatest number of trails, many of them easily accessed right from the road. **Banff Townsite**, situated on the TransCanada Highway, is the prominent centre of the Rockies, and Canada's most visited resort in both summer and winter. **Lake Louise** to the north is the single most famous location in the Rockies, and is also a major base for great hikes.

Many people miss the BC parks altogether, driving straight up the incredible Icefields Parkway to **Jasper**, by far the biggest and wildest of the parks, with many longer backcountry trails. Yet a short loop down through **Kootenay**, north on Highway 95, then up through **Yoho,** takes in both of these BC parks quickly and easily and sacrifices nothing. Yoho in particular justifies the diversion, with its wonderful scenery and first-class hikes. Many of these are centred on the beautiful **Lake O'Hara**, which connoisseurs often rate as the Rockies' finest base. In fact, if pushed for time, think about concentrating on Banff and Yoho, but be sure to take a driven excursion up the **Icefields Parkway** to the **Columbia Icefield** and back, as this strip of road is bordered by the most breathtaking scenery of all.

Flora and fauna

Fauna You are almost guaranteed a sighting of elk, deer and bighorn sheep, often on the roads or at campgrounds, causing a degree of excitement that after a while seems excessive. There's also a chance of seeing moose, black or grizzly bears, mountain goats and coyotes, as well as a host of smaller animals like otters, beavers, pikas and porcupines. Hoary marmots inhabit rocky slopes and make a distinctive whistling sound to warn each other of your presence. On rare occasions you'll catch a glimpse of a wolf, badger, wolverine, marten, cougar, caribou or lynx. Some first-class bird-watching spots attract all kinds of waterfowl, and there's a good chance of seeing jays, ptarmigans, finches, chickadees, ospreys, various eagles, and many other species.

There are only a couple of hundred grizzly bears left in the Rockies and the same number of black bears. As well as being much bigger, grizzlies have a dished face, a big, muscular shoulder hump, and long, curved front claws. You are more likely to see one by the side of the road than in the bush, but to minimize the chances of a scary encounter, take a few simple precautions (see page 478 and page 33. Any animal can be unpredictable and dangerous if scared, so keep a respectful distance. More people get attacked annually by elk than by bears. Female elks are most aggressive during the May-June calving season; males are especially dangerous during the September-October rutting season. According to a po-faced notice at Lake Louise ski hill, the greatest number of injuries in Banff National Park result from people getting too close to squirrels!

Small creatures are indeed the ones most likely to prove a nuisance. At lower elevations, especially on dry overcast days, mosquitoes are sure to bug you. From early to mid-June ticks are prevalent, especially on sunny, grassy slopes. Check vigilantly for them at the end of the day, and ideally remove them using fine-pointed tweezers: grab hold of the mouth without squeezing the body and gently pull back until the tick lets go. Pull out any remaining parts like a splinter. Then there are black flies, deer and horse flies, and no-see-ums, so named because they're too small to see (see Insects, page 474).

Hiking in the Rockies

It is important not to overstretch yourself. Start with gentle hikes and build up from there. If you're not used to hiking, an 11-km day-hike can be very tiring. Even experienced backpackers tend to stick to about 16 km per day.

Check the weather forecasts at a Visitor Centre (or T7622088), but do not trust it. Always be ready for the worst.

The best clothing is several thin layers that can then be added or taken away at will. Synthetic fabrics are the best as they take moisture away from the skin, insulate when wet, and dry rapidly. Wool and fleece are also good. Avoid jeans and anything else made of cotton. Always take a waterproof jacket (preferably something that breathes, like Goretex) and trousers, plus a hat and gloves.

If backpacking, travel light! Shed unnecessary items. Photocopy the pages of your guidebook or take notes. And keep everything in a plastic bag: most backpacks are not waterproof, and rain is practically guaranteed. Obviously good boots that fit well are essential for anything more than a stroll.

Take plenty of water, and only fill up from sources that are clearly safe, like glaciers or springs. All other water should be boiled, filtered or treated, since giardia lamblia (beaver fever) is widespread. Take more food than you think you'll need. Hunger adds to fatigue, clumsiness and risk of injury, and the risk of hypothermia should you get a soaking. During a six-hour hike, count on burning 1,800-3,000 calories. Food heavy with complex carbohydrates and relatively low in fat and protein is best. Take a few energy bars as a back-up. Since camp fires are usually prohibited, think about taking pre-cooked or raw foods instead of lugging a stove and pans. Pittas and tortillas, pre-cooked rice and pasta, granola, nuts, seeds, fruits and vegetables are all recommended.

A small first-aid kit should be taken, including anti-bacterial ointment, pain killers, bandages, sterile gauze and absorbent pads, adhesive tape, fold-up scissors, and maybe a compact manual. Always take matches in a plastic bag, and toilet paper! Consider taking a torch/flashlight, a compass, bug repellent, sunglasses, sunscreen and a hat with a brim.

From mid-July to mid-August, the Rockies' many meadows come alive with an exciting display of multicoloured **wild flowers**, including Indian paintbrush of all shades, alpine forget-me-nots, lousewort, western anemone, buttercups, daisies, alpine fleabane, false azalea, arnica, columbine, spring beauty, pearly everlasting, and many more. Several types of orchid bloom about a month earlier. Red and white heather, mosses and multicoloured lichens are present throughout the temperate months. In autumn, larches and deciduous trees brighten the predominantly evergreen forests with their spectacular golden hues. Other vegetation includes a host of berry bushes, rhododendrons, red elder, cinquefoil, and several species of saxifrage.

Flora

Sports

There are over 3,400 km of trails in the Rockies from the very short to the absurdly long. As a rule we have only mentioned the cream, chosen from personal experience with the help of two excellent trail guides: *The Canadian Rockies Trail Guide*, by Brian Patton and Bart Robinson is the standard choice, providing a great deal of useful information and a comprehensive overview; *Don't Waste Your Time in the Canadian Rockies*, by Kathy and Craig Copeland gives less details but in a structured manner that cuts to the chase and really helps you choose from the daunting range of options. Brochures issued by Parks Offices are useful but almost devoid of opinion, though the

Hiking
See also page 33

Canadian Rockies

staff there are usually knowledgable enthusiasts. They often have small reference libraries for detailed research. The trail descriptions in this book are not intended to be sufficient to guide you through the hikes.

Winter sports   There are six ski hills in the Rockies. **Lake Louise** is the most significant, with the largest terrain in Canada and awesome views (but cold!). Banff's **Sunshine Village** is the second biggest, and receives 10 m per year of first-class powder, Canada's biggest snowpack. **Mount Norquay** is small, close to town, and well respected for its advanced runs. **Marmot Basin** in Jasper is cheaper and noted for its friendly atmosphere and uncrowded slopes. In Kananaskis Country, **Nakiska** is one of Canada's newest resorts, combining a small, friendly size with state-of-the-art equipment, and **Fortress Mountain** is smaller still, a good start for beginners.

Canmore, Banff, Lake Louise and Jasper all have ample opportunities for quality **cross-country skiing**, while a wealth of operators and equipment renters can get you snowshoeing, skating, tobogganing, ice-climbing, canyon-crawling, dog-sledding, ice-fishing or curling.

Kananaskis Country

Phone code: 403
Colour map 2,
grid B3

Kananaskis Country covers a 4,000 sq km area of mountains and foothills along the Continental Divide to the southeast of Banff National Park. The scenery is not as spectacular as in the four big parks. Nor is this region conveniently placed unless coming from Highway 3, and there's no public transport. Should it fall into your itinerary, however, there are a few advantages to starting here. It provides a gentle introduction to the Rockies that puts the higher peaks into a proper perspective, and it's a cheaper, considerably less crowded opportunity to venture into undeniably beautiful terrain and get in shape for the more demanding hikes to come. The trails here are also lower and so likely to be clear of snow earlier and later in the season.

Several relatively uninteresting Albertan Provincial Parks fall under the Kananaskis Country umbrella, but the key focuses are Peter Lougheed Park and Kananaskis Village, both on Highway 40, which joins the TransCanada 23 km east of Canmore, and links (via PR541) with Highway 22 south of Calgary. A winter gate blocks access from this latter route until mid-June. For more information visit www.kananaskis-country.org

Peter Lougheed Provincial Park

About 50 km south of Highway 1, a road leads 3 km from Highway 40 to this park's **Visitor Information Centre**, T5916322, June-September 0900-1700 Monday-Friday, 0900-1800 Saturday-Sunday; May-June 0930-1600 Wednesday-Sunday. Trail maps can be bought for $1, topo maps for $10. Paved roads fan out from here to the attractive Upper and Lower Kananaskis Lakes, a number of decent hiking and cycling trails, and six campgrounds.

The best hikes are the short but stiff 7.8-km return climb to scenic **Rawson Lake**, the strenuous 4.6-km return grunt up to the views from **Mount Indefatigable**, and the gentle 16-km loop around the **Upper Lake**. For something truly first-class, however, head north along **Smith-Dorrien Highway**. Also known as PR 742, this rough but stunning gravel road is an alternative 52-km route to Canmore via the gorgeous **Spray Lakes** campgrounds, and holds trailheads for the southern section of Banff Park. Most are more easily accessed from

Canmore (see page 306), but a real delight, the trail, starts at Mud Lake just 12 km from here. This fairly easy 14.8-km hike, with an elevation gain of 451 m, leads to superb views of saber-tooth mountains in all directions, equal to almost anything in the Rockies. Opposite Mud Lake is a trail system with by far the best mountain biking in the region. **Whiskey Jack/Pocaterra**, starting from Boulton Creek, is another fine, much closer, biking route.

The nicest vehicle-accessible campgrounds are **F** *Interlakes* and **F** *Mt Sarrail*, both on   **Sleeping**
Lower Lake with many sites right on the water and gorgeous panoramic views. The latter has walk-in sites for tents only. There are also 5 backcountry campgrounds, including I on the *Point* trail, a 3-km hike round Upper Lake. Permits are $3 per person from the Information Centre, or T5917075. Others are on the *Three Isle Lake* and *Maude-Lawson Lakes* trails, 2 of the longer, better hikes in the park, both extendable into BC's Height of the Rockies Park. **Provisions** can be bought in the park at *Boulton Creek Trading Post*.

Kananaskis Village

This purpose-built tourist resort caters to those who like their wilderness tem-   *Colour map 2, grid B3*
pered with expensive luxury, and is also a handy base from which to exlore a network of trails. An **Information Centre** in the village, 0900-1730, T5917555, sells trail maps for $1.

The best trails start at the nearby Ribbon Creek parking lot. The **Skogan/Sunburts/High Level** trail is a 12.7-km loop with wonderful views throughout. Even better is the 20-km return **Ribbon Falls/Lake** trail with 594 m elevation gain to great views. This fun hike, which involves a bit of chain-assisted climbing, leads through massive cliffs past waterfalls and canyons. There are backcountry campgrounds ($3) at the lake and 2 km earlier at the falls. The **Galatea Creek** trail leaves Highway 40 about 10 km south of the village. This 13-km return hike (16 km to Upper Galatea Lake, set in a dramatic alpine cirque) leads past canyons, cascades and views to a campsite at Lillian Lake. These last two hikes are connected by the 3-km **Guinn's Pass** trail, making for a handy loop (with some hitching between trailheads).

Further north, some 10 km from the junction with Highway 1, is an Information Centre at Barrier Lake, T6733985, 0900-1700 daily. A few short hikes from here include the 5-km return **Jewel Pass** trail, which passes Jewell Falls and gives good views of the lake.

Dominating the village are 2 luxurious but expensive hotels, the **LL-AL** *Delta Lodge*,   **Sleeping**
T5917711, www.lodgeatkananaskis.deltahotels.com, and the **AL** *Kananaskis Mountain Lodge*, T5917500, www.kananaskismountainlodge.com Both have fitness rooms, hot tubs, restaurants and lounges. The alternative is the HI-affiliated **E** *Ribbon Creek Hostel*, T7624122, a homely little place with dorms and fairly basic common room and kitchen. **Camping** The nearest campsites are **F** *Eau Claire*, 10 km south, T5917226, and **F** *Sundance Lodges*, just north of the village, T5917122, who also rent large tepees and trapper's tents (**D**).

Boundary Ranch, T5917171, arrange guided horse riding and pack trips up to 6 days.   **Sports**
The spectacular *Kananaskis Country Golf Course*, T1877-5912525, is just south of the village. There are 2 small ski hills nearby. Just north is **Nakiska Ski Hill**, T5917777. Developed specifically for the 1988 Winter Olympics, this is one of Canada's newest resorts. **Fortress Ski Area**, T5917108, 15 km south, is a very small hill used mainly by locals and school groups, a good place for beginners to cut their teeth.

Canadian Rockies

Canmore

Phone code: 403
Colour map 2, grid B3
Population: 9,800
Altitude: 1,350 m

Though it's starting to be taken over by the 'condo explosion', Canmore still retains the comfortable feel of an authentic small town, making it an attractive and cheaper alternative to the insanely busy and commercially oriented Banff, just 21 km away. Centred on Main (8th) Street, the small Downtown has some decent, down-to-earth pubs and fine restaurants, with as many sports equipment shops as anyone could wish for. Many fine hikes into Banff and Mount Assiniboine Parks are most easily accessed from here, and all kinds of other outdoor activities are seriously pursued, especially climbing, Nordic skiing and mountain biking. See Sports, below.

Canmore's most worthwhile attraction, **Grassi Lakes**, is past the Nordic Centre on the way to Spray Lakes. Park just before the road's surface gives way to dirt, and follow the path. Due to glacial deposits, the colour of these two tiny lakes is extraordinary even by local standards, an unreal aquamarine/lime green. It's a lovely, relaxing place. North of the lakes is a very popular spot for rock climbing, well worth watching even if you don't partake. The lava cliff faces are riddled with holes perfect for placing hands and feet, and all levels of climb can be found with routes already anchored by locals.

Tourist information

For a map and trail information, call in at **Tourism Canmore** next to the bus station at Main St/7th Av, T6781295, www.tourismcanmore.com They can also provide a brochure for the self-guided *Historic Walking Tour* of the town. More useful for general enquiries is *Travel Alberta*, northwest of town at the junction of Hwy 1 and the Bow Valley Trail (Hwy 1A), T6785277, www.travelalberta.com May-Oct 0800-2000, winter 0900-1800. The national HQ of the *Alpine Club of Canada* is on Indian Flats Rd, T6783200, a short drive from town. They are very helpful and knowledgable about climbs and hikes and sell a good selection of maps and guidebooks. They also have a hostel (see below), and backcountry huts dotted throughout the parks. For locations visit www.AlpineClubofCanada.ca

Sleeping

Canmore has a dearth of decent hotels, but there are dozens of nice, reasonably priced B&Bs. Many are close to Downtown on 1st and 2nd St. Call the B&B Hotline at T6093399, or check the Information Centre website. **B** *McNeill Heritage Inn*, 500 Three Sisters Dr, T6784884. 5 en suite rooms in a historic home set in riverside woods. **C** *By the Brook*, 4 Birchwood Pl, T6784566. 2 big en suite rooms with TV, sauna, hot tub and sundecks. **C** *A Haven of Rest*, 814-3 St, T6785706. 3 en suite rooms. Large garden with patio. **C** *Riverview & Main*, 918-8 St, T6789777. 3 rooms with decks and mountain views. Private sitting room. Otherwise, the best bet in the centre is **C** *Drake Inn*, 99 Railway Av, T6785231, www.drakeinn.com Nice standard rooms, hot tub and sauna, pub with patio. **C** *Paintbox Lodge*, 629-10 St, T6783956. Reasonable rooms with balconies. **D** *Canmore Hotel*, 738 Main St, T6785181. Cheap but sleazy Downtown option.

E *Alpine Club of Canada*, Indian Flats Rd, a short drive east, no public transport, T6783200. Dorms, kitchen, lockers, sauna, internet, laundry. **Camping F** *Rundle Mountain Campground*, by *Travel Alberta*, T6782131, is horrible. **F** *Spray Lakes Campground*, T5915226, is 16 km away on a rough and sometimes steep dirt road, with no public transport. But it's a wonderful campground that hugs the lakeside for 6 km, making for private sites right on the crystal clear lake and surrounded by mountains.

Eating

Expensive *Sinclair's*, 637 Main St, T6785370. Sophisticated and mouthwatering West Coast menu, fancy interior, patio. *Tannin's Fine Food and Wine*, 838-10 St, T6099200. Eclectic international cuisine from fondue to buffalo penne. Varied wine list. **Mid-range** *Crazyweed Kitchen*, Main St. Espresso coffee and great food like Thai curries, gourmet sandwiches, pizzas and salads. Limited seating. *Grizzly Paw Brewing Co*, 622 Main St. Fine ales brewed on the premises. Superior casual food like fish'n'chips and burgers. *Sherwood House*, Main St/8th Av. Good selection of beers on tap. Patio with mountain views. Overpriced pub food. *Zona's*, 710-9 St, T6092000. *The* place to eat. International food with a creative edge, like Moroccan lamb and molasses curry. Cosy house setting with garden dining area. Licensed, open late. Very popular.

For good coffee, there's *Blends* at 637-10 St, who roast their own, and *The Coffee Mine*, **Cafés**
802 Main St, with light food and outdoor seating.

Hooligan's, at 103 Bow Trail, is the only nightclub, and the name speaks for itself. **Clubs**

Canmore Heritage Days Folk Festival, T6782524, in early **Aug** is the main annual **Festivals**
event, with lots of acts on 4 stages in Centennial Park. 3-day pass $60.

Books *The Second Story Used Books*, 713 Main St. Stock up, because used book stores **Shopping**
in the Rockies are a rarity. **Camping gear/sports** *Valhalla Pure*, 726 Main St, T6785610.
Sports Consignment, 718-10 St. Good deals on used sport and camping equipment.
Food *Nutter's*, 900 Railway Av, in front of the *IGA* supermarket. The perfect place to
stock up on healthy camping food. **Photography** *Canmore Film Lab*, 801 Main St.

Climbing is the local speciality, at **Grassi Lakes**, Yamanuska on Hwy 1A E, and **Cougar** **Sports**
Canyon for a more challenging climb. Ask at the Alpine Club. Access to excellent
long-distance **hikes**, mostly in the south of Banff Park, is via Spray Lakes Rd and its
extension, the Smith-Dorrien Hwy, a distance of some 40 km. Follow signs to the
Nordic Centre and keep going up the steep, rough road, ignoring the right turn to
Spray Lakes campground. Local hikes include the **Three Sisters** area, and **Ha Ling**
Peak across from the Goat Creek parking lot, both on Spray Lakes Rd; **Grotto Moun-**
tain is accessed from the Alpine Club. For **mountain biking**, there are excellent networks of trails at **Mt Shark** and **Mud Lake**, both on the Smith-Dorrien Hwy, and much
closer at *Canmore Nordic Centre*. *Rebound Cycle*, 902 Main St, rent mountain bikes
($25 per day), skis and snowboards.

The Bow River makes for fairly mellow **canoeing** or **floating**, while the Kananaskis
provides **whitewater rafting** and **kayaking**. See below for tour operators. *Gear Up*,
1302 Bow Valley Trail, T6781636, rent kayaks and canoes ($40 per day), climbing and
camping gear, and bikes ($20 per day). *Canmore Nordic Centre*, off Spray Lakes Rd,
well signed from town, T6782400, has some of the best **cross-country skiing** trails in
the Rockies, and hosts various sporting events. Visit their *Trail Sports*,
www.trailsports.ab.ca, for rentals and lessons. **Golf** *Canmore Golf Course*, 2000-8 Av,
T6784785. **Swimming** *Canmore Recreation Centre*, 1900-8 Av, T6785597. Indoor salt
water pool, hot tub, sauna, fitness room.

Bird-watching *Halfway to Heaven Bird-Watching*, T6732542. **Caving** *Canadian* **Tour operators**
Rockies Cave Guiding, T6783522. *Canmore Caverns*, T6788819. **Climbing** *MW*
Guide's Office, T6782642. Rock climbing, ice-climbing, heli-skiing and glacier travel;
Yamnuska, T6784164, www.yamnuska.com Ice and rock climbing, mountaineer-
ing, skiing. Mountain school and guide service. **Fishing** *Banff Fishing Unlimited*,
T7628222; *Mountain Fly Fishers*, T6789522. **Heli touring** *Assiniboine Heli Tours*,
T6785459. Flight-seeing and multi-day packages. **Hiking** Guided day-hikes and
backcountry treks with local experts, and cross-country skiing are offered by *Alpine*
Routes, T6780954; *Back of Beyond Advnture Co*, T6780910; and *White Mountain*
Adventures, T6784099. **Horse touring** *Cross Zee Ranch*, T6784171. Day trips.
Rafting *Canadian Rockies Rafting Co*, T6786535; *Mirage Adventure Tours*,

T6784919. 3-hr whitewater rafting trips from $55. **General** *Good Earth Travel Adventures*, T6789358. Hiking, rafting, canoeing and biking in summer. Skiing and dog-sledding in winter.

Transport   The *Greyhound* station is at 801 Main St, T6784465. *Sky Shuttle*, T7625200, stops in Canmore on its way from Calgary airport to Banff. *Link Transit*, T7623795, runs a daily service to/from Banff. For *Canmore Taxi*, call T6784465.

Directory   **Bank** *Bank of Montreal*, 701 8th St; *Royal Bank*, 1000 Railway Av. **Communications** Internet: free at the library. Canada Post: 801 Main St. **Laundry** *The Lost Sock Laundromat*, 1000-7 Av. **Library** *Canmore Public Library/Art Gallery*, 950 8th Av, T6782468. **Medical services** *Canmore Hospital*, 1100 Hospital Pl, T6785536. *Magic Fingers Clinic*, 749 Railway Av, T6783266. Massage and so forth. *Feel Your Best*, T6782747. Holistic healer and herbalist.

Mount Assiniboine Provincial Park

Phone code: 250
Colour map 2, grid B3

Canmore is the main jumping-off point for hikes into the south of Banff National Park. These are reached on the Smith-Dorrien Highway (No 742) beyond Spray Lakes. For the **Burstall Pass** trail from Mud Lake see page 305. Mount Shark trailhead is one of the starting points for hikes into Mount Assiniboine Provincial Park in BC. Turn right onto Watridge logging road past the south end of Spray Lakes reservoir and drive 5.3 km. Mount Assiniboine is one of the most instantly recognizable and visually gratifying peaks in the Rockies, a pyramid-shaped icon that has been compared to the Matterhorn in the Swiss Alps. The rest of the park is equally sensational, and certainly one of the top few backpacking destinations in the range.

From Mount Shark, the easiest route is via **Bryant Creek** and the Assiniboine Pass. It is 27.5 km one way, with an elevation gain of 480 m. A strong hiker can do it in a day. Otherwise there is a campground at Km 9.7, and a warden hut, campground and shelter at Km 13.6. To stay at either, make arrangements with the Banff Visitor Centre. The easiest route back to Mount Shark, making a nice loop, is over **Wonder Pass** and by Marvel Lake. This is also 27.5 km, with an elevation gain of 230 m then a lot of downhill. A second access route, and probably the best, is over **Citadel Pass** from **Sunshine Village** in Banff (see page 319). This is a delightful, slightly easier, 29 km hike with 450 m gain and 427 m loss. The ultimate trip would access this way and exit via Wonder Pass, but arranging a shuttle would be tricky. None of this should be done without a map and a more detailed trail description.

The core area of this triangular park is its southeast corner, which contains Mount Assiniboine, eight other peaks over 3,000 m, and several beautiful lakes. The main focus and campground is at **Lake Magog**. There is also a Park HQ/warden's cabin.

Some excellent one-day hikes give the chance to see some of the park and recover from the trek in. **Nub Peak**, a moderate 11.6-km round-trip (from Magog), offers excellent views of the surroundings. **Windy Ridge**, a moderate 17.4-km round-trip, is one of the highest trail-accessible points in the Rockies, with even better views, and wildflower meadows on the way. An easier excursion is the 8-km loop to **Sunburst**, **Cerulean** and **Elizabeth Lakes**, which can be extended to 18.6 km to take in the views from **Ferro Pass**. Whatever the skies are doing and the forecasts say, always come prepared for the worst the weather can throw at you.

Lake Magog The very expensive **LL** *Mt Assiniboine Lodge*, T6782883, and the much more basic **E** *Naiset Huts*, with bunks on a first-come first-served basis. Despite the long walk-in, don't expect to be alone. **Camping** As well as those mentioned above, there is a campground (**F**) at **Lake Magog**, and a quieter one 6 km north at **Og Lake**.

Sleeping

Banff National Park

Banff National Park, the oldest and most famous in the Canadian Rockies, and Canada's number one tourist attraction, receives some 4.7 million visitors per year. This is partly due to its 6,641 sq km of jaw-dropping scenery, which includes 25 peaks over 3,000 m. Equally significant is the ease with which visitors can get to such delightful spots. Banff Townsite is situated right on the country's main highway, a mere 128 km from the major city of Calgary, and offers all manner of services that cater to every budget. Over 1,500 km of trails lead into the backcountry, more than any other mountain park. Many of these are easily accessed from the highway and of a difficulty-rating that does not exclude the out-of-shape. In fact, there is a wealth of wonderful landscapes in the park to enjoy without ever having to leave your vehicle.

Phone code: 403
Colour map 2, grid B3

For Tourist information, see page 311

Banff the park struggles to keep up with its own popularity. The protection of wildlife, its first priority, has become an increasingly serious problem. Sometimes there isn't even enough space for the human invaders. It is not unknown on a midsummer weekend for every single bed and vehicle-accessible campsite in the park to be taken. There are enough trails that you can usually escape the hordes, but for true isolation think about going somewhere else: Banff does not have the monopoly on magnificent scenery.

The park's trails and services can be divided into four sections: **Banff Townsite**, the **Bow Valley Parkway**, **Lake Louise**, and the long **Icefields Parkway** that leads to Jasper National Park. Note that many trails into the southern portion of the park start on the Smith-Dorrien Highway accessible from Canmore.

Archaeological digs at Vermillion Lakes have unearthed evidence of a native presence in the area dating back 11,000 years. Stoneys, Cree, Ktunaxa (Kutenai), and the Plains Blackfoot all resided here at one time. The arrival of explorers David Thompson, Alexander Mackenzie and Simon Fraser, all seeking a route to the Pacific Coast, presaged the end of their tranquillity, and in the late 19th century the Canadian Pacific Railway was directed straight through the heart of the Rockies. It was three railway workers who, in 1883, stumbled over what are now the Cave and Basin Hot Springs. Shrewd railway investors were not slow in recognizing that thermal waters combined with outstanding scenery and some grandiose hotels could attract enough tourism to finance this incredibly expensive line. The springs were soon protected and enlarged to form the Rocky Mountains Park in 1885, Canada's first National Park. To retain a monopoly, cars were banned until 1916.

History

Banff Townsite

Banff enjoys a stunning location and was clearly once a pretty little village. Today, however, the 50,000 visitors it receives daily throughout the summer, which apparently makes it the busiest urban centre within a national park in the world, have taken their toll. The streets are perpetually heaving, the roads choked with tour buses. The crowds, expense and relentless commercialism become tiresome very quickly, and there is little to actually do but shop, eat and

Phone code: 403
Colour map 2, grid B3
Population: 7,000
Altitude: 1,384 m

Canadian Rockies

party, all of which can be fun after a few days in the bush. Those needing creature comforts are almost limited to here, Lake Louise and Canmore, but if you are camping or staying in hostels, there are countless nicer places to be. The one essential reason to visit is to use the excellent Banff Information Centre.

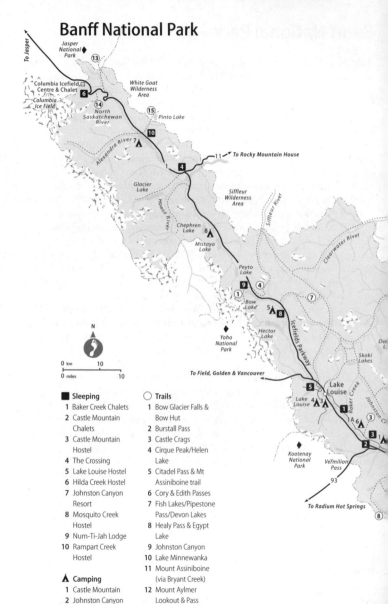

Banff National Park

Canadian Rockies

The closest major **airport** is in Calgary, 128 km to the east, with numerous flights from Canadian and US cities. Several shuttle services run directly to Banff. The *Greyhound* station is Downtown at 100 Gopher St, with regular **buses** to Vancouver, Calgary, Winnipeg, Jasper, and Lake Louise. The **TransCanada Highway** connects Banff with Vancouver to the west and all points east.

Ins & outs
For transport details see page 318

Banff townsite can be easily explored on foot. Almost everything in town is on or near Banff Av. 2 **shuttles** (*Happy Buses*) operated by *Banff Transit*, run to the more distant campgrounds and some local hikes. The *Canadian Rockies Hostel Shuttle* runs to Jasper stopping at all hostels on the way. *Link Transit*, runs daily to Canmore. *Brewster* have several tours going as far as Jasper. Bikes, mopeds and cars can all be rented in town.

The **Banff Information Centre**, 224 Banff Av, comprises the **Parks Canada** office, T7621550, www.parkscanada.gc.ca/ banff, and the Banff **Chamber of Commerce**, T7628421. The former is an excellent source of information about hikes and all other park activities, and issues 4 very useful maps: 1 for day-hikes, 1 for cycling, 1 for the Icefields Parkway, and 1 showing longer trails and backcountry campgrounds. To stay at one of these you must register here and buy a Wilderness Pass ($6 per person per night). The Chamber helps with sleeping arrangements and keep track of which hotels/B&Bs/campsites still have spaces; they will even call for you. They also give out brochures for the *Banff Historical Walking Tour*. The **Friends of Banff National Park**, T7628918, sell topographic maps, and run free guided walks throughout the summer. Free topical films are shown downstairs. Summer 0800-2000, spring and autumn 0800-1800, winter 0900-1700. All Park-run campgrounds in Banff National Park operate on a first-come, first-served basis. T7621550 for information.

Tourist information
Park radio is at 101.1 FM

Canadian Rockies

The nicest part of Banff lies at its west end, where a picturesque bridge over the Bow River gives an idea of how the village must have looked before its popularity got out of hand. Appropriately enough, this is the location for Banff's few sights, almost all of which look back to the park's formation.

Sights

Banff

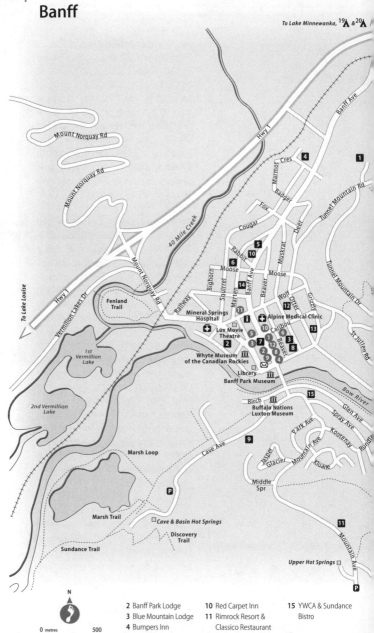

Sleeping

1 Banff International
  Youth Hostel
  & Cougar Pete's

2 Banff Park Lodge
3 Blue Mountain Lodge
4 Bumpers Inn
5 Global Village
  Backpackers Hostel
6 Holiday Lodge
7 King Edward
8 Mountain Home
9 Pension Tannenhof

10 Red Carpet Inn
11 Rimrock Resort &
  Classico Restaurant
12 Rocky Mountain
13 Tan-Y-Bryn
14 The Driftwood Inn,
  Arrow Motel &
  Caramba! Restaurant

15 YWCA & Sundance
  Bistro

Camping

16 Trailor Court
17 Tunnel Mountain I
18 Tunnel Mountain II
19 Two Jack Lakeside
20 Two Jack Main

The **Whyte Museum of the Canadian Rockies** is the best place to start. It was created by artists Peter and Catherine Whyte to preserve as much material relating to the Rockies as possible, and this includes literally thousands of volumes of archives and Alpine Club records of early expeditions. There is a fine permanent collection of mountain-related art, much of it by the founders, and temporary exhibitions by local and international contemporary artists. Most fascinating of all is the excellent collection of photos that vividly document the early days of the park and the radically changing attitudes that have prevailed regarding its wildlife. Countless black and white pictures depict fancily dressed Edwardian tourists standing next to their vintage cars, grinning stupidly as they feed a bear by hand; or a self-satisfied ranger standing smugly over some poor dead beast. The museum presents lectures and various tours, including horse-drawn carriage tours, and a Historic Banff Walk at 1100 and 1500 daily, $5. ■ *1000-1700. $7, $4.50 concessions. 111 Bear St, T7622291, www.whyte.org*

The nearby **Banff Park Museum** is housed in a splendid wood cabin built in 1895, its age explaining all the skylights, which compensated for the lack of electric light. Like the building itself, the interior is more a relic from the past than a place where the past is documented. A large collection of dusty old stuffed animals pay their politically incorrect tribute to a time when people's idea of wildlife watching was taking high tea in a room lined with animal heads, and even the official park approach to wildlife preservation was to shoot all predators like cougars, lynx and eagles so that innocents like elk, deer and sheep could multiply unhampered. ■ *Summer 1000-1800, winter 1300-1700. $2.50, $1.50 concessions. 91 Banff Av, T7621558.*

Canadian Rockies

● **Eating**
1 Aardvark Pizza & Sub
2 Cassis Bistro &
  Maple Leaf Grille
3 Coyotes,
4 Le Beaujolais
5 Magpie & Stump
6 Sushi House
7 Waldhaus &
  Henry VIII Pub

● **Bars & clubs**
8 Aurora Night Club
9 Barbary Coast
10 Rose & Crown
11 St James Gate
12 Tommy's
   Neighbourhood Pub

▶ ## Hikes around Banff Townsite

Fenland Trail *A 1.5-km loop through the wetlands near the first Vermilion Lake, a haven for birds and other wildlife. Access is from Mount Norquay Road.*

Marsh Loop *This 2-km trail from the Cave and Basin Hot Springs explores a similarly rich area for flora and fauna.*

Tunnel Mountain *(3.6 km return, 200 m elevation gain. Trailhead: St Julien Road) This short, steep but easily attainable hike leads to fine views of Banff Village.*

C-level Cirque *(8 km return, 455 m elevation gain. Trailhead: 3.5 km north on Lake Minnewanka Road) This is a short, easy hike leading to some moving mountain scenery. You'll also see mining remains and wild flowers.*

Lake Minnewanka *(6-60 km return with little elevation gain) This trail is suitable for anyone, and is open even in April and November when most others are closed. You can also go as far as you like. The **Ghost Lakes** are at Km 24, with frequent campgrounds along the way. At Km 7.8, you can turn left for the steep climb to **Mount Aylmer Lookout/Pass** (23.6 or 27 km, 615 or 845 m elevation gain). This route also enjoys a longer season than most. From the lookout are great views of the lake and mountains towering above the opposite shore. From the pass the views are bigger, but mostly limited to vast expanses of desolate grey rock.*

Cory and Edith Passes *(13-km circuit, 960 m elevation gain. Trailhead: 0.5 km on Bow Valley Parkway after it leaves Highway 1, turn right and continue 1 km) Cory Pass can usually be hiked by late June. An extremely tough trail involving steep sections and some scree slope scrambling, this is only for the fit and reasonably experienced, but if you can manage it, the rewards are an adrenalin-pumping quest and some exhilirating views. Edith is less exciting but makes for an easier descent and a neat loop.*

Across the river, the **Buffalo Nations Luxton Museum** has a small collection of First Nations artefacts like beadwork and headdresses, and a number of poorly executed tableaux. The gift shop is its best feature. Daily tour at 1130 in summer. ■ *Summer 0900-1900, winter 1300-1700. $6, $2.50 concessions. 1 Birch Av, T7622388.*

Further afield, the **Cave and Basin Hot Springs** is the site of the thermal waters whose discovery prompted the park's formation. The whole story is told through a collection of exhibits and the film *Steam, Schemes and National Dreams*. The cavernous atmospheric setting of that first pool is the highlight, making you wish it were still open for bathing. The outdoor 'basin' pool is only slightly less enticing. The grounds are also attractive, and contain a couple of short, popular walks. The 2-km interpretive **Marsh Loop** trail leads on boardwalks around a wetland area whose warm microclimate has made it unusually lush and flower-filled, a rewarding spot for bird-watchers. The easy and popular 3.7-km **Sundance Canyon** trail follows a paved path to the canyon mouth. ■ *Summer 0900-1800. $2.50, $1.50 concessions. 311 Cave Av, T7621566. Tours daily at 1100.*

After the discovery of the springs, the Canadian Pacific Railway quickly saw tourism as a means to pay for its expensive line, and went about building a series of luxurious hotels. First of these was the **Banff Springs Hotel**, the largest in the world when finished in 1888. Unfortunately, the Gothic giant was constructed back to front, with wonderful views from the kitchens and none at all from the guest rooms. Since then it has been rebuilt and developed, its 250 rooms expanded to 770, all of which are full in summer, mostly with Japanese tour groups. Known as the 'Castle in the Rockies' it is now more village than hotel, a vast, confusing labyrinth of restaurants, lounges, shops and facilities. Utterly over-the-top, its sheer excessiveness makes it the only unmissable sight in Banff. Be sure to pick up a map from reception before exploring. It's a boring walk up Spray Avenue, so take the *Happy Bus*.

If the Cave Springs have put you in the mood, head for the **Upper Hot Springs**, an outdoor thermal swimming pool with great views, whose very sulphurous water is cooled to 40° C. The Hot Springs Spa offers massage, aromatherapy, and a steam room. ■ *May-Oct 0900-2300, Oct-May 1000-2200. $7.50, $6.50 concessions, reduced rate in evening and winter. End of Mountain Av, T7621515.*

Just down the road is the **Sulphur Mountain Gondola**, which takes you up 700 m in eight minutes at a 51° angle. At the top is a restaurant, two observation terraces for taking in the exceptional panoramic views, and a couple of short trails leading to even more vistas. ■ *Peak season 0730-2100, spring and autumn 0830-2000, winter 0900-1600. $19, $9.50 concessions. T7622523. End of Mountain Av, T7626767, www.brewster.ca In summer, Brewster Grayline run a shuttle to the gondola from the town centre.*

The **Vermilion Lakes**, just west of town off Mount Norquay Road, are easily explored by bike or car. The marshes around them are home to a wide range of birds, such as ospreys and bald eagles, and animals like muskrat, beaver, elk and coyote. **Lake Minnewanka**, north of the eastern highway junction, is a focus for hiking, biking, fishing and boating, as well as organized boat tours.

Accommodation in Banff is expensive and heavily booked, so reservations are strongly recommended. You can book through *Canadian Rockies Reservations*, T1866-2202005, www.rockiesreservations.net If you turn up without a reservation, head straight for the Information Centre; they know exactly what is left.

Sleeping
■ *on map, page 312*

Canadian Rockies

LL-L *Fairmont Banff Springs Hotel*, Spray Av, T7622211, www.fairmont.com A great place to visit, this Gothic castle is more geared to tour groups and those for whom outward show is everything. The rooms themselves are rather small and nothing special. For true luxury, the place to stay is the **LL-L** *Rimrock Resort Hotel* on Mountain Av, T7623356, www.rimrockresort.com The rooms here are classy and spacious, with incredible views of the surrounding scenery and the *Banff Springs Hotel*. There's a health club with pool and sauna, and an excellent restaurant. Of the Downtown luxury hotels, probably the best is **L** *Banff Park Lodge*, 222 Lynx St, T7624433, www.banffparklodge.com Fairly nice rooms, and all the usual facilities including pool and steam room.

A *Bumpers Inn*, Banff Av/Marmot Cr, T7623386. Nice spacious room, balcony, quiet. **A** *The Driftwood Inn* and *Arrow Motel* 337 Banff Av, T7624496, www.banffcaribou properties.com Reasonable mid-range options, sharing facilities like hot tub, sauna and gym with the more expensive *Ptarmigan Inn*. **B** *Red Carpet Inn*, 425 Banff Av, T7624184. Small but nice room, great bed, TV and pool. **B** *King Edward Hotel*, 137 Banff Av, T7622202. No frills Downtown hotel.

As well as those below, check www.bbcanada.com **A** *Mountain Home*, 129 Muskrat St, T7623889, www.mountainhomebb.com 3 en suite rooms and common room in a renovated home with antique furnishings. **A-B** *Pension Tannenhof*, 121 Cave Av, T7624636, www.pensiontannenhof.com 10 rooms. **B** *Rocky Mountain*, 223 Otter St, T7624811. 10 rooms with kitchenettes, some with shared bath. **C** *Holiday Lodge*, 311 Marten St, T7623648, www.banffholidaylodge.com **C-D** *Blue Mountain Lodge*, 137 Muskrat St, T7625134. 10 en suite rooms in a centrally located turn-of-the-century building with period decor and shared kitchen. 6 small but good-value rooms.

D *Tan-Y-Bryn*, 118 Otter St, T7623696. 8 rooms, fake wood panelling, not great but cheap. **D-E** *Banff International Youth Hostel*, Tunnel Mountain Rd, T7624122. A little

As so often, B&Bs represent good value and are usually less likely to be full

inconveniently placed, 3 km from town, but the *Happy Bus* passes by. Otherwise, this is *the* budget option, with excellent facilities and lots of choices: en suite rooms in a beautiful wood beam structure with a gorgeous lounge area; regular private rooms with shared bath; or dorms, some with en suite. Laundry, nice kitchen, games room, lockers, deck, cheap restaurant with good food and big portions. Highly recommended. **D-E** *Global Village Backpackers Hostel*, 449 Banff Av, T7625521, www.globalbackpackers.com Not as well equipped as the HI, but closer to town and more geared to a young, party atmosphere. Mostly 6-bed dorms, plus 1 semi-private double bed loft. Kitchen, small TV room, internet, courtyard, hot tub, sauna, lockers. Bikes for rent $23.50 per day. **D-E** *YWCA*, alias *Y Banff Mountain Lodge*, 102 Spray Av, T7623560, info@ywcabanff.ab.ca A cheap reliable favourite (not just for women). Dorms or private rooms. Pleasant lounge, volleyball court, and a cheap restaurant with nice patio. There are 7 HI-affiliated *Banff & Mountain Chain Hostels* in the park. Central reservations is T7624122, banff@HostellingIntl.ca

Camping There are 5 campgrounds around Banff. Prices vary, but all fall within the **F** category. Sites cannot be reserved and fill up fast in summer; turn up in the morning to be sure. Information at T7621550. $4/night is charged for a campfire permit, which includes wood. On Tunnel Mt Road are the big and ugly *Tunnel Mountain I* and *Tunnel Mountain II*, with 618 and 188 crowded sites respectively, and showers. The latter is the only one open year-round. *Tunnel Mt Trailer Court*, is a big parking lot with full hook-ups for RVs. The nicest campground by far is *Two Jack Lakeside*, with 80 sites including some tent-only spots on the lake, and showers. *Two Jack Main*, across the road, has 381 fairly nice sites. Both are 12 km northeast of town on Lake Minnewaka Rd.

Eating
● on map,
page 312

Expensive Banff's expensive restaurants often have 'tasting menus' which are 4-8-course meals for $50-100 per person. *Le Beaujolais*, Banff Av/Buffalo St, T7622712. Set dinners from $50-72 as well as à la carte. Lots of game and seafood with delicious French sauces. Dress code and extensive wine list. *Classico*, in the *Rimrock Hotel*, T7621865. Tasting menu $95. Canadian cuisine with a great view and classy wine list. *Cassis Bistro*, 137 Banff Av, T7628289. Intimate and very stylish cocktail bar with excellent tapas and good wine list. Lunch and dinner specials, quality over quantity. *Waldhaus*, behind the *Banff Springs Hotel*, T7626860. Beautiful setting, very romantic German-style interior. Fondues are a speciality, or try the roast duck or trout. **Mid-range** *Aardvark Pizza & Sub*, 304 Caribou St. Take-out menu, good pizzas, open till 0400. *Caramba!* 337 Banff Av, T7623667. Homemade pastas with innovative toppings, wood oven pizza, free range chicken. Nice patio, but the lounge is more intimate. *Coyotes*, 206 Caribou St, T7623963. Sophisticated southwest-style food like orange chipotle prawns. Subtle decor with open kitchen, and some decent breakfast options. *Magpie & Stump*, 203 Caribou. An old Tex-Mex stand-by with a big menu and open till 0200. *Maple Leaf*,137 Banff Av, T7625511. True Canadiana with wood and leather and a genuine birch-bark canoe. Nice view from dining room. Salmon, steak and pasta, and a comfy lounge for a quiet drink. *Sushi House*, 304 Caribou St. Quaint place with reasonable prices and sushi riding by on a toy train. **Cheap** *Cougar Pete's*, at the *HI Hostel*. Large portions of diner-type food. *Sundance Bistro*, at the *YWCA*. Nice patio, best value breakfast in town, licensed, wraps and salads.

Cafés *Evelyn's Coffee Bar*, beside the cinema on Bear St and at the *Town Centre* on Banff Av. Good coffee and baking. The *Maple Leaf Grille* has a nice coffee corner but doesn't open until 1100.

Bars & clubs
● on map, page 312

Aurora Night Club, 110 Banff Av. Heaving DJ-led dancefloor, and an elegant Martini/cigar bar. *Barbary Coast*, 119 Banff Av. Bluesy/alternative music, starts at 2200. *Henry the VIII Pub*, under the *Waldhaus Restaurant* at the *Banff Springs Hotel*. An authentic German-style boozer with low ceilings and Becks on tap. Sunshine, views and a good pub menu. *Rose & Crown*, upstairs at 202 Banff Av. Good bands most nights, jam night Sun, pub food. *St James Gate*, 207 Wolf St. 31 beers on tap and upscale pub food. Really does feel like an Irish pub, right down to the smoke. *Tommy's Neighbourhood Pub*, 120 Banff Av. Small local hangout.

To find out what's going on, pick up *Wild Life*, a free monthly paper for the Banff/Canmore area, www.wildlifemag.com The *Banff Centre for the Arts* on St Julien Rd is one of the most highly respected art schools in North America with all sorts of cultural events happening constantly, including art exhibitions, theatre, music concerts of all kinds, dance, etc. Their calendar is available at Information Centres. Or call the box office, T7626301, www.banffcentre.ca/events Their *Walter Phillips Gallery* is open Tue-Sun 1200-1700. Free, T7626281. **Cinema** *Lux Movie Theatre*, 229 Bear St. **Entertainment**

The *Banff Centre for the Arts* hosts the *Banff Festival of the Arts* throughout the **summer** months. It will celebrate its 70th birthday in 2004. Dance, theatre, film, visual art, lectures, music. In **Nov** they also host the famous *Banff Mountain Film and Book Festival*, showcasing mountain/adventure films, the best 20 of which then tour the rest of Canada and abroad. **Festivals**

Freya's Collectables, 108 Banff Av. A non-tacky gift store with authentic native crafts, much like what can be seen in the *Luxton Museum* (but more of it!). **Shopping**

Mountain biking is possible on many of the local trails, though **Lake Louise** is better, and **Canmore** better still. Highest calibre is the **Brewster Creek** trail which extends the **Sundance/Healy Creek** trails from Cave and Basin Hot Springs to a possible 37-km one-way ride to Allenby Pass. An exciting 5.2-km downhill run is the **Lower Stoney Squaw** at Mt Norquay Ski Area. The **Rundle Riverside** is a 14-km rollercoaster ride to Canmore Nordic Centre and more trails. Good gentle cycling can be had at Lake Minnewanka, Vermilion Lakes or Sundance Canyon. For bike rentals, equipment and information there's *The Ski Stop*, 203A Bear St, T7601650, and *Bactrax*, 225 Bear St, T7628177, who also run tours. **Summer sports** *For hikes around Banff Townsite see above; those in Banff National Park are arranged geographically throughout this chapter*

  Canoeing is possible on **Two Jack Lake**, **Vermilion Lakes**, **Echo Creek**, **40 Mile Creek**, and **Bow River**. Rentals at *Bow River Canoe Docks*, end of Wolf St.

  Climbing *Mountain Magic Equipment*, 224 Bear St, T7622591, have a climbing wall and rent equipment. See also *Banff Centre*, below.

  Fishing gear and licences can be obtained from *Lake Minnewanka Boat Rentals*, T7623473.

  Golf *Banff Springs Golf Course*, Spray Av, T7626801. $165 in summer.

  Scuba diving in Lake Minnewanka, where an old mining town was flooded decades ago, but only for those with their own gear.

  Skateboarding *Banff Recreation Centre* on Norquay Rd, T7621147, has a skateboard park, 1100-2200, drop-in fee $8, $6 concessions.

  Swimming The *Sally Borden Building* in the *Banff Centre* at St Julien Rd, T7626450. Pool, exercise room, various indoor courts and a climbing wall. 1200-2200. $3.75 from 1430-1930, otherwise $9.50.

Skiing Banff is very much a year-round resort, with 2 ski hills right on its doorstep. **Mount Norquay Ski Area**, T7624421, just 6 km to the north, receives 300 cm of snow per year and employs a snow-maker. 5 lifts access terrain that is 11% beginner, 45% intermediate, 28% advanced and 16% expert. This has long been considered the domain of experienced skiers, with plenty of steep and deep runs. The season is early Dec to mid-Apr. Highest elevation is 2,133 m, with a vertical drop of 497 m. A lift pass is $35. **Winter sports**

Canadian Rockies

Rentals and lessons are available, and there's a free shuttle from major Banff hotels. It has the only night skiing in the Rockies on Fri 1600-2100. The greatly superior **Sunshine Village Ski Area**, T7627500, is 18 km southwest of Banff off Hwy 1 (see below).

Many local trails are groomed in winter for **cross-country skiing**. Pick up the *Nordic Trails* pamphlet from the Information Centre for details. *White Mountain Adventures*, T6784099, give skiing lessons and arrange **canyon icewalks** ($45) to the beautiful frozen waterfalls of Johnston Canyon. Also wildlife walks in snowshoes. **Dog sled tours** are offered by *Howling Dog Tours*, T6789588, and *Snowy Owl Sled Dog Tours*, T6784369. **Horse-drawn sleigh** rides are arranged by the *Trail Rider Store* at 132 Banff Av, T7624551. There is indoor **ice-skating** at *Banff Rec Centre*, Mt Norquay Rd, T7621235, and outdoor rinks at the *Banff High School*, Banff Av and Wolf St; *Bow River* at the end of Wolf St, and the *Banff Springs Hotel*. The latter also has a **tobogganing** hill. Equipment can be rented at *Performance Sports*, 208 Bear St. **Ice-fishing** is possible with *Banff Fishing Unlimited*, T7624936.

Tour operators **Boat** *Lake Minnewanka Boat Tours*, T7623473. Glass enclosed boat, $28, $12 concessions, for 1½-2 hrs. May-Oct 5 tours a day from 1030. **Bus** *Brewster Gray Line*, 100 Gopher St, T7626767, www.brewster.ca Motorcoach tours to most destinations in Banff and the park. **Fishing** *Banff Fishing Unlimited*, T7624936. **HI tours** *True North Tours Ltd*, T/F9120407, www.backpackertours.com/truenorth In association with HI. 3-day ($115) or 6-day ($215) tours of the park in a 15-passenger van, staying at hostels. Drop-off in Calgary an option. Price includes park entrance fee. Ends up being cheaper than the bus. **Hiking** *Great Divide Nature Interpretation*, T5222735. Interpretive hikes led by professional naturalists. **Horses** For guided tours, hiring of horses, or trips in a horse-drawn carriage ($20/30 mins), contact *Trail Rider*, 132 Banff Av, T7624551. **Rafting** *Adventures Unlimited*, 211 Bear St, T7624554. Whitewater trips on the Kicking Horse River. Also fishing. *Inside Out Adventure*, T1877-9997238. Various options with an emphasis on fun and learning. **Town** *Discover Banff Tours Ltd*, T7601299, www.DiscoverBanffTours.com $45, $25 concessions, 3½-hr tour of sites in immediate Banff area.

Rocky Mountain Rail Tours run prohibitively expensive 2-day, 1-night trips from **Vancouver** to Banff or Jasper, with an option to continue on to **Calgary**. Prices start at at $600 one-way.

Transport **Long distance** **Air**: The closest major airport is in Calgary, 128 km to the east. Several shuttle services run directly to Banff. *Banff Airporter (Brewster)*, T7626700, $40 one way, $75 return. *Sky Shuttle*, T7625200. **Bus**: *Greyhound*, T1800-6618747, www.greyhound.ca, have 5 daily **buses** to Calgary, also stopping at the airport ($20), and **Vancouver** ($110), with 4 daily to **Jasper** ($100), and **Winnipeg** ($170). **Car**: The TransCanada Highway connects Banff with Vancouver to the west, Calgary, Winnipeg, Toronto and beyond to the east. For road conditions call T7621450.

Local *Banff Transit*, T7608294, run 2 shuttle buses, known locally as the *Happy Bus*. One connects the *Banff Springs Hotel* (on the hour and half hour) with the *Tunnel Mountain Trailer Court* (on the quarter hour); the other connects the *Luxton Museum* (on the quarter) with *Village Campground* on Tunnel Mountain Rd (on the hour and half hour). Both run along Banff Av and cost $1, $0.50 concessions. The *Canadian Rockies Hostel Shuttle* leaves daily at 1300, stopping at all hostels on the way to **Lake Louise** ($12) and **Jasper** ($51). Call T1888-7863641 or the local hostel, T7624122. Bikes cost extra. *Link Transit*, T7623795, runs a daily service to **Canmore**. *Brewster*, T7626700, run all manner of bus tours with commentaries as far as **Jasper**. **Car rental** from *Hertz* at the *Banff Springs Hotel*, T7622027. **Moped rentals** at the *Shell* station on Wolf St and Lynx St, T7609363, $11-25 per hr. For **bike rentals** see Sports.

Directory

Banks *Foreign Currency Exchange*, Clock Tower Village Mall, 112 Banff Av, T7624698. But shop around. **Communications** Internet: kiosks all over town charge $2 for 15 mins. The library is cheaper. **Canada Post**: 204 Buffalo St. **Laundry** *Cascade Coin Laundry*, 317 Banff Av; *Johnny O's*, 223 Bear St. **Library** 101 Bear St, T7622661. **Medical services** *Mineral Springs Hospital*, 301 Lynx St, T7622222. *Alpine Medical Clinic*, 216 Banff Av, T7620460. **Useful numbers** For emergencies only: **Police** T7622226; **Medical** and **Fire** T7622000; *Banff Warden Office* T7624506.

Sunshine Village Ski Area

Bow Valley Parkway (see below) is the scenic route to Lake Louise and beyond. Highway 1 is still a beautiful drive, but much faster with less chances to stop and hike. After 8 km, a road heads from the latter to Sunshine Village Ski Area, T7627500, 18 km southwest of Banff, situated on the Continental Divide. The snow here is of a much higher calibre than that found at nearby Mount Norquay, with 10 m per year of first-class powder, Canada's biggest snowpack. The hill also has one of the longest seasons, running till late May. A high-speed gondola and 12 lifts whisk skiers up to 62 uncrowded runs (see box page 46). The highest elevation is 2,730 m, with a vertical drop of 1,070 m. Note that it's very cold up here

Phone code: 403
Colour map 2, grid B3

The shuttle bus fare from major Banff hotels is $15 return

As well as rentals and lessons, the hill has its own accommodation, the **LL** *Sunshine Inn*, T1877-5422633, www.skibanff.com Facilities (an exercise room) and rooms (decent enough, but smallish) fail to justify the price, but it's the only ski-in ski-out option.

Sleeping

The beauty of ski hills is the speed with which you can be whisked to elevations that would cost hours of sweat and grunt to reach otherwise. Then you can maximise your time and effort because the views are already fantastic. Unfortunately the Sunshine gondola no longer runs in summer, but there is a shuttle bus run by *White Mountain Adventures*, T6784099, costing $18 return ($9 concessions) from the Sunshine parking lot, or $35 ($17.50 concessions) from Banff townsite.

Hikes from Sunshine Village

At the top, the **Sunshine Meadows** stretch for 15 km along the Continental Divide, receiving copious amounts of rain and snow that feed one of the most glorious midsummer displays of wild flower you're ever likely to see. Naturally, such an easily accessible Eden draws crowds of visitors. Most go only as far as **Rock Isle Lake**, an easy 1.6-km trail to a beautiful viewpoint. To avoid the crowds set a brisker pace towards **Citadel Pass**, 18.6 km return, 343 m elevation gain. On a clear day many of BC's mighty and rugged peaks are visible, including Mount Assiniboine. Continue a little further towards Fatique Pass, 2.5 km away, for even better views. This is a popular way to begin a multi-day backpacking trip into Mount Assiniboine Provincial Park in BC. Lake Magog is almost 20 km from the pass. See page 308.

Healy Pass (18.4 km return, 360 m or 655 m elevation gain). There are two ways to reach Healy Pass: from Sunshine Village via the shuttle and Simpson Pass, or from the Sunshine parking lot via Healy Creek. The distance is the same, but the second option involves a lot more climbing, though at a gentle pace. If you're fit and are bothered by the shuttle fare/schedule, go via Healy Creek. Either way, the flowers are wonderful. The pass itself is unexceptional, but offers good views of Egypt and Scarab Lakes and the Pharaoh Peaks. You could also explore the Monarch Ramparts south of the pass. **Egypt Lake** campground and a basic, cheerless hut is 3 km further on. To stay here reserve at the Banff Visitor Centre, T7621550, $11 per person (including Wilderness pass). There are some worthwhile side-trips if you do. **Whistling Pass** is a fine 6.6-km round-trip, and could be extended to **Shadow Lake** beneath the lofty Mount Ball (26 km return from Egypt Lake).

The Bow Valley Parkway

Colour map 2, grid B3 The Bow Valley Parkway leaves Highway 1 just west of Banff. Its speed limit is a sometimes frustrating 60 kmph, but when drivers are liable to hit the breaks at any moment if a sheep appears, this is a good thing. Along the road are three campgrounds, a hostel, a few lodges, and numerous hikes and viewpoints. At Km 16 is Johnston Canyon.

Johnston **Johnston Canyon Trail** (11.6 km return, 215 m elevation gain) is the most Canyon worthwhile hike along the parkway. The chasms and waterfalls of this canyon are famous and perpetually flooded with tourists, but it's a charming walk that can be done in May or October when there are less people. The canyon is at its most beautiful in winter, when the waterfalls are frozen. See Banff winter sports, page 317, for details. You can continue beyond the falls to the multicoloured cold-water springs of the **Inkpots** and views of Johnston Creek Valley.

Sleeping B *Johnston Canyon Resort*, T7622971, www.johnstoncanyon.com, a good alternative to staying in Banff. Large 2-bedroom cabins are very nice, modern and fully equipped, including a kitchen, clawfoot tub, TV and VCR, porch and fireplace. A great deal for 2 couples sharing. Smaller cabins are less impressive, and they are all far too close together. There is a dining room, coffee shop and tennis court on site. **F** *Johnston Canyon Campground* has showers and 140 not very private sites.

Castle Castle Mountain, 30 km from Banff, marks the junction with Highway 93, Mountain which heads south through Kootenay National Park to Radium and the East Kootenays. The mountain itself is a magnificent and aptly named sight, worth pulling over to admire. The nearby **Rockbound Lake** trail is more trouble than it's worth, but **Silverton Falls** from the same trailhead is a nice 1.6-km jaunt.

Sleeping AL *Castle Mountain Chalets*, T5222783, wwwcastlemountain.com, are very nice but not as good value as *Johnston Canyon Resort* (see above). Some have hot tubs, all have kitchens. **E** *Castle Mountain Hostel* is opposite, T7624122. Fairly basic with 28 dorm beds, laundry and kitchen. With just 44 sites, **F** *Castle Mountain Campground* is one of the smaller, nicer sites in the park. No showers though.

Castle About 5 km to the west is the Castle Crags trail (7 km return, 520 m elevation Crags trail gain). This short but steep hike leads to an old fire lookout and an outstanding panorama of the Bow Valley from Banff to Lake Louise. It is also free of snow earlier and later than most trails. On the way up you'll pass wildflower gardens and a dilapidated old cabin.

Sleeping and eating Beyond the cabin, opposite the train tracks, the very basic **F** *Protection Mountain Campground* with 89 sites, is best avoided. Another 10 km brings you to **A** *Baker Creek Chalets*, T5223761, www.bakercreek.com Fairly nice 1- and 2-bedroom log cabins with kitchenettes. Good value. The *Baker Creek Bistro* is a very good if expensive restaurant, with a pleasant outdoor patio and a licensed lounge.

Lake Louise

Magnificent Lake Louise is the single most famous icon in the Rockies, and consequently receives far more visitors than any scene of natural beauty should have to endure. This is the only focus in the park other than Banff Townsite, with a much better assortment of trails and attractions, but far fewer facilities. There are actually four components to Lake Louise: the Lake, the Village, the Ski Hill, and Moraine Lake.

Colour map 2, grid B3
Phone code: 403,
Altitude: 1,540 m,
1,731 m at the lake.

Banff Airporter, T7626700, from Calgary airport ($45), *Greyhound, Brewsters*, and the *Hostel shuttle* all stop here (see Banff Transport). *Vista Lake Louise* is a free shuttle from the campground and village to Moraine Lake and Lake Louise. From Jun 26 to Sep 5 it leaves at least every hour, every half hour at peak times.

Getting there & around
See also Rockies introduction, page 300

You'll come to the village first, close to the important junction where Highway 1 veers west through Yoho towards Golden and Revelstoke. Highway 93 then becomes the sole route north, henceforth known as the Icefields Parkway. This 'village' is little more than the ugly, overpriced Samson Mall, though it does contain most of the limited local accommodation, including one of the best hostels in the country, and the excellent **Lake Louise Visitor Centre**, T5223833. June-September 0800-1800, rest of the year 0900-1600 or 1700. As in Banff, this Parks Office/Information Centre helps out with hikes and accommodation, handing out brochures and maps, and issuing backcountry permits. A number of interesting natural history exhibits explain some of the local geographical features, including displays on the Burgess Shale in Field.

The Village

There are many lakes in the Rockies whose water has an opaque, milky quality due to the presence of glacial silt known as 'rock flour', mineral deposits that glaciers have scraped from the mountain rock. These particles absorb all colours of the light spectrum except green and blue. Far and away the most famous is Lake Louise, whose milky water is of the most exquisite aquamarine colour (or colours, because the hue changes dramatically according to the time of year and angle of the sun). Add to this the lake's sheer size and dramatic location at the foot of an incredibly powerful, towering rock rampart, and it is not difficult to understand why this is *the* definitive picture postcard image of the Rockies, the single most popular sight in the range.

The Lake

Around 10,000 people come here every day in peak season, so if you want to see its shores uncrowded, arrive at sunrise. It comes as little surprise that this was the spot chosen by the CPR for the second of their giant hotels, originally built in 1890. Many visitors are shocked by the behemoth **Château**, and consider its monstrous presence on the shores of the heavenly water an outrage that would never be allowed today. The best thing is to ignore it and go for a walk, or hire a canoe and go for a paddle. **Lake Agnes Tea House** and **Plain of the Six Glaciers Tea House** are each situated on popular trails about one or two hours' hike above the lake.

Lake Louise is 4.5 km from the Village up a steep hill (2.7 km on foot). Halfway up, a left fork leads 12.5 km to Moraine Lake, another striking emerald product of rock flour. Half the size of its sister, equally beautiful, and almost as popular, its location is maybe even more dramatic. Stretching away from its shores is the

Moraine Lake

Canadian Rockies

▶ ## Hikes around Lake Louise

From the Lake

Saddleback/Fairview Mountain *(7.4-10.6 km return, 600-1,014 m elevation gain. Trailhead: by the canoe rental at northeast end of lake)* The hike to Saddleback, despite its steepness, is very popular, especially in September when the larches turn to gold. This is a great viewpoint. Even better is Saddle Mountain, 90 m straight up above it. Best of all is Fairview Mountain, a further steep 1.6-km climb. The panorama from here is to drool for, with gargantuan peaks all around Lake Louise 1,000 m below.

Mount St Piran *(11.4 km, 920 m elevation gain)* The ascent here is steep enough to discourage most visitors, and leads to magnificent views of the area's many lofty cliffs and peaks.

Plain of the Six Glaciers *(13.8 km, 380 m elevation gain)* This popular trail takes you up to the Teahouse, and is perpetually crowded. Go anyway, because the views are astounding, embracing the giant peaks of mounts Lefroy and Victoria, and their extensive glaciers and icefalls. Try starting after 1600 to minimize the company.

From Moraine Lake Road

Paradise Valley/Lake Annette *(18.2-km circuit/11.4 km return, 400 m/250 m elevation gain. Trailhead: 2.5 km from junction with Lake Louise Drive, 10 km before Moraine Lake.)* Though this is a valley hike, the views it offers are as good or better than most ridge walks, with plenty of peaks and sheer, awesome rock faces. A return hike to Lake Annette is phenomenal in itself, but the longer circuit is recommended, and best done in a clockwise direction. Shortly after Lake Annette, a short steep ascent leads to Sentinel Pass, for a possible 17-km one-way combination with the following hike. Otherwise, Horseshoe Meadow has a backcountry campground for those who want to take their time and extend it into a two-day trip. A possible worthwhile detour is to Giant Steps, where a river cascades slowly over some truly enormous slabs of quartzite. The paths there are confusing.

From Moraine Lake

Valley of the Ten Peaks/Sentinel Pass *(11.6 km return, 725 m elevation gain. Trailhead: past the lodge)* This wonderful, exhilarating trail leads through Larch Valley, a particularly popular spot in the autumn when the trees turn to gold. It is a fairly gentle hike most of the way until the final switchback ascent to the pass, which is not as hard as it looks. The view from the top is spectacular, taking in most of the ten peaks, and looking down on the other side into Paradise Valley. This hike can be combined with the Paradise Valley one to make a 17-km one-way trip ending 10 km down Moraine Lake Road. The best bet is to leave a vehicle here and hitch or take the shuttle up to Moraine Lake. This is a very popular trail but only takes four or five hours so think about starting early or late. **Consolation Lakes** *(6 km return, 60 m elevation gain)* Though no substitute for the above, this is a short and easy walk, and the cliffs that tower over the lakes are undeniably impressive. The rough trail beyond the first lake means that the second is always less busy.

From the Ski Area

Skoki Valley *(31.6 km, 785 m elevation gain. Trailhead: follow Whitehorn Road towards the Ski Area, turn right at Km 2 onto Fish Creek Road and follow for 1.1 km)* The high point of this hike are the alpine meadows, and numerous lakes surrounded by rugged mountains with a romantically desolate air. The down side is that many hikers come this way, meaning trails are muddy if it's been raining. At least the first 4 km are on a boring fire-road. Think of doing it as a day-trip and cycle that section. If camping, Merlin Meadows and Baker Lake are the best options, or you could stay at the Skoki Lodge, T5223555. A fine day-hike from here is the 6.2-km round-trip to the beautiful Merlin Lake. A 1.6-km scramble up Skoki Mountain leads to 360° views. This is also a very popular area for cross-country skiing.

Valley of the Ten Peaks, a wonderfully scenic cluster of mighty mountains, also known as the **Wenkchemna**, the Stoney word for ten. Some excellent trails lead into the valley and up to viewpoints. Expensive canoes can be rented for a paddle ($27 per hour). The lodge here (see Sleeping, below) is one of the few expensive Rockies resorts that can justify their elevated price, and would be a prime choice for a honeymoon or splurge. Parking is a problem, best avoided by leaving your car down at the village and catching the free *Vista* bus.

Just before the Bow Valley Parkway crosses Highway 1 on its way to Lake Louise, it passes the turn-off to the Ski Area, T5223555. This is the biggest ski hill in Canada, 40 sq km of terrain featuring vast open bowls. With excellent powder and stupendous views, it ranks for almost all ski aficionados as one of the best hills in North America. A high-speed gondola and 11 lifts service terrain that is 25% beginner, 45% intermediate and 30% expert. The top elevation is 2,637 m, with a vertical drop of 1,000 m. The only drawbacks are the low snowfall of 360 m, and the fact that it is bitterly cold up there, not helped by the fact that most runs are above the tree-line. The lodges at the bottom are open year round, with restaurants, pubs and lounges, a cappuccino bar, equipment rentals and lessons. A day pass is $45.

Lake Louise Ski Area

In summer, the **Lake Louise Sightseeing Gondola** runs people to the top of the hill to enjoy the views, though there's not much to do up there apart from that. The *Environmental Education Centre* runs free guided nature walks daily at 1000, 1230, 1430 and 1630. ■ *May 0900-1600, Jun-Sep 0800-1800.*

Canadian Rockies

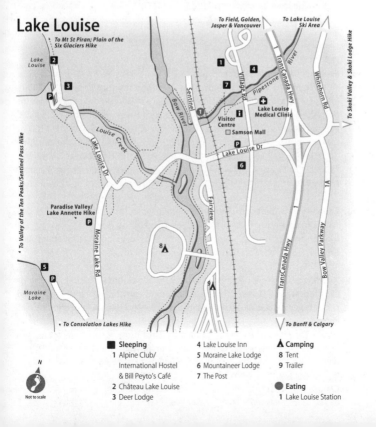

Lake Louise

To Field, Golden, Jasper & Vancouver
To Lake Louise Ski Area
To Skoki Valley & Skoki Lodge Hike

To Mt St Piran; Plain of the Six Glaciers Hike

Lake Louise

To Valley of the Ten Peaks/Sentinel Pass Hike

Louise Creek

Bow River
Sentinel Rd
Village Rd
Pipestone River
TransCanada Hwy
Whitehorn Rd

Lake Louise Medical Clinic

Visitor Centre

Samson Mall

Lake Louise Dr

Fairview

Lake Louise Dr
Moraine Lake Rd

Paradise Valley/ Lake Annette Hike

TransCanada Hwy
Bow Valley Parkway
1A

Moraine Lake

To Consolation Lakes Hike

To Banff & Calgary

N

Not to scale

■ **Sleeping**
1 Alpine Club/ International Hostel & Bill Peyto's Café
2 Château Lake Louise
3 Deer Lodge
4 Lake Louise Inn
5 Moraine Lake Lodge
6 Mountaineer Lodge
7 The Post

▲ **Camping**
8 Tent
9 Trailer

● **Eating**
1 Lake Louise Station

$17, $9 concessions, $2 extra for breakfast buffet, $6 extra for lunch buffet.
T5223555. A free shuttle bus to the hill leaves the Village every hour on the
hour from 0800-1700, leaving the *Château* 30 minutes earlier.

Sleeping
■ *on map,*
page 323

The Village LL *The Post Hotel*, 200 Pipestone Rd, T5223989, www.posthotel.com
The Village's luxury option, built in a Swiss Alpine style with lots of wood. Small but nice
rooms with patio or balcony, pool, sauna, pub, expensive restaurant. **L-A** *Lake Louise
Inn*, 210 Village Rd, T5223791, www.lakelouiseinn.com Poor value, standard
motel-style rooms. Better is the **A** *Mountaineer Lodge*, 101 Village Rd, T5223844,
www.mountaineerlodge.com Standard rooms, hot tub, steam room. **E** *Alpine
Club/International Hostel*, Village Rd, T5222200, www.hostellingintl.ca/alberta A
spacious, attractive, well-equipped hostel. Dorms and private double rooms ($6 per
person extra), some with en suite bath. Two kitchens, laundry, library, lots of common
places to relax, map access, internet, and an excellent cheap restaurant. Some guided
tours. Reservations well in advance are essential. **Camping** There are 2 campgrounds
in the Village, neither very nice. **F** *Lake Louise Tent* has 220 sites and showers. **F** *Lake
Louise Trailer* has 189 sites with hook-ups and is open year-round.

The Lake LL *Château Lake Louise*, T5223511, www.fairmont.com It is a piece of
history and has a location to die for, but the 497 rooms, 4 dining rooms and multiple facilities fail to justify these prices. Nearby is the **AL** *Deer Lodge*, 109 Lake Louise Dr,
T6096150, www.crmr.com Apparently built in 'vintage national-park gothic' style, with
antique furnishings, this hotel has plenty of character, but its rooms are very small and
rather ordinary. Roof top hot tub, expensive but decent restaurant with a nice patio.

Moraine Lake LL *Moraine Lake Lodge*, T5223733, www.morainelake.com Comfortable, attractive, nicely decorated and well-equipped cabins or lodge rooms. Genuine luxury and class in a prime location. Worth a splurge. Has a first-class, expensive
restaurant, and a pleasant little café.

Eating
■ *on map,*
page 323

Expensive *Deer Lodge*, Upper Lake Louise, T5223747. 'Rocky Mountain Cuisine'
including elk and wild mushrooms. Great patio. **Mid-range** *Bill Peyto's Cafe* in the
Hostel. Cafeteria-style. Great breakfasts, pastas, salads, large portions. *Lake Louise Station*, 200 Sentinel Rd in Village, T5222600. Pleasant interior with lots of wood, high ceilings and big windows. Steak, pastas, fish and game. Lovely garden patio with BBQ in
the summer, a fine spot for a drink. Open until midnight. There's also a vintage railway
car with an expensive menu, open 1800-2100. *Village Grill and Bar*, in Samson Mall,
T5223879. Family-style joint with all-day breakfast, sandwiches, etc. **Cheap** *Laggan's
Bakery*, in the Samson Mall. Good bakery items and cheap sandwiches to go.

Shopping

Camping and sports gear *Wilson Mountain Sports Ltd*, in the Village, T5223636,
www.lakelouisewilsons.com Bikes $29 per day, climbing equipment, camping and
fishing gear to buy or rent. $20 per day for tent, $9 per day for backpack. **Food** *Village
Grocery*, in Samson Mall. Overpriced, but essential.

Summer sports

For **hiking**, see below. Some local trails are ideal for **mountain biking**. The 14.6-km
return **Ross Lake** trail starts behind the *Château* and leads through forest to a small lake
beneath a steep rockwall. The more demanding 10-km **Moraine Lake Highline** leads
from the Paradise Valley trailhead to the scenic lake, sometimes closed due to grizzly
activity. The 13.4-km **Pipestone** trail starts off Slate Rd just west of the Village, and follows the Pipestone River to the valley. The 7 km **Bow River Loop** is a gentle trail on
both sides of the river. The 10.5-km one-way **Great Divide Path** is a paved but traf-
fic-free route starting at Km 3.6 on Lake Louise Drive and ending at Hwy 1 in Yoho.
Canoes can be rented at both lakes. **Horse riding** *Timberline Tours*, T5223743. All
day for $110, 3-day trip $400.

As well as top notch **downhill** at Lake Louise Ski Area, there is fine **cross-country ski-** **Winter sports**
ing in the Skoki Valley. A shuttle from behind the ski-hill takes you 10 km to the
trailhead for an 11 km ski-in to **B-C** *Skoki Lodge*, T5223555. The log cabins here make
an excellent base for getting into the backcountry, and have been used as such since
the 1930s when the lodge put Lake Louise on the Nordic ski map. Lake Louise (the lake)
provides an idyllic location for **ice-skating**. Skates can be rented at *Monod Sports* in
the *Château*. *Brewsters*, T5223522, organize **sleigh rides** on the lake.

Communications Canada Post: in Samson Mall, which also has internet machines **Directory**
and ATMs. **Medical Services** *Lake Louise Medical Clinic*, 200 Hector St, T5222184.
Also at the clinic is *Temple Mountain Therapeutic Massage*, T5223003, $60 per hr.

The Icefields Parkway

This 230-km road between Lake Louise and Jasper runs through some of the
Rockies' most spectacular scenery, bridging the two major parks, and must
qualify as one of the most exciting drives in the world. In fact, the endless
parade of lofty snow-capped peaks and vast glaciers is likely to push you
towards sensory overload. The climax comes just beyond the Sunwapta Pass
that separates Banff and Jasper National Parks. This is the Columbia Icefield,
the single largest and most accessible area of ice and snow in the Rockies.

Though it straddles the two major parks, the Parkway is treated here as an
entity in itself, with distances given from Lake Louise. Dotted along the road at
fairly regular intervals are five youth hostels, twelve campgrounds, and a
whole host of long and short trails. Pick up the *Icefields Parkway* map/guide
from a Visitor Centre in Banff, Lake Louise or Jasper. If making the journey by
bus, sit on the left-hand side coming from Banff, and tell the driver in advance
where you would like to be dropped. There are few services along what,
despite its heavy use, remains a region of extreme wilderness. Road closures
are common from October onwards. If cycling, note that Jasper is 500 m
higher than Banff. Bikes can be rented in Jasper for one-way trips.

Lake Louise to the Columbia Icefield

At Km 28 is Mosquito Creek. As the name suggests, bugs can be a problem. **Mosquito**
This is due to the proximity of the Bow River flats. Park here and walk across **Creek**
the road and over the bridge for the start of the **Fish Lakes/Pipestone**
Pass/Devon Lakes trail (29.6-62.8 km, 762 m-1,116 m elevation gain) This
trail leads through mostly open terrain with scenery that is consistently wonderful. There are a few possible itineraries. **North Molar Pass** would make a
good 23-km day-hike. On this route, a scramble east of the pass gives views of
the Fish Lakes and Pipestone River valley. **Upper Fish Lake** is reached at Km
14.8, a conceivable day-trip for fast hikers. But the campground, right on the
lake beneath a towering rock wall, is a fine spot for a night in the mountains.
To make it a four-day trip, continue to Pipestone Pass, with extensive views
that include 19 km of the **Siffleur River Valley**, through the rolling meadows
of **Clearwater Pass**, and on to the quiet and remote **Devon Lakes** at Km 31.4.

Sleeping The hostel at Mosquito Creek has 38 dorm beds in 4 log cabins, a kitchen,
common room and sauna. The small and basic year-round campground has 38 sites of
which 20 are walk-in only.

Canadian Rockies

Cirque Peak At Km 34 is the **Crowfoot Glacier** viewpoint, and trailhead for the **Cirque Peak/Helen Lake** trail (15 km return, 1,043 m elevation gain) This is one of the best hikes in the Rockies. You get pretty quickly to open sub-alpine meadows covered with heather and some of the most beautiful displays of wild flowers in the range, with views of the impressive surrounding mountains. The marmots at Helen Lake are among the most daring and entertaining anywhere. From the lake to Cirque Peak is a long, slow scramble up a scree slope, but it's not as difficult as it appears. The 360° views from the top, which take in the Dolomite Valley, Bow Lake, Peyto Lake, Crowfoot Glacier and Bow Glacier, more than justify the effort.

Bow Lake & Bow Lake, at Km 37, is a beautiful lake whose turquoise hue seems almost
Peyto Lake supernaturally vivid. A number of fine trails start here. **Bow Glacier Falls** (9 km return, 148 m elevation gain) is the easiest, little more than an excuse to stroll along the shore of the striking lake, and witness the birthplace of the Bow River. The **Bow Hut** trail (14.8 km return, 500 m elevation gain) follows the same trail almost to the falls, then heads uphill through a canyon to a mountaineering hut close to the edge of the vast Wapta Icefield. The rock and ice views are wonderful, but those scared of heights might baulk at the final ascent.

Bow Summit (2,069 m) at the 40-km mark is the highest pass in the Rockies and the highest highway crossing in Canada. Just beyond, a short side-road leads to the exceptional but very busy viewpoint above Peyto Lake, another of those Rockie mountain icons whose undeniable beauty can get lost among the throngs and clamour. It's named after Bill Peyto, a legendary Rocky pioneer who was as famous for his exploits around town as for his wilderness exploration. The **Bow Lookout** trail (6 km return, 260 m elevation gain) gets you away from the crowds and up to a former fire lookout. Commanding views take in the many lofty peaks that line the Parkway, and offer another perspective on the fabulous Bow Lake.

Sleeping and eating A *Num-Ti-Jah Lodge*, Bow Lake, T5222167, www.num-ti-jah.com enjoys a prime location on its shore. This octagonal construction, one of the oldest and most interesting in the range, was built in 1920 by Jimmy Simpson, a legendary pioneering guide and clearly a fascinating character. Age has lent a lot of charm to the rooms, which include some cheaper options with shared washroom. There is an outdoor sauna, a fine restaurant, and a coffee shop. Its excessive popularity is a little off-putting, and makes advance booking a necessity.

North to The **Mistaya Canyon** trail, at Km 71, is a pleasant 300-m stroll along a pretty
Rampart Creek canyon. At Km 77 is **Saskatchewan Crossing**, the junction with Highway 11 to Rocky Mountain House and Red Deer. This grim crossroads is a useful service centre, a rare chance to get gas and essential supplies like camera film.

At Km 89 is **Rampart Creek**. Just north is the **Sunset Pass** trail (16.4 km return, 725 m elevation gain). This long expanse of pretty meadows is usually snow-free by late June, but can be very wet and is prime grizzly habitat. The landscape opens up as you proceed, climaxing at the north end with views of the deep blue Lake Pinto.

Sleeping Km 57 F *Waterfowl Lake Campground*, 116 nice sites close to the lake. **Km 77 B-C** *The Crossing*, Saskatchewan Crossing, T7617000, is an overpriced but heavily booked standard motel. There is also a fast-food cafeteria, a restaurant, a grocery store and a tacky gift shop. **Km 89** The summer-only **hostel** (**E**)at Rampart Creek has 30 beds in 2 cabins. The basic but pleasant **F campground** has 50 sites on the river.

Some 25 km north of Rampart Creek, the road enters a dramatic giant switch-back known as the 'Big Bend'. The Saskatchewan Glacier trail at its foot is not recommended. At the top are the impressive **Panther Falls**, and a couple of viewpoints where you can stop and enjoy the sweep of mountains back to the south. Look out also for the **Weeping Wall**, where water plunges down from a series of cracks in the apparently solid rock face. At Km 113 is the **Nigel Pass** trail (14.4 km return, 365 m elevation gain) This is an easy, gentle hike suitable for anyone. The views are huge and constant. At the pass, look beyond to the more starkly beautiful, formidable peaks of the upper Brazeau Valley. This is the opening section of the multi-day backpacking trip to **Jonas Pass** and **Poboktan Pass** (80 km return, 1,913 m elevation gain) Among the best long hikes in the range, this network of trails presents many options and factors that require thought and research. The highlight of the trip is Jonas Pass, an 11-km high meadow valley with pristine mountain scenery. **Pobokton Pass** is also a delight to explore, but both the loop via Brazeau Lake and the one-way exit along Pobokton Creek have major drawbacks. Better is to camp at Jonas Cutoff, day-hike to Pobokton Pass, pass another night at the Cutoff, then hike out the same way. The lack of camping throughout Jonas Pass means either hiking 33 km to the Cutoff campground, then 33 km out on the third day, or breaking the journey by camping at Four Point (14 km), making it a five-day trip.

About 4 km further on is the **Parker Ridge** trail (4.8 km return, 270 m elevation gain) This is one of those hikes whose rewards far outweigh the effort expended. Breathtaking views take in the awesome expanse of the 9-km-long Saskatchewan Glacier, the longest tongue of the Columbia Icefield. Just 1 km further is the *Hilda Creek Hostel*, and shortly after **Sunwapta Pass** (2,023 m) marks the border between the national parks. Jasper is 108 km northwest, Banff is 189 km southeast.

Sleeping E *Hilda Creek Hostel* 21 beds in log cabins. Its marvellous location makes it one of the most sought after in the park.

The Columbia Icefield

The northern hemisphere's most extensive glacial area south of the Arctic Circle, the Columbia Icefield provides a dramatic introduction to Jasper National Park. As well as feeding three giant watersheds, its meltwaters are the source of some of the continent's mightiest rivers, including the Columbia, Saskatchewan and Athabasca, and drain into three oceans, the Atlantic, Pacific and Arctic. The only other icefield of equal scope and importance in the world is in Siberia. Most of the icefield's staggering 325 sq km terrain is high in the mountains out of view, but three of the six major glaciers are clearly visible from the road, including the huge **Athabasca Glacier** (6 km long, 1 km wide and 100 m thick), which you can walk or even be driven on (see below).

The ultimate way to see this spectacle is from the **Wilcox Pass** trail that starts just south of *Wilcox Creek Campground* (8 km return, 335 m elevation gain). This is one hike that everybody should do. Short and easy, it quickly whisks you to views that many longer hikes fail to equal. After a brief ascent through mature forest, the Columbia Icefield is suddenly visible in all its glory, and from an angle far more gratifying than you'll get taking the *Snocoach* (see below). Wildflower meadows and resident bighorn sheep complete the idyllic picture. With so much to be gained from so little effort, don't expect to be alone.

Many people choose to turn round at the icefield, and indeed this is the high point of the drive

Canadian Rockies

Sleeping F *Wilcox Creek* and F *Columbia Icefield* campgrounds enjoy one of the prime locations in the Rockies, and are both predictably very crowded. The latter is for tents only, with very nice walk-in sites.

The Icefield Centre A joint venture by *Brewster* and *Parks Canada* (open April-October), the Icefield Centre resembles an airport and totally takes the edge off the wondrous surroundings, although it is a fine vantage point from which to ogle the Athabasca Glacier. The **Glacier Gallery** contains well-mounted informative displays, explaining glaciation, the icefield, and the stories behind it. ■ *0900-2100. Free.* The **Parks Canada** desk is helpful, and can provide maps and leaflets for whichever park you are entering.

Brewster's Snocoach tours take you onto the glacier in a specially built bus (see Tour operators, below). Don't be tempted to walk on the glacier alone: people are killed and injured every year. Either they fall into one of its many crevasses, or injure themselves on the sharp sediment embedded in the ice.

Sleeping and eating AL *Columbia Icefield Chalet*, T1877-4237433, has nice, heavily booked rooms, spacious and comfy with high ceilings and loft. There is an expensive Chinese restaurant and a hamburger/hotdog cafeteria as well as a gift shop with photo gear and glacier water sold in vending machines.

Tour operators *Brewster's Snocoach* tours take you onto the glacier in a specially built bus that moves at a snail's pace, doing the 5-km round trip in 55 mins. Tours leave every 15 mins, May-Oct daily, and cost $27, $13.50 concessions. T7626767. *Parks Canada* also run 2 different guided walks on the Icefield. 1100 daily except Sun and Thu, 3 hrs, $40, $20 concessions, climbing 200 m; 1100 Sun and Thu, 6 hrs, $45, $22 concessions, climbing 600 m to get above the glacier. Crampons are provided if necessary, 20 people per hike, T8525595. Tickets can be bought at the Icefield Centre.

North to Jasper

Beauty Creek After so much rich fare, the easy 3.6-km Beauty Creek trail, which starts 15.5 km to the north, provides a nice change. This tiny chasm and its chain of pretty scaled-down waterfalls can be an uplifting sight. The mountains along this stretch of highway are striated at a 45° angle, and resemble cresting waves.

Sleeping and eating The summer-only E *Beauty Creek Hostel*, T8523215, is very basic with 24 beds in 2 cabins, outdoor toilets, no showers, and a small kitchen. All-you-can-eat pancake breakfast $4, some groceries for sale. F *Jonas Creek Campground*, 9 km further along, has 25 sites, some walk-in only.

Sunwapta Falls At 53 km from the Icefield Centre, a side road leads to Sunwapta Falls, which are mostly interesting for the canyon they have carved through the valley.

Sleeping A *Sunwapta Falls Resort*, T780-8524852, has small but nice and cosy rooms, a sun deck, and a reasonable restaurant. Bike rentals $6/hr or $18/day. A little further on F *Honeymoon Lake Campground* is one of the nicer places to camp, with 35 spacious sites, some right on the lake.

Athabasca Falls At this point Highway 93A, the old Parkway, branches off from Highway 93 and runs parallel for 30 km, providing access to a campground, a hostel, Marmot Basin ski hill and a number of hikes. These are covered in the Jasper section, below.

Jasper National Park

Jasper feels much closer to wilderness than Banff. Neither as world famous nor as convenient to reach, it receives far fewer visitors, and has 10,878 sq km over which to spread them, an area bigger than Banff, Yoho and Kootenay national parks combined. Vast tracts of this land are extremely remote and practically inaccessible, the overall emphasis being less on instant gratification, more on long backcountry hikes that account for much of Jasper's 1,000 km of trails. Apart from the trails on the Icefields Parkway that have already been covered, most are close to the pleasant town of Jasper, or around the attractive Maligne Lake, 48 km away.

For Hikes in Jasper National Park, see page 336

Jasper Townsite

Jasper is a far more relaxed base than Banff, having managed to hold on to its small-town charm despite a turnover of some three million visitors per year. There is little in the way of out-of-control commercialism, and not much to do. Almost everything is on Connaught Drive, the road in and out of town, or Patricia Drive which runs parallel to it. The only possible 'sight' in town is the **Yellowhead Museum and Archives**, with a number of predictable displays exploring the town's fur-trade and railway. ■ *Summer 1000-2100, winter Thu-Sun 1000-1700. $3, $2 concessions. 400 Pyramid Lake Rd, T8523013.*

Phone code: 780
Colour map 2, grid A2
Population: 5,000
Altitude: 1,067 m

Explorer David Thompson passed through the area on his way to opening up the Athabasca Pass, and left William Henry to establish Henry House, the first permanent European dwelling. Like most of the Rockies, however, white settlers were overwhelmingly outnumbered by Native Americans well into the 20th century. And as usual, it was the coming of the railway that proved the turning point. Following the success of the CPR with their route through Banff and Yoho, the Grand Trunk Pacific Railway routed its line through Jasper in 1902, and the Jasper Forest Park was created six years later. The first accommodation for tourists, a collection of tents on Lac Beauvert, were replaced in 1921 by the *Jasper Park Lodge*, which has continued to upgrade ever since.

The **Information Centre/Parks Canada** are nicely situated in the pretty 1914 stone building in the city park at 500 Connaught Dr, Sep-Jun 0900-1700, Jul-Aug 0800-1900. T8526176 for general information, T8526177 for trail information, www.jaspercanadianrockies.com They have information on accommodation and trails, issue Park and Wilderness Passes, and hand out a number of useful maps such as the *Backcountry Visitors' Guide*, the *Day-hiker's Guide* and a *Cycling Guide*. They also operate a voluntary safety registration system. All Park-run campgrounds operate on a first-come, first-served basis. **Parks Canada** gives guided walks around town leaving at 1000 and 1400, 2-3 hours, T8528487. **Friends of Jasper National Park** operate a number of free or cheap walking tours throughout the summer. For weather information call T8523185, www.tor.ec.gc.ca

Tourist information

Lakes Just 5 km east of town on Lodge Road are **Annette Lake** and **Edith Lake**, whose shallow waters are the warmest around in summer, making their beaches very popular for swimming and sunbathing. There is a wheelchair-accessible path around the former. The winding Pyramid Lake Road leads 8 km northwest of town to **Pyramid Lake** and **Patricia Lake**. Apart from good views of Pyramid Mountain, this duo offers a couple of alternatives to sleeping options in Jasper, plus fishing, boating and horse riding.

Excursions

Canadian Rockies

Jasper Tramway Canada's longest and highest tramway takes seven minutes to climb 1,000 vertical metres in 2.5 km. Expect to have to queue in the summer. At the top is an expensive restaurant, an interpretive centre, and excellent views. A steep trail gains another 600 m to reach **Whistlers Summit** at 2,470 m, and even more awe-inspiring vistas as far as Mount Robson 80 km away. ■ *Apr-Oct 0930-1630, till 2200 in summer. T8523093, www.jaspertramway.com 3 km south on Hwy 93, then 4 km west on Whistler Mountain Rd.*

Jasper National Park

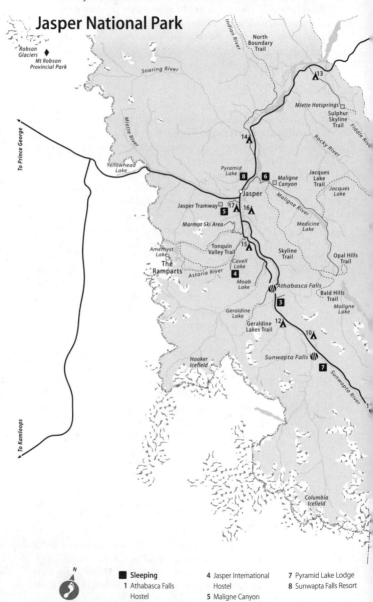

N

| 0 km | 10 |
| 0 miles | 10 |

■ Sleeping
1 Athabasca Falls Hostel
2 Beauty Creek Hostel
3 Hilda Creek Hostel

4 Jasper International Hostel
5 Maligne Canyon Hostel
6 Mt Edith Cavell Hostel

7 Pyramid Lake Lodge
8 Sunwapta Falls Resort

▲ Camping
9 Columbia Icefield

Maligne Lake Road This busy road branches off Highway 16 east of town, leading 48 km to the most popular attraction in the park, with a few major sights on the way. In summer it is perpetually crowded with a stream of vehicles. The *Maligne Lake Shuttle* makes the journey several times daily (see Transport, below). **Maligne Canyon**, 11.5 km from Jasper, is a spectacular gorge, 55 m deep and almost narrow enough to jump across. A number of short walking trails and footbridges lead to viewpoints. Unfortunately, the area is far too busy, and is taking on the unpleasant feel of a tourist trap. The canyon is at its most beautiful in winter, when the water freezes into an ice palace with 30-m icefalls and incredible blue ice caves. In winter a few operators (see below) run three-hour tours, with clampons, head lamps and other equipment provided ($35, $20 concessions). There is a hostel here, and the northern terminus of the famous **Skyline Trail**.

A further 21 km is the pretty **Medicine Lake**, whose water level fluctuates dramatically with the seasons because it fills and empties through sink-holes into an elaborate network of underground limestone caves. In summer the water is high, but in winter it sometimes disappears altogether. While such temporal variations fascinated Native Americans, the one-time visitor will see nothing but another lake.

Maligne Lake At 22 km long, beautiful Maligne Lake (pronounced 'maleen') is the largest lake in the Rockies, and the second largest glacier-fed lake in the world. Surrounded by white-peaked mountains, it is a sight to behold, but not of the Lake Louise magnitude. The best views open up from the middle of the lake. See Tour operators below for possible cruises and tours. Lots of hikes begin here (see box), including the Skyline Trail. For something shorter, the 3.2-km **Schäffer Viewpoint** loop leads along the east shore from Car Park 2. There is no accommodation at the lake apart from two backcountry campgrounds on the lakeshore that can only be reached by canoe (a four-hour trip), and must be booked at Jasper Information Centre.

To Edmonton

South Boundary Trail

Southesk Lake

Brazau Icefield

Brazeau Lake

Brazeau River

Stanley Falls

Nigel Pass/Jonas Pass/ Poboktan Pass Trail

Columbia Icefield, Icefield Centre & Chalet

Athabasca Glacier

Banff National Park

To Banff & Calgary

10 Honeymoon Lake
11 Jonas Creek
12 Mt Kerkeslin
13 Pocahontas
14 Snaring River
15 Wabasso
16 Wapiti
17 Whistlers
18 Wilcox Creek

Canadian Rockies

Miette Hot Springs   A favourite excursion from Jasper is to Miette Hot Springs, 60 km east on Highway 16, then 17 km south on Miette Road. **Ashlar Ridge Viewpoint** is 8.5 km down this road, with great views of this impressive rock wall. The springs are the hottest in the Rockies. Cooled from 54° C to 39° C, the water is chlorinated and runs into two large outdoor pools. Interpretive displays explain the local geology. ■ *Jun-Sep 0830-2230, $6, 5$ concessions, May-Jun and Sep-Oct 1030-2100. $5, $4 concessions. T8663939. Road closed winter.*

Sleeping
■ *on map*

Jasper's hotels are not much better value than Banff's, and are just as likely to be full in summer. **LL** *Jasper Park Lodge*, Lac Beauvert, off Maligne Lake Rd, T8523301, www.jasperparklodge.com More a village than a hotel, and more impressive than the other vast *Fairmont* complexes. The main lodge is modern, stylish and bustling with restaurants, lounges and shops. The rooms are in log buildings scattered over the vast grounds, chic and comfortable, with patios. There is a health club, tennis courts, a golf course, riding stables, boat, and mountain bike rentals, fishing, hiking and cross-country ski trails, a swimming pool and hot tubs. **LL-AL** Pyramid Lake Lodge, 5 km northwest on Pyramid Lake Rd, T8524900, www.pyramidlakeresort.com Attractive lakeside location. A variety of loft rooms, suites or cabins with fireplaces or balconies. Great restaurant and lounge. Boat and bike rentals. **L** *Sawridge Hotel Jasper*, 82 Connaught Dr, T8525111. Average rooms. Pool, hot tub, sauna, restaurant and lounge.

    AL *Amethyst Lodge*, 200 Connaught Dr, T8523394, www.mtn-park-lodges.com Big rooms with balcony, hot tub, lounge. Nicest of a chain which also includes the similarly-priced *Lobstick Lodge*, T8524431, and *Marmot Lodge*, T8524471. **AL** *Jasper Inn*, 98 Geike St, T8524461. Standard rooms with balcony, pool, laundry. **AL** *Whistlers Inn*,105 Miette Av, T8523361, www.WhistlersInn.com Hot tub, steamroom, in the heart of town. **A** *Mount Robson Inn* 902 Connaught Dr, T8523327. Slightly better than a motel room. **A** *Tekarra Lodge*, 1 km south off Hwy 93A, T8523058. Cabins or B&B lodge rooms set in the trees by the confluence of the Athabasca and Miette Rivers. Fireplaces or kitchens.

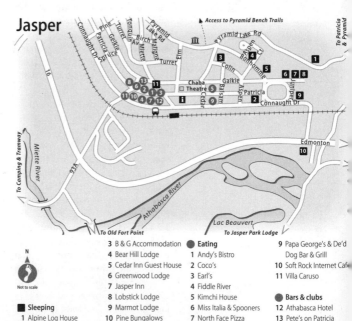

Jasper

	3 B & G Accommodation	9 Papa George's & De'd
	4 Bear Hill Lodge	Dog Bar & Grill
	5 Cedar Inn Guest House	10 Soft Rock Internet Cafe
	6 Greenwood Lodge	11 Villa Caruso
N	7 Jasper Inn	
	8 Lobstick Lodge	● **Bars & clubs**
Not to scale	9 Marmot Lodge	12 Athabasca Hotel
■ **Sleeping**	10 Pine Bungalows	13 Pete's on Patricia
1 Alpine Log House	11 Whistlers Inn	
2 Amethyst Lodge		

● **Eating**
1 Andy's Bistro
2 Coco's
3 Earl's
4 Fiddle River
5 Kimchi House
6 Miss Italia & Spooners
7 North Face Pizza
8 Nutters

B *Bear Hill Lodge*, 100 Bonhomme St, T8523209, www.BearHillLodge.com Good value bungalows, with kitchenette $20 extra, gas fireplace, full bath. **B-C** *Patricia Lake Bungalows*, 6 km north towards Pyramid Lake at Patricia Lake, T8523560, www.patricialakebungalows.com Motel room is a good deal, cottages are nicer, comfy and spacious with kitchen. Hot tub, laundry, canoe rentals. Good value. **B-C** *Pine Bungalows*, close to where Connaught Dr meets Hwy 16 at the east end of town, T8523491, pinebung@telusplanet.net Reasonable and economical motel-style rooms and cabins, some with kitchenettes, and nicer 3-room cabins for 4 people at $155.

There are plenty of private homes close to town with reasonably priced rooms (**C-D**) . Check at the tourist office for availability or call *Rocky Mountain Reservations*, T8529455, info@rockymountainreservations.com **C** *Alpine Log House*, 920 Pyramid Lake Rd, T8524420, patmarrek@hotmail.com 3 en suite rooms with private entrance. **C** *Castle Guest House*, 814 Miette Av, T8525768. Nice suites with big beds. **C** *Cedar Inn Guest House*, 209 Bonhomme St, T/F8525368. Small breakfast provided, shared bath. **D** *Greenwood Lodge*,104 Geike St, T8525099, gkb91@hotmail.com 1 room with balcony and private bath, 2 with shared bath, in town and very reasonable. **D** *B&G Accommodation*, 204 Colin Cr, T8524345. Shared bath, private entrance.

For all hostel reservations, call T8523215. **E** *Jasper International Youth Hostel*, 6 km south, near gondola on Whistlers Mountain Rd. Shuttles from Downtown. 80 beds, full kitchen, showers, laundry, bike rental. **E-F** *Maligne Canyon Hostel*, 11 km E, T8523584. 24 beds in 2 cabins near Canyon. Open year-round (closed Wed in winter). **E-F** *Mount Edith Cavell Hostel*, Edith Cavell Rd, 13 km off Hwy 93A, 26 km south. 32 beds in 2 cabins with views of the Angel Glacier. Sauna. Handy for trails, popular.

Camping Campsites close to Jasper fill up fast in summer, with queues starting about 1100. A $3 fire fee includes wood. **F** *Whistlers*, 3 km south off Hwy 93. 781 sites, including some with full hook-ups. Tenters should try to get a walk-in site. **F** *Wapiti*, 4 km south on Hwy 93. 362 sites, some with electric, showers. Open year-round. OK for being so close to town. **F** *Wabasso*, 15 km south on Hwy 93A. 228 sites. Its inconvenient location tends to mean it's the last one to fill up. **F** *Snaring River*, 15 km north off Hwy 16 on the road towards Celestine Lake. This is the nicest campground. When all others are full, there is overflow camping here with space for 500. Not a bad place to be stuck. **F** *Pocohontas*, 45 km east then 1 km on Miette Hot Springs Rd. 140 reasonable sites.

Jasper has over 100 backcountry sites. Wilderness Passes cost $6 per person per night, refundable up to 1000 on proposed date of departure. Reservation (with $10 fee) at Information Centre or T8526177, up to 3 months before departure.

Expensive *Fiddle River*, 620 Connaught Dr, T8523032. Nice variety of seafood dishes, big wine list. *Andy's Bistro*, 606 Patricia St, T8524559. European-influenced cuisine, mostly meat, cheese fondue. *The Pines* at Pyramid Lake, T8524900. Dishes like smoked trout chowder and seafood pasta flavoured with black sambuca, patio overlooking the lake. The prices seem reasonable. *Villa Caruso*, 640 Connaught Dr, T8523920. Steak and seafood, nice atmosphere with balcony seating. **Mid-range** *Earl's*, 600 Patricia St. Seating with views on the 2nd-floor balcony. *Kimchi House*, 407 Patricia St, T8525022. Actually in someone's little house, some outdoor seating in their backyard, a cultural experience. Korean BBQ dishes big enough for 2. *Miss Italia*, upstairs at 610 Patricia, T8524002. Sweet spot with little tables on the balcony, lots of plants, good pasta. *Papa George's*, 404 Connaught Dr, T8523351. 'Family' restaurant with good food and cream tea in the afternoon. **Cheap** *North Face Pizza*, 618 Connaught Dr. Pizza and burgers.

Eating
● *on map*

Coco's 608 Patricia St. Hang-out spot with good coffee and music, magazines. *Soft Rock Internet Café*, 622 Connaught Dr. Good breakfast and grilled sandwiches, internet $1/10 mins. *Spooners*, 610 Patricia St. Nice place on second floor, lots of light, balcony, organic coffee, delicious baking and sandwiches.

Cafés

Bars & clubs *Athabasca Hotel*, 510 Patricia St. Sleezy night club with DJs and occasional live music. *De'd Dog Bar and Grill*, 404 Connaught Dr. Fairly good ale on tap, pool table and darts. *Whistle Stop*, 105 Miette Av in *Whistlers Inn*. A smoky dive. *Pete's on Patricia*, 614 Patricia St. Occasional live music. Dancing. Most of the hotels have 'lounges' for a quiet drink (except for the big screen TVs).

Entertainment *Chaba Theatre*, 604 Connaught Dr. First-run movies.

Festivals *Children's Festival*, 1-day event at Jasper Activity Centre in **May**. *Heritage Folk Festival*, T8523615. Biennial music festival held in **Aug** (2003, 2005).

Shopping **Books and maps** *Friends of Jasper National Park*, across from the Information Centre on Connaught Rd, T8524767, friends@incentre.net **Camping and hiking gear** *Outdoor Supplies*, 625 Patricia St. **Food** *Bear Paw Bakery*, 4 Cedar Av. Fresh bread and rhubarb squares, coffee. *Nutters*, 622 Patricia St. Health food and bulk hiking snacks, good salamis and cheeses. *Super A Foods*, 601 Patricia St. Groceries. **Photography** *Tekarra Color Lab*, 600 Patricia St.

Summer sports *On-Line Sport*, 600 Patricia St, T8523630, are the best first stop for most sports equipment, rentals and tours. They rent bikes, snowshoes, fishing gear, canoes and boats, and backpacking gear. *Jasper Source for Sports*, 406 Patricia St, T8523654, is another good all-round store, renting bikes, canoes, ice-skates, etc. **Biking** Pick up the *Jasper Cycling Guide* at the Information Centre. There are several good trails right from town. Experienced bikers will enjoy the **Saturday Night Lake Loop**, 27 km, starting at the Cabin Lake Rd parking lot, west end of town. Views of Miette and Athabasca Valley. There is some good riding across the river at **Old Fort Point**, which is also the start of the 23-km **Trail No 7**, a good all-level ride passing through Maligne Canyon. *Freewheel Cycle*, 618 Patricia St, T8523898, www.freewheeljasper.com $24-$30 per day. Trail-maps, rentals, tours and information. **Climbing** *Gravity Gear*, 618 Patricia St, T8523155. Ask them about climbing at Maligne Canyon, Rock Gardens and Boulder Garden. Hidden Valley, 30 km east, is good for the experienced. **Golf** *Jasper Park Lodge*, T8526090. One of the finest and most scenic courses in the country. High-season fees are $95-119. **Swimming** *Jasper Aquatic Centre*, 401 Pyramid Lake Rd, T8523663. $6.

Winter sports **Skiing** Marmot Basin, T8523816, www.skimarmot.com, has a reputation for being one of the most spacious, friendly and uncrowded ski hills in the country. It receives 400 cm of powder per year, with no need for snow-makers. 8 lifts service 465 ha of skiable terrain, which breaks up evenly into 35% beginner, 35% intermediate and 30% expert. The top elevation is 2,601 m, with a vertical drop of 914 m and a longest run of 5.6 km. At Maligne Lake are 20 km of groomed **cross-country ski** trails. The Bald Hills up above offer plenty of space for telemarking and touring, but the 480 m elevation gain over 5.5 km makes it hard work getting there. The 5 km **Beaver/Summit Lake** trail, Km 27 on Maligne Lake Rd, gives easy access to the backcountry. There are 1-30-km trails at **Pyramid Bench** and around Patricia Lake. **Jasper Park Lodge** also has a network of groomed loops from 5-10 km. The 4.5-km **Whistlers Campground** loop is flat, easy and lit up at night. **Moab Lake** is a nice, easy 18-km trail with great views, 20 km south on Hwy 93A.

Beyond the Beaten Path, T8525650, run Maligne Canyon **icewalks**, and **snowshoe/cross-country** ski tours. *Walks and Talks*, T8524945, run guided ski and snowshoe tours. *Jasper Adventure Centre*, T8525595, arrange **dog-sled** packages. There is **ice-skating** on Lac Beauvert by *Jasper Park Lodge*, on Pyramid Lake, and on an indoor rink at *Jasper Activity Centre*, 303 Pyramid Av, T8523381.

Canadian Rockies

Bird-watching and wildlife *Birding Tours*, T8523630. 3-hr tour in Jasper, $49.
Half-day tour on a canoe, $149. *Alpine Art*, T8523709, www.aa.net **Carriage** *Jasper*
Carriage Co, T8523562. 4-seater horse-drawn carriage tours around town.
Climbing *Jasper Climbing School*, T8523964. **Fishing** *Currie's Guiding & Tackle*,
T8525650, www.curriesguiding.com Also run sightseeing van tours and wildlife
searching. **Flightseeing** *Air Jasper*, Hinton Airport, T8525595. Just over 1 hr's flight in
a Cessna, $175 including shuttle. **Hiking** *Beyond the Beaten Path*, T8525650. *Rocky
Mountain Hiking*, T8525015. *Walks and Talks Jasper*, T8524945. **Horse** *Happy Trails
Adventure Tours*, T8525493, www.sundogtours.com *Skyline Trail*, T8524215, Sky-
line@agt.net $465 for 3 days including accommodation and food. *Amethyst Lake
Pack Trips*, T8654417. 4-5-day trips into the Tonquin Valley, staying in cabins. *Tonquin
Valley Pack Trips*, T8521188, www.tonquinadventures.com, offer much the same. *Pyr-
amid Riding Stables*, T8523562. See also Maligne Lake.

   Mountaineering *Peter Amann Mountain Guiding*, T8523237. **Sightseeing** *Sun-
dog Tours*, T8524056. **Whitewater rafting** Athabasca River is for mellow runs, grade 2,
Sunwapta and Maligne Rivers offer scary grade-3 trips. Usually 2-3 hs, $40-65 per person.
Maligne Rafting Adventures, T8523370, www.discoverjasper.com Sunwapta trips, also
wilderness tours on the Kakwa/Smoky Rivers. *Raven Rafting*, T8524292,
www.explorejasper.com Mild to wild trips. *Rocky Mountain River Guides*, T8523777.
Whitewater Rafting Ltd, T8527238, www.WhitewaterJasper.com **Various** *Maligne
Tours* run 90-min narrated cruises to Spirit Island in glass-enclosed heated launches,
hourly 1000-1700, $35, $17.50 concessions. These fill up quickly, but can be booked in
Jasper at 626 Connaught Dr, T8523370, www.malignelake.com The same company
also rents out expensive fishing gear, canoes and rowboats ($15/hr, $70/day) and **kayaks**
($20/hr, $85/day), and arranges rafting trips, guided fishing, hiking, and 3½-hr horse
rides up to the summit of the Bald Hills, leaving at 1000 and 1400 ($55). *Ultimate Adven-
tures*, T780-4140537, www.canada-adventure.com Edmonton-based ecotourism outfit offering hiking, biking, caving, canoeing and rock-climbing. *Jasper Adventure Centre*,
T8525595. Rafting, horse riding, ice-walks, van tours, etc. 2-hr voyageur canoe trips.
Brewster Gray Line, T8523332, run tours to Banff, Lake Louise, Maligne Lake, Columbia
Icefield, and around town.

   Travel agent *Treks & Travel*, 400 Connaught Dr, T8525473. Local and international bookings.

Long distance Jasper's main port of access is **Edmonton**, 370 km to the west, about
4 hrs' drive. Just as many people arrive on the **Icefields Parkway** from Banff, 281 km
away. The **train** and **bus** stations are in the same attractive building, Downtown at 314
Connaught St. *Greyhound*, T1800-6618747, wwww.greyhound.ca, run 4 daily buses
from **Edmonton**, 4 from **Vancouver** via **Kamloops**, and 2 from **Prince George**. *VIA
Rail* operate 3 trains per week each from **Edmonton** and **Vancouver**. The *Canadian
Rockies Airporter*, T8523332, runs to Calgary ($71), and Banff ($51) daily at 1330.

Local Jasper is a small town, easy to walk round, with a fair number of hikes nearby.
However, most of its important trails are far removed, and for those without their own
transport the choices are to hitchhike or use one of the expensive shuttle services: *Jasper Adventure Centre*, T8525595; *Thompson Tours*, T8527269; *Walks and Talks Jasper*, T8524945. From May-Oct the *Maligne Lake Shuttle*, T8523370, connects Jasper
with Maligne Lake, leaving every 1½ hrs starting 0830 from Jasper, ending 1730 from
the lake. One way is $12, or $8 to Maligne Canyon. From 627 Patricia St or *Jasper Park
Lodge*. The *Canadian Rockies Hostel Shuttle* leaves daily at 1300, stopping at all hostels between Jasper and Banff ($51). Extra charge to take bikes. Call T1888-7863641 or
local hostel, T8523215.

Directory   **Communications** Internet: *Library* Internet access for a small fee. *More Than Mail*, 620 Connaught Dr. Internet, fax, shipping, laptop stations. Can also set you up with any kind of tour. *Soft Rock Internet Café*, 622 Connaught Dr. $1/10 mins. **Canada Post**: 502 Patricia St. **Laundry** *Coin Clean Laundry*, Patricia Av. Also coin-op showers. **Library** Jasper Municipal Library, Elm Av/Robson St. **Medical services** *Seton Hospital*, 518 Robson St, T8523344. *Cottage Medical Clinic*, 507 Turret St, T8524885. **Useful numbers** Police: T8524848.

Hikes in Jasper National Park

Around town
See also the Icefields Parkway section, page 325, and Jasper excursions, page 329

There are many loop day-hikes around the **Pyramid Bench** area, some leading to Pyramid Lake. Start at the Activity Centre, 401 Pyramid Lake Rd, and climb up to the bench. The **Old Fort Point** is a 3.5-km return trail leading to marvellous views of Athabasca River and Jasper. Take Highway 93A from town to the Old Fort Point access road. Turn left and cross the iron bridge. You can continue from here on signposted No 7 trail to **Maligne Canyon** (9.5 km one way), and return along the river for an easy 20.7-km loop.

From
Highway 93A

Tonquin Valley (43-km loop, 920 m elevation gain) Astoria trailhead: 7.2 km south on Parkway, turn west onto Highway 93A, continue 5.3 km south, then right onto Mount Edith Cavell Road and 12.2 km to parking area just past the hostel. Portal Creek: 2.5 km south on Highway 93A, right onto Marmot Basin Road, 6.5 km to car park. The Tonquin Valley is one of Jasper's most popular backpack trips, leading to the beautiful Amethyst Lakes and an incredible 1,000-m rock wall known as The Ramparts that shoots straight up from their shores. Before considering this hike, be aware that it could easily degenerate into a nightmare. There are two possible routes to the valley, and both of them are used by outfitters whose horses churn up the trails. If it rains, or has done so in the last few days, the hike in is likely to be a long, frustrating trudge through ankle deep mud. To do the trip by horse, see Tour operators. If it's not raining, the mosquitoes and other biting insects are ferocious. The easier, flatter route into the Valley is along the *Astoria River* trail, known as the Tonquin Expressway. The more satisfying route is the *Portal Creek* trail over Maccarib Pass, which is steeper but consequently offers better views. Ideally, hike in on one and out the other, arranging a shuttle or hitching between trailheads. There are plenty of campsites to choose from, Surprise Point being a good choice. Reserve sites well in advance. Nearby is the Wates-Gibson Hut, reserved through the Alpine Club, T6783200. The best day-hike side-trip is into the narrow Eremite Valley, leading to more glacier-bearing peaks. In winter, you can ski into the valley with *Jasper Tonquin Valley Pack and Ski Trips*, T8523909, and stay in their cabins.

Geraldine Lakes (10.5 km return to second lake, 13 km return to fourth lake, 407-497 m elevation gain. Trailhead: 1 km north of Athabasca Falls on Highway 93A, then 5.5 km up Geraldine Fire Road) The first lake is an easy hike to an unremarkable destination. After that, things get more difficult and more rewarding. It's a fairly tough climb to the second and biggest lake with ridgetop views and a waterfall as compensation. Beyond there is no trail and much bush-whacking to reach pristine pools set in wild, alpland meadows.

Cavell Meadows (8-km loop, 370 m elevation gain. Trailhead: 13 km south on Highway 93A, 14 km on Cavell Road) This easy hike leads to spectacular views of the giant Angel Glacier. In mid-summer, these are also some of the finest wildflower meadows in the Rockies. The pay-off is marching along with crowds of people.

Skyline (44.5 km, 820 m elevation gain, 1,350 m elevation loss) This is one of **From Maligne Lake** the all-time great backpack trips, offering everything you come to the Rockies for: drool-inducing views of lofty peaks, including some of the range's highest, and sweeping meadows full of wild flowers. Fast hikers can do it in two days, but three is more realistic. It is a one-way hike best started at Maligne Lake. If driving, leave your vehicle at the terminus, Maligne Canyon, and hitch or bus to the lake. Book sites in the backcountry campgrounds well ahead, because this is one hike that is almost impossible to get onto at short notice. Plan your trip for after late-July, when the steepest section of the trail, known as 'the Notch', should be snow-free. This is the only steep section of a hike that is surprisingly level, considering that almost all of it is above the treeline. This last fact means you're particularly at the mercy of the weather, so go prepared for anything.

Bald Hills (12.6 km return, 610 m elevation gain) The Bald Hills are actually a 7 km-long ridge. The lack of trees that gave them their name makes for excellent views of the surroundings, including Maligne Lake and the Queen Elizabeth Ranges, with razorback ridges, gleaming glaciers, rugged rock faces, green forests, alpine meadows, and extraordinary rock formations. After about 45 minutes, take the cut-off trail through the trees, and look out for wild flowers. Most people stop at the old fire lookout, but you can continue for greater panoramas and less company.

Opal Hills (8.2 km, 460 m elevation gain) This trail is short but very steep with no switchbacks. The rewards are gorgeous views of mountains and the lake, and a host of tiny wild flowers.

From the Beaver Creek Picnic Area, 28 km along Maligne Lake Road are: **The South Boundary** trail, a 166-km epic taking 10-14 days, ending at the Nigel Pass trailhead on the Icefields Parkway. Its rewards do not justify such efforts, but it might appeal to those with a strong urge to push *their* boundaries. There is also a **North Boundary Trail**, which is over 173 km long and would equally only appeal to those seeking extremes. Ask at the Parks Office for details. **Jacques Lake** (25.8 km, 90 m elevation gain) is an easy but unexceptional hike that might be worth considering in the shoulder season or on a rainy day.

Sulphur Skyline (8 km return, 700 m elevation gain) Another short but **From Miette Hot Springs** steep hike whose mighty views are far out of proportion to the energy expended. It is also a good early-season destination.

Mount Robson Provincial Park

The Yellowhead Highway (Highway 16) accompanies the railway west from *Phone code: 250* Jasper to the Yellowhead Pass (1,131 m), which has been used as a route across the Continental Divide by fur-traders and gold-seekers for over 150 years. This is the border between Alberta and British Columbia, Mountain and Pacific time zones (BC is one hour behind) and Jasper and Mount Robson Parks. There are few facilities in the latter, so if planning to do the overnight hike discussed below, stock up in Jasper. The next closest town is **Tête Jaune Cache**, 16 km beyond the park's western boundary.

More than any other of the Rocky Mountain Parks, this one is utterly dominated by its crowning feature. At 3,954 m, Mount Robson is the highest peak in the Canadian Rockies and possibly the most spectacular. It was one of the last mountains in the Rockies to be climbed, and even today represents a difficult challenge. Whether you're approaching on Highway 16 or from Kamloops on Highway 5, the first sight of this colossal rock pyramid is likely to take your

Canadian Rockies

breath away. It's not just the sheer size, but the perfection of its shape, highlighted by the pointed triangle of ice at its apex and the distinct layering of rock, which inspired the native name *Yuh-hai-has-hun*, 'Mountain of the Spiral Road'. The only way to fully appreciate the peak's awesome beauty is by doing the hike, which reveals the incredible vast glaciers that cover its north side.

The only public transport into the park is the *Greyhound*. Ask to be dropped at the Mount Robson viewpoint, also site of the **Visitor Centre**, T5669174, May-early September. This is the place to register and pay for backcountry camping ($6). The nearby café/garage is about the only place to get food.

Sleeping

Camping There are 2 park campgrounds (**F**, T5664325) close to the Visitor Centre, *Robson River* and *Robson Meadows*, with 144 sites between them, and showers. Another is just west of the park's eastern boundary on Hwy 16. **F** *Emperor Ridge Campground*, T5668538, is within walking distance of the Visitor Centre on Kinney Lake Rd. It has 37 sites, and hot showers. **C** *Mount Robson Guest Ranch*, T5664370, is the next closest, 2 km from the highway on Hargreaves Rd, with 10 cabins and 10 campsites (**F**).

Outside the park boundary, 5 km west on Hwy 16, is **F** *Robson Shadows Campground*, with nice sites on the river and showers; and **C** *Mount Robson Lodge*, T5664821, with log cabins, standard rooms, and offering various tours.

Tour operators

Mount Robson Adventure Holidays, T5664351, arrange canoeing and hiking day-trips, rent camping gear, and have cabins (**C**) 16 km east of the Visitor Centre.

Hikes in Mount Robson Provincial Park

Mount Robson/Berg Lake (39.2 km return, 786 m elevation gain. Trailhead: 2 km north of the Visitor Centre on a side road) This is the most popular and one of the very best backpacking trips in the range, and can be attempted by mid-June when most other trails are still snowed under. Most people reach Berg Lake in a day, spend a day exploring, then hike out on the third. The trail is extraordinary and varied, leading through lush, flower-dotted rainforest, past open gravel flats, over suspension bridges in a rugged river gorge, through the Valley of a Thousand Faces, and past three powerful waterfalls, including the 60-m Emperor Falls. At Berg Lake, Mount Robson rises 2,316 m directly from the shore, its cliffs wrapped in the vast ice-cloaks of Mist and Berg Glaciers. Huge chunks of ice regularly crash from the latter into the lake, explaining its name. There is a campground right here, a more private one 0.6 km further, and another 1.4 km further still. A recommended 9-km day-hike is to **Snowbird Pass**. The path leads to the toe of Robson Glacier and for the next 3 km the views of the glacier are stupendous. From the pass, views are of the Coleman Glacier and the 10-km-long Reef Icefield. A more demanding possibility is the big loop that includes the wildflower meadows of **Mumm Basin**, **Toboggan Falls** and **Hargreaves Glacier**.

Yellowhead Mountain (9 km return, 715 m elevation gain. Trailhead: 8.5 km west of the pass on Highway 16, 1 km on a gravel road across Yellowhead Lake on an isthmus. Park below the railway where road splits) Passing through meadows and aspen forest, this trail is particularly attractive in autumn. The best day-hike in the park, it offers wonderful views of the Yellowhead Pass.

Mount Fitzwilliam (26 km return, 945 m elevation gain. Trailhead: 7 km west of the pass at Yellowhead Lake Boat Launch) This trail starts off easy and boring but towards the end becomes demanding and ill-defined, involving route-finding skills and some scrambling. The reward at the top for strong hikers is a glorious alpine basin studded with lakes and meadows beneath the eastern wall of Mount Fitzwilliam.

Yoho National Park

Phone code: 250
Colour map 2, grid B3

Yoho is a Cree exclamation of awe and wonder, something like 'Wow!' The scenery in this park is indeed astounding, with many waterfalls, and 28 peaks over 3,000 m. Banff may be the most famous of the four contiguous parks, and Jasper may be the biggest, but get any Rocky Mountain aficionado talking and pretty soon they will start to wax passionate about Yoho. A comparitively small park, it contains possibly the greatest concentration of quality hikes in the range, most of them clustered in two major areas and one minor one.

Yoho National Park

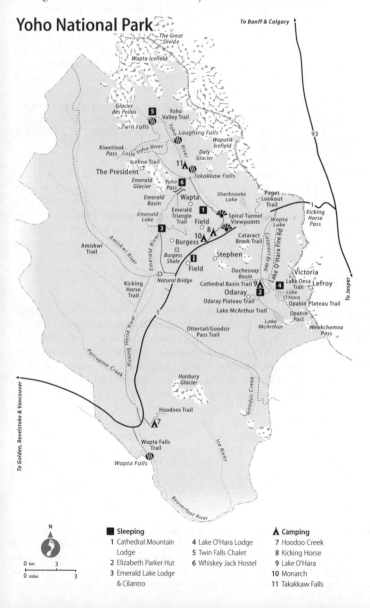

Canadian Rockies

■ Sleeping		▲ Camping
1 Cathedral Mountain Lodge	4 Lake O'Hara Lodge	7 Hoodoo Creek
2 Elizabeth Parker Hut	5 Twin Falls Chalet	8 Kicking Horse
3 Emerald Lake Lodge & Cilantro	6 Whiskey Jack Hostel	9 Lake O'Hara
		10 Monarch
		11 Takakkaw Falls

Most important, famous and busy of these is **Lake O'Hara** which has proved so popular that a complete ban on traffic to the area has been imposed, and visitor numbers are strictly limited. A good second choice, if that's too much hassle, is the **Yoho Valley**, which has the park's only hostel and a fabulous campground. **Emerald Lake** is a pretty destination and offers one very good hike. Otherwise, there are a few trails straight from the highway.

History   As throughout the Rockies, it was the arrival of the railway that kick-started Yoho National Park. The high and steep Kicking Horse Pass was chosen over the much easier and more logical Yellowhead Pass to the north for the simple reason that so northerly a route would bypass the valuable prairie land in the south. But negotiating the 1,643-m pass and its 4% grade was an unprecedented engineering challenge. The answer came in the form of two enormous figure-of-eight galleries blasted out of the mountains, known as the **Spiral Tunnels**. For railway buffs, the sight of a long goods train twisting its way through is an extraordinary phenomenon not to be missed. There are two viewpoints for witnessing the spectacle: 8 km east of Field on Highway 1, and 2 km up the Yoho Valley Road. Despite the frequent runaways that occurred on the 'Big Hill', a 6-km descent at a 4.5% grade between Wapta Lake and Field, the line pushed its way through, and the first hotel was built by the Canadian Pacific Railway in 1886. In 1911, Yoho became Canada's second National Park, after Banff.

Park   The TransCanada runs right through the middle of the park, sharing the valley bottom
information   with the railway and the Kicking Horse River. Unless you know specifically what you want to do, a sensible first port of call is to the village of Field which is close to all of these bases and contains the excellent **Visitor Centre/Parks Office**, see below, who can help with camping arrangements, give sound advice on what hikes to choose, and issue very useful backcountry guide and maps. They also take backcountry camping reservations ($6) up to three months ahead, a must for Lake O'Hara.

Field

Phone code: 250   Field is a remarkably attractive one-horse town of 300 people built on the side
Colour map 2, grid B3   of a mountain, and it makes a delightful base for day-hikes around the park.
Altitude: 1,301 m   There are no sights as such, but Field Mountain, visible across the valley, is the site of the **Burgess Shale**, an ancient sea-bed that has yielded a host of 515 million year-old fossils. Remains of more than 120 species of soft-bodied marine animals have been found, some so well preserved that scientists can tell what they ate just before they died. This is one of only three places in the world where such fossils are found. An excellent exhibit recreating the sea and explaining its inhabitants is one of the highlights of the Royal Tyrell Museum in Drumheller, Alberta (see page 366). There are also displays at the Field and Lake Louise Visitor Centres. Long and strenuous guided hikes to the fossil beds are run between July and mid-September by the Yoho Burgess Shale Foundation, T1800-3433006. Numbers are limited to 15 per hike. The **Field Visitor Centre/Parks Office**, T3436783, is open summer 0800-1900, rest of the year 0900-1700.

Sleeping   The only hotel in town is the **B** *Kicking Horse Lodge* at the end of Kicking Horse/Stephen Av, T3436303, www.kickinghorselodge.net Large rooms, kitchenettes for an extra $14, a nice restaurant and patio, and laundry facilities. Otherwise, there are many guesthouses in private houses, usually offering 1 or 2 self-catering suites with kitchen for about $95. **C** *Alpenglow B&B*, T3436356, has 4 rooms with shared bath and no kitchen. **C** *Mt. Burgess Bungalow*, T3436480, has 2 rooms with kitchens, private bath and TV. **C** *Mt Stephen Guesthouse*, T3436441, has 2 en suite rooms with kitchen. Contact the Visitor Centre for more.

Camping The nearest campgrounds are 3.7 km northeast at the Yoho Valley turn-off. **F** *Kicking Horse* has 86 very nice private sites and good showers. Across the way, the cheaper **F** *Monarch* has 46 ugly parking lot-style sites and no showers. All Yoho campgrounds are first-come, first-serve, T3436783 for information.

Siding General Store and Truffle Pigs Cafe on Kicking Horse/Stephen Av, T3436462, is just about the only store and has a small but excellent and quite expensive restaurant. The food is fresh, they do gourmet dinner specials, very good coffee, and there's outdoor seating. Food at the hotel is also good. **Eating**

If you want to go paddling, canoes can be rented at *Emerald Sports Boat Dock and Horse Stables*, T3436000. **Sports**

Lake O'Hara

Exquisitely framed by the two lofty mountains, Victoria and Lefroy, that tower over Lake Louise on the other side of the Continental Divide, Lake O'Hara is a rare jewel even in the overflowing treasure chest of the Rockies. When it was first discovered by Canada's hiking fraternity, news of its extraordinary natural beauty and network of quality day-hikes spread like wildfire, and soon the area was too popular for its own good. *Parks Canada* have taken measures to protect it, so visiting can be difficult unless you book ahead. No traffic is allowed into the region, not even bikes. *Colour map 2, grid B3*

Hiking in the Lake O'Hara region is among the most popular and rewarding in the Rockies. On the Continental Divide between here and Lake Louise are a number of the highest, most awe-inspiring peaks in the range. Within a relatively small area are 25 named lakes and an extensive, well-maintained network of trails that radiate out from Lake O'Hara like the spokes of a wheel. There are five main sub-regions that can be combined in any number of ways. **Hikes from Lake O'Hara**

Lake Oesa (5.8-km loop, 240 m elevation gain) This is a short and easy hike to a stunning turquoise lake set in a rugged cirque. Towering above are the Continental Divide summits of Mounts Lefroy and Victoria, the other side of the stunning massif that towers so dramatically over Lake Louise.
Opabin Plateau (7.2-km loop, 250 m elevation gain) Set in a beautiful hanging valley, this easy hike offers many temptations for casual exploration among small flower-filled tundra meadows. The loop follows the east and west sides of the same valley. A 0.6-km side-trail leads from the west side to outstanding views from Opabin Prospect. From the east side, a detour leads along Yukness Ledge, a possible highline traverse to Lake Oesa.
Lake McArthur (7 km return, 315 m elevation gain) This half-day hike is one of the area's finest. The 1.5-km-long lake is the biggest in the area, and an exquisite deep blue colour due to its 65-m depth. Sheer cliffs rising straight up more than 600 m above the water make for a dramatic location.
Odaray Plateau (7-10-km loops, 290-655 m elevation gain) This is one of the most spectacular routes in the park, but is often closed, or visitor numbers are limited due to grizzly bears. The trail climbs quickly and sometimes steeply. Odaray Prospect offers a 180° panorama centred on Lake O'Hara, backed by the wall of high peaks that comprise the Great Divide. Further along, the trail branches off to **Odaray Grandview**, the only spot in the park from which all of

Canadian Rockies

its major lakes can be seen simultaneously. To achieve this prize you have to face a difficult 1.1-km scramble over talus that requires endurance and some experience. At Km 4.5 a junction at McArthur Pass leads back to the start making a 6.5-km loop, or on to Lake McArthur as part of a 9.5-km loop.

Cathedral Basin (13-15 km return, 300 m elevation gain) This is one of the longest and least crowded day-hikes in the area, but is also one of the lowest and least dramatic. However, after skirting the pretty Linda and Cathedral Lakes, the trail starts to climb towards the mouth of the Cathedral Basin. The wonderful views all along this stretch peak at Cathedral Prospect, which offers one of the most complete overviews of the whole Lake O'Hara region. The climb to the Prospect is fairly steep on a poor, rocky surface.

Alpine Circuit (9.8-12.4 km, 495 m elevation gain) The classic way to combine some of the area's sights, this is one of the highlights of the Lake O'Hara region, but it's a fairly tough circuit, more route than trail, following cairns and paint-marks across scree slopes and along exposed ledges. Those scared of heights, worried about getting lost, or not in tip-top condition should probably choose another hike. Use a good trail description and carry a good map. Starting the circuit with the toughest section, the ascent to Wiwaxy Gap, is a good idea. Views from the gap are exceptional. The loop can be extended or shortened in a couple of places. The short detour to Opabin Prospect is worth the effort, while the ascent to All Souls' Prospect is an excellent conclusion to the hike.

Sleeping There are 3 possibilities. **LL** *Lake O'Hara Lodge*, T3436418, is expensive and luxurious and must be booked well in advance. The Alpine Club's *Elizabeth Parker Hut*, T6783200, sleeps 24, is open year round, and is also heavily booked. Most people stay at the **campground (F**) which is, of course, for tents only. To reserve a place, which is essential, call the Field Visitor Centre, T3436783, with precise details of dates, numbers, etc. Between 3-5 sites per day are available on a first-come first-serve basis, but to get one of these you need to be lining up at the Field Visitor Centre the day before at 0700.

Transport Entry is by foot on the 13-km **Cataract Brook** trail, or on the **shuttle bus** which runs between 19 Jun and 8 Oct from the Lake O'Hara Fire Road parking lot. Turn onto Hwy 1A 3 km south of the Continental Divide sign or 1.6 km north of the lodge at Wapta Lake, cross the tracks, turn right and proceed 0.8 km. **Buses** leave at 0830, 1030, 1630 and 1930, departing from *Lake O'Hara Lodge* at 0730, 0930, 1530 and 1830. To get a place on the bus it is essential to reserve at T3436433 as early as 19 Mar. The fare is $12 return, with $10 reservation fee (non-returnable upon cancellation). Once up there, a place on the return bus is guaranteed at either 1530 or 1830. Bus seats can sometimes be booked at the Field Visitor Centre, but priority goes to those who have reserved accommodation.

The Yoho Valley

Colour map 2, grid 3 Logistically easier than Lake O'Hara and almost equally wonderful is the Yoho Valley, which is lined with waterfalls, including the dramatic **Twin Falls** and the 380-m **Takakkaw Falls**, one of Canada's highest, whose name comes from a Stoney Indian word meaning 'magnificent'. This is also one of the most exceptional areas for glaciers: the enormous Wapta and Waputik Icefields are both easily visible, as is the beautiful Emerald Glacier. The valley is ringed with monster peaks. To get there, drive 3.7 km northeast of Field, or 12.5 km southwest of the Continental Divide, turn north on Yoho Valley Road and drive about 13 km up a very steep, winding road, not siutable for RVs or trailers.

On the way up is **B** *Cathedral Mountain Lodge*, T3436442, www.cathedralmountain.com Small close-together cabins with good beds, kitchenette, pretty setting, bistro with sandwiches and buffalo stroganoff. At the top is the park's only hostel, and one of the best in the Rockies, **E** *Whiskey Jack Hostel*, T403-7624122, open mid Jun-mid-Oct. Great views, 27 beds in 3 dorms, kitchen, common room. A little further a group of car parks signal the end of the road. **F** *Takakkaw Falls Campground* is a 500-m walk from here, and therefore for tents only (and on a first-come first-serve basis). It combines the excitement of the backcountry with much of the convenience of front-country camping, because there are wagons on which you can cart in as much food and equipment as you wish. The sites are fairly private and very beautifully located close to the falls, with a view of the Wapta Icefield. Some excellent hikes also begin here. At Twin Falls, a boring 10-km hike to the other end of the valley, is a small backcountry campground, and the **D** *Twin Falls Chalet*, T403-2287079, with rooms and meals in Jul-Aug. Halfway there is the 8-site *Laughing Falls* backcountry campground.

Iceline (12.8-21.3 km, 690 m elevation gain. Trailhead: *Whiskey Jack Hostel*) The steep ascent of this popular hike takes you up to the Emerald Glacier, on a level with truly extraordinary scenery that includes the Daly Glacier and Takakkaw Falls opposite, and the vast Wapta Icefield to the north. Once at the top, the hiking is high, easy and scenically uplifting. A return journey to the highpoint is 12.8 km. Circuits can be made by continuing to the Yoho Valley and possibly the Little Yoho Valley as well, though neither option adds anything that compares to the views from the top. A two-day backpack trip would entail a night at Little Yoho campground or the nearby Stanley Mitchell hut (reserve with the Alpine Club, T5222200), a possible diversion to Kiwetinok Pass, and a return via the stupendous vantage point of the Whaleback.

Yoho Valley (16.4 km, 290 m elevation gain) This flat trail through the trees leads to a few waterfalls, ending at the dramatic Twin Falls. It is a nice enough stroll and good for a rainy day, but otherwise there seems no point if you're capable of doing the spectacular Iceline trail, which offers so much more.

This is another pretty spot whose name is acccurate if lacking in imagination. To get here, drive 2.6 km southwest of Field, then 8 km on Emerald Lake Road, passing on the way the **Natural Bridge**, a giant rock that has been carved out by the powerful Kicking Horse River.

The clearcut choice for a day-hike is the **Emerald Triangle** (19.7 km, 880 m elevation gain). This is a satisfying loop, best done clockwise. The climb that way is gentle, but the descent at the end is rapid. As well as the lake, views are of the glaciated ramparts of The President, the sheer cliffs of Wapta Mountain, the Kicking Horse Valley, and the fossil-fields of the Burgess Shale.

Sleeping and eating Dominating the lake is the **LL** *Emerald Lake Lodge*, T403-6096199, www.crmr.com Beautiful setting with a warm earthy feel and burning wood smell, cosy furniture, billiards, lounge and expensive restaurant serving lots of game and fish. Luxurious townhouse-style suites, all with private balconies overlooking the lake. Next door in an impressive wood building is *Cilantro Restaurant*. The food is expensive and a bit predictable, but it's a perfect spot for a cold drink on a hot day.

Sports Canoes can be rented on the lake for $20/hr, and *Emerald Lake Stables* offer pack trips.

Hikes from the TransCanada

These are arranged north to south. Note that there are two front-country campgrounds on the southern edge of the park (see below).

Paget Lookout (7.4 km return, 520 m elevation gain. Trailhead: Wapta Lake Picnic Area, 5.5 km southwest of BC/Alberta border) This short but steep climb leads to astounding views that include the mountains encircling Lake O'Hara and the Kicking Horse Valley. Scramblers can ascend a further 430 m to Paget Peak for even better views.

Ottertail Trail/Goodsir Pass (50.4 km return, 1,110 m elevation gain. Trailhead: 8.4 km southwest of Field, 150 m northeast of Ottertail River Bridge) Goodsir Pass is up there with the most sublime locations in the Rockies. This vast, flower-crested alpine meadow sits beneath some strapping monster peaks, including the twin-towered Goodsir that is Yoho's highest mountain. It would probably be a far more popular destination if the trail there were not so long and boring. The answer is to do the first 14.5 km on a mountain bike, gaining just 360 m, then slogging up 770 m in 10.7 km on foot. It is a hard day, only for the very fit, but the rewards are considerable, and you're likely to have them to yourself. There are two backcountry campgrounds on the way, the more useful being McArthur Creek with 10 sites.

Hoodoos (3.2 km, 455 m elevation gain. Trailhead: 22.7 km southwest of Field, right before campground entrance, 1.5 km to parking area) A short but very steep hike leads to these fascinating elongated-mushroom-shaped rock formations. They're far more impressive than the ones around Banff. Follow the trail above them for the best views. This can be enjoyed whatever the weather, and combines nicely with **Wapta Falls** (4.8 km, 45 m elevation gain. Trailhead: 25 km southwest of Field, 1.8 km down Wapta Falls access road), a powerful waterfall in a raw setting. The short, level hike is good for spring or autumn, a rainy day, or just a leg-stretch to see the cascade.

Mountain biking　Hiking is clearly the most popular pastime here, but a number of the longer trails are better suited to mountain biking. **Amiskwi** trail, 35 km one way, follows a river, starting at Emerald Lake Road. The 19.5-km **Kicking Horse** trail starts at the same point or at the now-closed Chancellor Peak campground.

Camping F *Hoodoo Creek* has 30 sites and no showers.

Kootenay National Park

Phone code: 250
Colour map 2, grid B3

The park is on Mountain Time, an hour ahead of most of BC

Situated on the other side of the Continental Divide from Banff, and bounded to the north by Yoho, it would be wrong to expect anything but spectacular scenery from Kootenay National Park, yet it is far and away the least visited of the big four. The park's boundaries neatly parallel the winding course of the Kootenay or Banff-Windermere Parkway (Highway 93) as it makes its way from Castle Junction on Highway 1 to Radium Hot Springs in the East Kootenays (see page 259). Most people reject this route, preferring to continue north to Lake Louise, Yoho and the Icefields Parkway. This is totally understandable, especially for those short on time or reliant on public transport which does not service this park. Yet a short, easy and very satisfying loop can be made by driving through Kootenay, shooting up Highway 95 to Golden, then following the TransCanada through Yoho to Lake Louise, losing little in the process and gaining a much more comprehensive overview of the Rockies.

Those entering from the Radium end are treated to a fine introduction as the road snakes its way through the steep and narrow **Sinclair Canyon**, its

Kootenay National Park

Yoho National Park

Kaufmann Lake

Vermilion Pass

1 1A

Ottertail River

Ottertail Pass

Ochre Creek

Tokumm Creek

⑥

②

Stanley Ck.

Helmet

⑤

⑧

3 ⚑

⑪

Washma-Wapta Icefield

⑩

Tumbling Ck.

⑨

Banff National Park

Egypt Lake

Healy Pass

ALBERTA

Wolverine Pass

⑫

Numa Ck.

Vermilion River

④

Verdant Creek

BC

⑩

Numa Pass

③

Floe Lake

The Monarch

Vermilion Crossing

1

Vermilion Crossing Visitor Centre

Canadian Rockies

Simpson River

Kootenay River

Kootenay Parkway

Mount Assiniboine Provincial Park

Kootenay Crossing

93

N

0 km 2
0 miles 2

Dolly Varden Ck.

2 ⚑

Pitts Creek

Kootenay River

Dog Lake

①

4 ⚑

■ Sleeping
1 Kootenay Park Lodge

⚑ Camping
2 Dolly Varden
3 Marble Canyon
4 McLeod Meadows
5 Redstreak

○ Trails
1 Dog Lake
2 Fireweed Trail
3 Floe Lake / Numa Pass
4 Hawk Creek / Ball Pass
5 Helmet Falls / Tumbling Creek
6 Kaufmann Lake
7 Kindersley Pass / Sinclair Creek
8 Marble Canyon
9 Paint Pots
10 Rockwall
11 Stanley Glacier Trail
12 Tumbling Pass

To Golden ▶

⑦

Sinclair Pass

95

Sinclair Canyon

Radium Hot Springs

Radium Hot Springs Visitor Centre

5 ⚑

93

95

To Cranbrook ▼

cliffs a rich red due to the high iron content. Otherwise, Kootenay has two major assets: the **Rockwall**, which is one of the top five backpacking trips in the range and, at the other end of the scale, a great number of very short but decent nature walks right from the highway, that are ideal for the less athletic.

The only Visitor Centre actually in the park is a privately run and not very helpful concern about 40 km south of the park boundary at **Vermilion Crossing**. They hand out the *Backcountry Guide*, whose map and trail descriptions are all you really need, and issue backcountry passes ($6 per person per night). Summer 0900-2100, spring and autumn 1100-1800. There is another privately run, more helpful but less conveniently situated Visitor Centre in the village of **Radium Hot Springs** at 7556 Main Street East, T3479505. June 0930-1630, July-August 0900-1900.

History

In contrast to the other parks, it was not the railway but a road that gave birth to Kootenay National Park. Up to the start of the 20th century, the area was solely occupied by the Ktunaxa or Kootenai natives (meaning 'people from beyond the hills'). Explorer David Thompson was the only white man to have set foot in the region when in 1910 a businessman named Randolph Bruce talked the Canadian government into building a road from Banff to connect the prairies with the port of Vancouver. To help funding, BC was persuaded to donate a corridor of land around the road to promote tourism, and in 1920 the land acquired national park status.

Hikes in Kootenay National Park

Short hikes
From north to south

Fireweed Trail (1 km. Trailhead: just south of park boundary) In 1968 a forest fire started by a single lightning bolt laid waste a 24 sq-km area just south of Vermilion Pass (1,651 m). This short trail talks you through the regeneration process, and reveals how such fires are an integral part of the forest's natural cycle, to the point that lodgepole pine cones actually require the heat of a forest fire in order to open and spread their seeds.

Marble Canyon (800 m or more. Trailhead: 7 km south of park boundary) An easy trail takes you to this lovely 600-m-long, 37-m-deep canyon which Tokumm Creek has carved out of the white dolomite limestone that was once mistaken for marble. The highlight is a striking view of a powerful waterfall where the creek forces its way through a narrow opening. In winter, the whole canyon turns into a magical palace of blue and green ice. This trail can extend 2.7 km to connect with the following.

The Paint Pots (3 km return. Trailhead: 9.5 km south of park boundary) This trail leads to a series of fascinating pools where iron-laden mineral springs push through clay sediments to create shades of red, orange and yellow. Native Americans came from far and wide to collect these coloured clays, which were then baked, ground into powder, and added to fat or oil to make paint, which was then used in a number of creative and ceremonial ways. According to ancient lore, the pools are the dwelling places of animal and thunder spirits.

Dog Lake (5.2 km return. Trailhead: 500 m south of Mcleod Meadows Campground) About the best of the short hikes in the southern half of the park. This shallow, marsh-edged lake sits in one of the Rockies' most temperate valleys, making it a good spot for wildlife. Orchids also abound in early summer.

The Rockwall (54.8 km, 1,490 m elevation gain, 1,440 m loss. Trailhead: **Longer hikes**
22.5 km south of park boundary) The Rockwall is the name of the Vermillion
Mountains' eastern escarpment, a solid sheet of grey limestone whose sheer
cliffs run for 35 km along the Great Divide. Instead of leading you along a
ridge like some highline trails, this one goes up and down like a rollercoaster,
crossing three alpine passes then plunging down into valleys, passing on the
way a number of hanging glaciers, flower-strewn meadows, breathtakingly
gorgeous lakes, and stunning waterfalls. It is one of the most demanding but
rewarding hikes in the Rockies, and is comfortably done in four days. Four
trails lead to the Rockwall, along Floe, Numa, Tumbling and Helmet Creeks.
The optimum approach is to hike up Floe Creek, spending night one at Floe
Lake campground (10.5 km), night two at Tumbling Falls (27.9 km), and
night three at Helmet Falls (39.7 km).

A few one- or two-day hikes take in sections of the Rockwall, although the
greatest reward is hiking the whole thing. **Floe Lake/Numa Pass** (21-26.4
km, 715-1,030 m elevation gain. Trailhead: 22.5 km south of park boundary).
This is the best of the Rockwall day-hikes. Floe Lake is one of the most majestic
sights in the Rockies: sheer cliffs rise 1,000 m straight up from the azure blue
waters, their ice floes mirrored on its crystal surface. In autumn, the surrounding larches turn golden to further elevate the sublime scene. The ascent
is long, quite steep and mostly through forest, making this more suited to an
overnighter than a day-hike. Views from Numa Pass, 2.7 km (1 hr) away, are if
anything even more striking, another reason to spend an extra day. It's the
best place to take in the lake and the rockwall that towers above it. From here,
it is possible to descend to the highway via Numa Creek, making a total loop of
27.3 km, though it means hitching 8 km back to the trailhead.

Tumbling Pass (24.4-km loop, 800 m elevation gain, 840 m loss.
Trailhead: 9.5 km south of park boundary) As a day-hike, this is extremely
long and tough. It starts pleasantly enough by passing by the Paint Pots, but
soon sets into a steady ascent with little reward until you reach Tumbling Falls
at 9.4 km, where there is a nice campground. The pass is a tough 3.6 km further, but worth it for the awesome sight of the Rockwall and Tumbling Glacier. A 6-km detour to #**Wolverine Pass** is also worth the effort, but as a
day-hike there's no time. From the pass, return to the trailhead along Numa
Creek, a steep but pleasant descent.

Helmet Falls/Tumbling Creek (37-km loop. Trailhead: 9.5 km south of
park boundary) As a two-day trip, it is worth hiking up Ochre/Helmet
Creeks to Helmet Falls at the north end of the Rockwall. This impressive cascade is one of the highest in Canada. It is possible to stay at the campground
here then ascend through Rockwall Pass and exit to the trailhead along Tumbling Creek, though this is a tough second day.

Stanley Glacier Trail (11 km return, 395 m elevation gain. Trailhead:
3 km south of park boundary) This hike leads through the Vermilion Pass
and switchbacks up to a hanging valley below Stanley Peak, ending at a plateau
with fine views of a waterfall and the glacier.

Kaufmann Lake (30 km return, 570 m elevation gain. Trailhead: 7 km
south of park boundary) This is a popular and rather overrated hike. It starts
off flat and boring, until the last few kilometres head steeply up into Prospector's Valley. The lake itself is surrounded by steep cliffs on the southern slopes
of the Wenkchemna (Ten) Peaks which are so much more glorious over in the
valley alongside Moraine Lake (which is only 6 km away as the crow flies).
This is a good one to do on a bad-weather day and there is a nice campground
on the lakeshore.

Hawk Creek/Ball Pass (19.4 km return, 885 m elevation gain. Trailhead: 22.5 km south of park boundary) Follow the gravel path 400 m northwest beside the highway, then follow the trail right. The views on this hike are good rather than spectacular, but nicely varied and relatively unspoilt by excessive crowds.

Kindersley Pass/Sinclair Creek (16.5-20.5-km loop, 1,055 m elevation gain. Trailhead: Across the highway from the parking area 9.5 km from the west gate at Radium) This is one of the park's most scenic and most strenuous hikes. The trail ascends steadily for 8.4 km with little reward. From Kindersley Pass, views start to appear northward of the countless peaks of the Brisco Range. For the next 1.4 km to Kindersley Summit, vistas of this ocean of summits keep getting better, giving ample reward for the earlier effort. It's worth following the faint path just below the ridgeline on a 4-km diversion around the head of the Sinclair Valley to Nixon Creek Summit. Alpine walking doesn't get much better than this. From Kindersley Summit, the indistinct trail along Sinclair Creek makes for a convenient loop back to the Highway, though it leaves you 1.2 km northeast of your vehicle.

Sleeping & eating
On map, page 345
For camping information contact Radium Visitor Information Centre, T3479331

The only beds in the park are in **Vermilion Crossing** at the **C** *Kootenay Park Lodge*, T7629196, www.kootenayparklodge.com Very small, basic cabins, poor value. Restaurant. Far more extensive facilities are found at Radium Hot Springs, an unpleasant little town just beyond the park's southern border (see page 259). **Camping** Also at this southern end is the park's biggest campground, the 242-site **F** *Redstreak*, which has showers and full hook-ups, open May-Oct. **F** *McLeod Meadows* is about 25 km north, with 98 basic sites on the river, open Jun-Sep. Just to the north, and only open in winter, is the tiny (free) *Dolly Varden*. In the more interesting upper two-thirds of the park there is just one campground, the newly repaired **F** *Marble Canyon*. There are 8 backcountry campgrounds, mostly on the *Rockwall* and *Kaufmann Lake* trails.

Canadian Rockies

Alberta

Introducing Alberta

Whereas British Columbia is defined by its mountainous landscapes, the presence of the Rockies in Alberta feels like a total anomaly. Soon enough the peaks descend to meet their antithesis, flat prairie land, which then continues unabated for thousands of kilometres. The province's true personality is here: grain farms and cattle ranches; saloons, cowboys, country and western; world-renowned beef is the food of choice, stetsons and boots the outfit. It seems fitting that Alberta has boomed with the discovery of oil, since it has much more in common with Texas than genteel Victoria or Pacific Rim Vancouver. The politics are right-wing, the beer light, the churches fundamentalist, the taxes low, the people wealthy.

All this may be of cultural interest to visitors, but it soon wears thin. The only exciting landscapes outside the Rockies are the **Badlands** east of Calgary, which also harbour one of the world's biggest caches of dinosaur skeletons, and best palaeontological museums. Touching the US border is **Waterton Lakes National Park**, whose landscapes and hikes are almost as impressive as the much bigger parks to the north, and considerably less crowded. Nearby is the important native site **Head-Smashed-In Buffalo Jump**, and a handful of lesser attractions.

Unless entering from BC, access to the Rockies will involve one of Alberta's two cities, **Calgary** or **Edmonton**, which service the south and north respectively. Neither are towns you would necessarily bother with otherwise. Big, brash and wealthy, they have neither the culture of cities further east nor the scenic splendour of Vancouver. A fierce rivalry has existed between the two ever since Calgary mushroomed into existence little more than a century ago. Today the younger city retains the upper hand, if only for its proximity to Banff (a mere 90 minutes away) and for the hosting of Alberta's ultimate festival, the raucous **Stampede** in July.

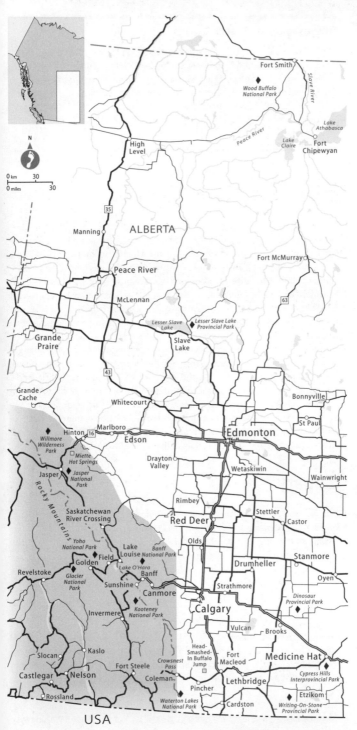

Things to do in Alberta

- Time your visit to coincide with the outstanding Calgary Stampede.
- Experience Badlands scenery and dinosaurs galore around Drumheller.
- Visit the historic site of Head-Smashed-In Buffalo Jump.
- Enjoy the first-class collection at Edmonton's Art Gallery.
- Go on a pub and restaurant crawl round Edmonton's lively Old Strathcona.
- See herds of bison and flocks of whooping crane in Wood Buffalo National Park.

Southern Alberta

Dominated by flat ranching country, Southern Alberta has little to offer compared to British Columbia. The greatest attraction east of the Rockies is the Drumheller Badlands, a day trip from Calgary, which combines weird and wonderful landscapes with an exceptional museum that houses one of the world's greatest collections of dinosaur skeletons. Most of these were found in Dinosaur Provincial Park to the southeast, another example of outstanding Badland scenery. The latter represents the only worthwhile excursion from the TransCanada Highway. While this road is the most important route across Southern Alberta, connecting its greatest attraction, Banff, with its key city, Calgary, it is the less convenient Highway 3 that gives access to the remainder of Southern Alberta's prime attractions. After passing through the depressing coal-mining towns either side of the Crowsnest Pass, this road soon settles into flat Prairie landscapes that make a change from the hilly forests of BC, until the novelty wears off. As far as Fort Macleod, the region's limited charms are further diminished by almost continual strong winds, but by way of compensation there are at least two unmissable attractions on this stretch: Waterton Lakes National Park and Head-Smashed-In Buffalo Jump, both of them UNESCO World Heritage Sites.

Calgary

Phone code: 403
Colour map 2, grid B4
Population: 878,866
Altitude: 1,048 m

One of North America's youngest and most modern cities, Calgary possesses a kind of youthful energy and optimism. The Downtown area is a grid of sleek glass, chrome and granite skyscrapers, a testament to the oil boom of the 1970s. While there's not much in terms of sights beyond the fine Glenbow Museum, Calgary has a good selection of restaurants, bars and entertainment, and a friendly population who during the famous Stampede demonstrate how much they love to party.

Ins and outs

Getting there
For transport details see page 364

Calgary International **Airport** is about 10 km northeast of Downtown on Barlow Trail, with regular shuttle buses running to town or directly to Banff. The *Greyhound* Station is at 850 16th St SW, with several daily **buses** from east and west. A free shuttle runs regularly to the 7th Av/10th St C-train from Gate 4.

Getting around

Calgary as a whole is a vast ever-expanding metropolis that is difficult to negotiate. The **Downtown** area, however, is small enough to tackle on foot. The **Plus 15 Walking System** is a maze of walkways connecting the many shopping centres, designed to avoid the

24 hours in Calgary

Start your day gently in laid-back **Kensington**, taking breakfast at *Georgina's*, and coffee at the *Heartland Café*. Soak up the atmosphere for a while, then stroll downriver and cross the bridge onto **Prince's Island**, then over to the **Eau Claire Market**. Walk to **Chinatown** and visit the small but fascinating museum in the Cultural Centre. Head **Downtown** and take the lift to the top of the **Calgary Tower** to see views of the surrounding flatlands all the way to the Rockies. Then head to the excellent **Glenbow Museum**, which is particularly strong on First Nations culture. You may be ready for another coffee, either downstairs or at *Caffé Mauro*. The pedestrianized streets of **Stephen Avenue** (8th Avenue) should by now be heaving with colour and incident, buskers and entertainers, so stroll around taking in the shops and the gleaming buildings, looking for somewhere for lunch. *Teatro* would be a fine choice. If you want to get out of the sun, visit the indoor **Devonian Gardens** or the **Art Gallery**.

Take the C-train to **St George's Island** and spend the rest of the afternoon in the **Calgary Zoo and Botanical Gardens**. Calgary's focus of evening activity is 17th Avenue and 4th Street. Have a pre-dinner drink at the *Ship and Anchor*, then do some menu-browsing, probably ending up at *Wildwood Grill*, *Bistro Jo Jo* or *Fourth Street Rose*. For live music head to *Kaos Jazz & Blues Bistro*, or to experience an authentic cowboy saloon with live country bands, make the trek out to *Ranchman's*. *Ming's* is a great place for a post-dinner Martini, and you're in the right place to check out the best of Calgary's clubs. Dance till dawn, and head to *Nellie's* for breakfast.

outside in winter. *Calgary Transit* run a cheap and efficient system of buses and the electric 'C-Train'. The grid of streets is divided into quadrants, with Centre St dividing east from west, and the river dividing south from north. In a 3-digit street number, the first digit refers to the block, so 130 9th Av SE means that the building is No 30 on 9th Av in the block between 1st and 2nd Streets SE.

Driving in Calgary is difficult and not recommended, and parking is always a problem. Drivers should be aware that the TransCanada Hwy runs north of Downtown as 16th Av NE. Hwy 2, the major north-south artery, splits the town in two. Macleod Trail is Hwy 2 heading south, Deerfoot Trail is Hwy 2 heading north. In town, signs often confusingly refer to the highway's name and not its number.

Tourist information Calgary's 2 **Visitor Service Centres**, T1800-6611678, are situated in *Riley & McCormack* stores Downtown at 220 8th Av, and Eau Claire Market, and are frankly inadequate for such a large city. There are also desks at the Arrivals and Departures levels at the airport. *Where Calgary*, www.wherecalgary.com, is a useful monthly magazine usually found at the Service Centres or posher hotels. Also worth checking are www.tourismcalgary.com, the official site, www.calgaryplus.ca, which is impartial and therefore more trustworthy, and www.downtowncalgary.com

Best time to visit Calgary is too cold to visit in the winter. The best month is Jul, which has the Stampede, a microbrewery festival, the folk festival, and Shakespeare in the Park. Sep, which is also a great time to visit the nearby Rockies, has Art Week and the International Film Festival, and enjoys a climate that is midway between the too-cold winters and too-hot summers.

History

Recent archaeological finds have confirmed that the Blackfoot have resided in the area for some 10,000 years, joined about 300 years ago by the Stoney and Sarcee. Fort Calgary was built in 1875 as part of a North West Mounted Police

Alberta

(NWMP) effort to control the trouble caused by rogue whisky traders, and particularly to protect the natives from such lawlessness. A railway and township followed, attracting ranchers drawn by the 'open grazing' policy of the

Alberta

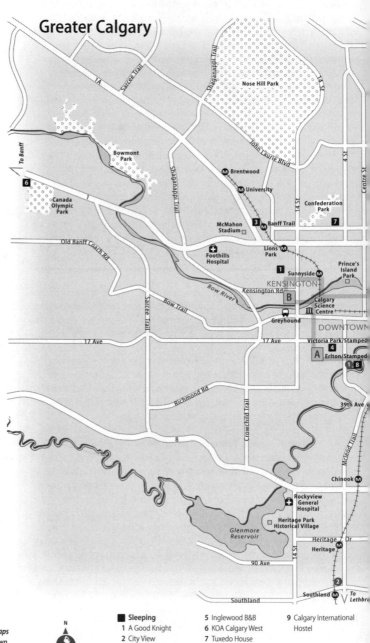

Greater Calgary

Nose Hill Park

To Banff

Bowmont Park

Canada Olympic Park

Old Banff Coach Rd

John Laurie Blvd

Shaganappi Trail

Sarcee Trail

1A

14 St

4 St

Centre St

Brentwood M

University M

Confederation Park

McMahon Stadium

Banff Trail M 3

Foothills Hospital

Lions Park M

Sunnyside M 1

Prince's Island Park

KENSINGTON

Kensington Rd B

Calgary Science Centre

Greyhound

DOWNTOWN

17 Ave

17 Ave

Victoria Park/Stamped

Erlton/Stamped A 4

8 1

Bow River

Bow Trail

Sarcee Trail

Richmond Rd

Crowchild Trail

39th Ave

8

Chinook M

Rockyview General Hospital

Heritage Park Historical Village

Glenmore Reservoir

Heritage Dr

Heritage M

90 Ave

14 St

McLeod Trail

Southland

Southland M

To Lethbr

Detail maps	N
A Downtown, page 358	
B Kensington, page 360	

0 km 1
0 mile 1

Sleeping
1 A Good Knight
2 City View
3 Comfort Inn (Banff Trail)
4 Hillcrest House
5 Inglewood B&B
6 KOA Calgary West
7 Tuxedo House
8 Westways Guesthouse
9 Calgary International Hostel

Bars & clubs
1 Blind Monk
2 Ranchman's

Alberta grasslands. From 1886 onwards, much of the town was rebuilt in sandstone after a number of fires had destroyed its wooden houses. Expansion was fairly fast, but accelerated rapidly after oil was struck and a refinery opened in 1923. The oil crisis of the 1970s caused the city to explode, and for a while it enjoyed the highest per capita income in Canada. The confidence of prosperity is still very much a part of the city's atmosphere today.

Sights

The majority of Calgary's sights are close together in Downtown. At the south end, the unmissable Glenbow Museum, a few other cultural venues, and the Calgary Tower cluster around the pedestrian-only Stephen Avenue Walk. Most of the other sights are north, scattered along the banks of the Bow River, including the Zoo, considered one of the country's best. The best places to escape the hustle and bustle are Prince's Island, in the middle of the river, and Kensington on the other side, the closest Calgary gets to a Bohemian quarter.

The large and varied collection of the **Glenbow Museum** Glenbow Museum provides a great introduction to Western Canada, especially for those who have just arrived in the country. It spreads over four floors, including the ground level, which is taken up with the lobby, gift shop and the *Lazy Loaf and Kettle Café*. The next floor contains a changing feature exhibition, a hands-on zone for children called the **Discovery Room**, the wonderful **Art of Asia** permanent collection, and an **art gallery**. Indigenous art here is cleverly placed alongside European works which illustrate the white man's varied responses to first contact with the aboriginal people.

The third floor takes up the story of Western Canada's past, starting with an excellent **First Nations** exhibit. Artefacts from the many different native cultures underline the easily forgotten fact that this word 'native' attempts to lump together a vast array

▶ ## Chinooks

The Chinook is a type of wind found around the world where long mountain chains lie at right-angles to prevailing wind patterns. In Canada, such gusts of warm, dry air blow down from the Rockies to the western prairies. In southwestern Alberta, most notably Calgary, one in three winter days is a chinook day, with temperatures rising by as much as 27°C in as little as two minutes.

There are two main reasons for this. First, Arctic air is replaced by maritime air, which is about 22°C warmer. Secondly, if it has rained in the mountains, the heat that would normally change water into vapour is returned to the air parcel, which is further warmed by its flow down the mountainside. Capable of gusting to 100 kph, the chinook melts snow and dries soil.

of radically varied groups. All kinds of arts and crafts are displayed, with fine examples of carving, beadwork, textiles and even music, such as the eerie throat music of the Inuit. Elsewhere a number of **pioneer** displays deal with many familiar topics: the fur trade, the early history of the Mounties, the railway, farming and, inevitably in Calgary, oil. The fourth floor has an educational and fun **West African** exhibit, with videos of dances, and lots of cultural items such as headdresses. There is also an extensive display of **rocks and minerals**, and a large collection of military paraphernalia such as armour and guns.

■ *Sat-Wed 0900-1700, Thu-Fri 0900-2100. $10, $6 concessions, $2 Sun morn, $3 Sep-May. 130 9th Av SE, T7775506, www.glenbow.org*

Around Stephen Avenue Walk After the museum, those hungry for more culture could check out the nearby **Art Gallery** or **Performing Arts Centre** (see Entertainment), or stroll down to the 1905 sandstone **Cathedral Church of the Redeemer** at 9th Avenue and 1st Street Southeast, one of Calgary's most attractive constructions. Those who don't object to the unreasonable fee could ride the lift up **Calgary Tower**, the city's most distinctive landmark since it was built in 1968. At that time, its 190-m (approximate) height was unchallenged by the surrounding structures, and even today great views of the city, with the Rockies as a backdrop on a clear day, can be enjoyed from the Observation Terrace, where there are snack and cocktail bars and an expensive revolving restaurant. ■ *0800-2300. $8, $5 seniors, $3 children. 9th Av/Centre St, T2667171.*

Otherwise, the obvious thing to do is wander down **Stephen Avenue Walk** (8th Avenue), a lively pedestrian street that is certainly Calgary's day-time focal point. Between Macleod Trail Southeast and 3rd Street southwest, it is also the most intact turn-of-the-20th-century Downtown street in Western Canada, with many of Calgary's finest and oldest buildings rubbing shoulders with the brand new. At ground level are pubs, restaurants, street vendors, buskers and some funky shops. Up above is a murky world of department stores, such as the massive Toronto Dominion Square between 2nd and 3rd streets, a block now dominated by a new set of odd steel sculptures called *The Trees*. Bizarrely enough, inside on the 4th floor are some real full-sized trees, as well as 20,000 varieties of plants, plus fountains, ponds, bridges and art exhibitions. Known as the **Devonian Gardens**, this is a perfect place to escape whatever the Calgary weather is up to. ■ *0900-2100. By donation. T2685207.*

Eau Claire Market & Prince's Island Park Pleasantly situated on the Bow River between 2nd and 3rd Streets, the Eau Claire Market brings together fruit and vegetable stalls, a food hall of fast-food joints, a few cinemas including an IMAX theatre ($11, $9 concession), and some tacky craft shops. Brash and garish, this is a failed attempt to emulate places like The Forks in Winnipeg or Vancouver's Granville Market. Outside is an open area surrounded by pubs, which offers a welcome respite from Downtown Calgary's teeming streets, as well acting as a meeting place and venue for cultural events. Across a pedestrian bridge is **Prince's Island Park**, a nice place for a stroll.

A few blocks east of the market, Calgary's Chinatown is small but clean, and packed with cheap bakeries and restaurants offering dim sum. The **Chinese Cultural Centre and Museum** is its main attraction, featuring a magnificent dome copied from the c1420 Temple of Heaven in Beijing. Its interior features 561 individually crafted gold dragons and 40 phoenixes. There is an **art gallery** upstairs and a very worthwhile **museum** downstairs with a number of fascinating exhibits, such as a big picture of tigers made entirely of feathers, a 'transparent bronze mirror', and a bronze bowl from which water jumps straight up when it's rubbed. ■ *1100-1700. $2, $1 concessions for museum. Dome interior 0900-2100. 197 1st St SW, T2625071, www.culturalcentre.ab.ca Bus No 31.*

Chinatown

On the north bank, reached via a footbridge from Prince's Island Park or more directly from the 10th Street bridge, Kensington is a pleasant neighbourhood focused on 10th Street Northwest and Kensington Road Northwest. Colourful and culturally stimulating, the area has a bohemian flavour, with tasteful restaurants, lots of pubs, some interesting shops and the closest this town gets to an alternative scene. Those who dislike cities but are obliged to spend a day in Calgary should head here.

Kensington

Situated on the river west of Downtown, this centre is aimed mostly at kids, with lots of hands-on stuff, mini experiments, and intriguing information, as well as some interesting exhibits. The so-called Amazement Park is half-hearted, however, and the whole affair fails to compete with the Odyssium in Edmonton (see page 386). The **Shaw Millennium Park** next door is a giant purpose-built skateboard park which also has a few volleyball courts. ■ *May-Jan 1000-1700. $9, $7 seniors, $6 children, includes Discovery Dome show. 701 11th St SW, T2213700. C-Train to 10th St Stn.*

Calgary Science Centre

This is a reconstruction of the 1875 North West Mounted Police fort, staffed by costumed guides who supplement the exhibitions by telling the story of Calgary's roots. ■ *May-Oct 0900-1700. $5.75, $3.25 concessions. 750 9th Av SE, T2901875, www.fortcalgary.com Bus No 1, 75 or 41 from Downtown.* Within walking distance is **Inglewood Bird Sanctuary** with 32 ha of paths, and an interpretive centre. ■ *Centre 1000-1700, paths open year-round till dark. By donation. 2425 9th Av SE, T2696688. Bus No 411 from Downtown, No 1 back.*

Fort Calgary

Across from the fort, situated on St George's Island between two branches of the Bow River, is the Calgary Zoo, Botanical Gardens and Prehistoric Park. With over 1,200 animals from all over the world, including the usual favourites, this is a nice place to spend the day, with lots of facts about the animals dotted around to make it an educational experience. The Prehistoric Park, entered via a suspension bridge across the river, has plastic life-sized dinosaurs in rather unconvincing settings. The Conservatory, containing tropical, arid and butterfly gardens, is well worth a visit. ■ *0900-1700. $11, $5.50 concessions. 1300 Zoo Rd, via Memorial Dr, T2329372, www.calgaryzoo.ab.ca Take the C-Train.*

Calgary Zoo

Alberta

Downtown Calgary

Related map
A Kensington,
page 360

0 metres   150
0 yards   150

■ **Sleeping**
1 Calgary International
   Hostel C6
2 Fairmont Palliser D4
3 Lord Nelson Inn C1
4 Regis Plaza C5

5 Sandman C2

● **Eating**
1 Athens By Night, Bad
   Ass Coffee Co, & Wired
   Cyber Café E1
2 The Belvedere &
   Latin Corner
   Cantina C4
3 Bistro Jo Jo E1
4 Bodega D2
5 Bookers B6

6 Buchanan's B2
7 Caffe Mauro C4
8 Cannery Row &
   McQueens D3
9 Cilantro E3
10 Divino Bistro & Wine
   Bar C4
11 Fourth Street Rose F3
12 Good Earth Café C4
13 Indochine C3
14 Kaos Jazz & Blues
   Bistro E2

15 La Chaumière E4
16 Nellies E2
17 Piq Niq Café & Beat
   Niq Jazz & Social
   Club C4
18 River Café A4
19 Sultan's Tent E1
20 Sushi Hiro B2
21 Teatro C4
22 Thai Sa-On D3
23 Wildwood Grill &
   Brewing Co F3

With 150 replicated 1914 prairie **Heritage Park**
buildings, this is one of the biggest and **Historical**
most complete heritage towns in the **Village**
country, absolving you from the
responsibility of visiting any others.
The only drawback is that, unlike
many examples such as Barkerville in
BC, this is a total fabrication, not the
renovation of a town that actually
existed. As elsewhere, the whole thing
is brought to life by costumed staff
who really do what their roles entail:
the baker makes bread, the restaurant
serves meals, the blacksmith shoes
horses and so on. There are also lots of
rides, including a steam train, wagon
and ferris wheel. Free pancake breakfast daily from 0900-1000.
■ *May-Sep 0900-1700. $11, $7 con-*
cessions; $19, $15 with all rides; or
$4.50 SS Moyie, $3 train, $3 horse
wagon, $3 most amusement rides. Her-
itage Dr SW, T2591900. Bus No 502
from the Heritage C-Train stop.

17th Avenue Southwest, just south **Other**
of Downtown between 2nd Street and **Neighbour-**
14th Street, is the most interesting **hoods**
night-time area, with lots of good restaurants and pubs, and the highest
concentration of clubs. While there,
check out the adjacent St Mary's
Church at 1st Street and 17th Avenue,
one of the latest Gothic revival
churches in Western Canada, with an
incredibly striking symmetrical brick
tower best appreciated at night. **Mission District** on 4th Street, southwest
from 12th Avenue going south, was
originally settled by French Canadian
priests, and now has some classy restaurants and art galleries. **Inglewood**,
9th Avenue, southeast from 10-12th
streets, is Calgary's oldest district, and
contains some of its grandest houses
and cottages, as well as antique shops.

The tourist board tries to tempt visi- **Excursions**
tors with self-guided tours. One is the
Cowboy Trail, most of it on Highway
22 to the west of Calgary, stretching
from Rocky Mountain House
National Historic Site in the north to

Alberta

● **Bars & clubs**
24 Auburn Saloon *C4*
25 Barley Mill *A4*
26 Blue Rock Wine &
   Cigar Bar *F2*
27 Cherry Lounge *D4*
28 Darby O'Gill's *C1*
29 Don Quijote *B3*
30 Embassy *C3*
31 James Joyce *C4*
32 Ming's *E2*
33 Night Gallery *D4*
34 Palace *C3*
35 Pongo Noodle Bar
   & Beerhouse *E2*
36 Roxy Nightlife *E3*
37 Ship & Anchor *E2*
38 Underground *D2*
39 Vicious Circle *D4*

Cardston in the south, via a number of ranches and heritage sites, including Cochrane's **Western Heritage Centre**, Longview's **Bar U Ranch**, and the **Kootenai Brown Heritage Village** in Pincher Creek. For more information, T1800-6611678, www.thecowboytrail.com

Essentials

Sleeping

■ *on maps,*
pages 354, 358 & below
There are
disappointingly few
options in
Downtown Calgary.
The major routes into
town are lined with
cheap chain motels,
especially Banff Trail
NW, which is known as
Motel Village

LL-AL *The Fairmont Palliser*, 133 9th Av SW, T2621234, www.fairmont.com Calgary's most upmarket hotel with a castle-like exterior in the heart of town. As usual, all the added extras are there, and the lounges, restaurants and lobbies are beautiful, the rooms full of class but not especially big. **LL-L** *Kensington Riverside Inn*, 1126 Memorial Dr NW, T2284442, www.kensingtonriversideinn.com Smaller, more personal choice by the river, close to but away from the noise of Downtown. Nice rooms, breakfast, balconies. **A-D** *Westways Guesthouse* 216 26th Av SW, T2291758, www.westways.ab.ca Antiques, oriental carpets, en suite baths and TVs.

B *Lord Nelson Inn*, 1020 8th Av, T2698262. Reasonable mid-range choice with balconies. **B** *Sandman*, 888 7th Av SW, T2378626. Best mid-range choice Downtown. **B-C** *A Good Knight*, 1728 7th Av NW, T2707628, www.agoodknight.com 3 themed rooms with private bath in an old house close to Kensington. **B-C** *Comfort Inn*, one of the more reliable motel choices, has branches at 2369 Banff Trail NW, T2892581, south on Macleod Trail SW, T2877070, and at the airport at 3111 26th St NE, T7351966. **B-C** *Hillcrest House*, 600 Hillcrest Av, T2286164, www.hillcresthouse.com 1914 home with en suite baths and TV in rooms. **C** *City View*, 2300 6th St SE, T8705640. Panoramic view of Rockies from balcony. **C** *Inglewood*, 1006 8th Av SE, T2626570. Victorian-style house near town and river. **C** *Regis Plaza*, 124 7th Av SE, T2624641. About the cheapest option Downtown, and rather run down. Some rooms have shared bath. **C** *Tuxedo House*, 121 21st Av NE, T2775298. Gardens, deck and patio. Guest lounge. Shared bath.

E *Calgary International Hostel*, 520 7th Av SE, T2698239. Close to Downtown. Dorms and private rooms, kitchen, laundry. In the summer, for extended stays, try the **E** *University of Calgary*, 3330 24th Av, T2203203. **Camping** There's little choice for campers. All the following are far from Downtown around the edge of the city limits. **E** *KOA Calgary West*, on south side of Hwy 1 near Olympic Park, T2880411. Shuttle service to Downtown. Games room and laundry. **F** *Pine Creek RV Campground*, Hwy 2 210th Av S, T2563002. Games, laundry. **F** *Symons Valley RV Park*, Symons Valley Rd/144th Av N, T2744574. Restaurant, laundry.

Eating

● *on maps,*
pages 354, 358 & right

Downtown Expensive *The Belvedere*, 107 8th Av SW, T2659595. Upmarket New York-style dining room. Romantic atmosphere, international cuisine. *Divino Bistro and Wine Bar*, 817 1st St SW, T2635869. Stylish, intimate space with candles and wooden tables. California- style cuisine. *Indochine*, 2nd Floor Bankers Hall, 315 8th Av, T2636929. Highly rated Vietnamese-French cuisine in elegant surroundings. *Sushi Hiro*, 727 5th Av SW, T2330605. Classy, very large, very Japanese. *Teatro*, 200 8th Av, T2901012. Fine dining in an elegant vintage bank building with an upmarket but lively ambience.

⇨ *Related map*
A Downtown
Calgary,
page 358

Kensington

3	Jug O Juice
4	Lido Café
5	Marathon
6	Stromboli Inn
7	Take 10
8	Tandoori Hut
9	The Roasterie Too
10	Trawlers & Fish Market

■ **Sleeping**
1 Kensington Riverside Inn

● **Eating**
1 Georgina's
2 Heartland Café

● **Bars & clubs**
11 Kilberry's Celtic Pub
12 Molly Malone's

Alberta

Mid-range *Bodega* 720 11th Av SW, T2628966. Flamenco guitar and tapas in an intimate setting. *Buchanan's*, 738 3rd Av, T2614646. Old-fashioned chop house with good steaks and range of malt whiskies. *Latin Corner Cantina*, 109 8th Av, T2627248. Good value home-cooked Latin American food. *River Café*, Prince's Island Park, T2617670. Tasty Canadian dishes cooked in a wood-fire oven, set in a gorgeous location. *Thai Sa-On*, 351 10th Av SW, T2643526. For 10 years rated the best Thai food in town.

17th Av and 4th St Expensive *La Chaumière*, 139 17th Av SW, T2285690. Haute cuisine in extremely opulent surroundings. **Expensive-mid-range** *Bistro Jo Jo*, 917 17th Av SW, T2452382. More down-to-earth but very highly regarded French dishes in a classic bistro setting. *Cilantro*, 338 17th Av, T2291177. A long-standing favourite. California-fusion eclectic cuisine in a brick and wood setting. Outdoor patio. *Wildwood Grill and Brewing Co*, 2417 4th St SW, T2280100. Stylish restaurant upstairs, pub that brews its own great beers downstairs. Food is eclectic West Coast fusion, using local ingredients like buffalo and rabbit. Saffron halibut, caribou ragout. Good wine list.
Mid-range *Athens By Night*, 17th Av/11th St SW, T2441771. Casual, modest, decent Greek food. *Brava Bistro*, 723 17th Av SW, T2281854. French/Canadian cuisine with organic and vegetarian dishes, an excellent wine list and a patio. *Fourth Street Rose*, 2116 4th St SW, T2285377. Popular and longstanding local haunt with an international touch. Tasteful unpretentious decor and patio. Tapas, salads, gourmet burgers and pizzas. *Nellies*, 2308 4th St SW and 738 17th Av SW. Great breakfast option with big portions. *Sultan's Tent*, 909 17th Av, T2442333. Moroccan cuisine such as couscous and *tagine*, decor based on a Berber tent, with floor seating.

Kensington Mid-range *Georgina's*, 10th St NW. Huge and varied menu, 10 types of eggs benedict, old world cuisine. *Marathon*, 130 10th St NW, T2836796. Delicious Ethiopian curries. Popular and intimate. *Stromboli Inn*, 1147 Kensington St, T2831166. Fresh pasta made to order in an old favourite with a lovely patio. *Tandoori Hut*, 201 10th St NW, T2704012. Good food at better prices, great lunch buffet. *Trawlers Restaurant and Fish Market*, 10th St NW/Memorial Dr. Incredibly varied choice of fresh and first-class seafood in a bistro atmosphere. **Cheap** *Take 10*, 304 10th St NW. Small, no-nonsense spot for Chinese food and breakfast. *Lido Café*, 144 10th St NW. Run-down diner with tableside jukeboxes and stools. Cheap breakfast, burgers and Chinese food.

Cafés *Bad Ass Coffee Co*, 1103 17th Av. *Caffe Mauro*, 805A 1st St SW. Good coffee and sandwiches in an elegant interior. *Good Earth Café*, several locations including Eau Claire Market and 119 8th Av SW. Casual atmosphere, speciality coffees, baking and vegetarian snacks. *Heartland Café*, 940 2nd Av NW. Pleasant local hang-out with a wholefood attitude. *Jug O Juice*. Funky building on Kensington St, outdoor seating, fresh juice. *The Roasterie Too*, 227 10th St NW. Fresh roasted coffee, comfy, outdoor seating.

Downtown *Auburn Saloon*, 712 1st St. Handily placed, arty spot with cosy couches and cocktails. *Darby O'Gill's*, 803 8th Av SW. Irish boozer with a pleasant terracotta interior and live music at weekends. *The James Joyce*, 114 8th Av SW. More of the same. Good food and a patio. *Vicious Circle*, 1011 1st St. Cosy café/lounge with varied music. **Eau Claire Market** has many pubs with pleasant summer patios, such as *Barley Mill*. A great reprieve from the Downtown traffic, with an absurd range of beers on tap.

Bars
● *on maps, pages 358 & 360*

17th Avenue SW *Ming's*, 520 17th Av SW. A cosy, trendy Martini lounge with dim lighting and serving good food. *Ship and Anchor*, 534 17th Av SW. Very popular with locals, arguably the best pub in town, with outside seating and an unbeatable selection of draught beers, including the whole range by excellent local brewers *Big Rock*. *Pongo Noodle Bar & Beerhouse*, 524 17th Av SW. Stylish joint open until 0400 on Fri-Sat.

Alberta

Kensington has far too many British-style pubs, all with very slight variations and vast selections of good draught beer. Happy hour 1600-1900. *Kilberry's Celtic Pub*, 302 10th St NW. Very nice menu features upscale pub food with a French twist, and lots of salads. Great selection of Scotch, live music Thu-Sat. *Molly Malone's*, 1153 Kensington Cres. Irish pub with seating on the rooftop, live music.

Entertainment

Check the listings in FFWD, www.ffwdweekly.com and Straight, free from cafés and elsewhere

Cinemas As well as the usual multiplexes, Calgary has 3 cinemas showing mainly first-run indie, foreign and art-house films: *Globe*, 617 8th Av SW, T2623308; *Plaza*, 1133 Kensington, T2833636, the oldest; and *Uptown* 612 8th Av SW, T2650120. There are *IMAX* cinemas at Eau Claire Market, T9744629, and 6455 Macleod Trail S, T2128994.

Clubs *The Blind Monk*, 2500 4th St SW. Deep house and ambient grooves. *The Cherry Lounge*, 1219 1st St SW. Different DJs and music every night. Underground funk, hip hop, electronica, etc. Popular. Minimalist interior with cosy Martini lounge upstairs. *Don Quijote*, 309 2nd Av SW. Spanish restaurant and tapas bar that turns into a Latin dance club with tango/salsa every Thu-Sat. *The Embassy*, 516 9th Av SW. Cosy underground dance club playing disco/retro or hip hop. Cheap drinks Wed. Chill-out room and rooftop patio. On **1st St** between 12th & 13th Av is a small but very busy club scene including *The Night Gallery*, 1209 1st St SW. Small and crowded dance spot, with a wide range of DJ music and live bands. *The Palace*, 219 8th Av SW. Plush, high-class club with serious sound/laser system, 2 main dance floors and an intimate atmosphere. Hip hop/R&B/house. *The Roxy Nightlife*, 214 17th Av SW. Upmarket nightclub for 25s and older. Sushi, best dressed prizes, etc. *The Warehouse*, 733 10th Av SW, entrance down a back alley, T2640535. Long-lasting yet progressive rave-culture favourite. Trance, jungle, house, etc. Cover charge. Till 0600 weekends.

Galleries *Art Gallery of Calgary*, 117 8th Av SW, T2662674, www.artgallery.com A variety of artists exhibited in 4 different spaces. Tue-Sat 1000-1800, Sun 1200-1600. By donation. *Centennial Gallery*, 125 9th Av SE, T2666783; and *Centre Gallery*, 924 6th Av SW, T2370383, are 2 of the better artist-run galleries.

Live music venues *Beat Niq Jazz and Social Club*, downstairs at *Piq Niq* Café, 811 1st St SW, T2631650. Small, vocal-led acts, cover charge. *Blue Rock Wine and Cigar Bar*, 512 23rd Av SW, T2299366. Lounge and restaurant with jazz duos Wed, Fri and Sat. *Bookers*, 316 3rd St SE, T2646419. Cajun food. Blues Fri and Sat. *Cannery Row*, 317 10th Av, T2698889. R&B Fri and Sat. Upstairs is *McQueens*, T2694722, with jazz and blues Wed-Sat. *Centre for the Performing Arts*, 205 8th Av SE, T4947455. Main venue for classical concerts. *Kaos Jazz & Blues Bistro*, 718 17th Av SW, T2289997. Best jazz venue, with first-rate acts. Large bar but usually crowded with an interesting clientele. Broad menu of good food. *The King Eddie*, 438 9th Av SE, T2623500. Blues. *Ranchman's*, 9615 Macleod Trail S, T2531100. Authentic cowboy saloon with live country bands Mon-Sat.

Spectator sports The *Calgary Stampeders* play **Canadian football** at McMahon Stadium, across from the NW Banff Trail C-ṭrain, T2890258. The *Calgary Cannons* play **baseball** at Burns Stadium, across Crowchild Trail from the NW Banff Trail C-train. **Show-jumping** at Spruce Meadows, 3 km west of Macleod Trail on Hwy 22X, T9744200. **Horse racing** at Stampede Park, 17th Av/2nd St SE, T2610214.

Theatre *Pleiades Theatre*, 701 11th St SW, T2213735. Mystery plays. *Shakespeare in the Park*, see Festivals. *Centre for the Performing Arts*, 205 8th Av SE, T4947455, www.theartscentre.org Calgary's premier venue, containing 5 theatres and concert halls. Home to the Calgary Philharmonic, Theatre Calgary and other major companies.

Alberta

The Calgary Stampede

◀

In early July, the whole city goes cowboy crazy for 10 days during the Calgary Stampede. Locals don ten-gallon hats, leather boots and Wrangler jeans, and start affecting a John Wayne drawl. Shop windows are covered with cowboy cartoons, free breakfasts are offered throughout Downtown every morning, and the streets are choked with parties and drunken revellers. If you don't want to throw yourself whole-heartedly into this all-consuming affair, the best advice is get out of town well before it begins, because there is no middle road. And don't even think about driving!

Festivities begin with the Stampede Parade, which takes about two hours to pass the bleachers set up along 6th and 9th Avenues. Even for this, seating needs to be reserved, T2577115. Thereafter, the serious action takes place at the Stampede Grounds on Macleod Trail South. The two major events are the Rodeo at 1330 and the Rangeland Derby at 2000, both involving nine days of heats building up to the final on the tenth day. Participants come from as far away as Australia to compete. The Rodeo is one of the biggest in the world, with $50,000 for winners in each of the six major competitions. These are: saddle bronc, where riders have to keep their feet in the stirrups; bareback, where points go to riders who spur their horses on to greater heights; bull riding, in which they try to stay on a furious 1,000-pound bull; steer wrestling, which involves jumping from a racing horse onto the horns of a running steer and forcing it to the ground; calf roping; and barrel racing, a

glorified sprint, and the only event in which women participate. There is also a host of minor events, such as wild cow milking, and at the end of the day spectators watch replays of the most exciting moments and elect a winner of the 'Wild Ride of the Day'.

The Rangeland Derby is a crazy race between four chuckwagons, each with four outriders. This is followed by a variety show and fireworks. Also on the grounds, and included in the admission price, is an agricultural exhibition, an amusement park with rides, various cowboy-related competitions, a casino, cowboy poetry recitals, and two major stages for live music, including some very big names, not all of them Country artists. At the Indian Village is a Bannock Booth, demonstrations of beadwork, meat cutting, teepee raising, and a Pow Wow featuring dancers from all over the continent. A second venue is the Olympic Plaza (renamed Rope Square) where free live entertainment and Wild West shows take place every morning but Sunday.

Gate Admission to the Stampede Grounds is $10, $5 concessions. On top of this, tickets for the Rodeo and Rangeland Derby range from $24-54 per event, reservable at the Box Office, T2699822, or TicketMaster, T7770000. Rush tickets for $10, $5 concessions, are available at the Box Office 90 minutes before the event. For general information, T2610101, www.calgarystampede.com Getting there: C-Train to Victoria Park or Erlton Stampede Stations; bus No 10 or 433.

Alberta

Calgary is famous far and wide for its sensational *Stampede* (see box), but there are **Festivals** plenty of other events scattered through the calendar. The *Winter Festival*, T5435480, in **Feb** is an 11-day celebration of the cold. *International Children's Festival*, T2947414, runs for 5 days in late **May**. *International Jazz Festival*, T2491119, in late **Jun** is a major 10-day event. During the *Calgary Stampede* in early **Jul** the 3-day *Microbrewery Stampede*, at Telus Convention Centre, T2549204, adds to the revelry with samples of countless brews from across North America. Later that month is the 4-day *Folk Music Festival*, T2330904, held in Prince's Island Park. *Shakespeare in the Park*, T2406821, runs from early **Jul** to early **Aug**, with free performances of the Bard's plays in Prince's Island Park, Tue-Sun at 1900. A couple of good musical events take place in **Aug** in nearby towns: *Big Valley Country Music Jamboree* in Camrose, T6720224; and the *Shady Grove Bluegrass Music Festival* in High River, T6525550.

Later in the month *Calgary Summer Festival of Art and Crafts*, 2862632, brings over 100 artists to the Olympic Park. Late **Sep** is a good time for culture, with the *Art Week*, and the 6-day *International Film Festival*.

Shopping   **Antiques**   There are several stores in Inglewood, 9th Av SE between 11th St and 13th St. **Art** *Fosbrooke Fine Arts*, 2nd Floor, Penny Lane, 8 Av/4 St. Rotating selection showcasing 15-20 artists. **Books** *Pages Books on Kensington*, 1135 Kensington Rd. *The Hostel Shop and Abbot Pass Trading Co*, 1414 Kensington Rd NW, T2838311. **Boots** *Alberta Boot Co.*, 614 10th Av SW, T2634623. One of the best things to buy in town is an authentic, handmade pair of cowboy boots. **Music** *Tramp's Music*, 109 10th St NW. Loads of new and used CDs. **Photography** *ABL Imaging*, 238 11th Av SE, T2666300. **Sports** *Mountain Equipment Co-op*, 830 10th Av SW. massive store, with all the sport and camping equipment you need. *Mountain Sport Exchange*, 1249 Kensington Rd NW. **Western Wear** *Lammle's*, 11 stores including 209 8th Av SW, T2665226; *Riley and McCormack*, 220 8th Av SW, airport, or Eau Claire market.

Sports   Calgary has many fine **golf** courses. Among the best are *Elks Golf Club*, 2502 6th St N, T5432899; *Inglewood Golf Club*, 34th Av/Barlow Trail SE, T2724363; and *McKenzie Meadows*, 17215 McKenzie Meadows Dr SE, T2572255. The *YMCA* in Eau Claire has an excellent **swimming** pool, plus fitness room, squash courts, sauna. Daily 0530-2230. $8.

Tour operators   *Brewster*, 808 Centre St SE, T2218242, www.brewster.ca Day-trips to Banff, overnight to Jasper, ½-day tour around Calgary, etc. Tour of University of Calgary, T2203147. *Chinook River Sports*, T2637238. Whitewater rafting on the Kicking Horse, Red Deer, Kananaskis and others. *Travel Cuts*, 1414 Kensington Rd NW, T5312070. Travel agent offering student discounts.

Transport   **Local** *Calgary Transit* has its own **Information Centre** at 240 7th Av SW, T2621000, 0830-1700 Mon-Fri. As well as information, they hand out very helpful maps. Tickets costing $1.60 ($1 concessions) or $5 ($3 for a day-pass) can be bought here, on C-train platforms, or from shops with the Calgary Transit sticker. If you need to take more than one bus to complete a journey, ask the driver for a transfer. The C-train is free on 7th Av between Macleod Trail and 8 St SW. **Taxis** *Calgary Cab Co*, T7772222. *Associated Taxi*, T2991111. **Car hire** *Budget*, 140 6th Av SE, T2261550; *Discount*, 444a 9th Av SW, T2991224; *Rent-a-wreck*, 1012 16th Av NW, T2308502. **Motorbike rentals** *All Season Rentals*, 17a-416 Meridian Rd SE, T2041771. **RV rentals** *Alldrive Canada*, 1908 10th Av SW, T1888-7368787, www.aldrive.com *Canadream Campers*, 2508 24th Av NE, T2911000, www.canadream.com *Cruise Canada*, 2980 26th St NE, T2914963, www.cruisecanada.com

Long distance   **Air** Calgary International Airport, T7351372, is about 10 km northeast of Downtown on Barlow Trail. International flights with *Air Canada* and *Air Transat*. National flights with *West Jet*, *Air Tango* and *Peace Air*. The *Airporter* shuttle, T5313909, leaves for Downtown every half hour from Bay 3 outside Arrivals (0630-2330, $8.50 one way). The *Airport Shuttle Express*, T5094799, goes door to door. *Banff Airporter (Brewster)*, T7626700, runs directly to Banff ($40 one way). *Sky Shuttle*, T7625000, runs directly to Banff, Canmore, Lake Louise, and Red Deer, and in winter to ski hills in Fernie, Kimberley and Invermere. *Yellowhead Transportation and Tours*, T780-8650007, run to and from all airports and hotels in Alberta.

Bus The *Greyhound* station is at 850 16th St/8 Av SW, T2659111, www.greyhound.ca A free shuttle runs regularly to the 7th Av/10th St C-train from Gate 4. There are several daily buses to **Edmonton** ($42); 5 to **Banff** ($21); 5 to **Vancouver** ($122); 2 to **Prince George** ($138). Weekly services: 5 to **Yellowknife** ($230); 4 to **Regina** ($94); 4 to

Winnipeg ($150), 3 to Toronto ($280). *Red Arrow Motorcoach*, T5310350, www.redarrow.pwt.ca have regular daily departures direct to **Edmonton** ($46), **Red Deer** ($32), and **Fort McMurray** ($100).

Airline offices *Air Canada*, T2659555; *Air Transat*, T514-9871616; *Peace Air*, T780-6243060; *West Jet*, T2505839. **Banks** *Canada Trust*, 751 3rd St SW; *TD Bank*, 902 8th Av SW. For **foreign exchange**: *Royal Bank Foreign Exchange*, T2923938. *Western Currency Exchange*, T2639000. **Communications** Internet: *Library*, see below; *Wired Cyber Café*, 1032 17th Av SW. Hip spot with good food. **Canada Post**: 315 8th Av S; 1702 4th St SW. **Embassies and consulates** American, T2668962; **Danish**, T2455755; **French**, T5083831; **Finnish**, T2999805; **German**, T2695900; **Hungarian**, T2524502; **Italian**, T2376603; **Netherlands**, T2662710; **Norwegian**, T2632270; **Swedish**, T5410354; **Swiss**, T2338919. **Laundry** *Avenue Coin Laundry*, 333 17th Av SW. **Library** WR Castell Central Library, 616 Macleod Trail, T2602605, www.calgarypublic library.com **Medical services** *Rockyview General Hospital*, 7007 14th St SW, T5413000; *Foothills Hospital*, 1403 29th St NW, T6701110; *Wild Rose College of Natural Healing and Holistic Clinic*, 1228 Kensington Rd NW, T2700891.

Directory

The Drumheller Badlands

Apart from the Rockies, the most worthwhile destination in Alberta focuses on the small, unexceptional town of Drumheller, an easy day excursion from Calgary. The Badlands scenery in this region is truly exceptional, easily enjoyed thanks to a circular driving route that connects some great vantage points, and takes in one of the finest palaeontology museums in the globe.

Colour map 2, grid B5

As melt-waters flowing from the BC highlands to the giant inland Bear Paw Sea carved out the Red Deer River Valley at the end of the last ice-age, their ever-changing courses resulted in a crazy jumble of oddly sculpted rock and steep coulees (deep, narrow ravines). Such bizarre shapes are thrown into sharp relief by the shades of purple, red, orange and brown that colour this arid, forbidding and strangely beautiful landscape. Layers of sandstone, mudstone and ironstone are clearly visible, adding horizontal stripes of colour to the extraordinary twisted shapes. The area is also dotted with hoodoos, those odd, elongated mushroom-shaped pillars that are created when an ironstone cap protects the eroding sandstone beneath it.

Geological evidence suggests that 75 million years ago, at the time of the dinosaurs, this area was a lush coastal plain, supporting a wealth of plant and animal life. The glaciers whose waters gouged out the landscape's features also scraped away the upper layers of rock, and as erosion continues, fossils are revealed buried in the Cretaceous layers beneath. So it is that one JB Tyrell, looking for the coal deposits that fuelled a successful mining industry in these parts, stumbled instead across the skull of an Albertasaurus, thus sparking off the 'Great Canadian Dinosaur Rush'. More than 20 species of dinosaur, including many complete skeletons, have since been unearthed in one of the most fruitful beds of dinosaur remains in the world. Though these have found their way to museums around the world, a large number are housed in the excellent Royal Tyrell Museum just outside Drumheller.

On the way to Drumheller, you will pass **Horseshoe Canyon**, one of the most dramatic viewpoints for admiring the Badlands. Just before town Reptile World cashes in on the dominant theme, with a collection of snakes and toads that can be handled, and the 270-kg alligator, Fred. ■ *Summer 0900-2200, spring/autumn 1000-1700. $4.50, $3.50 concessions.* T8238623.

Drumheller
Phone code: 403

Alberta

Drumheller itself remains hidden in the canyon until the last moment, no bad thing as it's a drab town full of cement dinosaurs that look like dogs. The nicest part of town is on its north side just over the bridge. As well as a wading pool, which offers some relief from the intense summer heat, and the 'World's Biggest Dinosaur' ($2 to climb to the top), this is where you'll find the **Visitor Information Centre**, 60 1st Avenue West, T8238100, www.dinosaurvalley.com 0900-2100. If here in June or July, ask about the celebrated **Passion Play** held at 17th Street Southwest/Dinosaur Trail, T8232001. Six shows per year.

Royal Tyrell Museum of Palaeontology
Half a million visitors per year flock to the Royal Tyrell Museum to see the world's largest collection of complete dinosaur skeletons: over 35 in all, including the ever-popular Tyrannosaurus Rex. With this many people you can expect it to be very crowded in summer, so think about arriving early or late. The building's exterior has been cleverly designed to blend into its arid surroundings. The interior too is intelligently managed. Every state-of-the-art technological trick available has been used to talk visitors through the difficult lessons of natural history. Displays explain such matters as evolution, plate tectonics and geology, as they trace the history of the world from the primordial soup to the present, discussing how fossils are created, and demonstrating how they are found and prepared. A new and engrossing exhibit deals with the findings at **Burgess Shale** in Yoho National Park, using a stunning display set in a dark tunnel to represent a deep sea scene from 500 million years ago, with the bizarre prehistoric creatures blown up to 12 times their original size and floating around in a surreal, illuminated landscape.

The whole experience builds you up to the climax of the **Dinosaur Hall**, where a mind-blowing collection of extremely varied skeletons are displayed in front of artistic backdrops that do a good job of evoking the deltas, swamps and lush vegetation that would have constituted this valley's scenery 75 million years ago. Before entering, take a moment to wander through the palaeoconservatory, where a number of plants unchanged since that time give a better idea of how the vegetation would have looked back then.

The story is completed with a series of displays that deal with the extinction of the dinosaurs, the dawn of the Age of Mammals, and the occurrence of ice ages. As well as a museum, this is one of the world's premier palaeontological research facilities, and runs many educational programmes. In the summer, you can assist the experts (for a fee) on one of their Day Digs. Two trails, a 1-hour and a 2½-hour loop, lead from the museum through the Badlands in Midland Provincial Park. ■ *Summer 0900-2100 daily, winter 1000-1700 Tue-Sun. $8.50, $4.50 concessions. T8237707, www.tyrellmuseum.com Located 6 km northwest of Drumheller on Hwy 838 (North Dinosaur Trail).*

The Dinosaur Trail & Hoodoo Trail
A perfect complement to the museum is the well-signed 48-km road circuit known as the Dinosaur Trail, an excellent way to see the stunning Badlands. Highway 838 is the North Dinosaur Trail, Highway 837 the South Trail. They join at the Bleriot Ferry. Which way you drive the loop depends on whether you want to visit the museum at the beginning or end. It's the first stop if you follow Highway 838. The next key attraction is **Horsethief Canyon**, which has superb views. Thereafter the road drops down to cross the river, with a lovely campground on the south bank. Views from this side have a different quality, so be sure to stop at the **Orkney Hill Viewpoint** on the way back to town.

The less essential Hoodoo Trail runs 25 km southeast along Highway 10 to a minor collection of hoodoos: mushroom-shaped sandstone pillars that would have appealed to Dr Seuss. On the way you pass yellow canola fields dotted

Alberta

with nodding donkeys, a suspension bridge, and the **Atlas Coal Mine**, one of the many remnants of the once-booming local mining industry. You can hike up to the mine, tour the site and visit the museum. ■ *1000-1800, $5.* A nice detour to **Wayne**, with 11 bridges along the way, is a pretty drive and essential on the first weekend in July, when the village hosts its annual **Harley Davidson Rally**, a huge biker party with 4,000 people and free camping everywhere. For information call the *Last Chance Saloon*, T8239189.

B *Best Western Jurassic Inn*, 1103 Hwy 9 S, T8237700. The most reliable choice in town. **Sleeping** Otherwise, go for one of the B&Bs. **C** *Newcastle Country Inn*, 1130 Newcastle Trail, T8238356, has pleasant rooms. **C** *Taste the Past*, 281 2nd St, T8235889, is an old brick home with 3 rooms and shared bath. **D** *McDougall Lane B&B*, 71 McDougall Lane, T8235379, has the best rooms of all, and a suite for $99. Garden, bath. In town are some standard motels including **D** *Badlands Motel*, Hwy 838 on way to museum, T8235155; and **D** *The Lodge*, 392 Centre St/Railway Av, T8233322, close to the bus station.

   Camping The best campsite in town is **E-F** *River Grove Campground and Cabins*, 25 Poplar St, T8236655, in town off the highway on the north side of bridge. Semi-private sites on the river. On the Dinosaur Trail are **E-F** *Dinosaur Trail RV Resort*, 11 km west on Hwy 838, T8239333. Reservations necessary in summer, swimming pool, canoe rentals; **F** *Bleriot Ferry Provincial Rec Area*, 23 km west on the south side of the ferry crossing, T8231753. Great views of the landscape, pleasant little site, river for swimming; **F** *Little Fish Lake Provincial Park*, T8231749, 25 km east of the Hoodoos off Hwy 10 on Hwy 573. Great campground down a dirt road, lake setting.

Eating choices in Drumheller are mostly family-dining joints catering to tour buses. Best **Eating** bet is *Sizzling House*, 160 Centre St, T8238098. Excellent cheap Szechuan and Thai food minus the MSG and sugar. Great value, veggie selection. *Whif's Flapjack House*, 801 North Dinosaur Trail in the *Badlands Motel*, does mostly breakfast but also lunch specials. **Cafés** *Molly Brown's*, 233 Centre St, good desserts, or *Our Place Cappuccino House* at 35 3rd Av. **Bars** The local bar is *Octane Nightclub* on Railway St and Centre St.

Badlands Adventure Tours, T8222200, offer trail rides, raft tours, canoe and mountain **Sports** bike rentals. *Mukwah Tours*, 202 17th St NW, T8230456, run whitewater rafting trips on the Red Deer, Highwood and Ram Rivers. The *Dinosaur Trail Golf Club*, across from the museum, T8235622, has one of the most interesting settings imaginable.

Roughly 150 km northeast from Calgary, Drumheller is reached on Hwy 9 north from **Transport** the TransCanada. Daily **buses** from **Calgary** leave at 0745, 1745, and 2300. If not driving, even getting to the museum is a problem, as it is further than most people would want to walk, especially given how hot the days tend to be here in summer. For a **taxi** call T8237433. There are so many cars that **hitching** should not be a problem.

Dinosaur Provincial Park

About 174 km southwest of Drumheller, set within a striking landscape of Red River Badlands, is Dinosaur Provincial Park, site of the **Royal Tyrell Museum Field Station**, and the place where most of the dinosaurs in that and many other world museums were found. Over 300 intact skeletons have been found to date, including 37 species, 5% of all those known. It seems that most of them were swept downriver, their corpses quickly buried in shifting sands and mud. In 1979, UNESCO declared it a World Heritage Site. There is no public transport to the park, but for drivers it is a short diversion from Highway 1.

Alberta

Though there is a Visitor Centre with various displays, the scenery is the real attraction here, its subdued colours best appreciated at sunset. The Badlands are different from those further north, not so vast but containing more details. There are some short walks, but most of the park is out of bounds, accessible only on official hiking and bus tours (May-September daily, September-mid-October Friday-Sunday). At $4.50, $2.25 concessions, for two hours, these are excellent value and highly recommended. Reservation by phone (T3784344) with a VISA or Mastercard is essential, especially in summer when the park struggles to keep up with demand. Last-minute tickets, if available, are posted the evening before and sold at 0830. ■ *Mid-May to Aug 0830-2100 daily, Sep-mid May 0900-1600 Mon-Fri. Free. T3784342, www.gov.ab.ca/ env/parks/ prov_parks/dinosaur* Eight kilometres southeast of here, with signs from Highway 1, is an impressive large **aqueduct**. ■ *Summer 1000-1800. T3624451.*

Sleeping & eating At the park is a lovely campsite by a slow-moving creek (**F** , T3783700), and a service centre with basic food, coin-op showers, and a laundromat. **Patricia** is the closest place for rooms. The pub, a slice of life in itself, has 9 small but acceptable rooms upstairs (**E** , T3784647). More pleasant is **D** *Conners' Country B&B*, call for directions, T3784633. A number of standard motels and restaurants can be found in the dull town of **Brooks**, just off Hwy 1, about 40 km away.

Tour operator *River Getaways*, T2355995, www.cadvision.com/getaways, offer 2-day all-inclusive self-guided canoe tours down the Red Deer River into the park.

Crowsnest Pass

Colour map 2, grid C4
Phone code: 403

The introduction to Alberta for those heading east on Highway 3 inspires little confidence. A collection of half-dead and unattractive ex-mining communities, under the collective name The Municipality of Crowsnest Pass, tempts passing tourists with a morbid litany of historic disasters and calamities. In 1903, part of the face of Turtle Mountain sheared clean off, spreading 82 million tonnes of limestone over about 3 sq km, wiping out part of Frank, and killing 70 inhabitants. In 1910, 30 miners in nearby Bellevue were suffocated following a methane explosion. And four years later, neighbouring Hillcrest saw the worst mining disaster in Canadian history when 189 men were killed in a blast.

On a thoroughly different note, a couple of minor pursuits are well catered for locally. The province's most elaborate network of caves, including Canada's second deepest, are in the area, which has also been voted the best overall spot for snowmobiling. There are two summer-only **Visitor Information Centres**, one on Highway 3 in Bellevue, the other just west of Coleman.

Frank Slide The only 'attraction' most people would want to stop for is the Frank Slide Interpretative Centre. With limestone rocks and boulders scattered over the whole valley, the slide is impossible to miss from the highway, but up at the centre its full extent can be appreciated, along with an inevitable sense of awe at the powers involved. The fee to peruse the small centre seems money wasted when the view is the key attraction, though it's worth picking up a self-guiding brochure if taking the 1.5-km walk around the site. There is still debate over what caused the disaster. While a network of mines no doubt added to the problem, it is significant that the natives' name for Turtle Mountain was 'the mountain that moves'. The more interesting mystery is how some of the giant boulders managed to move so far. Most scientists apparently accept that the material moved like a thick liquid, though the theory of rocks surfing on a layer of air compressed by their own mass is more attractive. ■ *May-Sep 0900-2000, Oct-Apr 1000-1700. $6.50, $3 concessions. T5627388.*

Enthusiasts might also want to experience the dark, damp reality of **Belle-vue Mine**, complete with miner's lamp, battery pack and hard hat. ■ *May-Sep 1000-1730. Tours every 30 mins. $6, $5 concessions. T5644700.* Those still not mined-out could stroll round the scant remains of **Leitch Collieries** a little to the east, though there's more information than things to see. ■ *Open year round. Free to wander at any time. Guided tours only by prior arrangement. T5627388.*

This dying area has few options for those who need to stop. By far the best is **C** *Eckardt Tecumseh Mountain Guest Ranch*, 8 km west from Coleman then 2 km north from the highway, T5633900. Nice log cabins with kitchenette, shower, bedroom. Meals by reservation. About 6 km from here (bear left) is a campground at **F** *Allison/Chinook Lake*, T5635395, a nicer choice than **F** *Lundbreck Falls* at the Hwy 22 intersection, T6271116. | **Sleeping & eating**

A dirt road from Coleman heads north through the foothills of the Rockies, passing a number of campsites and Livingstone Falls, eventually reaching Kananaskis Park and Highway 40. This is as good a way as any to enter the Range, as it builds up slowly to the more dramatic scenery further north. Those short on time should at least make a 51-km diversion south on Highway 6 from Pincher to Waterton Lakes National Park, whose magnificent scenery compares favourably with the more famous parks to the north. | **Into the Rockies**

Along this stretch of Highway 3 countless elegant white windmills range across the undulating hills. This is the Cowley Ridge Windplant, a successful alternative energy project. With just 52 of these turbines, almost 300 tons of noxious emissions are avoided each year. A mere two hours of production from one turbine will power a local home for a month, the extra power being sold to California. Two more windpower companies are planning to set up shop in Pincher Creek in the near future. This is a very windy part of the country!

Waterton Lakes National Park

Despite its modest size – a mere 525 sq km – the most southerly of Canada's Rocky Mountain parks delivers landscapes and hiking to rival just about anything further north, without the rampant commercialism that can take the edge off those more famous locations. When the Rockies were formed, Waterton's mountainous mass moved as a single piece instead of rupturing, with rocks over 1.5 billion years old appearing on the surface, the oldest exposed bedrock in the range. This also resulted in some distinctive scenery: a juxtaposition of prairies and mountain with little in between. The park is open from the long weekend in May until Labour Day weekend in September, though many of the hikes are still under snow until well into June. | *Colour map 2, grid C4*

Ins and outs

Southwest Alta Bus Lines, 1015 Hewetson Av in Pincher Creek, T6275205, connects with the closest *Greyhound* station. $102.50/single or day-return. 3 daily in summer, 0715, 1030 and 1600 from Pincher Creek, returning 0905, 1430 and 1905 from Waterton Park Lodge. They also run shuttles to trailheads. The nearest US border crossing is at Chief Mountain on the park's eastern edge, Jun-Aug 0700-2200, late May and Sep 0900-1800. At other times, the closest border crossing is east on Hwy 2 at Carway Alberta/Peigan Montana, 0700-2300 daily year-round. | **Getting there** *For transport details, see page 374*

Alberta

▶ ## Kootenai Brown

Born in England, John George Brown had already been a soldier in India, a gold prospector in BC, and a pony express rider in the US, when he was attacked by Blackfoot natives in the Waterton region and held captive by Chief Sitting Bull. Escaping at night, he joined the Ktunaxa – or Kootenai – natives, and lived as one of them until he married in 1869. He then built a cabin on Waterton Lake, becoming the region's first permanent white resident, and began campaigning for its protection. The fight was taken up by his friend Frederick Godsal, who succeeded in having it named a Federal Reserve in 1895, with Brown as Warden. In 1911, when the reserve became Canada's fourth National Park, Brown was given the job of superintendent.

Getting around
There are 4 main routes around the park to the trailheads: Upper Waterton Lake; Akamina Parkway, which ends at Cameron Lake; Red Rock Canyon Parkway, which ends at Red Rock Canyon; and Chief Mountain International Hwy, which skirts the eastern edge of the park, leading to the US border.

A *Hiker Shuttle Service* will take you to Cameron Lake, Red Rock Canyon and other trailheads. *Crypt Lake Water Shuttle Service*, at the marina, delivers hikers to Crypt Lake trailhead and other points such as Goat Haunt Overlook, Rainbow Falls and Francis Lake.

A park permit is required costing $4 per person per day
The **Parks Visitor Centre** is on Entrance Rd on the way into town, T8592445, Jun-Aug 0800-2100, May and Sep 0900-1700. The rest of the year, information is available Mon-Fri 0800-1600 at the **Parks Administration Office**, 215 Mt View Rd, T8592477, or from the Chamber of Commerce, T8592224, www.watertonchamber.com Also useful is the *Waterton Heritage Centre* at 117 Waterton Av, T8592624, which has exhibits, an art gallery, a museum, and sells park-related books and maps. Serious hikers can buy a 1:50,000 map here or at the Visitor Centre, though for most people the free Parks map will suffice.

History

Over 200 archaeological sites in the park trace a native presence going back 11,000 years. Traditionally this territory was used by the Ktunaxa (Kootenai), who crossed the mountains from their home in BC to hunt. During the 18th century, however, this annual pilgrimage was disrupted by the arrival of the Blackfoot, whose use of horses extended their ambitions and mobility. By the mid-19th century, the Blackfoot were driven back east by white homesteaders, and the area remained practically uninhabited until the arrival of an extraordinary character known to history as 'Kootenai Brown' (see box). Visit the **Kootenai Brown Heritage Village** in Pincher Creek to learn more. ■ *T6273684.*

Sights

The park's remarkable diversity of geographic zones – prairie, wetlands, aspen parkland, montane forest, sub-alpine, and alpine – has led to a far greater variety of flora and fauna than any of Western Canada's other national parks, with about 1,200 plant species, including 55% of Alberta's wild flowers. Prairie flowers bloom in the spring and early summer, while higher elevation wild flowers arrive in the late summer and early autumn, also the best time to see large animals such as bears and elk. As a tribute to the herds that once roamed freely on this land, a **Bison Paddock** is maintained just north of the park entrance off Highway 6. The park lies on two migration routes, so many species of bird can be spotted, especially in autumn around **Maskinonge Lake**.

At the park's heart are the picturesque **Upper** and **Middle Waterton Lakes**, crystal blue expanses of water surrounded by towering snowy peaks. Fishing (with a licence) and canoeing are very popular activities, as is wind-surfing, thanks to the strong local winds. The best place to catch them is **Cameron Bay**. Scuba diving is popular in **Emerald Bay**, where an old paddle-wheeler sits in 18 m of water. Wonderful views are quickly and easily attained and a few of the many day-hikes lead right from the townsite. For horse riding, contact *Alpine Stables*, T8592462. There is also the possibility to hike into the adjoining much bigger Glacier National Park in the United States. Though technically separate, with Customs between them for motorists, the two were designated an International Peace Park in 1932 and a UNESCO World Heritage Site and Biosphere Reserve in 1995.

Hikes in Waterton Lakes National Park

There are over 200 km of trails in the park, and 13 designated wilderness campgrounds. Limited spaces have resulted in a quota system, with reservations possible 90 days in advance, T8595133. Passes are issued at the Visitors Centre and a per person fee is charged.

Check for ticks in spring and early summer

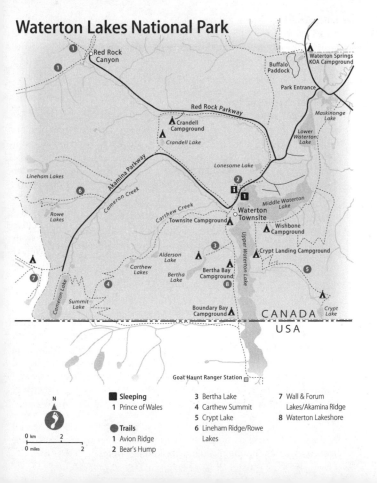

Waterton Lakes National Park

Alberta

Sleeping
1 Prince of Wales

Trails
1 Avion Ridge
2 Bear's Hump
3 Bertha Lake
4 Carthew Summit
5 Crypt Lake
6 Lineham Ridge/Rowe Lakes
7 Wall & Forum Lakes/Akamina Ridge
8 Waterton Lakeshore

N

0 km   2
0 miles   2

From town **Crypt Lake** (17.2 km return, 685 m elevation gain. Trailhead: by boat) This is one of the most popular and exciting trips in the park, with a bit of everything thrown in. You start with a boat trip across the lake, hike an undulating trail through **Hell Roaring Valley**, pass four waterfalls including the stunning **Crypt Falls**, stoop through a dark 20-m tunnel, then ascend a mountainside using a safety cable. The views are fine throughout, and the emerald lake itself sits in a steep and dramatic cirque. You can expect to have plenty of company. There is a backcountry campground at Km 8.

Bear's Hump (1.4 km, 200 m elevation gain. Trailhead: above Information Centre) Short but steep, leading to great views of mountains, lake and townsite. One of the earliest to be snow-free.

Bertha Lake (11 km return, 460 m elevation gain. Trailhead: car park opposite the town campground) The popularity of this hike is due mainly to it being easy and conveniently located. The views of the lake and distant prairie, at Km 1.5, is the trail's highlight. A fork here leads right to Bertha Lake. The left fork descends to the **Waterton Lakeshore** trail. This leads to the decent beach at **Bertha Bay**, and beyond to **Goat Haunt** (15 km in all), where you can catch a boat back. This is only really recommended as a spring or autumn hike, as it's usually snow-free from April to October.

From the Akamina Parkway **Lineham Ridge/Rowe Lakes** (17-20 km return, 920-1,060 m elevation gain. Trailhead: Km 10.5 on the parkway) This trail follows a creek up gentle slopes with valley views and through mature forest before cutting up bare, rocky slopes to the ridge. The pretty Row Lakes are a worthwhile side-trip best saved for the return leg if time and energy allow, because the highlight is Lineham Ridge, which offers excellent views of many of the jagged peaks in Waterton and Glacier Parks.

Wall and Forum Lakes/Akamina Ridge (10/12/20 km return, 915 m elevation gain. Trailhead: at Km 14.6 on the parkway) There are three possible hikes in Akamina-Kishinena Provincial Park, adjacent to Waterton in British Columbia. Forum and Wall Lakes are distinct, easy hikes to pretty lakes at the base of sheer rock walls. Between the two is Akamina Ridge, the real prize for those not averse to a bit of scrambling, with great views into Waterton and Glacier Parks. The Forum-Ridge-Wall circuit is best done in this order. Be sure to get full details before attempting it, and be ready for strong winds on the ridge.

Carthew Summit (20 km one-way, 700 m elevation gain, 1,070 m loss. Trailhead: at Km 15.7, the end of the road) This is a one-way hike from Cameron Lake to Cameron Falls on the edge of Waterton Townsite, so is best done using a shuttle to the trailhead. The highlight is the view from Carthew Summit itself, with the steep peaks of Glacier National Park to the south and the curious sight of endless Alberta prairies stretching off to the northeast horizon. From here it's all downhill in every respect.

From Red Rock Parkway **Avion Ridge** (22.9-km loop, 944 m elevation gain. Trailhead: canyon carpark at road's end) This long, high, narrow ridge has few truly inspiring viewpoints, but offers panoramas whose very size makes an impression. The loop is best done clockwise, past Snowshoe Campground, over the ridge and down past Goat Lake. Strong hikers could dispatch it as a day-trip. Otherwise, take the worthwhile 7-km detour from Snowshoe to Twin Lakes, whose campground is much nicer.

Alberta

Waterton Townsite

The first thing you see approaching the core of the park is the grandiose **Prince** *Colour map 2, grid C4*
of Wales Hotel set high on a bluff overlooking the aquamarine lake. Waterton *Phone code: 406*
Townsite cannot live up to this opening gambit, but it's a pleasant enough spot
with a picturesque lake setting. More resort than genuine village, it still feels
rather quaint compared to the likes of Banff, with mule deer and bighorn sheep
wandering freely over the lawns, and Cameron Falls just on the edge of town.

Accommodation in Waterton is more expensive than it should be, but embraces a few **Sleeping**
budget options. Call the Central Reservations Office for package deals, T1800-2152395. ■ *on map below*
LL *Prince of Wales Hotel*, T2363400, www.glacierparkinc.com/pow1 A must for those *and page 371*
who can afford it, this beautiful timber-frame building is brimming over with character
and a sense of history, and the views are to die for. Ask for a lake view. **A-B** *Aspen Village*
Inn, Windflower Av, T8592255, www,aspenvillageinn.com Small rooms with balcony,
hot tub. **A-B** *Bayshore Inn*, 111 Waterton Av, T8592211, www.bayshoreinn.com Nicer

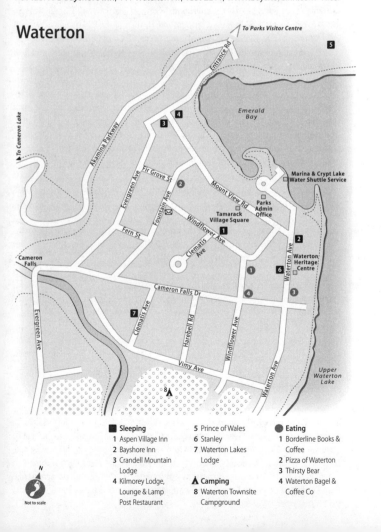

Waterton

Alberta

■ Sleeping
1 Aspen Village Inn
2 Bayshore Inn
3 Crandell Mountain
  Lodge
4 Kilmorey Lodge,
  Lounge & Lamp
  Post Restaurant

5 Prince of Wales
6 Stanley
7 Waterton Lakes
  Lodge

Å Camping
8 Waterton Townsite
  Campground

● Eating
1 Borderline Books &
  Coffee
2 Pizza of Waterton
3 Thirsty Bear
4 Waterton Bagel &
  Coffee Co

N
Not to scale

than it looks. Large comfortable rooms, balcony with lake views for $10 extra. **A** *Crandell Mountain Lodge*, Mountain View Rd, T8592288, www.crandell mountainlodge.com Country cottage with 17 pleasant rooms and some suites with kitchenette and fireplace. **B** *Kilmorey Lodge*, Mountain View Rd, T8592334, www.kilmoreylodge.com Large rooms, old-fashioned but comfortable, big windows. Common room with TV. **B** *Rocky Ridge Country Resort*, about 20 km east on Hwy 5, T6532350. 6 nice rooms. Common room, hot tub, sauna, billiards, breakfast included.

E *Stanley Hotel*, Waterton Av, apply at *Waterton Pharmacy* above building, T8592335. 9 small but not unpleasant rooms with shared bath. **E** *Waterton Lakes Lodge International Hostel*, 101 Clematis Av, T8592151. Small dorms, kitchen, lounge, private rooms available with shared baths (**D**).

Camping in order of proximity to town: **F** *Waterton Townsite Campground* is like an ugly parking lot with 238 sites. **F** *Crandell Mountain Campground*, 8 km west on Red Rock Canyon Rd. 129 sites, water, firepits, camp kitchen. There are several walk-in sites and some private campgrounds north on Hwy 6 and east on Hwy 5. **F** *Waterton Springs KOA*, 3 km north of gate on Hwy 6, T8592247. 190 sites. Showers, laundry, swimming pool. **F** *Payne Lake Campground*, 18 km east, 3 km off Hwy 5. Grassy sites on the lake, nice views. **F** *Belly River Campground*, by the border, 29 km away, 1 km off Chief Mountain Hwy, T8592224. 24 sites, camp kitchen. **F** *Great Canadian Barn Dance*, near Hillspring, half way to Pincher Creek, T6263407. A 16-ha campground and B&B with a celebrated country dance every Fri night.

Eating
● *on map page 373*

The better choices for food in town are hotel dining-rooms. Those in the *Prince of Wales* are the most upmarket. The *Bayshore Inn* restaurants have lake views, but the best choice for fine dining is the **expensive** *Lamp Post* in the *Kilmorey Lodge* (see Sleeping), whose menu includes some exotic options like ostrich, caribou and elk. It's also the best bet for breakfast. Otherwise, the **mid-range** *Pizza of Waterton* on Fountain Av is a nice option, with good pizzas, an outdoor patio, and a decent selection of beers.

Cafés   For coffee and snacks there's *The Waterton Bagel and Coffee Co* and *Borderline Books and Coffee*, both on Windflower Av.

Bars   The bar locals choose is *The Thirsty Bear* on Waterton Av, which can get a bit rowdy. *The Kilmorey Lounge* in the *Lodge* is the nicest spot for a quiet drink, though the posher lounge at the *Prince of Wales* is the place for views.

Sport   *Waterton Spa and Rec Centre* in the *Waterton Lakes Lodge*, 101 Clematis Av, T8592151. Fitness equipment, hot tub, indoor swimming pool. *Waterton Sports and Leisure*, Tamarack Village Sq, T8592378. Outdoor apparel, equipment and maps.

Tour operators   *Alpine Stables*, T8592462. Horse riding. *Waterton Outdoor Adventures*, Tamarack Village Sq, T8592378. Guided hikes and scrambles. *Waterton Shoreline Cruises*, T8592362. Interpretive tours of the lake. *Jammer Tours*, T8592231. Transport into Glacier Park in a touring bus.

Transport   A *Hiker Shuttle Service* to Cameron Lake, Red Rock Canyon and other trailheads is operated by *Waterton Visitor Services*, Tamarack Village Sq, Mount View Rd, T8592378. *Crypt Lake Water Shuttle Service*, at the marina, T8592362, delivers hikers to Crypt Lake trailhead (daily 0900, 1000, 1300 and 1400, $21 return), and other points on the lake such as Goat Haunt Overlook, Rainbow Falls and Francis Lake. *Pat's Cycle Rental*, 224 Mount View Rd, T8592266, rents **mopeds** ($18/hr) and **bicycles** ($6/hr). *Cameron Lake Boat Rentals* at Cameron Lake, 17 km west, rents canoes, rowboats and paddleboats (all $17/hr), open 0730-1930.

Banks Exchange and ATM in Tamarack Village Sq. ATM in *Rocky Mountain Food* on Windflower Av. **Communications** Canada Post: corner Fountain Av/Windflower Av. **Laundry** 301 Windflower Av. **Medical services** Closest hospitals are in Cardston, T6534931, and Pincher Creek, T6273333. **Useful numbers** Police: T8592244; **Ambulance**: T8592636.

Cardston

Colour map 2, grid C4

The obvious route between Waterton Lakes National Park and Fort Macleod is via Highways 6 and 3, passing through Pincher Creek. An alternative route (and about the same length) is on Highways 5 and 2, which meet at Cardston, a small town with a couple of worthwhile attractions.

The **Remington-Alberta Carriage Centre** has over 250 horse-drawn carriages from around the turn of the 20th century are displayed in a superbly equipped, purpose-built museum. Most of the carriages are original and in top condition. Videos, panels, displays, and live demonstrations deal with the carriage business from factory to blacksmith to fire station. ■ *May-Sep 0900-1800, Sep-May 1000-1700. $6.50, $3 concessions. Free guided tours leave every hour on the hour in summer, a 14-min film is shown every hour on the half-hour, and rides can be taken mid-May to mid-Jun, $3/$1.50 for 15-20 mins. 623 Main St, T6535139, www.remingtoncentre.com*

While in town, the amazing **Alberta Temple** of the Latter Day Saints is well worth seeing. Built in 1912 from 3,680 tons of premium white gold-bearing granite quarried around Kootenay Lake, this geometric structure successfully blends ancient and modern styles, with traces of the Temple of Solomon, Mayan-Aztec pyramids, and the Prairie School of Frank Lloyd Wright. The inside sounds equally impressive, but non-Mormons cannot enter. ■ *Information Office May-Sep 0900-2100. 348 3rd St, T6533552.*

Sleeping Cardston is one of the best places to stay on a genuine working horse and cattle ranch. There are 3 in the area, all **B-C**: *Badger Valley Ranch*, T6532123; *Echo Hill Horse Haven Ranch*, T6532508; and *Rangeview Ranch*, T6532292, www.rangeviewranch.com In town are a couple of standard motels and the fairly nice **F** *Lee Creek Campground*, T6533734, adjacent to the Carriage Centre, with trees, a pool and showers.

Fort Macleod

Colour map 2, grid C4

After a gruelling 1,280-km trek, the North West Mounted Police (NWMP) established their first fort in 1873 on an island in the Oldman River, naming it after the man that led them, Colonel James F Macleod. Today the extremely dull and horribly windy town of Fort Macleod contains a reconstruction of that fort, but is mainly busy due to its proximity to Head-Smashed-In Buffalo Jump and Waterton Lakes National Park, and famous as the birthplace of Joni Mitchell.

The **Fort Museum** tries to give an impression of life in the original NWMP fort, as well as exploring the influence the men in red had on the settlement of Western Canada. Exhibits include a chapel, dispensary and trading post. Galleries deal with topics such as transport, ranching and First Nations artistry. The most popular spectacle, the Musical Ride, happens four times daily in July and August, weather permitting. This is a traditional demonstration of horsemanship, now performed by students in uniform. ■ *Jul-Aug 0900-2000, Mar-Jun and Sep-Dec 0900-1700. $5, $3 seniors, $2 children. Tour $4.50, $2.50 seniors, $1.50 children. 219 25th St, T5534703, www.nwmpmuseum.com*

Sleeping & eating Everything of use in town is located on or around Main St, which has some old stone buildings and antique signs to offset the ugly string of motels. Of these, which are often full, the **D** *Red Coat Inn* at 359 Main St, T5534434, is the best. Decent rooms, sauna, a nice indoor pool, and hot tub. Also has some spacious suites (**C**). Reservations recommended. Away from the strip, **D** *Sunset Motel*, 104 Hwy 3 W, T5534448, has spacious rooms and a much needed windbreaker in front.

The best place to eat is the **mid-range** *Johnny's*, 225 Main St, serving decent, authentic Chinese food. *Ildiko's Bistro* next to the bus station on 2nd Av, is good for coffee.

Transport The *Greyhound* station at 2302 2nd Av, T5533383,

Head-Smashed-In Buffalo Jump

Colour map 2, grid C4 Native Americans had thousands of years to refine their techniques for the large-scale slaughter of bison, their ultimate method being the coldly efficient 'buffalo jump'. Situated 18 km northwest of Fort Macleod on the paved secondary Highway 785, Head-Smashed-In Buffalo Jump was named a UNESCO World Heritage Site because it is one of the oldest and best preserved of its kind in the world. Over 11 m of bone deposits at the base of the cliff bear witness to at least 5,500 years of continual use. Countless artefacts found here have also provided invaluable clues concerning the lifestyles of the ancient people.

A masterpiece of invention that blends into the sandstone cliff over which the herds were driven, the **Interpretive Centre** uses archaeological evidence and the verbal records of the local Blackfoot to explain the functioning of the jump. After the ground-floor reception, restaurant and gift shop, four storeys lead you back in time. First the science of archaeology itself is discussed using a recreated dig and a slide show. Then comes the recent history of the white man's arrival, which brought guns, horses, new diseases and the near extinction of the buffalo.

The whole process of the buffalo hunt is revealed on the second floor: the pre-hunt ceremonies; the **Gathering Basin**, a 40-sq-km grazing area of plentiful grass and water to attract the herds; the network of **Drive Lanes**, particularly well preserved here, consisting of stone cairns that helped hunters to funnel the bison towards the cliff; the **Kill Site**, which is just north of the centre, with another visible 1 km north; and the **Campsite/Processing Area**, where the meat was sliced into thin strips and hung on racks to dry, much of it pounded with grease, marrow and berries to make pemmican. The next floor presents the lifestyle of prehistoric **Plains people**, their techniques of food gathering, social life and ceremonies. Finally it is all put into an ecological context, with an exposition of the geography, climate, flora and fauna of the northwest plains.

A couple of trails at the lower and upper level allow you to explore the site and have a good look at the Drive Lanes and cliff. Tours are conducted by Blackfoot guides. In late July is the 3-day **Buffalo Days Pow Wow and Tipi Village**, featuring native dancers from across North America.

■ *Mid-May to mid-Sep 0900-1800, rest of the year 1000-1700. T5532731, www.head-smashed-in.com There is no public transport to the site. Taxis from Fort Macleod cost about $25.*

Sleeping & eating Head-Smashed-In-Buffalo-Jump run their own tepee camps, May-Aug, which include accommodation, food and activities. *Pure West Adventures*, T1877-8949378, arrange trips to **Eagle's Nest Indian Village** – $200-250 per person per day depending on itineraries – which include tepee accommodation, all meals, pick-up and drop-off in Calgary, activities and entertainment, and entry to HSIBJ. *Buffalo Plains RV Park and Campground*, T5532592, 3 km east of HSIBJ, has 30 pleasant sites with views and laundry but no showers.

Lethbridge

Originally a coal-mining town, Lethbridge is now the supply centre for a region booming with oil, gas and some of Southern Alberta's more useful agricultural land. The largest city south of Calgary, it comes as a relief after the windy dry plains and one-horse towns further west. The Downtown, roughly 3rd to 5th Avenues and 5th to 10th Streets, is indistinct and disappointing, but elsewhere are wide, tree-lined streets, and some varied and interesting architecture. The **Visitor Information Centre** is at 2805 Scenic Drive, Junction of Highway 5 and Highway 4, T1800-6611222, www.albertasouth.com Summer 0900-2000, winter 0900-1700. Also at Brewery Gardens, 1st Avenue South off Highway 3, same hours.

Phone code: 403
Colour map 2, grid C5
Population: 67,374

The only main attraction in Lethbridge is the **Alexander Galt Museum** which, despite its grand exterior, contains little beyond the typical small-town offerings. This is the place to pick up a brochure to the town's many heritage buildings. ■ *Mon-Fri 1000-1630. Free. Special exhibits $5. Scenic Dr/5th Av, T3203898.* The museum's best feature is as a vantage point from which to appreciate the region's harsh but compelling scenery. The outstanding **University** building was designed by architect Arthur Erickson (see page 455) to blend into this landscape of dry plains and steep coulees (deep narrow ravines). Nine stories high and 300 m long, it was cleverly built into the side of a hill, inspired, apparently, by the elegant **High Level Railway Bridge** which spans a broad valley to the west, and is probably the town's most distinctive feature.

Situated in a valley below this bridge, and sheltered by 90-m-high coulee walls, is **Indian Battle Park**, the most central and important of a string of parks that forms an almost uninterrupted green belt along the Oldman River, covering some 1,620 ha. This was the suitably dramatic site of the last armed battle between First Nations tribes, namely the Cree and the Blackfoot. Third Avenue South runs west into the heart of the park. As well as 10 km of walking trails which connect (sometimes by underpasses) with other parks, it contains a number of attractions. **Fort Whoop-Up** is a reconstruction of the most infamous whisky trading post of all. It was founded in 1869 by Montana outlaws, who did business exchanging booze with the Blackfoot natives for buffalo robes and furs. So successful were they that the government in Ottawa became nervous, finally establishing the North West Mounted Police, whose primary mission was the fort's eradication. At the end of their 94-day march across 1,500 km of prairie wilderness, these prototype Mounties arrived to find that the whisky traders had already flown the coop. Costumed staff do their best to bring those lawless days back to life. ■ *Jun-Aug 1000-1800 Mon-Sat, 1200-1700 Sun. Sep-May 1300-1600 Tue-Fri and Sun. $2.50, $1.50 concessions. T3290444.*

The **Helen Schuler Coulee Centre**, situated in Lethbridge Nature Reserve, has displays about the local flora and fauna, three self-guided nature trails, and information about the **Elizabeth Hall Wetlands** to the west, where a Wildlife Viewing Blind provides a perfect vantage point for spotting birds and other fauna. ■ *Free. T3203064.*

On the east side of town, just off Mayor Magrath Drive, is the very pleasant **Henderson Lake Park**, which has a pretty walking trail around the lake, an outdoor pool, tennis courts, a decent campground, and the **Nikka Yuko Japanese Gardens**. Touted as Lethbridge's chief tourist attraction, these five gardens covering 1.6 ha combine traditional Japanese elements such as a pavilion, bridges, gates, trees, rocks, lanterns and water. ■ *Jun-mid-Sep 0900-2100 daily, May and mid-Sep-mid-Oct Thu-Sun only. $5, $3 concessions. T3283511.*

Alberta

Sleeping Lethbridge has the best accommodation for many miles. The number one luxury option is the **B** *Lethbridge Lodge Hotel*, 320 Scenic Dr, T3281123, www.lethbridge lodge.com, which has a lovely central tropical garden containing a pool, hot tub and lounge. Rooms are comfortable and intelligently equipped. Ask for one facing inwards. It also has a dance club and fine restaurant.

D *Heritage House B&B* 1115 8th Av, 15-min walk from town, T3283824. Art deco-style house built in 1937, a museum in itself with all the original decor, stained glass, glass tiles, antiques. Only 2 rooms (with shared bath), so reserve. Most of the motels are around Mayor Magrath Dr (Hwy 5 S), including the **D** *Super 8*, 2210 7th Av, T3290100. Standard, but best location, opposite Henderson Lake Park. **D** *Pepper Tree Inn*, 1142 Mayor Magrath Dr, T3284436. Small rooms but cheapest. Both the **E** *University of Lethbridge*, T3292793, and the **E** *Lethbridge Community College*, T3292244, have rooms available May to mid-Aug in student residences. Shared kitchen, no TV or phone. **Camping F** *Henderson Lake Campground*, T3285452, has nice wooded sites close to town. Showers, laundry.

Eating **Expensive** *Anton's*, in the *Lethbridge Lodge* (see Sleeping above), T3281123. Best food in town. Upmarket steak, seafood and European-style favourites. **Mid-range** *Coco Pazzo Italian Café*, 1264 3rd Av S, T3298979. Wood-oven pizza, antipasti and delicious pastas in a bright, colourful setting. Recommended. *O-Sho Japanese*, 311 4th St S, T3278382. Sushi, etc. *Cheesecake Café*, 904 2nd Av S, T3942253. Sandwiches and larger than life cheesecake.

Cafés For great coffee and atmosphere head to *The Penny Coffee House*, 331 5th St. Very popular and friendly.

Bars & clubs *Duke of Wellington*, 132 Columbia Blvd W. The liveliest pub in town, favoured by students. For dancing try *Esmeralda's Tavern* in the *Lethbridge Lodge* or the *Roadhouse Bar and Grill*, 1016 1st Av, more popular with a younger clientele.

Entertainment **Art** *Southern Alberta Art Gallery*, 601 3rd Av, T3278770, www.saag.com Regularly changing contemporary exhibitions, from local to international. Tue-Sun 1000-1700, Sun 1300-1700. Free. Alternative films Wed at 1900. *Bowman Arts Centre*, 811 5th Av S, T3272813. Modern art shows, weekdays 0900-1700. *University of Lethbridge Gallery*, 4401 University Dr, T3292666. **Cinema** *Paramount Movie Theatre*, 4th Av/8th St S, T3275100. *The Movie Mill*, 1710 Mayor Magrath Dr S, T3816455. **Theatre** *Yates Centre*, 1002 4th Av S, T3204973. Live theatre and home of the Lethbridge Symphony Orchestra.

Festivals In **Jul** is the *Whoop-up Days Rodeo*, T3284491, a 4-day event featuring chuckwagon races, a funfair, etc. In **Aug** is the *Lethbridge International Air Show*, T3804245.

Sports There's an indoor **climbing** wall at the *Ascent Climbing Centre*, 2510 Scenic Dr, T3287673. The *YMCA* at 515 Stratford Dr/6th Av has a **swimming** pool and fitness room, $1 showers. *Ascent Cycle*, 1022 2nd Av S is the place for **bike** rentals.

Shopping **Books** *Adam's Book Corner*, 606 3rd Av S. New and used. *Chapters*, 701 1st Av S. Biggest selection of new books.

Transport The *Greyhound* station is at 411 5th St S, T3271551, with 3 daily **buses** to **Calgary**, 4 to **Fort MacLeod**, and 2 slow services to **Vancouver** via **Cranbrook** and **Kelowna**. For details of **local transport**, call T3203885. *Lethbridge Cabs*, T3274005.

Directory **Communication** Internet: at the library and *Adams Book Corner*, 606 3rd Av S, T3209131, free. **Canada Post:** 704 4th Av S. **Laundry** *King Koin Laundry*, 1263 3rd Av S.

Alberta

Library Lethbridge Public Library, 810 5th Av S. **Medical services** *Lethbridge Regional Hospital*, 960 19th St S, T3826111.

Close to the US border, about 125 km southeast of Lethbridge, this out-of-the-way park is an attractive, relaxing spot to spend a day or two exploring the fantastical features of the local landscape: bizarre rock formations, buttes, coulees and hoodoos. Most of the park is open to the public year-round. The self-guided **Hoodoo Trail**, 2.5 km each way, has some examples of rock art, but most of the 50 or so sites featuring petroglyphs (carvings) and pictographs (paintings) are in the **Archeological Preserve**, accessible only on free tours. Non-reservable tickets are handed out one hour ahead at the interpreter's office. ■ *Tour times vary, but generally run May-Sep 1400 daily, with an extra morning tour on Sun and daily Jul and Aug. Less tours the rest of the year. Call T6472364 for information.* There is a **campground** (**F**) in a river valley, with trees, bushes and flowers, and a natural sand beach. Showers. By taking Highway 61 route to or from Medicine Hat, you can visit the **Windmill Museum** at Etzikom, a reconstruction of a pioneer Main Street, with lots of artefacts and a self-guided tour through displays about the history of windpower in Canada. It's only worth the diversion if you're interested in windmills. ■ *May-Sep 1000-1700 Mon-Sat, !200-1800 Sun. $4, $3.50 seniors, children free. T6663737*

Writing-On-Stone Provincial Park
Colour map 2, grid C6

Milk River Raft Tours, T6473586, offer walking tours and 2-6 hour raft trips on the Milk River that runs through the park.

Tour operators

Medicine Hat

There is little of note between Lethbridge and Medicine Hat, though long diversions could be made to Dinosaur Provincial Park near Brooks to the north (see page 367), or Writing-on-Stone Provincial Park to the south (see above). From Seven Persons, a 26-km detour south on Highway 887 leads to **Red Rock Coulee Natural Area**, a landscape of badlands and hoodoos, where large round red sandstone boulders are seen emerging from the bedrock beneath.

Phone code: 403
Colour map 2,
grid C6
Population: 46,000

Alberta

There's not much to do in Medicine Hat, unless you catch the **Exhibition and Stampede** in late July, T5271234. Yet its position on the banks of the South Saskatchewan River, and its many interesting buildings both old and new, make for an unexpectedly attractive little town. The town's name probably comes from the Blackfoot word for 'hat worn by medicine man', Saamis. This headpiece was traditionally made from otter skin, weasel skin, owl feathers, magpie tail feathers and the stuffed body of a crow.

The large natural-gas field right beneath the town, together with its location at the junction of Highways 1 and 3, has brought Medicine Hat a degree of prosperity which is positively flaunted by the new **City Hall**, a striking glass structure which contrasts nicely with the spires of St Patrick's Church on the opposite side of the bridge. Many other handsome churches, including the United Church on Fifth Avenue, can be visited on a self-guided **Historic Tour**. There's a map in the *Downtown Directory* available at the **Visitor Centre**, east of town just off the TransCanada Highway, T1800-4812822, www.albertasouth.com Summer 0800-2100 Mon-Fri, 0800-1800 Sat-Sun; winter 0900-1700 Mon-Fri. Bikes can be rented in **Strathcona Island Park**, across the rail tracks on Fifth Street, to cruise round the town's 70 km of connected trails and into the pleasant 16-ha **Police Point Park** to the northeast. From late November to early January, 'the Hat' becomes the 'City of Lights', with electric light displays in Kin Coulee Park, and gas lamps illuminating Downtown.

Sleeping **B** *Medicine Hat Lodge*, SE of Downtown at 1051 Ross Glen Dr, T5292222. The luxury offering, but a disappointment after the *Lodge* in Lethbridge (see page 378). **D** *Medicine Hat Inn*, 530 4th St, Downtown, T5261313. Big rooms. **D** *Nestle Inn B&B*, 271 1st St. 3 small rooms with shared bath in a house built by the city's first mayor. **Camping** **F** *Gas City Campground*, 580 1st St SE, off Hwy 1 W, T5260644. Showers, laundry.

Eating **Mid-range** *Mario's Restorante*, 439 5th Av, T5292600. Homemade pasta, steak and seafood. Or try the *Mad Hatter Roastery* at 513 3rd St.

Cafés & bars For coffee there's *Café Mundo* at 579 3rd St. An inordinate number of places serving cheap booze include *The Bar* under *Mario's* (see above), and the enticing *Ottoman Empire Cocktail and Martini Lounge*, 502 S Railway St. Martinis and occasional live music.

Shopping Medicine Hat is overflowing with second-hand **bookshops**, including *Mad Hatter*, 399 Aberdeen St, and *Woody's Book Shack*, 669 2nd St. For new books there's *The Book Shop*, 435 3rd St.

Transport The *Greyhound* station at 557-2 St, T5274418, receives a daily bus from **Calgary** via Fort Macleod and Lethbridge, and 4 each way between **Calgary** and **Winnipeg**, 3 continuing east to **Toronto**.

Directory **Communications** Internet: *Café Mundo*, 579 3rd St. **Canada Post**: 406 2nd St SE. **Laundry** *Kingsway Coin Laundry*, 1023 Allowance Av. **Library** 414 1st St SE. **Medical services** *Medicine Hat Regional Hospital*, 666 5th St, T5298000.

Cypress Hills Interprovincial Park

Colour map 2, grid C6

About 30 km east of Medicine Hat, Highway 41 heads south to the border, passing through the village of Elkwater and the western section of Canada's only interprovincial park. This chain of three hills forms a 130-km plateau from east to west, rising like a green island from the surrounding prairie flatness. The Blackfoot Indians called these unexpected heights *Ketewius Netumoo*, or the 'hills that should not be'. At about 1,400 m, their elevation is modest compared to the ranges further west, yet this is the highest point between the Rockies and Labrador way to the east, a fact that hints at the mindboggling vastness of Canada's interior flatlands. Indeed, this is the best place to absorb the extent of the endless prairie horizons, and understand how between 30 and 60 million bison were nourished by the Great Plains.

Thanks to the anomaly of its sudden elevation, this was one of only two regions in Western Canada (the other being Haida Gwaii, the Queen Charlotte Islands, see page 284) to avoid glaciation during the last ice age. The result is an ecosystem whose mild, wet climate supports a wide variety of vegetation. Described by Captain John Palliser as "an oasis in the desert", this mixture of woodland, wetland and grassland contains over 700 species of plant and orchid, and a wealth of fauna that includes elk, lynx and bobcat, as well as over 220 species of bird. While not likely to generate much excitement for those coming from the Rockies or British Columbia, these landscapes are about the best the prairies have to offer.

Elkwater

Bikes and boats can be rented around the lake

Pleasantly situated on Elkwater Lake, this tiny tourist resort is the only base for exploring the park's western section. Facilities are scant but cover all the necessities. There is a **Park's Office**, T8933777, and a summer-only **Visitor Centre** which runs guided walks in the summer and hands out maps and trail guides.

1000-1800, T8933833, www.cypresshills.com Most of the park's **trails** begin at the campgrounds (see below), winding up through the pine and spruce forests. The best for views is the **Horseshoe Canyon Trail**, 4 km one-way from Old Baldy to the Lookout point.

Sleeping and eating D *Green Tree Motel*, T8933811, is the only place. Rooms are small and grotty. Go for one of the nicer cabins, with kitchenette. Reasonable restaurant with a broad menu. **Camping** There are 11 campgrounds around town and deeper into the park. All fill up in summer. For reservations call T8933835. F *Elkwater Campground* is the closest but its sites are crowded. Those at **F** *Ferguson Hill* are much nicer.

Edmonton

Desperately cold in winter, and gateway to nothing more appealing than the flat and underpopulated north, Alberta's capital loses out in many ways to its rival to the south, yet it is older and has a better selection of sights and restaurants. The problem is that Edmonton is far too big and its attractions are scattered. Despite some interesting architecture, Downtown Edmonton is a sprawling, soulless affair, with only one point of interest, Sir Winston Churchill Square. In summer this is the principal focus for a constant stream of major cultural events that justifies Edmonton's claim to be 'The Festival City'. Maybe as a reaction to the Calgary Stampede, the quintessential Albertan celebration, Edmonton tries hard to be fun, and was recently upset when a British journalist labelled it 'Deadmonton'. An unfair judgement, since Whyte Avenue in Old Strathcona is the liveliest street west of Toronto. In fact, it's too brash for its own good, a judgement that could be extended to Edmonton's most visited attraction, the dreaded West Edmonton Mall.

Phone code: 780
Colour map 2, grid A5
Population: 666,104,
Greater Edmonton:
937,845

Alberta

Ins and outs

Edmonton International Airport is 29 km north of Downtown. Two shuttles run from the Arrivals terminal into town. The train station is at 12360 121st S, while the *Greyhound* bus station is Downtown at 10324 103rd St. *Red Arrow* buses arrive at 10014 104th St, walking distance from Downtown.

Getting there
For transport details, see page 393

Edmonton is not an easy city to negotiate on foot. The confusing **Pedway** is a godsend in winter, but best avoided otherwise. There is an extensive bus network and a very useful light railway system (LRT). Transport information kiosks are at Jasper Av/100A St and the Churchill LRT station.

Edmonton is divided by the broad North Saskatchewan River, its Downtown just to the north, Old Strathcona to the south. The grid system is easy and logical: streets run north-south with numbers larger as you go west. Avenues run east-west with numbers larger going north. The last 2 digits of an address denote the location within a block, the first 2 or 3 digits tell you what block it is in. So 14825 102nd Av means No 25 in the block north of 148th St. Problems begin around the river, whose course interrupts the grid, with further confusion caused by a tangle of overpasses and by certain roads that unexpectedly head down to the river. The best advice is to rely on the High Level Bridge on 109th Av. And don't drive!

Getting around

Edmonton Tourism has its very useful main **Visitor Information Centre** one floor below ground level in the Shaw Conference Centre, 9797 Jasper Av, T4968400, Mon-Fri 0800-1700. There are others on the way into town at 2404 Calgary Trail SW (northbound), T4968400, summer 0800-2000, winter 0900-1700; and summer-only on

Tourist information

24 hours in Edmonton

Start the day **Downtown** with breakfast at the atmospheric *Silk Hat*, then coffee at *Baraka Café*. If it's summer, the chances are that something is going on in Sir William Churchill Square. Be sure not to miss the **Art Gallery**. Catch a bus to the **Muttart Conservatory**, then go on a **cruise** along the North Saskatchewan River on the *Edmonton Queen* riverboat. Heading back to the north bank, take in the **Legislature Building**, then enjoy the views as you eat lunch at *Devine's*. The afternoon could involve a trip west to the **Provincial Museum of Alberta** and, if curiosity gets the better of you, join the hordes at the **West Edmonton Mall**. Those with kids should definitely make for the **Odyssium** Science Centre, and could take in an IMAX film.

The best place for evening atmosphere is Old Strathcona. Whyte Avenue is perfect for bar-hopping, and has many choices for dinner, including *Packrat Louie's* and *Unheardof*. *Devlin's* is a great spot for a post-dinner Martini. *Yardbird Suite* and *Blues On Whyte* are good local venues for live music, and the *Princess* shows worthwhile rep movies. There are also a few decent clubs around, but for the best of these, head back **Downtown**. Having bopped till you drop, you'll also be in the right place for coffee at the 24-hr *Naked on Jasper*, and back to breakfast at the *Silk Hat*.

Hwy 16A West. *Where Edmonton*, www.whereedmonton.com is a handy bi-monthly magazine, though their opinions are not always to be trusted. Also useful are: **www.tourism.ede.org**, the official information site, and **www.govedmonton.ab.ca**, the government site; **www.edmontonplus.ca** which has impartial reviews of restaurants, bars, etc; and **www.discoveredmonton.com**, good for sights, events, etc.

Best time to visit   Winters in Edmonton are bitterly cold, with average temperatures of -15° C. Summer is the obvious time to visit, not just for the average temperature of 17° C, and 17 hrs of sunshine per day, but because of the perpetual festivals. Despite everything, the mammoth *Folk and Fringe Festivals* in **Aug** make this one of *the* places to be in that month.

History

In 1795 the Hudson's Bay Company established its trading post, Edmonton House, near the present site of Fort Saskatchewan. By 1826 it was one of the major distribution centres for the western prairies. Incorporated as a town in 1892 with a population of 700, Edmonton only boomed when newspapers, prompted by town officials, duped stampeders on their way to the Klondike Gold Rush into taking the allegedly safer 'All Canadian Route' to the Yukon. This non-existent route entailed 3,000 km of unbroken wilderness, a nightmare that proved fatal for hundreds of hapless hopefuls. A note written by one, just before he shot himself, read: "Hell can't be worse than this trail. I'll chance it".

Named provincial capital in 1905, Edmonton's Legislature Building and High Level trestle bridge across the river were completed in 1912-13. Construction of the Alaska Highway in 1942 solidified Edmonton as *the* transportation and supply hub of the north, and the 1947 discovery of oil in nearby Leduc made it the Oil Capital of Canada. Things have boomed ever since, with zero unemployment and a very healthy standard of living.

Sights

The potentially attractive North Saskatchewan River carves a major valley right through the middle of town, but its scenic possibilities are largely squandered.

Alberta

Downtown is inexplicably focused a few blocks to the north, where the natural light and sense of space fail to penetrate. In the valley are a number of parks and the attractive glass pyramids of the Muttart Conservatory. On the south bank, again removed from the views, is Edmonton's historic district and Party Central, Old Strathcona. Many of the town's key sights are irritatingly far afield.

The undisputed focus for Downtown Edmonton is **Sir Winston Churchill Square**. Almost everything of any importance is here, and in summer it is constantly alive with music, street performers and festival events. Bounded by 99-100 Streets and 102-102A Avenues, it features a great statue of the man himself wearing his classic British Bulldog expression. On the northeast corner is the exceptional **Edmonton Art Gallery**, with seven separate exhibition spaces, and an excellent 5,000-piece rotating collection that includes many modern works of varied media, such as *Wayne Gretzky #99* by Andy Warhol. Predominantly contemporary works are by Albertan, Canadian and international artists, in that order. There is also a children's gallery, a nice gift shop, and a coffee bar. ■ *Mon-Wed 1030-1700, Thu 1030-2000, Sat-Sun 1100-1700. $5, $3 seniors, $2 children. Free Thu after 1600. T4226223, www.edmontonartgallery.com* A block north is the **City Hall**, an eight-storey glass pyramid, well worth exploring for its great collection of art, pleasant atmosphere and useful information. Its tower has a 23-bell carillon that plays 99 tunes. ■ *Mon-Fri 0700-2200, Sat-Sun 1100-1700. Free. T4968200.*

On the square's east side is the **Francis Winspear Centre for Music**, one of the best concert halls in the west, with the splendid **Stanley A Milner Public Library** on the southern edge, and the **Citadel Theatre** on the corner between them. A block east, a distinctive gate marks the start of the small and unimpressive **Chinatown** that seems to share a border with the city's red-light district. Streets lead south from here to Jasper Avenue, with views of the river valley and the Muttart Conservatory's glass pyramids (see below). The **Shaw Conference Centre** (home of the Information Centre) is a striking building whose glass tiers complement those structures, descending the valley like giant steps. Other moments of architectural interest include **Grant McEwan College** on 109th Street and 104th Avenue, an eye-catching structure of thin monolithic cement towers and a glass dome.

The **Muttart Conservatory**, a collection of four glass pyramids laid out in the river valley, represents Edmonton's most distinctive feature. Each contains the flora of a different environment, such as orchids, hibiscus and passion flowers in the Tropical Pyramid, Japanese maples, oaks and magnolias in the Temperate, cacti, jojoba and aloe in the Arid. The Show Pyramid's displays change eight times through the year, usually following a theme. ■ *Mon-Fri 0900-1800, Sat-Sun 1100-1800. $5, $4 seniors, $2.50 children. 9629-96A St, T4968755. Bus No 64-69.*

The easiest way to get to Old Strathcona is on the LRT or by driving west on Jasper Avenue then south on 109th Street. Either way, you go across the **High Level Bridge**, which is equipped with a manmade waterfall that cascades dramatically into the river below on special occasions. In summer, the historic **High Level Streetcar**, T4335866, travels from Grandin Station (109th Street/98th Avenue) to Old Strathcona ($3 return). Just north of the bridge is the **Alberta Legislature Building**. Completed in 1912 on the site of one of the original Fort Edmontons, this grand sandstone building is far more impressive from the outside than it is inside. The grassy lawn that surrounds it offers some of the best views of the river valley, and an enormous wading pool that

Downtown

South of Downtown

Alberta

can be a godsend on a hot day. Free tours of the interior – which has a few dull displays of chairs and uniforms – start at the interpretive centre. ■ *Tours daily from 0900-1700, hourly in the morning, every 30 mins in the afternoon. 97th Av/107th St, T4272826. LRT Government Centre station.*

Old Strathcona Old Strathcona is Edmonton's historic quarter, with buildings dating back to 1891. To learn all about it, contact the **OS Foundation**. ■ *Summer Mon-Fri 0900-1700, winter Tue-Wed only, 10324 Whyte Av www.osf.strathcona.org* These days the area is more renowned for its party atmosphere, with an astounding quantity of restaurants, bars and clubs packed into a few blocks of **Whyte Avenue** (82nd Avenue) between 106th and 103rd Streets. There is something here for everyone, but the clientele is young, and the atmosphere intense. At times of celebration, the presence of thousands of drunk revellers in so small an area can get out of hand. In August, this is the venue for the biggest **Fringe Theatre Festival** in North America, well worth while if you happen to be around.

The **C&E (1891) Railway Museum** is a local favourite, with steam engines and assorted train paraphernalia. ■ *Summer Wed-Sun 1000-1600. $2. 10447 86th Av, T4339739.* The popular **Saturday Farmer's Market** is the city's best, with over 130 vendors selling produce, arts and crafts, baking, preserves, etc. ■ *Sat 0800-1500. 10310 83rd Av.*

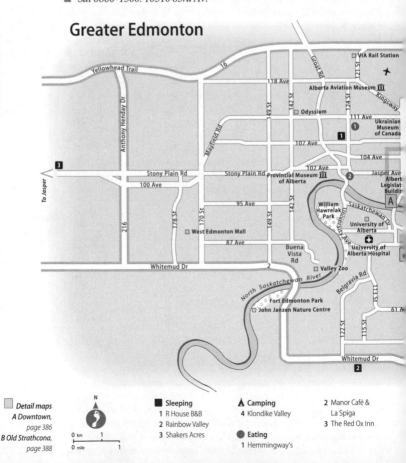

Greater Edmonton

N

0 km   1
0 mile   1

■ **Sleeping**
1 R House B&B
2 Rainbow Valley
3 Shakers Acres

▲ **Camping**
4 Klondike Valley

● **Eating**
1 Hemmingway's

2 Manor Café &
   La Spiga
3 The Red Ox Inn

The south bank gives easier access into this green belt, which has the longest expanse of urban parkland in North America, with 97 km of hiking, biking, and ski trails covering 7,400 ha. The **River Valley Centre** provides brochures and information, T4967275. From Whyte Avenue walk a few blocks north to Saskatchewan Drive. Steep staircases from here descend into the park.

The North Saskatchewan River Valley

Situated on the river west of Old Strathcona, Alberta's main university was established in 1908, and contains some of the city's older buildings. At 11153 Saskatchewan Drive is **Rutherford House**, a 1911 Edwardian mansion that was home to Alberta's first premier. Tours are conducted by costumed guides. ■ *May-Sep 0900-1700. $2. T4273995.* The **Fine Arts Building Gallery** has exhibitions of modern Canadian artists ■ *Tue-Fri 1000-1700, Sun 1400-1700. Free. T4922081.*

The University of Alberta

The river winds its way southwest passing William Hawrelak Park, venue for many festivals, on the way to two out-of-the-way riverside attractions. Valley Zoo, fairly small compared to the one in Calgary, is aimed at kids, with camel rides and a miniature train. ■ *Summer 0930-2000, rest of the year 0930-1600. $5.75, $3.25 concessions. 13315 Buena Vista Rd/134th St, T4696911.*

Valley Zoo & Fort Edmonton Park

Fort Edmonton Park contains reconstructions of the 1846 fort and three streets representing the years 1885, 1905 and 1920, all brought to life by costumed performers, with period retail shops and food outlets. There are plenty of activities, such as a steam train and streetcar rides, and pioneer children's games, all included in the price. ■ *May-Sep 1000-1800. $7.75, $4 concessions. Fox Dr/Whitemud Dr, T4968787. LRT to University then bus No 32, 39 or 139.* The **John Janzen Nature Centre** next door, T4962939, has an exhibit room and a number of nature walks.

Provincial Museum of Alberta dotted with cafés and quaint gift shops, and containing the city's largest concentration of private art galleries, 124th Street, between 110th and Jasper Avenues, is one of Edmonton's only genteel neighbourhoods. You'll pass it on the way to the Provincial Museum of Alberta, which is in the upmarket district of Old Glenora. Spread over two spacious floors, the collection is well organized and sets high standards. On the ground floor is a gallery given over to temporary exhibitions of a featured artist, the space adapted to fit in with the displays, and complemented by a

West of Downtown

Alberta

related big-screen video presentation. The **Habitat Gallery** contains reconstructions of many different Alberta landscapes, complete with the (stuffed) animals that inhabit them.

Upstairs is the **Natural History Gallery**, with an amazing collection of minerals including a mammoth amethyst, a Chinese jade bowl and a copper boulder. Equally extensive is the delightful and fascinating **Bug Room**. The **Adaption and Survival Room** has more stuffed animals, including lots of birds, and then there are fossils and dinosaur reproductions. A smaller feature gallery has space for another temporary exhibition, followed by the **Syncrude Gallery of Aboriginal Culture**, which uses exhibits and artefacts to explore 11,000 years of native history. ■ *Mon-Fri 0900-2100, Sat-Sun 0900-1700. $8, $4 children, Tue half-price. 12845 102nd Av, T4539100, www.pma.edmonton.ab.ca Bus No1 to Jasper Place.* The grounds also contain **Alberta Government House**, a heritage building full of antique artefacts. ■ *Sun only, with free tours every half hour.*

Odyssium North of here is the Odyssium, Edmonton's Science Centre, and one of the best of its kind. A whole range of different galleries use any tricks available to make science interesting to kids. This involves a lot of hands-on stuff, games, sports, puzzles and brain-teasers, but also areas like **Mystery Avenue**,

Downtown Edmonton

Sleeping
1 Alberta Place Suite
2 Comfort Inn & Suites
3 Delta Edmonton Centre Suite
4 Econolodge
5 Edmonton House Suite
6 Fairmont Hotel Macdonald
7 Howard Johnson
8 Union Bank Inn
9 YMCA

Eating
1 Baraka Café
2 Bistro Praha
3 Bohemia Cyber Café
4 Café Select
5 The Crêperie
6 Devine's
7 Donna at the Citadel
8 Hardware Grill
9 Khazana Tandoori
10 La Ronde
11 Mikado
12 Naked on Jasper
13 Rivo Tapas
14 Silk Hat

0 metres 200
0 yards 200

where they have to gather clues and use forensics to solve a crime. There is a free **Observatory**, **Discoveryland** for two to eight year-olds, live demonstrations on the **Science Stage**, a computer lab, a giant planetarium dome (included in admission) and an IMAX theatre. ■ *1000-2200. Admission or IMAX $10, $8 seniors, $7 children; combined ticket $16, $13 seniors, $11 children. 11211-142nd St, T4529100, www.odyssium.com Bus No 5 or 135 from Jasper Av.*

West Edmonton Mall It says a lot about Edmonton that its number one tourist attraction is a mall; the biggest mall in the world, in fact, covering 48 city blocks, with 800 stores, 110 restaurants, the world's largest indoor amusement park, largest indoor lake, largest indoor wave pool, and so on. There's a waterpark with 2 ha of slides, dolphin shows, a submarine, a galleon, an amusement park with a huge rollercoaster, 26 movie theatres including the ubiquitous IMAX, mini-golf, a skating rink, a casino, clubs and bars on the tacky Bourbon Street, restaurants on Europa Boulevard, and so on.

For all that, it's still a mall, and if malls excite you, join the hordes. But be warned that it's a long way from Downtown, and most of the above will be overpriced ($29 to enter the waterpark). You can stay in the **LL-A** *Fantasyland Hotel*, T1800-737 3783, which has theme rooms. Free tours of these rooms leave daily at 1400. ■ *170-178th St/87-90th Av, T4445300, www.west edmontonmall.com Buses No 2, 109 or 112 from Churchill Sq.*

A great way to spend an afternoon, and a useful antidote to the mall, is to walk around the beautiful **Devonian Botanic Garden**, where 10,000 different species of plant are arranged over 30 ha, including Japanese, native and alpine Gardens, and an indoor display of orchids and butterflies. There are also 45 ha of nature trails and wetland. ■ *Summer 1000-1900, spring and autumn 1000-1600. $5.75, $3.50 concession. 25 mins from the mall on Hwy 60 S.*

Excursions

About 30 km east of Edmonton, Elk Island National Park was established in 1906, and has one of the highest densities of living things in the world. Over 40 species of mammal include 470 plains bison, 300 wood bison, 950 elk and 400 moose, all roaming freely, safari-style. Over 230 species of bird visit the park, including the rare trumpeter swan, and over 300 flowering plant species have been identified. The park's southern gate and **Information Centre**, T9225790, is 1 km

Elk Island National Park

Alberta

● Bars & clubs

15 Caliente Latin Club
16 Cristal Lounge
17 Fly
18 Halo
19 Lush/Rev Cabaret
20 Majestik
21 Mezza Luna
22 New City Suburbs
23 Rose & Crown
24 Sherlock Holmes Pub
25 Therapy
26 Zenari's

from Highway 16. A further 14 km north is the main focus of facilities at **Astotin Lake**. This includes an Interpretive Centre and several campgrounds. There are over 100 km of trails of every length.

Ukranian Cultural Heritage Village A living-history museum with 30 historic buildings and costumed role players recreating life as a Ukranian pioneer in Alberta from the 1890s to 1930s. ■ *Summer 1000-1800, autumn 1000-1600. $6.50, $3 concessions. T6623640. 25 mins east of Edmonton off Hwy 16.*

Reynolds-Alberta Museum An important museum celebrating the 'Spirit of the Machine', with a huge collection of machines and vehicles from aircraft to tractors. Some of them can even be ridden. ■ *Summer 0900-1900, rest of the year 0900-1700. $9, $5 concessions. T1800-6614726. Halfway to Red Deer, 1 km west of Wetaskiwin on Hwy 13.*

Essentials

Sleeping
■ *on maps, pages 384, 386 & below*

Downtown There are many plush hotels in Downtown Edmonton, all offering many facilities and most affording grand views from high rooms. Their prices tend to be greatly reduced for Fri and Sat nights. **L** *Delta Edmonton Centre Suite Hotel*, 10222 102nd St, T4293900, www.deltahotels.com A variety of decent rooms. All facilities except pool. **L** *Fairmont Hotel Macdonald*, 10065 100th St, T4245181, www.fairmont.com The town's most impressive building. Squash courts. Expensive restaurant.

Old Strathcona

N

Not to scale

■ Sleeping
1 Commercial & Blues On Whyte
2 Edmonton HI Hostel
3 Strathcona
4 Varscona

● Eating
1 Albert's Family
2 Benny's Bagels
3 Block I912-European Café
4 Chianti Café
5 Da-De-O
6 French Meadow Bakery
7 Funky Pickle
8 Julio's Barrio
9 The King & I
10 Naked Cyber Café & Blackbyrd Myoosik
11 Netwerks Internet Café
12 New York Bagel Café
13 Packrat Louie Kitchen & Bar
14 Polo's Café
15 Sorrentino's Bistro
16 Two Rooms Café & Backroom Vodka Bar
17 Unheardof
18 Yiannis Taverna

● Bars & clubs
19 The Attic
20 Black Dog
21 Cook County Saloon
22 Devlin's
23 Lola's
24 The Next Act
25 O'Byrnes Irish Pub
26 Parliament
27 Savoy
28 Urban Lounge & Whiskey Grill

A-B *Alberta Place Suite Hotel*, 10049 103rd St, T4231565, www.albertaplace.com Fairly nice rooms with large kitchen. **A** *Edmonton House Suite Hotel*, 10205 100th Av, T4204000, www.edmontonhouse.com Spacious and well equipped with kitchen, lounge and bedroom. Good value. **A** *Union Bank Inn*, 10053 Jasper Av, T4233600, www.unionbankinn.com A small hotel, half of whose rooms follow the vision of different selected designers. Breakfast and wine and cheese tasting, down duvets, fireplaces.

C *Comfort Inn and Suites*, 10425 100th Av, T4235611, www.comfortinnedmonton.com Good value. Pool, hot tub and sauna. Continental breakfast included. **C** *Howard Johnson*, 10010 104th St, T4232450, www.hojo.com Comfy rooms with big beds. Pool, hot tub, sauna. **D** *Econolodge*, 10209 100th Av, T4286442. Quietly stylish, comfortable rooms. None of the extras, but great value. **D** *R House B&B*, 10804 125th St, T4482723. 3 rooms in heritage home northwest of Downtown. **D** *YMCA*, 10030 102A Av, T4219622. Basic single rooms. Shared bath and TV lounge. Pool and fitness room.

Old Strathcona/University AL-B *Varscona*, 8208 106th St/Whyte Av, T4346111, www.varscona.com Very plush and comfy, huge beds, free evening wine and cheese tasting. **B** *Campus Tower Suite Hotel*, 11145 87th Av, T4396060, www.campuStower.com Very nice suites in a good part of town. **B** *McLellan House*, 11135 84th Av, T4338707. Attractive B&B in nicely furnished 1913 house. En suite bath, library, balconies, porch. **B** *The Understudy*, 11329 University Av, T4350662. 2 rooms with full kitchen and en suite bath, wood house, nice garden. **C** *This is it*, Hinton House, 11013 87th Av, T4398481. En suite, guest lounge, friendly and helpful owner. **C** *University B&B*, 11027 86th Av, T4390837. 2 en suite rooms.

E *Commercial Hotel*, 10329 Whyte Av, T4393981. Sleazy but cheap, with a bar downstairs, with or without bath. **E** *Edmonton International Youth Hostel*, 10647 81st Av, T9886836. Dorms and some double rooms, big kitchen, laundry, games room, internet, courtyard, big and clean. **E** *Strathcona Hotel*, 10302 Whyte Av, T4391992. Run down and old but acceptable, shared bath unless getting the more expensive room which is larger with 2 beds.

Camping F *Klondike Valley*, 1660 Calgary Trail S, T9885067. Large, quiet site on Blackmud Creek. **F** *Rainbow Valley*, in Whitemud Park, off Whitemud Drive at 119th St, T4365479. **F** *Shakers Acres*, 21530 103rd Av, W of city at Winterburn exit from Highway 16A, T4473564.

Downtown Expensive *Hardware Grill*, 9698 Jasper Av, T4230969. Set in a heritage building. First-class Canadian cuisine that changes with the seasons. *The Harvest Room* at the *Fairmont Hotel Macdonald* (see Sleeping, above). Fancy dining at its best. Meat and fish dishes with a local bias, such as Alberta buffalo flank or native pepperberry-crusted Arctic char. Impeccable service. *La Ronde*, in the *Crowne Plaza Hotel*, 10111 Bellamy Hill, T4822277. First rate food in a revolving restaurant with the only panoramic views in town. *Mikado*, 10350 109th St, T4258096. Oldest Japanese restaurant in town, sushi bar with large selection of fish. *The Red Ox Inn*, 9420 91st St, T4655727. Small, intimate venue, quiet but popular. Eclectic gourmet menu with some veggie dishes.

Mid-range *Bistro Praha*, 10168 100A St, T4244218. Czech-inspired cuisine in comfortable, romantic surroundings. *Café Select*, 10018 106th St, T4230419. International French-influenced cuisine in a romantic, sophisticated setting. Fondue, salads, extensive wine list. Recommended. *The Crêperie*, 10220 103rd St, T4206659. Mainly crêpes plus French-inspired main courses in an intimate cellar setting. No smoking. *Devine's*, 9712 111th St, T4826402. An old brick house overlooking the river, with gorgeous views from patio and upstairs lounge. West Coast-style food, some nice salmon dishes and 4-5 specials a night. Brunch on Sat and Sun. *Donna at the Citadel*, 10177 99th St, T4293338. Fine international cuisine in a great location, with patio. *Khazana*

Eating

● *on maps, pages 384, 386 & 388*

Edmonton's culinary scene could well be the city's best feature, and is certainly far ahead of Calgary's

Tandoori, 10177 107th St, T7020330. Best Indian food in town, full marks for selection, decor and service. *Rivo Tapas*, 9707 110th St, T4827277. Great view of river, international tapas. **Cheap** *The Silk Hat*, 10251 Jasper Av. Oldest restaurant in town. Generous breakfasts, lots of character, booths.

Over 50 restaurants fight for business in a few short blocks

Old Strathcona Expensive *Packrat Louie Kitchen and Bar*, 10335 83rd Av, T4330123. Popular, candlelit dining, casual but sophisticated. Creative gourmet selections. *Sorrentino's Bistro*, 10612 Whyte Av, T4397700. A chain-style fancy Italian place, very nice lounge, delicious homemade pastas, patio. *The King and I*, 8208 107th St, T4332222. A haunt of the Rolling Stones and other stars when in town. Good reputation for food but rather cramped. *Unheardof*, 9602 82nd Av, T4320480. Excellent food, service and ambience. Varied menu. East of busiest section.

Mid-range *Chianti Café and Restaurant*, 10505 Whyte Av, T4399829. Cheap pasta on Mon-Tue, patio, large and lively interior. *Da-De-O*, 10548 Whyte Av, T4330930. Classic diner decor, creole food such as catfish and oysters. *Julio's Barrio*, 10450 Whyte Av, T4333654. Mexican joint which is often the focus of attention on this busy street. Large portions. Patio and margueritas. *Polo's Café*, 8405 112th St, T4321371. Eclectic Oriental fusion cuisine, highly renowned. *Yiannis Taverna*, 10444 Whyte Av, T4336768. Very popular, upmarket Greek joint with pleasant decor and patio.

Cheap *Albert's Family Restaurant*, 10370 Whyte Av. A favourite breakfast spot. *Funky Pickle*, 10441 82nd Av and 10815 Jasper Av. Great reputation for its pizza, available by the slice, open till 0230.

West of Downtown Expensive *Hemmingway's*, 10942 124th St, T4510330. Exquisite fine dining in an elegant old house. Emphasis on local produce and wild game. *La Spiga*, 10133 125th St, T4823100. Best Italian food in town in attractive setting. Nice patio. **Mid-range** *Manor Café*, 10109 125th St, T4827577. A renovated mansion with an upbeat, innovative menu at reasonable prices.

Cafés **Downtown** *Baraka Café*, 10168 Jasper Av. Comfy decor. Cakes, chocolates and snacks. *Bohemia Cyber Café*, 11012 Jasper Av. *Naked on Jasper*, 10354 Jasper Av. 24-hr internet café. **Old Strathcona** *Benny's Bagels*, 10461 Whyte Av. Relaxed spot for coffee and snacks. *Block 1912-European Café*, 10361 Whyte Av. Large, plush and comfy, open till midnight. *French Meadow Bakery*, 10732 Whyte Av. Good coffee and expensive pastries, nice cheese store attached. *Naked Cyber Café*, 10442 Whyte Av. 24-hr espresso and internet. *New York Bagel Café*, 8209 104th St. Cosy with lots of character. *Two Rooms*, 10324 Whyte Av. Arty café with salads, good desserts and a well-located patio.

Bars **Downtown** *Rose and Crown*, 10235 101st St, in the *Sheraton Grande*. Good selection

● *on maps, pages 386 & 388*

of draught, pool tables. *Sherlock Holmes Pub*, 101A Av, behind Scotia Place. Mock Tudor-style English pub with red phone booth, nice patio, good beer and food but a bit overpriced. *Zenari's*, 10117 101st St. Live jazz most nights, cover charge.

The 25 pubs and clubs in this four-block radius are mostly obnoxious meat-markets, but there are a few exceptions

Old Strathcona *Black Dog*, 10425 Whyte Av. One of a few down-to-earth English-style pubs. Narrow and crowded. Mixed clientele. Rooftop patio. *Blues On Whyte*, 10329 Whyte Av. Rough and ready spot for live music. *Devlin's*, 10507 Whyte Av. Elegant Martini and tapas lounge playing good music. *The Next Act*, 8224 104th St. Beer garden frequented by thespians. *O'Byrnes Irish Pub*, 10620 Whyte Av. Irish and English beer on tap, live Celtic music. *Savoy*, 10401 Whyte Av. Trendy Martini bar with lurid red walls, futuristic bar and acid jazz music. Good food too.

Downtown *Caliente Latin Club*, 10815 Jasper Av. Eclectic music with a Latin bias, but embracing electronica. Special DJ nights. Mixed but slightly older crowd. *Cristal Lounge*, 10336 Jasper Av. Edmonton's premier spot for electronic dance music, attracting top DJs playing anything from hip hop to R&B and reggae. *Fly Bar*, 10314 104th St. Difficult-to-spot gay club playing dance music. *Halo*, 10538 Jasper Av. Dance club for the wealthy and well-heeled. Lounge rooms, expensive drinks. *Lush/Rev Cabaret* 10030A 102nd St. 2 venues in 1: the former a cutting-edge dance club with an industrial feel playing hip hop/trance/house, the latter an alternative rock institution. *Majestik*, 10123 112th St. Hardcore dance club. House, trance, etc. *Mezza Luna*, 10238 104th St. Best Latin club in town for serious dancing. DJs and live acts. Martinis and shooters. Open till 0300. *New City Suburbs*, 10161 112th St. Alternative spot for up-and-coming bands and dance-club rolled into one. *Therapy*, 10028 102nd St. High energy techno club with a subterranean feel.

Old Strathcona *The Attic*, 10407 Whyte Av. Busy dance-club with a 20-something clientele. *Backroom Vodka Bar*, 10324 82nd Av. A big vodka menu and house music. *Cook County Saloon*, 8010 103rd St. An authentic cowboy club, with line dancing, Wranglers, stetsons and big hair. *Lola's*, 8230 103rd St. Martini lounge for a well-heeled clientele, with dance music till 0200. *Parliament*, 10551 Whyte Av. The alternative club option. Jungle and hip hop. Bands upstairs, DJ's downstairs. *Urban Lounge and Whiskey Grill*, 8111 105th St. Big dance club with *Latin Tuesdays*.

Clubs
● *on maps, pages 386 & 388*

Vue Weekly and *See* are the free weekly entertainment magazines. The former also has some good articles. Both come out Thu. An easy way to get tickets is at *Tix on the Square*, in the Chancery Hall on Churchill Sq, T4201757.

Entertainment

Cinema *Garneau Theatre*, 8712 109th St, and *Princess*, 10337 82nd Av, T4330728, both show repertoire and foreign films. *Metro Cinema* in the *Citadel theatre* on Churchill Sq, T4259212, shows independent, international and Canadian films, weekends only, $5.

Live music *Blues On Whyte*, 10329 Whyte Av. Rough and ready spot for live music, mostly **blues**. *Francis Winspear Centre for Music*, 99th St/102nd Av, T4281414, is the main venue for **classical** music, and home of the Edmonton Symphony Orchestra. Great acoustics. *Yardbird Suite*, 10203 86th Av, T4320428. The city's number one **jazz** club, operated by serious jazz fans. *Zenari's*, 10117 101st St, has live jazz most nights, cover charge. *Jubilee Auditorium*, 11455 87th Av at the University, T4272760. Hosts a lot of **opera** as well as other acts.

Spectator sports Edmonton regularly plays host to major world sporting events, and is home to a few big league sports teams. **Baseball**: The *Edmonton Trappers* play at Telus Field, T4144450. **Football**: The *Edmonton Eskimos* play at the Commonwealth Stadium, T4483757. **Hockey**: Wayne Gretzky's first NHL team, the *Edmonton Oilers*, play at Skyreach Centre, 118th Av/74th St, T4518000. **Horse racing**: The Spectrum at Northlands Park is a major venue, 116th Av/73rd St, T4717210.

Theatre *Celtic Hall Medieval Dinner Festival*, 10104 32nd Av, T4303663. Interactive **Celtic** feasts, dinner with dancers, fire juggling, and sword fighting. *Citadel Theatre*, 9828 101A Av on Churchill Sq, T4251820. Huge complex housing 5 theatres, a bookstore and restaurant. *Catalyst Theatre*, 8529 103rd St, T4311750. Modern theatre productions. *Jubilee Auditorium*, 11455 87th Av at the University, T4272760. Home to theatre companies as well as Alberta **Ballet** and Edmonton **Opera** companies. *The New Varscona Theatre*, 10329 83rd Av, T4333399. Venue for the world's

Alberta

▶ **The Great One**

Wayne Gretzky, born in Brantford Ontario, 1961, is undoubtedly the greatest ice hockey player of all time. At the age of 17 he joined the Edmonton Oilers as the youngest player in a major league team in North America. In his first season he tied for the leading NHL scorer, and won the Hart Trophy as the league's most valuable player. The following year, he broke the former single-season record by 123 points, and the assist record by seven. The following year, he shattered his own points record and scored 92 goals, 16 more than the previous record, and led the Oilers to the first of four Stanley Cup championships in five years. Many Canadians still mourn the day he was traded to the Los Angeles Kings in 1988, and despite raising the profile of the American game, Gretzky

never equalled the glory of the Edmonton days. In the 1993-94 season, he won his 10th scoring record in 15 NHL seasons, and scored his 802nd goal to break the all-time scoring record.

Gretzky has broken all records thanks to his agility, speed, accuracy of shot and incredible passing. He is a tremendous reader of the game, as instinctive as he is creative. Despite such success, he has remained humble throughout his career, and in a game so given to thuggery and brawling, has always managed to keep his hands clean and has won over spectators as much with his nice-guy persona as with his obvious prowess. Now reduced to advertising breakfast cereals and the like, he is still practically deified in Canada, spoken of reverently as 'The Great One'.

longest-running live improvised soap opera, over 10 years old. Mon nights Oct-May. *The Walterdale Playhouse*, 10322 83rd Av, T4392845. Community theatre that has presented a variety of Canadian and International plays for 42 years.

Festivals   In late *May* is the *International Children's Festival*, T4591542. 5 days of music, theatre, dance, storytelling and puppetry, held at the Arden Theatre in the suburb of St Albert. *Jazz City International Jazz Festival*, T4327166, in late *Jun* is a major 10-day event with concerts all over town, including free evening shows in Churchill Sq. Also this month is *The Works Visual Arts Festival*, T4262122. 50 free exhibits and 250 special events. In early *Jul* Churchill Sq comes alive again with the *Street Performers Festival*, T4255162, featuring over 1,000 free outdoor shows. Later that month is *Edmonton Klondike Days*, T4717210, 10 days of Gold Rush celebrations, much of it aimed at kids.

Aug, the busiest month in the calendar, kicks off with the *Heritage Festival*, T4883378, a celebration of cultural diversity, with international music, arts and food in Hawrelak Park. Then come the 2 events for which Edmonton is most famous: *Folk Music Festival*, T4291899, www.edmontonfolkfest.org, 4 days of events at Gallagher Park; and the *Edmonton Fringe Theatre Festival*, T4489000, www.fringe.alberta.com, the first and biggest in North America, attracting 500,000 visitors a year. Over 100 performances per day for 11 days from noon to midnight. Various inside and outside venues all in Old Strathcona. Great food and craft vendors. Later that month is the *Blues Festival*, T4400333, 4 days in Hawrelak Park; and *Symphony under the Sky*, T4281414, 5 days of classical music in Hawrelak Park.

Shopping   **Arts and crafts**   *Alberta Craft Council Gallery and Shop*, 10186 106th St. Quality handmade crafts. *Fort Door*, 10308 81st Av. First Nations art and crafts including West Coast jewellery. *Treasure Barrel*, 8216 104th St. Handmade gifts. **Books**   *Audrey's Books*, 10702 Jasper Av. Large selection of new books. *Greenwood's Bookshoppe*, 10355 Whyte Av. New books. *Hub Cigar and Newstand*, 10345 Whyte Av. Good selection of magazines and foreign newspapers. *Wee Book Inn*, 10310 Whyte Av and 10428 Jasper Av. Used books at reasonable prices. **Camping gear**   *Totem Outdoor Outfitters*, 7430 99th St,

T4321223. Anything you need for camping, and used sports equipment. **Music** *Blackbyrd Myoosik*, 10442 Whyte Av. Good range of used music. *Southside Sound*, 10362 Whyte Av. New and used, biggest selection. **Travel** *Geo*, 10237 109th St, T7023256. Books, maps, passport photos, internet café. *The Travel Shop*, 10926 88th Av, T4393089. HI-operated. Guide books, maps, gear.

Budget Sports Rentals, 6504 104th St, T4514546. *Instant Mountain Bike Rentals*, T9056066. Drop-off and pick-up service, $25/day, $45/weekend. *Moon Shadow Adventures*, T9050110. **Canoe** trips, rentals and shuttles.

    There are over 70 **golf** courses in Greater Edmonton, including the oldest city course in Canada. The *Highlands Golf Course*, T4794713, gives good views of Downtown. *MacEwan Centre for Sport and Wellness*, 108 St/ 104-105 Av, T4795300. Fitness room, **swimming** pool and steam room. $4.25, $7 peak hrs.

    Sport

Out An' About, 9127 77th Av, T9098687, www.outanabouttours.com Walking and driving tours of Old Strathcona. *Edmonton Queen Riverboat*, 9734 98th Av, T4242628. Daily cruises on North Saskatchewan River. *Edmonton Ghost Tours*, T4693187. Tour of Old Strathcona, Mon-Thu 2100 in front of the *Walterdale Playhouse*, 10322-83 Av. $5. *Too-Loose Latreks*, T4877184. 2-3-day trips on the Red Deer and North Saskatchewan Rivers. *Edmonton Discovery Tours*, T4825300. Sightseeing hiking tours around Edmonton.

    Discount Travel Warehouse, 7125 109th St, T9449433. *Geo/Uniglobe*, 10237 109th St, T4248310. Also has maps, books and currency exchange. *Travel Cuts*, 10127A 124th St, T4888487. Student discounts.

Tour operators & travel agents

Local Unlike most towns, Edmonton is not easy to negotiate on foot, unless you stay around Churchill Sq. The **Pedway**, much of it underground, is a system that allows you to walk all over Downtown without getting wet or freezing cold in the winter. Otherwise, like the Calgary version, it is far too confusing to bother with. *Edmonton Transit Service* operate an extensive bus network and the very useful LRT rapid transit system. This runs through Downtown, connecting the Commonwealth Stadium with Churchill Sq, Jasper Av and the University. Information kiosks are at Jasper Av/100A St, and the Churchill LRT station. Call T4961600 for schedules, T4961611 for personalized trip planning. One ticket per journey, $1.75 adult, $1.25 child, $6 day pass. From town to Old Strathcona take the LRT to University Station, then transfer to bus No 8, 43 or 46. **Taxi** *Alberta Co-op Taxi*, T42552525; *Yellow Cab*, T4623456.

Transport

Long distance **Air** Located 29 km north of Downtown, Edmonton International **Airport**, T8908382, is served by several local airlines, with direct scheduled flights to several US cities and **London Heathrow**. The *Sky Shuttle Bus*, T4658515, runs to Downtown and the University, $11 one way. *Airport Shuttle*, T4134090, charges $20 into town.

    Train The *VIA Rail* station is at 12360 121st St, T1800-5618630. *The Canadian* runs 3 times weekly east to **Saskatoon**, **Winnipeg** and **Toronto**; and 3 times west to **Jasper**, **Kamloops** and **Vancouver**.

    Bus The *Greyhound* station is Downtown at 10324 103rd St, T4138747, www.greyhound.ca 16 daily services to **Calgary**; 13 to Red Deer; 4 to **Saskatoon**; 2 to **Winnipeg**; 2 to **Vancouver** via Jasper and Kamloops; 2 to **Prince George** and **Prince Rupert** via Jasper; 2 to **Dawson Creek**, with 1 continuing to **Whitehorse**; 3 to **Peace River**; and 3 to **Fort McMurray**. *Red Arrow*, 10014 104th St, T4243339, run services to Calgary, Red Deer and Fort McMurray.

Airlines *Air Canada/Air BC*, T1888-2472262; *Horizon*, T1800-5479308, *WestJet*, T1800-5385696. **Banks** *Custom House*, 10250 101st St, T4236000; *Thomas Cook*, Manulife Place, 10165 102nd St, T4483660. **Communications** Internet: free at the

Directory

Alberta

library; *Netwerks Internet Café*, 8123 103rd St. See also under Cafés. **Canada Post**: 9808 103A Av, T9443271. **Laundry** *Whyte Av Laundromat*, 9904 82nd Av. **Library** *Stanley A Milner Library*, 7 Sir Winston Churchill Sq, T4967000. **Medical services** *University of Alberta Hospital*, 8440-112th St, T4078822. *Medical Walk–in Clinic*, 9121 82nd Av, T4651370. *New Life Clinic*, 10155 102nd St, T4258185. Acupuncture, massage. *Travellers' Health Services*, 10320 100th St, T4135745. **Pharmacy**: *Shoppers Drug Mart*, 24-hr delivery, T4332424. **Useful numbers** Police: T4234567; Ambulance: T4263232.

Northern Alberta

The impossibly vast distances north of Edmonton stretch through unexciting prairie landscapes dotted with lakes, rivers and farms, gradually melding into equally dull expanses of boreal forest. With nothing but functional and unattractive towns to break the monotony, it is hard to imagine why anyone would venture into this region except on their way somewhere else.

From Edmonton, the two key escape routes are west to **Jasper** on **Highway 16**, and northwest on **Highway 43** to **Dawson Creek**, BC, and the Alaska Highway. **Highway 35** passes through the Peace River district en route to the **Northwest Territories**, its provincial capital Yellowknife, and the **Wood Buffalo National Park**. Huge even by Canadian standards, this park is of limited appeal to all but hardcore wilderness fans. Though mostly in Alberta, its only year-round road access is through the Northwest Territories. Finally, **Highway 63** ploughs northeast from Edmonton to the oil-sands boomtown of **Fort McMurray**. In winter, an ice road continues north to Fort Chipewyan and a possible southern entry to Wood Buffalo, though such an expedition would require careful thought and research even for experienced travellers.

Highway 16 to Jasper

This 357-km journey is easily done in a day by car, bus (four or five per day) or train (three per week). The scenery only gets interesting when the Rockies start to appear in the distance. Plenty of campsites and motels line the highway, but the obvious place for those who need to break the journey is halfway at **Edson**.

By the time you get to **Hinton** there seems little reason not to keep going, unless you want to stay on a working guest ranch (see Sleeping, below). The **Athabasca Tower**, 20 km north of Hinton on Highway 40, gives excellent views of the Rockies. **William A Switzer Provincial Park** is 3 km further, offering plenty of recreation opportunities.

Along with Grand Cache 120 km further north, Hinton is one of the jumping-off points for **Willmore Wilderness Park**. This continuation of the Rocky Mountain Parks borders Jasper to the south, and is far more remote and untouched. *Rock Lake Lodge*, T8653295, and *Rocky Mountain Escape*, T8655559, are both close to the park and arrange horse-riding trips.

Sleeping **Edson** **B** *Best Western*, 300 52nd St, T7122378. The most comfortable option in town, with swimming pool, fitness centre, jacuzzi suites and restaurant. **E** *Commodore Hotel*, Main St, T7231883. Little to recommend it but the price. Some rooms have shared bath. Campers should hang on for the basic but attractive **F** *Hornbeck Creek Recreation Area*, 15 km west, T7236209, though RVers might prefer **F** *East of Edson RV Resort*, 8 km east, T7232287, with full service, pull-throughs and showers.

Hinton Among many others guest ranches are **A** *Black Cat Guest Ranch*, 25 km northwest on Hwy 40, T1800-8596840. 16 en suite lodge rooms with views of the Rockies. Price includes all meals. Guest living room with fireplace, games room. Patio and hot tub. Trail riding, hiking, fishing, canoeing, dog sledding and skiing. **C** *Entrance Ranch*, 12 km from Hinton on Hwy 40, T8657549. The closest of its kind. Rustic cabins, lodge rooms, tepees and tent camping. Meals available. Horse riding and hiking.

William A Switzer Provincial Park *Blue Lake Adventure Lodge*, about 35 km northwest of Hinton on Hwy 40, T8654741. Right in the middle of the park. Cabin and chalet rooms with private bath and family cabins. Bunkhouse (**E**) and camping (**F**). Hot tub, sauna, games room, restaurant, rental of canoes, kayaks, bikes, camping and fishing gear, skis and snowshoes.

Willmore Wilderness Park **C** *Rock Lake Lodge*, on Rock Lake at the edge of Willmore and Jasper Parks, just over an hour from Hinton, T8653295, www.rocklakelodge.com Rustic log cabins that sleep up to 6 (**B**), and simple lodge rooms. $40 per person per day for meals. Trail rides, fishing, canoeing, hiking, biking and bird-watching. **A** *Rocky Mountain Escape*, 50 km up Hwy 40, then 25 km on Rock Lake Rd. T8655559, www.ecolodge.com Price includes all meals. Same activities as *Rock Lake Lodge*. Many possible activity packages.

Highway 43 to Dawson Creek

Two daily buses cover the 590 remarkably dull kilometres from Edmonton to Dawson Creek. On the way is the oil boomtown of Grande Prairie, an ugly, sprawling place. The biggest city north of Edmonton, it's good for provisions and has a better value selection of accommodation than Dawson Creek.

Grande Prairie

Sleeping and eating Several standard motels line 100th Av W and 100th St N, including **C** *The Grande Prairie Inn*, 1163 100th St, T5325221, www.gpinn.com Pool, hot tub, sauna, restaurant, lounge and dance club. **D** *Westport Inn*, 11301 100th Av, T5324100. Standard but clean rooms, best value. Note that due to seasonal workers, summer here is the low season. The best place for food and beer is *Earl's* at 101st Av/100th St.

Highway 35 to the Northwest Territories

Those heading due north need to take Highways 43, 49 and 2. The latter passes **Lesser Slave Lake Provincial Park**, which has some of the finest sand beaches in the province, and **McLennan**, where the Kimiwan Birdwalk, T3242004, helps visitors to observe the many thousands of shore birds and waterfowl that pass through annually. The Mackenzie Highway (Highway 35) is finally picked up at Peace River. Passing through the more remote reaches of Alberta's northern hinterland, Highway 35 still retains a degree of adventure: only the intrepid would consider taking so long and boring a route with so little reward. It's a good, straight road, but services are few and far between, so be prepared. Two daily *Greyhounds* make the journey to Peace River, one continuing to Hay River, NWT, for connections to Yellowknife and Wood Buffalo National Park.

The first and last town of any consequence is Peace River, 486 km from Edmonton, at the confluence of the Peace, Smoky and Heart rivers. The undeniably pretty valley provides the scenic highlight of the entire journey, so savour it. Ask the summer-only **Tourist Office** at 9309 100th St, T6242044, how to get up to Sagitwa Lookout, Judah Hill or Grouard Hill, which have the best views.

Peace River

Alberta

Sleeping Of several standard mid-range hotels in town, the best is **D** *Traveller's Motor Hotel*, 9510 100th St, T6243621, www.travellershotel.com Price includes passes to the local pool and sports centre. **F** *Lion's Club Park Campground*, on the river's west bank, T6242120, is the only real choice for campers, with showers, a playground and a store.

Tour operators Cruises down the river are arranged by *Peace Island Tours*, T6244295.

Manning & High Level

It's worth covering an extra 100 km to reach Manning, far and away the prettiest town on this route, though there's nothing much to do but sleep. By the time you get to High Level, fuel and motel prices are becoming unreasonable, and all the buildings are looking more like trailers.

Sleeping Manning: The 2 motels, **C** *Garden Court*, T8362801, and **C** *Manning Motor Inn*, T8362801, are equally unexceptional and overpriced, 2 qualities that become increasingly exaggerated the further north you go, along with the lack of good food. **C** *Whispering Winds Ranch*, T8362689, have 2 cabins by the river with a sauna, and organize hiking tours and trips on the Peace River. **Camping** There's a small municipal campground right in town (**F**) but campers would do well to hold on for another 65 km to reach **F** *Twin Lakes Rec Area* which has nice big private sites right on the lake, fishing off a dock, and swimming.

High Level: Probably the best value of a handful of hotels, all of them mysteriously prone to be full, is the **D** *Four Winds Hotel*, T9263736. **Camping** Campers can go another 25 km north to the pleasant, small and basic **F** *Hutch Lake Rec Area*, T9262201, or plump for the more luxurious and expensive **F** *Aspen Ridge*, 3 km south of town, T9264540.

Wood Buffalo National Park

Colour map 4, grid A5

Created in 1922 to protect the largest free-roaming buffalo herd in the world, Wood Buffalo is the largest national park in Canada, and was named a UNESCO World Heritage Site in 1983. Much of its 44,807 sq km is covered by boreal plains and forest, and a mosaic of muskeg, meandering streams, shallow lakes and bogs. This is one of the world's most productive ecosystems, home to many species of flora and fauna, including plenty of large mammals and a proliferation of voracious insects. Be warned also that such landscapes are rarely attractive to most people's tastes: what appeal they have comes from sheer scale and the power of such utter remoteness. The park does contain many interesting features, however, including salt plains and some fine examples of gypsum karst landforms. The Peace-Athabasca Delta is one of the largest freshwater deltas in the world, and a major nesting and staging area for migrating waterfowl from all four North American flyways. The park also contains Canada's only nesting area for the rare and endangered whooping crane. There are about 130 here, half of the world population.

The 2,500 or so bison that remain in the park are mostly hybrids of the originally pure herds of plains and wood buffalo. The herd is at the centre of a great deal of controversy, because it is infected with tuberculosis and brucellosis. Government scientists on the Environmental Advisory Board, backed up by Alberta's powerful beef lobby, have suggested that the herd should be exterminated to prevent these contagious diseases spreading to the province's valuable cattle. Those opposed to such extreme measures argue that the bison have kept the disease to themselves for 80 years, showing no outward signs of discomfort. The logistics and ramifications of wiping out the whole herd also speak for themselves. Ironically, a large increase in the farming of game animals, such as elk, has led to serious outbreaks of those very diseases the wood buffalo harbour. The argument continues, but so far the buffalo seem to be winning.

Near the park entrance is the **Angus fire-tower**, good for views and wildlife spotting. Also on Highway 5 on the way to Fort Smith are the whooping crane pull-off, with a trail and lookout tower, and the **Salt Plains** overview and trail. In Fort Smith is the **Northern Life Museum**, which has a fine selection of native crafts and artefacts, fur-trading items and archive photos. On Marine Drive is the **Slave River Lookout**, with a telescope trained on the white pelicans' nesting site. Halfway to Pine Lake at Salt River are two 1-km trails, and a 21-km loop. **Canoeing** on the Peace and Slave rivers can be extremely gratifying, but experience is required. The Visitor Centre can provide a River Guide, and tell you where to rent canoes and boats in Fort Smith. **Pine Lake** is the main recreation centre, with swimming, canoeing and a 6-km hiking trail to Lane Lake.

Sweetgrass Station, located between Peace River and Lake Claire, is the park's most popular backcountry destination. Access is via a 13-km hiking trail from Sweetgrass Landing, which is 66 km downstream from Peace Point, or 14 km upstream from Carlson's Landing, accessible only by canoe or boat. **Fort Chipewyan** on the shores of the massive Lake Athabasca, is great for fishing, and bird-watching in spring and autumn. Insane adventurers might also think about trying to make it to **Athabasca Sand Dunes Provincial Wilderness Park** in neighbouring Saskatchewan, where the world's most northerly sand dunes stretch for about 100 km along the lake's southern shore. As the park brochure bluntly states: "There are no communities, permanent residents, services or facilities of any kind in the park".

Wood Buffalo is a remote wilderness area with very few services, so any trip into the **Park** park should be preceded by much planning and preparation. The best time to visit is **information** late Aug-Sep, when the vegetation has taken on its autumn colours and there are fewer insects. Contact **Parks Canada**, T6973662, www.parkscanada.pch.gc.ca, or the **Park Hotline**, T867-8722878, which has recorded messages on programmes, facilities and road conditions. The main **Visitor Reception Centre** is in Fort Smith at 126 McDougal Rd, T867-8723910. Summer 0900-1200 and 1300-1700 daily, rest of the year Mon-Fri only. The centre offers a slide show, and a fairly useful free map/brochure is also available. A second **Visitor Centre** is in Fort Chipewyan on Angus Rd, T780-6973560, same hours. Both centres have exhibit areas, films and videos.

Fort Smith **B** *Pelican Rapids Inn*, T867-8725214, F867-8724727. Probably the nicest **Sleeping** option, with 31 rooms and suites, cocktail lounge and restaurant. **C** *Pinecrest Hotel*, **& eating** T/F867-8722320, is the cheapest in town, and has what's probably the best restaurant. **B** *Portage Inn*, T867-8722276, www.auroranet.nt.ca/portageinn, has mostly single rooms, kitchenettes, and restaurant. **Camping** **F** *Queen Elizabeth Park* is a provincial campground in town. There is a primitive campground at **F** *Little Buffalo Falls*, 25 km northwest of town, off Hwy 5, and **F** *Thebacha Campground* at Salt River, 19 km northwest of town, also off Hwy 5. The park's main campground is at **F** *Pine Lake*, 61 km south. Almost halfway, a 6-km hike leads to a backcountry campground situated beside a sinkhole at *Rainbow Lakes*.

Fort Chipewyan **B** *Fort Chipewyan Lodge*, T780-6973679. You can request to camp on the lake front by calling T780-6973682, or there's a free, primitive campground at *Dore Lake*, 12 km away. Note that a permit is required for all backcountry camping and fires.

Tour operators The way to get the most out of this rather intimidating park is by taking a tour with a professional operator. There are plenty in Fort Smith, the most highly recommended being *Subarctic Wilderness Adventures*, T867-8722467, who offer excellent 9- and 12-14-day tours, day bus trips, and 6-hr rafting trips. Also in Fort Smith are *River Trails North*, T867-8722060, who run 2-7-day river tours, *Taiga Tour Co*, T867-8722060, and *Woodbison Tours*, T867-8723418.

Transport **Air** The easiest access is by plane from **Edmonton** (800 km) with *Canadian North*, T1800-6611505; from **Yellowknife** (400 km) with *Northwestern Air*, T1877-8722216, or from **Fort McMurray** to Fort Chipewyan with *Mikisew Air*, T1800-2687112. *Air Canada* and *WestJet* fly from Edmonton to Fort McMurray.

Car From mid-Dec to late Mar, a packed-ice winter road runs north 228 km from Fort McMurray to Fort Chipewyan. It is a further 300 km to Fort Smith. The usual year-round access is on Hwy 5. From Alberta, follow Hwy 35 across the border, fork east at Enterprise, continue through Hay River, which has motels and stores for supplies, then eventually fork south onto Hwy 5. It is about 250 km from the border to this junction, then a further 268 km on a gravel road to Fort Smith, which contains the Park HQ. Edmonton to Fort Smith is 1,360 km by road. From here a rough gravel road leads 120 km to Peace Point, deeper within the park, from where a winter-only road connects with Fort Chipewyan and on to Fort McMurray, making a winter round-trip a distinct possibility for the truly adventurous.

Highway 63 to Fort McMurray

Another crushingly boring drive is the 439-km trip to Fort McMurray, a strange anomaly in the middle of a wilderness, owing its prosperous existence to the oil sand deposits that apparently hold over 30% of the world's petroleum reserves. A surprisingly popular three-hour **Mine Tour** follows every step of the extraction process. ■ *$15. Reservations from the Visitor's Bureau, T7914336.* The whole story is also told at the **Oil Sands Discovery Centre**. ■ *May-Sep 0900-1700. $3, $1.50 concessions. T7437167.* To find out more about this obscure place and its fur-trading history, visit the inevitable **Heritage Park and Museum**. ■ *$2. T791757.*

Sleeping **B** *Nomad Inn*, 10006 McDonald Av, T7914770, Pool, exercise room, parking, airport shuttle. **D** *Twin Pine Motor Inn*, 10024 Biggs Av, T7433391, the cheapest place in town, pretty basic but quiet.

Tour operators Most people will be here to hunt or fish, with plenty of outfitters around to help them, such as *Majic Country Wilderness Adventures*, T7430766, who also do river tours and rent canoes. Others will be flying into Fort Chipewyan for access to the vast **Athabasca Lake** and the southern portion of Wood Buffalo National Park. *Air Mikisew*, T7438218, is the main operator, with daily scheduled flights to Fort Chipewyan and Edmonton. The extraordinary **Athabasca Sand Dunes** can also be reached from here. *Northern Lights*, T7913893, lead guided 3-4-day quad tours there. *Points North*, T7439350, organize guided canoe tours on the Clearwater River. This is also a good place for seeing the **northern lights**.

The Yukon

Introducing The Yukon

The landscapes of the Yukon are wide, magnificent, and often utterly unspoilt. **Kluane National Park** is part of the largest protected area on earth, containing the highest mountains in North America, the most extensive non-polar icefields in the world, and the greatest concentration of grizzly bears. Hiking here is unbeatable and uncrowded, and the park's Tatshenshini River is famed for its whitewater rafting. The province as a whole is criss-crossed with rivers that are perfect for canoeing, particularly the Yukon River, whose Loucheux Native name *Yu-kun-ah*, meaning 'great river', gave the territory its name.

But to enjoy the Yukon scenery, all you have to do is drive. Backcountry roads take you off the beaten track into pristine wilderness where wildlife such as bears, Dall sheep, moose, Arctic foxes and caribou abounds. One such route provides the only access south to the unfeasibly picturesque village of **Atlin**, across the state border in British Columbia. The **Dempster Highway** is the most adventurous remaining frontier road on the continent, crossing the Arctic Circle and a series of desolate mountain ranges. From the road's end, excursions to fly-in communities offer sights of rare wildlife and hundreds of odd volcano-shaped 'pingoes'.

All the while you will be regaled with tales of the past. The greatest **Gold Rush** of all time occurred here, as hundreds of thousands stampeded to the goldfields of the Klondike. You can retrace their steps by hiking the **Chilkoot Pass**, or by visiting the renovated but still-living Wild West town of **Dawson City**, where boardwalk dirt streets are lined with false-fronted clapboard houses and saloons. **First Nations** culture is also far more prominent here than further south. What keeps many visitors coming back though is the overwhelming friendliness of the Yukon people. The demands of life in the north break down all barriers and pretentions, making the people here curious, talkative, open, and often delightfully eccentric.

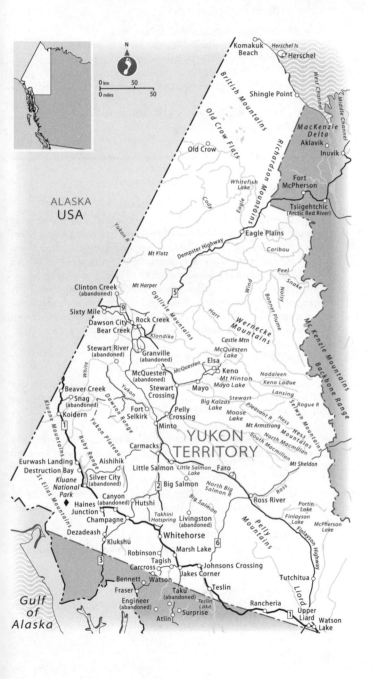

The Yukon

Things to do in the Yukon

- Canoe the Yukon River from Whitehorse to Dawson City.
- Visit the picturesque village of Atlin, BC, and go for a hike up Monarch Mountain.
- Take a whitewater rafting trip on the Tatshenshini River.
- Drive the wild and colourful Dempster Highway to the Land of the Midnight Sun.
- Hike the Slims West Trail in Kluane National Park for a taste of North America's highest mountain range.
- See 1,400 volcano-like pingoes on an Arctic flight from Inuvik to Tuktoyaktuk.

Whitehorse

Phone code: 867
Colour map 5, grid B4
Population: 19,058

Although it's the provincial capital, Whitehorse is a very small, friendly town that's unlikely to evoke any kind of strong reaction. Its location on the Yukon River is pleasant enough, but there's little of the atmosphere and excitement generated by the even smaller Dawson City to the north. For most visitors, this is a good place to organize an excursion and pick up supplies, or to enjoy the advantages of civilization after days or weeks in the bush. The canoe trip from here to Dawson City is the most popular in the Yukon, easily arranged, and suitable even for beginners. Most of Whitehorse's sights are inspired by its river and history, and there's a lot of very good art, much of it by local First Nations.

Ins and outs

Getting there
For transport details, see page 409

Whitehorse **Airport** is situated between town and the Alaska Hwy, with regular local buses to Downtown. Scheduled daily flights connect with **Vancouver** and **Dawson City**. *Greyhound* buses leave daily for Edmonton and Dawson Creek.

Getting around

Whitehorse is small enough to explore on foot. Most **buses** leave from the corner of Ogilvie and 3rd Av, running through town on 4th and 2nd Av. Downtown is centred on 2nd Av and Main St.

Tourist information

Maps ($1.50) can be bought at the **Visitor Reception Centre** on 2nd Av and Hanson, T6673084, www.city.whitehorse.yk.ca May-Sep 0800-2000. This is a very helpful and professional office, with much information on the whole province. Every hour they show an absurdly gushing film about the Yukon. Try not to laugh. Drivers should ask for a 3-day complimentary parking pass. The **Yukon First Nations Tourism Association** is at 1109 1st Av, T6677698, www.yfnta.org

Best time to visit

In Jan the average temperature is -19° C with 6 hrs of daylight; in Jul it's 19° C with 19 hrs of daylight. Winter would certainly be the time to experience the northern lights and the incredible resilience and friendliness of the Yukon people, but Jun is the best month for festivals.

History

For centuries, Southern Tutchone First Nations lived well off the abundant fish, plant and animal reserves of the Yukon River watershed. The first Hudson's Bay Company traders arrived in 1843, followed 40 years later by men

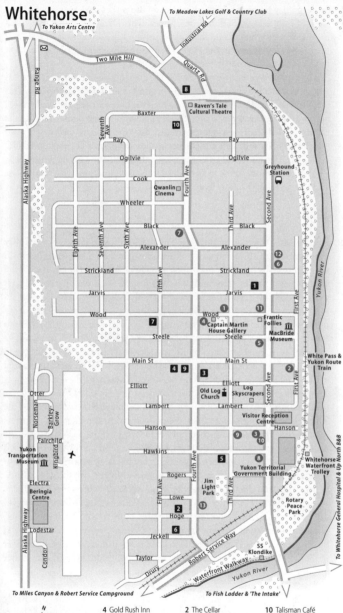

Whitehorse

To Meadow Lakes Golf & Country Club

To Yukon Arts Centre

Industrial Rd

Two Mile Hill

Quartz Rd

Range Rd

8

Raven's Tale
Cultural Theatre

Baxter

10

Seventh Ave

Ray

Ray

Ogilvie

Ogilvie

Greyhound
Station

Cook

Fourth Ave

Qwanlin
Cinema

Second Ave

Wheeler

Black

Third Ave

Black

7

Eighth Ave

Seventh Ave

Sixth Ave

Alexander

Alexander

12

Strickland

Fifth Ave

Strickland

6

Jarvis

Jarvis

Wood

1

1

Wood

11

7

4

Captain Martin
House Gallery

Frantic
Follies

Steele

Steele

MacBride
Museum

First Ave

Yukon River

Main St

4 **9**

3

Main St

Second Ave

2

White Pass &
Yukon Route
Train

Elliott

Elliott

Old Log
Church

Log
Skyscrapers

First Ave

Lambert

Lambert

Otter

Norseman

Barkley

Grow

Hanson

Visitor Reception
Centre

Hanson

Fairchild

Kingbird

Hawkins

9

3

10

To Whitehorse General Hospital & Up North B&B

Yukon
Transportation
Museum

Rogers

Fourth Ave

5

Whitehorse
Waterfront
Trolley

Electra

Beringia
Centre

Fifth Ave

Third Ave

8

Yukon Territorial
Government Building

Lodestar

Jim
Light
Park

Rotary
Peace
Park

Lowe

2

13

Alaska Highway

Hoge

6

Condor

Jeckell

SS
Klondike

Taylor

Drury

Robert Service Way

Waterfront Walkway

Yukon River

To Miles Canyon & Robert Service Campground

To Fish Ladder & 'The Intake'

The Yukon

N

| 0 metres | 200 |
| 0 yards | 200 |

■ Sleeping
1 2-0-2 Motor Inn &
Giorgio's Cuccina
2 Beez Kneez Hostel
3 The Bonanza Inn

4 Gold Rush Inn
5 Hawkins House
6 Hide On Jeckell
Guesthouse
7 Historical House
8 Pioneer Inn
9 Town & Mountain
10 Yukon Inn

● Eating
1 Blackstone Café

2 The Cellar
3 The Deli
4 Java Connection
5 Klondike Rib &
Salmon BBQ
6 The Little Dutch
Bakery
7 Midnight Sun Coffee
Roasters
8 North Dragon
9 Sanchez Mexican Deli

10 Talisman Café

● Bars & clubs
11 Backwater Pub
12 Roadhouse Inn
Saloon
13 Yukon Mining Co

toting gold-pans. After that lucky strike on Bonanza Creek sparked the Gold Rush of 1898, a flood of stampeders travelled upriver in makeshift boats, and for the next fifty years, until the building of the Alaska Highway in 1942 and the Klondike Highway in the 1950s, the Yukon River remained the foremost means of transportation in the province.

The city of Whitehorse was named after a set of fierce whitewater rapids whose thrashing waters resembled the manes of galloping horses. This treacherous stretch of water, which claimed the lives of many men and vessels, began 7 km above today's city at Miles Canyon. Those wary of facing the rapids hauled their belongings around the obstruction on horse-drawn tramways. Makeshift tent settlements quickly developed at either end of the rapids, the one above called Canyon City, the one below called Whitehorse. The latter only truly came to flourish after the construction of the White Pass and Yukon Route Railway from Skagway in 1900.

Sights

Yukon River Approaching Whitehorse from the south, 3 km before Robert Service Way heads into town, Miles Canyon Road leads down to the site of the rapids, which were removed by the damming of the Yukon River in 1958. The diversion is still worthwhile, as **Miles Canyon** is a beautiful spot, lined with fantastic basalt walls. A footbridge crosses to a network of trails that are popular for mountain biking and skiing. One leads 3.5 km to the site of Canyon City, though there's nothing left to see. Rather than returning to the highway, follow the river into town, passing the dam, Schwatka Lake, and a parade of colourful seaplanes.

Either way, entering town on Robert Service Way, you won't be able to miss the hulking **SS Klondike**, largest of the sternwheelers that played so vital a role in the Yukon's early life. As in BC's West Kootenays, these shallow-bottomed vessels proved invaluable for transporting men, supplies and gold over the treacherous rock-strewn waters. As many as 250 such boats once plied the Yukon River, its banks dotted with woodcamps at 50-km intervals, its forests quickly razed for fuel. Launched in 1929 to transport ore to Whitehorse, the *Klondike*'s cargo capacity of 300 tons was 50% larger than any other vessel on the river. Today this key historical monument has been restored to its condition prior to hitting a reef in 1936. Displays within recount the whole story. ■ *May-Sep 0900-1900, tours every half hour. $4, $2.25 concessions. T6677039.*

Across the river from here, Lewes Blvd leads to Nisutlin Drive and access to the dam. About 1 km below this is the **intake**, a tiny remainder of whitewater, whose surfing waves are popular in summer with kayakers and canoers. At 95 Nisutlin Drive is **Whitehorse Fish Ladder**, the longest wooden fish ladder in the world. You can tour the fishway and watch salmon through underwater viewing windows. ■ *Summer 0830-2100. By donation.*

Downtown The sights of Downtown Whitehorse are mostly historical. **MacBride Museum**, housed in a group of log cabins, is the obvious first stop. Exhibits and artefacts reveal the stories of the Yukon's First Nations, the Gold Rush, the North West Mounted Police, and early pioneers. There's also the usual stuffed animals, rocks, and mining items. Highlights include a replica of a 9.1-m Tlingit canoe, and a carving shed where demonstrations are given through the summer. ■ *Summer 1000-1800 daily, winter 1200-1600 Thu-Sat. $5, $3.50 concessions. 40 1st Av, T6672709, www.macbridemuseum.com* The **Yukon Archives** at 500 College Drive, T6675321, contain much material relating to Yukon First Nations history and culture, including original films, manuscripts, photos, and over 3,000 hours of recordings, many of which are interviews with elders. You can even do genealogy research to find out if any of your relatives took part in the Gold Rush.

Many Klondike enthusiasts travel to Skagway on the **White Pass and Yukon Route Train**, T6683225, though the first leg to Fraser is actually on a bus. Tickets are US$95 one way, available from the old depot on the waterfront at the bottom of Main Street. For a cheaper step back in time, the **Whitehorse Waterfront Trolley** runs along the riverfront from behind the Information Centre ($2). In summer, the Yukon Historical and Museums Society, T6674704, organizes daily **heritage walks** led by guides in period costumes, starting at Donnenworth House, 3126 3rd Avenue. One of the town's oldest buildings is the **Old Log Church**, constructed in 1900. It contains exhibits on Anglican missionaries, a small collection of Inuvialuit artefacts, and some interesting historic photos that document the impact of the white man's arrival on the native people. ■ *Jun-Sep 1000-1800. $2.50, $1 concessions. 303 Elliott St, T6682555.* The **Log Skyscrapers** on Lambert Street are another much-touted example of pioneer architecture.

Whitehorse has a lot of good art on display. The best venue is the **Yukon Arts Centre** in the Yukon College, which has a 390 sq m gallery that hosts between 10 and 17 exhibitions per year of works by provincial, national and international artists. ■ *Mon-Fri 1100-1700, Sat-Sun 1200-1700. By donation, www.yukonartscentre.com North of town on Range Rd off Two Mile Hill.* The **Yukon Territorial Government Building** opposite the Visitor Centre has a rotating exhibit from the permanent Yukon art collection, and some nice tapestries and murals. **Captain Martin House Gallery**, at 305 Wood Street, T6674080, is home of the Yukon Art Society, and represents 150 provincial artists. A free **Art Walk** brochure, available at the Visitor Centre, has a map guiding you round the many locations where art can be seen.

Beringia Centre

During the last ice-age, when widespread glaciation caused sea levels to drop dramatically, Siberia was joined to Alaska by a great corridor of land that today is again submerged beneath the Bering Sea. While most of North America was buried under ice, a vast continent stretching from the Asiatic Steppes across Northern Yukon to the Mackenzie Delta avoided glaciation, thus becoming a last refuge for thousands of species of plant and animal. Among these were the giant woolly mammoth, scimitar cat, steppe bison, and of course man. It has long been proposed that most, if not all of the ancestors of today's Native Americans entered the continent across this land bridge and moved south as the ice retreated. The Beringia Centre uses a lot of dioramas, murals, and life-sized reproductions of long-extinct wildlife to paint a picture of that frozen land and the people who managed to survive it. Highlights are a half-hour film and a giant mastodon skeleton. ■ *Summer 0830-1900 daily, winter 1300-1700 Sun only. $6, $4 concessions. T6678855, www.beringia.com Located near the airport on the Alaska Hwy.*

Yukon Transportation Museum

Just up the road, the Yukon Transportation Museum documents provincial methods of movement, from mooseskin boats to modern aircraft. As well as many displays and a lot of information, enthusiasts could spend all day watching hour-long videos on the White Pass Railway, Alaska Highway, Sternwheelers, and the Yukon Dog Sled Race. For most, the highlight is a scale model of the White Pass and Yukon Railway. ■ *May-Sep 1000-1800, tours 1130 and 1600. $4.25, $2 concessions, combo pass with Beringa Centre $7. T6684792. Beside the airport.*

The Yukon

Takhini Hot Springs About 10 km north, the Alaska Highway veers west towards Haines Junction and Kluane National Park, while the Klondike Highway continues north to Dawson City. Almost 10 km beyond the junction, a road heads 10 km west to Takhini Hot Springs. The waters of this commercial operation are odorless and range from 47° C at one end to 30° C at the other, an especially welcome treat in winter. There's a campground, restaurant, and trail rides. ■ *Summer 0800-2200, winter 1000-2200. $4.50, $3.50 concessions. T6332709, www.Takhinihotsprings.yk.ca*

Essentials

Sleeping
■ *on map, page 403*

There are over 20 B&Bs in town. Check www.bbaa.alaska.com for more

A *Hawkins House*, 303 Hawkins St, T6687638, www.hawkinshouse.yk.ca 5 beautifully decorated theme rooms, balcony. Breakfast not included. They also have some longer-stay rooms with kitchens. **B** *Town and Mountain Hotel*, 401 Main St, T6687644, www.townmountain.com Comfy rooms with good beds. **B** *2-0-2 Motor Inn*, 206 Jarvis St, T6684567. Spacious rooms with big TVs, good value. **C** *Historical House*, 5128 5th Av, T6683907, www.yukongold.com 3 rooms in a wooden home with lots of character, 2 blocks from centre. Kitchen available, stocked fridge to make your own breakfast. **C** *Up North B&B*, 86 Wickstrom Rd, on the other side of the river, T6677905. 5 rooms, shared bath, lively atmosphere, deck, full breakfast, nice location on river. **C** *Yukon Inn*, 4220 4th Av, T6672527, www.yukoninn.yk.ca Fairly nice, quiet. **C-D** *Gold Rush Inn*, 411 Main St, T6684500, goldrush@yknet.yk.ca Economical rooms are small but nice, bigger rooms are good value. **D** *The Bonanza Inn*, 4109 4th Av, T6684545, and **D** *Pioneer Inn*, 2141 2nd Av, T6682828, both have small but reasonable rooms.

Whitehorse has 2 first-class hostels, close together and 15 mins' walk from the bus station: **E** *Beez Kneez Hostel*, 408 Hoge St, T4562333, www.bzkneez.com More of a relaxed, homey atmosphere. Garden, laundry, free internet and bikes. **E** *Hide On Jeckell Guesthouse*, 410 Jeckell, T6334933, www.hide-on-jeckell.com Very well organized. Each of the 4 dorms and 2 private rooms represents a different continent. Lots of books everywhere. Games in the living room. A nice kitchen. Free internet, coffee and bikes. Lockable drawers. Small deck, garden and BBQ. Lots of little extras.

Camping F *Robert Service Campground*, 2 mins' drive or 20 mins' walk on Robert Service Dr, T6672846. Tents only, nice atmosphere, shower, sushi take away. **F** *Wolf Creek Territorial Campground*, 16 km south of town. Quite nice with a creek running through, salmon spawning Jul and Aug. There are plenty of grim RV parks on the highway south of town, all resembling gravel parking lots. Best of a bad bunch is **F** *MacKenzie's RV Park*, 18 Azure Rd, T6332337.

Eating
● *on map, page 403*

Expensive *The Cellar*, 101 Main St, T6672572. The best eatery, serving steak and seafood type dishes. Low lighting and soft music make for a romantic atmosphere. **Mid-range** *Giorgio's Cuccina*, 206 Jarvis St, T6684050. One of the most popular choices with locals. Pastas, pizza, and fish dishes. Decor has a Classical Rome theme. *Klondike Rib and Salmon BBQ*, 2nd Av/Steele St, T6677554. Huge portions of halibut and chips or ribs, no pretentions. *North Dragon Restaurant*, 2058 2nd Av. Best of the many Chinese restaurants. *Sanchez Mexican Deli*, 211 Hanson St, T6685858. Authentic Mexican dishes such as *pollo con mole*, in a nice, colourful setting. *Talisman Café*, 2112 2nd Av. Large portions of international vegetarian food. Recommended. **Cheap** *The Deli*, 203 Hanson St. Great sandwiches with sausages made from buffalo, caribou, reindeer, etc. *The Little Dutch Bakery*, 2nd Av/Strickland. Local greasy spoon that oozes atmosphere, with all day breakfast, burgers, soup, etc.

Cafés *Blackstone Café*, 302 Wood St. Good coffee and breakfast and a nice place to hang out. *Midnight Sun Coffee Roasters*, 4168 4th Av/Black St. A local institution.

Canoeing the Yukon River

The 735-km canoe trip from Whitehorse to Dawson City is the most famous and popular route in the Yukon. It takes about two weeks to complete, and though the water is fast-flowing there are few rapids, making this a fairly safe trip even for beginners. Along the way is some great scenery and lots of First Nations and Gold Rush relics, as well as the wooden remains of settlements and trading posts from the 50-odd years when the river was the province's main transportation corridor. The so-called Thirty-Mile River from **Lake Laberge** *to the confluence of the Teslin River, many of whose features are named after wrecked riverboats, is famous for its bald eagle population.* **Hootalinqua** *at the Teslin confluence is the site of an old NWMP post established in 1898.*

The river crosses the Klondike Highway at **Carmacks***, a good place to stock up with provisions. The famous* **Five Finger Rapids***, the river's biggest these days, are 38 km downstream, followed 8 km later by* **Rink Rapids***. Below the confluence of the Pelly River is the important historic site of* **Fort Selkirk***, the first white settlement on the upper Yukon, accessible only by river (see page 420). Those who are still not satisfied can continue 155 km beyond Dawson City to the next take-out at Eagle, Alaska, accessed on the Top-of-the-World Highway. But a number of operators in both cities make it very easy to do the Whitehorse-Dawson City run. It costs about $325 to rent a canoe, which can then be left in Dawson. Transport back can also be negotiated.*

Bars & clubs

Every hotel in Downtown Whitehorse has its own pub, but most are either sleazy or sterile. *Backwater Pub*, 102 Wood St. Decent low-key place with Yukon beer on tap, and regular live music. The locals' pub is the *Roadhouse Inn Saloon* on 2nd Av/Strickland. Full of character, country and western music. The nicest all-round spot is the very popular *Yukon Mining Co* in the *High Country Inn*, 4051 4th Av. Excellent, locally made Yukon Brewing Co beers on tap. Heated patio seating, pricey pub-style food.

Entertainment

Pick up the daily Whitehorse Star for listings

Cinema *Qwanlin Cinema*, 4th Av/Wheeler; *Yukon Theatre*, 3rd Av/Wood, both T6686644. **Performing arts** For many people, one of Whitehorse's key highlights is the old-time musical revue, *Frantic Follies*. Held in the *Westmark Whitehorse Hotel* at 27 2nd Av, this tribute to the gold-rush era is aimed squarely at tourists, but it's good fun and well-executed. Every night at 2030 in summer. $19, $9.25 concessions. *Raven's Tale Cultural Theatre*, held in the *Trapper's Lounge* of the *Westmark Klondike Inn*, 2288 2nd Av, T6684747. An Aboriginal theatre company whose first couple of years of cultural performances has met with success and acclaim. Thu-Sat 1900. $19, $9.50 concessions. Call for details. To find out what the native *Nakai Theatre Ensemble* are up to, call T6674626, nakai@yukon.net The *Yukon Arts Centre* on College Dr has a theatre and art gallery, and plays host to major visiting acts of all kinds.

Festivals

Many of Whitehorse's festivals take place in Rotary Park on the Yukon River. *Frostbite Music Festival*, T6684921, www.frostbite.net, in **Feb** features 3 nights of cold entertainment, music and dance. *Yukon Quest International Sled Dog Race*, www.yukonquest.yk.ca, is a 1,600-km race along trap lines ending in Fairbanks, Alaska. Later that month is the *Sourdough Rendezvous Festival*, T6672148, www.rendezvous.yukon.net Winter sports, games, entertainment: a huge party Yukon-style. In early **Jun** is the *Yukon International Storytelling Festival*, T6337550. Story-telling is an important part of native culture, and a favourite pastime of the people of Yukon. Probably the most unmissable event of the year, closely followed by the *Commisioner's Potlatch*, T3938142, a couple of weeks later. This is the main annual aboriginal event. Later in the month is the *Yukon River Quest Canoe and Kayak Race*, T6684711,

The Yukon

www.polarcom.com/~riverquest, from Whitehorse to Dawson City. The *Yukon River Bathtub Race*, T6672148, www.tubrace.yukon.net in **Aug** is apparently the longest bathtub race in the world, 776 km from Whitehorse to Dawson.

Shopping   **Books**   *Mac's Fireweed Books*, 203 Main St. Maps, travel books, large selection about the north, open till midnight in summer. *Well-Read Books*, 4194 4th Av. Used books. *Zack's New and Used Books*, 2nd Av/Hawkins. **Camping/sport gear**   *Coast Mountain Sports*, Main St. **First Nations art/craft**   Best of all is *Indian Craft Shop Ltd*, 504 Main St. *Captain Martin House*, 305 Wood St. Run by the Yukon Art Society, local art/craft and revolving exhibition space. *Folkknits* 2nd Av/Strickland St. Beautiful hand-knitted garments, some made of musk ox. *Yukon Gallery*, 2093 2nd Av. **Food**   *The Deli*, 2nd Av/Hanson. Home-made game sausages, 30 different mustards, all sorts of pickles etc. *3 Beans Natural Foods*, 308 Wood St. Bulk foods, fresh juice, organic produce. *Wharf On Fourth*, 4040 4th Av. Fresh fish. **Photography**   *Photovision*, 205 Main St.

Sports   **Canoeing**   On top of the 2-week trip to Dawson City, a number of short **canoe** excursions can be made to or from town. It is 40 km, or 1 day, from Marsh Lake to the south via Miles Canyon. Another 1- or 2-day trip could be made to Lake Laberge to the north. Carmacks is 320 km, or 5-6 days. **Golf**   *Meadow Lakes Golf and Country Club*, 121 Copper Rd, T6684653. **Hiking**   There are plenty of short hikes around Whitehorse. You can drive to Grey Mountain then follow a ridge trail with views of the city. Pick up a copy of the trail map from *Mac's Fireweed Bookstore*. For walks closer to town, the Information Centre has a pamphlet, *Whitehorse Trails*. A useful book is *Hikes and bikes: Whitehorse and area*, available at *Mac's*. The **Yukon Conservation Society**, T6685678, runs free guided nature walks. Local **mountain bike** trails are particularly good, and there's also good **rock-climbing**. For details on both ask at *Fireweed Hikes and Bikes* (see below). **Cross-country ski trails** are all over, including Miles Canyon and Chadburn Lake Rec Area. The tiny ski hill nearby at Mount Sima, T6684557, has one lift, a tow rope, and snowshoeing trails. For **swimming** there's *Lion's Pool* at 4th Av/Hoge St.

Tour   **Bike and hike**   *Fireweed Hikes and Bikes*, T6687313, www.yukonhikes.com Bike rent-
operators   als $25/day. 1-7-day hiking trips in Kluane and around. **Boat**   *MV Schwatka River Cruise*, T6334716, call ahead, $21, $10.50 concessions to the Miles Canyon. *Canadian Yukon Riverboat Family*, T6334414, www.riverboat.yknet Riverboat trips on the Yukon River to or from Dawson City (3-4 nights), meals provided. **Bus**   *Gray Line Yukon*, T6683225, run bus tours of the city and surroundings. **Canoe**   Most of the canoe places are around 2nd/1st Av and Strickland, by the river. Some rent by the trip and some by the day, $25-35. They sell maps and all gear/supplies, and offer a shuttle/pick-up service (about $1/km). Some can arrange air transport to remote put-ins. Of the many, the following are recommended: *Access Yukon*, 1st Av, T6686158, ayukon@internorth.com; *Big Bear Adventures*, T6335642, www.bigbear.yk.net Guided tours only, all kinds of trips, $175 per day all-inclusive; *Kanoe People*, 1st/Strickland, T6684899, www.kanoe.yk.ca Also rent bikes; *Up North Adventures*, 103 Strickland St, T6677035, www.upnorth.yk.ca **Dog-sled**   *Cathers Wilderness Adventures*, T3332186, www.cathersadventures.com *Muktuk Kennels*, T3931799, www.muktuk.com, both offer year-round tours. **Fishing**   *Wild Water Heli-fishing*, T4293999. Guided helicopter trips to remote salmon and steelhead waters. **Flightseeing**   *Trans North Helicopters*, 20 Norseman Rd, T6682177, www.tntaheli.com **Horse riding**   *Yukon Horsepacking Adventures*, T3931947. **Motor bikes**   *Arctic Motorcycle Tours and Rentals*, T6333344, www.arcticmoto.yk.net Rentals and 4-10-day tours. **Rafting**   *Gold Rush Float Tour*, T6334716. Tours of the Miles Canyon in a real wooden raft . $52, $29 concessions.

Local   For local transit information call T6687433. **Taxis**: *Global Taxi*, T6335300. *Yellow*   **Transport**
Cab, T6684811.

Long distance   Air: Scheduled daily flights connect Whitehorse with **Vancouver** and
Dawson City. Bus: The *Greyhound* station is in town at 2191 2nd Av, T6672223. 1 bus
daily leaves Edmonton at 0015, Dawson Creek at 0800. *Alaskon Express*, T6683225.
Service to Skagway, Haines, Anchorage. *Atlin Express*, T6517617. To Carcross and Atlin.
Mon, Wed and Fri from the *Bonanza Inn* at 1215, $40 return to Atlin. **RV rent-
als** *Canadream*, 110 Copper Rd, T6683610, www.canadream.com   All sizes of unit.
1-way rentals available to Vancouver, Calgary, Winnipeg, Toronto, etc.

Airlines   *Air Canada*, T1800-6651177; *Air North*, T6682228, www.airnorth.yk.net *Alkan*   **Directory**
Air, T6682107, www.alkanair.yk.net Charters. **Banks** *Thomas Cook*, 2101A 2nd Av,
T6682867. **Communications** Internet: free at the library; *Internet Emporium*, 412 4th
Av. Open till midnight. **Canada Post**: Main office with General Delivery is at the top of
Two Mile Hill. Otherwise, *Shoppers Drug Mart*, 211 Main St.   **Laundry** *Norgetown
Laundry*, 4213 4th Av. **Library** Whitehorse Public Library, Govt Building, 2nd Av.
Medical services *Whitehorse General Hospital*, Hospital Rd, south side of river.
East-West Health Centre, T6336157. Acupuncture, massage, nutritional counselling.

Watson Lake to Whitehorse

*The Alaska Highway enters the Yukon just south of Watson Lake and follows the   Alaska Highway Road
border westwards until the long finger of Teslin Lake forces it northwest towards   Report, T250-7747447
Whitehorse. The first section of the highway, which begins in Dawson Creek BC,
is covered in the Northern BC section. Before reaching the provincial capital, a
lengthy but highly recommended detour heads back south to Atlin. This gorgeous
village sits on the shore of Atlin Lake, the largest natural lake in BC, in a setting
that is barely equalled even in this incredible country. It is an honorary member of
the Yukon chapter as its only access is through the territory. A second, less enticing
detour heads into the region of the Southern Lakes, whose prime attraction is the
role it played in the Klondike Gold Rush, when thousands weathered the challenge of the famous Chilkoot Pass.*

The Yukon

Watson Lake

The Cassiar Highway (Highway 37) enters the Yukon 22 km west of Watson   *Phone code: 867*
Lake, with a useful gas station at the junction. This is a relatively dull little town   *Colour map 5, grid C6*
with a handful of sights that do not necessarily justify a 44-km diversion,   *Population: 912*
unless you can make it in mid-July for the **Watson Lake Rodeo**. One reason
to visit is the extremely useful **Visitor Information Centre**, T5367469,
www.watsonlake.net, May-Sep 0800-2000, whose knowledgable staff can
provide all the information you need plus guides and maps. There are also
interesting displays and a twice-hourly 18-minute slide-show about the
Yukon and specifically the construction of the Alaska Highway.
   Watson Lake was just a tiny airport, part of the Northwest Staging Route
Programme that tried to create a Great Circle Route connecting Alaska, Siberia and China, when 30,000 US Army personnel arrived in 1942 to work on
the highway. One homesick soldier put up a sign showing the distance and
direction to his home town, and unknowingly began a collection that now
includes 50,000 such signs. This 'world famous' **Sign Post Forest**, next to the
Information Centre, is the town's number one attraction. Across the highway

is the only other. The **Northern Lights Space and Science Centre** shows 50-minute films that present the myths and reality of the aurora borealis, and animal photos set to music. ■ *6 shows daily starting in the afternoon. $10, $6 concessions. T5367827, www.northernlightscentre.com*

Sleeping & eating All of Watson Lake's motels are are on the highway. Most have restaurants we could not recommend. **C** *Big Horn Hotel*, T5362020, has the nicest rooms. **C** *Gateway Motor Inn*, T5367712, has acceptable rooms, a second-rate pizza restaurant and a bar that's full of Yukon character. **D** *Belvedere Motor Hotel*, T5367712, has some cheap, unpleasant rooms, yet the most appealing restaurant. **Camping F** *Liard Canyon Campground*, 12 km east, is a pretty spot to spend the night. **F** *Campground Services*, just east of town, is not great but has showers and laundry and is much nicer than the RV parking lot in town. Far better is the **F** *Watson Lake Campground*, just west then 1.5 km on an access road, with 55 sites on the lake. For coffee and down-to-earth food, hang on for the *Wolf It Down Restaurant*, 26 km west.

Sports There are 80 km of **hiking** and **skiing** trails in and around town. To get out into the wilderness for **boating**, **horse riding** and **whitewater rafting**, contact *Ceasar Lake Outfitters*, T4435390, www.ceaserlake.com One of the Yukon's 5 **golf** courses, *Greenways Greens*, is 10 km west.

The Robert Campbell Highway The Robert Campbell Highway (Highway 4), a fairly rough gravel road, heads north from Watson Lake, joining the Klondike Highway just above Carmacks. This alternative route to Dawson City could be taken on the way up or down to create a loop, always a good idea in a land whose prime asset is its scenery. Having said that, the landscapes are fairly uneventful until the junction with the Canol Road at Ross River. Since the South Canol Road is one of the most beautiful stretches in the territory, it makes more sense to make a smaller loop from Johnson's Crossing to Ross River to Carmacks or vice versa.

Teslin

Colour map 5, grid B5 After a brief, barely noticeable foray back into BC, the road joins the attractive shores of Teslin Lake at the town of the same name. A kilometre before the long and stately bridge that crosses the lake is a viewpoint where the water and its backdrop of mountains can be savoured. A number of panels also provide an introduction to local wildlife, geography and First Nations history. Teslin is home to a thriving community of Native Tlingit, originally of coastal origin, who moved permanantly to their inland summer home in the early 1900s, prompted by the quest for furs. The arts and crafts of their West Coast heritage migrated with them, and provide a couple of good reasons to stop.

The largest collection of Tlinget artefacts is found at the small but splendid **George Johnston Museum**. This successful Tlingit trapper and entrepreneur opened the first aboriginal-owned store in town, and brought its first car, a 1928 Chevrolet exhibited in the museum. Of far greater interest is a fine collection of black and white prints taken by this self-taught and clearly gifted photographer, that candidly document 50 years of Teslin's history. For those with time to spare, there are also some interesting videos available to view at no extra charge. ■ *May-Sep 0930-1730. $5, $3 concessions. T3902550. Off the Highway on the north side of town.* On the same road is an interesting tepee-shaped church, adorned with stained-glass windows.

The best place to witness the work of talented local mask and totem carvers is further north on the highway at the new **Teslin Tlingit Heritage Centre**. Interpretive and audiovisual displays introduce the history and culture of the Tlinget, with an outdoor carving shed and their works are on display. ■ *May-Sep 0900-2100. $5. T1866-8546438, www.teslintlingits.ca*

Sleeping & eating

C *Yukon Motel*, on the highway, T3902575. Tidy rooms in a log building. F *Teslin Lake Campground*, 10 km north, has 27 fairly nice sites on the lake. The best place to eat locally is *Mukluk Annie's*,13 km north of town, T3902600. Salmon bake, made with delicious wild sockeye, is their specialty and is served with all-you-can-eat salad and tasty baked beans, a bargain at $17. And what's more, it comes with a free houseboat cruise on Teslin Lake at 2000! All-you-can-eat breakfast until 1100 for $8. Free overnight parking for anyone, or very primitive cabins to rent for $45. Showers and laundry available.

Sports

Teslin Lake is noted for its **fishing**. Chinook salmon run late Jul-mid Aug, whereas Spring and autumn are the best times for whitefish, trout, northern pike, Arctic grayling and inconnu. The Nisutlin Delta National Wildlife Area at the north end of Teslin Lake is a major **waterfowl** staging area, visited in autumn by thousands of ducks, swans and geese, and predators like peregrine falcon, fox, coyote and wolf who come to hunt them. It is also a prime spot for viewing larger **wildlife**, particularly moose. You can canoe there on Nisutlin River or the lake. A fairly easy 4-5-day **whitewater canoe/kayak** trip on the **Lower Nisutlin River** starts 69 km up the South Canol Rd and ends in Teslin. *Nisutlin Outfitting*, T3902123, www.nisutlinoutfitting.bigstep.com rent canoes for $25/day, $125/week and will shuttle for $1/mile. *Big Bear Adventures*, T6335642, run 7-day excursions on the much wilder *Wolf River*, also ending in Teslin, ($200/day all-in).

Johnson's Crossing

As well as a popular put-in spot for people canoeing the Teslin River to access the Yukon, Johnson's Crossing is the junction with the **Canol Road** (Highway 6). The controversial Canol (Canadian Oil) Pipeline was built by the US in 1942 to pump oil from Norman Wells NWT to a refinery in Whitehorse. It was dismantled after just one year of use. Today its southern section provides a chance to sample some of the Yukon's remote backcountry. The surface can be pretty rough, but the effort is well rewarded by the last stunning stretch before Ross River, when the road skirts close to picturesque Pass Peak, then winds its way through the **Lapie River Canyon**. On the way are three small campgrounds, the second on the shore of **Quiet Lake**, a pristine body of water favoured by anglers and paddlers.

The road continues northeast past increasingly remote lakes and rivers to the NWT border. It's very rough, often washed out, and has no services. The MacMillan Pass at the border marks the start of the **Canol Heritage Trail**, a long-distance trek the sheer logistics of which render it an almost unthinkable proposition. From Ross River, Highway 4 heads northwest through Faro to connect with the Klondike Highway near Carmacks, a very worthwhile alternative route to or from Dawson City, bypassing Whitehorse. The brand new **Dena Cho Trail**, T9692278, is an 80-km hike from Ross River to Faro, with campsites and cabins along the way.

Sleeping and eating AL-A *Inn on the River*, T6605253, www.exceptionalplaces.com A handsome log building with luxurious en suite rooms. Price includes breakfast, bikes, canoes, kayaks, etc. Delicious but expensive dinner for guests by arrangement. D *Johnson's Crossing Motel and Campground*, T3902607. Small but nice rooms, and campsites (F). There is a good bakery, famous for its cinnamon buns, that also has fast food like chicken and ribs sold by the kilo. F *Squanga Campground* is 22 km further north.

The Yukon

**Jake's Corner
& Marsh Lake**
There is little of note between Johnson's Crossing and Whitehorse. At Jake's Corner, two possible diversions present themselves. Easily the more worthwhile follows Highway 7 south for 95 km to the Atlin, BC. The other provides a loop on Highways 8 and 2, which takes in Carcross, a dull little village that nevertheless played an important role in the Klondike Gold Rush and today is gateway to the Chilkoot Trail and Skagway, Alaska. Beyond Jake's Corner, the northern end of Marsh Lake, known as McClintock Bay, is a critical habitat for migrating waterfowl in April and May. The arrival of thousands of Tundra and Trumpeter swans is heralded annually by the **Celebration of Swans Festival**. There is a viewing deck, Swan Haven Interpretive Centre, and a **F** campground.

Atlin, BC

Phone code: 250
Colour map 5, grid C4
Highway 7 to Atlin is a rough gravel and dirt road that mostly hugs the shore of BC's largest natural lake, which is also the headwater of the Yukon River. There are a few campgrounds along the way, and at Km 6 is the trailhead for the **Mount White** trail, one of the Yukon's most rewarding day-hikes. The path starts on the left at the back of a gravel pit by an orange generator, and climbs to a plateau that offers views over Little Atlin Lake and the Southern Lakes.

Atlin itself is a ramshackle little frontier-style village of funky houses full of friendly, arty and eccentric characters. It makes a relaxing spot to hang out, but don't expect entertainment, especially at the tiny museum. What is extraordinary about Atlin is its setting. As in the Yukon, to which it belongs in spirit, the landscapes here are unimaginably vast and offer a glimpse into true timeless wilderness. Rearing up behind the broad swath of Atlin Lake is a string of giant glaciated mountains belonging to the always impressive Coast Range. The sight defies description; it is primal, ancient, raw and magnificent.

For **information**, go straight to Heather at *Atlin's Happy Trails* (see Tour operators, page 411).

The mountain closest to town is actually on the enormous **Teresa Island**, a bear sanctuary and apparently the world's tallest freshwater island. The area behind it, around the lake's southern shore, is protected by **Atlin Provincial** and **Wilderness Parks**. Both are accessible only by boat, and a third of the latter is covered in glaciers. The biggest of these, Llewellen Glacier, can be seen from along Warm Bay Road, which follows the lake to the south. The best views of all are from the top of **Monarch Mountain**. This stiff 12-km return hike starts 5 km down Warm Bay Road, where there is also a beach. On the way up, stop at the **Atlin Centre for the Arts**, T6517659, www.atlinart.com, for a tour of their great studios. They offer three-week workshops that are highly renowned. The **Warm Springs**, about 24 km down this rough gravel road, are not hot enough to enjoy, but it's a pretty spot with camping and a small clear pool surrounded by watercress. Atlin is actually connected to Telegraph Creek by a bushwhacking, 362-km, 25-day trail. Bart de Haas guides hikers on this trail every year. Contact **Atlin Visitors Association**, T6517522.

Sleeping   **B** *Brewery Bay Chalet*, McBride Blvd, on the lake, T6510040, www.brewerybay.com 8 nice suites with 2 bedrooms and kitchenette. **B** *Win's Place*, T6517550. An entire charming and spacious cottage on the lake. Lower rent for longer stays. **C** *Atlin Inn* on Lake St, T6517546, atlininn@atlin.net, is the most likely place to have vacancies. Small but attractive and comfortable rooms, and some slightly cheaper but rather shabby cabins close to the water. They also have a restaurant with burgers, steak, fish, and great views, a pub and an expensive coffee shop. **C** *Quilts & Comforts B&B*, Pillman Rd, T6510007, www.quiltsandcomforts.com 3 very small and twee rooms. Good

The Chilkoot Pass

◀

The most common method for the 100,000 or so stampeders to get to the Klondike Gold Fields (see page 421) was to catch an ocean liner to Skagway, then trek over the dreaded Chilkoot Pass to the bottom end of Bennett Lake, from where they could proceed by boat. To make it infinitely worse, the Canadian authorities, feeling threatened by this mass migration of unruly Americans, established a North West Mounted Police post at the pass to collect duty and make sure that every American had enough supplies to last them for a whole year. Together with tents and mining equipment, this usually added up to a load of over a ton.

It took the average strong man as many as 40 ascents to the pass to do it, at least 90 days of tough, soul-destroying hiking.

*Today, the **Chilkoot Trail** is Canada's largest National Historic Site, and a very popular hike. The 55-km route, which takes three tough days to complete, is lined with remnants of abandoned mining equipment and interpretive signs. There is often still snow at the pass well into July. A permit is required to hike the trail, and the number of hikers departing each day is limited. Call Parks Canada at T6673910, or write to/visit them at Rm 205, 300 Main St, Whitehorse, YT Y1A 2B5, www.harbour.com/parkscan/ct*

breakfast. Beautiful perennial garden with deck and views. For the best views of Llewellyn Glacier stay at **D** *Glacier View Cabins*, 12 km on Warm Bay Rd, T6517691. 2 simple but lovely cabins with bedroom and living room/kitchen.

Camping There are a couple of campgrounds north of town, but the best bet is along Warm Bay Rd to the south. **F** *Pine Creek*, at 5 km, is handy but not as nice as the forestry sites further on like Como Lake, Surprise Lake and Warm Bay. A particularly nice spot right on the lake is at Km 24.

The *Atlin Inn* is the best for food. *Pine Tree Café* on Discovery Av, is a diner-style joint. **Eating**
The Garret Store on Pearl Av has good **coffee** in the back with couches and magazines, local crafts and some good used books. Be sure to try the local **smoked salmon**, available almost everywhere.

Go first to Heather at *Atlin's Happy Trails*, on the lake at McBride Blvd. She is very help- **Tour**
ful with information about trails and boat trips, rents bikes ($7 per hour, $27 per day), **operators**
sells topo maps and can set you up with any kind of tour. *Atlin Lake Houseboat Tours*,
T6510030, www.AtlinLakeHouseboatTours.com, run trips from the central dock to
Teresa Island. *Atlin Quest*, T6517659, www.atlinquest.com Boat tours, glacier walks,
guided hikes. *Atlin General Store*, on Lake St, and *Sidka Tours*, sidkatours@
atlin.net, rent out canoes ($25), the latter also kayaks ($30).

The *Atlin Express*, T6517617, leaves Mon, Wed and Fri, from the *Bonanza Inn* in White- **Transport**
horse at 1215, and leaves Atlin from the *Atlin Inn* on the same days at 0615. $40 return.
With your own transport you could explore the mining roads that cross the area. Otherwise you'll have to rely on tours or rent a canoe. Hitching in might entail a long wait.

Atlin is part of a region touted as the **Southern Lakes**, which contains more **Carcross**
than 600 linear kilometres of thin lakes within an area of some 100 sq km.
Canoeing, boating and fishing are major local activities, and the winds are
often strong enough for windsurfing. A loop on Highways 8 and 2 from Jake's
Corner leads to the heart of this area, adding just 38 km to the journey to
Whitehorse. Despite a lack of real attractions, many visitors make the diversion thanks to the important role the area played in the Klondike Gold Rush
(see page 421). Skookum Jim Mason, who first sparked the stampede with his

The Yukon

discovery of gold on what became known as Bonanza Creek, was a member of the Tagish First Nation, but there is little reason to stop in **Tagish**.

The hub of the region is Carcross, whose name was shortened from the more evocative Caribou Crossing. It sits at the north end of Bennett Lake, which has some large sandy beaches and is a favourite with windsurfers. Prospectors that made it over the Chilkoot Pass travelled up the lake to here. The town has clearly remained almost unchanged since those heady days, and is of interest mainly for its many historical buildings and general run-down frontier town atmosphere. There is practically nothing to do but stroll around and dream of the past, unless you are here to retrace the steps of the many hopefuls on the **Chilkoot Trail** (see box). There is nowhere worth mentioning to stay or eat in Carcross. Ask at the **Visitor Centre**, T8214431, www.yukonsoutherlakes.com, situated in the restored train station, May-September 0800-2000.

Onwards from Carcross
The train played its own part in transporting prospectors, a role celebrated today by the **White Pass and Yukon Railway** which carries tourists along the historic route to Skagway, a six-hour train ride. ■ *1300, US$90 (if bought in advance, otherwise more), T907-9832217, www.whitepassrailroad.com* Non-Americans must clear custom in advance or get off at **Fraser** (US$30 one way). Buses also continue to **Skagway**, which is a busy and expensive Alaskan town where many ferries and cruise boats unload. A short but costly ferry runs down the Taiya Inlet to the extremely pretty community of **Haines**, part of a popular circuit that is continued by taking US Highway 7/Canada Highway 3 north to Haines Junction in Kluane Country, a beautiful drive through some of the Yukon's most extravagent mountain landscapes.

Appropriately known as the Klondike Highway, Highway 2 follows the Gold Rush trail north from Carcross through Whitehorse to Dawson City. The southern leg soon passes **Carcross Desert**, really a dried out lake bottom, very small and not especially impressive. A little further are the pretty **Emerald and Spirit Lakes**, where there is a very primitive private campsite, along with an unpleasant motel/cabin. **Annie Lake Road** branches west at the Robinson Roadhouse historic site and winds its way up the scenic Wheaton River Valley. There are lots of opportunities for hiking and mountain biking along here, such as the **Red Ridge** and **Two Horse Creek** trails, and experienced paddlers can canoe down the Wheaton or Watson Rivers to Bennett Lake.

Kluane Country

Some 10 km beyond Whitehorse, the Klondike Highway continues north towards Dawson City, while the Alaska Highway veers westwards to some of Canada's most outstanding mountain scenery around Kluane National Park. The unavoidable service centre of this sublime region, and its only town of any size, is Haines Junction, from where two roads skirt along the park's eastern boundary. Both are part of worthwhile loops from Whitehorse. The Alaska Highway passes the lovely Kluane Lake, and the park's main focus at Sheep Mountain, which has the best visitor centre and the greatest concentration of hikes. The road continues into Alaska before heading north and then east to connect with the wonderful Top of the World Highway to Dawson City. The Haines Highway heads south over the Chilkat Pass, through scenery exceptional even by local standards, to BC and Haines, Alaska. From this delightful little town, US ferries and water taxis make the short journey to Skagway. The road back to Whitehorse via Carcross then parallels the route taken by the Gold Rush stampeders in 1898.

Seventy kilometres west of Whitehorse, a good dirt road heads 20 km south to **Kusawa Lake**, a local favourite for hiking, fishing and canoeing. There is a small eight-site campground at Km 14.5, and a bigger one on the lake at Km 22.5. The latter is the put-in for the 25-km, one-day canoe trip up the Takhini River, the most popular day-paddle from Whitehorse. Rated class II-III, with one easily portaged set of rapids, this is ideal for beginners/intermediates. **Kwaday Dan Kenji** (Long Ago People's Place), 23 km further on, is a traditional First Nations camp with displays on the history and culture of the Southern Tutchone people, guided tours, and a campground. Another 26 km on the highway, then 42 km on a dirt road, leads to the quiet and remote **Aishihik Lake**, a local fishing hole with a small campground. **Otter Falls**, on the way at Km 30, is home to a small herd of bison and some good mountain bike trails.

West to Haines Junction

Haines Junction

Haines Junction, 92 km further on, is an ugly little town, but a vital stop for organizing excursions and picking up supplies. The principal **Visitor Reception Centre** for **Kluane National Park** is here (follow signs). The **Parks Office**, T6347207, Summer 0900-1900 daily, winter 1300-1600 Monday-Friday only, gives out maps and key information on trails and backcountry routes, takes the essential registrations, and hands out a calendar of interpretive events such as guided walks and hikes. **Yukon Tourism**, T6342345, in the same building, May-September 0800-2000, deals with provincial enquiries.

Phone code: 867
Colour map 5, grid B3
Population: 800

The junction itself, marked by what looks like a giant cupcake with cement animals crawling out of the icing, is an important one: Whitehorse is 158 km east, Kluane Lake some 60 km northwest, and Haines, Alaska, is 241 km south via one of the region's most stunning roads.

B *Raven Hotel and Gourmet Dining*, T6342500, www.yukonweb.com/tourism/raven The nicest place to stay. Good food, breakfast included in room, nice and new. **C** *Laughing Moose B&B*, T6342335, has a self-contained apartment with kitchen and large living room. **D** *Cozy Corner Motel*, on the Alaska Hwy at the north end of town, T6342119, is about the best of the many standard motels, and has a restaurant. Campers should stop at the lovely *Pine Lake Campground*, 7 km east of town. *Village Bakery and Deli*, across from the Visitor Centre, has good bread, muffins, pizza, quiche, espresso and smoked salmon.

Eating & sleeping

The *Alsek Music Festival* in early **Jun** is a 3-day outdoor event featuring music mainly from the Yukon. Later that month, the *Kluane Chilkat International Bike Rally* is a 238-km relay race for up to 8 people from HJ to Haines.

Festivals

A number of tour operators based in town run trips into the park. A good first stop is *Paddle/Wheel Adventures*, across from the Visitor Centre, T6342683, www.paddlewheel adventures.com They rent bikes and canoes, run shuttles to trailheads, and can book you onto tours with guiding companies. **Hiking/ kayaking** *Kluane Ecotours* on Haines Rd, T6342626, www.kluaneco.com Personalized 2-10-day trips with a naturalist and guide. **Rafting** *Tatshenshini Rafting Expeditions*, T6332742. 1-11-day trips, leaving daily, through scenery on a river that has the best reputation for whitewater rafting in the Yukon, if not Canada. $100 for 1 day. **Horse riding** *Yukon Trail Riding*, T6342386. Excursions of varying lengths. **Flights** *Kluane Glacier Tours*, T6342916, www.kluane glaciertours.com *Kluane Helicopters*, T6342224, khmi@yknet@yk.ca and *Trans North Helicopters*, TT6682177, www.tntaheli.com, all run glacier tours, providing a way of getting into the most striking landscapes for hiking, fishing, skiing or just flightseeing.

Tour operators

The Yukon

Kluane National Park

This extraordinary park is part of the largest internationally protected area in the world, which also embraces Alaska's massive Wrangell-St Elias National Park to the west, Tatshenshini-Alsek Wilderness Park in BC to the south, and Glacier Bay National Park further south in Alaska. Together they are recognized by UNESCO as a World Heritage Site. Everything in Kluane National Park (pronounced Kloo-ah-nee) is of an exaggerated scale. The Saint Elias Range is the second highest set of coastal mountains in the world after the Andes, containing Mount McKinley, North America's highest peak at 6,193 m, and Mount Logan, Canada's highest at 5,959 m. Bearing sheets of ice over 1.5 km thick, this rugged, awesome range contains the largest non-polar icefields in the world, with glaciers extending up to 112 km down its broad valleys. Together with the surprisingly lush lower valleys of the front ranges, these landscapes contain the greatest diversity of flora and fauna in northern Canada, including mountain goats, moose, rare silver-blue glacier bears, wolves, Dall sheep and the world's greatest concentration of grizzly bears. This may well be the only protected area in North America large enough to ensure the long-term survival of the grizzly, and the chance of stumbling upon one here is far greater than in the more famous parks to the south.

Ins and outs

Getting there & around   Access to the bulk of the park is virtually impossible except by air. Only its eastern edge is bordered by roads. The southern section, reached from the Haines Highway, tends to be greener and lusher; the northern part, accessed from the Alaska Highway, has the greater concentration of trails, and is more arid. Stunning as the views may be, the really big mountains of the St Elias Range are almost perpetually hidden by the lower front ranges, with only the occasional glimpse offering the motorist a hint of what is being missed. Helicopter tours, rafting trips, and overnight hikes are the only real ways to get closer.

Park information   *Kluane National Park Hiking Guide* by Vivien Lougheed can be picked up at the Visitor Centre. As well as the bear situation, hikers should be aware that most routes in the park often involve difficult creek crossings, with no bridges and extremely cold, fast-flowing water. It is not a good idea to go bare-footed and you are advised to take a pair of creek-crossing shoes, such as old sneakers or well-fitting sandals. Registration for backcountry hiking is obligatory. A fee of $5 per person per night is charged for camping, which is allowed anywhere, except on the Cottonwood trail which has designated sites. The normal no-trace ethical rules apply (see page 33).

Hiking in Kluane National Park

Day-hikes   **From Haines Highway: King's Throne** (10 km return, 4 hours, 1,220 m elevation gain. Trailhead: Kathleen Lake day use area, 26 km south of Haines Junction) A well-defined trail switchbacks fairly steeply to a saddle at Km 5, offering expansive views. The hike can be continued along a ridge, with ever-greater views as the peak is approached, a possible 10-hour hike in all, and one of the park's most popular.

Rock Glacier (1.5 km, 30 minutes. Trailhead: 44 km south of Haines Junction) Short and easy hike on a former glacier, leading to good views.

St Elias Lake (7.6 km, 3 hrs, 120 m elevation gain. Trailhead: 60 km south of Haines Junction) A fairly easy but rewarding hike, with the chance of scrambling to better views.

From Sheep Mountain: **Sheep Creek** (10 km, 4-5 hours, 430 m elevation gain. Trailhead: Visitor Centre) Exceptional views for so short a hike.

Sheep-Bullion Plateau (24 km, 7-8 hours, 880 m elevation gain. Trailhead: Visitor Centre) A beautiful area with diverse plant life as well as views of the valley, a glacier toe, and the striking Red Castle Ridge. Home to bear families, so potentially dangerous. Could be treated as a two-day trip.

Soldiers Summit (1 km, 30-40 minutes, 90 m elevation gain. Trailhead: 1 km north of the Visitor Centre) Easily the best very short hike.

Sheep Mountain Ridge (11-km loop, 6-10 hours, 1,310 m elevation gain. Trailhead: 2 km north of Visitor Centre) Wonderful views of the lake, Slims River Valley, mountains and glaciers, and the chance to see up to 200 sheep.

Cottonwood (83-km loop, 4-6 days, 520 m elevation gain. Trailhead: 27 or 55 km south of Haines Junction) A well-marked trail through more lush surroundings giving great views of towering mountains. Lots of creek crossings.

Overnight hikes
From north to south

Alsek (52 km, 2-3 days, 90 m elevation gain. Trailhead: 10 km north of Haines Junction on Alaska Highway) Long but fairly easy trek down a spectacular valley. Good introduction for the inexperienced hiker.

Slims East (46 km, 2-4 days, 910 m elevation gain. Trailhead: 3 km south of the Visitor Centre) Not quite as spectacular as the Slims West, but a better trail, and certainly recommended. Also has lots of grizzlies.

Slims West (60 km, 3-5 days, 1,340 m elevation gain. Trailhead: Sheep Mountain Visitor Centre) Most popular overnight hike in the park, leading to Observation Peak and probably the best views of glaciers and mountains to be had without a guide, backcountry expertise or dishing out lots of money. High concentration of grizzlies causes frequent closures.

Donjek Glacier (96-km loop, 6-10 days. Trailhead: Duke River, 9 km north of Burwash Landing) A long, demanding hike, very popular with experienced hikers, many of whom come to Kluane just to do it.

The park's two main rivers, the Tatshenshini and Alsek, both run south through BC's Wilderness Reserve and into Alaska. Their forested valleys provide the only two green corridors through the towering icy realm of the St Elias Mountains. Not only are these two of the most beautiful, pristine rivers in North America, but they also provide access to a remote world few people ever get to see. The most popular way to get there, highly recommended for anyone, is on a whitewater rafting tour of the Tatshenshini. See Sports, below, and Haines Junction (see page 415 for details).

Rivers in Kluane National Park

Tatshenshini River (215 km, 10-14 days, class III-IV. Put-in: Dalton Post. Take-out: Dry Bay, near Yakutat, Alaska) **Upper Tatshenshini** (40 km, 1-2 days, class III-IV. Put-in: 110 km south of Haines Junction. Take-out: Dalton Post) The Yukon's most popular day-trip for rafters and experienced kayakers/canoeists. This short trip can act as a prelude to the former, or can be reached via **Blanchard River** (26 km, including 15 km on the Tatshenshini. Day-trip. Class II-III. Put-in: 105 km south on the Haines Hwy. Take-out: Dalton Post). **Alsek River** (290 km, 10-14 days, featuring class IV rapids. Put-in: Dezadeash River, Haines Junction. Take-out: Dry Bay, near Yakutat, Alaska) A tough trip for experienced kayakers only.

Rafting, kayaking & canoeing
Both rivers draw experienced kayakers and canoeists

There are some excellent **mountain biking** routes in the park. **Mush Lake Road** and the Alsek trail are recommended. **Cross-country skiing** in winter is also first class, especially on the **Cottonwood** and **Dezadeash** trails, or around the Chilkat Pass, where you can ski as late as June. The 15-km **Auriol** trail, 7 km south of Haines Junction is over-rated for

Other sports

The Yukon

hiking, but good for its groomed ski trails. Ski touring is great in the Mt Decoeli area. Mts Logan, St Elias, Steele, etc, are magnets for world-class **mountaineering**.

Haines Highway	Highway 3, the Haines Highway, heads south through glorious alpine terrain that slowly builds over a distance of 144 km to the crescendo of Chilkat Pass. At Km 26 is **Kathleen Lake**, the start of a number of hikes, whose facilities include the only campground within the park. At Km 62 is **Klukshu**, meaning 'coho place' in Tlingit (coho being a kind of salmon). Klukshu is a traditional First Nations salmon-fishing village that welcomes visitors with a small museum, a craft shop, smokehouses, and signs detailing the people's traditional way of life. Slightly more authentic is **Dalton Post** (Shäwshe), 22 km further on then 5 km down a dirt road. Situated on the Tatshenshini River, this is a key put-in/take-out for rafts and kayaks (see above). In British Columbia, the road follows the eastern boundary of Tatshenshini-Alsek Wilderness Park, almost inaccessible except on a guided rafting trip. The **US Customs** post at Km 170 is open from 0800-2400.

Anyone considering doing the Haines-Skagway-Whitehorse loop should be aware that the short journey by Alaskan ferry is expensive by Canadian standards. Skagway is a particularly touristy place inundated with cruise-ship passengers and, Gold Rush paraphernalia aside, the drive north is of limited interest compared to the Haines Highway. It almost makes more sense to drive Highway 3 to Haines *and back*, enjoying the exquisite views a second time, and continuing on to Kluane Lake and Sheep Mountain.

Sleeping C *The Cabin B&B*, just south of Kathleen Lake, T/F6342626. 5 guest cabins in the woods with kitchenettes and sauna. **Camping** The only campground actually in the park is F *Kathleen Lake*, at Km 26, with 39 sites. At Km 50 is F *Dezadeash Lake*, with 20 sites. At Km 79 is F *Million Dollar Falls*, with 35 sites including 8 tent-only.

Haines, Alaska	Haines is a delightfully attractive, laid-back little town, very different from the bigger, overtly touristy and expensive Skagway. The **Visitor Bureau** is at 2nd Avenue near Willard Street, T1800-4583579, Monday-Friday 0800-1800, Saturday-Sunday 1000-1600, www.haines.ak.us There are some good hikes from town, notably those to **Mount Ripinsky** and **Seduction Point**.

Sleeping and eating The best rooms are in the old army officers' quarters of the **B-C** *Fort Seward Lodge*, Haines Hwy, T7662009, www.ftsewardlodge.com For food, head to the *Bamboo Room*, 2nd Av, near Main, and for a drink try the *Fog Cutter Bar*.

Transport Regular **ferries** up the Taiya Inlet to Skagway are operated by *Fast Ferry*, T1888-7662103, www.chilkatcruises.com *Haines-Skagway Water Taxi*, T1888-7663396, www.alaskafjordlines.com and *Alaska Marine Highway*, T1800-6420066, www.alaska.gov The 35-min crossing costs roughly US$24 one-way, US$35 return.

Alaska Highway	Interpretive panels are dotted along this highway, but few are of real interest except to hard-core history enthusiasts. The first reason to stop west of Haines Junction is the **Kluane Lake** viewpoint at Km 60, with winning views over the Yukon's largest lake. Anglers should note that Kluane is a Southern Tutchone word meaning 'lake with many fish'. Another 11 km brings you to the only **Visitor Centre** in the park at **Sheep Mountain**, mid-May to September 0800-2000. Information here tends to be that much sharper than at Haines Junction, because the staff are generally young, enthusiastic rangers who actually get out regularly onto the trails. Sheep Mountain itself is often dotted with

the herd of Dall sheep after which it is named, but they are most easily seen from September to early June when there are no people around. Many of the park's hikes start conveniently close to the Visitor Centre. Nearby on the lake the **Arctic Institute** has an interpretive room with details on expeditions and research in the St Elias icefields.

Burwash Landing, 72 km past Sheep Mountain, is an old community of 100 people, home to the **Kluane Museum of Natural History**. As well as fossils and minerals from the area, there is a decent collection of First Nation artefacts and a number of wildlife dioramas. ■ *Mid-May to mid-Sep. By donation. T8415561.* The **Icefield Ranges viewpoint**, 57 km further on, is one of the best places to stop for views of those elusive St Elias Mountains, as well as the dramatic Donjek River Valley.

C *Kluane B&B*, 11 km south of Sheep Mountain at Destruction Bay, Mobile Operator 867 2M 3924, Destruction Bay channel. Cabins on the beach, with kitchen, shower, bike rentals. On the lake close to Sheep Mountain is **B-E** *Kluane Mun*, T/F8414551. Lakeside lodge rooms, dorms, camping. Hot tub and one of the only restaurants around. They arrange fishing, hiking, rafting and snowmobile trips. **C** *Burwash Landing Resort*, off the highway on the lake, T403-8414441. Standard rooms with old beds, restaurant with reasonable if predictable menu. **Camping** **F** *Congdon Creek*, 17 km west of Sheep Mountain with 81 sites. **F** *Lake Creek*, 131 km further with 27 sites. **F** *Snag Junction*, 59 km further with 15 sites. | **Sleeping & eating**

Just before the border with Alaska is the tiny and grim village of Beaver Creek. The coldest temperature ever recorded in Canada was measured close to here at a place called Snag. It was minus 62.8°C. There is a summer-only **Visitor Centre** here, T8627321, open daily 0800-2000. | **Beaver Creek**

Sleeping and eating **B** *Westmark Hotel*, T8627501. The best place to stay. Small but pleasant rooms with no TVs. Bar, recreation room and restaurant with theatre in the evening. Typical of the motley gang of motels is **D** *1202 Motor Inn*, T8627600. Ugly and basic rooms, some hostel-style for **E** .

Those looping straight to Dawson City still have to pay US$6 at the border, which is open 24-hours. Unless you want to sample the limited charms of Tok, bear north at Teslin Junction onto Taylor Highway 5, a windy dirt road through a narrow valley, where gold panners can still be seen at work. The drive is unexceptional until you cross back into the Yukon at **Little Gold Creek**. The border here is only open 0900-2100, with the US side an hour behind. From here the aptly-named Top of the World Highway affords unspeakably gorgeous views, with bare, multicoloured hills in the foreground and mountain peaks lining up on the horizon. This is the ultimate way to enter Dawson City, 105 km away. | **Top of the World Highway**

Klondike Highway

*By Yukon standards, the Klondike Highway north of Whitehorse is a pretty dull drive. The minor towns of **Carmacks** and **Pelly Crossing** offer little reason to stop. A worthwhile side-trip off the beaten track is down the **Silver Trail** (Highway 11) to Faro and the tiny, quaint, artist-dominated village of **Keno**. Just south of the turn-off, a dirt road leads to **Ethel Lake**, a beautiful camping and fishing spot for those seeking tranquility. Remainders of very large forest fires along the highway offer the chance of hunting for morel mushrooms.* | *For Camping on the Klondike Highway see page 421*

The Yukon

Carmacks
Phone code: 867
Colour map 5, grid A4
Population: 500
Native band:
mid-way between
the Southern and
Northern Tutchone

The Yukon River crosses the highway at Carmacks, 176 km from Whitehorse, making it a useful provisions stop. Camping and fishing supplies can be picked up at **Tatchun Centre Store** (0700-2300). A pleasant 2-km boardwalk runs along the river from the summer-only **Carmacks Visitor Centre**, T8636271. Ask here about local trails leading to areas good for seeking agates and other semi-precious stones. The town's main sight is the **Tage Cho Hudan Interpretive Centre**, which has displays on First Nations culture and history, an interpretive trail and local handicrafts. ■ *T8635576. Free.*

Sleeping About the only places to stay are **C** *Hotel Carmacks*, T8636171, with standard rooms, cabins and a restaurant; and **C** *Northstar B&B*, 130 Dawson Dr, T9942243. 5 rooms with shared bath, kitchen, living room.

Tour operators *Experience Yukon*, T8636021, rent canoes and run tours to **Five Finger Rapids** and **Fort Selkirk**.

Robert Campbell Highway to Faro

The region west of Carmacks is named Campbell after Robert Campbell, a Hudson's Bay Company employee who was sent here in the 1840s to open up new fur trading routes. Following established trails blazed by the Native Kaska Dena people, Campbell built a chain of trading posts culminating in Fort Selkirk (see below). Sent back to England after a decade of exploration, he (to quote the *Yukon Tourism* brochure) "publicized grandiose memoirs of his travels, despite more private reflections of a north he hated and feared".

The highway that bears his name (Highway 4) heads east just north of Carmacks and connects with the South Canol Road at Ross River, a fine alternative route that bypasses Whitehorse and Carmacks. The Tatchun/Frenchman Road cuts the corner between this and the Klondike Highway, offering a remote diversion lined with small lakes and several lovely campgrounds. Further east, Little Salmon Lake is a pleasant fishing spot with two tiny picturesque campgrounds.

Faro

The only town before the junction at Ross River, Faro is situated in the remarkably broad Tintina Trench, an important wildlife corridor that attracts millions of migrating birds and harbours one of the highest concentrations of moose and wolves in the province. A breed of sheep unique to Faro, the Fannin, can be seen at Mount Mye Sheep Centre, a 10-km hike from the 1.5-km **Van Gorder Falls** trail. The summer-only **Campbell Region Interpretive Centre**, T9942728, www.faro.yk.net, has some displays of marginal interest, but will provide information. The *Farrago Revival* in mid-August, T9942728, is a newly resuscitated music festival, mostly featuring Yukon artists. A week later is the jamboree bag of the *Fireweed Festival*. The new **Dena Cho** trail, T9692278, follows a historic gold prospector route between Faro and Ross River. Still a work in progress, it will soon feature five overnight cabins.

Five Fingers Rapids & Fort Selkirk

Just north of Carmacks is a viewpoint looking down on Five Fingers Rapids, one of the most treacherous spots on the Yukon River, with many a sunken sternwheeler to its name. A 1-km boardwalk leads to an observation deck with better views of the five whitewater channels that funnel between four small islands. At Pelly Crossing is **Big Jonathan House**, T5373331, which contains displays of native artefacts, arts and crafts. It's a replica of a building still standing in Fort Selkirk, due west at the confluence of the Yukon and Pelly Rivers, accessible only by water. For centuries before the fort was established by Robert Campbell in 1848, this spot was a gathering and trading place for various

◀

The Klondike Gold Rush

The Klondike bonanza began when George Washington Carmack and his native brothers-in-law Skookum Jim and Tagish Charley prospected on Rabbit Creek, a tributary of the Klondike River, following a tip from a Nova Scotian named Robert Henderson. Legend has it that on 17 August 1896, at the spot now named Discovery Claim on the creek now renamed Bonanza, Carmacks pulled out a nugget the size of his thumb, later talking about layers of gold between slabs of rock "like cheese sandwiches". The trio staked their claim, and when word got out miners already in the vicinity staked every creek in the Klondike and Indian River watersheds, including the unthinkably bountiful Eldorado. By that winter, when snow and ice quarantined the region from the rest of the world, all the big money had already been secured by the fortunate few. A second wave of West Coast prospectors arrived the following spring to fight for the remaining scraps, but the real story was yet to begin.

In mid-July 1897, some of the newly rich were seen in San Francisco struggling from the Excelsior with more gold than they could carry. When the Portland docked in Seattle, the press were waiting, and the Post-Intelligencer's description of "a ton of gold" effectively sparked off the stampede. In an atmosphere of great econmomic depression, thousands suddenly sold off their possessions or used their hoarded funds to answer the call to

adventure and fortune. It has been estimated that over a million souls left their homes, of which only 100,000 made it to the Yukon. Only 20% of these ever panned for gold, a fifth of that number actually found some, and very few made that elusive fortune. The rich pickings had, after all, been snapped up long since.

In retrospect, it seems that the real point for many, like writer Jack London, was not finding the gold but being part of the quest. And what a crazy journey it was. The richest travelled up the coast to the mouth of the Yukon in Alaska, and upriver from there. The unfortunate and gullible were hoodwinked into taking the bogus 'All Canadian Routes' through Edmonton and BC, spending two years on hellish trails, if they made it at all. The majority took ocean liners to Skagway, laboured their way over the fearsome Chilkoot Pass (see page 413) and waited out the winter somewhere between Carcross and Whitehorse. They then constructed makeshift boats to cover the last 800 treacherous kilometres down the Yukon River. Those who could afford it took one of the 60 sternwheelers that plied the river. Between them, the goldseekers spent some $50 million reaching the Klondike, about an equal sum to what was extracted from the creeks in the first five years of mining. Almost every town in Western Canada was affected by the stampede, and the Yukon Territory itself was created in 1898 to assert sovereignty over the region.

The Yukon

native bands. Later used by Gold Rush stampeders and the RCMP, the settlement was practically abandoned following the completion of the highway in the 1950s. Today about 40 buildings stand in good repair, with renovation projects ongoing. There is a campground, and in summer staff talk visitors through its long history. Other than paddling down by canoe, you can go with operators from Carmacks (see above).

The following are all Yukon Government sites and non-reservable. They tend to be in attractive locations, usually situated right on lakes or creeks, good for fishing and paddling. From south to north: **F** *Lake Laberge*, 36 km north of Klondike/Alaska junction, 22 sites. At Km 58 is **F** *Fox Lake*, 33 sites, 3 tent-only. At Km 119 is the very small and pretty **F** *Twin Lakes*, with 8 sites. *Pelly Crossing* has a free campground, left just before the bridge. 62 km north a side-road leads 24 km to the particularly idyllic **F** *Ethel Lake*,

Camping on the Klondike Highway

with 14 sites. **F** *Tatchun Creek*, 26 km north of Carmacks, has 12 sites. **F** *Moose Creek*, 25 km beyond Stewart Crossing, has 36 sites, 6 tent-only.

The Silver Trail

The Yukon's first small Gold Rush occurred on the Stewart River in 1883, but ultimately the area proved more successful with its high-grade lead-silver ore. Better known as the Silver Trail, Highway 11 from **Stewart Crossing** is one of the Yukon's more worthwhile side-tracks, leading past abandoned home-steads and mining equipment to the sleepy, ramshackle communities of Mayo (Km 53), Elsa (Km 96) and Keno (Km 112).

Mayo & Elsa
Phone code: 867
Colour map 5, grid A4/5
Population: 500

Watch for moose on the first 15 km of the Silver Trail, as this is a calving habi-tat. The road is paved as far as Mayo, whose **Visitor Centre**, T9962926, www.silvertrail.net, is housed in historic Binet House, which also has a col-lection of historic photos and displays on local natural history, flora and fauna. There's a viewing deck overlooking the river, but not much to do. Minto Lake Road is a good place for genuine **gold panning**. Ask the Mayo Mining Recorder which streams are open, T9962256. **Elsa** is now essentially a ghost town, though its United Keno Mine continued to operate until 1989.

Sleeping Mayo: **D** *Bedrock Motel*, T9962290, has a licensed lounge and continental breakfasts. **D** *North Star Motel*, T9962231, has kitchenettes and private showers. **Camping F** *Whispering Willows* in town, T9962284, caters to RVers, but tenters should hold on for **F** *Five Mile Lake Campground* 7 km further on, with 20 sites, swim-ming, fishing, and a trail around the lake.

Keno
Phone code: 867
Colour map 5, grid A5
Population: about 30

The dirt road deteriorates towards Keno, but this funky little village is the highlight of the trip, one of the Yukon's quirky little gems. A small cluster of log cabins mainly populated by artists, miners and eccentrics, Keno's authen-tic character remains as yet uncompromised. Housed in a boom-time dance hall, **Keno City Mining Museum** has an extensive collection of old photo-graphs, mining artefacts and local alpine butterflies. ■ *Jun-Aug 1000-1800*, T9952792. A huge number of butterflies are to be found at **Keno Hill**, along with wild flowers, a famous milepost and great views. A network of hiking trails criss-crosses the surrounding area. Ask in Mayo, or visit www.kenocity.yk.net

Sleeping and eating C *Keno Cabins*, T9952892, www.kenocity.info/cabins, have 2 very nice, cosy units. The summer-only **F** *Keno City Campground* consists of 7 sites on Lightning Creek. *Keno City Snack Bar* has pizza and light meals. *Mooseberry Bakery* serves delicious homemade treats and coffee in a renovated 1922 cabin.

Sports
The Silver Trail provides easiest access to the **Peel Wilderness**, one of the most remote areas on earth. Experienced local paddlers know that some of the Yukon's very best **canoeing** is down the pristine rivers of the Peel watershed, particularly the Wind, the Snake and the Bonnet Plume. The sanctity of these waters, which flow through the heart of the Mackenzie Mountains and harbour large animal popula-tions, has been preserved by their very remoteness. Access is by floatplane, difficult and expensive. Trips lasting about 2 weeks, with class II-III waters, are organized by a couple of well-respected operators. *Subarctic Wilderness Tours*, T9952412, www.keno city.yk.net, is a local company that tailors tours to suit people wanting to get off the tourist trail. Average $150 per person per day, including canoes and all

equipment. *Big Bear Adventures*, T6335642, www.bear.yk.net, is a reliable outfit arranging all kinds of trips on these rivers, $200 per day all in.

There is great **hiking** and **mountain biking** off the Silver Trail, with many mining roads to explore. A trail map is available at the Mayo Visitor Centre. For the best views, hike the **Mount Haldane** trail, 6 hrs return, from Halfway Lakes between Mayo and Keno. **Wind River Adventures** in Mayo, T99622273, www.windriveryukon.com, offer guided **horse-riding** trips into the wilderness.

Back on the Klondike, 121 km north of Stewart Crossing, is the Tintina Trench viewpoint, with vistas of the Klondike River and a valley so big that it stands out clearly on satellite photos. The product of the largest geological fault in North America, the trench apparently provides visible proof of the concept of plate tectonics. The Dempster Highway branches off 20 km later (see page 430), and 39 km beyond you roll into the ultimate apotheosis of Gold Rush memorabilia, Dawson City.

Tintina Trench

Dawson City

All the unavoidable Gold Rush paraphernalia in every village and roadside in the province culminates in Dawson City. To visit the Yukon and not come here is like going to Agra and failing to see the Taj Mahal. Dawson was the ultimate boom-town, site of the biggest stampede to the most productive gold fields of all time. Canadian history doesn't get any more exciting than this.

Phone code: 867
Colour map 7, grid C3
Population: 1,251

To get the most out of this evocative throwback to an adventurous era, you have to submerge yourself in the history. Reading a work like Pierre Berton's bestseller Klondike (1958) certainly helps. You also have to enter into the spirit of the place. At the heart of summer, when the streets throng with thousands of tourists and the atmosphere is more that of theme-park than museum, you may decide that Dawson has been saved at the expense of its character and soul. But its soul remains that of a party town, so go gambling at Diamond Tooth Gertie's, *catch the Gas-light Follies show at the* Palace, *have a few drinks in the saloon, and dream of gold.*

The Yukon

Ins and outs

The **airport**, 19 km southeast on the Klondike Hwy, receives flights from Whitehorse and Fairbanks. A shuttle service runs to town ($10). A taxi costs $23 for the same jour-ney. Shuttle **buses** from Whitehorse and Fairbanks arrive Downtown.

Getting there

Most people arrive in Dawson in their own vehicle. Entering on the Klondike High-way gives an idea of the extent to which the land hereabouts has been plundered. For almost 10 km you pass through a valley that has been turned into a desolate waste-land, littered with huge boulders and abandoned mining equipment. Hidden until the last moment, the town swings abruptly into view. An equally fine introduction is on the Top of the World Highway (see page 419). A free ferry runs 24-hrs daily from late May to mid-Oct across the Yukon River to connect the town with the highway, the best campground and a hostel.

The best place to start a tour of town is at the **Visitor Reception Centre** by the river on Front Street, www.dawsoncity.com, mid May-mid Sep 0800-2000. Jointly operated by Tourism Yukon, T9935566, and Parks Canada, T9937200, this first-class facility has all the information and photos you could want on the town's historical buildings, plus some fine archive and contemporary films dealing with aspects of its heady past. Parks Canada manage 35 National Historic Sites, of which 7 sights/tours cost $5 each, $10 for

Tourist
information

3, $15 for 4 or $25 for all 7. One of these is the popular 90-min **walking tour** of town, conducted by guides in period costume, daily at 0930, 1100 and 1300. Another is the **waterfront tour** (daily 1030 and 1530), which talks you through the history of First Nations and river transportation, ending with a tour of the *SS Keno*, one of the last sternwheelers to travel the Yukon and Stewart rivers. There is a handy bulletin board outside the centre if you're looking for a ride somewhere. Across the road is the **Northwest Territories Visitor Centre**, T9936456, open daily 0900-2000, a key stop for anyone planning on travelling up the Dempster Highway.

Best time to visit Dawson City hibernates in winter, when average temperatures drop to -30° C. Most sights are only open mid-May to mid-Sep. The hottest months are Jul and Aug, when mean temperatures rise to 15° C and the sun shines almost round the clock. Unfortunately the streets throng with hordes of tourists, many of them RVers stopping en route from the US to Alaska. Jun is a good compromise, with the bonus of an excellent festival (see below). In late Aug and Sep the crowds begin to dwindle and the scenery takes on the magnificent colours of autumn.

History

When the motley bunch of gold prospectors arrived, the population of Dawson City swelled to 30,000, making it the biggest city west of Winnipeg and north of Seattle. Today the rebuilt town harbours the ghosts of what must have been the most exciting place on earth. There were casinos and cabarets, show-girls and saloons, brothels and rag-time tunes. Projected motion pictures were shown just three years after their invention. Telephones, fancy hotels, running water and electricity were all available for those who could pay. The North West Mounted Police kept a degree of order amid the chaos, religiously closing everything down on Sundays. Prices ran amok, with gold dust used as currency. You hear stories about barkeepers who sifted the saloon floor sawdust and came away with $300 worth; down-and-outs panning $40 of dust from the dirt beneath the boardwalks; $1,000 of dust panned when the Orpheum theatre was rebuilt in the 1940s.

For most, the reality was a harsh squalour. Prospectors would have to build fires to thaw the frozen ground, then spend weeks on end wallowing in the icy, rocky mud. Men outnumbered women 25 to one, so prostitutes could pretty much name their price. Overnight the Native Americans were reduced to strangers in their own land, their culture almost completely destroyed. Hunting areas were overrun, forests burned away. In the midst of such wealth and decadence many literally starved to death. The land too has continued to suffer, the Gold Rush having catalyzed a string of later mineral discoveries.

No more than a year after the masses arrived, all the accessible gold had been extracted. As individuals moved out, big businesses moved in, using great monster machines such as Dredge #4 to scrape away at bedrock and boulders. The last of these shut down in 1966, returning the fields again to a small number of dreamers and die-hards. Dawson City, which had remained the territorial capital until 1953, sank into a terminal decline until Parks Canada began to intervene in the 1960s. They named the town a National Historic Site and set about restoring its century-old buildings. Today the whole place is like one big living museum, a fossilized remnant of the Wild West, complete with false-fronted wooden houses, boardwalks, saloons and dirt streets. There are some fine old structures to see, the best being broken-down ramshackle hovels, buckled by time and temperatures that can drop to -60°C in winter.

The Yukon

Sights

Most of the town's century-old buildings are still in use as hotels and saloons. The first to be renovated (in 1960) was the wonderful **Palace Grand Theatre** on King Street. It was originally built by Gold Rush legend, Arizona Charlie Meadows, from the hulks of two beached paddlesteamers. Every night in summer at 2000 it hosts the **Gaslight Follies** show, a two-hour Vaudeville musical comedy aimed squarely at tourists, but good fun for all that. ■ *$15 floor, $17 balcony. T9936217.*

Heritage Buildings

The grandest building in town is the **Commissioner's Residence** at the east end of Front Street. This elegant former home of the Queen's representative to the Yukon has been renovated to reflect the 1912-16 era. ■ *Tours by costumed guides run daily Jun to mid-Sep at 1400. $5. Unguided walk-throughs*

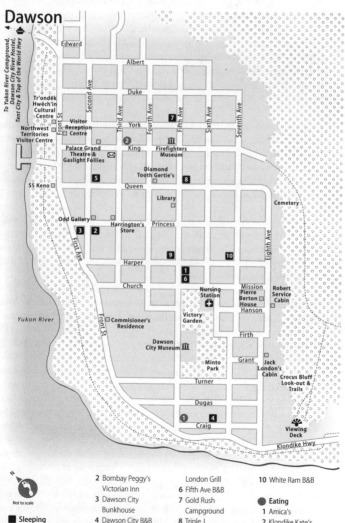

Dawson

The Yukon

Not to scale

Sleeping
1 Aurora Inn

2 Bombay Peggy's Victorian Inn
3 Dawson City Bunkhouse
4 Dawson City B&B
5 Downtown & Jack

London Grill
6 Fifth Ave B&B
7 Gold Rush Campground
8 Triple J
9 Westmark Inn

10 White Ram B&B

● **Eating**
1 Amica's
2 Klondike Kate's

are free, daily at 1500-1700. Many of the best structures are on 3rd Avenue, such as the 1901 **Post Office** at 3rd Avenue and King Street, which is still in operation. **Harrington's Store**, nearby at 3rd Avenue and Princess Street, displays a collection of rare original photos and journal excerpts from the Gold Rush era entitled *Dawson as they saw it.* Also worth seeing is the **Firefighters Museum** at 5th Avenue and King Street. ■ *Summer Mon-Sat 1230-1830. By donation.* The town's **cemeteries** make for interesting meandering: ask for a free brochure at the Visitor Centre.

Dawson City Museum Housed in the old territorial administration building, the town museum is an essential stop for soaking up some history. It's jam packed full of artefacts and photos, First Nations items, old diaries and newspaper cuttings. One key highlight is the 27-minute *City of Gold*, a moving black and white documentary made by Pierre Berton (see Literature, page 461), which underlines the town's sad demise and helped spur the federal government to action. If you think some relatives may have taken part in the stampede, this is the place to conduct some geneological research. Tours of the museum building (daily at 1100, 1300 and 1700) take in the old court chambers, the archives and the Visible Storage area, where a fifth of the museum's 30,000 artefacts are displayed. A second tour, at irregular hours, takes in the government buildings at the south end of town. ■ *Jun-Sep 1000-1800. $5, $2.50 concessions. 5th Av/Church St, T9935291.*

Diamond Tooth Gertie's Gambling Hall An absolute must is a visit to Canada's first legal casino, housed in the old Arctic Brotherhood Hall, which was built in 1899. The atmosphere is wonderful, with three can-can based Follies shows staged nightly. The midnight performance is a little more risqué. There are great Yukon beers on tap; happy hour starts at midnight. Gambling proceeds go to the continued development of town. ■ *1900-0200. $6 for all three shows. 4th Av/Queen St, T9935575.*

Tr'ondëk Hwëch'in Cultural Centre Displays, photos, dioramas, artefacts, arts and crafts, theatre and slide shows bring alive the history and culture of the Native Hän people. You can arrange to stay at a wilderness camp on the river, or take a tour to Mooseshide Island on a restored paddlewheeler. ■*1400-1700, slide show at 1500. $5 donation. Front St, T9936564, www.trondek.com*

Authors' Avenue These days Parks Canada offer daily tours at 1000 and 1530 that take in three cabins on Eighth Avenue, all former homes of famous writers. Born in Preston, England, Robert Service (1874-1958) became one of the most successful poets of his day, writing verses that romanticized the north but immortalized much of its mystique, charm and eccentricity. Ironically, most of his Gold Rush verse was written before he even set foot in the Yukon. The **Robert Service Cabin** is a renovated version of the poet's abode when he worked here as a bank clerk in 1908. The cabin can be viewed and there's a tour which includes a brief recital of verses like *The Cremation of Sam McGee* and *The Shooting of Dan McGrew.* ■ *1300-1500 daily. Free.* A much longer recital was formerly given here by Irish-born actor and eccentric Tom Byrne, but this became so popular that it now takes place in a small theatre on Front Street/Princess. Service's poems are far more effective when read aloud, so this is a recommended experience. ■ *1500 and 2000 daily. $8.*

The tours move across the road to the home of local author **Pierre Berton** (see page 461), whose best-seller *Klondike* is the best introduction to the era, then head to **Jack London's Cabin**, which was built with 'a few' logs from the original in which the writer lived. Jack London also fell in love with the north, and made it over the Chilkoot Pass during the stampede. As for many others, his journey's real quest was for something more ephemeral than gold, and he never really did any panning. Ultimately finding Dawson too expensive, he left penniless after just a year, having gathered enough inspiration to win fame and acclaim with stories like *Call of the Wild* and *White Fang*. His version of the Yukon is tougher and more realistic than that of Service, and his writing has reached a much wider audince.

The Gold Fields

An integral part of the Dawson City experience is to witness **Bonanza** and Eldorado creeks, where most of the gold was mined. You can take a car or bike, or join one of the many tours. The action begins at Km 4 on the Klondike Highway, the start of Bonanza Creek Road which runs through scenes of chaos and cataclysm. Near the turning is **Bear Creek**, a 25-ha site that supported the dredge teams until 1966. Parks Canada run tours of the site ($5) at 1230, 1400 and 1500, taking in the machine shops and the gold room where the dust was processed. On Bonanza Creek Road, also managed by Parks Canada, is the fascinating **Dredge #4**, the largest bucket-line, wooden-hulled dredge in North America. Tours (on the hour from 0900-1600, $5) take you inside this three-storey leviathan, whose control room feels more like the bridge of a ship, full of levers and controls. Monsters like this one scooped up copious quantities of mud and rock, passed the material through their insides where it was sifted for gold, then left the debris behind them in long caterpillar-like ridges. Though it cost a small fortune in its day, the machine paid for itself in a few years. Operated by just four men, it extracted a remarkable 25 kg of gold per day between 1913 and 1966. At Km 12 on this road is the cairn marking **Discovery Claim**, where the original lucky strike occurred. Every 150-m claim on this stretch went on to yield around 3,500 kg of gold, worth about $25 million at 1900 prices.

The road forks here, the east spur leading along **Eldorado Creek**, which proved even more bountiful than Bonanza. The other branch runs up to the summit of **King Soloman Dome**. From here you can take in the network of trails and roads behind the major creeks, all of them littered with interpretive signs, ramshackle buildings, and the rusting remains of mining equipment. Hunker Road runs back from the summit to the highway. Enthusiasts could spend hours exploring these desolate landscapes. To take a tour of a still-operating placer mine on Hunker Creek Road, contact *Gold Bottom Mine Tours* (see Tour operators, below). Or you could try your hand at gold-panning. There are plenty of operators who will take you out, or show you where to go for a fee. At about Km 15 km on Bonanza Creek Road is **Claim #6**, where you can usually pan for free. Ask at the Visitor Centre, or call T9935575. Pans can be rented at several places in town.

Hikes

Midnight Dome, the hill that rises behind Dawson City, is so named because it's a great place to watch the sun drop to the horizon then rise again at midnight on 21 June, an occasion causing for much drinking and festivity. A stiff 8-km return hike to the summit is rewarded with superb views of the city, goldfields, Yukon River and rows of mountains. Ask at the Visitor Centre for directions. *Gold City Tours* (see page 429) run regular trips up here in the day and evening. The **Crocus Bluff Lookout** trail is a short walk leading to good views of the town. Follow King Street southeast above town to the trailhead. The 32-km **Ridge Road Recreation** trail starts in Upper Bonanza Creek and follows the ridge tops back to the Klondike Valley, with views all the way. It's a three-day hike with two campsites along the way.

The Yukon

Essentials

Sleeping
■ *on map, page 425*

There is a very good listing of accommodation with prices and photos in the Tourist Information Centre

AL-B *Aurora Inn*, 5th/Harper, T9936860, www.wildandwooly.yk.net 10 very nice en suite rooms with big beds in a large pine-finished house, very new and clean. Great leisure area. 2 deluxe rooms with jacuzzi tubs at the more expensive end. Open year-round. **A** *Bombay Peggy's Victorian Inn*, 2nd/Princess, T9936969. The nicest place to stay in town. A handful of elegant, classy rooms in a house full of historic character. TV and video library. **B** *Bear Creek Bed & Bannock*, 11 km east of Dawson City in Bear Creek subdivision, T9936765. 4 rooms with wood and native craft decor, laundry, kitchen. **B** *Dawson City B&B*, 451 Craig St, T9935649. 7 rooms with shared bath in a comfy home with a reputation for great hospitality. **B** *Downtown Hotel*, 2nd/Queen, T9935346, www.downtown.yk.net Acceptable rooms. Those across the road from the office open out on to a plant-filled courtyard with hot tub. **B** *Triple J Hotel*, 5th/Queen, T9935323, www.triplejhotel.com Avoid the cabins and motel, go for the nice, spacious hotel rooms. **B-C** *Fifth Avenue B&B*, next to the museum on 5th Av, T9935941. 7 ordinary rooms in a nice house. **B-C** *Klondike Kate's*, 3rd/King, T9936527, www.klondikekates.ca 15 pretty log cabins, newly renovated and understandably popular.

C *White Ram B&B*, 8th/Ram, T9935772. 10 small but tasteful rooms in a nice house with a good atmosphere. Guest kitchen, hot tub, internet, bikes. $10 more for private bath. **C-D** *Dawon City Bunkhouse*, Front/Princess, T9936164, www.bunkhouse.ca Tiny and simple but cute rooms with shared bath in a nice building. Rooms with baths are more expensive. **E** *Dawson River City Hostel*, across the river (on ferry), T9936823, www.yukonhostels.com HI-affiliated. Basic, rustic accommodation, dorms or private rooms, kitchen, deck with good views of town, lockers. Rents canoes and bikes for $20 per day. Also has some ugly tent sites.

Camping E-F *Gold Rush Campground*, right in town on 5th Av/York St, T9935247. The only place for RVs, but utterly devoid of charm. Showers $2. **F** *Yukon River Campground*, across the ferry, walking distance from town. By far the nicest campground, with sites right on the river. Fills up, so secure a spot in the morning. Even cheaper camping is opposite at **F** *Tent City*, a chaotic place with a set-up-wherever policy. **F** *Klondike River Campground*, 15 km east of town, is not as nice as the Yukon River site.

Eating
● *on map, page 425*

Expensive *Amica's*, east end of 5th Av. Italian cuisine, a bit pricey but highly regarded. **Mid-range** *Klondike Kate's*, 3rd/King St, T9936527. Very popular and reasonably priced. Heated patio, pastas, fish, etc. *Jack London Grill*, 2nd/Queen, T9935346. Burgers, steak, fish. *Ruby's Hideaway*, in the Callison subdivision off the Klodike Hwy, T9935721. An old shack in an unlikely spot, but with a great reputation for French/Cajun cuisine. Reservations recommended. *Westmark Inn* has a decent restaurant with a nice deck. **Cheap** Everywhere seems to have good breakfast deals for $5. *Grubstake*, 2nd Av. Pizza, patio, internet. *Riverwest Cappucino Bistro*, Front St across from the *SS Keno*. Organic fair trade coffee, European atmosphere, sandwiches, bagels, treats.

Bars & clubs

Bombay Peggy's Lounge, 2nd/Princess. Best, most relaxed place for a pint. Some small snacky food, great atmosphere. *Diamond Tooth Gertie's Gambling Hall*, see Sights, above. Yukon beers on tap and a fun atmosphere. Open till 0200. Happy hour at midnight. *Sourdough Saloon*, in the *Downtown Hotel*. An atmospheric, smoky, reasonably authentic place frequented by locals and visitors. Pool table, and a strange ritual involving the Sourtoe Cocktail, that involves a real petrified human toe. *Westmark Inn* has a nice lounge with a deck and Martinis. *Westminster Hotel*, on 3rd Av, aka *the Pit*, houses the *Beer Parlour* and the *Pink Palace*. This is the rough-edged drinking place for genuine local miners, who don't necessarily want to share it with tourists.

6

See Diamond Tooth Gertie's and *Palace Grand Theatre* under Sights, above. The *Odd **Entertainment** Gallery* on 2nd/Princess, www.kiac.org, features visual and performing arts, always Canadian and usually very good.

The year's biggest event, and rated as one of the best in the West, is the *Dawson City **Festivals** Music Festival*, T9935584, www.dcmf.com, in late **Jun**. Thousands of people drop in to enjoy 3 days of various musical acts on 6 outdoor stages around town. Usually the best up-and-coming Canadian talent is featured. Extra camping laid on, and the atmosphere is fantastic. There's late night dancing under a big-top in the centre of town. *Dawson International Short Film Festival*, T9935838, www.dawsonarts.com, in **mid-Jul** runs for 3 evenings and 2 afternoons. *Discovery Days*, T9931996, in **mid-Aug** is a weekend of events including live music, bathtub races and the inevitable gold panning.

Camping and fishing gear *Dawson Trading Post*, Front St. **Food** *Bonanza Market*, **Shopping** 2nd/Princess. Groceries, deli, bakery. *Dawson City General Store*, Front St. Bakery, groceries, film, newspapers. *Riverwest Cappucino Bar*, Front St. Some health food items. **Jewellery** *The Gift Box*, 2nd Av. Jewellery made from the gold nuggets that are still found in local creeks, and worth much more than processed stuff. **Photography** *Peabody's*, 2nd/Princess. Sepia portraits, photofinishing.

Canoeing *Castle Rock Canoe*, Front St, T9935919, castlerockcanoe@yahoo.com **Sports** Rentals $30 per day. Rock Creek to Dawson, $59, 3 hrs; Dempster Highway to Dawson, $79, 6 hrs. Includes rental and shuttle. **Golf** *Top of the World Golf Course*, T9935443, gives the rare opportunity to tee off in the middle of the night and play a round beneath the midnight sun. 9 holes. Rentals available.

Ancient Voices Wilderness Camp, T9935605. First Nations camp with cabins and tents, **Tour operators** offering cultural day trips. *Canadian Yukon Riverboat Family*, T6334414, www.riverboat.yknet Riverboat trips on the Yukon River to or from Whitehorse (3-4 nights), meals provided. *Gold Bottom Mine Tours*, T9935023. Tours of a still-operating placer mine on Hunker Creek Rd, 1100-1900, $15. *Gold City Tours*, Front St, T9935175, www.goldcitytours.com Your best first stop for most types of tour, including town, the goldfields, Midnight Dome, gold-panning, etc. They also arrange all transport tickets, charters and airport limo. *River of Culture Tours*, T9935482. 2-hr First Nations tours on a small paddlewheeler. $47, $35 concessions, including salmon BBQ. *Trans North Helicopters*, T9935494, www.tntaheli.com Flightseeing tours of the gold fields or Tombstone Mtns. *Yukon Queen*, T6683225. Cruises to Eagle, Alaska, in a 110-passenger catamaran.

Air Dawson City's airport is 19 km southeast of town on the Klondike Hwy. *Gold City* **Transport** *Tours* run a shuttle-bus Downtown, meeting all scheduled flights. A *Dawson Courier* taxi, T9936688, costs $23 from the airport. *Alkan Air*, T6682107, www.alkanair.yk.net, fly regularly to **Whitehorse** and **Inuvik**. *Air North*, T6682228, www.airnorth.yk.net, fly to **Whitehorse**, **Watson Lake**, **Inuvik**, **Fairbanks** and **Juneau**.

Bus *Dawson Courier*, T9936688, run a bus to **Whitehorse** at 1315 daily except Sat, $82.50 one way; and to **Inuvik** if 5 people reserve, Wed only, $238 one-way. *Parks Highway Express*, T1888-6006001, www.alaskashuttle.com, run a regular scheduled shuttle service to **Fairbanks**, continuing on to **Anchorage**.

Boat You could also cruise to **Eagle**, Alaska, on the *Yukon Queen* (see above).

Car For car rentals there's *Budget*, 451 Craig St, T9935644. Drivers should gas up at *MacKenzie Petroleum*, off the Klondike Hwy in Callison, which is far cheaper than those in town.

The Yukon

Directory **Banks** *CIBC*, Queen St between Front/2nd. 24-hr ATM. **Communications** Internet: at the library (see below), or *Grubstake*, 2nd Av. **Canada Post**: across from library on 5th St; 1901 heritage building at 3rd Av and King. **Laundry** *The Wash House*, 2nd/Queen and Princess. **Library** 5th Av/Queen and Princess. **Medical services** *Nursing Station*, behind the museum on Mission, T9934444. **Useful numbers** Ambulance: T9934444. Police: T9935555.

Dempster Highway

The 740-km Dempster Highway is the great frontier road to the frozen north, and Canada's only year-round public road to cross the Arctic Circle. Construction of a highway across the tundra was a great challenge, eventually solved by using a raised gravel pad to insulate the permafrost and keep it from melting. Driving the length of this rough road is also a challenge and an adventure, not to be entered into without adequate preparation (see below). The effort is amply rewarded by ever-changing, wide-open views. Three very different mountain ranges are crossed, and the continuous freeze and thaw adds a host of unusual features to the landscapes, with names like hummocks, tussocks, frost boils, ground slumping and polygons. In summer, perpetual sunshine causes the vegetation to burst into a riot of colour. Mid-August ushers in the autumn, the most beautiful time of all, when the scenery is filled to the horizon with vivid shades of red, orange, gold, purple and brown, and hosts of berries are ready to pick.

Preparations First stop at the **NWT Visitor Centre** in Dawson City, T4567623. They provide details on road conditions, weather, and which gas stations are open. Drivers should fill up at *Mackenzie Petroleum* in Callison off the Klondike Hwy, which is much cheaper. Gas stations are scarce on the highway, so drivers must fill up every time they get the chance. Those with a small tank should take a jerry can and keep it filled. Note that tyre repair and mechanics in Dawson don't work weekends. Make sure your tyres are good and take at least 2 spares, preferably 6-ply. Do any routine maintenance before heading out. Gas and tyre repairs are usually only available at Eagle Plains (369 km), Fort McPherson (542 km) and Inuvik (740 km). There is no drinking water available until Fort McPherson.

Flora & fauna The wildlife of the north includes old favourites like grizzly bears and Dall sheep, and some unique species such as musk oxen, polar bears, Arctic foxes and barren ground caribou. The most famous caribou herd is the 120,000-strong **porcupine caribou herd**, which migrates each year from forested wintering grounds in central Yukon to calving grounds on the Beaufort Coast, returning south in the autumn. Their migration path crosses the Dempster, and many people travel the road around the beginning of September in the hope of seeing them. It can take hours for the whole herd to cross the road, and they have right of way. In summer, the smaller Hart caribou herd can be seen in the Tombstone area. Some of the parks reached from Inuvik (see below) are renowned for marine wildlife. Creatures of the Arctic Ocean include bowhead and beluga whales, ringed and bearded seals. More accessible (and tasty) are the fish that live in multitudes in pristine creeks and lakes all along the highway.

Plants have a particularly hard life up here. The average temperature is so low that the ground never thaws, with only a thin top layer melting enough to sustain vegetation. Moreover, Arctic precipitation is so low that technially it's classified as desert. Yet a surprising amount of vegetation such as sedges and dwarf birch survives, and goes absolutely crazy every summer. The growing

The Land of the Midnight Sun

At the Arctic Circle on the summer solstice (21 June) the sun never sets; on the winter solstice (21 Dec) it never rises. The further north you go from here, the higher the midnight sun remains above the horizon, and the longer its season. At the North Pole, the sun is ever present for six months, then utterly absent for the next six. Everybody adjusts to this strange phenomenon in different ways. Sleeping patterns are utterly disrupted, while the whole concept of night and day and time in general fly out the window. It can be an invigorating experience.

It is easy to forget that the islands north of the Canadian mainland, one of which contains magnetic north, are part of this vast country. In fact, the Arctic Circle is more or less Canada's mid-point. One third of the country's land mass lies in the frozen tundra north of the tree-line. Half of it – and one fifth of the world – is underlain by permafrost. Up to 80% of the sun's energy is reflected back into space by ice and snow. The people of the north do not refer to themselves as Eskimo, and find the term offensive. In the east and centre they are known as Inuk (one person), Innuk (two people), or Inuit (three or more). In the west, they call themselves Inuvialuk (singular) and Inuvialuit (plural). The words Inuit and Inuvialuit literally mean 'people'.

---

season may be short, but it's rendered particularly intense by the constant sunshine. Millions of birds are drawn north to feed on this nutrient-rich vegetation. Birders can expect to see, among many others, long-tailed jaegar, arctic tern and snowy owls.

You don't have to go far to get the most out of the Dempster Highway. In fact its most beautiful and well-paved section is the first 100 km. A perfect destination is the Tombstone Mountain Campground at Km 72, a lovely spot and home to the **Dempster Highway Interpretive Centre** (mid-June to early September). They can give you all the information you need on local wildlife, geology, natural history, First Nations culture and some of the most rewarding hikes in the West. The spectacular Tombstone Mountain Range, well known for its jagged black granite peaks and idyllic alpine lakes, is a long day's hike away, but plenty of shorter trails lead to gorgeous views, with no trees to get in the way, and there's a good chance of spotting Dall sheep, grizzlies and the Hart caribou herd. Ask to have a look at the Visitor Centre's copy of the useful *Yukon's Tombstone Range and Blackstone Uplands: A Traveller's Guide.*

The Tombstone Mountains

The shortest hike is the 30-minute self-guided interpretive trail from the Visitor Centre. **Goldensides** (2½ hours, 610 m elevation gain. Trailhead: 3 km north of the Centre, turn right and drive to the radio tower) From the top are views of the Klondike River Valley and Tombstone Mountains.

Angelcomb Mountain (10 km return, 3 hours, 580 m. Trailhead: 9.5 km north of the Centre, park at the gravel pit on the east side of the highway) A fairly easy and gradual ascent to the first peak, with wonderful views and a fair number of Dall sheep and caribou around. You can keep on going at will.

Grizzly Valley (8 km round trip, 2-4 hours, 640 m elevation gain. Trailhead: 12.5 km north of the Centre on the west side) This, the fastest route into the Tombstone Range, leads to a lookout with great views. To go all the way in is at least a 58.5-km return hike, with possible additional diversions to Divide Lake, Talus Lake or Tombstone Mountain itself (2,192 m). A first-class adventure.

The Yukon

The Arctic Circle By the West Blackstone River at Km 115, look upstream: the two low, cone-shaped mounds about 8 km away are not volcanoes but *pingoes*, strange phenomena caused by mass movements of frost. These ones are thought to be more than 5,000 years old. Further on, the highway eventually leads through a set of Ogilvie Mountain peaks very different from the scenic Tombstones. These bare, grey-black piles of shale make for bizarre, other-wordly landscapes. Beyond, you enter the broad flat horizons of the **Eagle Plains**, arriving eventually at the service centre of the same name (Km 371), where you can get gas, tyre repairs and even a bed for the night (see Sleeping, below).

Just north, at Km 402, the road crosses the 66°33' latitude line that marks the Arctic Circle. This is a second worthy destination, not just for the symbolic value of entering the Arctic realm, nor for the inevitable but quite interesting interpretive panels. It's a little over halfway up the Dempster, with the best of the scenery already gone. The stretch from Km 408 to the Richardson Mountains is part of the porcupine caribou herd's winter range, should you be passing between September and May.

Into the Northwest Territories **Wright Pass**, at Km 465, marks the Continental Divide and the border with the Northwest Territories. The **Richardson Mountains** are softer and rounder than those further south. A moderate hike up to the obvious summit via the ridge on its south side offers a chance to admire their gentle contours. On the other side, the road sweeps down to the Peel River Valley. Near the top, a viewing platform provides equally outstanding vistas. At Km 542 a free ferry crosses the river on demand from 0900-0100 June to mid-Oct. The small native village of **Fort McPherson**, 10 km further, has a mechanic, a hotel (see below) and usually gas for tanking up, but don't depend on the latter. From here the road gets even rougher and far less interesting. At Km 608 is the impressively broad **Mackenzie River**, the small village of Arctic Red River, and another free ferry which leaves hourly from 0900-0100. The end of the road is Inuvik, a grim little town best used as a jumping-off point for even more remote northern communities and parks that can only be reached from here and by plane.

Essentials

Sleeping & eating
There are just two stops for beds, food and even fuel on the Dempster Highway

Eagle Plains, more gas station than village, has the **B** *Eagle Plains Hotel*, T9932453, a standard but reasonably priced restaurant, basic campground (**F**), and showers.

Fort McPherson has the **B** *Tet'lit Service Co-op*, T9522417, with beds, a restaurant, and gas pumps. Also **C** *Bell River Bedrooms*, T9522465, and **C** *Tetlichi B&B*, T9522356.

Camping Campgrounds on the highway, all **F**, are as follows: *Tombstone Mountain* at Km 72, 31 sites; *Engineer Creek*, at Km 194, 15 sites; *Rock River*, at Km 447, 20 sites, 3 tent-only; *Nitainlaii Campground*, at Km 547, 5 km from the Peel River ferry; *Gwich'in Territorial Campground*, at Km 705, which should be open but is usable anyway.

Inuvik, NWT

Phone code: 867
Colour map 7, grid B6
Population: 3,300

Inuvik is an unattractive little town that may come as a disappointment after 740 km on a dirt road. Most visitors who come this far are planning on continuing to one of the arctic parks and isolated communities that can be reached only from here by plane. Note the corrugated steel ducts that snake bizarrely through the streets, carrying piping that would normally go underground. The houses, identical but painted bright colours to add some character, are built with steel poles drilled through to the stable layer of permafrost so that they don't buckle during the spring frost heaves.

The Northern Lights

Theories as to the exact science behind the aurora borealis, or northern lights, continue to evolve. Apparently, streams of charged particles from the sun are carried toward the earth by cosmic winds. As these interact with lines of the earth's magnetic field energy is produced. The result for those spectating, is a light show, with eerie patterns projected over the sky, often seeming to spread out from a point, shifting like a kaleidoscope. The main colours are green, which comes from oxygen, and pink from nitrogen. Deep red auroras are rare, and were once seen as evil omens.

The aurora appears around the north and south poles simultaneously and symmetrically, though obviously it can only be witnessed at one as the other will always be in daylight. There is a 27-day cycle between the most brilliant displays, and also an 11-year cycle, which last peaked in 2002. Strong auroras can cause problems with radio signals and even pipelines and transmission lines. Natives of the north were capable of hearing swishing sounds accompanying the lights, though these have never been recorded. They may be related to radio waves or static electricity.

Almost everything of interest is within four blocks on Mackenzie Road, including Inuvik's only real sight, the striking **Igloo Church**, which unfortunately is not usually open to the public. On the way into town is the **Western Arctic Visitor Centre**, T7774727, www.nwttravel.nt.ca, www.town.inuvik.nt.ca, July-September 0900-2000, May-June and early September 1000-1800. They have a display about four different native cultures, and a collection of videos that represent about the entertainment in town. If flying out on an excursion, it's worth watching the video first. You also have to register at the **Parks Canada** office on MacKenzie Avenue, T7778822, william_hurst@pch.gc.ca, open year round Monday to Friday 0800-1700.

Sleeping

Beds in Inuvik are overpriced, because the 3 main hotels are owned by the same company. **A** *Finto Motor Inn*, at the south entrance to town, T7772647, finto@permafrost.com, is the nicest. **A** *Mackenzie Hotel*, Mackenzie St, T7772861. Spacious. **B-C** *Arctic Chalet*, just before town on the highway, T7773535, www.arcticchalet.com 7 rooms, most with bath, kitchenette, laundry, TV. Also 2 spacious cabins. **C** *Polar B&B*, 75 Mackenzie Rd, T7772554. 4 rooms that share a kitchen, bathroom, and laundry. **C** *Delta Vista*, 37 Dolphin St, T7774010. 1 double and 2 single rooms. Use of kitchen, but no breakfast.

Camping There are 2 campgrounds in town. **F** *Happy Valley*, northwest end of town on Franklin Rd. Showers, views of surroundings, nice sites. **F** *Juk Park*, south of town on the highway. Quieter, nicer in many ways, and high enough to give good views. Coin-op showers. Both have drinking water. **F** *Gwich'in Territorial Campground*, 30 km to the south, is big and brand new.

Eating

While in the north, fish lovers should be sure to try the delicious Arctic char

Expensive *Peppermill Restaurant*, in the *Finto Motor Inn*, T7772647. The nicest environment, with specialities like Arctic char and caribou. **Mid-range** *To Go's*, 71 Mackenzie. Musk ox and caribou burgers. *The Roost*, across the road, serves the same kind of thing. Each hotel has a restaurant. *The Sunrise Café*, in the *Mackenzie*, has basic food, good for breakfast. *Café Gallery*, on Mackenzie, is a nice spot for coffee and baked treats.

Bars & clubs

Cabin Lounge in the *Finto* is nice for a drink, and sometimes has live music. *The Mad Trapper* on Mackenzie is reasonable. With a pool table and occasional live music.

Festivals

Great Northern Arts Festival, T7773536, www.greatart.nt.ca, is a 10-day bonanza in mid-Jul, featuring over 100 artists from north of the Arctic Circle.

The Yukon

Shopping *Boreal Books*, 181 Mackenzie. Maps and books about the north. *Inuvik Sports*, 75 Mackenzie. Sporting goods, film developing. *Northern Images*, 115 Mackenzie. Inuit sculpture, sealskin slippers, prints, etc. *Northern Store*, 160 Mackenzie. One-stop department store. Groceries, clothing, tacky souvenirs, pharmacy.

Tour operators & travel agents *Arctic Nature Tours*, T7773300, www.arcticnaturetours.com The biggest, most reliable operator for tours and the excursions listed below, usually offering whatever is available at the time. Tours to **Tuktoyaktuk** ($159-259), **Herschel Island** ($285), **Mackenzie Delta** by boat ($65-$100) and smaller communities. Also occasional but expensive hiking tours to some of the parks like **Tuktuk Nogait**, 10 days ($2000). *Beaufort Delta Tours*, T/F7773067, www.permafrost.com/beauforttours, run most of the same trips, naturalist safaris, fishing, hiking and canoeing. *Eagle Tours*, T7773465. Naturalist tours on the Mackenzie River. *Western Arctic Adventure and Equipment*, 38 Spruce Hill, T7772594, www.inuvik.net/canoenwt Canoe and kayak outfitters. Can arrange fly-in trips. *Mackenzie Delta Sled Dog Tours*, T7773253; and *White Husky Outfitters*, T7773535, run dog-sled tours. **Travel agents** *Mack Travel*, 151 Mackenzie Rd, T7772941, www.macktravel.ca

Transport **Air** Flights from **Dawson City** with *Alkan Air*, and *Air North* are $380 return (less with advance booking). Flights from **Whitehorse** start at $410 if booked a week in advance. *First Air*, run scheduled flights from Whitehorse.
    Car *MGM*, T7774295/T6686497, mgm@permafrost.com, sometimes make chartered van journeys from **Whitehorse**, $250 one-way, and **Dawson City**, $200. For **car hire**: *Norcan Rentals*, 60 Franklin Rd, T7772346. *Delta Auto Rentals*, T7773535.

Directory **Airline offices** *Air North*, T1800-6610407, www.airnorth.yk.net *Alkan Air*, T6682107, www.alkanair.yk.net. *First Air*, T1800-2671247, www.firstair.ca *Arctic Wings*, T7772220; *Aklak Air*, T7773777; and *BeauDel Air*, T7772333, service the fly-in communities. **Banks** *CIBC*, Mackenzie. 24-hr ATM; *Bank of Montreal*, in the post office. **Communications** Internet: free at the library. **Canada Post**: on Mackenzie Rd. **Laundry** *Happy Valley Campground*. **Library** *Inuvik Centennial Library*, 100 Mackenzie Rd, T7772749. Videos about the North, book exchange, national newspapers. **Medical services** *Regional Hospital*, Inuvik Access Rd, on the way into town, T9792955.

Excursions from Inuvik

When making plans, remember that flights are at the mercy of the changeable Arctic weather. Don't keep your schedule too tight

A number of small communities and large parks are accessible only by air from Inuvik. These are places where the 'true North' can still be experienced, and relatively easily, with animals such as musk oxen, rugged but minimal landscapes, and people who still live off the land. Don't expect to see any igloos though. *Arctic Wings* and *Aklak Air* are the main airlines for those who want to make their own arrangements, but it's easier and often cheaper to go with a tour company.

Tuktoyaktuk Sitting on a sandspit 137 km due north of Inuvik on the icy Beaufort Sea, 'Tuk' is the most popular excursion. Most people go more for the plane-ride than the village, which these days is mainly supported by the oil and gas industries. From the air there's a good chance of spotting pods of beluga and bowhead whales, and you're guaranteed to see the world's greatest concentration of **pingoes**. Utterly conspicuous on the delta's otherwise flat expanses are 1,400 of these strange volcano-like cones, which are created by frost heaves. In winter the village can be reached on a 194-km ice road. Tours cost from $140 for half a day to $259 for a full day. Supplies can be bought at *Northern Supermarket*. In town is an artist cooperative. For more information call T9772286, F9772110.

Sleeping **A-B** *Hotel Tuk Inn*, T9772381, F9772566, has 18 rooms with private bath and laundry. **A-B** *Pingo Park Lodge*, T9772155, F9772416, has 18 rooms with private bath. Both have restaurants open to non-guests. **B** *Arctic Tour Company*, T9772230, F9772276, has 3 rooms with shared bath. **Camping** Campers should be able to find a spot near the beach.

Those going it alone should reserve accommodation before buying a plane ticket

Tour operators Hiking, fishing, wildlife viewing, pingo tours and boat trips from Inuvik, are all run by local operator *Ookpik Tour Co*, T9772170, F9772399. *Arctic Tour Co*, T9772230, F9772276, run community and cultural tours of the village.

Transport See Inuvik Transport, above. For a taxi call T9772474.

The closest trip from Inuvik is to Aklavik, situated on the Mackenzie Delta 55 km west on the other side of the river, and connected by a 116-km ice road in winter. Aklavik was seen as a no-hope town, and Inuvik was actually created in the 1950s to replace it. Many of the inhabitants refused to leave, however, prompting the nickname 'the town that wouldn't die'. In 1931, Aklavik briefly captured the world's attention thanks to the 'Mad Trapper of Rat River', one of the north's most legendary figures. Mystery still shrouds the identity, origin and motives of this bizarre character, who arrived one day out of nowhere, paid cash for suspicious quantities of arms and ammo, and built himself a fortified cabin here on the Delta. Believed to be killing trappers for the gold in their teeth, he shot the constable who was sent to check him out, then resisted a 15-hour siege laid by seven heavily armed RCMP officers. He managed to hide out in the Arctic's frozen wastes through the worst of a harsh winter for 40 days.

Aklavik

Today his unconsecrated grave can be visited in town, as can a Hudson's Bay post, and a former mission church turned museum. Flights and tours from Inuvik are easily arranged, the latter usually involving just an hour here, long enough to see everything. Again, the beautiful 20-minute flight in is the major highlight. For a little more you can take a two- or three-hour boatride back out, a recommended option.

Sleeping and eating Those going alone can stay at **C** *Bessie's Boarding House*, T9782461, F9782815, which has 15 rooms. There is one store and no restaurant.

Tour operators *Aklavik Tours*, T9782527, F9782521, run boat trips and a water taxi from Inuvik. *Red Mountain Adventures*, T9782747, F9782071, run wildlife viewing trips in the Richardson Mountains.

Situated some 250 km northwest of Inuvik in the Beaufort Sea, Herschel Island is renowned for its summer displays of wild flowers. At least 150 species turn the flat plains into a sea of colour throughout the short summer. There are also 70 species of bird, plus musk ox, Arctic fox, the odd polar bear and whales. People have been travelling through the area for 9,000 years, but the first settlement was by the whale-hunting Thule people 1,000 years ago. The first whaling camp established by white men resulted in the death of most of the Inuvialuit from the island's three villages, as well as the near extinction of local whale populations The whaling stopped in 1907, one of the last such stations to close. The next inhabitants were the North West Mounted Police, who raised their sled dogs here until 1964. The island was declared a Territorial Park in 1987.

Herschel Island Territorial Park

Herschel is a remote destination with few services. Park Rangers are present at **Pauline Cove** in the summer, and will give a one-hour tour to visitors. Contact *Parks and Outdoor Recreation Branch*, T7774058, www.renres. gov.yk.ca/

The Yukon

protect/park Before setting out, register at the Parks Office in Inuvik, and pick up a free camping permit. The campground at Pauline Cove has a wind shelter and a fire ring for burning beach wood, and there's a trapper's cabin that can be used for free. Fish can be caught from the shore, but drinking water is in short supply, so bring plenty, as well as the essential mosquito repellent.

Ivvavik National Park Situated on the northwestern tip of the Yukon just below Herschel Island, Ivvavik National Park was created to protect the calving grounds of the 120,000-strong porcupine caribou herd (see page 430) who migrate through the park each summer. Most visitors to this remote park are there to raft or kayak the spectacular **Firth River**, which flows 130 km through steep, colourful canyons from Margaret Lake to the Beaufort Sea and Herschel Island, with up to Class 5 rapids on the way. With no facilities, a very hostile climate and no firewood, this is no place for amateurs. All visitors must register with the Parks Office in Inuvik, and pay a fee of $100 per person. There's a stiff fine for those who fail to deregister, as search and rescue parties are deployed.

Vuntut National Park & Old Crow To the south across the British Mountains is the remote Vuntut National Park, covered by shallow lakes and marshes that are visited each summer by some half a million nesting birds. This tundra was part of the ice-age continent of Beringia (see page 438). The park is most easily accessed from Old Crow, an isolated fly-in community of 300 or so Van Tat-Gwich'in, meaning 'people of the lakes'. The village is reached from Inuvik, and with *Air North* six times per week from Dawson City and Whitehorse. Operators organize bird- watching tours and guided river trips. There's a café, a general store and two places to stay.

Sleeping C *Ch'oo Deenjik*, T9963008. 6 rooms with shared bath and kitchen. Pick-up from airport; C *Harold and Teresa Frost B&B*, T9963913, also have 6 beds and will pick up.

Sachs Harbour & Aulavik National Park **Banks Island**, 525 km northeast of Inuvik, is rarely visited, and mostly by those keen to see musk oxen, of which there are some 70,000, the world's largest population. Other wildlife includes caribou, Arctic fox, beluga whales, polar bears, and lemmings. The main community, Sachs Harbour, is a functional place geared towards hunting and fishing, the island's biggest draws. Those wishing to observe rather than kill animals would do better to visit Aulavik National Park, a further 250 km to the north. Visitors need to register in Inuvik and pay a fee of $100 per person. The only way to get there is by charting a plane, and as there are no facilities, total self-sufficiency is required. For more information call T6903904, F6904808. Quite flat, easy canoeing can be enjoyed on the Thomsen, the world's most northerly navigable river. The average temperature here in July is 5° C.

Sachs Harbour AL *Kuptana's Guesthouse*, T/F6904151, has 5 rooms. Price includes 3 meals a day. They also run naturalist, wildlife and cultural tours.

Paulatuk Situated 394 km east of Inuvik on Darnley Bay in the Amundsen Gulf, the tiny community of Paulatuk is another popular hunting destination, and noted for its Arctic char fishing. Operators run bird-watching trips north to **Cape Parry Bird Sanctuary**, while bigger fauna can be spotted at **Tuktut Nogait National Park**, 50 km to the east. Visitors can hike there or hire a local boat. To the west are the **Smoking Hills**, where coal seams ignited years ago are still smouldering away. The name Paulatuk means 'place of coal'.

Sleeping and eating L *Paulatuk Visitor Center Hotel*, T5803051/F580 3054, has 10 over-priced rooms, a kitchen and restaurant. B *Marlene's Guest House*, T5803812, and B *Sharon's B&B*, T580 3904, sharonkirby@excite.com have a few rooms and provide meals.

Background

History

First Nations

Beringia The generally accepted explanation of how North America's very first people arrived is that they crossed a temporary land bridge between Asia and Alaska. Though some sites in Alaska and the Yukon hint at occupation as long as 25,000 years ago, the most common theory is that this migration occurred about 15,000 years ago, when ice-age glaciation had lowered the world's sea levels dramatically, creating a whole continent called Beringia. Animals now long extinct, such as the woolly mammoth and giant beaver, fled to this vast oasis of green within a desert of ice looking for food, and human hunters with the same motives followed them.

Pre-history At least 14,500 years passed before the first Europeans 'discovered' this New World, by which time aboriginal societies had spread throughout North and South America. In Canada alone, over 50 languages were spoken, a fact that prompted historian Olive Dickason to comment: "Canada has 55 founding nations rather than just the two that have been officially recognized". It is certainly useful to band Canada's First Nations together according to language groups or broad geographical areas, but to generalize about them is about as useful as speaking of Europeans as a single cultural unit.

The Iroquoian The Iroquoian people who lived in the St Lawrence-Great Lakes region of Eastern Canada were the continent's northernmost farmers. They enjoyed a stable and complex social life, based in relatively large, heavily fortified towns consisting of huge longhouses inhabited by as many as 50 members of an extended family. Most notable in this language group was the Iroquois Confederacy, or Five Nations, whose Great Law of Peace is often cited as a key inspiration behind the US Constitution. It represents an astounding system of political equality and democracy, practised at a time when Europe was still locked in a feudal economy. Masters of a vast territory, the Iroquois have also been called 'the Romans of the New World.

Algonquian Nations speaking languages derived from the Algonquian group, including the **Cree** and the **Ojibwa**, occupied most of southeastern Canada, much of it covered in the inhospitable forests of the Canadian Shield. The soil there is thin, rendering agriculture unfeasible and wildlife scarce. These people lived a tough, nomadic life based around small kinship groups. The Ojibwa in particular are renowned as inventors of the birchbark canoe, an ingenious craft that was to open up most of the country's interior to trade and expansion.

Athapascan The Athapascan language was spoken by nations such as the Chipewyan, Dogrib and Beaver, all referred to as **Dene**. They occupied the rugged northwest section of the Canadian Shield, corresponding today to the north of Manitoba, Saskatchewan and Alberta, and the Nothwest Territories. This was an equally tough region to survive, allowing for little social unity or cultural self-expression.

People of the Plains The stereotypical Hollywood-style image of the painted 'Red Indian' warrior with his eagle-feather headdress, buffalo outfit, horse and rifle is based entirely on the tribes that lived on the Great Plains of Central Canada. Of these, the most militant and powerful were the Blackfoot Confederacy, who waged almost continual war with the Plains Cree and Assiniboine to the north and east, the Sioux and Crow to the south, and tribes such as the Kootenay and Shuswap who occupied the interior valleys of southern BC, but crossed the Rockies to hunt at certain times of year.

The whole way of life of the Plains Indians depended on the herds of buffalo that roamed the prairies in staggering numbers. Their meat provided the people with food; their hides were used to make clothes, blankets, rafts, and tepees that could be quickly dismantled and carried away when whole villages left to follow the buffalo's migrations.

Ironically, the heyday of the Plains dwellers only came with the arrival of the Europeans and introduction of horses and rifles. But the white settlers also introduced the systematic and wholesale slaughter of the buffalo herds which they used as a means to rid themselves of the aboriginals.

The Pacific Northwest

By far the most densely populated area in Canada when the Europeans arrived, with about half of the country's inhabitants, was the Pacific Northwest. About 16 languages were spoken here, including two that were utterly unrelated to any others, making this one of the most linguistically rich regions in the history of the world. Radically different as they may have been, the West Coast nations had many cultural similarities, although the Haida, from the isolated Queen Charlotte Islands, in Northern BC, were the fiercest, wealthiest, most extravagant and artistically gifted nation of all.

Thanks to a relatively mild climate and an abundant supply of food and materials, the coastal people had enough time and wealth to evolve into incredibly rich and complex societies. Extended families lived in vast, elaborately carved and decorated cedar plank houses, before which stood tall cedar poles covered in rich, anthropomorphic symbolism. People wore weavings, furs, leather footwear and exquisite jewellery, kept their possessions in sumptuously carved cedar boxes, and travelled in long dugout canoes that made them masters of the turbulent ocean and formidable fishermen. They dined on a rich diet of salmon, game, fruit, berries and roots, and enjoyed gambling, dancing, games, ceremonies, music and celebrations (see Culture, page 455). The coastal First Nations has a firmly entrenched sense of social class, with ranks including chiefs, commoners and slaves who were usually prisoners from conquered neighbours. Private ownership covered everything, even such essentials as fishing and hunting rights.

The Inuit & Inuvialuit

The people of Canada's Arctic occupy the very last region on earth to be inhabited by humans. The Inuit arrived from Siberia about 4,000 or 5,000 years ago, and speak the Inuktitut language in an area that stretches from Eastern Siberia to Greenland. Their survival is a testament to their formidable skills as hunters, and a triumph of human ingenuity and perseverance. The traditional Inuit abode, rarely seen today, is the igloo, a strong, elegant, complex structure that can be erected in little over an hour. Seals and whales were the buffalo of these Arctic dwellers, from which they crafted almost every tool for survival. Among other things, they invented the fur-lined parka, snowshoes, dog-sleds and the kayak. These incredible little vessels, made from skins stretched over a frame, are waterproof and virtually unsinkable.

The white man cometh

A complex network of trade had long-since been practised by most First Nations, and far from being easily duped innocents, they were from the start notoriously shrewd and tough in their dealings with the white man, and greatly appreciative of the iron, weapons and various tools that revolutionized their lives. The big problem originally was those other imports, the infectious diseases. Most European germs were utterly alien in the New World, so the natives had never developed a resistance to them. Smallpox, measles, influenza, even the common cold, decimated aboriginal populations. It has been estimated that the population of North America before the Europeans arrived was between 10 and 18 million, a number that fell by 95% in a mere 130 years.

Native bands were continually at war with their neighbours over territorial disputes and hunting and fishing rights; they raided and looted each other, taking slaves from

Background

▶ The Northwest Passage

An interesting footnote in Canadian history is the story of Britain's obsession with finding the Northwest Passage which, it was originally hoped, would provide an alternative trade route to the Orient. One of the first to fall to the challenge was **Martin Frobisher**, a big, blustering, larger-than-life professional adventurer who made three voyages into the Arctic.

Henry Hudson set sail in 1610 to find the passage. He made it through the Strait that separates Québec from Baffin Island, and headed south across the vast bay that now bears his name. At the bottom of James Bay he hit a dead end, and spent what remained of the summer looking for a way through, before finally getting frozen in and passing the winter on starvation rations, eating moss to survive. When in the spring he wanted to continue rather than

return, his crew mutinied and set him adrift, tied up, in a small boat.

Some two centuries later, despite the fact that the geography of the continent had been established, and it was clear that any existing Northwest Passage would be utterly unsuitable as a trade route, Captain **John Franklin** took up the old challenge. Having already made two attempts, one of which had ended in death, murder and cannibalism, he set off again in 1845, loading up the ships Terror and Erebus with 129 men. They were never seen again. The expeditions that followed rank as the longest, most extensive search in human history, and though Franklin was never found, a possible Northwest Passage was, by **Robert McClure** in 1851. Even then it was only conquered by ship in 1905 byNorwegian explorer **Roald Amundsen**.

among the defeated, and in some cases practised ritual cannabilism and torture. However, this situation only got out of hand with the introduction of European weapons, a problem further exacerbated by Christian missionaries, who divided bands, villages, even families, between those who had converted and those who had not.

First contacts The debate is still open concerning which Europeans first reached the so-called New World. It may well have been a group of Irish monks led by St Brendan in AD 565. They almost certainly reached Iceland before the Vikings, and may well have visited the Northeast American Coast, but proof is yet to arrive. The Norsemen had island-hopped their way to Greenland by AD 1000, when sailors on a lost supply ship caught a glimpse of an unknown shore. Eric the Red's son Leif went in search of this mysterious land, stopping first at Baffin Island, then Labrador, then a heavily forested and pastured land, probably on Newfoundland, which he named Vinland, Land of Wine. His brother later returned and spent the winter getting into a battle with the people they called *skraelings*, meaning 'barbarians'. Little more came of it.

In 1497 John Cabot, searching for the 'backdoor' route to China, arrived in Newfoundland, or maybe Cape Breton, where he found so many cod that "they sometimes stayed his shippes". From then on hundreds of ships from all over Europe prowled the Newfoundland waters, but nobody was interested in settling the land.

Jacques Cartier The motivation behind Jacques Cartier's 1534 expedition to the new land was much simpler: gold. Stumbling across a group of Iroquoian Natives on a fishing expedition, he set up a wooden cross in their presence, and claimed the land for France, a symbolic act understood despite the language barrier by their chief Donnacona, who was enraged. On his third voyage Cartier returned to set up a colony, but the understandable antagonism of the natives, together with the harshness of the weather, made him leave again for home, this time with a handful of 'gold', that turned out to be the fool's variety, and 'diamonds' that were merely quartz.

In 1608 Samuel de Champlain set up his *habitation* at the site of today's Quebec City, and refused to give up, even when 20 of his 28 men died of scurvy in the first winter. Determined and energetic, this true founding father of Canada explored the waterways of the St Lawrence and Great Lakes, criss-crossing the ocean to promote his struggling colony. In 1609 the Montagnais Indians asked Champlain to accompany them on an expedition against the Iroquois to the south. It was the first time European weapons had been used against the natives, and began a feud with the Iroquois, particularly the Mohawk, that would continue for generations, keeping the future land of New France in a state of almost constant siege until a peace treaty was finally signed in 1701.

Samuel de Champlain

As early as 1615, Champlain invited the Récollet missionaries to come over and start converting the natives. He said it would "cement their commercial ties with the French as well as save them from eternal hell-fire in the next world". Their tactic was to relocate the natives on farms, dress them in European clothes, and teach them French. It failed utterly. The Jesuits, however, lived among the natives, learned *their* language, and sought to convert them one at a time. The tactic was far more successful and ultimately perilous for the natives. Chief Dan George later lamented: "When the white man came, we had the land and they had the Bibles. Now they have the land and we have the Bibles".

Men (and women) with a mission

Despite many vicissitudes, and thanks largely to the fur trade, New France survived, but it remained little more than a trading post until 1617, when Champlain asked one Louis Hébert to settle the land properly, by farming it. The first century was a tenuous time, during which the colony's very existence was constantly threatened by the powerful Iroquois Confederacy. In 1667, Louis XIV sent over 1,100 of his best soldiers, whose very presence led to a truce and 20 years of peace during which the young colony flourished. At the same time, the king sent about 800 young female settlers, known as *Filles du Roi*, to redress the balance between males and females. This helped spark a population explosion, and today the majority of Canada's six million Québecois can trace their roots back to these adventurous women, who were mainly orphans, prostitutes and widows.

The fur trade

It was the humble beaver that really allowed the colony to survive and expand. In Europe, top hats were all the rage, and the best felt for their fabrication came from the soft underpelt of the beaver. Since the best fur came from the coldest regions, pursuit of the beaver led directly to the colonization of the north and west of this vast new continent. At first native trappers brought furs to trade with the French, but Champlain shrewdly began sending men to live among his native allies, learn their language and customs, and become familiar with the geography. As well as bridging a gap between the cultures, he wanted these *coureurs de bois*, runners of the woods, to help him chart the interior. They were forerunners of the *voyageurs*, intrepid adventurers who paddled deep into the continent each year in flotillas of canoes to collect furs.

Coureurs de bois & voyageurs

Background

Two *coureurs de bois* named Radisson and Groseilliers, maybe at the suggestion of the Cree trappers in the north, realized that instead of taking the longer route to the northwest via the St Lawrence River, ocean-going vessels could sail right into Hudson Bay and load up with furs brought straight to them by native trappers, thus cutting out the middlemen entirely. The French were not interested in the idea, so they took it to the English, whose only prior interest in the continent had been a colony established on Newfoundland in 1610, which was soon driven away by neighbouring pirates. In 1668, the English sent out two ships to test the idea, one of which, the *Nonsuch*, made it through to the bottom of James Bay and set up a small trading post. Word got out, 300 Cree suppliers turned up laden down with furs, and the ship went home to turn a terrific profit. Canadian history had been changed overnight.

The Hudson's Bay Company

A Royal Charter was issued for a 'Company of Adventurers', who were given exclusive trading rights over the lands that drained into Hudson Bay. Named Rupert's Land, this vast area covered 40% of Canada's present territory. Founded in 1670, the Hudson's Bay Company (HBC) was the world's first corporation, very much in the shape of things to come. Historian Peter C Newman has pointed out that "at the peak of its expansion (the HBC) controlled nearly 3 million square miles of territory – nearly a twelfth of the earth's land surface and an area 10 times that of the Holy Roman Empire at its height".

The Conquest of New France

The Fur Wars   Montréal, which had hitherto established itself as the centre of the fur trade and consequently outgrown Québec City, had been seriously outflanked. Its merchants responded in 1682 by banding together to form the Company of the North. An unofficial war began, the French drawing first blood when master tactician Pierre de Troyes led a daring commando-style raid, capturing three Hudson Bay forts against tremendous odds. In an even more spectacular endeavour, Pierre Le Moyne, Sieur d'Iberville, captured the main English trading post of York Factory, which remained in French hands for 16 years. Some kind of showdown was clearly inevitable.

The Seven   The battle for supremacy between the French and English continued for over 150
Years' War   years, often during times of official peace, finally culminating in the so-called Seven Years' War (which lasted nine years in North America). The conflict began on the American frontier and eventually spread to Europe and beyond, spawning a web of alliances that fought on four continents, making this the first true World War. Though outnumbered three to one in ships, four to one in troops, and ten to one in money, the French actually seemed to be winning the war, until Britain was rescued by the election of Prime Minister William Pitt, for whom the war became an obsession.

The Plains   The tide turned when the British rained cannonballs down on Québec City from across
of Abraham   the river, firing over a distance the French had fatally considered impossible. Later, as winter approached and time was running out, General James Wolfe spotted a break in the cliffs west of the city. The French General Montcalm, previously warned of the danger, had written in his journal: "We do not need to imagine that the enemy has wings so that in one night they can cross the river, disembark, and climb the obstructed cliffs". But in a daringly imaginative assault, Wolfe managed to get 4,500 of his men, along with two cannons, to do just that. In the morning, Montcalm looked out at the rows of Redcoats lining up on the Plains of Abraham and lamented, "they have no right to be there".

Chevalier de Lévis, ablest of the French officers, waited out the winter and prepared to counterattack in the spring. The Second Battle of the Plains of Abraham was a victory for the French, but little did Lévis know as he waited for help to arrive from France that the English had defeated the French Navy in Europe. The war had ultimately been decided on foreign fields, and New France finally had to capitulate in Montréal on September 8, 1760. Three years later in the Treaty of Paris, they ceded control of all their North American lands other than two small islands off the coast of Newfoundland. The same year the Royal Proclamation created the Provinces of Québec and Nova Scotia, and declared the land west of the Appalachian Mountains off-limit to settlers, reserved as 'Indian territory'.

The American   The war against France had pushed Britain to the brink of financial ruin. Attempts to
Revolution   make the American colonies contribute towards clearing the imperial debt was the last straw for a people already ripe for self-dominion: the Thirteen Colonies of the Eastern Seaboard broke free from British rule and formed a new political union, the United States of America. The question is not why did they want to break free, but why did the northern colonies not choose to seize the moment. A very important part of the answer is that

they were wary of the Americans, a factor that has recurred perennially throughout Canadian history to this very day. English settlers in Canada were happy to have access to so much land, the territory of Québec having just been expanded to include the Great Lakes and the Ohio Valley. The French had so far been well-treated by the English, who had done little to undermine their institutions and culture. As Henri Bourassa later put it: "It was all very simple; we had to choose between the English of Boston and the English of London. The English of London were farther away and we hated them less". Both sides considered their neighbours to the south a much less tolerant prospect than the present regime, so when the Americans attempted to take Québec by force in 1775, they were duly resisted, and the attempt degenerated into a fiasco.

Go West, Young Men!

The differing styles of the opposing fur trading companies was apparent from the very beginning. While the English HBC encouraged native traders to bring furs to them, the French *voyageurs* went out into the land and learned to live like the natives. The first Canadian explorer to be born in Canada, Pierre de La Vérendrye, was also the first to push west of the Great Lakes and the Canadian Shield into the great Central Plains. In the 1730s and 40s, he and four of his sons discovered the Saskatchewan River, whose twin branches turned out to be the key to the interior. They went on to found a string of trading posts, including Fort Rouge at the fork of the Red and Assiniboine Rivers, a junction now known as The Forks in the heart of Winnipeg.

Pierre de la Vérendrye

With the Company of the North destroyed by Britain's victory over France, a trading vacuum appeared that was quickly filled by Scottish and American merchants, who hired seasoned *voyageurs* and picked up where the French had left off. An American named Peter Pond had established a trading post near Lake Athabasca in Northern Alberta, opening up the deep north to the fur trade. Establishing themselves as the NorthWest Company, the Montréal traders dedicated themselves to expanding the fur trade still further, as far as the Pacific and the Arctic. It was their explorers who travelled, charting almost all of the vast land north and west of Ontario, opening it up to later settlement. Of these, three in particular have become household names.

The NorthWest Company

Alexander Mackenzie mistakenly followed the river later named after him, which he called the 'River of Disappointment', all the way to the Arctic Ocean. On his next expedition he became the first person to cross the continent north of Mexico. Following the Peace River into the Rockies, he battled his way across the mountains to the Pacific, where on a large boulder he left Canada's most famous bit of graffiti: *Alexander Mackenzie, from Canada, by land, 22nd July 1793.* **Simon Fraser** was chosen to expand trade into the land west of the Rockies, and explore the Columbia River. Between 1805 and 1807 he accomplished the first of these goals, establishing four forts at McLeod, Stuart and Fraser lakes, and Fort George, naming this vast and hitherto unexplored wilderness New Caledonia. The following year, believing it to be the Columbia, he followed the treacherous river that now bears his name all the way to the Pacific. **David Thompson** founded a series of important trading posts along BC's windy rivers (including the one named after him) in his pursuit to follow the Columbia River to the Pacific. He finally succeeded in 1811, only to find that the Americans had beaten him by a few weeks.

Mackenzie, Fraser & Thompson

Background

While the English were fighting the 1812 war against Napolean, the Americans saw their chance of capturing Canada. With Britain preoccupied and the US population at 7.5 million compared to Canada's 80,000, Thomas Jefferson advised President Madison that it was "a mere matter of marching". On 18 June 1812 they promptly declared war on Britain and made plans for the Conquest of Canada. It was General Isaac Brock and

A mere matter of marching

the great Shawnee Chief Tecumseh who were to save Canada. In a series of battles in which they were greatly outnumbered, this dynamic duo scared the Americans into submission by exploiting their irrational fear of those wild Indian braves.

The capture of Detroit is a case in point. Brock sent a false communiqué along enemy lines, where it was duly intercepted, advising his superiors that he needed 'only' 5,000 more native warriors for the assault on Detroit. Tecumseh then marched his troops along the edge of a forest that was just out of range of the Americans but in full view. Once past, the warriors slipped into the woods and hurried back to the end of the line, each of them passing by three times. American estimates judged their number as reaching up to 3,000, when there were actually only 600. The US General in charge was so afraid that he surrendered with barely a shot fired.

In the treaty that followed, Canada and the First Nations were excluded from negotiations, while Britain agreed to return the frontiers to their original positions, allowing the Americans to extend their borders into the Indian Territory that had previously been reserved as native lands. The First Nations had been shafted again, this time for good. No longer needed by the British as allies or a buffer zone, they were destined to be 'civilized' and assimilated, or slowly wiped out.

The Red River Colony By 1812, the Nor'westers were gaining the upper hand in the fur wars to such an extent that the HBC sold a controlling interest to a group of Scottish investors led by nobleman Lord Selkirk. Having taken up the cause of Highland crofters, kicked off their land to make way for sheep rearing, Selkirk bought 116,000 square miles of land from the company, including the whole Red River Valley from the US border to Lake Winnipeg. Much to the alarm of both fur-trading companies, he then shipped over a contingent of 105 Scottish immigrants and created the first settlement on the prairies, named the Red River Colony. A significant force on the Prairies at the time was the Métis, those of mixed blood, often the result of unions between native women and the French *voyageurs*. Seeing its access routes to the Northwest compromised by the settlers, the NWC encouraged the Métis to view this settlement as a violation of their right to the land. This bit of stirring led to the death of 21 settlers in a clash that became known as the Seven Oaks Massacre.

Ultimately, the settlement survived, and the struggle for supremacy between the fur companies exhausted them both to the point that a ceasefire had to be called. A merger under the HBC name led to a total monopoly. The real losers once again were the natives, whose bargaining power was now greatly reduced.Once upon a time in the West

First landings The first European to arrive on the Pacific Northwest coast was a Danish sea captain, named Vitus Bering, after whom the Strait was later named. Working for the Russian Czar he reached the islands off the coast of Alaska, and his crew returned with otter pelts whose value soon inspired the Russians to set up trading posts in the area. Hearing of this, the Spanish, who had claimed the whole Pacific Ocean for themselves, sent their own expedition to the region, and began trading with the Haida in 1774. Next to arrive were the British, in the form of Captain James Cook, who began charting the west coast of Vancouver Island. He traded with the friendly natives for otter pelts, which his crew later sold in China at a great profit. Cook himself had by then been killed by Hawaiian Polynesians. Word was out and the sea otter, like the beaver, would be hunted to the brink of extinction.

A Perfect Eden Despite the burgeoning sea otter trade, and Captain George Vancouver's extensive charting of the coast, no attempt was made to settle the West until the HBC established Fort Langley (near today's Vancouver) in 1827, and Fort Victoria in the 1840s. The latter was a purely strategic manoeuvre. The border with the US had been drawn along the 49th parallel from the Great Lakes to the Rockies, but the HBC shrewdly recognized that if this line were ever extended, it would clip the south end off Vancouver Island. In an attempt to get there first, James Douglas was sent to survey prospective sites for a new fort and trading post, and chose a site which he called 'a perfect Eden'. Douglas was named governor of Vancouver Island on top of his title as Chief Factor of the HBC.

The Company's fears were soon vindicated. In 1844, US President James Polk was elected on the cry of "54.40 or fight", a brazen threat that the Union would claim the whole of the mountainous Oregon territory, including most of today's BC, right up to Alaska, taking it by force if necessary. The matter was ultimately decided by the 1846 Treaty of Oregon, signed by the US and Britain, which extended the 49th parallel straight across, ignoring the natural geography of north-south river valleys. The HBC was obliged to relocate its western HQ to the new Fort Victoria, greatly bolstering its importance.

If Canada as a whole owes its existence to the beaver, British Columbia came about **Gold fever** thanks to the more obvious incentive of gold, the 1858 discovery of which in the Fraser Valley changed Fort Victoria almost overnight. For 25,000 stampeders en route to the gold fields, this was the only possible stop-over, and the town quickly swelled with stores and hotels, bars and brothels, politicians and newspapermen. Afraid of an American takeover, Governor Douglas issued a public proclamation that the gold fields were Crown property, forcing all miners to register and pay a fee. In doing so he had assumed control of the mainland, a blatant bluff. Britain pointed out that he was overstepping his authority, then backed him up anyway, creating a second Crown Colony called British Columbia in 1866, with Douglas as governor of both.

Soon the new colony was littered with desperate hopefuls panning every creek for traces of the yellow metal. When large deposits of gold were found in the Cariboo, Douglas commissioned the Cariboo Road, a 650-km marvel of engineering and daring, eventually used to haul out millions of tons of ore, much of it from the boomtown of Barkerville, which for many years took its turn as the biggest settlement north of San Francisco. More importantly, the road opened up the grassland valleys and rolling basins of the interior plateau to ranching.

Dominion from sea to sea

Many of Canada's problems can be traced back to the Constitutional Act of 1791, which **Two nations** cut the large province of Québec in two: Upper Canada in the west (now Ontario) would **warring…** be English, Lower Canada in the east (now Québec once again) would be French. The problems caused by this apartheid smouldered for 40 years before flaring up as two minor rebellions in the 1830s which, though quickly smothered, had far-reaching effects. The British sent over Lord Durham, whose liberal leanings had earnt him the name 'Radical Jack'. He recommended that Upper and Lower Canada be united under one government in order to assimilate the French; that leaders of the elected assembly should henceforth assume the role of the governor's ruling advisors; and that the colonies be given authority over their own internal affairs. He blamed the unrest on an outdated colonial system in Upper Canada, and in Lower Canada talked of "two nations warring in the bosom of a single state". The two provinces were joined under one government by the 1841 Act of Union, and the 1848 election saw the victory of one of the greatest political alliances in Canadian history: Louis-Hippolyte La Fontaine and Robert Baldwin. The capital of the new single province of Canada was eventually decided by Queen Victoria. She chose a small unknown lumbertown called Ottawa. Strategically located on the river border between French and English Canada, it was inland from a possible American attack on the St Lawrence, yet linked to the Great Lakes by the defensive Rideau Canal.

During the 1860s, several key elements came together to make the union of the north- **Confederation** ern colonies a reality. The emphasis in Britain had shifted to trade and profits rather than military glory and monopolies. The colonies were coming to be seen as financial

Background

burdens that had to grow up and take responsibility for themselves. At the same time, Britain's clear sympathy and tacit support of the southern states during the brutal Civil War of 1861-65 had angered the northern states, at times bringing Britain and the US to the brink of war, with Canada as the battlefield. Newspapers in Chicago and New York were warning Canada: "Just wait till this war is over. You're next!"

The Treaty of Reciprocity with the US that had helped Canada to survive when Britain ended its protective colonial tariff and began moving towards freer trade seemed unlikely to be renewed, so Canada had to look elsewhere, namely towards the land to the west. In this respect, the railways offered great promise, a possible response to the US threat, and also great profits. It is no coincidence that the leading proponents of Confederacy were also railway promoters. And one of the arguments they used was that of glory, the glory of expansion.

A federal system was eventually agreed on that borrowed from the British and American systems. Like the latter, it would have two levels of government, federal and provincial. But rather than electing a President by a separate vote, they chose to be led by a Prime Minister, who would be the leader of the party with the most seats in the House.

The Province of Canada said yes to union, though there was only a small majority among the French. New Brunswick eventually said yes. The Nova Scotia premier said yes, though without the consent of his people who were basically tricked into the deal. Newfoundland said no. Ironically, the first Canadian land to be inhabited by Europeans, or so we believe, was the last to join the union, holding out until 1949. Canada was called a Dominion after the Psalm 72 phrase "His dominion shall be from sea to sea", which also provided the national motto *A Mari Usque Ad Mari*. The very day after Queen Victoria signed the British North America Act in 1867, the Americans ominously purchased Alaska from the Russians.

The Canadian Pacific Railway Asked to join the Confederation, BC requested a wagon trail from Manitoba to the coast. Cartier extravagently offered them a full-scale Trans-Continental railway instead, an offer they couldn't refuse. The Liberals called the building of the Canadian Pacific Railway (CPR) "an act of insane recklessness", and they were right, but glory knows no bounds. The railway skirted the edge of bankruptcy on several occasions. Crossing 5,000 km it would become the longest railway on earth, and a marvel of modern engineering. Historian Will Ferguson says: "Ours was a country forged not in revolution but in a landscape traversed. Ours was a victory over sheer geography". In places the railway had to be blasted out of rock, costing thousands of lives. It has been estimated, for instance, that the Hell's Gate section of Fraser Canyon cost about three Chinese workers for every kilometre of line that was laid.

Home on the Range

The Red River Resistance Two years after Confederation, the HBC agreed to sell the vast Northwest Territories to Canada for $1.5 million, but the deal included some land concessions by which they kept the most valuable parts. No one bothered to consult the people who lived there, most of whom lived around the Red River. This fertile region now had a cosmopolitan population of 12,000, including a large number of Métis, who were furious when news of the sell-out surfaced. Led by one Louis Riel, a group of Métis confronted a team of surveyors. Literally putting their foot down on a surveying chain, they spoke the momentous words, "You shall go no further!" On a roll, they seized the HBC post of Upper Fort Garry, and declared a provisional government. His fragile new union under threat, Macdonald had little choice but to meet most of their demands. In 1870, on the same day that the Northwest Territories were purchased, the Province of Manitoba was born, its name taken from the word *Manitou* meaning 'Great Spirit'.

A number of sad changes had meanwhile afflicted the Prairies. Estimated numbers of **The Plains** bison fell from 60 million in 1800 to about 800 in 1889, and only concerted efforts have **truth** prevented them going the same way as the prehistoric horse. A parallel fate overtook the Plains Indians, whose traditional way of life depended so utterly on the great herds. Ravaged by foreign diseases, half-starved through want of buffalo, and denied of their traditional way of life, the remnant of the once-proud indigenous nations was coerced into signing a series of numbered treaties that transferred their land rights to the Confederation in return for life on reservations. The government, who shrewdly sought to arrange land treaties before the arrival of the railway and settlers, used a number of low-down divide-and-conquer tactics to cajole them into signing, first going to Christian Natives and those in serious dire straits.

The Cypress Hills that straddle the Alberta/Saskatchewan border were the scene of a **The North** four-year war between the Blackfoot and the Cree, some 3,000 of whom arrived in **West Mounted** 1865 following the failure of their own hunting grounds further east. Both sides were **Police** ravaged by fighting and smallpox epidemics when a new threat arrived in the form of whisky traders. Trading out of stockaded outposts such as the infamous Fort Whoop-up near Fort McLeod, these American outlaws preyed on the Indians, getting them hooked on gut-rot liquor, which they exchanged for furs and buffalo robes. In June 1873, following a heated disagreement over a missing horse, a group of drunk white wolf-hunters opened fire on an Assiniboine camp, killing between 20 and 70 natives (depending on whose account you believe).

Known as the **Cypress Hills Massacre**, this event catalyzed the detachment of the North West Mounted Police (NWMP), a law-keeping force that Macdonald had been planning for some time. Distinctive in their red jackets, these were the prototypes for today's Royal Canadian Mounted Police (RCMP) or 'Mounties'. The joint Canadian-American Boundary Commission had set out in 1872 to establish the international border, an invisible line which soon became known by natives as the Medicine Line, as it could be crossed by those seeking sanctuary. The following year, that route was retraced by 300 brave members of the fledgeling NWMP on their legendary 800-mile 'March West'. Contrary to expectations, the journey turned into a desperate struggle. Water was scarce, rations were low, men were sick with dysentery and the horses and cattle were dying. When Troop A arrived at Edmonton, they completed the longest march on record of any force carrying its own supplies. When the other units arrived at Fort Whoop-up, the American bandits had already fled.

As white settlers flooded into Manitoba, the Métis were pushed further west into Sas- **The North-** katchewan, occupying land to which they had no legal claim. History began to repeat **west Rebellion** itself with the arrival of surveyors, and the cry went up for Louis Riel, who had fled to Montana and become a school teacher. Round two began with Riel sending Macdonald a petition and later declaring a provincial government at Batoche. Two breakaway bands of Cree plus some Sioux and Assiniboine joined the Métis in the Northwest Rebellion, which culminated at the Battle of Batoche.

Ironically, it was the Canadian Pacific Railway that defeated them. Whereas in 1870 it had taken three months for the army to reach the Red River, in 1885 it was just 10 days before 5,000 soldiers turned up, armed with US-made Gatling guns capable of firing 500 rounds per minute. Riel was tried in Regina, and found guilty of treason, a hangable offence. Prime Minister John A MacDonald refused to pardon him, saying "He will hang, though every dog in Québec barks in his favour". Margaret Atwood has since described Riel as "the perfect all-Canadian failed hero". The real victor was the railway, suddenly considered a vital aspect of national defense, its future guaranteed. The last spike was driven home on 7 November 1885.

Background

How the West was won

British Columbia joined the Confederation in 1871, but the union was for some time an unhappy one. Governing a large mountainous area with few people was an expensive business, revenue from resources was low, and the hoped-for expansion of trade with East Asia following completion of the Canadian Pacific Railway was slow to arrive. The railway did, however, bring people to the port of Vancouver, which in 15 years already surpassed the population it had taken Victoria almost 60 to accrue.

The kind of settlers attracted to BC were very different from those drawn to the East and Prairies. Entrepreneurs with capital to invest came West around the turn of the 20th century to exploit the province's vast resources. A salmon-cannery industry was established along the coast. Sawmills sprang up around the shores of Georgia Strait and along eastern Vancouver Island. The first pulp and paper mill at Powell River wasn't completed until 1912 and significant expansion of the forest industry only occurred after the First World War, when the Panama Canal gave access to markets in the North Atlantic.

Missionary Father Pandosy's successful cultivation of apples in Kelowna had led to a string of orchards down the Okanagan Valley by the 1890s, and around the same time the discovery of gold, silver, copper and lead around Kootenay Lake led to a new wave of gold fever and subsequent settlement. Responding to railways that extended northward into the region from the US, the CPR built a line through the Crowsnest Pass in 1899 to extract coal from Fernie, constructed the Kettle Valley Railway from Hope, and blazed the Dewdney Trail, much of which was later converted into Highway 3. Throughout the mayhem of gold fever, which created or affected almost every community in BC, the province never turned into the kind of lawless free-for-all that California had earlier become. Much credit for this goes to the NWMP, and to the famous figure of Matthew Begbie, also known as 'the hangin' judge'.

The Gold Rush to end them all led tens of thousands of mostly Americans to the Klondike River near the overnight boomtown of Dawson City. For a full account, see page 421 . The Yukon Territory was created in 1898 to assert Canadian sovereignty over the region. The building of the Grand Trunk Pacific Railway west from Edmonton through the Upper Fraser, Bulkley and Skeena valleys in 1907-14 was intended to give Canada a second gateway through the mountains to the Pacific Coast. Prince George then became a minor sawmill centre, servicing the growing housing market in the Prairies to the east.

From sea to frozen sea Britain had meanwhile transferred jurisdiction over the Arctic Islands to Canada in 1880, but it wasn't until the early 20th century that Canada officially extended its boundary to the North Pole. A single mariner claimed the entire Arctic Archipelago for Canada in 1909, but it meant nothing until the area was surveyed in the mid-1930s. As a senior Ottawa bureaucrat noted: "The history of the Canadian North can be divided into two periods – before and after the airplane".

The 20th century

First World War Canada catapulted itself onto the world stage with the accomplishments of its soldiers in the Great War, most famously at Vimy Ridge, Passchendaele, Amiens and the Hindenburg Line. Canada's contribution of over 620,000 men, 60,000 of whom died, with over 172,000 injured, was extremely high in relation to its population, a fact that further strengthened its international voice. In 1917, Prime Minister Robert Borden, along with South African Prime Minister Jan Smuts, demanded that the dominions be given full recognition as "autonomous nations of an Imperial commonwealth". He also insisted that Canada put its own signature on the Treaty of Versailles, and when the League of Nations was formed, Canada and the other dominions were given seats of their own, much to the annoyance of the US, who saw it as a British ploy to secure more votes.

The inglorious side of the war, often glossed over, was the mass arrest of over 8,500 'enemy aliens', including over 5,000 Ukrainians who were interred and used as labour in the steel mills of Nova Scotia. In other respects the war years and following decade were a time of positive reform. The Labour and Women's movements in particular made great leaps forward: in 1916, women won the right to vote in Manitoba, Alberta and Saskatchewan, with BC and Ontario following the next year and Nova Scotia a year later. Other provinces followed suit, although Québec women were denied their rights until 1940.

Wrongs & rights

It's clear today that the prosperity of the 1920s was a colossal house of cards which provoked a domino effect of crises when it came tumbling down in 1929. When panic ensued, countries followed the example of the US and retreated behind walls of protectionist tariffs. As a nation whose economy was largely built on exports, Canada was one of, if not *the* worst-hit countries in the West. The Prairies suffered the most. A bumper crop flooded the market just as demand dried up, pushing prices to an all-time low, then a severe drought began with almost no rain at all for seven years. The whole Plains region became a dust bowl, afflicted with dirt storms, darkened skies and plagues of grasshoppers. More than 200,000 people were forced to leave their farms. Income in Canada as a whole fell by almost 50%, with 20% of the population living on relief handouts. The jobless rate rose from 4 to 27%. With warmer weather on the West Coast, many of the homeless gravitated towards Vancouver, where they seem to have set up permanent residence on Hastings Street. At this time a new party was formed in Calgary from farmers and unions. Called the Co-operative Commonwealth Fed (CCF) it later merged in 1961 with the Canadian Labour Congress to form the NDP.

The Great Depression

The most striking aspect of Canada's involvement in the Second World War was the way in which Canadian troops were so often used as cannon fodder. Churchill sent 1,900 of them into Hong Kong as a hopeless 'symbolic' defense against the Japanese, 'like lambs to the slaughter'. In 1942, in what could be seen as a farcical dress-rehearsal for the D-day landings, 6,000 troops, including 5,000 Canadians, were sent on an ill-conceived mission into Dieppe that turned into a bloody fiasco. Over a million Canadians served in all, of which 45,000 died and 55,000 were wounded.

Second World War

The war had made Canada, along with the US, one of the two richest nations on earth, with the third largest navy and fourth largest air force. At the same time as the Citizenship Act of 1946 defined the people of Canada as Canadian citizens rather than British subjects, discriminatory immigration laws were set up to preserve "the fundamental character" of the country, making it very hard for blacks, Arabs, Asians and Jews to get in.

Surprisingly enough, Canada was where the Cold War began. It was a clerk at the Soviet Embassy in Ottawa, Igor Gouzenko, who revealed to British intelligence officers just how many spies had infiltrated their embassies, governments, and atomic research facilities. He had tried to approach Canadian officials, who refused to take him seriously. But the Cold War was a serious business for a country which, as one Soviet ambassador put it, was "the ham in the Soviet-American sandwich". During the 1950s, a series of expensive radar lines were built across Canadian Territory, including the Distant Early Warning line, which was entirely paid for by the US, who would not allow Canadian officials even to approach the sites without prior approval. In 1956, Canada's reputation as a peace-keeping force was cemented when diplomat (and later Prime Minister) Lester Pearson almost single-handedly defused the highly explosive Suez Crisis, for which he earnt the Nobel Peace Prize.

The Cold War

John Diefenbaker was elected in 1957, the only Prime Minister to come from Saskatchewan. A powerful and big-hearted man committed to social progress, and a dangerously inept bungler when it came to international and economic matters. His 1960 Canadian

Dief the Chief

Bill of Rights declaring equality of race, religion and beliefs, ended up as an empty gesture because he failed to give it any authority in provincial courts. He did, however, grant the vote to natives in 1960; appoint Canada's first native senator in 1958; appoint Canada's first female cabinet minister in 1957; end the discriminatory immigration quotas in 1962; support the inclusion of the first African state, Ghana, in the Comon- wealth; force South Africa out of the Commonwealth for apartheid. The TransCanada Highway was also completed during his office, in 1962, though it had been started in 1949.

Trudeaumania   Pierre Elliott Trudeau was perhaps the all-time most famous icon of Canadian politics, and dominated the scene from 1968-84. Young, suave and free-spirited, he captured the optimistic spirit of the Sixties.

Though prone to be coldly intellectual, Trudeau mostly lived up to his purported liberalism. As Minister of Justice he had already brought in key changes that relaxed divorce laws and ended restrictions on homosexuality and access to abortion. In 1971 he introduced the Canadian Multicultural Act, emphasizing the equality of all 'cultural and ethnic groups'. A few years later, in a landmark piece of legislation, a proposed gas pipeline from Alaska to Alberta was shelved due to native land rights and environmental issues. And in a reversal of former policy, nearly 60,000 Indo-Chinese were allowed into Canada during the Vietnamese boat crisis.

With a great deal of squabbling and difficulty, Trudeau drew up a Canadian Constitution in 1982. Until then the Constitution was still under British jurisdiction. Included within it was the Charter of Rights and Freedoms, which delineates freedom of conscience and religion; freedom of expression (including that of the press); freedom of peaceful assembly; and freedom of association.

Separatism   Perhaps Trudeau's key contribution to Canadian politics, though, was his firm stance against separatism in Québec, a position that has been upheld by his colleague and fellow Québecois, Jean Chrétien.

In 1976 the Parti Québecois (PQ) was elected as Québec's government. The following year they passed Bill 101, which banned English on commercial signs and severely restricted access to English-language education. Ironically, a federal bill had already been passed making it compulsory for the rest of the country to have labels in both languages on items as trivial as a jar of jam. In 1980, the PQ held a referendum on separation in which 60% of Québecois voted against sovereignty, but this was far from the end of the affair. During the term of Albertan PM Brian Mulroney, the separatists' position strengthened due to the premier's constant pandering to Québec, which was cited as a major reason why dissatisfied conservatives from the West broke away to form the Reform Party in 1987.

The stakes were raised in 1990 when the Bloc Québecois was formed to campaign on a federal level. Another referendum was arranged by the PQ for 1995, and this time the nation held its breath. Just 50.6% of Québec voted against separation, the narrowest of escapes. The issue of two warring nations has been a perennial thread in Canada's political tapestry, and doesn't look like going away any time soon.

During and after the Second World War, a trend began by which Canada became more and more linked to the US both militarily and economically. The Ogdensburg Agreement of 1940 established a Permanent Joint Board to integrate North American defences, while the government started courting American money to a degree that was considered shameless. By signing the North American Air Defense Agreement (NORAD), John Diefenbaker pretty much put Canada's air defences under US control.

Trudeau became more and more concerned by US penetration into the Canadian economy, and made real efforts to increase ties to Britain and Europe, introducing some of the most unabashed examples of economic nationalism since Macdonald. But matters took a dramatic turn with the election of Brian Mulroney, an Albertan Conservative who actually started *Investment Canada* to encourage American investment. In 1987 he proposed the Free Trade Agreement with the States, removing almost every trade barrier between the countries, even though 80% of Canada's exports were already going south. He then won the 1988 election on a platform of closer economic ties with the US, the first time that had ever happened. The White House saw the FTA as "a major victory for the United States", one US trade rep even saying, "The Canadians don't understand what they have signed. In 20 years they will be sucked into the US economy".

By 1993, Mulroney's popularity had fallen to a record low of 9%, and he was replaced in 1993 by Kim Campbell, Canada's first female prime minister, who only lasted a few months. Trudeau's old henchman Jean Chrétien was voted in, and has remained in power ever since. In January 1994, months after taking office, he signed the NAFTA agreement that greatly expanded the Mulroney agenda he claimed to oppose. The effects were immediate: while the US retail giant Walmart moved into every mall in the country, the ancient Canadian stalwart Eatons filed for bankruptcy.

The third strand that has persisted throughout Canada's history is the plight and strug- **Return of** gles of its First Nations. The Indian Act that followed the First World War aimed at nothing **the natives** short of complete assimilation, forcing natives to relinquish all rights and status in order to vote or even own property. This once proud people had been racked by alien diseases, restricted to reserves, deprived of their traditional hunting grounds, taught in schools where they were discouraged from speaking their own languages, forbidden to continue ceremonies like the potlatch (see page 457), and denied basic rights such as a vote. In the 1920s it seemed that they were a dying breed.

Yet somehow they survived, and with many of their traditions and languages intact. After the Second World War the government decided to revise the Indian Act, and for the first time natives were involved in the discussions. Little came of it, but at least they got the vote in 1960.

The struggle for native land claims began in the 1890s in British Columbia, where no treaties had ever been drawn up as they were further east. Nations like the Nisga'a of the Nass Valley near Terrace never signed their land away and were never conquered, so technically their land still belongs to them. Only in the last 25 years have such claims begun to be taken seriously. When the government of Québec wanted to build a hydro project in the north, they had to negotiate terms with the James Bay Cree and Inuit, who surrendered their rights to a million square kilometres of land in exchange for self government within their own communities, hunting, trapping and fishing rights, and a trust fund of $225 million. In 1987, the Sechelt Inlet Band became the first native group in Canada to be granted self-government within their own reserve lands.

In 1990, Mohawk protesters in the Oka region outside Montréal barricaded roads to a forest that was slated to be cut down, and in the resistance killed a police officer. This led to the formation in 1991 of the Royal Commission on Aboriginal Peoples. The report took five years to complete, and included 400 proposed changes, including the creation of an individual tribunal for land claims. It was finally recognized that the government could hardly be impartial in cases filed against itself. In 1999 the UN Human Rights Committee ruled that Canada was in violation of international law in its treatment of aboriginal rights. In 1999 the new territory of Nunavut was created. More than twice the size of BC it covers two million square kilometres, about a fifth of Canada's land mass. One of the most thinly populated areas on earth, it has just 25,000 people, 83% of whom are Inuit, who were allowed to retain ownership of 18% of the land. The territory was given self-government and a $1 billion cash settlement. It is the first time any single First Nations group will have a majority presence in a provincial or territorial government.

Modern Canada

An overview   Like most of the First World, Canada has become a consumer society, dominated by bad television, suburbs and malls. Fortunately, in Western Canada that grim summary only really applies to the two comparitively small pockets where the vast majority of people live: the Lower Mainland around Vancouver in BC, and the corridor between Calgary and Edmonton in Alberta. Elsewhere, life moves at a slower pace, and people still have time to ponder the age old mysteries and enjoy the natural beauty that surrounds them. The air is fresher, the water cleaner, the people more friendly, the atmosphere more relaxed. In June 2000, the UN declared Canada the best country in the world in which to live for the seventh year running.

Politics

Canada's political scene has been dominated by Jean Chrétien for far too long, leading to an inevitable level of complacency and corruption. Chrétien originally promised to axe the GST and Free Trade, but has done the opposite: he has pursued Brian Mulroney's unpopular policies even more than Mulroney himself. At the top of most Canadians' list of concerns and complaints, however, is health care, which is in dire straits across the country and desperately needs to be addressed. On the positive side, the Liberals have balanced the budget for the first time in 20 years, have ended the annual deficit, and have even begun paying off the national debt. Much of this is thanks to Chrétien's colleague but eternal opponent, Finance Minister Paul Martin, who has made it only too clear that he wants the Prime Minister's seat. In August 2002, Chrétien decided that he would not run again, and declared that he intends to use the rest of his time in office spending some of the federal surplus funds on worthy causes such as the environment. He is also trying hard to ratify the Kyoto Accord, despite strong opposition, particularly from Alberta. Martin is favourite to replace him.

The official Opposition is currently the Canadian Alliance, which was formed in 1987 as the Reform Party by Conservative politicians in the west who were fed up with Mulroney.

Sleeping with the elephant   In an address to the National Press Club of Washington, DC in March 1969, Pierre Elliot Trudeau said, "Living next to you is in some ways like sleeping with an elephant. No matter how friendly and even-tempered is the beast, if I can call it that, one is affected by every twitch and grunt". Canada continues to be defined by the fact that it is not the United States and it is unsure how long it can retain its national identity when it is so completely overwhelmed by the centrifugal force of US money and ideology. Living next door to the world's number one superpower has never been easy, and though a land-grab seems less likely now than in the past, the threat of a more insidious cultural and economic takeover is as real as ever. Some 200 million people cross the border every year, and over $1 billion of trade crosses it every day.

Focus on the West   While Alberta's economy continues to boom, its Conservative premier has gone on a spree of privatization, cutting the public health service and welfare to practically nothing. The province's wealthy are laughing all the way from oil-field to bank, but the have-nots are in an extremely jeopardised position. British Columbia, meanwhile, voted in a nominally Liberal premier, Gordon Campbell, whose policies bear a striking resemblance to those pursued by Margaret Thatcher in Britain's 1980s. First he cut taxes, then he used financial deficits as an excuse to cut just about every service, benefit and facility in the province. Hospitals have been closed down at an alarming rate across the province, leaving all but city-dwellers in a precarious position. Schools are closing down or facing serious under-staffing. Thousands of civil servants have lost their jobs. Even tourist offices are being closed. Together with the crisis in the forestry industry, upon which BC's economy depends more than any other province, this has resulted in much hardship and gnashing of teeth.

Economy

Forestry has been the main component of BC's economy throughout this century. About 64% of the province is forested, and thanks to excellent growth conditions BC produces nearly 60% of Canada's sawn lumber, most of its plywood and 30% of its chemical pulp. Recently this over-dependence on its softwood has caused the province major problems following tariffs introduced by the US, where most of the wood goes. **British Columbia**

A wide range of metals has been discovered throughout the Cordilleran part of the province, including lead, zinc, gold, silver, copper and iron. The Peace River Lowland has a different geological base consisting of younger, sedimentary rocks which have been the sources of petroleum, natural gas and coal. **Mining** and mineral processing employ about 3% of the labour force but yield nearly 20% of the product value of BC's major industries. Most consumer-goods **manufacturing**, as well as management and financial activities concerned with resource developments, has remained concentrated in or near the ports of the southwest, whose activities contrast ever more clearly with the primary activities of the north coast and interior.

In 1994, $685 million worth of fish were harvested in BC and 25,000 were employed in the industry. The most valuable fishery is for the five species of Pacific salmon, which are caught by large, modern **fishing** vessels mostly near the mouths of the Fraser and Skeena Rivers, a method of harvesting that has resulted in disastrously depleted fish stocks. Other important seafood include herring, halibut, cod and sole, and a large variety of shellfish, particularly oysters. In cultivated land as a percentage of total provincial area, BC ranks second lowest in Canada, behind Newfoundland. Its most productive official crops are vegetables, tobacco and, recently, ginseng, but these are probably dwarfed by the incalculable market value of BC's marijuana industry. The most important regions for **agriculture** are the Peace River area, which accounts for about 90% of BC's grain, the Okanagan Valley, one of Canada's three main fruit-growing regions, and the small but fertile farms of the Lower Fraser River. Cattle ranching on the grasslands of the southern Interior Plateau is relatively small-scale.

BC is well endowed with steep and rugged landforms and ample precipitation, which together produce enormous seasonal runoffs in numerous rivers and vast amounts of potential **hydroelectric** power. Dams along the Kootenay, Columbia, and Peace Rivers in particular are among the country's most productive, producing energy for the Lower Mainland and the United States. The physical environment of BC is itself a valuable resource, attracting visitors from throughout the world. Above all, the province is renowned internationally for the extent and diversity of its opportunities for outdoor recreation. In 1994 **tourism** generated 4.3% of BC's GDP, employing 105,000 directly and 185,000 indirectly.

Like the other Prairie provinces, Alberta was struggling with an economy reliant on the vicissitudes of the world's grain and cattle markets, until the discovery of **oil** in the Leduc field in 1947 transformed it overnight into Canada's most energy-rich province. A rapid rise in the world price of oil in the early 1970s drove the Alberta economy to unprecedented and frantic growth. While Edmonton became the centre for petroleum servicing, production and transmission, Calgary remained the exploration, administrative and financial centre. After a decade of financial boom, the nationwide recession of the 1980s was particularly severe in Alberta. The mid-1990s saw its fortunes rise again **Alberta** with higher world prices for oil and natural gas. The value of fuels in 1993 reached $18.5 billion, or 79.9% of total national value.

While proven remaining recoverable oil reserves are still considerable, Alberta holds some other aces. About 70% of Canada's proven remaining **coal** reserves lie within the province, estimated in 1995 at $34 billion. The **natural gas** industry is older than oil, dating from 1883 discoveries near Medicine Hat, and in 1994 Alberta's production was still 83% of the Canadian total. Two-thirds of the world's **bitumen** is located in the Fort McMurray region of Northern Alberta in the form of oil sands that cover more than 78,000 sq km, an area almost as large as Scotland. The 1.7 trillion barrels of bitumen represents one of the largest known hydrocarbon accumulations in the world. As conventional production declines, the oil sands could become the future for Canada's energy security in the next century. Alberta also has vast heavy oil reserves which exhibit the same general chemical characteristics as bitumen from the oil sands.

The success story of the petroleum industry had a knock-on effect that further benefitted Alberta's economy. As Canada's balance of financial power shifted westward, Calgary emerged as the third-largest head-office location after Toronto and Montreal for major Canadian companies and foreign **banks**. Between 1978 and 1986 the Calgary-based Alberta **Stock Exchange** increased its number of company listings by nearly 400, reaching 491. The construction industry in the two major cities also rides high on the province's booms.

Forests cover nearly three-quarters of Alberta, 67% of which is considered productive for **forestry**. Owing to the boom and bust cycle of the oil industry, the Alberta government has been aggressively promoting this sector of the economy since the late 1980s, and it now ranks as the province's second-largest primary industry. **Agriculture** and **livestock** husbandry also remain of vital importance. The black and brown soils of the mixed-grass prairie and parkland regions possess great potential for mixed farming. Away from this fertile crescent, especially in the southeast, lie the more specialized ranching and wheat operations, which compensate for their marginal soils with their large size. Over $40 billion worth of product is exported each year.

Tourism has become an increasingly important sector of Alberta's economy, thanks to the spectacular scenery and year-round recreational facilities of the Rocky Mountain National Parks, particularly Banff and Jasper, which attract hundreds of thousands of tourists annually from all over the world. The next most significant sector of the economy is **manufacturing**, principally food and beverages, chemical products, forest products, and petroleum products. Other sectors include the processing of minerals such as sulphur, and commercial fishing in the northern lakes.

The Yukon Having been originally put on the map by the greatest Gold Rush the world has known, it comes as no surprise that **mining** has continued to play a vital part in the Yukon's survival, comprising more than 30% of the territory's economic base. This has made it extremely vulnerable to reversals. The closure of all the Yukon's major mines in the 1980s because of depressed world markets and depleting resources resulted in a serious economic crisis, but this trend reversed in 1986 with the re-opening of the Yukon's major lead-zinc mine and the setting of a 30-year record in placer gold production. Many large mineral deposits still remain, and new mines have recently been developed which will bring significant increases in the production of copper, zinc, lead, gold and silver.

Tourism is the second most important industry in the Yukon, and continues to grow steadily. Other secondary but expanding sectors include agriculture, forestry, manufacturing and fishing.

Background

Culture

Architecture

Apart from the cedar longhouses that can still occasionally be seen, particularly in Northern BC, most of Western Canada's architectural interest resides in Vancouver and Victoria. The former features a handful of undeniably innovative structures, while the latter is dominated by hulking Victorian-England style structures and streets lined with attractive brick and stone buildings. Otherwise, only the occasional town is of interest: some, like Nelson, for their turn-of-the-20th-century heritage buildings; others, like Stewart, for their appealing ramshackle eccentricity.

Francis Rattenbury

The man responsible for almost all of Victoria's important buildings, including the Empress Hotel and the Parliament Building was Francis Rattenbury. A first-class draftsman, Rattenbury was a master at manipulating the Château and Beaux-Arts styles that were so popular at the time. This brought him a great deal of work from employees such as the Canadian Pacific Railway, for whom he finished many buildings. He also completed a number of provincial courthouses, such as the ones at Nanaimo (1896), Victoria (1899), Nelson (1905-06) and Vancouver (1906-1911), this last one adapted by Arthur Erickson in 1978-83 for the Vancouver Art Gallery. His main contribution to architecture in BC was not in the originality of his designs but rather his ability to bring a new level of sophistication to building technology and craftsmanship. After a scandal over his divorce and remarriage, Rattenbury returned to Britain in 1929, only to be murdered by his second wife's lover, who was also his chauffeur.

Arthur Erickson

If there is such a thing as a Vancouver style of architecture, Arthur Erickson is the man who invented it. Born in the city in 1924, he rose to prominence by winning the design competition for Simon Fraser University in 1963, and has many key buildings dotted around town. In keeping with the frequently overcast climate of the West Coast, which he believed could not take bright colours, Erickson became famous for creating dramatic structures out of potentially dull, mute colours, and concrete and glass canopies. Part of the secret of his success is a strong ability to blend a building into its landscape, as best evidenced by the extraordinary University building in Lethbridge. He also displays a rare knack for designing a building so as to make a statement about its purpose, as demonstrated by the Native Big House design of the UBC Museum of Anthropology (1973-6), and the deliberate openness of the Law Courts complex at Robson Square.

Background

Arts and crafts

Native arts

The native people of Canada, and particularly the Pacific Northwest, excelled and continue to excel in all forms of art, but most particularly in the field of carving. The genius of recently deceased master Bill Reid (see page 74), can be seen in various venues around Vancouver. Throughout Western Canada there are many opportunities to experience native art, particularly in the UBC Museum of Anthropology in Vancouver, the Glenbow Museum in Calgary, the Kwagiulth Museum on Quadra Island, around the Hazeltons in Northern BC, and on Haida Gwaii (Queen Charlotte Islands). A number of stores in Vancouver and Victoria also carry works by contemporary native artists, and a particularly fine private collection is on display in *Swans Pub* in Victoria.

▶ ## Canada: an alternative view

"For some reason, a glaze passes over people's faces when you say Canada." Sondra Gotlieb.
"The beaver, which has come to represent Canada as the eagle does the United States and the lion Britain, is a flat-tailed, slow-witted, toothy rodent known to bite off its own testicles or to stand under its own falling trees." June Callwood.
"Canada could have enjoyed: English government, French culture and American know-how. Instead it ended up with: English know-how, French government, and American culture." John Robert Colombo.
"Very little is known of the Canadian country since it is rarely visited by anyone but the Queen and illiterate sport fishermen." PJ O'Rourke.

The Group of Seven   While the turn of the 20th century art scene was marked by such major figures as James Wilson Morrice, considered the father of Canadian modernism, a truly Canadian form of painting only arrived with the ascension of the Toronto-based Group of Seven, who sought to draw inspiration directly from the Canadian landscape. Like the European *fin de siècle* symbolists and post-impressionists, they steered clear of the naturalism that had defined the previous generation, attempting to capture nature's grandeur through the use of bold colours and decorative patterning.

The original members – Franklin Carmichael, Lawren Harris, AY Jackson, Franz Johnston, Arthur Lismer, JEH Macdonald and FH Varley – befriended each other in Toronto between 1911 and 1913, and often painted together, their work, romantic and with mystical tendencies, developing along somewhat similar lines. Tom Thomson, who died in 1917 before he could become a member of the group, also left behind a remarkable collection of paintings and oil sketches.

If the group had a leader it was Harris, who began to radically simplify the colour and layouts of his canvasses. By the mid-1920s he had reduced his paintings to a few simplified and nearly monochromatic forms. Ten years later he became the only member of the group, and one of the first Canadian artists, to turn to abstraction. By the time the group disbanded in 1933, however, it had in many ways become as entrenched and conservative as the art establishment it had overthrown.

Emily Carr   Born and raised in a disciplined, middle-class Victoria household, Emily Carr (1871-1945) was orphaned in her teens, and went in 1891 to study art at the California School of Design in San Francisco. Her most important of many early travels was to France in 1910, from where she returned with a post-impressionist style of painting. She then continued a tour of Native Canadian sites, rendering a service to humanity by capturing on canvass, ancient villages, longhouses and totem poles that would soon fall into complete neglect.

It wasn't until 1928 that she slowly began to receive the kind of national exposure and critical recognition that she deserved, though financial success remained elusive. Most people agree that her late work is her best, when she returned to painting nature scenes inspired by the rugged West Coast, in a style that was more free-flowing and expressive. Large collections of her work are held at both the Vancouver and Victoria Art Galleries, and her Victoria house, where she lived with all kinds of animals, can also be visited.

First Nations Culture

Society   The most formidable of the First Nations was the Haida of Haida Gwaii, whose artwork is so distinctive as to be instantly recognizable. For more information about them, see page 286, and visit the Gwaii Haanas National Park to see their long-abandoned villages, one of the most moving experiences in Canada.

Extended families of 50 or more lived together in large, elaborately decorated longhouses, whose interiors were divided by hanging mats, with communal fires and cooking areas shared by all. Containers, clothing and utensils were fashioned from cedar bark, roots, reeds and animal skins and furs, while specialized equipment was designed for catching salmon, hunting deer and elk, snaring birds, and harpooning sea mammals such as seals and porpoises. These, along with gathered shellfish, fruits and roots, provided the people with a fairly broad diet. Ritual dancing, singing and drumming were a major part of life, as were feasts, story-telling and games. Spiritually, as has been well documented, the great animist tradition of the First Nations perceived the whole of Nature as alive with sacred significance.

Their complex social system divided people into two clans: Eagle and Raven among the Haida, Crow and Wolf in many other nations. These are further divided into hereditary kin groups. Marriage within a clan was considered incestuous, so Eagles would seek a Raven and vice versa. In this way there are always ties between clans and between people from distant places. Descent was through the female line, meaning that if a chief wanted to keep his property within the clan, he had to pass it on to his sister's sons.

The potlatch

Native Americans were (and are) fun-loving people. They would travel long distances to gather and socialize, and today's native pow-wows are always wonderful celebrations. The most famous ceremony of the coastal people was the potlatch, a celebration that marked major events, from births, deaths and marriages to the raising of a totem pole. The word potlatch derives from the verb 'to give', and this was an excuse for an individual to display their wealth by giving things away, be it art, land deeds or slaves. This was a means by which wealth was redistributed, but it was also an investment and a challenge, as those who received would be shamed if they failed to respond with a potlatch where they gave away even more. With the arrival of the Europeans, inequality between tribes and villages escalated to the point that the receivers were ruined both financially and symbolically by their own inability to respond. As a result of these and less noble considerations, like fear and ignorance, the Government outlawed the potlatch from 1884 to 1951. Many items were returned, on the condition that they be stored and displayed in museums. A collection of items resides at the Kwagiulth Museum on Quadra Island.

Mythology

West Coast mythology is rich and complex, far too involved to treat with any justice here. A wealth of tales passed on verbally from one generation to the next served to provide the spiritual and social foundation of the group, imbuing existence with meaning and mystery, and helping each individual through the natural trials and rites to which every lifetime is subject. Most of these stories involved animals such as the bear or wolf, but the most important character is the raven or crow. Raven is the creator, as well as a trickster and transformer, making people laugh at themselves and cry simultaneously, by revealing how human greatness is tempered with pride and vanity, and subject to the whims of fate and chance. After the great flood, having gorged himself on shellfish, Raven discovered the remnant of the human race hiding in a clam shell on Rose Spit, Haida Gwaii, and coaxed them out with his voice, helping them to build their culture. A sculpture of the scene by Bill Reid can be seen in the UBC Museum of Anthgropology.

Background

Art and crafts

Native art around Western Canada
A gallery of native art can be found at www.lights.com/sicc2/keepinghouse

The principal art of the **Dene** or Athapaskan people involved decoration of personal gear and clothing, such as caribou and moose hides embellished with porcupine quills, moosehair embroidery, and beads arranged in geometric and floral patterns. The Blackfoot and other **Plains** dwellers specialized in paintings on leather. This included tipis lavishly decorated with naturalistic and geometric motifs, rawhide shields symbolically painted with guardian spirits that would protect the warrior, and buffalo robes whose motifs ranged from the abstract to concentric sunburst patterns to representational images. The interior **Salish** of central BC's plateau region left behind a major body of prehistoric pictographs. The Lillooet, Thompson, Okanagan and Shuswap are noted for their finely crafted, watertight baskets made by the coiling technique and decorated with geometric motifs.

Pictographs, paintings executed with the finger in red ochre, and **petroglyphs**, carvings incised, abraded or ground by means of stone tools upon cliff walls, boulders and flat bedrock surfaces, have been discovered throughout Canada, and may constitute the continent's oldest and most widespread artistic tradition. The BC coast has many petroglyph sites, primarily on Vancouver Island, including Nanaimo and Gabriola Island. Other sites have been discovered as far north as Prince Rupert and along the Nass and Skeena River system, and there is an extensive series of small-scale petroglyphs incised on sandstone bluffs at Writing-On-Stone Provincial Park in southern Alberta.

Northwest Coast Art
Northwest Coast societies were unique in their ability to sustain a whole sub-class of professional male artists who were commissioned by wealthy patrons to produce works for potlatches and winter dances. Such artists were trained from youth as apprentices by master artists, usually their uncles or fathers. All men and women, however, would produce works of art and craft for their own home. For at least 2,500 years native men have created **carvings** from a variety of media, including wood, stone, horn, copper, bone, antler, leather, ivory and abalone shells. The finest and best known of these are large-scale works in red cedar, including totem poles, house posts and canoes. Sadly though, much of Canada's prehistoric art has been lost. On Haida Gwaii a type of soft shale called argillite is used, which can only be found in one spot, its location a jealously guarded secret. Silver and gold were used in historic times, and works in bronze have been made in recent years. Knives, adzes, chisels, gouges and awls were made of stone, shell and beaver teeth, with sculptural hafts. Bowls, dishes and ladles were fashioned from stone and wood. Boxes were made by a kerfing technique in which a single board is steamed and bent in three corner folds with a bottom and fourth corner attached by pegs. In **weaving**, almost every technique found elsewhere in North America was used.

Crests
Crests were usually, but not always, composed of animal images (including some imaginary ones like the thunderbird), whose representation was given a conventional, stylized form. Details of the crest images vary widely, according to personal and stylistic preferences. Families and bands jealously guarded their crests, which were a legacy from the ancestors, acquired in mythic time from supernatural beings, and to be held in perpetuity by their descendants. Common crest-bearing artefacts are totem poles, painted housefronts and screens, ceremonial robes and headdresses, staffs, feast dishes, spoons and ladles. To display a crest of another group is an insult to their integrity and identity. As well as displaying crests, totem poles portrayed actual characters, often enemies of the family who were depicted to provoke ridicule and contempt from those passing by.

Formlines
Objects made in the Northwest Coast traditions are so distinctive as to be instantly recognizable. The primary design element on which their artforms depend is called the formline, and by the turn of the 20th century its use had spread to the southern regions as well. Formlines are continuous, flowing, curvilinear lines that turn, swell and diminish in a prescribed manner. They are used for figure outlines, internal design elements and in abstract compositions. Traditionally figures were strongly coloured with primary black lines (charcoal and lignite), secondary red lines (ochres) and tertiary blue-green elements (copper minerals), though the colour palette has exploded since the 1980s to embrace the full spectrum. Pigments were mixed with a medium derived from dried salmon eggs, and paint brushes were made of porcupine hairs. Designs were rendered freehand, although templates were frequently used for the recurring ovoid shapes.

Native art, like the people themselves, has enjoyed a recent resurgence, and covers the full spectrum from commercial and often trashy tourist kitsch to traditional artworks. Besides the legacy of Bill Reid, many key artists such as Robert Davidson, Joe David, Norman Tait, Tony Hunt Sr., Freda Diesing, Susan Point, and Dorothy Grant are training a new generation of artists who both sell to the collectors' market and make masks, blankets and other traditional objects and regalia, including totem poles, for use by their own people. Many new materials are utilized, including ceramics, glass, and clothing, with objects in the latter category ranging from sweatshirts to haute couture. To a large extent, tourist art only pretends to represent authentic native culture, catering as it does to the stereotypical expectations of the non-Native tourist market, and has been shown more often than not to misrepresent that culture. In fact many native artists see themselves primarily as artists, whose ancestry is secondary if not incidental.

Contemporary Native Art

Language

Of the 50 or so Native Canadian languages that existed when the Europeans arrived, only a few are still widely spoken enough to ensure a long-term future. To hear an aboriginal dialect spoken is sadly rare, but most likely in remote areas of Northern BC or the Yukon, especially among older people. Canadian English is roughly half way between that spoken in Britain and the United States. Québecois French, which you are likely to encounter at some point in the west, is very different from that spoken in France, riddled with slang, and almost incomprehensible when spoken at full speed. Vancouver is celebrated for its multiculturalism, with immigrants accounting for about a third of the population, and over half of the city's school-age children having been raised speaking a language other than English. The top 10 languages spoken in the city, in order, are: English, Cantonese, Punjabi, German, French, Tagalog (Phillipine), Italian, Spanish, Vietnamese and Polish.

Cinema

Many films are shot in Vancouver, but most of them are a) American and b) second-rate tosh. Some of the best are: *The Accused*, *Little Women*, *The X-Files*, *McCabe and Mrs Miller*, and Schwarzenegger's *The Sixth Day*. Films made *by* Canadians are less famous but often a lot better. The best-known are by Toronto director **David Cronenberg**, whose films tend to combine conventional elements of horror and science fiction with a wry commentary on contemporary life that hints at profound questions involving the relationship between mind and body, and the role of technology and science in modern life. These include: *Scanners* (1980); *Videodrome* (1980); *The Dead Zone* (1983); *The Fly* (1986), a hugely successful remake of the classic B-movie, starring Jeff Goldblum; *Dead Ringers* (1988), starring Jeremy Irons, considered by many to be his masterpiece; *Naked Lunch* (1991), based on the William Burroughs novel of the same name; *M Butterfly* (1993), based on the play by David Henry Hwang; and his most controversial film yet, *Crash* (1996), modelled on the novel by JG Ballard, which won a Special Jury Prize at the Cannes Film Festival for 'originality, daring and audacity'.

A generation of writer-directors to emerge in the 1980s included **Guy Maddin**, **Denys Arcand** (*Jesus of Montréal*), **Bruce McDonald** (*Road Kill*, *Last Night*), and **Patricia Rozema** who came to international recognition with her first feature film *I've Heard the Mermaids Singing* (1987), one of Canada's most successful films both critically and commercially. Probably the most acclaimed and influential is **Atom Egoyan**, who grew up in Victoria. *Speaking Parts* (1989) and *The Adjuster* (1991) were both invited to debut at the Cannes Film Festival in France. *Exotica* (1994) became the most successful English-Canadian movie export since *Porky's* in 1981. For most people his finest work to date is *The Sweet Hereafter*. Made by the Inuit collective *Igloolik Isuma Productions*, under the self-effacing leadership of director **Zacharias Kanuk**, prize-winning *Atanarjuat- The Fast Runner* (2002), is an epic in the old sense of the word: the enactment of primal, archetypal human issues on a mythic stage; set in real time but utterly timeless. The camerawork is exceptional, the story compelling and sometimes surreal.

Canadians you always thought were American

Dan Ackroyd
Pamela Anderson
Jim Carrey
Michael J Fox
Christopher Plummer
Keanu Reeves
Donald Sutherland

Literature

Up to the mid-20th century In the first century of Canadian writing, techniques tended to reflect literary fashions in England. The best-known book by an early settler is **Susanna Moodie**'s *Roughing It in the Bush* (1852), which opens with a warning to prospective immigrants that Canada is not the Eden it is widely promoted as in England, and that the settlers' lot is a harsh one. Lurking behind the young lady's steadfast moral vision is a fascination with characters, an acute attention to detail, considerable psychological insight, and a good dose of genuine wit. Those writers best known for their portraits of the Northwest around the time of the Gold Rush were both foreigners: the British poet **Robert Service**, who romanticized the frozen north, and the American writer of short novels and stories, **Jack London**.

With Confederation came a quickened interest in the growth of a national culture, most often expressed through romantic rewritings of Canadian history. The most successful turn-of-the-20th-century works were both written for children: **Margaret Marshall Saunders'** *Beautiful Joe* (1894) and **LM Montgomery**'s international best-seller *Anne of Green Gables* (1908). Around the same time, **Stephen Leacock** established an international reputation as a comic writer and lecturer in the Dickensian tradition with works such as *Sunshine Sketches of a Little Town* (1912) and *Arcadian Adventures with the Idle Rich* (1914). And native poet **E Pauline Johnson** produced a timeless work, *Legends of Vancouver*, a collection of stories based on legends recounted to her by Chief Joe Capilano of Vancouver.

Hugh McLennan, who won the prestigious Governor General's award an unequalled five times, is credited as the first major English-speaking writer to attempt a portrayal of Canada's national character. His 1941 novel *Barometer Rising* introduced a period of optimism towards the country's own culture, progress and role on the world stage. His classic *The Watch that Ends the Night* (1959) summarizes a new faith in the land, if not the politicians it spawns. Such themes, given impetus by the humanist and anticlerical stances of francophone writers such as **Gabrielle Roy**, were picked up by the likes of Pierre Berton, **Roderick Haig-Brown** and Farley Mowat.

Following a heart attack in 1937, renowned Victoria artist **Emily Carr** began devoting more of her time to writing. *Klee Wyck* (1941) won her a Governor General's Award, followed by *The Book of Small* (1942), and *The House of All Sorts* (1944). Her very readable journals *Growing Pains*, *The Heart of a Peacock*, *Pause*, and *Hundreds and Thousands* were published posthumously. **Morley Callaghan**'s novels deal with two apparently irreconcilable worlds, the self-seeking empirical jungle, and the spiritual realm of trust and faith. Such heady themes are most timelessly treated in *Such is My Beloved* (1934), and *The Loved and the Lost* (1951), which is often considered his masterpiece. In 1960, American critic Edmund Wilson identified him as "unjustly neglected" and compared him to Chekhov and Turgenev. **Ethel Wilson** was born in South Africa, but lived in Vancouver, and is one of the first Canadian writers to truly capture the rugged and unsurpassed beauty of the BC landscape. A strong sense of place is evoked in the unpretentious and lucid style of books such as *Swamp Angel* (1954), while her characters consistently struggle with the paradox of the human condition. Around the same time, **William Mitchell** achieved instant recognition with his classic *Who has seen the Wind* (1947), which magically captures the characters and eccentrics, but especially the beauty and power of the Prairies.

Margaret Atwood is probably Canada's most celebrated late 20th-century writer, and has written 15 novels, 13 books of poetry, and numerous other miscellaneous works. She first gained critical and popular acclaim, as well as a number of literary prizes, with *The Handmaid's Tale* (1985). A disturbing dystopia set in a post-nuclear wasteland run by a right-wing monotheocracy, it was made into a film in 1990. *Cat's Eye* (1988), shortlisted for the Booker Prize, broke literary ground in its exploration of the realm of childhood, replete with shifts of power, secrecies and betrayals. *The Robber Bride* (1993) focuses on the characters of three very different Toronto women and their evil nemesis. In *Alias Grace* (1996), which was very popular in Britain, Atwood looked back into the life and mind of one of the most enigmatic and notorious women in 19th-century Canada, Grace Marks. In 2000, Atwood finally won the Booker Prize with *The Blind Assassin*.

Margaret Atwood

Pierre Berton, who was born and lived in Whitehorse, Yukon, and grew up in Dawson City amid the debris of the Stampede, is one of Canada's best-known living writers. Above all, he is renowned for his serious but highly readable popularizations of Canadian history, which combine patriotic verve, colourful detail, and a strong, driving narrative. His first important book was *Klondike* (1958), a classic account of the 1898 Gold Rush, whose left-overs he grew up with. Among other key moments in Canadian history, he turned his hand to the building of the CPR in *The National Dream* (1970) and *The Last Spike* (1971); the settling of the West in *The Promised Land* (1984); and the Canadian army's glorious First World War victory in *Vimy* (1986). *Winter* (1994), is a celebration of that season and the strength of character that allows Canada as a nation to overcome its harshness.

Pierre Berton

Canadian fiction's most rumbustious, larger-than-life character, Robertson Davies is best remembered as a prolific novelist, but for years he was an actor, playwright, essayist and teacher. His work demonstrates Canadian humour at its best, with wry social comment and witty observations on life often carrying greater importance than the slow-paced plot development. His breakthrough came with *Fifth Business* (1970), which remains one of *the* Canadian classics. In this and its two sequels *The Manticore* (1972) and *World of Wonders* (1975) (known collectively as *The Deptford Trilogy*), he uses a deep knowledge of Jungian psychology and archetypes to show that matters of the spirit inform and transcend mere worldly concerns. The most highly recommended of Davies' vast oeuvre is the *Cornish Trilogy*, comprising *The Rebel Angels* (1981), a Rabelaisian satire of academia, *What's Bred in the Bone* (1985), a profound study on artistic inspiration, and *The Lyre of Orpheus* (1988). Published posthumously, *The Merry Heart* (1996) is a charming selection of speeches, reminiscences, parodies, book reviews and essays.

Robertson Davies

Background

The recently deceased, openly gay, and greatly loved writer Timothy Findley lived much of his life on Salt Spring Island. He was equally succesful as a playwright, and his novels were eclectic. *The Wars* (1977) is one of the greatest fictional treatments of the First World War; *Famous Last Words* (1981) deals with the rise of fascism and an international conspiracy during the Second World War; *Not Wanted on the Voyage* (1984) is a witty and inventive reworking of the Noah myth; *Headhunter* (1993) pictures a Toronto replete with upper-class violence and evil; *The Piano Man's Daughter* (1995) focuses on a young piano tuner forced to face the questions of his father's identity and his mother's madness.

Timothy Findley

Farley Mowat On a field trip as a student biologist, Farley Mowat became outraged at the problems of the Inuit, all of which he attributed to white misunderstanding and exploitation. Such observations led to his first book, *People of the Deer* (1952), which made him an instant, albeit controversial, celebrity. Since then he has spent a lot of time living in the Arctic with the Inuit people, and has written 26 books, whose views are bitterly attacked by some and highly praised by others. The most famous are *Never Cry Wolf* (1963), which was made into a moving film, and the novel *Lost in the Barrens* (1956), written for younger readers. He has also written some very readable accounts of those crazy explorers who obsessively sought the Northwest Passage. Reputedly Canada's most widely read author, Mowat is a natural storyteller with a graceful, personal, and conversational tone, and his narratives and anecdotes are always fast-paced and compelling.

Alice Munro Alice Munro is mostly a writer of short stories, but her best-known work is the novel *Who Do You Think You Are?* (1978), which concerns the tough life of a girl growing up in the Prairies. It was runner-up for the Booker Prize, and winner of the Governor General's Award, which she also received for *Dance of the Happy Shades* (1968), and *The Progress of Love* (1986). The latter represented a major distillation of her work thus far, exploring with increased profundity the problems of time, and the narrator's relation to it, in an instinctive prose that perfectly balances senses of wonder and compassion. Her two subsequent collections of stories, *Friend of My Youth* (1990) and *Open Secrets* (1994), built on these strengths and extended her fame far beyond Canada's borders. The latter won the 1995 W.H. Smith Award as the best book in any category published in Britain throughout the previous year. Her latest collection of stories, *Hateship, Friendship, Courtship, Loveship, Marriage* (2001), has also won a number of key awards.

Michael Ondaatje Born in Sri Lanka, Michael Ondaatje was the forerunner of a burgeoning multicultural strata in Canadian literature. An editor, film-maker and teacher, Ondaatje was originally more a poet than novelist, with 11 books of verse to his name, including *The Cinnamon Peeler* (1992). His prose style also has an extremely poetic quality: lilting, dream-like, extremely cinematic at times, and textured with richly exotic imagery that gravitates towards the bizarre, the exaggerated, and the unlikely. Earlier works often combine documentary and fictional elements, such as *Coming Through Slaughter* (1976), which tells of real and imagined events in the life of New Orleans jazz cornetist Buddy Bolden. *In the Skin of a Lion* (1987), a novel set in Toronto's golden age, received great critical and national acclaim, but Ondaatje only reached international stardom with *The English Patient* (1992), which earned him a share of the prestigious Booker Prize (the first ever awarded to a Canadian), and was made into a film that garnered nine Oscars at the 1997 Academy Awards. *Anil's Ghost* (2000), set amidst the civil war that tore Sri Lanka apart, also won a handful of major literary prizes, and became an international bestseller.

Other key players The late **Mordecai Richler** established himself as one of Canada's foremost novelists with the publication of *The Apprenticeship of Duddy Kravitz* (1959) about a young Montréal-Jewish entrepreneur. Its dramatic scenes are complemented by a lively narrative pace, and profound characterisation. Other works include *St. Urbain's Horseman* (1971), *Joshua Then and Now* (1980), and *Solomon Gursky Was Here* (1990), which won the Commonwealth Writers' prize. **Thomas King** is the best-known of Canada's First Nations writers. His most celebrated works are *Green Grass, Running Water* (1993), and a collection of short stories, *One Good Story, That One* (1993). He has also edited *The Native in Literature* (1987), a collection of critical essays, and *All My Relations* (1990), an anthology of native Canadian fiction. In Canada he is equally famous for penning the hilarious CBC radio show *Dead Dog Café* – a perfect introduction to native humour and issues.

Margaret Laurence's many novels, of which *The Stone Angel* (1964) is the most highly regarded, are wonderful treatments of life in rural Canada. The fiction of **Jack**

Hodgins, while sometimes experimental, displays a playful love of narrative. His novels, such as *The Resurrection of Joseph Bourne* (1979), deal with characters reconstructed from the his Vancouver Island childhood. In his hands, they are eccentric but realistic characters, deployed with stylistic suppleness in life-affirming situations. **Leonard Cohen** is best known as a singer, but he started life as an exceptionally gifted poet. *Stranger Music* (1993) gives a good overview of his verse and lyrics. He also wrote two very fine novels, *The Favourite Game* (1963) and *Beautiful Losers* (1966).

The New Breed

At the start of the new millennium, a fresh breed of Canadian writers is winning international awards and conquering the international market. The trend began with **Douglas Coupland**'s *Generation X: Tales for an Accelerated Culture* (1991), which came to crystallize the entire post-boomer generation born in the late 1950s and the 1960s. Most popular of the follow-ups are *Girlfriend In A Coma* (1998), and *All Families are Psychotic* (2001). Recently he put together an interesting book of anecdotes and photos about his native Vancouver, *City of Glass* (2001). Since then the floodgates have opened. **Jane Urquhart** has been tremendously successful with *The Underpainter* (1997), which won the Governor General's Award and *The Stone Carvers* (2001), also a world-wide bestseller. But her best work is probably still *Away* (1993), in which she juxtaposed the Irish potato famine of the 1840s with pioneer homesteaders in 19th-century Ontario to explore the transplanting of Old World myths to the new land. She has also published a book of short stories, *Storm Glass* (1987) and three books of poetry.

    Carol Shields won several prizes, including the Pulitzer Prize with her classic *The Stone Diaries* (1993). Other favourites are *Larry's Party* (1997), and *Unless* (2002), which has received rave reviews. **Rohinton Mistry** has been greeted with tremendous international acclaim. Set in India, his novels *Such A Long Journey* (1991), *A Fine Balance* (1995) and *Family Matters* (2002) have won many literary awards, including a nomination for the Booker Prize. **David Adams Richards** has built a reputation as one of the country's most gifted writers with novels like *Nights Below Station Street* (1988), and *Mercy Among the Children* (2000). **John Ralston Saul** caused quite a stir in the intellectual world with *Voltaire's Bastards* (1992), a brilliant treatise on the problems caused by modern man's excessive devotion to reason. Other highly recommended recent international bestsellers are *The Cure For Death By Lightning* (1996) and *A Recipe for Bees* (1998) by Alberta novelist **Gail Anderson-Dargatz**, *At the Full and Change of the Moon* (1999) by the highly gifted **Dionne Brand**, and **Anne-Marie MacDonald**'s fashionably miserable *I Fall On My Knees*. Popular on the home front are **Anne Michaels'** *Fugitive Pieces*, **Nino Ricci**'s superb *Lives of the Saints* (1990), and novels by Galiano Island resident **Jane Rule**, including *Memory Board* (1987) and *After the Fire* (1989). And most recent of all is **Yann Martel**'s *Life of Pi*, which won the 2002 Booker Prize.

    For a collection of short modern fiction by BC writers, there's *West by Northwest: BC Short Stories* (1998), edited by D Stouck and M Wilkinson (Polestar). An finally *George Bowering, Selected Poems 1961-92* is an overview of the work of a Vancouver poet who was named Canada's first poet laureate in 2002.

Music

It comes as no surprise that those Canadian musicians and bands who have achieved a degree of international recognition are usually mistaken as Americans. Many of these are singer-songwriters such as **Joni Mitchell**, **Neil Young**, **Leonard Cohen**, **Tom Cochrane**, **Bruce Cockburn**, **Paul Anka**, **Ann Murray**, **Gordon Lightfoot**, and **Buffy Sainte-Marie**. Certain others, utterly unknown abroad, are veritable institutions here in

Canada, especially **Valdi** and the irrepressible **Stompin' Tom Connors**. There have also been a few big rock groups such as **Bachman Turner Overdrive**, **Steppenwolf**, **The Guess Who**, **Rush**, and most of **The Band**, including **Robbie Robertson**.

The trend of solo artists has continued more recently with big names like **Sarah McLachlan**, **KD Lang**, **Alanis Morissette**, **Jann Arden**, **Jane Siberry**, **Céline Dion**, and **Loreena McKennitt**. The latter is the most internationally successful of a large number of musicians who delve into their Celtic roots. To these should be added Vancouver-boy **Brian Adams**, and **Daniel Lanois**, who is more famous for producing bands like U2, and national favourites like **Bif Naked**, **Veda Hille** and **Kinnie Starr**. Some of the more successful modern Canadian bands include **The Tragically Hip**, **Crash Test Dummies**, **Cowboy Junkies**, **The Rankin Family**, **Spirit of the West**, **Blue Rodeo** and **Barenaked Ladies**. The best-known singer in the Country genre that dominates Alberta and the Prairies is **Shania Twain**. Canadian jazz musicians include the hugely popular singer **Diana Krall**, maestro pianist **Oscar Peterson**, the ebullient big band-style trumpeter **Maynard Ferguson**, superb ECM trumpeter **Kenny Wheeler** and alto-sax master **David Sanborn**. **Metalwood**, a modern, funky quartet from Vancouver, have five very good albums to their name. **Roots** is the real music of Canada, enjoying a resurgence today thanks to artists like BC's excellent **Zubot** and **Dawson**.

Religion

Most people in Canada are of British national origin and English-speaking, so it's not surprising that they are predominantly Christian, belonging to the United, Anglican or Roman Catholic churches. The variety of other cultures and second languages can be seen in the relative significance of other religions such as Buddhism, Sikkhism and Islam, which are far more significant in Vancouver than anywhere else in Western Canada. It must also be remembered that Canada, and the Prairies in particular, has in certain eras received large influxes of minor religious groups such as the Mormons, Mennonites, Hutterites and Doukhobours. The latter group are particularly well-represented in the Okanagan-Boundary and West Kootenay regions of BC (see page 226). Many native people converted to Christianity and often take the religion more seriously than their white neighbours, but it should not be forgotten that the older, animist-style spirituality of Canada's First Nations is still alive and in a position to make a come-back.

Land and environment

Geography

The Canadian Shield   Canada consists of six geological regions, five of which are arranged roughly concentrically around, and partly on top of, the sixth. Far older than the others this central core is the Canadian Shield, which is of Precambrian age, more than 570 million years old. Itself a mosaic of geological sub-regions centred around Archean age rocks (more than 2.5 billion years old), the Shield covers an area of about 4.8 million sq km stretching in a broad band from the Northwest Territories down to the Great Lakes of southern Ontario. Repeated advances of glacial ice have scoured its surface and left it covered with hundreds of lakes and rivers, including the biggest on the continent, making it very easily identified on any map. Also dominating this vast region's landscapes are slabs of protruding basement rock. Originally formed during rounds of mountain-building activity, these are now among the most stable, and oldest, on Earth. This bare rock, together with its thin soils, muskeg, and insects, has presented a constant barrier to settlement. The agricultural frontier of the prairie provinces and eastern Canada end abruptly at its perimeter. The railway link to the West literally had to be blasted through Shield rock, which also revealed its treasures of gold, silver, nickel, cobalt, zinc, copper and iron ore.

Of the younger geological regions that border the Shield, almost all of the area covered in this book is part of the Canadian Cordillera, meaning the landscapes are utterly dominated by mountain ranges. British Columbia has two main regions, loosely called the **Coast** and the **Interior**, each containing many contrasting sub-regions. The Peace River Lowland of the northeast is the only part of BC not on the Cordillera. An extension of the Interior Plains, it belongs in character to neighbouring Alberta. **The Canadian Cordillera**

The western section of the Cordillera is dominated by the lofty Coast Mountains and the offshore Insular Mountains. The **Cascade Mountains** of Washington State end at the Fraser River, then the high, snow- and ice-covered peaks of the **Coast Mountains** extend northward along the Alaskan Panhandle into the Yukon. These gloriously scenic mountains have peaks, rising to 3,000 m in the southern part, while northern peaks such as Mount Waddington rise to over 4,000 m. Numerous long, twisting, deep fjords penetrate into the mountain mass along the coast. Only three major rivers, the Fraser, Skeena and Stikine, have managed to cut through the Coast Mountain barrier, the first two of which have provided vital funnels for the only roads and railway lines to reach the Ocean. Northwest of the Coast Range the St Elias Mountains straddle BC, the Yukon and Alaska, containing North America's mightiest peaks, including the highest in BC, Fairweather Mountain (4,663 m), and the highest in Canada, Mount Logan (6,050 m). The offshore **Insular Mountains**, whose highest peak is Strathcona Park's Golden Hinde at 2200 m, are the partially submerged northern continuation of the Olympic Mountains and Coast Ranges of Washington State. They provide the land mass for both Vancouver Island and the Queen Charlotte Islands. **The Coast**

Almost all of BC's population resides in its southwestern corner. The so-called **Lower Mainland**, dominated by metropolitan Vancouver, contains almost half of the province's population, and represents its commercial, cultural and industrial core. Together with Victoria and the southeast coast of Vancouver Island, this zone is also sometimes called the **Georgia Strait** region, which holds a whole 70% of BC's population.

British Columbia's vast interior is equally dominated by mountains. In the south are three parallel, north-south oriented ranges known collectively as the **Columbia Mountains**. The backbone is the **Selkirk** Range, flanked by the **Purcells** to the east and the **Monashees** to the west. Between them, carved out by lakes and rivers, are great valleys such as the Okanagan and the Kootenay, along which most of the population is strung. These tend to have radically differing characteristics of landscape and climate dependant on such factors as the rain-shadows which keep the Okanagan and Thompson Valleys so very dry. **The Interior**

Further northwest is a fourth range of the Columbias, the **Cariboo Mountains**. Between these and the Coast Range lie the broad, gently rolling uplands of the **Interior Plateau** that covers much of central BC. This region can be considered a basin because it is surrounded by higher mountains, though its average elevation is still about 1,000 m above sea level. Some of BC's bigger but less interesting towns, such as Kamloops and Prince George, have grown as transportation and service hubs for the isolated subregions that surround them. The **northern** half of the province is barely inhabited away from the Yellowhead Highway, and beyond Prince Rupert is cut off from the Pacific by the Alaska Panhandle. The Cassiar-Omineca Mountains run between the Coast and Rocky Ranges, broken up by a second relatively flat expanse, the Spasizi Plateau.

Background

The Canadian Rockies The Rocky Mountains rise abruptly about 1,000-1,500 m above the foothills of Alberta, and some of their snow-capped peaks tower more than 3,000 m above sea level, the highest being BC's Mount Robson at 3,954 m. The range ends south of the Liard River in northeastern BC, its western boundary marked by the Rocky Mountain Trench, which extends 1,400 km from Montana to the Yukon, making it the longest valley in North America. Out of the trench flow the headwaters of many rivers, including the Kootenay, Columbia, Fraser and Liard. For details on the formation of the Rockies, see Geology.

The Yukon The Yukon constitutes the northernmost part of the Cordilleran region. Much of its area is covered by a high subarctic plateau with an average elevation of 1,200 m, frequently interrupted by predominantly northwest-southeast oriented mountain ranges and deep valleys. To the east the Yukon Plateau is bounded by the Selwyn and Mackenzie mountains. To the south an area of lower terrain near the 60th parallel separates it from the mountainous areas of northern BC. The territory's southwest is dominated by the spectacular St Elias and Coast mountains mentioned above, many of them covered by extensive permanent ice caps, including the largest nonpolar icefields in North America. These mighty peaks cut off direct access to the Pacific Ocean, despite its relative proximity. The 2,400 m Ogilvie Mountains in the north separate the Yukon and Porcupine Plateaus, the latter hemmed in by the British Mountains to the north and Richardson Mountains to the east. The Arctic Coastal Plain is a narrower eastward continuation of the same region in Alaska, which slopes down to the Beaufort Sea from the British Mountains inland. Much of the north and northwest was part of the Ice Age continent of Beringia, which escaped glaciation despite its northern latitude.

The Interior Plains East of the Rockies, the foothills quickly slope down to the broad, comparitively flat eco-region of the Interior Plains, which stretches right across Saskatchewan and Manitoba. **Alberta** can be divided into into four biophysical regions according to physiography, climate, soil and vegetation. The **prairie** region includes most of southern Alberta, more precisely the land south and east of an arc stretching from Waterton in the southwest to a point along the Saskatchewan border east of Red Deer. This gently rolling grassland is relatively dry and mostly treeless. The terrain varies locally, in places broken by deep river valleys, and rising from less than 300 m in the northeast to over 1,460 m in the southeastern Cypress Hills. The **parkland** region predominates in central Alberta, forming a crescent to the west and north of the prairie region and including most of the North Saskatchewan River drainage basin. This area varies from the flatland of old lake bottoms to rolling landscapes with numerous lakes and depressions. It contains both forested and grassy terrain, with soil and climatic factors favourable to agriculture. West of the plains an area of **foothill ridges** rises fairly rapidly towards the Rockies. The northern half of the province is covered by **boreal forest**. Here great rivers and lakes dominate the landscape, draining northward to the Arctic Ocean. Soil and climatic factors make agriculture unprofitable except in the northwestern Peace River region that extends into BC, where parkland conditions create the world's most northerly grain-growing area.

In sociocultural terms, the province's more populated lower half can be further divided into two distinct regions, with Calgary and Edmonton as their respective focal points. This is a long-standing division dating to the times when the powerful Blackfoot Confederacy dominated the south, with the Cree and Assiniboine inhabiting the north. In the early days of white settlement, grain farmers opened up the central fertile zone, while the south was more suitable for cattle-rearing on large-scale ranches, a fact that has led to the cowboy culture of Calgary, its nickname of Cow-town, and the famous Stampede. Calgary and southern Alberta were first linked to the east by the Canadian Pacific Railway, Edmonton and the north by the Grand Trunk Pacific and Canadian Northern railways. Later, Calgary became the administrative and financial headquarters for the province's petroleum industry, Edmonton its exploration and production centre.

Geology

The continent now known as North America was covered by vast granite mountains
up to roughly 600 million years ago. The greatly eroded lake-dotted remains of this
rock now constitute the **Canadian Shield**, which stretches from Great Bear Lake in the
Northwest Territories to the Great Lakes of Ontario. As the Shield had a slight tilt, all the
eroded debris was carried westward by streams and rivers, and dumped into the
Ocean, slowly building up a 'continental slope' that reached a depth of 20 km over 400
million years. The weight of this sediment turned mud to stone, sand to sandstone,
and the lime-heavy sea-debris into limestone.

The Cordillera

Roughly 200 million years ago, two distinct, equally vast chains of volcanic islands
were carried eastwards by the shifting **Pacific Plate** towards the continent's west
coast. When this 50-km thick platform eventually collided with the **North American
Plate**, it slid underneath it, plunging into the earth's molten interior. At the same time,
the first island chain was broken apart from the heavier plate and smashed violently
into, over and through the continental rock, causing it to lift, crumple, buckle and twist
itself into the myriad fascinating shapes of BC's interior mountain ranges. Over a period
of 75 million years, the aftershock of this awesome collision caused further ripples of
upheaval, as the incoming islands continued to smash into the ancient rock, creating
the Western Ranges of the Rockies that are mostly contained in Yoho and Kootenay
National Parks. Eventually, they bulldozed their way still further east, building the Eastern Ranges, such as those around Lake Louise.

When the second Pacific island chain smashed into the continent, further chaos
was unleashed: a new round of lifting, distorting, rupturing and co-mingling resulted
in the Rockies' easternmost Front Ranges, the rockwall that rears up from the Albertan
Prairies, together with the lower foothills. A series of ice-ages (at least three) in the last
240,000 years, have added their own contributions to this on-going work of art, sculpt-
ing, shattering, eroding and re-shaping of the mountain contours.

The Columbia Mountains consist mainly of sedimentary and intrusive rocks of Cretaceous, Triassic and Jurassic ages, and they have been well mineralized. The exception is
the Cariboo Range, which is composed of sedimentary rocks of Proterozoic age that
appear to be less mineralized. Many of the rocks of the interior plateau are lavas of Cretaceous and Tertiary geological ages with apparently little mineralization except around
the plateau edges. The Coast Mountain rocks are mostly granitic intrusions of Cretaceous
and Tertiary ages and there are some recent volcanoes. The Yukon is geologically very
complex but includes three parallel sectors oriented northwest-southeast. In the east,
folded sedimentary Paleozoic and Mesozoic formations are set off sharply from the Mackenzie Valley by great faults. The middle sector includes sedimentaries, metamorphics
and volcanics ranging from Precambrian to Mesozoic age. Massive plutonic Mesozoic
and Tertiary granites make up the core of the western sector.

Alberta's oldest surface landscape is a small outcrop of the Canadian Shield in its extreme
northeastern part. This does not end in the northeast, for its rocks form a basement under
the rest of the province, sloping down to 6,000 m in the southwest. During the Paleozoic
era (544-250 million years ago), Alberta alternated between dry land and sea, and life
evolved from simple plants and animals to vertebrates and dryland vegetation. The
decay of this plant and animal life, especially during the Devonian period (410-353 million years ago), formed the basis of most of the province's oil and natural gas deposits.
Alternating upraisings of the land and infloodings of ocean waters affected the province
during the Mesozoic era (250-65 million years ago). This was the era of the dinosaurs, the
period that shaped the **badland** formations of the Red Deer River valley, and laid down
most of the province's coal resources. The Cenozoic era (65 million years ago to the present) saw the uplifting of the Rocky Mountains, then about 25,000 years ago the last

Alberta

advance of continental ice scoured the terrain, covering the entire province apart from the highest parts of the Rockies, the Cypress Hills and the Porcupine Hills. The final retreat of the ice age, created the current river systems and soils.

Glaciation   During the last ice age, almost all of Western Canada was covered by a thick sheet of ice until about 12,000-15,000 years ago in the coastal lowlands and some interior valleys, and as late as 7,000 years ago at higher elevations. The results of continental and alpine glaciation are seen throughout the region in coastal fjords, mountain cirques, ground moraines across the Interior Plateau, and terraces and benches along the interior rivers. Many features commonly produced by glaciers can be observed on or near the Athabasca Glacier in the Rocky Mountains. These include: crevasses; fissures that form from tensile stress in the glacier surface; icefalls, resulting from crevasses formed where the glacier hangs over a bedrock protuberance; and a medial moraine, composed of debris and ice, which is formed where two valley glaciers coalesce. Other features that were formed during the retreat of the glacier (and can be seen nearby) include lateral moraines, formed by debris deposited along the glacier terminus. In addition, glacier meltwater carries and deposits debris, forming such features as deltas and glacial-outwash plains composed of sand and gravel. The Bow Valley itself is also a classic example of the kind of U-shaped valley caused by glaciation as opposed to the more steep, rugged, narrow valleys that were carved out by rivers such as the Fraser.

Climate

Western Canada is a vast region of complex geography, with many different microclimates. The single most obvious variable at play is latitude, which has a great effect on the quantity and strength of sunlight. In December, southern Canada receives eight hours of daylight, whereas the far north gets none at all. The north compensates for its short summer season with almost continuous sunshine.

British Columbia and the Rockies   The second most crucial factor for climate is distance from the ocean, with the most marked differences existing between the coast and interior. Relatively warm air masses from the Pacific Ocean keep **coastal** temperatures **mild** in the **winter**, while cold water keeps it **cool** in the **summer**. The barrier of the Coast Mountains prevents such moderating conditions from reaching the **interior**, which tends to have **cold winters** and **hot summers**. Average January temperatures are above 0° C at most coastal stations – the mildest in Canada – and July averages are about 15° C in the north and 18° C in the sheltered Georgia Strait region. In contrast, the interior may be covered in winter by cold air masses pushing south from the Yukon or Alaska, particularly in the northern part of the province. Average daily January temperatures are -10° C to -15° C across the central interior and are a cold -20° C or more on the northeastern plains. The southern interior valleys tend to heat up during the summer, with average July temperatures of more than 20° C, sometimes considerably more. The frost-free season on the coast is the longest in Canada, averaging more than 200 days, whereas the central Interior Plateau receives only about 75-100 frost-free days.

The air masses which cross the Pacific also bring ample **rainfall** to the coast, particularly in the autumn and winter. Much of this is dumped on the western slopes of mountain ranges, with the eastern (lee) sides often sitting in what is called a rain shadow, deprived of moisture. The western slopes of the Coast Mountains, for instance, accumulate 1,000 to 3,000 mm of precipitation annually, of which a high percentage is snowfall, whereas the Okanagan Valley receives a mere 250 mm per year. Weather in the Rockies and BC's various mountain ranges is notoriously unpredictable, with snow and hail always possible at high elevations even on the hottest days of July.

As a whole, Alberta is characterized by cold winters and relatively short, cool summers. **Alberta**
The most important factors in determining both temperatures and precipitation are the
height and width of the Rocky Mountains and the direction of the prevailing winds. As
the Rockies' eastern slopes sit in a rain shadow, Alberta's skies are predominantly clear.
Precipitation is generally low, ranging from about 300 mm annually in the southeast to
400-450 mm in the north, with a little more in the foothills region. The dry clear air provides Albertans with plenty of sunshine, ranging from 1,900 annual hours in the north to
2,300 in the south. Air funnelling through the Rockies also produces the warm, dry *chi-*
nook winds (see box page 356) which can raise temperatures dramatically within hours.
In eastern Alberta, the influence of the Pacific air mass gives way to continental conditions originating in the Arctic and mid-western US. These air masses bring mean temperatures in January ranging from -8° C in the south to -24° C in the north, and July mean
temperatures ranging from 20° C in the south to 16° C in the north. The growing season
lasts about 120 days in southern Alberta, decreasing to 60 days in the north.

The climate of the Yukon is continental, as its steep mountain ramparts seal it off from the **The Yukon**
moderating Pacific Ocean. Winters are very cold most of the time, with Canada's lowest
ever recorded temperature (-62.8° C) occurring at Snag, northwest of Kluane Lake, in
1947. At times, Pacific air may edge into the southwestern sectors resulting in short intervals of milder temperatures. Summers are warm and frequently hot (35° C has been
recorded at Dawson City) but cooler air from the Arctic can push southward. Precipitation is generally low because the high mountains in the southwest seal off access to the
moister air. The Arctic receives so little moisture that it technically qualifies as a desert.

Vegetation

The coniferous trees of coastal British Columbia are the tallest, broadest trees in Can- **West Coast**
ada. The outer island and exposed mainland coasts are predominantly covered in giant **forest**
Douglas fir, western red cedar, western hemlock, yellow cypress, Sitka spruce, shore
pine, and occasionally western yew. The principal deciduous hardwoods are red alder
and Scouler willow. The main undergrowth shrubs in these regions are salal, skunk
cabbage, salmonberry, bilberry and huckleberry, along with assorted mosses, ferns,
lichens, liverworts, and orchids. The Georgia Strait area on the east coast of Vancouver
Island and the adjacent mainland have a drier, Mediterranean climate, with a hot, dry
summer spell that can last up to eight weeks. Vegetation here is characterized by a
colourful spring flora with several annual herbaceous species. Arbutus, western flowering dogwood and Garry oak reach their northern limits in this region. Other forest species include Douglas fir, western hemlock, grand fir, bigleaf maple, western red cedar
and bitter cherry. The copious undergrowth includes thimbleberry, red elderberry,
blackberry, Nootka rose, ocean spray, snowberry, western sword fern and deer fern.

Vegetation of the Canadian Cordillera is very diverse, depending on differences in eleva- **Cordillera**
tion and latitude. Many additional variations in vegetation are the result of parallel
mountain ranges that run at right-angles to the easterly flow of weather systems, causing 'rainshadows' that keep the mountains' eastern slopes dry. The lower slopes of BC's
interior mountains and the Rockies, known as **Columbia** (or Interior) **forest** are mostly
dominated, like the coast, by Douglas fir, western red cedar and western hemlock,
though you will also see many pines, larch and spruce, as well as deciduous trees such as
alder, birch, aspen, and giant cottonwood. The undergrowth here includes devil's club,
azaleas, black and red twinberry, salmonberry and redberry alder. Common flowers
include mountain lily, columbine, bunchberry and heartleaf arnica. The more southerly
and sheltered reaches of the Rockies, and the plateaux of interior BC, are covered by less

attractive **montane forest** comprised mostly of ponderosa and lodgepole pine, along with more spindly Douglas fir and western larch. Most of the hillsides in the Thompson and Okanagan Valleys have a sparse scattering of occasional trees, between which grows vegetation typical of such arid landscapes: sage, antelope grass and even cacti.

The next major zone is the **sub-alpine**, from 1,300 to 2,200 m, where forests are typically made up of lodgepole and whitebark pines, subalpine larch, Engelmann spruce, and subalpine fir. Common understorey plants are white-flowered rhododendron, false azalea, black huckleberry, Sitka alder, oak fern, mountain arnica and leafy liverwort. The zone above the treeline, known as the **alpine**, is mainly covered with grasses, sedges, dwarf willows, mosses, lichens and other low woody and herbaceous plants. Meadows at this elevation compensate for the lack of forest with dazzling displays of wild flowers throughout the summer, including lilies, anemones, Indian paintbrush, lupins, arnica, cinquefoil, and glacier lily.

Grasslands
The **prairie** region of southern Alberta includes both short-grass and mixed-grass characteristics. The short-grass area of the southeastern corner features short, drought-resistant grasses such as blue grama. The mixed-grass area, forming an arc to the west and north of the short-grass region, contains more fertile, dark brown soil, with western wheat grass and other taller grasses providing the natural vegetation. The **parkland** regions of central Alberta and the Peace River country are characterized by a natural vegetation cover of tall grasses and aspen tress.

Boreal forest
The boreal forest that runs in a broad band across Northern Canada is dominated by plants that are capable of surviving cool, short summers and long, cold winters. The southern half is typified by canopied forests composed of both pure and mixed stands of deciduous and coniferous trees, mostly aspen, balsam poplar and white spruce. The undergrowth is usually a mixture of herbs and deciduous shrubs, while dry sites with less tree cover have a ground storey dominated by bearberry, blueberry and lichens. The northern boreal forest tends to be composed of stunted (5-7 m tall) coniferous trees of which black spruce and balsam fir are the most common, with white spruce, paper birch and jack pine occurring on warm dry sites. Between the dwarfed trees grow shrubs such as dwarf birch and Labrador tea or mats of lichens and mosses. About a quarter of the boreal forest is covered in poorly drained areas, sometimes filled with organic deposits (peatlands). These ecosystems are called fens or bogs depending upon whether they are nutrient-rich or poor. Species such as black spruce, larch, eastern red cedar (eastern and southern portion only), willows, Labrador tea, bog rosemary, cloudberry, sedges, sphagnum and mosses are typical members of wetland communities. Sedges, horsetails and spike rushes are common plants in peatlands.

Tundra
The arctic tundra which covers much of the Yukon is the second-largest vegetation region in the country, with a greater range of latitude than any other. Only a few birch, willow and trembling aspen can survive the cold temperatures and short growing season this far north, and these rarely reach more than a metre in height. Grasses and sedges abound, along with small flowering annuals, mosses, lichens and shrubs. Wild flowers include purple mountain saxifrage, yellow Arctic poppy, and Jacob's Ladder. Purple wild crocuses arrive in May, followed by lupine, wild rose and wild sweet pea in June. Mountain meadows break out in rashes of alpine forget-me-nots, pink moss campion and yellow mountain avens the following month, then August brings an explosion of reds and purples as the provincial flower, fireweed, sets every roadside ablaze. In summer and autumn, these treeless expanses represent some of the most beautiful landscapes in Canada, bursting into colourful life, encouraged by the sheer lack of time and the lengthy hours of sunshine. The transition zone from boreal forest to tundra consists of ribbons or islands of stunted black and white spruce trees in a sea of tundra vegetation.

Most of the Arctic region covered by this book, called Low Arctic, is characterized by nearly complete plant cover and abundant low and dwarf woody shrubs. Along rivers, streams and lakeshores, and on steep slopes the major plant communities include tall (2-3 m) shrub tundra of alder, scrub birch and willows. On medium-drained slopes the vegetation is lower (30-60 cm), consisting of willow, dwarf birch, dwarf heath shrubs, numerous sedges and small herbaceous species, and abundant lichens and mosses. The poorly drained soils of low rolling hills are covered in tussock sedge, dwarf heath shrubs, mosses and lichens, while various combinations of sedges, a few grasses and herbs, and abundant mosses dominate the poorly drained flatland soils. Again, this vegetation celebrates its short life with dazzling displays of colour in July and August.

Wildlife

Western Canada is one of the least disrupted regions in the world, with vast areas of remaining wilderness covered by diverse forests and lakes. Some of the planet's most productive ecosystems are found here, including great swaths of wetlands and temperate rainforest. The Pacific Ocean region has the largest number of marine mammal species in Canada, while British Columbia contains the country's greatest number of terrestrial mammal species and bird species. To the latter must be added a large number of migrating or 'accidental' species. Below is a brief look at what animals you are most likely to see in the key eco-regions, but as many creatures are found throughout much of Western Canada, this is preceded by an A-Z of the most important species.

Visit Environment Canada at www.ec.gc.ca

A-Z of species

The beaver was the obvious choice as Canada's national animal, as it had a greater impact on the country's history than any other animal or plant. The reason: beaver underfur is warm, soft and waterproof, the perfect material for making the kind of felt used in top hats. To make the fur softer still, hatters used nitrate of mercury, continued exposure to which made them go mad, hence the expression. With beaver pelts fetching the highest prices, pursuit of the rodents was the leading motive of early colonizers, and led to explorations which opened up most of the northwestern hinterland to settlement. In the process, the beaver population was reduced from ten million to near extinction.

Ten thousand years ago, Beringia was inhabited by giant beavers the size of bears with lower incisors 25 cm long. Today they are still the largest member of the rodent family. Beavers are monogamous and mate for life. Their tails are horizontal, flattened, paddle-shaped and scaly. As well as eye membranes and ear valves, they have structural adaptations at the back of their mouths to stop water from entering the lungs, meaning they can gnaw and carry branches when submerged. They typically inhabit slow-moving streams, where they construct dams, making them one of the only animals beside humans that can build their own environment. Beaver lodges are made of intricately interlaced branches, with mud and grass plastered on the outside, and are almost impenetrable. Rather than hibernating, they stay in their lodges, whose clever design keeps temperatures at an even 8-12° C even when it is -40° C outside. A cache of food is kept nearby, submerged to preserve it. Mainly nocturnal, this most hard-working of animals can usually be seen swimming busily around at dusk.

Without beaver dams, much of Canada's water would flow unchecked. The beavers thin out dense woods, creating opportunities for a variety of animals and plants. They are therefore a keystone species in temperate and boreal forest aquatic ecosystems.

Beaver
For an illustrated overview of Canadian species, www.cws-scf.ec.gc.ca/ hww-fap

The list of birds native to Western Canada is extensive. This is a summary of the most notable species. **Waterbirds** Common and red-throated loon, horned and

Birds

red-necked grebe, cormorant, various species of swan including the trumpeter, geese, American widgeon, mallard, northern pintail, green-winged teal, common eider, various ducks including the harlequin, Barrow's goldeneye, merganser. **Raptors** Osprey, northern harrier, bald and golden eagles, various hawks and kestrels, peregrine falcon, gyrfalcon. **Shorebirds** American golden plover, lesser yellowlegs, wandering tattler, spotted and upland sandpiper, whimbrel, red-necked pharalope, long-tailed jaegar, various gulls, Arctic tern, black guillemot, belted kingfisher. **Owls** Great grey, snowy, northern hawk, short-eared. **Perching birds** Various jays including blue and grey, raven, numerous swallows including tree, violet-green, bank, barn and cliff, chickadees, American dipper, ruby-crowned kinglet, northern wheater, Townsend's solitaire, various thrushes including grey-cheeked and Swainson's, American pipit, Tennessee, Wilson's and yellow warblers, common yellowthroat, numerous sparrows, junco, snow bunting, Lapland and Smith's longspur, redpolls. **Other** Spruce and sharp-tailed grouse, ptarmigan, sora, American coot, sandhill crane, northern flicker, assorted woodpeckers and many hummingbirds.

Bears **Black bears** Black bears are bulky, thickset animals about 150 cm long and 100-120 cm high at the shoulder. Adult males weigh about 135 kg, although exceptionally large animals weighing over 290 kg have been recorded. Females are much smaller, averaging 70 kg. Although black is the most common colour, other colour phases such as brown, dark brown, cinnamon, blue black, and even white also occur. A black bear walks like a human being with the entire bottom portion of the foot touching the ground, and will often stand on two legs with its nose in the air. Since the eyesight of bears is poor, they rely heavily on well-developed senses of hearing and smell, and will usually attempt to get downwind from an intruder to make an identification by smell. Contrary to common misconceptions, bears are shy, timid animals who want nothing more than to be left alone. They are mostly vegetarians, particularly fond of berries, though they will also happily devour a whole nest of ants.

Black bears appear awkward as they shuffle along, but can move with amazing speed when necessary. For short distances they have been clocked at speeds of up to 55 kmph. They are good swimmers and frequently cross rivers and small lakes. Climbing is second nature to a black bear. Young animals readily take to trees when frightened. They climb with a series of quick bounds, grasping the tree with their forepaws and pushing with their hind legs. The black bear has several distinct calls, including a growl of anger, a whining call, and sniffs of many sorts. A female with cubs may warn them of danger with a loud woof-woof and call them in with a whining or whimpering sound. The cry of a young cub in trouble is similar to the crying of a human baby.

Grizzly bear The brown, or grizzly, bear has always been something of a feared, misunderstood and mythologized enigma, its habits only becoming known following extensive studies in Canada and the United States during the 1960s. As human populations have grown, the grizzly's range has gradually shrunk back to northwestern North America, and even here you are far more likely to see a black bear. Although grizzly bears have been known to weigh as much as 500 kg, the average male weighs 250-350 kg and the female about half that. Like black bears, grizzlies are mostly vegetarian, though they have a great love of salmon. Watching them fishing during salmon season, at places like Hyder near Stewart, is a particularly rewarding experience. Despite their reclusive tendencies, grizzlies are much feared by many people, the more ignorant of whom will shoot them for pleasure or 'sport'. As a result, the grizzly is becoming a greatly endangered species, and a moratorium (suspension of hunting) was recently declared to protect them. This, however has been lifted by BC premier Gordon Campbell.

The usual obvious way to distinguish between black and grizzly bears is by size and colour. Such methods are unreliable, not accounting for big black bears, younger, smaller grizzlies, and the tendency of both bears to come in a variety of shades. To be certain, look at the faces: black bears have a 'Roman' (straight) facial profile, whereas Grizzlies have dish-shaped (concave) profiles. Grizzlies have a large shoulder hump lacking in black bears, and much longer front claws which prevent them from climbing trees. You are most likely to see a grizzly where there are few humans, such as in the Yukon's Kluane National Park, or very remote spots such as Bella Coola. Sadly, the most reliable place of all to see either bear is around municipal garbage dumps.

Buffalo (bison)

The bison is the largest land animal in North America. A bull can stand 2 m high and weigh more than a tonne. It has curved black horns on the sides of its head, a high hump at the shoulders, a short tail with a tassel, and dense shaggy dark brown and black hair around the head and neck. Another distinctive feature of the buffalo is its beard. Two hundred years ago, the Great Plains aboriginal people relied heavily on the great herds of 30 to 70 million bison that roamed free in North America. By the end of the 1800s, the species was on the verge of extinction. Since then numbers have increased, but the great free-ranging herds have gone forever. Today's wild herds move freely only within parks and fenced wildlife sanctuaries.

There are two living subspecies of wild bison in North America: the plains bison and the wood bison. Today, there are few **plains bison**, though some of their traditional routes are still visible from the air in the form of deep paths worn over the years by millions of passing hooves. A herd of about 600 lives at Elk Island National Park, 64 km east of Edmonton, and there are small numbers at Waterton Lakes National Park in Alberta. Some commercial ranchers have bred the plains buffalo with cows, resulting in 'beefalo'.

In historic times, the range of the **wood bison** was further north, centred in northern Alberta and adjacent parts of BC, the Northwest Territories, and Saskatchewan. In general, the wood bison is darker in colour, less stocky and long-legged, but heavier. Never as abundant as its southern cousin, the total number in North America was probably never more than 170,000. Today the largest free-roaming herds of both breeds is in Wood Buffalo National Park, on the Alberta/NWT border, where there are about 2,000 animals. Bison have keen senses of smell and hearing, able to distinguish smells from 3 km away, and are quick to detect changes in their environment.

Caribou

One of Canada's most widely distributed large mammals, the caribou is the only member of the deer family whose males and females both carry antlers. They are similar to and belong to the same species as the reindeer of Eurasia. Their ability to use lichens as a primary food distinguishes them from all other large mammals, and has enabled them to survive on harsh northern rangeland. An excellent sense of smell enables them to locate lichens under the snow. Large, concave hooves splay widely to support the caribou in snow or muskeg, and also function well as paddles, making them excellent swimmers. In fact, a herd of caribou will often swim across even the widest of lakes rather than walk around them, and often do so to gain some respite from the swarms of insects that make their lives a misery in summer.

Woodland caribou are large, dark animals usually found in small herds in northern boreal forests. Average weights are 180 kg for bulls and 135 kg for cows. In the mountainous areas of Western Canada, they make seasonal movements from winter range in forested valleys to summer range on high, alpine tundra. Clearing of land for agriculture has sadly destroyed much of their habitat, with new growth forest a much more suitable environment for moose and deer. **Barren-ground caribou** are smaller and lighter coloured, and spend much or all of the year on the tundra. Most of those in Western Canada belong to the porcupine and bluenose herds which migrate seasonally across the Yukon from the tundra to the sparsely wooded northern coniferous forests, known as taiga. They are excellent navigators, unerringly walking hundreds of kilometres in spring to their relatively small calving areas, led by the pregnant cows. In fact, their migration routes have always been so well established that, in past years, native hunters would lay in wait at certain places, knowing the caribou would come. The annual crossing of the Dempster Highway by the porcupine herd in autumn is one of the most spectacular sights imaginable.

Cougar   The cougar's range has decreased since European settlement, but is still the most extensive of any terrestrial mammal in the western hemisphere, extending from the Yukon to Patagonia. In Canada this large predator, which can also go my the names mountain lion, puma, and panther, is now common only in western forested regions, where three subspecies occur: one in southwestern Alberta and interior BC, one in the Coast Mountains, and one only on Vancouver Island. The cougar is the second largest cat in the New World after the jaguar, with a body length of around 2 m, and weights of about 71 kg and 41 kg for males and females respectively. One of the cougar's distinctive characteristics is its long tail, which is useful for balance. Like all cats, cougars are formidable hunters, very secretive, and almost entirely nocturnal, so the chances of seeing one are almost nil.

Deer   Of all North America's large animals, the **white-tailed deer** is the most widely distributed and the most numerous. Its range extends from the southern tip of the continent well into the northern boreal forest. Far from being endangered, these deers are excessively numerous, and you are almost guaranteed to see their distinctive white rears bouncing away into the bush, or running out in front of your vehicle. Even more common west of the Continental Divide is the almost identical **black-tailed deer**, which has similar antlers and will sometimes show the characteristic 'flag' of the white tail, though usually with less flare. **Mule deer** can be distinguished by a small white tail with a black-tip, antlers that divide and redivide into paired beams and points, and large ears that resemble those of their namesake.

Elk   In general appearance elk, also known as *wapiti*, are obviously kin to these deer, but considerably larger. An adult bull elk stands about 150 cm tall at the shoulder and weighs around 300-350 kg, with some large bulls approaching 500 kg in late summer. The colour of the elk's coat ranges from reddish brown in summer to dark brown in winter. They have long, blackish hair on the neck that is referred to as a mane. Male elk are notable for their impressively large antlers, which are grown new each year in just a few months. In summer these are encased by a protective layer of 'velvet'. Elk are sociable and talkative animals, communicating through frequent grunts and squeals. They are also long-lived, with males surviving to an average of 14 years, and females living as long as 24 years. In autumn the males go into rut as they prepare to mate, at which time they can be extremely aggressive, and should be avoided. While elk inhabit almost the entire region covered by this book, you are most likely to see them wandering through campgrounds in the Rockies, or grazing in northern wetlands.

Insects   Unfortunately, the creatures you are most likely to encounter are voracious biting insects. Though the Tropics are more famous for their mosquitoes, nowhere in the world has bugs worse than those found in Canada. Naturally, such beasties only thrive at certain temperatures, so the further north you go the shorter their season, and places like the Okanagan are too hot for them in summer. Most of Western Canada has horrible bugs for at least a few weeks of the summer. Central BC is particularly brutal, and the whole of the north is afflicted with appallingly vicious insects for a shorter time span. **Mosquitoes** are annoying mostly for their persistence and whining sound, but **black flies** can be an even greater torment as they are numerous, harder to kill, and like to go for your eyes. They can be horrible in the Coast Mountains. **No-see-ums** are so named because you can't see them, making these a formidable enemy. They're small enough to get through protective netting, and their bites are extremely painful. Towards the end of the summer, **deer**

flies and **horse flies** have a brief season. Both are big enough to take a nasty chunk out of you, but they're slow and fairly easy to kill. For a couple of weeks in spring, the most heinous bugs of all have a brief season in certain regions that includes the Rockies: **ticks**. Ticks attach themselves to your flesh and suck your blood. They particularly like to hang out in long grass. Signs normally warn hapless hikers of the danger, so do a full body (and hair) check at the end of the day, and wear long trousers. The best way to remove them is very delicately with a pair of tweezers, making sure that no parts of the insect break off inside. The very tiny ticks that carry Lymes disease are practically non-existent in Canada.

Of the three Canadian wild cats, the lynx and bobcat are most alike and most closely related, both probably having descended from the Eurasian lynx. They resemble a large domestic cat, with a short tail, long legs, large feet, and prominent ear tufts. Both cats have large eyes and ears, and depend on acute sight and hearing when hunting. Secretive and nocturnal, these too are rarely seen in the wild, generally inhabiting forested wilderness areas, particularly old-growth boreal forests with a dense undercover of thickets and windfalls. The lynx preys almost exclusively on the snowshoe hare, and numbers of lynx are known to fluctuate dramatically due to this hare's 10-year population cycle.

Lynx and bobcat

Moose are the largest members of the deer family. An estimated half to one million of them live throughout Canada's forests, though you are most likely to see them in boreal forest, or marshy areas of Northern BC. A bull moose with a full rack of antlers is arguably the continent's most formidable animal, standing taller than the largest horse, and weighing up to 600 kg, or 800 kg in the Yukon. For all that, the moose is an ungainly, rather whimsical looking beast. Its body is deep at the shoulders, where massive muscles result in a humped appearance. The slim hindquarters and spindly legs look inadequate for the task of supporting so massive a bulk. The head is heavy and huge, its ears similar to a mule's, its long nose lending the beast a perpetual mournful expression. The upper lip is drooping and flexible, and from its throat hangs a pendant of fur-covered skin, some 30 cm long, called a bell. In colour the moose varies from dark brown, almost black, to reddish or greyish brown, with grey or white leg 'stockings'.

Moose

In late summer and autumn, a mature bull carries a great rack of antlers which may reach a span of 180 cm. The heavy main beams broaden into large palms which are fringed with a series of spikes usually less than 30 cm long. At this time, like the elk, bull moose enter their rutting season, at which time they are extremely dangerous. The eyesight of the moose is extremely poor, but its senses of smell and hearing compensate for this. On obscure forest roads, moose have a habit of getting in front of a car and walking or running along the road for long distances. Few motorists seem to mind.

Background

Mountain goats are found throughout the mountain ranges of the Cordillera, at elevations where they feel safe from humans and other predators. Their ability to negotiate steep, rocky terrain is unequalled. Pure white of colour, with short, pointed horns, these bearded goats have long, thin faces that seem to wear perpetual expressions of benign intelligence and mild amusement, no doubt one of the reasons for their great popularity with visitors. Though they do not stoop to begging at roadsides like the sheep, your chances of encountering these creatures in the Rockies are very high.

Mountain goat

The wild, or mountain, sheep is a stocky, hoofed mammal, about one and a half times as large as a domestic sheep. The most distinctive characteristic of the males is their massive horns, which spiral back, out, and then forward, in an arc. Adult females have slightly curved horns about 30 cm long. North American wild sheep are related both to domestic sheep, which were imported from Europe by early settlers, and to the native sheep of Asia, which is thought to have migrated across the Bering land bridge about half a million years ago. As the great ice-age glaciers moved south from the pole, those

Mountain sheep

animals became isolated in two ice-free areas, one in central Alaska, the other in the United States. The former evolved into the slender-horned **Dall sheep**, those farther south into the heavy-horned **Rocky Mountain** and desert **bighorns**. Today the white Dall sheep is found in mid and north Yukon, while its almost black cousin, the Stone, or black Dall sheep, makes its home in northern BC and southern Yukon. In the Pelly Mountain area of the Yukon, the two breeds merged gradually with each other, resulting in the Fannin sheep of the Faro region.

The southern sheep evolved into seven races, two of which returned to Canada after the retreat of the glaciers. Rocky Mountain bighorns moved north into the Rockies of BC and Alberta. California bighorns expanded into southwestern BC, colonizing the arid mountains and river valleys of the Okanagan and Chilcotin areas. Once a year, around about June or July, the bighorns shed their hair, resulting in a scruffy, bedraggled appearance until the new coat grows in.

Musk ox Superficially the musk ox resembles the bison, its humped shoulders and long black coat accentuating the shortness of its legs. In fact, it is more closely related to sheep and goats. Although not very tall, musk oxen are relatively heavy owing to their stocky and compact build. Adult bulls weigh 270-315 kg and cows about 90 kg less. Both have impressive, very distinctive horns, which curve downward toward the face then out and up at the slender tips. On the bulls, the base of each horn extends across the forehead to meet as a solid 'boss' of horn and bone up to 10 cm thick. Superbly equipped to withstand frigid temperatures, the musk ox remains on the Arctic tundra year round. Fossil evidence suggests that their ancestors crossed the Bering land bridge to North America about 90,000 years ago. An ability to function normally in temperatures of -40° C in high winds and blowing snow is mainly due to the muskox's amazing coat, which has layers of wool and hair. The insulating woolly layer next to the animal's skin is stronger than sheep's wool, eight times warmer, and finer than cashmere. The coarser hairy layer that covers and protects the wool grows to be the longest hair of any mammal in North America. The Inuit name for muskox is *omingmak*, "the animal with skin like a beard".

Polar bear The polar bear is North America's largest land carnivore. Adult males measure 240-260 cm in total length and usually weigh 400-600 kg, although they can weigh up to 800 kg, about as much as a small car. Adult females weigh 150-250 kg. Polar bears have longer necks, skulls and bodies than their southern cousins, and a 'Roman' nose like black bears. Though it looks white, or lemon yellow under a rising sun, polar bear hair is translucent, and reflects the heat from the sun down to the base of the hair, where it is absorbed by the black skin. It sheds water easily, so that after a swim the bear can shake itself dry like a dog. Polar bears are considered to be marine mammals because they depend upon seals and the marine environment for their existence. They feed mostly on ringed seals, but they also catch bearded seals, harp seals, hooded seals, and harbour seals, occasionally also killing walruses, belugas or white whales, and narwhals.

Along with eyesight and hearing believed to be similar to those of a human, polar bears have an exceptional sense of smell, and sniff constantly, testing the air for scent from ringed seal breathing holes, which they can detect through layers of ice and snow 90 cm or more thick up to a kilometre away. When the seal comes up to the breathing hole for air, the polar bear kills it and flips it out of the water with a single blow of its large front paws, which also double up as powerful oars. During spring and early summer, when seals are most accessible, a bear may catch one every 4-5 days. Whatever the time of year, they can slow down their metabolism at will if food is short. Polar bears can be seen around the Beaufort Sea in winter, but the best place to see them is Churchill, Manitoba.

Few people, even those who spend a lot of time outdoors, have seen wolverines in the wild. This contributes to their mysterious reputation and explains why they are the most misunderstood of Canada's wild animals. The wolverine belongs to the weasel family, and has been described as the fiercest creature on earth, a fearlessly aggressive fighter that will drive bears away from their kills. The wolverine is not long and lean, like a weasel, but short and thick, like a small bear. An adult is about the size of a medium-sized dog, and weighs 12-18 kg, 8-12 kg for females. The typically glossy, dark brown pelt of the wolverine is striking.Two yellow stripes originate at the nape of its neck and sweep along each flank to merge at the base of its long, bushy tail.

Wolverine

Wildlife by region

When Captain Cook first visited these shores, the waters teemed with the kind of cute **sea otters** that like to lay around on their backs adroitly opening up shellfish with their skillful little hands. Alas, the brisk trade in their pelts that followed this first sojourn of a European led the otters to be hunted to near extinction, a crisis from which they have recovered less well than the inland beaver. They can still be seen, though the Vancouver Aquarium is the most likely spot. Colonies of **seals** and **sealions** are a more likely specta-cle, especially for sea kayakers off the West Coast of Vancouver Island or Haida Gwaii.

Pacific Ocean

Some 22,000 **grey whales** migrate past the West Coast every year from March to May. **Orca** (killer whales) are year-round residents, and can often be seen from the Van-couver Island shore, especially in Victoria. The world's third largest residence of orca pods is in the Johnstone Strait close to Telegraph Cove. **Humpback** whales are also frequently seen in the Pacific, and further north are blue, beluga and right whales. **Dolphins** are also spotted. Of the many fish species, the most remarkable is **salmon**. Divers come to these shores to see the likes of **giant octopuses** and massive **wolf eels**. At low tide a large number of colourful critters can be seen in tide pools, especially in sheltered waters such as on the Gulf Islands. The starfish are big, numerous, and come in many colours.

As well as bears, cougars, deer and elk, and the usual collection of smaller mammals, the temperate rainforests of the West Coast are home to many bird species, including a wealth of woodland species, such as Townsend's, Wilson's and orange-crowned war-blers, junco, Swainson's thrush, and golden-crowned kinglet. Rarer birds include the rufous hummingbird. The Gulf Islands are very good places to see golden and bald eagles, but the best place for the latter is Brackendale near Squamish, which plays host to thousands of the salmon-hungry birds every January.

West Coast forest

The lower slopes of BC's interior mountains and the Rockies also support healthy popu-lations of the widespread large mammals, as well as many smaller creatures such as coyotes and weasels, porcupines, red and grey squirrels, and chipmunks. Birds are numerous, especially hawks and owls.

Columbia forest

The more southerly and sheltered reaches of the Rockies and the dry plateaux of interior BC are home to a lot of coyotes, who thrive on the large numbers of voles and small rodents. Parts of the Okanagan are home to desert species such as the rattle-snake and certain rare amphibians. This is a good area for birds such as warblers, woodpeckers, nut-hatches, chickadees and the ruby-crowned kinglet. Birds of prey include goshawks and Swainson's hawks. Ducks such as mallard, shoveler, and widgeon are common, and rarer birds such as the cinnamon teal can also be seen.

Montane forest

Forests between 1,300-2,200 m throughout the Rockies' interior ranges in BC are teeming with deer and elk. Smaller mammals include the golden-mantled ground squirrel. Bird species include Clark's nutcracker.

Sub-alpine forest

▶ Bear essentials

Bears are shy, reclusive creatures who will usually take off if warned of your presence. Your voice is the best way to do so. In areas where forest or brush limits visibility, especially if you are hiking into the wind or close to a stream, sing and shout loudly. The little bells you see some people wearing are not loud enough to be effective. Be particularly wary in areas where bears are known to live, if there are lots of berry bushes around, or if you have seen bear droppings (it looks like what it is: mushed up berries). When camping, never leave food in or close to your tent (see Responsible tourism page 33).

Only in very rare cases have bears preyed on humans, or attacked in a premeditated way. If you catch a bear by surprise, however, it may attack out of fear, especially if it's a sow with cubs to defend. If you see a bear, avoid looking it in the eyes, which could be construed as a challenge. Resist the temptation to run: like most animals, bears are more likely to pursue a fleeing target, and they run much faster than humans. They are also strong swimmers, and black bears are consummate climbers of trees. Generally the best advice is to stay calm and still, moving in slow motion if at all. Stand your ground making soothing, non-threatening sounds, then retreat slowly. If a lone black bear attacks, fighting back and screaming at it might be effective. If it's a grizzly, try climbing a tree, otherwise lie face down with your legs apart and your hands clasped behind your neck. This position makes it hard for the bear to flip you over. Once the bear feels you are no longer a threat it is likely to leave you alone. Only move when you are sure the bear has left the area, then get up slowly and quietly and walk away.

Alpine Alpine zones above the treeline are less inhabited by man, and so popular with animal species. Elk and mule deer are resident only in summer, whereas Dall and bighorn sheep and mountain goats can be seen year-round. Among smaller mammals, a particular favourite is the **marmot**, a large rodent that often lives on rock-slides in the mountains. These can become tame and curious, approaching humans for hand-outs. Often seen, they are more frequently heard, producing a shrill whistle to warn each other of intruders. The pika is a seldom seen little relative of the rabbit. Birds at this elevation include rosy finches, pipits, and blue grouse. The white-tailed ptarmigan, similar to a partridge, is resident throughout the year.

Grasslands The grasslands of Alberta and BC's Peace River district are the traditional home of **bison** and the **pronghorn**, a tawny-gold species of antelope. The size of a large dog, but with a heart twice the size and eyes larger than a horse, pronghorns are the fastest animals in North America, capable of speeds over 100 kmph. The traditional predators of such cattle are wolves and coyotes, both of which you are much more likely to hear than see. What you are guaranteed to witness are large numbers of small mammals such as gophers, groundsquirrels and jackrabbits, which have bred out of control and are much hated by farmers. Occasional ponds or 'sloughs' on the plains are important breeding grounds for ducks, grebes, herons, pelicans, rails and many more. Other common birds are the marbled godwit, the curlew, and the prairie falcon, which is a close relative of the peregrine falcon.

Boreal forest The boreal forest that runs in a broad band across much of Canada is one of the best places to see many of the species mentioned above, particularly caribou and **moose**. Thanks to their unmerited reputation, most of the west's population of **wolves** has been driven back to these sparsely populated northern forests. **Beavers** can be seen in any wet forest environment, but are especially common here. Small mammals include muskrat, varying hare, red squirrel, deer mouse and red-backed vole. Frequently seen birds are jays, ravens and grouse. Forest wetlands offer a refuge to ducks, geese and herons, including the great blue heron, with loons, grebes and songbirds attracted to the surrounding undergrowth. There are also plenty of raptors, including numerous types of hawk, and Canada's largest owl, the great grey. There is a good chance of seeing ruffed and spruce grouse, belted kingfisher, grey jay, robin and other thrushes, black-capped and boreal chickadees, waxwings and finches, several nuthatches, vireos and grosbeaks, and many species of warblers and sparrows. The zone is also justly infamous for supporting some of the world's most voracious and copious biting insects, including the ubiquitous mosquitoes, black flies and no-see-ums.

The apparently harsh environment of the Arctic tundra is nevertheless rich in animal life. This is the best place to see caribou and smaller mammals such as Arctic ground squirrels, and lemmings, ermines and weasels, Arctic white foxes and Arctic hares. **Tundra**

The far north is home to Muskoxen and polar bears, while the Beaufort Sea is home to ringed and bearded seals, and the incredibly graceful beluga whales. Lots of ravens inhabit the north, earning their reputation as crafty tricksters. Predators including the gyrfalcon, the largest falcon in the world, jaegars, hawks, gulls and owls, including the snowy owl. Of the hundred or so bird species to be spotted, most are migratory, including numerous swans, geese and loons. The Arctic tern makes a 32,000 km return migration from the Antarctic, the longest annual migration of any creature.

Conservation

The first European explorers and settlers in Canada found wildlife in abundance. Believing natural resources to be unlimited, they saw no need to practise conservation. Wildlife, fish and timber were free for the taking. The result of this attitude became apparent in the latter half of the 19th century with the near extinction of animals like buffalo and elk that once numbered many millions. Even then, western and northern Canada were still held to be boundless frontiers. The British North America act of 1867 assigned resource-management responsibilities to governments, with wildlife conspicuous by its omission, lumped under 'matters of private and local nature'. Wildlife enthusiasts of the 1880s solemnly predicted the extinction of most large North American mammals, but the next two decades marked a significant turning point in Canadian wildlife history. Following Confederation and the assumption of resource- management control by the original provinces, a move was made to develop wildlife conservation laws. Banff National Park, the first in Canada (established 1885), was created to make money rather than protect wildlife, but this would become one of its significant functions. Others, such as Wood Buffalo National Park, were created solely for that purpose.

From 1920 to 1970, the concerns of society led to the formation of non-profit organizations such as the Canadian Wildlife Federation, Canadian Nature Federation, Ducks Unlimited (Canada), World Wildlife Fund (Canada), and the Nature Conservancy of Canada, as well as government conservation agencies like the Canadian Wildlife Service of Environment Canada. Many parks and conservation areas were created to protect particular animals and ecosystems, and thanks to the wide distribution of most species, relatively few have actually been lost compared with what has occurred in tropical regions. The most significant exceptions were the great auk, passenger pigeon, Labrador duck, Dawson caribou, and sea mink.

Many forms of wildlife are more abundant now than they were a century ago, but a number of species have continued to decline to threatened levels or are in danger of extinction, and this includes some very significant animals such as the grizzly bear. Over-hunting or harvesting is often to blame, but the real problem is usually the extensive alteration of ecological regions because of competing land uses such as forestry, agriculture and urbanization. Despite its obvious importance and irreplacable status,

Background

the unlogged temperate West Coast rainforest keeps shrinking; hardly any of Canada's only living desert around Osoyoos has survived the wholesale conversion of land into orchards and vineyards; and only a few hectares of the resilient tallgrass prairie remain intact, the rest having been degraded to the point of increasing worthlessness by short-sighted agricultural methods. Wetland drainage permanently removes the habitat required by many species.

Western Canada is lucky because it has only been subjected to a century and a half of abuse by modern man. Given time and increasing over-population of the globe, however, there is no reason to believe that its vast tracts of wilderness will not eventually go the same way as most of Europe, which has lost almost all of its forests and indigenous wildlife, unless a fundamental shift in human priorities occurs. Pollution of rivers and estuaries will render them unfit for wildlife survival; acid rain will sterilize vast tracts of land and waterways; marine birds and mammals will increasingly face the threat of offshore oil spills, general pollution of the oceans, and the gradual depletion of marine life due to over-fishing. The direct threat of uncontrolled harvests, so devastating in the 19th century, has been replaced by the indirect, insidious but permanent threat of environmental degradation that is characteristic of the 20th century. Certainly, provincial governments seem just as happy to sell off chunks of priceless and irreplacable temperate rainforest to the big money of logging companies unless their people kick up enough of a fuss to deter them. So often, such environmental trouble-makers have been led by native people whose relatives have witnessed the undoing in little more than a century of a happy natural balance their ancestors had managed to sustain more or less intact for some 15,000 years.

Protected areas

National parks Following the discovery of the Cave and Basin Hot Springs by railway workers in today's Banff National Park, the government was flooded with offers but chose not to grant private title to the lands. Instead, it was decided that the region should be preserved for the benefit of all Canadians. A report by the commissioner of Dominion Lands that "a large tract of country lying outside of the original reservation presented features of the greatest beauty, and was admirably adapted for a national park" led to the creation of Canada's first national park in 1887. Within eight years, three new mountain reserves were set aside, unavailable for "sale, settlement or squatting". These later became Yoho, Glacier and Waterton Lakes National Parks.

The world's first distinct bureau of national parks, the Dominion Parks Branch, was formed in 1911, and led by JB Harkin from 1911-36. During this time nine national parks were established, including Elk Island (1913), Mount Revelstoke (1914), Kootenay (1920), and Wood Buffalo (1922), and "hereby dedicated to the people of Canada, for their benefit, education and enjoyment". Further park establishment was sporadic until, in 1961, John I. Nicol became director of the National and Historic Parks Branch. Under his administration, 10 new national parks were created, and the emphasis shifted to the preservation of natural ecological processes above all else. Current policy has continued this shift in emphasis and now stresses the importance of minimal interference from people. These days, if a grizzly mother wants to set up home with her cubs in a Banff campsite that normally caters to 200 people, the campsite closes. National parks are also protected by federal legislation from all forms of extractive resource use such as mining, forestry, agriculture and sport hunting, though fishing is still allowed with a special licence.

By 1970, 20 national parks had either been established or negotiated, but opportunistically, without a vision or long-term goal. This vision was provided in the early 1970s by the National Park System Plan, which sought to develop a system of national parks using the principle of 'representativeness'. Canada is thus divided into 39 natural regions, each containing a unique set of geological, biological and ecological

Greenpeace

Greenpeace was born in Vancouver. It was 1969, a few days after the US detonated a nuclear bomb at Amchitka Island in the Alaskan Aleutians. A small group, varied in age and profession, but equally concerned for the environment, formed the Don't Make a Wave Committee. At the end of a meeting one of the oldest members is said to have uttered the traditional 'Peace' as he left, and one of the youngest replied "Make it a Green Peace". At first the name was *given to the fishing boat which the group chartered to head for the detonation site, but which bad weather forced to turn back. A bigger boat, Greenpeace Too! suffered the same fate, and the bomb was detonated. The foundation persisted, however, adopting its new name, and expanding its efforts to combat whaling, sealing and eventually such broader concerns as toxic pollution and the destruction of rainforests.*

characteristics, each to be represented by at least one national park. By 1998, 24 natural regions were thus represented.

In October 2002 Jean Chrétien announced his intention to give the national parks a massive shot in the arm, and came very close to completing the National Park System Plan. So far $218 million of federal funds have been promised over the next five years, and the system is set to expand by almost 50%. There will be 10 new national parks, five new marine conservation areas, and three park expansions, as well as restoration and protection of the existing parks.

British Columbia's national parks are: Pacific Rim, Gwaii Haanas, Mount Revelstoke, Glacier, Yoho, and Kootenay. Alberta's are Banff, Jasper, Waterton lakes, Elk Island, and Wood Buffalo. In the Yukon are Kluane, Ivvavik and Vuntut. All of these have their own fees. An annual pass valid for all of them currently costs $38. An annual pass for all Parks-run historic sites is $30. The two combined, called a Discovery package, is $48.

UNESCO recognizes the responsibility of all nations to protect places of such unique natural and cultural value and that they are considered part of the heritage of all mankind. In Western Canada Kluane, Nahanni (NWT), Wood Buffalo, the Burgess Shale of Yoho National Park, and Anthony Island (Gwaii Haanas Park National Park Reserve) have been designated World Heritage Sites. The combined boundaries of Yoho, Jasper, Banff and Kootenay national parks and Mount Robson, Mount Assiniboine and Hamber PPs (BC) make up the Canadian Rocky Mountain Parks World Heritage Site. Waterton Lakes National Park has been chosen as a Biosphere Reserve, which designates outstanding examples of natural ecosystems throughout the world. **UNESCO World Heritage Sites**

The term provincial park is misleading as it can equally refer to a five-site campground by a strip of highway or a vast area of outstanding wilderness which is every bit the equal of one of the more high profile national parks. This is especially true in British Columbia, the first western province to create provincial parks. Strathcona on Vancouver Island gained park status in 1911 as a result of public support from such groups as the Alpine Club of Canada. Attention then focused on the mountains and glaciers of eastern BC, Mount Robson being declared a provincial park in 1913, followed by Garibaldi in 1920, and Mount Assiniboine and Kokanee Glacier in 1922. The province's largest park, Tweedsmuir (9,810 sq km) , gained park status in 1938; Wells Gray, in 1939. By 1996, BC had 443 provincial parks, 131 ecological reserves and one wilderness area, totalling 78,000 sq km; Alberta had 67 provincial parks, 3 wilderness areas, over 300 recreation areas, 14 ecological reserves and Willmore Wilderness, together encompassing over 10,000 sq km. **Provincial Parks**

Background

Books

Guide books
& reference
See also Literature,
page 460

Devine, B. *Western Canada: National Geographic Guide to America Outdoors* (2002) National Geography. Full of gorgeous photos. **Spalding, D and A et al.** *Southern Gulf Islands* (1995) Altitude. Useful guide to the islands with lots of pictures. **Bushnell, V.** *Kids' Vancouver* (2000) Raincoast Books.

History

Vogel, A and Wyse, D. *Vancouver: A History in Photos* (1993) Altitude. A visual approach to the city's past, captured in vintage black and white.

Natural history
& environment

Baron, N and Acorn, J. *Birds of the Pacific Northwest Coast* (1997) Lone Pine. Thorough and illustrated with great pictures.
Sheldon, I. *Seashore of British Columbia* (1998) Lone Pine. An exploration of coastal flora and fauna with decent drawings.
Lamb, A and Edgell, P. *Coastal Fishes of the Pacific Northwest* (1986) Harbour.
Kramer, P. *Gardens of British Columbia* (1998) Altitude. Lots of sumptuous photos.

Outdoor
activities

Wainwright, J. *Canoe Trips BC* (1994) Wainbay. **Ed McGee, P.** *Kayak Routes of the Pacific Northwest Coast* (1998) Greystone. **Hanna, D.** *Easy Hikes and Walks of Southwest BC* (2002) Lone Pine. A useful resoource for those who want to home in on less demanding hiking. **Dunn, S.** *Mountain Biking BC* (2001) Rip It Up Pub. **Cousins, J.** *Easy Hiking around Vancouver* (1980, updated 2001). Greystone. **Cousins, J and N.** *Easy Cycling Around Vancouver* (2002) Greystone. **Stedham, Glen.** *The Vancouver Paddler* (1999) Self-published.

Pictorial

Over Beautiful British Columbia. Beautiful BC Pub. A coffee-table book with stunning pictures. **Hines, Sherman.** *British Columbia* (1988) Nimbus. Coffee-table book with some nice photos. **Leighton, D.** *The Canadian Rockies* (1993) Altitude. One of a few similar coffee-table offerings of the range. **McAllister, I & K.** *The Great Bear Rainforest: Canada's Forgotten Coast* (1997) Harbour. Stunning shots of the wild and rugged coast from north of Vancouver Island to Alaska. **Pistolesi, Andrea.** *Vancouver: Sunrise to Sunset* (1998) Bonechi. Best collection of glossy photos depicting this photogenic city. **Coupland, D.** *City of Glass* (2001) Douglas & MacIntyre. An interesting book of anecdotes and photos about Vancouver by this celebrated local. *Souvenir of Canada* (2002) Douglas & MacIntyre. This time the author presents a collection of quirky photos and observant witicisms about the country as a whole.

Travelogues
& biographies

Gordon, Charles. *The Canada Trip* (1997) Douglas Gibson. About the only example of humourous travel writing on the country, but only a few chapters on Western Canada. **Coffey, M and Goering, D.** *Visions of the Wild: A Voyage by Kayak around Vancouver Island* (2001) Harbour. An account of a personal odyssey laced with beautiful photos.

Footnotes

Glossary

Geographical features
Hoodoo Odd, elongated mushroom-shaped pillar created when a hardstone cap protects the eroding soft stone beneath it.
Pingo Volcano-shaped mound caused by frost heaves, and found on the Arctic plains (especially near Tuktoyaktuk).
Coulee A steep-sided ravine with sloping sides.
Butte A conspicuous, isolated hill, usually with steep, cliff-like sides. Especially found in Badlands landscapes.
Badlands Extensive tracts of heavily eroded land.
The boonies The middle of nowhere.
Old growth Ancient forest that has never been logged.

Activities
Powder Deep, fresh snow.
Toque Winter hat, usually woollen.
Bouldering Climbing boulders, a safe but challenging practice for rock-climbers.
Scrambling Literally scrambling up scree slopes, often to reach a mountain peak that has no path.
Nordic skiing Cross-country skiing, often on groomed, track-set trails.
Backcountry skiing Getting out to mountain slopes that aren't groomed ski hills. More invigorating, but also more dangerous.
Cat-skiing Accessing remote terrain using a snow cat (a tank-like all terrain vehicle).
Heli-skiing Accessing even more remote terrain with a helicopter.

Food and drink
Appies Appetizers.
Entrée Main course.
Microbrew Homemade beer from a small batch brewery.
Poutine French fries with cheese curd and gravy on top. A Québec speciality.
Perogy Pale Ukrainian dumpling usually filled with potato, fried and served with sour cream and onion.
Prairie oysters Testicles of a young bull, fried and served up after a day of branding and castration.
Sleeve Glass of beer slightly smaller than a pint.

Index

Shorts index

Map index

Credits

Footprint credits
Text editor: Felicity Laughton
Map editor: Sarah Sorensen

Publishers: James Dawson and
Patrick Dawson
Editorial Director: Rachel Fielding
Editorial: Alan Murphy, Sophie Blacksell,
Sarah Thorowgood, Claire Boobbyer,
Caroline Lascom, Davina Rungasamy,
Laura Dixon
Production: Mark Thomas, Jo Morgan
Cartography: Claire Benison,
Kevin Feeney, Robert Lunn
Proofreading: Jenny Piening
Design: Mytton Williams
Marketing and publicity:
Rosemary Dawson, La-Ree Miners
Advertising: Debbie Wylde,
Lorraine Horler
Finance and administration:
Sharon Hughes, Elizabeth Taylor,
Leona Bailey

Photography credits
Front cover: gettyone Stone
Back cover: Alison Bigg
Inside colour section: Alamy,
Alison Bigg, gettyone Stone

Print
Manufactured in Italy by LegoPrint
Pulp from sustainable forests

Footprint feedback
We try as hard as we can to make
each Footprint guide as up to date as
possible but, of course, things always
change. If you want to let us know
about your experiences – good, bad or
ugly – then don't delay, please email
wcan1_online@footprintbooks.com

Publishing information
Footprint Western Canada Handbook
1st edition
© Footprint Handbooks Ltd
June 2003

ISBN 1 903471 56 7
CIP DATA: A catalogue record for this
book is available from the British Library

® Footprint Handbooks and the Footprint
mark are a registered trademark of
Footprint Handbooks Ltd

Published by Footprint Handbooks
6 Riverside Court
Lower Bristol Road
Bath BA2 3DZ, UK
T +44 (0)1225 469141
F +44 (0)1225 469461
discover@footprintbooks.com
www.footprintbooks.com

Distributed in the USA by
Publishers Group West

Complete title listing

Footprint publishes travel guides to over 120 countries worldwide. Each guide is packed with practical, concise and colourful information for everybody from first-time travellers to travel aficionados. The list is growing fast and current titles are noted below.

Available from all good bookshops

www.footprintbooks.com

Latin America & Caribbean

Argentina Handbook
Barbados (P)
Bolivia Handbook
Brazil Handbook
Caribbean Islands Handbook
Central America & Mexico
  Handbook
Chile Handbook
Colombia Handbook
Costa Rica Handbook
Cuba Handbook
Cusco & the Inca Trail Handbook
Dominican Republic Handbook
Ecuador & Galápagos Handbook
Guatemala Handbook
Havana (P)
Mexico Handbook
Nicaragua Handbook
Peru Handbook
Rio de Janeiro Handbook
South American Handbook
Venezuela Handbook

North America

Vancouver (P)
Western Canada Handbook

Africa

Cape Town (P)
East Africa Handbook
Libya Handbook
Marrakech & the High Atlas
  Handbook
Morocco Handbook
Namibia Handbook
South Africa Handbook
Tunisia Handbook
Uganda Handbook

(P) denotes pocket Handbook

Middle East

Egypt Handbook
Israel Handbook
Jordan Handbook
Syria & Lebanon Handbook

Australasia

Australia Handbook
New Zealand Handbook
Sydney (P)
West Coast Australia Handbook

Asia

Bali Handbook
Bangkok & the Beaches
  Handbook
Cambodia Handbook
Goa Handbook
India Handbook
Indian Himalaya Handbook
Indonesia Handbook
Laos Handbook
Malaysia Handbook
Myanmar (Burma) Handbook
Nepal Handbook
Pakistan Handbook
Rajasthan Handbook
Singapore Handbook
South India Handbook
Sri Lanka Handbook
Sumatra Handbook
Thailand Handbook
Tibet Handbook
Vietnam Handbook

Europe

Andalucía Handbook
Barcelona Handbook
Berlin (P)
Bilbao (P)
Bologna (P)
Copenhagen (P)
Croatia Handbook
Dublin Handbook
Dublin (P)
Edinburgh Handbook
Edinburgh (P)
England Handbook
Glasgow Handbook
Ireland Handbook
London Handbook
Madrid (P)
Naples (P)
Northern Spain Handbook
Paris (P)
Reykjavik (P)
Scotland Handbook
Scotland Highlands & Islands
  Handbook
Spain Handbook
Turkey Handbook

Also available

Traveller's Handbook (WEXAS)
Traveller's Healthbook (WEXAS)
Traveller's Internet Guide (WEXAS)

Footnotes

Map symbols

Administration
- **- - -** International border
- **—·—·** Provincial border
- ○ City/town

Roads and travel
- **━━** Highway
- **—** Main road
- **—** Other road
- **- - -** Track
- **······** Footpath
- **←━** Railway with station
- **❺** Vancouver SkyTrain station

Water features
- River
- ⬭ Lake
- ▦ Beach
- Ocean
- ⦙⦙ Waterfall
- ⛴ Ferry

Cities and towns
- ▫ Sight
- **1** Sleeping
- **1** Eating
- Building
- Main through route
- Main street
- Minor street
- ⊐⊐⊐ Pedestrianized street
- Σ ⊏ Tunnel
- → One way street

⧓ Bridge
Park, garden, stadium
⦀⦀⦀⦀ Steps
✈ Airport
🚌 Bus station
✚ Hospital
Ⓜ Market
🏛 Museum
Ⓟ Police
✉ Post office
🅻 Tourist office
✝ ⛪ Cathedral, church
🛕 Sikh Temple
🛕 Buddhist Temple
Ⓟ Parking
@ Internet
Ⓐ Detail map
◀Ⓐ Related map

Topographical features
- ⛰ Mountain
- ⛰ Mountain pass
- ⸺ Escarpment
- Gorge
- Glacier

Other symbols
- ◆ National park/wildlife reserve
- ❀ Viewing point
- ⋀ Campsite
- ⛳ Golf course
- ❧ Winery

Western Canada

Beaufort Sea

7

ALASKA
USA

1

Dawson City

*Yukon
Plateau*

YUKON
TERRITORY

Atlin

Mackenzie Mountains

Great Bear
Lake

NORTHWEST
TERRITORIES

6

Great Slave
Lake

5

BRITISH
COLUMBIA

*Haida Gwaii/
Queen
Charlotte
Islands*

Prince
Rupert

Coast Mountains

Interior Plateau

Fort
Saint John

ALBERTA

Prince
George

Rocky Mountains

3

Bella
Coola

4

Edmonton

Pacific Ocean

Kamloops

Calgary

*Vancouver
Island*

Kelowna
Naramata

Lethbridge

Medicine Hat

1

Vancouver

Victoria

2

N

USA

0 km   100

0 miles   100

	3,350
	2,130
	1,530
	920
	610
	305
	0

Altitude in metres

Neighbouring
Country

Expressway

principal highway

other highway

major road

major winter road

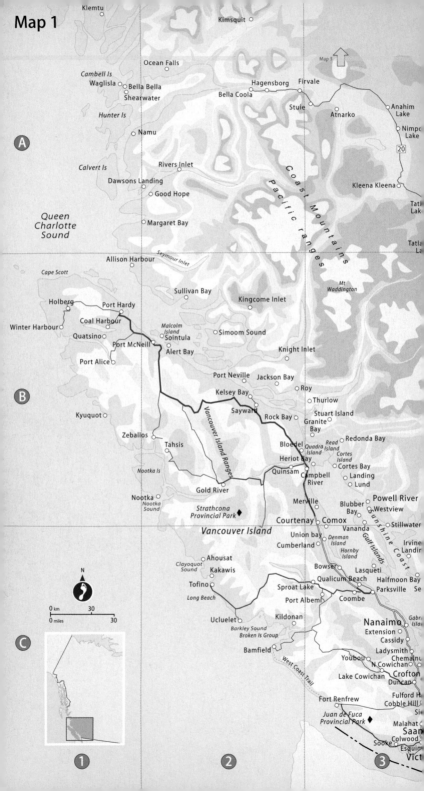

Manola Thorhild Smokey Lake Bellis Burney Mine

Highridge Virny Egremont Vilna Ashmont Gurneyville

Sangudo Busby Legal Waskatenau Saint Paul Lindbergh

thorpe Cherhill 43 Gibbons Red water Andrew Elk Point

chefort Morinville Brue;derheim Willingdon Duvernay Heinsburg

ridge Namao Lamont Two Hills Myrnam Clandonald

Wabamun Saint Albert Fort Saskatchewan Map 4 Vermillion

16 Spruce Grove Edmonton 16 Mundare Vermillion River

Seba Wabamun Lake Sherwood Park Vegreville Vermillion

Beach Duffield Stony Plain North Cooking Lavoy Ranfurly Mannville

Valley Devon Beaumont Tofield Ryley Holden A

Sunnybrook Leduc New Sarepta Hay Lakes Round Hill Viking

Breton Calmar Kavanagh Millet Irma

Winfield Pigeon Lake Wetaskiwin Bittern Lake Camrose Daysland Wainwright Edgerton

Hoadley Hobbema Rosealind Killam Lougheed

Bluffton Ferintosh Donalda Heisler Forestburg Hardisty

Rimbey Gull Lake Ponoka Bashaw Red Willow Galahad Czar

ky Bentley Lacombe Clive Buffalo Lake Alliance Sounding Lake

tain Sylvan Lake Sylvan Lake Alik Stettler Battle River

se Benalto Blackfalds Joffre Gadsby Fleet Gooseberry Lake Veteran Consort

stleville Red Deer Halkirk Castor Coronation Monitor

Penhold Delburne Fenn Kirkpatrick Lake Hemaruka

Innisfail Lousana Big Valley Endiang Sullivan Lake

Eagle Hill Bowden Wimborne Trochu Rumsey Gough Lake Dowling Lake Stanmore Sounding River B

Olds Torrington Three Hills Morrin Craigmyle 9

Carstairs Didsbury Acme Munson Michichi Hanna Sheerness Youngstown Cereal

Crossfield Beiseker Carbon Drumheller Coleman Lake Rose Lynn Oyen

Aidrie Irricana Rosebud River Rosebud Rosedale Dorothy Sunnynook Big Stone

Cochrane Balzac Keoma Nightingale East Coulee Red Deer River Pollockville

Montgomery Chestermere Standard Finnegan Wardlow Dinosaur Provincial Park Buffalo

Bowness Forest Lawn Langdon Hussar Gem Jenner

Calgary Midnapore Strathmore Gleichen Rosemary

Black Diamond Carseland Bow Bassano Duchess Iddesleigh

Turner Valley Okotoks Mossleigh Majorville Patricia

High River Blackie Milo Cassils Brooks

ong View Cayley Ensign Lomond Tilley Trans-Canada Ralston

Parkland Vulcan Champion Enchant Scandia Suffield 1

Claresholm Barons Vauxhall Bow Island Redcliff Medicine Hat C

Granum Nobleford Picture Butte Turin Grassy Lake Whitla Dunmore

Head-Smashed-In Buffalo Jump Monarch Oldman Taber Seven Persons Cypress Hills Provincial Park

Coleman Cowley Fort Macleod Coaldale Barnwell 3 Purple Springs Saskatchewan

Bellevue Brocket Lethbridge Crowsnest Highway

Pincher Creek Pincher Stirling 4 Wrentham Skiff Foremost Etzikom Orion Manyberries

Waterton Lakes National Park Glenwood Raymond New Dayton Warner

Twin Butte Magrath Cardston Spring Coulee Milk River Writing On Stone Provincial Park

Waterton Park Mountain View 4 5 6

Map 3

Map 5 ↑

ALASKA
USA

N

| 0 km | 30 |
| 0 miles | 30 |

Sheslay

Mountains

Glenora · Grand Canyon of
Teleg
Cre

Stikine R

Stikine

Bob Quinn
Lake

Premi
Bear Glacier
Hyder · Stewa

Anyox

Kincolith · Aiy

Greenville

Ross

Dixon Entrance

Dundas Is · Lax Kw'alaams
(Port Simpson)

Portland Canal

Chatham Sound

Masset

Graham Is

Queen Charlotte Mountains

Juskatla · Port Clements

Tlell

Lawnhill

*Haida Gwaii/
Queen
Charlotte
Islands*

Queen
Charlotte · Skidegate

Alliford Bay · Sandspit

Sewell Inlet

Tatsu · ◆ *Gwaii Haanas
National Park*

Moresby Is

Jedway

Metlakatla
Stephens Is · Prince Rupert
Port Edward

Hunts Inlet

Porcher Is · Skeena · Exstew
Cop
Skeena R
Port Essington · La

Oona River

Kitkatla

Kitimat
Kitimat

Pitt Is

Hartley Bay

Banks Is · *Principe Channel*

Inside Passage

Gill Is

Kitimat Range

Estevan Group · Campania Is · Butedale

Princess Royal Is

Hectate Strait

Aristazabal Is · King Is

Klemtu
Swindle Is

Price Is

Oc

Waglista · Bella

A

B

C

1   2   3

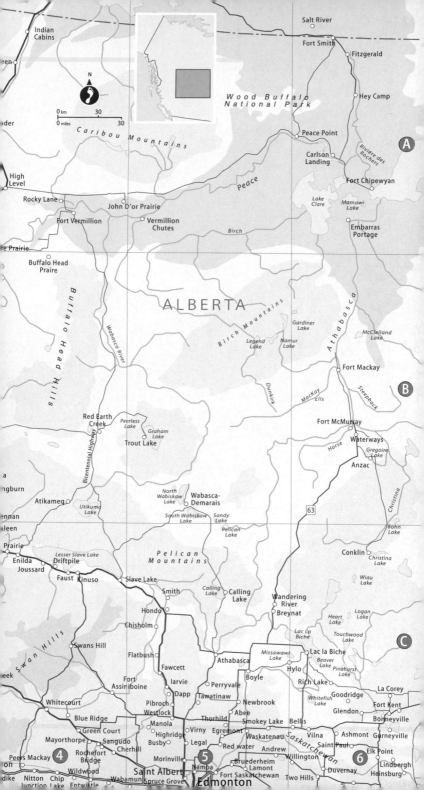

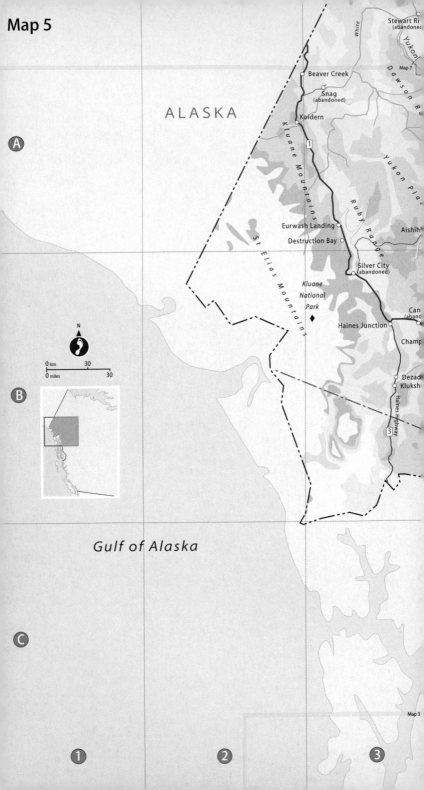

Map 5

ALASKA

Stewart Ri
(abandoned

White

Map 7

Beaver Creek

Snag
(abandoned)

Koidern

Yukon

Dawson R

A

Kluane Mountains

1

Yukon Pla

Ruby Range

Eurwash Landing

Destruction Bay

Aishih

St Elias Mountains

Silver City
(abandoned)

Kluane
National
Park

Can
(aband

Haines Junction

Champ

N

0 km   30
0 miles   30

B

Dezad
Kluksh

Haines Highway

3

Map 3

Gulf of Alaska

C

1   2   3

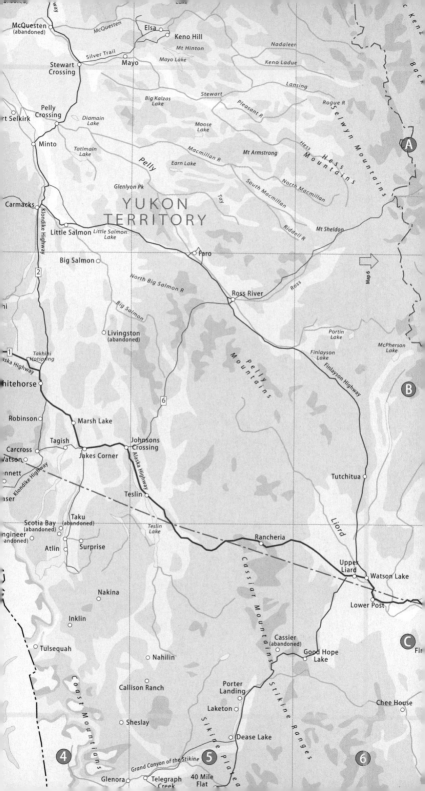

Map 6

Map 5

Map 4

NORTHWEST
TERRITORIES

Canol
Norman Wells
Délįr
(Frank
Great Bear
Fort Norman
Carcajou Range
Heritage Trail
Stewart
Lake
Wrigley
Lake
Canyon Range
Mackenzie Mountains
Backbone Range
ountains
Franklin Mountains
Black
Le
Wrigley
Hic
1
McPherson
Lake
South Nahanni
Nahanni
National Park
Nahanni Butte
7
Liard
a
Watson Lake
ower Post
Smith River
Fireside
Coal River
Fort Halkett
Liard River
Chee House
Liard
Hot Springs
Toad River
Post
Nelson
Forks
Fort Liard
Tro
Trou
Petitot
Snake
River
Yoyo
Muncho Lake
Toad River

Map 7

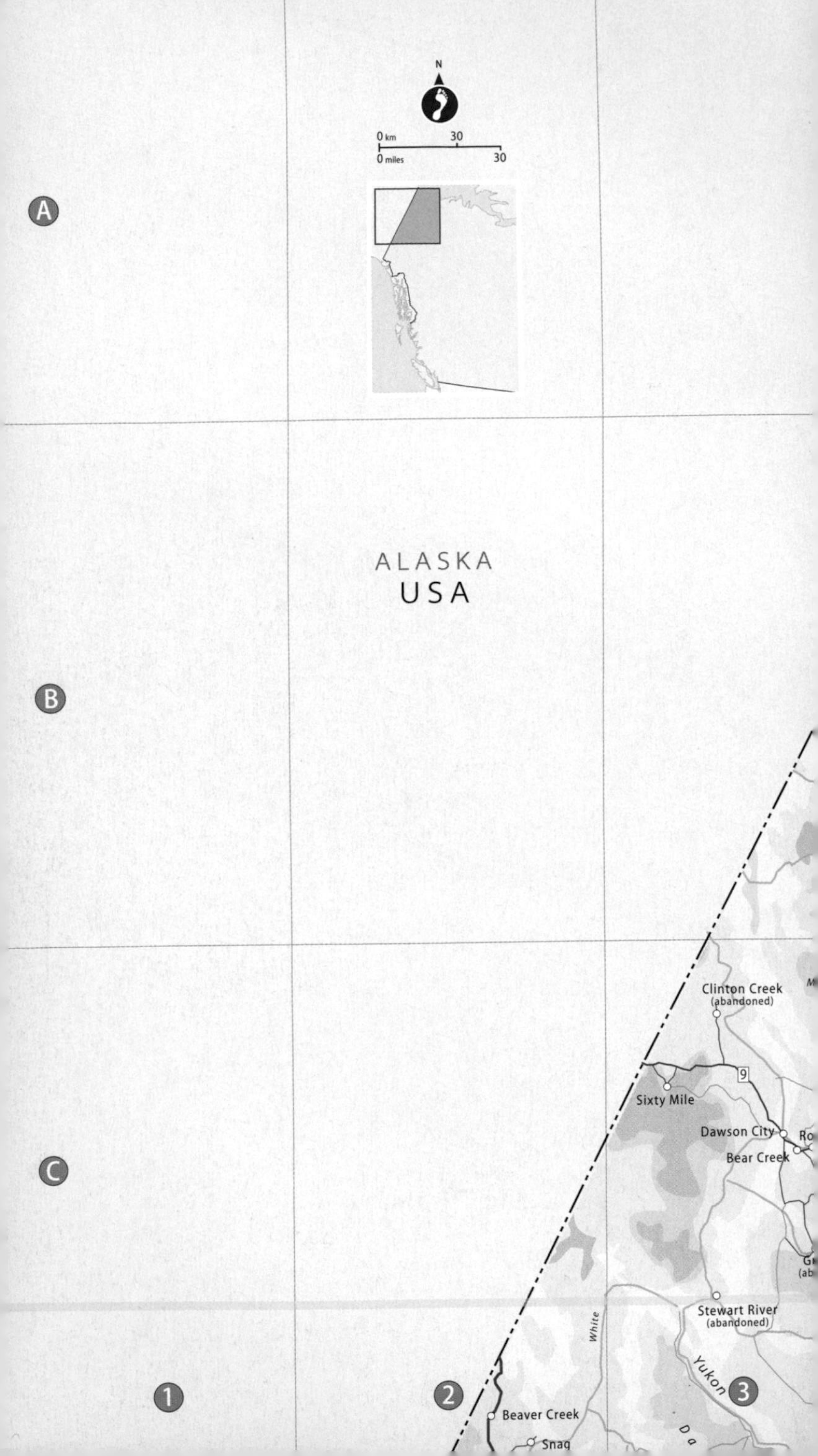

N

0 km   30
0 miles   30

ALASKA
USA

Clinton Creek
(abandoned)

9

Sixty Mile

Dawson City   Ro

Bear Creek

G
(ab

Stewart River
(abandoned)

White

Yukon

Beaver Creek

Snag

A

B

C

1

2

3

For a different view of Europe, take a Footprint

New pocket Handbook series:
Berlin, Bilbao, Bologna, Copenhagen, Dublin, Edinburgh, Lisbon, Madrid, Naples, Paris, Reykjavik, Seville, Turin, Verona.
Also available: Barbados, Cape Town, Havana, Hong Kong, Marrakech, Sydney, Vancouver

Discover so much more...
Listings driven, forward looking and up to date. Focuses on what's going on right now. Contemporary, stylish, and innovative approach providing quality travel information.